Course	Financial Accounting Theory
Course Number	**ACCT 5331**

Dr. Ramaswamy
University of Saint Thomas
Cameron School of Business

http://create.mheducation.com

ISBN-10: 1308382073   ISBN-13: 9781308382074

Contents

Credits

CHAPTER

1

Environment and Theoretical Structure of Financial Accounting

OVERVIEW ———————— The primary function of financial accounting is to provide useful financial information to users who are external to the business enterprise, particularly investors and creditors. These users make critical resource allocation decisions that affect the global economy. The primary means of conveying financial information to external users is through financial statements and related notes.

In this chapter you explore important topics, such as the reason why financial accounting is useful, the process by which accounting standards are produced, and the conceptual framework that underlies financial accounting. The perspective you gain in this chapter serves as a foundation for a more detailed study of financial statements, the way the statement elements are measured, and the concepts underlying these measurements and related disclosures.

LEARNING ———————— After studying this chapter, you should be able to:
OBJECTIVES

- **LO1–1** Describe the function and primary focus of financial accounting. (p. 4)
- **LO1–2** Explain the difference between cash and accrual accounting. (p. 6)
- **LO1–3** Define generally accepted accounting principles (GAAP) and discuss the historical development of accounting standards, including convergence between U.S. and international standards. (p. 8)
- **LO1–4** Explain why the establishment of accounting standards is characterized as a political process. (p. 13)
- **LO1–5** Explain factors that encourage high-quality financial reporting. (p. 15)
- **LO1–6** Explain the purpose of the conceptual framework. (p. 19)
- **LO1–7** Identify the objective and qualitative characteristics of financial reporting information, and the elements of financial statements. (p. 21)
- **LO1–8** Describe the four basic assumptions underlying GAAP. (p. 25)
- **LO1–9** Describe the recognition, measurement and disclosure concepts that guide accounting practice. (p. 27)
- **LO1–10** Contrast a revenue/expense approach and an asset/liability approach to accounting standard setting. (p. 33)
- **LO1–11** Discuss the primary differences between U.S. GAAP and IFRS with respect to the development of accounting standards and the conceptual framework underlying accounting standards. (pp. 15 and 21)

FINANCIAL REPORTING CASE

Misguided Marketing Major

During a class break in your investments class, a marketing major tells the following story to you and some friends:

The chief financial officer (CFO) of a large company is interviewing three candidates for the top accounting position with his firm. He asks each the same question:

CFO:	What is two plus two?
First candidate:	Four.
CFO:	What is two plus two?
Second candidate:	Four.
CFO:	What is two plus two?
Third candidate:	What would you like it to be?
CFO:	You're hired.

After you take some good-natured ribbing from the non-accounting majors, your friend says, "Seriously, though, there must be ways the accounting profession prevents that kind of behavior. Aren't there some laws, or rules, or something? Is accounting based on some sort of theory, or is it just arbitrary?"

By the time you finish this chapter, you should be able to respond appropriately to the questions posed in this case. Compare your response to the solution provided at the end of the chapter.

── QUESTIONS

1. What should you tell your friend about the presence of accounting standards in the United States and the rest of the world? Who has the authority for standard setting? Who has the responsibility? (p. 8)

2. What is the economic and political environment in which standard setting occurs? (p. 13)

3. What is the relationship among management, auditors, investors, and creditors that tends to preclude the "What would you like it to be?" attitude? (p. 15)

4. In general, what is the conceptual framework that underlies accounting principles? (p. 19)

FINANCIAL ACCOUNTING ENVIRONMENT

PART **A**

In 1984 an undergraduate student at the University of Texas used $1,000 of his own funds to found a company called PC's Limited. The student's vision was to capitalize on the emerging personal computer (PC) business by selling directly to customers rather than through traditional retail outlets. The customer's PC would not be manufactured until it was ordered. This just-in-time (JIT) approach to production combined with the direct sales model would allow the company to better understand customer needs and more efficiently provide the most effective computing solutions.

4   SECTION 1   The Role of Accounting as an Information System

In 1985, the first full year of company operations, the student's family contributed $300,000 in expansion capital, and revenue topped $73 million.[1] These were the humble beginnings for a visionary student named Michael Dell and a company eventually renamed Dell Inc. that has become the world's largest PC manufacturer. Company profits for the year ended January 28, 2011, exceeded $2.6 billion and revenue topped $61 billion.

Many factors have contributed to the success of Dell Inc. The company's founder was visionary in terms of his approach to marketing and production. Importantly, too, the ability to raise external capital from investors and creditors at various times in the company's history was critical to its growth. Funding began with Michael Dell's initial $1,000 outlay and his family's $300,000 investment. In 1988, an initial public offering of the company's stock provided $30 million in equity financing.

> "Michael S. Dell built the multibillion-dollar company that bears his name not by inventing new products or services, but by constantly looking for ways to sell technology 'better, faster, cheaper,' as the company's mantra goes."[2]

Investors and creditors use many different kinds of information before supplying capital to business enterprises like Dell. The information is used to assess the future risk and return of their potential investments in the enterprise.[3] For example, information about the enterprise's products and its management is of vital importance to this assessment. In addition, various kinds of financial information are extremely important to investors and creditors.

● LO1–1

The primary focus of *financial accounting* is on the information needs of investors and creditors.

Think of accounting as a special "language" used to communicate financial information about a business to those who wish to use the information to make decisions. Financial accounting, in particular, is chiefly concerned with providing relevant financial information to various *external* users.[4] The chart in Illustration 1–1 lists a number of financial information supplier groups as well as several external user groups. Of these groups, the primary focus of financial accounting is on the financial information provided by *profit-oriented companies to their present and potential investors and creditors.* The reason for this focus is discussed in a later section of this chapter. One external user group, often referred to as *financial intermediaries,* includes financial analysts, stockbrokers, mutual fund managers, and credit rating organizations. These users provide advice to investors and creditors and/or make investment-credit decisions on their behalf.

Illustration 1–1

Financial Information Providers and External User Groups

PROVIDERS OF FINANCIAL INFORMATION	EXTERNAL USER GROUPS
• Profit-oriented companies	• Investors
	• Creditors (banks, bondholders, other lenders)
	• Employees
	• Labor unions
• Not-for-profit entities (e.g., government entities, charitable organizations, schools)	• Customers
	• Suppliers
	• Government regulatory agencies (e.g., Internal Revenue Service, Securities and Exchange Commission)
• Households	• Financial intermediaries (e.g., financial analysts, stockbrokers, mutual fund managers, credit-rating organizations)

[1]"Dell, Inc.—Company History," www.fundinguniverse.com.

[2]Elizabeth Schwinn. "A Focus on Efficiency," *The Chronicle of Philanthropy* (April 6, 2006).

[3]Risk refers to the variability of possible outcomes from an investment. Return is the amount received over and above the investment and usually is expressed as a percentage.

[4]In contrast, managerial accounting deals with the concepts and methods used to provide information to an organization's *internal* users, that is, its managers. You study managerial accounting elsewhere in your curriculum.

The primary means of conveying financial information to investors, creditors, and other external users is through financial statements and related disclosure notes. The financial statements most frequently provided are (1) the balance sheet, also called the statement of financial position, (2) the income statement, also called the statement of operations, (3) the statement of cash flows, and (4) the statement of shareholders' equity. Also, starting in 2012, companies must either provide a statement of other comprehensive income immediately following the income statement, or present a combined statement of comprehensive income that includes the information normally contained in both the income statement and the statement of other comprehensive income.[5] As you progress through this text, you will review and expand your knowledge of the information in these financial statements, the way the elements in these statements are measured, and the concepts underlying these measurements and related disclosures. We use the term financial reporting to refer to the process of providing this information to external users. Keep in mind, though, that external users receive important financial information in a variety of other formats as well, including news releases and management forecasts, prospectuses, and reports filed with regulatory agencies.

Dell Inc.'s 2011 financial statements and related disclosure notes are provided in Appendix B located at the back of the text. You also can locate the 2011 statements and notes online at www.dell.com. To provide context for our discussions throughout the text, we occasionally refer to these statements and notes. Also, as new topics are introduced in later chapters, you might want to refer to the information to see how Dell reported the items being discussed.

The Economic Environment and Financial Reporting

In the United States, we have a highly developed free-enterprise economy with the majority of productive resources privately owned rather than government owned. For the economy to operate efficiently, these resources should be allocated to private enterprises that will use them best to provide the goods and services desired by society and not to enterprises that will waste them. The mechanisms that foster this efficient allocation of resources are the capital markets. We can think of the capital markets simply as a composite of all investors and creditors.

The capital markets provide a mechanism to help our economy allocate resources efficiently.

Businesses go to the capital markets to get the cash necessary for them to function. The three primary forms of business organization are the sole proprietorship, the partnership, and the corporation. In the United States, sole proprietorships and partnerships outnumber corporations. However, the dominant form of business organization, in terms of the ownership of productive resources, is the corporation. Investors provide resources, usually cash, to a corporation in exchange for an ownership interest, that is, shares of stock. Creditors lend cash to the corporation, either by making individual loans or by purchasing publicly traded debt such as bonds.

Corporations acquire capital from investors in exchange for ownership interest and from creditors by borrowing.

Stocks and bonds usually are traded on organized security markets such as the New York Stock Exchange and the NASDAQ. New cash is provided by initial market transactions in which the corporation sells shares of stock or bonds to individuals or other entities that want to invest in it. Subsequent transfers of these stocks and bonds between investors and creditors are referred to as secondary market transactions. Corporations receive no new cash from secondary market transactions. Nevertheless, secondary market transactions are extremely important to the efficient allocation of resources in our economy. These transactions help establish market prices for additional shares and for bonds that corporations may wish to issue in the future to acquire additional capital. Also, many shareholders and bondholders might be unwilling to initially provide resources to corporations if there were no available mechanism for the future sale of their stocks and bonds to others.

Initial market transactions involve issuance of stocks and bonds by the corporation.

Secondary market transactions involve the transfer of stocks and bonds between individuals and institutions.

What information do investors and creditors need when determining which companies will receive capital? We explore that question next.

---

[5]FASB ASC 220: Comprehensive Income (originally "Presentation of Comprehensive Income," *Accounting Standards Update No. 2011–05* (Norwalk, CT: FASB, June 2011)).

The Investment-Credit Decision—A Cash Flow Perspective

Investors and creditors are interested in earning a fair return on the resources they provide.

While the decisions made by investors and by creditors are somewhat different, they are similar in at least one important way. Investors and creditors are willing to provide capital to a corporation (buy stocks or bonds) only if they expect to receive more cash in return at some time in the future. A corporation's shareholders will receive cash from their investment through the ultimate sale of the ownership shares of stock. In addition, many corporations distribute cash to their shareholders in the form of periodic dividends. For example, if an investor provides a company with $10,000 cash by purchasing stock at the end of 2012, receives $400 in dividends from the company during 2013, and sells the ownership interest (shares) at the end of 2013 for $10,600, the investment would have generated a rate of return of 10% for 2013, calculated as follows:

$$\frac{\$400 \text{ dividends} + \$600 \text{ share price appreciation}}{\$10,000 \text{ initial investment}} = 10\%$$

The expected rate of return and the uncertainty, or risk, of that return are key variables in the investment decision.

All else equal, investors and creditors would like to invest in stocks or bonds that provide the highest expected rate of return. However, there are many factors to consider before making an investment decision. For example, the *uncertainty,* or *risk,* of that expected return also is important. To illustrate, consider the following two investment options:

1. Invest $10,000 in a savings account insured by the U.S. government that will generate a 5% rate of return.
2. Invest $10,000 in a profit-oriented company.

A company will be able to provide a return to investors and creditors only if it can generate a profit from selling its products or services.

While the rate of return from option 1 is known with virtual certainty, the return from option 2 is uncertain. The amount and timing of the cash to be received in the future from option 2 are unknown. The company in option 2 will be able to provide investors with a return only if it can generate a profit. That is, it must be able to use the resources provided by investors and creditors to generate cash receipts from selling a product or service that exceed the cash disbursements necessary to provide that product or service. Therefore, potential investors require information about the company that will help them estimate the potential for future profits, as well as the return they can expect on their investment and the risk that is associated with it. If the potential return is high enough, investors will prefer to invest in the profit-oriented company, even if that return has more risk associated with it.

The objective of financial accounting is to provide investors and creditors with useful information for decision making.

In summary, the primary objective of financial accounting is to provide investors and creditors with information that will help them make investment and credit decisions. More specifically, the information should help investors and creditors evaluate the *amounts, timing,* and *uncertainty* of the enterprise's future cash receipts and disbursements. The better this information is, the more efficient will be investor and creditor resource allocation decisions. But financial accounting doesn't only benefit companies and their investors and creditors. By providing key elements of the information set used by capital market participants, financial accounting plays a vital role by providing information that helps direct society's resources to the companies that utilize those resources most effectively.

Cash versus Accrual Accounting

● LO1–2

Even though predicting future cash flows is the primary goal of many users of financial reporting, the model best able to achieve that goal is the accrual accounting model. A competing model is cash basis accounting. Each model produces a periodic measure of performance that could be used by investors and creditors for predicting future cash flows.

CASH BASIS ACCOUNTING.   Cash basis accounting produces a measure called net operating cash flow. This measure is the difference between cash receipts and cash payments from transactions related to providing goods and services to customers during a reporting period.

Net operating cash flow is the difference between cash receipts and cash disbursements from providing goods and services.

Over the life of a company, net operating cash flow definitely is the variable of concern. However, over short periods of time, operating cash flows may not be indicative of the company's long-run cash-generating ability. Sometimes a company pays or receives cash in one period that relates to performance in multiple periods. For example, in one period a company receives cash that relates to prior period sales, or makes advance payments for costs related to future periods. Therefore, net operating cash flow may not be a good predictor of long-run cash-generating ability.

To see this more clearly, consider Carter Company's net operating cash flows during its first three years of operations, shown in Illustration 1–2. Over this three-year period Carter generated a positive net operating cash flow of $60,000. At the end of the three-year period, Carter has no outstanding debts. Because total sales and cash receipts over the three-year period were each $300,000, nothing is owed to Carter by customers. Also, there are no uncompleted transactions at the end of the three-year period. In that sense, we can view this three-year period as a micro version of the entire life of a company.

	Year 1	Year 2	Year 3	Total
Sales (on credit)	$100,000	$100,000	$100,000	$300,000
Net Operating Cash Flows				
Cash receipts from customers	$ 50,000	$125,000	$125,000	$300,000
Cash disbursements:				
Prepayment of three years' rent	(60,000)	–0–	–0–	(60,000)
Salaries to employees	(50,000)	(50,000)	(50,000)	(150,000)
Utilities	(5,000)	(15,000)	(10,000)	(30,000)
Net operating cash flow	$ (65,000)	$ 60,000	$ 65,000	$ 60,000

Illustration 1–2

Cash Basis Accounting

At the beginning of the first year, Carter prepaid $60,000 for three years' rent on the facilities. The company also incurred utility costs of $10,000 per year over the period. However, during the first year only $5,000 actually was paid, with the remainder being paid the second year. Employee salary costs of $50,000 were paid in full each year.

Is net operating cash flow for year 1 (negative $65,000) an accurate indicator of future cash-generating ability?[6] Clearly not, given that the next two years show positive net cash flows. Is the three-year pattern of net operating cash flows indicative of the company's year-by-year performance? No, because the years in which Carter paid for rent and utilities are not the same as the years in which Carter actually consumed those resources. Similarly, the amounts collected from customers are not the same as the amount of sales each period.

Over short periods of time, operating cash flow may not be an accurate predictor of future operating cash flows.

ACCRUAL ACCOUNTING. If we measure Carter's activities by the accrual accounting model, we get a more accurate prediction of future operating cash flows and a more reasonable portrayal of the periodic operating performance of the company. The accrual accounting model doesn't focus only on cash flows. Instead, it also reflects other resources provided and consumed by operations during a period. The accrual accounting model's measure of resources provided by business operations is called *revenues,* and the measure of resources sacrificed to earn revenues is called *expenses.* The difference between revenues and expenses is *net income,* or net loss if expenses are greater than revenues.[7]

Illustration 1–3 shows how we would measure revenues and expenses in this very simple situation.

Revenue for year 1 is the $100,000 sales. Given that sales eventually are collected in cash, the year 1 revenue of $100,000 is a better measure of the inflow of resources from company operations than is the $50,000 cash collected from customers. Also, net income of $20,000 for year 1 appears to be a reasonable predictor of the company's cash-generating ability, as total net operating cash flow for the three-year period is a positive $60,000. Comparing the three-year pattern of net operating cash flows in Illustration 1–2 to the three-year

Net income is the difference between revenues and expenses.

Net income is considered a better indicator of future operating cash flows than is current net operating cash flow.

---

[6]A negative cash flow is possible only if invested capital (i.e., owners contributed cash to the company in exchange for ownership interest) is sufficient to cover the cash deficiency. Otherwise, the company would have to either raise additional external funds or go bankrupt.

[7]Net income also includes gains and losses, which are discussed later in the chapter.

Illustration 1–3
Accrual Accounting

The accrual accounting model provides a measure of periodic performance called *net income,* the difference between revenues and expenses.

	CARTER COMPANY Income Statements			
	Year 1	Year 2	Year 3	Total
Revenues	$100,000	$100,000	$100,000	$300,000
Expenses:				
Rent	20,000	20,000	20,000	60,000
Salaries	50,000	50,000	50,000	150,000
Utilities	10,000	10,000	10,000	30,000
Total expenses	80,000	80,000	80,000	240,000
Net Income	$ 20,000	$ 20,000	$ 20,000	$ 60,000

pattern of net income in Illustration 1–3, the net income pattern is more representative of Carter Company's steady operating performance over the three-year period.[8]

While this example is somewhat simplistic, it allows us to see the motivation for using the accrual accounting model. Accrual income attempts to measure the resource inflows and outflows generated by operations during the reporting period, which may not correspond to cash inflows and outflows. Does this mean that information about cash flows from operating activities is not useful? No. Indeed, one of the basic financial statements—the statement of cash flows—reports information about cash flows from operating, investing and financing activities, and provides important information to investors and creditors.[9] The key point is that focusing on accrual accounting as well as cash flows provides a more complete view of a company and its operations.

The Development of Financial Accounting and Reporting Standards

● LO1–3

FINANCIAL Reporting Case

Q1, p. 3

Accrual accounting is the financial reporting model used by the majority of profit-oriented companies and by many not-for-profit companies. The fact that companies use the same model is important to investors and creditors, allowing them to *compare* financial information among companies. To facilitate these comparisons, financial accounting employs a body of standards known as generally accepted accounting principles, often abbreviated as GAAP (and pronounced *gap*). GAAP is a dynamic set of both broad and specific guidelines that companies should follow when measuring and reporting the information in their financial statements and related notes. The more important broad principles underlying GAAP are discussed in a subsequent section of this chapter and revisited throughout the text in the context of accounting applications for which they provide conceptual support. Specific standards, such as how to measure and report a lease transaction, receive more focused attention in subsequent chapters.

Historical Perspective and Standards

Pressures on the accounting profession to establish uniform accounting standards began to surface after the stock market crash of 1929. Some felt that insufficient and misleading financial statement information led to inflated stock prices and that this contributed to the stock market crash and the subsequent depression.

The 1933 Securities Act and the 1934 Securities Exchange Act were designed to restore investor confidence. The 1933 Act sets forth accounting and disclosure requirements for

---

[8]Empirical evidence that accrual accounting provides a better measure of short-term performance than cash flows is provided by Patricia DeChow, "Accounting Earnings and Cash Flows as Measures of Firm Performance: The Role of Accrual Accounting," *Journal of Accounting and Economics* 18 (1994), pp. 3–42.
[9]The statement of cash flows is discussed in detail in Chapters 4 and 21.

initial offerings of securities (stocks and bonds). The 1934 Act applies to secondary market transactions and mandates reporting requirements for companies whose securities are publicly traded on either organized stock exchanges or in over-the-counter markets.[10] The 1934 Act also created the Securities and Exchange Commission (SEC).

In the 1934 Act, Congress gave the SEC the authority to set accounting and reporting standards for companies whose securities are publicly traded. However, the SEC, a government appointed body, has *delegated* the task of setting accounting standards to the private sector. It is important to understand that the power still lies with the SEC. If the SEC does not agree with a particular standard issued by the private sector, it can force a change in the standard. In fact, it has done so in the past.[11]

> The *Securities and Exchange Commission (SEC)* was created by Congress with the 1934 Securities Exchange Act.
>
> The SEC has the authority to set accounting standards for companies, but has delegated the task to the private sector.

EARLY U. S. STANDARD SETTING.   The first private sector body to assume the task of setting accounting standards was the Committee on Accounting Procedure (CAP). The CAP was a committee of the American Institute of Accountants (AIA). The AIA, which was renamed the American Institute of Certified Public Accountants (AICPA) in 1957, is the national professional organization for certified professional public accountants. From 1938 to 1959, the CAP issued 51 *Accounting Research Bulletins (ARBs)* which dealt with specific accounting and reporting problems. No theoretical framework for financial accounting was established. This piecemeal approach of dealing with individual issues without a framework led to criticism.

In 1959 the Accounting Principles Board (APB) replaced the CAP. The APB operated from 1959 through 1973 and issued 31 *Accounting Principles Board Opinions (APBOs),* various *Interpretations,* and four *Statements.* The *Opinions* also dealt with specific accounting and reporting problems. Many *ARBs* and *APBOs* have not been superseded and still represent authoritative GAAP.

> The *Accounting Principles Board (APB)* followed the CAP.

The APB suffered from a variety of problems. It was never able to establish a conceptual framework for financial accounting and reporting that was broadly accepted. Also, members served on the APB on a voluntary, part-time basis, so the APB was not able to act quickly enough to keep up with financial reporting issues as they developed. Perhaps the most important flaw of the APB was a perceived lack of independence. Because the APB was composed almost entirely of certified public accountants and supported by the AICPA, critics charged that the clients of the represented public accounting firms exerted self-interested pressure on the board and inappropriately influenced decisions. A related complaint was that other interest groups lacked an ability to provide input to the standard-setting process.

THE FASB.   Criticism of the APB led to the creation in 1973 of the Financial Accounting Standards Board (FASB) and its supporting structure. There are seven full-time members of the FASB.[12] FASB members represent various constituencies concerned with accounting standards, and have included representatives from the auditing profession, profit-oriented companies, accounting educators, financial analysts, and government. The FASB is supported by its parent organization, the Financial Accounting Foundation (FAF), which is responsible for selecting the members of the FASB and its Financial Accounting Standards Advisory Council (FASAC), ensuring adequate funding of FASB activities and exercising general oversight of the FASB's activities.[13] The FASB is, therefore,

> The *FASB* was established to set U.S. accounting standards.

---

[10]Reporting requirements for SEC registrants include Form 10-K, the annual report form, and Form 10-Q, the report that must be filed for the first three quarters of each fiscal year.

[11]The SEC issues *Financial Reporting Releases (FRRs),* which regulate what information companies must report to it. The SEC also issues *Staff Accounting Bulletins* that provide the SEC's interpretation of standards previously issued by the private sector. To learn more about the SEC, consult its Internet site at www.sec.gov.

[12]The FASB reduced its membership from seven to five members in 2008, but returned to seven members in 2011.

[13]The FAF's primary sources of funding are fees assessed against issuers of securities under the *Public Company Accounting Reform and Investor Protection Act of 2002,* commonly referred to as the *Sarbanes-Oxley Act.* The FAF is governed by trustees, the majority of whom are appointed from the membership of eight sponsoring organizations. These organizations represent important constituencies involved with the financial reporting process. For example, one of the founding organizations is the Association of Investment Management and Research (formerly known as the Financial Analysts Federation) which represents financial information users, and another is the Financial Executives International which represents financial information preparers. The FAF also raises funds to support the activities of the Government Accounting Standards Board (GASB).

an independent, private sector body whose members represent a broad constituency of interest groups.[14]

> The *Emerging Issues Task Force (EITF)* identifies financial reporting issues and attempts to resolve them without involving the FASB.

In 1984, the FASB's Emerging Issues Task Force (EITF) was formed to improve financial reporting by resolving narrowly defined financial accounting issues within the framework of existing GAAP. The EITF primarily addresses implementation issues, thereby speeding up the standard setting process and allowing the FASB to focus on pervasive long-term problems. EITF rulings are ratified by the FASB and are considered part of GAAP.

Illustration 1–4 summarizes this discussion on accounting standards. The graphic shows the hierarchy of accounting standard setting in order of authority.

Illustration 1–4

Accounting Standard Setting

HIERARCHY OF STANDARD-SETTING AUTHORITY

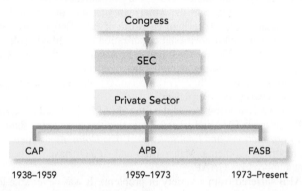

CODIFICATION.   Present-day GAAP includes a huge amount of guidance. The FASB has developed a conceptual framework (discussed in Part B of this chapter) that is not authoritative GAAP but provides an underlying structure for the development of accounting standards. The FASB also has issued over 160 specific accounting standards, called *Statements of Financial Accounting Standards (SFASs)*, as well as numerous FASB *Interpretations, Staff Positions, Technical Bulletins* and *EITF Issue Consensuses.*[16] The SEC also has issued various important pronouncements. Until 2009, determining the appropriate accounting treatment for a particular event or transaction might require an accountant to research several of these sources.

> The Codification does not change GAAP; instead it reorganizes the thousands of U.S. GAAP pronouncements into roughly 90 accounting topics, and displays all topics using a consistent structure.[15]

> The *FASB Accounting Standards Codification* is now the only source of authoritative U.S. GAAP, other than rules and interpretive releases of the SEC.

To simplify the task of researching an accounting topic, in 2009 the FASB implemented its *FASB Accounting Standards Codification.* The Codification integrates and topically organizes all relevant accounting pronouncements comprising GAAP in a searchable, online database. It represents the single source of authoritative nongovernmental U.S. GAAP, and also includes portions of SEC accounting guidance that are relevant to financial reports filed with the SEC. When the FASB issues a new standard, it is called an Accounting Standards Update (ASU) and becomes authoritative when it is entered into the Codification. The Codification is organized into nine main topics and approximately 90 subtopics. The main topics and related numbering system are presented in Illustration 1–5.[17] The Codification can be located at www.fasb.org.

---

[14]The major responsibility of the FASAC is to advise the FASB on the priorities of its projects, including the suitability of new projects that might be added to its agenda. FASAC includes approximately 35 representatives from auditing firms, private companies, various user groups, and academia.

[15]"FASB Accounting Standards Codification™ Expected to Officially Launch on July 1, 2009," *FASB News Release* (Norwalk, Conn.: FASB, December 4, 2008).

[16]For more information, go to the FASB's Internet site at www.fasb.org.

[17]FASB ASC 105–10: Generally Accepted Accounting Principles—Overall (previously "The FASB Accounting Standards Codification™ and the Hierarchy of Generally Accepted Accounting Principles—a replacement of FASB Statement No. 162," *Statement of Financial Accounting Standards No. 168* (Norwalk, Conn.: FASB: 2009)).

FASB Accounting Standards Codification Topics	
Topic	**Numbered**
General Principles	100–199
Presentation	200–299
Assets	300–399
Liabilities	400–499
Equity	500–599
Revenues	600–699
Expenses	700–799
Broad Transactions	800–899
Industry	900–999

Illustration 1–5
FASB Accounting Standards Codification Topics

Throughout the text, we use the Accounting Standards Codification System (ASC) in footnotes when referencing generally accepted accounting principles (FASB ASC followed by the appropriate number). Each footnote also includes a reference to the original accounting standard that is codified in ASC. Your instructor may assign end-of-chapter exercises and cases that ask you to research the FASB's Accounting Standards Codification.

Additional Consideration

Accounting standards and the standard-setting process discussed above relate to profit-oriented organizations and nongovernmental not-for-profit entities. In 1984, the Government Accounting Standards Board (GASB) was created to develop accounting standards for governmental units such as states and cities. The FAF oversees and funds the GASB, and the Governmental Accounting Standards Advisory Council (GASAC) provides input to it.

INTERNATIONAL STANDARD SETTING. Most industrialized countries have organizations responsible for determining accounting and reporting standards. In some countries, the United Kingdom, for instance, the responsible organization is a private sector body similar to the FASB in the United States. In other countries, such as France, the organization is a governmental body.

Accounting standards prescribed by these various groups are not the same. Standards differ from country to country for many reasons, including different legal systems, levels of inflation, culture, degrees of sophistication and use of capital markets, use of financial reports by taxing authorities or government planners, and political and economic ties with other countries. These differences can cause problems for multinational corporations. A company doing business in more than one country may find it difficult to comply with more than one set of accounting standards if there are important differences among the sets. These differences also cause problems for investors who must struggle to compare companies whose financial statements are prepared under different standards. It has been argued that different national accounting standards impair the ability of companies to raise capital in international markets.

In response to this problem, the International Accounting Standards Committee (IASC) was formed in 1973 to develop global accounting standards. The IASC reorganized itself in 2001 and created a new standard-setting body called the International Accounting Standards Board (IASB). The IASB's main objective is to develop a single set of high-quality, understandable, and enforceable global accounting standards to help participants in the world's capital markets and other users make economic decisions.[18]

The *International Accounting Standards Board (IASB)* is dedicated to developing a single set of global accounting standards.

As shown in Illustration 1–6, the way international standard setting is structured is similar in many respects to the way standard setting is structured in the U.S.

[18]www.iasb.org.

Illustration 1–6

Comparison of Organizations of U.S. and International Standard Setters

	U.S. GAAP	IFRS
Regulatory oversight provided by:	Securities Exchange Commission (SEC)	International Organization of Securities Commissions (IOSCO)*
Foundation providing oversight, appointing members, raising funds:	Financial Accounting Foundation (FAF): 20 trustees	International Accounting Standards Committee Foundation (IASCF): 22 trustees
Standard-setting board:	Financial Accounting Standards Board (FASB): 7 full-time members	International Accounting Standards Board (IASB): 14 members (12 full-time; 2 part-time)
Advisory council providing input on agenda and projects:	Financial Accounting Standards Advisory Council (FASAC): 30–40 members	Standards Advisory Council (SAC): 30–40 members
Group to deal with emerging issues:	Emerging Issues Task Force (EITF): 15 members	International Financial Reporting Interpretations Committee (IFRIC): 14 members

*Each country's security regulator has authority. IOSCO includes representatives from numerous regulators, including the SEC, to facilitate coordination among those regulators and other organizations and encourage effective capital markets.

International Financial Reporting Standards are gaining support around the globe.

The IASC issued 41 International Accounting Standards (IASs), and the IASB endorsed these standards when it was formed in 2001. Since then, the IASB has revised many IASs and has issued new standards of its own, called International Financial Reporting Standards (IFRSs). More and more countries are basing their national accounting standards on IFRS. By late 2011, over 115 jurisdictions, including Hong Kong, Egypt, Australia, and the countries in the European Union (EU), require or permit the use of IFRS or a local variant of IFRS.[19]

EFFORTS TO CONVERGE U.S. AND INTERNATIONAL STANDARDS

Should the U.S. also adopt IFRS? Many argue that a single set of global standards will improve comparability of financial reporting and facilitate access to capital. However, others argue that U.S. standards should remain customized to fit the stringent legal and regulatory requirements of the U.S. business environment. There also is concern that differences in implementation and enforcement from country to country will make accounting under IFRS appear more uniform and comparable than actually is the case. Another argument is that competition between alternative standard-setting regimes is healthy and can lead to improved standards.[20]

Regardless, the FASB and IASB have been working for many years to converge to one global set of accounting standards. Here are some important steps along the path to convergence:

- **September 2002:** The FASB and IASB sign the Norwalk Agreement, pledging to remove existing differences between their standards and to coordinate their future standard-setting agendas so that major issues are worked on together.
- **December 2007:** The SEC signaled its view that IFRS are of high quality by eliminating the requirement for foreign companies that issue stock in the United States to include in their financial statements a reconciliation of IFRS to U.S. GAAP. As a consequence, those companies have access to U.S. capital markets with IFRS-based financial statements.
- **April 2008:** The FASB and IASB agreed to accelerate the convergence process and focus on a subset of key convergence projects. Already-converged standards that you will encounter later in this textbook deal with such topics as earnings per share, share-based compensation, nonmonetary exchanges, inventory costs, and the calculation of fair value. Where We're Headed boxes throughout the text describe additional projects that are ongoing, and Where We're Headed supplements to chapters 5, 12, and 15 describe proposed converged standards relevant to revenue recognition, investments, and leases.
- **November 2008:** The SEC issues a *Roadmap* that listed necessary conditions (called "milestones") that must be achieved before the U.S. will shift to requiring use of IFRS by public companies. Milestones include completion of key convergence projects,

[19]See www.iasplus.com/country/useias.htm.
[20]For a comprehensive analysis of the pros and cons of U.S. adoption of IFRS, see L. Hail, C. Leuz and P. Wysocki, "Global Accounting Convergence and the Potential Adoption of IFRS in the US (Part 1): An Analysis of Economic and Policy Factors", *Accounting Horizons* 24 (No 3.), September 2010, pp. 355–394, and " . . . (Part 2): Political Factors and Future Scenarios for U.S. Accounting Standards", *Accounting Horizons* 24 (No. 4), December 2010, pp. 567–588.

improving the structure and funding of the IASB, and updating the education and licensing of U.S. accountants.

- **May 2011:** The SEC issues a discussion paper describing a possible approach for incorporating IFRS into U.S. GAAP. That approach, since labled "condorsement", involves continuing the convergence process coupled with endorsement of additional International Financial Reporting Standards by the FASB for inclusion in U.S. GAAP if those standards are of sufficiently high quality. Under this approach, the SEC and FASB still have sovereignty over U.S. accounting standards, but those standards should largely converge to IFRS over time.

- **November 2011:** The SEC issued two studies comparing U.S. GAAP and IFRS and analyzing how IFRS are applied globally. In these studies, the SEC identifies key differences between U.S. GAAP and IFRS, and notes that U.S. GAAP provides significantly more guidance about particular transactions or industries. The SEC also notes some diversity in the application of IFRS that suggests the potential for non-comparability of financial statements across countries and industries.

- **December 2011:** The SEC postpones making a final determination concerning whether and how to incorporate IFRS into U.S. GAAP until sometime in 2012.

At the time this text is being written, it still is unclear whether or how IFRS will be incorporated into U.S. GAAP. The SEC might require (a) whole-scale adoption of IFRS by U.S. companies, (b) a standard-by-standard endorsement of IFRS standards in the U.S., or (c) a condorsement process like the SEC has suggested. Regardless, convergence already is gradually occurring through cooperation between the FASB and IASB.

SEC Chairman Schapiro has indicated that the first time U.S. companies could be required to report under IFRS would be no earlier than 2015. In the meantime, although U.S. companies continue to follow U.S. GAAP, you should be aware of important differences that exist between U.S. GAAP and IFRS. In fact, beginning in 2011, IFRS are tested on the CPA exam along with U.S. GAAP. Therefore, International Financial Reporting Standards boxes are included throughout the text to highlight circumstances in which IFRS differs from U.S. GAAP. Your instructor may assign end-of-chapter IFRS questions, exercises, problems, and cases that explore these differences. Throughout the remainder of the text, IFRS-related material is marked with the globe icon that you see to the left of this paragraph.

The Establishment of Accounting Standards

● LO1–4

DUE PROCESS. When developing accounting standards, a standard setter must understand the nuances of the economic transactions the standards address and the views of key constituents concerning how accounting would best capture that economic reality. Therefore, the FASB undertakes a series of elaborate information-gathering steps before issuing an Accounting Standards Update. These steps include open hearings, deliberations, and requests for written comments from interested parties. Illustration 1–7 outlines the FASB's standard-setting process.

FINANCIAL Reporting Case

Q2, p. 3

Step	Explanation
1.	The Board receives requests/recommendations for possible projects and reconsideration of existing standards from various sources.
2.	The FASB Chairman decides whether to add a project to the technical agenda, subject to oversight by the Foundation's Board of Trustees and after appropriate consultation with FASB Members and others.
3.	The Board deliberates at one or more public meetings the various issues identified and analyzed by the staff.
4.	The Board issues an Exposure Draft. (In some projects, a Discussion Paper may be issued to obtain input at an early stage that is used to develop an Exposure Draft.)
5.	The Board holds a public roundtable meeting on the Exposure Draft, if necessary.
6.	The staff analyzes comment letters, public roundtable discussion, and any other information. The Board redeliberates the proposed provisions at public meetings.
7.	The Board issues an Accounting Standards Update describing amendments to the Accounting Standards Codification.

Illustration 1–7
The FASB's Standard-Setting Process

The FASB undertakes a series of information-gathering steps before issuing an Accounting Standards Update.

These steps are the FASB's attempt to acquire information to help determine the preferred method of accounting. However, as a practical matter this information gathering also exposes the FASB to much political pressure by various interest groups who want an accounting treatment that serves their economic best interest. As you will see later in this chapter, the FASB's concepts statements indicate that standards should present information in a neutral manner, rather than being designed to favor particular economic consequences, but sometimes politics intrudes on the standard-setting process.

POLITICS IN STANDARD SETTING. A change in accounting standards can result in a substantial redistribution of wealth within our economy. Therefore, it is no surprise that the FASB has had to deal with intense political pressure over controversial accounting standards, and sometimes has changed standards in response to that pressure.

One example of the effect of politics on standard setting occurred in the mid-1990's with respect to accounting for employee stock options. The accounting standards in place at that time typically did not recognize compensation expense if a company paid their employees with stock options rather than cash. Yet, the company was sacrificing something of value to compensate its employees. Therefore, the FASB proposed that companies recognize compensation expense in an amount equal to the fair value of the options, with some of the expense recognized in each of the periods in which the employee earned the options. Numerous companies (particularly in California's Silicon Valley, where high-tech companies had been compensating employees with stock options to a great extent) applied intense political pressure against this proposal, and eventually the FASB backed down and required only disclosure of options-related compensation expense in the notes to the financial statements. Nearly a decade later, this contentious issue resurfaced in a more amenable political climate, and the FASB issued a standard requiring expense recognition as originally proposed. This issue is discussed at greater length in Chapter 19.

Another example of politics in standard setting relates to accounting for business combinations. GAAP used to allow two separate and distinct methods of accounting for business combinations: the pooling of interests method and the purchase method. A key issue involved goodwill, an intangible asset that arises only in business combinations accounted for using the purchase method. Under the then-existing standards, goodwill was amortized (expensed) over its estimated useful life. To avoid that amortization expense, many companies incurred costs to structure their business combinations as a pooling of interests. The FASB proposed eliminating the pooling method. As you can guess, that proposal met with strong opposition. Companies that were actively engaged in business acquisitions argued that they would not undertake business combinations important to economic growth if they were required to use the purchase method, due to the negative impact on earnings caused by goodwill amortization. Eventually the FASB compromised.[21] In the final standard issued in 2001, only the purchase method, now called the acquisition method, is acceptable, but to soften the impact, the resulting goodwill is *not* amortized.[22] We discuss goodwill and its measurement in Chapters 10 and 11.

A recent example of the political process at work in standard setting is the controversy surrounding the implementation of the fair value accounting standard issued in 2007. Many financial assets and liabilities are reported at fair value in the balance sheet, and many types of fair value changes are included in net income. Some have argued that fair values were estimated in a manner that exacerbated the financial crisis of 2008–2009 by forcing financial institutions to take larger than necessary write-downs of financial assets in the illiquid markets that existed at that time. As discussed further in Chapter 12, pressure from lobbyists and politicians influenced the FASB to revise its guidance on recognizing investment losses in these situations, and ongoing pressure remains to reduce the extent to which fair value changes are included in the determination of net income.

---

[21] Jonathan Weil, "FASB Backs Down on Goodwill-Accounting Rules," *The Wall Street Journal* (December 7, 2000).

[22] FASB ASC 805: Business Combinations (previously "Business Combinations," *Statement of Financial Accounting Standards No. 141 (revised)* (Norwalk, Conn.: FASB, 2007)), and FASB ASC 350: Intangibles—Goodwill and Other (previously "Goodwill and Other Intangible Assets," *Statement of Financial Accounting Standards No. 142* (Norwalk, Conn.: FASB, 2001)).

CHAPTER 1 Environment and Theoretical Structure of Financial Accounting **15**

International Financial Reporting Standards

Politics in International Standard Setting. Political pressures on the IASB's standard-setting process are severe. One source of pressure comes from the international business community. Unlike the FASB, which is funded through fees paid by companies listing securities on stock exchanges, the IASB receives much of its funding through voluntary donations by accounting firms and corporations, and there is concern that this financial support may compromise the IASB's independence. In fact, one of the milestones specified by the SEC for the eventual adoption of IFRS in the U.S. is that the IASB's independence be increased by creating a funding mechanism more like the FASB's.

● LO1–11

Another source of political pressure arises from the fact that politicians from countries that use IFRS lobby for the standards they prefer. The European Union (EU) is a particularly important adopter of IFRS and utilizes a formal evaluation process for determining whether an IFRS standard will be endorsed for use in EU countries. Economic consequences for EU member nations are an important consideration in that process. For example, in 2003 and 2004 French banks lobbied against some aspects of accounting for financial instruments stridently enough that the EU eventually "carved out" two key provisions before endorsing the relevant accounting standard (IAS 39).[24] Similarly, in 2008 the EU successfully pressured the IASB to suspend its due process and immediately allow reclassification of investments so that EU banks

> **Charlie McCreevy, European Commissioner for Internal Markets and Services**
> Accounting is now far too important to be left solely to . . . accountants![23]

could avoid recognizing huge losses during a financial crisis.[25] Highlighting the importance of politics in the IASB, as of July 1, 2011, the chairman of the IASB is Hans Hoogervorst, a Dutch securities regulator with much diplomatic experience but no formal accounting background. Although the IASB's vice-chairman, Ian Mackintosh, has a long career in accounting and standard setting, the appointment of a nonaccountant as IASB Chairman perhaps signals a priority on political considerations.

Encouraging High-Quality Financial Reporting

Numerous factors affect the quality of financial reporting. In this section, we discuss the role of the auditor, recent reforms in financial reporting, and the debate about whether accounting standards should emphasize rules or underlying principles.

● LO1–5

The Role of the Auditor

It is the responsibility of management to apply GAAP appropriately. Another group, auditors, serves as an independent intermediary to help ensure that management has in fact appropriately applied GAAP in preparing the company's financial statements. Auditors examine (audit) financial statements to express a professional, independent opinion about whether the statements fairly present the company's financial position, its results of operations, and its cash flows in compliance with GAAP. Audits add credibility to the financial statements, increasing the confidence of those who rely on the information. Auditors, therefore, play an important role in the capital markets.

The report of the independent auditors of Dell Inc.'s financial statements is in the annual report information in Appendix B located at the back of the text. In that report, the accounting

FINANCIAL Reporting Case

Q3, p. 3

Auditors express an opinion on the compliance of financial statements with GAAP.

---

[23]Charlie McCreevy, Keynote Address, "Financial Reporting in a Changing World" Conference, Brussels, 5/7/2009.
[24]Stephen A. Zeff, "IFRS Developments in the USA and EU, and Some Implications for Australia," *Australian Accounting Review* 18 (2008), pp. 275–282.
[25]Sarah Deans and Dane Mott, "Lowering Standards," www.morganmarkets.com, 10/14/2008.

firm of PricewaterhouseCoopers LLP stated that "In our opinion, the consolidated financial statements listed in the accompanying index present fairly . . . , in conformity with accounting principles generally accepted in the United States of America." This is known as a clean opinion. Had there been any material departures from GAAP or other problems that caused the auditors to question the fairness of the statements, the report would have been modified to inform readers. Normally, companies correct any material misstatements that auditors identify in the course of an audit, so companies usually receive clean opinions. The audit report for public companies also provides the auditors' opinion on the effectiveness of the company's internal control over financial reporting. We discuss this second opinion in the next section.

Auditors offer credibility to financial statements.

In most states, only individuals licensed as certified public accountants (CPAs) can represent that the financial statements have been audited in accordance with generally accepted auditing standards. Requirements to be licensed as a CPA vary from state to state, but all states specify education, testing, and experience requirements. The testing requirement is to pass the Uniform CPA Examination.

Certified public accountants (CPAs) are licensed by states to provide audit services.

Financial Reporting Reform

Sarbanes-Oxley

The dramatic collapse of Enron in 2001 and the dismantling of the international public accounting firm of Arthur Andersen in 2002 severely shook U.S. capital markets. The credibility of the accounting profession itself as well as of corporate America was called into question. Public outrage over accounting scandals at high-profile companies like WorldCom, Xerox, Merck, Adelphia Communications, and others increased the pressure on lawmakers to pass measures that would restore credibility and investor confidence in the financial reporting process.

> **Paul Sarbanes—U.S. Senator**
> We confront an increasing crisis of confidence with the public's trust in our markets. If this continues, I think it poses a real threat to our economic health.[26]

Driven by these pressures, Congress acted swiftly and passed the *Public Company Accounting Reform and Investor Protection Act of 2002,* commonly referred to as the *Sarbanes-Oxley Act* or *SOX* for the two congressmen who sponsored the bill. SOX applies to public securities-issuing entities. It provides for the regulation of auditors and the types of services they furnish to clients, increases accountability of corporate executives, addresses conflicts of interest for securities analysts, and provides for stiff criminal penalties for violators. Illustration 1–8 outlines key provisions of the Act.

Section 404 is perhaps the most controversial provision of SOX. It requires that company management document internal controls and report on their adequacy. Auditors also must express an opinion on whether the company has maintained effective control over financial reporting.

No one argues the importance of adequate internal controls, but many argued that the benefits of Section 404 did not justify the costs of complying with it. Research provides evidence that 404 reports affect investors' risk assessments and companies' stock prices, indicating these reports are seen as useful by investors.[27] Unfortunately, it is not possible to quantify the more important benefit of potentially avoiding business failures like Enron by focusing attention on the implementation and maintenance of adequate internal controls.

The costs of 404 compliance initially were quite steep. For example, one survey of Fortune 1,000 companies estimated that large companies spent, on average, approximately $8.5 million and $4.8 million (including internal costs and auditor fees) during the first two years of the act to comply with 404 reporting requirements.[28] As expected, the costs dropped significantly in the second year, and likely continued to drop as the efficiency of internal control audits increased. Fortunately, many companies now perceive that the benefits of these internal control reports exceed their costs.[29]

We revisit Section 404 in Chapter 7 in the context of an introduction to internal controls.

---

[26]James Kuhnhenn, "Bush Vows to Punish Corporate Lawbreakers," *San Jose Mercury News* (July 9, 2002), p. 8A.
[27]Hollis Ashbaugh Skaife, Daniel W. Collins, William R. Kinney, Jr., and Ryan LaFond. "The Effect of SOX Internal Control Deficiencies on Firm Risk and Cost of Equity," *Journal of Accounting Research* 47 (2009), pp. 1–43.
[28]"Sarbanes-Oxley 404 Costs and Implementation Issues: Spring 2006 Survey Update," CRA International (April 17, 2006).
[29]Protiviti, Inc., *2011 Sarbanes-Oxley Compliance Survey* (June, 2011).

Key Provisions of the Sarbanes-Oxley Act:

- **Oversight board.** The five-member (two accountants) Public Company Accounting Oversight Board has the authority to establish standards dealing with auditing, quality control, ethics, independence and other activities relating to the preparation of audit reports, or can choose to delegate these responsibilities to the AICPA. Prior to the act, the AICPA set auditing standards. The SEC has oversight and enforcement authority.

- **Corporate executive accountability.** Corporate executives must personally certify the financial statements and company disclosures with severe financial penalties and the possibility of imprisonment for fraudulent misstatement.

- **Nonaudit services.** The law makes it unlawful for the auditors of public companies to perform a variety of nonaudit services for audit clients. Prohibited services include bookkeeping, internal audit outsourcing, appraisal or valuation services, and various other consulting services. Other nonaudit services, including tax services, require pre-approval by the audit committee of the company being audited.

- **Retention of work papers.** Auditors of public companies must retain all audit or review work papers for seven years or face the threat of a prison term for willful violations.

- **Auditor rotation.** Lead audit partners are required to rotate every five years. Mandatory rotation of audit firms came under consideration.

- **Conflicts of interest.** Audit firms are not allowed to audit public companies whose chief executives worked for the audit firm and participated in that company's audit during the preceding year.

- **Hiring of auditor.** Audit firms are hired by the audit committee of the board of directors of the company, not by company management.

- **Internal control.** Section 404 of the act requires that company management document and assess the effectiveness of all internal control processes that could affect financial reporting. The PCAOB's *Auditing Standard No. 2* (since replaced by *Auditing Standard No. 5*) requires that the company auditors express an opinion on whether the company has maintained effective internal control over financial reporting.

Illustration 1–8

Public Company Accounting Reform and Investor Protection Act of 2002 (Sarbanes-Oxley)

A Move Away from Rules-Based Standards?

The accounting scandals at Enron and other companies involved managers using elaborately structured transactions to try to circumvent specific rules in accounting standards. One consequence of those scandals was a rekindled debate over **principles-based**, or more recently termed **objectives-oriented**, versus **rules-based** accounting standards. In fact, a provision of the Sarbanes-Oxley Act required the SEC to study the issue and provide a report to Congress on its findings. That report, issued in July 2003, recommended that accounting standards be developed using an objectives-oriented approach.[30]

An objectives-oriented approach to standard setting emphasizes using professional judgment, as opposed to following a list of rules, when choosing how to account for a transaction. Proponents of an objectives-oriented approach argue that a focus on professional judgment means that there are few rules to sidestep, and we are more likely to arrive at an appropriate accounting treatment. Detractors, on the other hand, argue that the absence of detailed rules opens the door to even more abuse, because management can use the latitude provided by objectives to justify their preferred accounting approach. Even in the absence of intentional misuse, reliance on professional judgment might result in different interpretations for similar transactions, raising concerns about comparability. Also, detailed rules help auditors withstand pressure from clients who want a more favorable accounting treatment, and help companies ensure that they are complying with GAAP and avoid litigation or SEC inquiry. For these reasons, it's challenging to avoid providing detailed rules in the U.S. reporting environment. Given ongoing efforts to converge FASB and IASB standards, it is likely that this debate will continue.

Regardless of whether accounting standards are based more on rules or on objectives, prior research highlights that there is some potential for abuse, either by structuring

A principles-based, or objectives-oriented, approach to standard-setting stresses professional judgment, as opposed to following a list of rules.

---

[30]"Study Pursuant to Section 108 (d) of the Sarbanes-Oxley Act of 2002 on the Adoption by the United States Financial Reporting System of a Principles-Based Accounting System," Securities and Exchange Commission (July 2003).

transactions around precise rules or opportunistically interpreting underlying principles.[31] The key is whether management is dedicated to high-quality financial reporting. It appears that poor ethical values on the part of management are at the heart of accounting abuses and scandals like Enron and WorldCom, so we now turn to a discussion of ethics in the accounting profession.

Ethics in Accounting

Ethics **deals with the ability to distinguish right from wrong.**

Ethics is a term that refers to a code or moral system that provides criteria for evaluating right and wrong. An ethical dilemma is a situation in which an individual or group is faced with a decision that tests this code. Many of these dilemmas are simple to recognize and resolve. For example, have you ever been tempted to call your professor and ask for an extension on the due date of an assignment by claiming a pretended illness? Temptation like this will test your personal ethics.

Accountants, like others in the business world, are faced with many ethical dilemmas, some of which are complex and difficult to resolve. For instance, the capital markets' focus on near-term profits may tempt a company's management to bend or even break accounting rules to inflate reported net income. In these situations, technical competence is not enough to resolve the dilemma.

ETHICS AND PROFESSIONALISM.   One characteristic that distinguishes a profession from other occupations is the acceptance by its members of a responsibility for the interests of those it serves. Ethical behavior is expected of those engaged in a profession. That expectation often is articulated in a code of ethics. For example, law and medicine are professions that have their own codes of professional ethics. These codes provide guidance and rules to members in the performance of their professional responsibilities.

Public accounting has achieved widespread recognition as a profession. The AICPA, the national organization of certified public accountants, has its own Code of Professional Conduct that prescribes the ethical conduct members should strive to achieve. Similarly, the Institute of Management Accountants (IMA)—the primary national organization of accountants working in industry and government—has its own code of ethics, as does the Institute of Internal Auditors—the national organization of accountants providing internal auditing services for their own organizations.

ANALYTICAL MODEL FOR ETHICAL DECISIONS.   Ethical codes are informative and helpful, but the motivation to behave ethically must come from within oneself and not just from the fear of penalties for violating professional codes. Presented below is a sequence of steps that provide a framework for analyzing ethical issues. These steps can help you apply your own sense of right and wrong to ethical dilemmas:[32]

Step 1.   Determine the facts of the situation. This involves determining the who, what, where, when, and how.

Step 2.   Identify the ethical issue and the stakeholders. Stakeholders may include shareholders, creditors, management, employees, and the community.

Step 3.   Identify the values related to the situation. For example, in some situations confidentiality may be an important value that might conflict with the right to know.

Step 4.   Specify the alternative courses of action.

Step 5.   Evaluate the courses of action specified in step 4 in terms of their consistency with the values identified in step 3. This step may or may not lead to a suggested course of action.

---

[31]Mark W. Nelson, John A. Elliott, and Robin L. Tarpley, "Evidence From Auditors About Managers' and Auditors Earnings Management Decisions," *The Accounting Review* 77 (2002), pp. 175–202.

[32]Adapted from Harold Q. Langenderfer and Joanne W. Rockness, "Integrating Ethics into the Accounting Curriculum: Issues, Problems, and Solutions," *Issues in Accounting Education* (Spring 1989). These steps are consistent with those provided by the American Accounting Association's Advisory Committee on Professionalism and Ethics in their publication *Ethics in the Accounting Curriculum: Cases and Readings, 1990.*

Step 6. Identify the consequences of each possible course of action. If step 5 does not provide a course of action, assess the consequences of each possible course of action for all of the stakeholders involved.

Step 7. Make your decision and take any indicated action.

Ethical dilemmas are presented throughout the text. These dilemmas are designed to raise your awareness of accounting issues with ethical ramifications. The analytical steps outlined above provide a framework you can use to evaluate these situations. In addition, your instructor may assign end-of-chapter ethics cases for further discussion and application.

Ethical Dilemma

You recently have been employed by a large retail chain that sells sporting goods. One of your tasks is to help prepare periodic financial statements for external distribution. The chain's largest creditor, National Savings & Loan, requires quarterly financial statements, and you are currently working on the statements for the three-month period ending June 30, 2013.

During the months of May and June, the company spent $1,200,000 on a hefty radio and TV advertising campaign. The $1,200,000 included the costs of producing the commercials as well as the radio and TV time purchased to air the commercials. All of the costs were charged to advertising expense. The company's chief financial officer (CFO) has asked you to prepare a June 30 adjusting entry to remove the costs from advertising expense and to set up an asset called *prepaid advertising* that will be expensed in July. The CFO explained that "This advertising campaign has led to significant sales in May and June and I think it will continue to bring in customers through the month of July. By recording the ad costs as an asset, we can match the cost of the advertising with the additional July sales. Besides, if we expense the advertising in May and June, we will show an operating loss on our income statement for the quarter. The bank requires that we continue to show quarterly profits in order to maintain our loan in good standing."

THE CONCEPTUAL FRAMEWORK

PART B

● LO1–6

FINANCIAL Reporting Case

Q4, p. 3

The conceptual framework does not prescribe GAAP. It provides an underlying foundation for accounting standards.

Sturdy buildings are built on sound foundations. The U.S. Constitution is the foundation for the laws of our land. The conceptual framework has been described as an "Accounting Constitution" because it provides the underlying foundation for U.S. accounting standards. More formally, it is a coherent system of interrelated objectives and fundamentals that is intended to lead to consistent standards and that prescribes the nature, function, and limits of financial accounting and reporting. The fundamentals are the underlying concepts of accounting that guide the selection of events to be accounted for, the measurement of those events, and the means of summarizing and communicating them to interested parties.[33] The conceptual framework provides structure and direction to financial accounting and reporting but does not directly prescribe GAAP.

The FASB disseminates this framework through Statements of Financial Accounting Concepts *(SFACs)*. *SFAC 1* and *SFAC 2* deal with the Objectives and Qualitative Characteristics of financial information, respectively. *SFAC 3,* describing the elements of financial statements, was superseded by *SFAC 6*. The objectives of financial reporting for nonprofit organizations are the subject of *SFAC 4* and are not covered in this text. Concept Statements 5 and 7 deal with recognition and measurement.

Earlier in the chapter we discussed the ongoing efforts of standard setters to converge U.S. GAAP and International Financial Reporting Standards. As part of that process, the FASB and the IASB are working together to develop a common and improved conceptual

---

[33]"Conceptual Framework for Financial Accounting and Reporting: Elements of Financial Statements and Their Measurement," *Discussion Memorandum* (Stamford, Conn.: FASB, 1976), p. 2.

framework that will provide the foundation for developing principles-based, common standards. Only the first phase of the project is complete. That phase contains two chapters which replace *SFAC 1* and *SFAC 2,* and was issued as *SFAC 8* in 2010.[34] As the project progresses, prior Concepts Statements will be replaced by new chapters in *SFAC* 8. It likely will take several years before the entire project is completed.

In the remainder of this section we discuss the components of the conceptual framework that influence financial statements as depicted in Illustration 1–9. The financial statements and their elements are most informative when they possess specific qualitative characteristics. Proper recognition and measurement of financial information rely on several assumptions and principles that underlie the financial reporting process.

Illustration 1–9

The Conceptual Framework

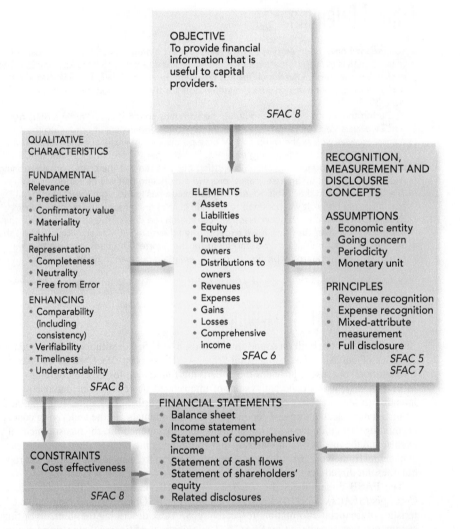

Our discussions of the objective and qualitative characteristics of financial reporting information are based on *SFAC 8,* while the remainder of our conceptual framework coverage relies on the relevant FASB Concept Statements still in effect. We discuss and illustrate the financial statements themselves in subsequent chapters.

---

[34]"Conceptual Framework for Financial Reporting: Chapter 1, The Objective of General Purpose Financial Reporting, and Chapter 3, Qualitative Characteristics of Useful Financial Information," *Statement of Financial Accounting Concepts No. 8* (Norwalk, Conn.: FASB, 2010).

International Financial Reporting Standards

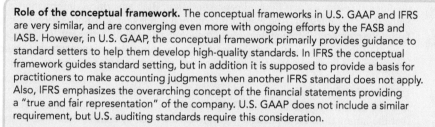

Role of the conceptual framework. The conceptual frameworks in U.S. GAAP and IFRS are very similar, and are converging even more with ongoing efforts by the FASB and IASB. However, in U.S. GAAP, the conceptual framework primarily provides guidance to standard setters to help them develop high-quality standards. In IFRS the conceptual framework guides standard setting, but in addition it is supposed to provide a basis for practitioners to make accounting judgments when another IFRS standard does not apply. Also, IFRS emphasizes the overarching concept of the financial statements providing a "true and fair representation" of the company. U.S. GAAP does not include a similar requirement, but U.S. auditing standards require this consideration.

● LO1–11

Objective of Financial Reporting

● LO1–7

The objective of general purpose financial reporting is to provide financial information about companies that is useful to capital providers in making decisions. For example, investors decide whether to buy, sell, or hold equity or debt securities, and creditors decide whether to provide or settle loans.[35] Information that is useful to capital providers may also be useful to other users of financial reporting information, such as regulators or taxing authorities.

Both investors and creditors are directly interested in the amount, timing, and uncertainty of a company's future cash flows. Information about a company's economic resources (assets) and claims against resources (liabilities) also is useful. Not only does this information about resources and claims provide insight into future cash flows, it also helps decision makers identify the company's financial strengths and weaknesses and assess liquidity and solvency.

Qualitative Characteristics of Financial Reporting Information

What characteristics should information have to best meet the objective of financial reporting? Illustration 1–10 indicates the desirable qualitative characteristics of financial reporting information, presented in the form of a hierarchy of their perceived importance. Notice that these characteristics are intended to enhance the decision usefulness of information.

Illustration 1–10   Hierarchy of Qualitative Characteristics of Financial Information

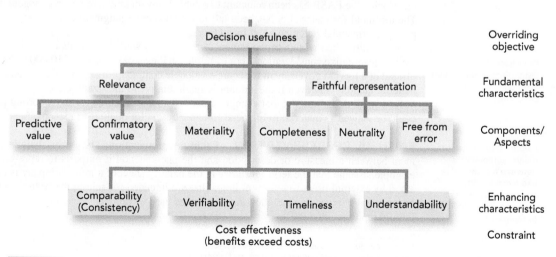

QUALITATIVE CHARACTERISTICS

_____
[35]Ibid., par. OB2.

Fundamental Qualitative Characteristics

To be useful for decision making, information should possess the qualities of *relevance* and *faithful representation*.

For financial information to be useful, it should possess the fundamental decision-specific qualities of relevance and faithful representation. Both are critical. Information is of little value if it's not relevant. And even if information is relevant, it is not as useful if it doesn't faithfully represent the economic phenomenon it purports to represent. Let's look closer at each of these two qualitative characteristics, including the components that make those characteristics desirable. We also consider other characteristics that enhance usefulness.

RELEVANCE.   Obviously, to make a difference in the decision process, information must be relevant to the decision. Relevance in the context of financial reporting means that the information must possess predictive value and/or confirmatory value, typically both. For example, current-period net income has predictive value if it helps users predict a company's future cash flows, and it has confirmatory value if it helps investors confirm or change their prior assessments regarding a company's cash-flow generating ability.

Predictive and confirmatory value are central to the concept of "earnings quality," the ability of reported earnings (income) to predict a company's future earnings. We revisit this concept frequently throughout this textbook in order to explore the impact on earnings quality of various topics under discussion. For instance, in Chapter 4 we discuss the contents of the income statement and certain classifications used in that statement to help analysts separate a company's transitory earnings from its permanent earnings. This separation is critical to a meaningful prediction of future earnings because it's permanent earnings that are likely to recur. In later chapters, we look at how various financial reporting decisions affect earnings quality.

Information is *material* if it has an effect on decisions.

Financial information is material if omitting it or misstating it could affect users' decisions. Materiality is an aspect of relevance that depends on a company's particular situation and is based on the nature or magnitude of the item that is being reported. If information is immaterial, it's not relevant.

One consequence of considering materiality is that GAAP need not be followed if an item is immaterial. For example, GAAP requires that receivables be measured at their "net realizable value." If bad debts are anticipated, they should be estimated and subtracted from the face amount of receivables for balance sheet measurement.[36] However, if the amount of anticipated bad debts is not considered to be large enough to affect decisions made by users, it's OK to wait and just record the effects of bad debts when the receivable has gone bad rather than having to estimate bad debts for existing receivables.[37]

The threshold for materiality often depends on the *relative* dollar amount of the transaction. For example, $10,000 in total anticipated bad debts for a multibillion dollar company like Dell would not be considered material. This same $10,000 amount, however, might easily be material for a neighborhood pizza parlor. Because of the context-specific nature of materiality, the FASB has been reluctant to establish any quantitative materiality guidelines. The threshold for materiality has been left to the subjective judgment of the company preparing the financial statements and its auditors.

Professional judgment determines what amount is material in each situation.

Materiality often relates to the nature of the item as well. It depends on qualitative as well as quantitative considerations. For example, an illegal payment of a $10,000 bribe to an official of a foreign government to secure a valuable contract probably would be considered material qualitatively even if the amount is small relative to the size of the company. Similarly, a small dollar amount that changes a net loss to a net income for the reporting period could be viewed as material to financial statement users for qualitative reasons.[38]

Faithful representation means agreement between a measure and a real-world phenomenon that the measure is supposed to represent.

FAITHFUL REPRESENTATION.   Faithful representation exists when there is agreement between a measure or description and the phenomenon it purports to represent. For example, assume that the term *inventory* in the balance sheet of a retail company is understood by external users to represent items that are intended for sale in the ordinary course of business. If inventory includes, say, machines used to produce inventory, then it lacks faithful representation.

---

[36]This is called the *allowance method* of accounting for bad debts.
[37]This is called the *direct write-off method* of accounting for bad debts.
[38]Conceptual Framework for Financial Reporting: Chapter 1, The Objective of General Purpose Financial Reporting, and Chapter 3, Qualitative Characteristics of Useful Financial Information, Statement of Financial Accounting Concepts No. 8 (Norwalk, Conn.: FASB, 2010).

To break it down further, faithful representation requires that information be *complete, neutral,* and *free from error.* A depiction of an economic phenomenon is complete if it includes all the information necessary for faithful representation of the economic phenomena that it purports to represent.[39] Omitting a portion of that information can cause it to be false or misleading and thus not helpful.

> A depiction is *complete* if it includes all information necessary for faithful representation.

A financial accounting standard, and the standard-setting process, is "neutral" if it is free from bias. You learned earlier that changes in accounting standards can lead to adverse economic consequences for certain companies and that political pressure is sometimes brought to bear on the standard-setting process in hopes of achieving particular outcomes. Accounting standards should be established with the goal of providing high-quality information, and should try not to achieve particular social outcomes or favor particular groups or companies. The FASB faces a difficult task in maintaining neutrality in the face of economic consequences and resulting political pressures.

> *Neutrality* implies freedom from bias.

Representational faithfulness also is enhanced if information is free from error, meaning that there are no errors or omissions in the description of the amount or the process used to report the amount. Uncertainty is a fact of life when we measure many items of financial information included in financial statements. Estimates are common, and some inaccuracy is likely. An estimate is represented faithfully if it is described clearly and accurately as being an estimate, and financial statement users are given enough information to understand the potential for inaccuracy that exists.

> Representational faithfulness is enhanced if information is *free from error.*

Many accountants have recommended that we deal with the potential for error by employing conservatism. Conservatism means that accountants require greater verification before recognizing good news than bad news. The result is that losses are reflected in net income more quickly than are gains, and net assets tend to be biased downwards.

> *Conservatism* is inconsistent with neutrality.

SFAC 8 explicitly rejects conservatism as a desirable characteristic of accounting information, stating that conservatism undermines representational faithfulness by being inconsistent with neutrality. Nevertheless, some accounting practices, such as the lower-of-cost-or-market method for measuring inventory (Chapter 9), appear to be generated by a desire to be conservative. One justification for these practices is that investors and creditors who lose money on their investments are less likely to sue the company if bad news has been exaggerated and good news underestimated. Another justification is that conservative accounting can trigger debt covenants that allow creditors to protect themselves from bad management. So, despite the lack of support for conservatism in the conceptual framework, it is likely to persist as an important consideration in accounting practice and in the application of some accounting standards.

Enhancing Qualitative Characteristics

Illustration 1–10 identifies four *enhancing* qualitative characteristics, *comparability (including consistency), verifiability, timeliness,* and *understandability.*

Comparability helps users see similarities and differences between events and conditions. We already have discussed the importance of investors and creditors being able to compare information *among companies* to make their resource allocation decisions. Closely related to comparability is the notion that consistency of accounting practices over time permits valid comparisons *among different reporting periods.* The predictive and confirmatory value of information is enhanced if users can compare the performance of a company over time.[40] In the Dell financial statements and disclosure notes, notice that disclosure Note 1 includes a summary of significant accounting policies. If Dell were to change one of these policies, new numbers might not be comparable to numbers measured under a previous policy. To be sure readers are aware of the change, Dell would need to provide full disclosure in the notes to the financial statements.

> Accounting information should be *comparable* across different companies and over different time periods.

> Accounting information is *consistent* if it is measured and reported the same way in each time period.

Verifiability implies that different knowledgeable and independent measurers would reach consensus regarding whether information is a faithful representation of what it is intended to

> Information is *verifiable* if different measurers would reach consensus about whether it is representationally faithful.

---

[39]Ibid., par. QC13.

[40]Companies occasionally do change their accounting practices, which makes it difficult for users to make comparisons among different reporting periods. Chapter 4 and Chapter 20 describe the disclosures that a company makes in this situation to restore consistency among periods.

depict. Direct verification involves observing the item being depicted. For example, the historical cost of a parcel of land to be reported in a company's balance sheet usually is highly verifiable. The cost can be traced to an exchange transaction, the purchase of the land. On the other hand, the fair value of that land is much more difficult to verify. Appraisers could differ in their assessment of fair value. Verification of their estimates would be indirect, involving examination of their valuation models and assessments of the reasonableness of model inputs. The term *objectivity* often is linked to verifiability. The historical cost of the land is objective and easy to verify, but the land's fair value is subjective, and may be influenced by the measurer's past experience and biases. A measurement that is subjective is more difficult to verify, which may make users doubt its representational faithfulness.

> Information is *timely* if it is available to users before a decision is made.

Timeliness also is important for information to be useful. Information is timely when it's available to users early enough to allow them to use it in their decision process. The need for timely information requires that companies provide information on a periodic basis. To enhance timeliness, the SEC requires its registrants to submit financial statement information on a quarterly as well as on an annual basis for each fiscal year.

> Information is *understandable* if users can comprehend it.

Understandability means that users must be able to comprehend the information within the context of the decision being made. This is a user-specific quality because users will differ in their ability to comprehend any set of information. The overriding objective of financial reporting is to provide comprehensible information to those who have a *reasonable understanding* of business and economic activities and are diligent in studying the information.

Key Constraint: Cost Effectiveness

Most of us learn early in life that we can't get everything we want. The latest electronic gadget may have all the qualitative characteristics that current technology can provide, but limited resources may lead us to buy a model with fewer bells and whistles. Cost effectiveness constrains the accounting choices we make. The benefits of endowing financial information with all the qualitative characteristics we've discussed must exceed the costs of doing so.

> Information is *cost effective* only if the benefit of increased *decision usefulness* exceeds the costs of providing that information.

> The costs of providing financial information include any possible adverse economic consequences of accounting standards.

The costs of providing financial information include those of gathering, processing, and disseminating information. There also are costs to users when interpreting information. In addition, costs include possible adverse economic consequences of implementing accounting standards. For example, consider the requirement that companies that have more than one operating segment must disclose certain disaggregated financial information.[41] In addition to the costs of information gathering, processing, and communicating that information, many companies feel that this reporting requirement imposes what could be called *competitive disadvantage costs*. These companies are concerned that their competitors will gain some advantage from having access to the disaggregated data.

The perceived benefit from this or any accounting standard is increased *decision usefulness* of the information provided, which, ideally, improves the resource allocation process. It is inherently impossible to quantify this benefit. The elaborate information-gathering process undertaken by the FASB in setting accounting standards is an attempt to assess both costs and benefits of a proposed accounting standard, even if in a subjective, nonquantifiable manner.

Elements of Financial Statements

> The 10 elements of financial statements defined in *SFAC 6* describe financial position and periodic performance.

SFAC 6 defines 10 elements of financial statements. These elements are "the building blocks with which financial statements are constructed—the classes of items that financial statements comprise."[42] They focus directly on items related to reporting financial position and measuring performance. The *accrual accounting* model actually is embodied in the element definitions. For now, we list and define the elements in Illustration 1–11. You will learn much more about these elements in subsequent chapters.

---

[41]FASB ASC 280: Segment Reporting (previously "Disclosures about Segments of an Enterprise and Related Information," *Statement of Financial Accounting Standards No. 131* (Norwalk, Conn.: FASB, 1997)).

[42]"Elements of Financial Statements," *Statement of Financial Accounting Concepts No. 6* (Stamford, Conn.: FASB, 1985), par. 5.

Elements of Financial Statements	
Assets	Probable future economic benefits obtained or controlled by a particular entity as a result of past transactions or events.
Liabilities	Probable future sacrifices of economic benefits arising from present obligations of a particular entity to transfer assets or provide services to other entities in the future as a result of past transactions or events.
Equity (or net assets)	Called shareholders' equity or stockholders' equity for a corporation, it is the residual interest in the assets of an entity that remains after deducting its liabilities.
Investments by owners	Increases in equity of a particular business enterprise resulting from transfers to it from other entities of something of value to obtain or increase ownership interests in it.
Distributions to owners	Decreases in equity of a particular enterprise resulting from transfers to owners.
Comprehensive income	The change in equity of a business enterprise during a period from transactions and other events and circumstances from nonowner sources. It includes all changes in equity during a period except those resulting from investments by owners and distributions to owners.
Revenues	Inflows or other enhancements of assets of an entity or settlements of its liabilities during a period from delivering or producing goods, rendering services, or other activities that constitute the entity's ongoing major or central operations.
Expenses	Outflows or other using up of assets or incurrences of liabilities during a period from delivering or producing goods, rendering services, or other activities that constitute the entity's ongoing major or central operations.
Gains	Increases in equity from peripheral or incidental transactions of an entity.
Losses	Represent decreases in equity arising from peripheral or incidental transactions of an entity.

Illustration 1–11

Elements of Financial Statements

Underlying Assumptions

● LO1–8

Though not emphasized in the FASB's concepts statements, four basic assumptions underlie GAAP: (1) the economic entity assumption, (2) the going concern assumption, (3) the periodicity assumption, and (4) the monetary unit assumption. These assumptions identify the entity that is being reported on, the assumption that the entity will continue to exist, and the frequency and denomination in which reports occur.

Economic Entity Assumption

An essential assumption is that all economic events can be identified with a particular *economic entity*. Investors desire information about an economic entity that corresponds to their ownership interest. For example, if you were considering buying some ownership stock in Google, you would want information on the various operating units that constitute Google. You would need information not only about its United States operations but also about its European and other international operations. The financial information for the various companies (subsidiaries) in which Google owns a controlling interest (greater than 50% ownership of voting stock) should be combined with that of Google (the parent) to provide a complete picture. The parent and its subsidiaries are separate *legal* entities but one *accounting* entity.

The *economic entity assumption* presumes that economic events can be identified specifically with an economic entity.

Another key aspect of this assumption is the distinction between the economic activities of owners and those of the company. For example, the economic activities of a sole proprietorship, Uncle Jim's Restaurant, should be separated from the activities of its owner, Uncle Jim. Uncle Jim's personal residence, for instance, is not an asset of the business.

Going Concern Assumption

Another necessary assumption is that, in the absence of information to the contrary, we anticipate that a business entity will continue to operate indefinitely. Accountants realize that the going concern assumption does not always hold since there certainly are many business failures. However, this assumption is critical to many broad and specific accounting principles. For example, the assumption provides justification for measuring many assets based on their historical costs. If it were known that an enterprise would cease operations in the near future, assets and liabilities would be measured at their current liquidation values. Similarly, when we depreciate a building over an estimated life of 40 years, we assume the business will operate that long.

Financial statements of a company presume the business is a going concern.

Periodicity Assumption

The periodicity assumption relates to the qualitative characteristic of *timeliness*. External users need *periodic* information to make decisions. This need for periodic information requires that the economic life of a company (presumed to be indefinite) be divided into artificial time periods for financial reporting. Corporations whose securities are publicly traded are required to provide financial information to the SEC on a quarterly and annual basis.[43] Financial statements often are prepared on a monthly basis for banks and others that might need more timely information.

The periodicity assumption allows the life of a company to be divided into artificial time periods to provide timely information.

For many companies, the annual time period (the fiscal year) is the calendar year. However, other companies have chosen a fiscal year that does not correspond to the calendar year. The accounting profession and the SEC advocate that companies adopt a fiscal year that corresponds to their natural business year. A natural business year is the 12-month period that ends when the business activities of a company reach their lowest point in the annual cycle. For example, many retailers, Walmart for example, have adopted a fiscal year ending on January 31. Business activity in January generally is quite slow following the very busy Christmas period. We can see from the Dell financial statements that the company's fiscal year ends at the end of January. The Campbell Soup Company's fiscal year ends in July; Clorox's in June; and Monsanto's in August.

Monetary Unit Assumption

The monetary unit or measurement scale used in financial statements is nominal units of money, without any adjustment for changes in purchasing power. In the United States, the U.S. dollar is the monetary unit used in financial statements. In the EU, the euro is the monetary unit. Other countries use other currencies as their monetary units.

The monetary unit assumption states that financial statement elements should be measured in a particular monetary unit (in the United States, the U.S. dollar).

One problem with use of a monetary unit like the dollar or the euro is that it is presumed to be stable over time. That is, the value of the dollar, in terms of its ability to purchase certain goods and services, is assumed to be constant over time. This assumption obviously does not strictly hold. The U.S. economy has experienced periods of rapidly changing prices. To the extent that prices are unstable, and machines, trucks, and buildings were purchased at different times, the monetary unit used to measure them is not the same. The effect of changing prices on financial information generally is discussed elsewhere in your accounting curriculum, often in an advanced accounting course.

Illustration 1–12 summaries the four assumptions underlying GAAP.

---

[43]The report that must be filed for the first three quarters of each fiscal year is Form 10-Q and the annual report is Form 10-K.

Assumptions	Description
Economic entity	All economic events can be identified with a particular economic entity.
Going concern	In the absence of information to the contrary, it is anticipated that a business entity will continue to operate indefinitely.
Periodicity	The life of a company can be divided into artificial time periods to provide timely information to external users.
Monetary unit	In the United States, financial statement elements should be measured in terms of the U.S. dollar.

Illustration 1–12
Summary of Assumptions Underlying GAAP

Recognition, Measurement, and Disclosure Concepts

Now that we have identified the various elements and underlying assumptions of the financial statements, we discuss *when* the elements should be recognized (recorded) and how they should be *measured* and *disclosed.* For example, an asset was previously defined as a probable future economic benefit obtained or controlled by a company as a result of past transactions or events. But *when* should the asset be recorded, at *what* amount, and what other important information about the asset should be provided in the financial statements? *SFAC 5* addresses these issues. Recognition refers to the process of admitting information into the financial statements. Measurement is the process of associating numerical amounts with the elements. Disclosure refers to the process of including additional pertinent information in the financial statements and accompanying notes.

● **LO1–9**

Recognition

GENERAL RECOGNITION CRITERIA.   According to *SFAC 5,* an item should be recognized in the basic financial statements when it meets the following four criteria, subject to a cost effectiveness constraint and materiality threshold:

1. *Definition.* The item meets the definition of an element of financial statements.
2. *Measurability.* The item has a relevant attribute measurable with sufficient reliability.
3. *Relevance.* The information about it is capable of making a difference in user decisions.
4. *Reliability.* The information is representationally faithful, verifiable, and neutral.[44]

Recognition criteria

These obviously are very general guidelines. *SFAC 5* provides further guidance with respect to revenue and expense recognition, and you will learn about more specific guidelines throughout this book.

REVENUE RECOGNITION: REALIZATION.   Revenues are inflows of assets resulting from providing a product or service to a customer. An income statement should report the results of these activities only for the time period specified in the financial statements. Therefore, the *timing* of revenue recognition is a key element of earnings measurement. Not adhering to revenue recognition criteria could result in overstating revenue and hence net income in one reporting period and, consequently, understating revenue and net income in another period.

    The realization principle requires that two criteria be satisfied before revenue can be recognized:

According to the *realization principle*, revenue should be recognized when the earnings process is virtually complete and collection is reasonably assured.

1. The earnings process is judged to be complete or virtually complete.
2. There is reasonable certainty as to the collectibility of the asset to be received (usually cash).

---

[44]"Recognition and Measurement in Financial Statements," *Statement of Financial Accounting Concepts No. 5* (Stamford, Conn.: FASB, 1984), par. 63. *SFAC 8* has replaced reliability with faithful representation as the second primary qualitative characteristic of financial information.

Financial Accounting Theory

These criteria help ensure that a company doesn't record revenue until it has performed all or most of its earnings activities for a financially capable buyer. Notice that these criteria allow for the implementation of the accrual accounting model. Revenue should be recognized in the period it is earned, *not necessarily in the period in which cash is received.*

The timing of revenue recognition also affects the timing of asset recognition. When revenue is recognized by crediting a revenue account, the corresponding debit typically increases some asset, usually cash or an account receivable.

Both revenue recognition criteria usually are met at the point-of-sale.

The primary earnings activity that triggers the recognition of revenue is known as the *critical event.* The critical event for many businesses occurs at the point-of-sale. This usually occurs when the goods or services sold to the buyer are *delivered* (i.e., title is transferred). However, some revenue-producing activities require revenue recognition over time, rather than at one particular point in time. For example, banks earn interest revenue associated with loans outstanding with the passage of time. We discuss revenue recognition in considerable depth in Chapter 5, and discuss upcoming changes to revenue recognition requirements in the Addendum to Chapter 5.

EXPENSE RECOGNITION: MATCHING. Expenses were defined earlier in the chapter as "outflows or other using up of assets or incurrences of liabilities." When are expenses recognized? In practice, expense recognition often matches revenues and expenses that arise from the same transactions or other events. There is a cause-and-effect relationship between revenue and expense recognition implicit in this approach. In a given period, revenue is recognized according to the realization principle, and the matching principle then requires that all expenses incurred in generating that revenue also be recognized.[45] The net result is a measure—net income—that identifies the amount of profit or loss for the period provided by operations.

According to the matching principle, expenses should be recognized in the period in which they produce revenues.

Although these concepts are straightforward, their implementation can be difficult, because many expenses are not incurred *directly* to produce a particular amount of revenue. Instead, the association between revenue and many expenses is indirect. Therefore, expense recognition is implemented by one of four different approaches, depending on the nature of the specific expense:[46]

- Based on an exact cause-and-effect relationship. This approach is appropriate for *cost of goods sold,* as one example. There is a definite cause-and-effect relationship between Dell Inc.'s revenue from the sale of personal computers and the costs to produce those computers. Commissions paid to salespersons for obtaining revenues also is an example of an expense recognized based on this approach.

- By associating an expense with the revenues recognized in a specific time period. Many expenses can be related only to periods of time during which revenue is earned. For example, the monthly salary paid to an office worker is not directly related to any specific revenue event. Instead, the employee provides benefits to the company for that one month that *indirectly* relate to the revenue recognized in that same period.

- By a systematic and rational allocation to specific time periods. Some costs are incurred to acquire assets that provide benefits to the company for more than one reporting period, so we recognize expenses over those time periods. For example, straight-line depreciation is a "systematical and rational" way to allocate the cost of equipment to the periods in which that equipment is used to produce revenue.

---

[45]Although the term *matching principle* is used frequently to refer to this expense recognition practice, the conceptual framework does not include that term. Rather, *SFACs 5* and *6* discuss matching as a result of recognizing expenses and revenues that arise from the same underlying transactions or events. Standard setters are reluctant to apply matching more broadly, because they are concerned that doing so could result in inappropriately recognizing as assets some amounts that do not provide "probable future economic benefits," and therefore don't meet the definition of an asset. We discuss this topic more in the "Evolving GAAP" section at the end of this chapter.

[46]"Elements of Financial Statements—a replacement of FASB Concepts Statement No. 3 (incorporating an amendment of FASB Concepts Statement No. 2)" *Statement of Financial Accounting Concepts No. 6* (Norwalk, Conn.: FASB, 1985).

- **In the period incurred, without regard to related revenues.** Sometimes costs are incurred, but it is impossible to determine in which period or periods, if any, related revenues will occur. For example, let's say Google spends $1 million for a series of television commercials. It's difficult to determine when, how much, or even whether additional revenues occur as a result of that particular series of ads. As a result, we recognize advertising expenditures as expenses in the period incurred.

The timing of expense recognition also affects the timing of asset and liability recognition and de-recognition. When we debit an expense, the corresponding credit usually either decreases an asset (for example, decreasing cash because it was used to pay an employee's salary) or increases a liability (for example, increasing salaries payable to accrue wages that will be paid at a later date).

Measurement

If an amount is to be recognized, it also must be measured. As indicated in *SFAC 5,* GAAP currently employs a "mixed attribute" measurement model. If you look at a balance sheet, for instance, you might see land measured at historical cost, accounts receivable at net realizable value, a liability at the present value of cash payments, and an investment at fair value. The attribute chosen to measure a particular item should be the one that maximizes the combination of relevance and representational faithfulness. *SFAC 5* lists five measurement attributes employed in GAAP:

1. Historical cost
2. Net realizable value
3. Current cost
4. Present (or discounted) value of future cash flows
5. Fair value

These different measurement attributes often indicate the same amount, particularly when the amount is initially recognized. However, sometimes they differ in important ways.

HISTORICAL COST.   We often measure assets and liabilities based on their *original transaction value,* that is, their *historical cost.* Some accountants refer to this practice as applying the *historical cost principle.* For an asset, historical cost equals the value of what is given in exchange (usually cash) for the asset at its initial acquisition. For liabilities, it is the current cash equivalent received in exchange for assuming the liability. Historical cost for long-lived, revenue-producing assets such as equipment typically is adjusted subsequent to its initial measurement by recognizing depreciation or amortization.

> *Historical cost* bases measurements on the amount given or received in the exchange transaction.

Why base measurement on historical costs? First, historical cost provides important cash flow information as it represents the cash or cash equivalent paid for an asset or received in exchange for the assumption of a liability. Second, because historical cost valuation is the result of an exchange transaction between two independent parties, the agreed-upon exchange value is objective and highly verifiable.

NET REALIZABLE VALUE.   Some assets are measured at their *net realizable value,* which is the amount of cash into which an asset is expected to be converted in the ordinary course of business. For example, if customers purchased goods or services on account for $10,000, and if $2,000 in bad debts were anticipated, net receivables should be valued at $8,000, the net realizable value. Departures from historical cost measurement such as this provide useful information to aid in the prediction of future cash flows.

> *Net realizable value* bases measurements on the amount of cash into which the asset or liability will be converted in the ordinary course of business.

CURRENT COST   Some inventories are reported at their current replacement cost, which is measured by the cost that would be incurred to purchase or reproduce the goods. This topic is discussed further in Chapter 9.

Present value bases measurement on future cash flows discounted for the time value of money.

PRESENT VALUE. Because of its importance to many accounting measurements, *present value* is the focus of an FASB concept statement, *SFAC 7,* which provides a framework for using future cash flows as the basis for accounting measurement and also asserts that the objective in valuing an asset or liability using present value is to approximate its fair value.[47] We explore the topic of present value in more depth in Chapter 6 and the application of present value in accounting measurement in subsequent chapters.

Fair value bases measurements on the price that would be received to sell assets or transfer liabilities in an orderly market transaction.

FAIR VALUE. We measure many financial assets and liabilities at *fair value* (called *current market value* originally in *SFAC 5*). Also, we use fair values when determining whether the value of nonfinancial assets like property, plant, equipment and intangible assets has been impaired. Given the complexity and growing importance of this measurement attribute, we discuss it in some detail.

Fair value is defined as:

The price that would be received to sell assets or paid to transfer a liability in an orderly transaction between market participants at the measurement date.

A key aspect of this definition is its focus on the perspective of *market participants.* For instance, if a company buys a competitor's patent, not intending to use it but merely to keep the competitor from using it, the company still will have to assign a value to the asset because a market participant would find value in using the patent.

The FASB has provided a framework for measuring fair value whenever fair value is called for in applying generally accepted accounting principles.[48] The IASB recently converged to use the same framework.[49] In the framework, three types of valuation techniques can be used to measure fair value. *Market approaches* base valuation on market information.

Fair value can be measured using:
1. Market approaches.
2. Income approaches.
3. Cost approaches.

For example, the value of a share of a company's stock that's not traded actively could be estimated by multiplying the earnings of that company by the P/E (price of shares/earnings) multiples of similar companies. *Income approaches* estimate fair value by first estimating future amounts (for example, earnings or cash flows) and then mathematically converting those amounts to a single present value. You will see how to apply such techniques in Chapter 6 when we discuss time value of money concepts. *Cost approaches* determine value by estimating the amount that would be required to buy or construct an asset of similar quality and condition. A firm can use one or more of these valuation approaches, depending on availability of information, and should try to use them consistently unless changes in circumstances require a change in approach.

To increase consistency and comparability in applying this definition, the framework provides a "hierarchy" that prioritizes the inputs companies should use when determining fair value. The priority is based on three broad preference levels. The higher the level (Level 1 is the highest), the more preferable the input. The framework encourages companies to strive to obtain the highest level input available for each situation. Illustration 1–13 describes the type of inputs and provides an example for each level.

Companies also must provide detailed disclosures about their use of fair value measurements. The disclosures include a description of the inputs used to measure fair value. For recurring fair value measurements that rely on significant *unobservable* inputs (within Level 3 of the fair value hierarchy), companies should disclose the effect of the measurements on earnings (or changes in net assets) for the period.

You are not yet familiar with some of the examples mentioned in Illustration 1–13, but as you progress through the book, you will encounter many instances in which we use fair value for valuation purposes. Refer back to this discussion and speculate on the level of input that would be available to a company in these situations. When a company has the option to measure financial assets or liabilities at fair value (discussed next), we address the choices available to the company in those situations.

---

[47]"Using Cash Flow Information and Present Value in Accounting Measurements," *Statement of Financial Accounting Concepts No. 7* (Norwalk, Conn.: FASB, 2000).

[48]FASB ASC 820: Fair Value Measurements and Disclosures (previously "Fair Value Measurements," *Statement of Financial Accounting Standards No. 157* (Norwalk, Conn.: FASB, 2006)).

[49]"Fair Value Measurement," *International Financial Reporting Standard No. 13* (London, UK: IASCF, 2011).

Illustration 1–13 Fair Value Hierarchy

Fair Value Hierarchy		
Level	**Inputs**	**Example**
1 **Most Desirable**	Quoted market prices in active markets for identical assets or liabilities.	In Chapter 12 you will learn that certain investments in marketable securities are reported at their *fair values*. Fair value in this case would be measured using the quoted market price from the NYSE, NASDAQ, or other exchange on which the security is traded.
2	Inputs other than quoted prices that are *observable* for the asset or liability. These inputs include quoted prices for *similar* assets or liabilities in active or inactive markets and inputs that are derived principally from or corroborated by observable related market data.	In Chapter 10 we discuss how companies sometimes acquire assets with consideration other than cash. In any noncash transaction, each element of the transaction is recorded at its *fair value*. If one of the assets in the exchange is a building, for instance, then quoted market prices for similar buildings recently sold could be used to value the building or, if there were no similar buildings recently exchanged from which to obtain a comparable market price, valuation could be based on the price per square foot derived from observable market data.
3 **Least Desirable**	*Unobservable* inputs that reflect the entity's own assumptions about the assumptions market participants would use in pricing the asset or liability developed based on the best information available in the circumstances.	Asset retirement obligations (AROs), discussed in Chapter 10, are measured at *fair value*. Neither Level 1 nor Level 2 inputs would be possible in most ARO valuation situations. Fair value would be estimated using Level 3 inputs to include the present value of expected cash flows estimated using the entity's own data if there is no information that indicates that market participants would use different assumptions.

The use of the fair value measurement attribute is increasing, both under U.S GAAP and IFRS. This trend, though, is controversial. Proponents of fair value cite its relevance and are convinced that historical cost information may not be useful for many types of decisions. Opponents of fair value counter that estimates of fair value may lack representational faithfulness, particularly when based on inputs from Level 3 in the fair value hierarchy, and that managers might be tempted to exploit the unverifiability of such inputs to manipulate earnings. They argue that accounting should emphasize verifiability by recognizing only those gains and other increases in fair value that actually have been realized in transactions or are virtually certain to exist.

FAIR VALUE OPTION. Usually the measurement attribute we use for a particular financial statement item is not subject to choice. However, GAAP gives a company the option to report some or all of its *financial* assets and liabilities at fair value.[50] For example, in Chapter 14 you will learn that a company normally would report bonds payable at historical cost (adjusted for unamortized premium or discount), but the fair value option allows that company to choose instead to report the bonds payable at fair value. If a company chooses the fair value option, future changes in fair value are reported as gains and losses in the income statement.

GAAP gives a company the option to value financial assets and liabilities at fair value.

Why allow the fair value option for financial assets and liabilities, and not for, say, buildings or land? Financial assets and liabilities are cash and other assets and liabilities that convert directly into known amounts of cash. These include investments in stocks and bonds of other entities, notes receivable and payable, bonds payable, and derivative securities.[51] Some of these financial assets and liabilities currently are *required* under GAAP to be reported

---

[50]FASB ASC 825–10–25–1: Financial Instruments—Overall—Recognition—Fair Value Option (previously "The Fair Value Option for Financial Assets and Financial Liabilities," *Statement of Financial Accounting Standards No. 159* (Norwalk, Conn.: FASB, 2007)).

[51]The fair value option does not apply to certain specified financial instruments, including pension obligations and assets or liabilities arising from leases.

at fair value, and others are not, leading to some potential inconsistencies in how similar or related items are treated. The fair value option provides companies a way to reduce volatility in reported earnings without having to comply with complex hedge accounting standards. It also helps in the convergence with international accounting standards we discussed earlier in the chapter as the IASB also has adopted a fair value option for financial instruments.

It is not necessary that the company elect the fair value option to report all of its financial instruments at fair value or even all instruments of a particular type at fair value. Companies can "mix and match" on an instrument-by-instrument basis. However, a company is not allowed to switch methods once a method is chosen.

We will revisit the fair value option in subsequent chapters that address the key financial assets and liabilities that now can be measured at fair value. You'll find it easier to understand the concepts introduced in this chapter in the context of the financial assets and liabilities affected: investments (Chapter 12) and bonds payable (Chapter 14).[52]

Disclosure

The *full-disclosure principle* requires that any information useful to decision makers be provided in the financial statements, subject to the cost effectiveness constraint.

Remember, the purpose of accounting is to provide information that is useful to decision makers. So, naturally, if there is accounting information not included in the primary financial statements that would benefit users, that information should be provided too. The full-disclosure principle means that the financial reports should include any information that could affect the decisions made by external users. Of course, the benefits of that information, as noted earlier, should exceed the costs of providing the information. Such information is disclosed in a variety of ways, including:

1. Parenthetical comments or modifying comments placed on the face of the financial statements.
2. Disclosure notes conveying additional insights about company operations, accounting principles, contractual agreements, and pending litigation.
3. Supplemental schedules and tables that report more detailed information than is shown in the primary financial statements.

We find examples of these disclosures in the Dell Inc. financial statements in Appendix B located at the back of the text. A parenthetical or modifying comment is provided in the stockholders' equity section of the balance sheet with disclosure of the number of shares of stock authorized, issued, and outstanding, and the statements include several notes. We discuss and illustrate disclosure requirements as they relate to specific financial statement elements in later chapters as those elements are discussed.

Illustration 1–14 provides an overview of key recognition, measurement and disclosure concepts.

Evolving GAAP

Earlier in this chapter you learned that the convergence of accounting standards with international standards is having a profound effect on financial reporting in the United States. More broadly, U.S. and international GAAP have been evolving over time from an emphasis on revenues and expenses to an emphasis on assets and liabilities. Of course, you know from introductory accounting that the balance sheet and income statement are intertwined and must reconcile with each other. For example, the revenues reported in the income statement depict inflows of assets whose balances at a particular point in time are reported in the balance sheet. But which comes first, identifying revenues and expenses, or identifying assets and liabilities? That emphasis can affect accounting standards in important ways. To help you understand the changes taking place, we start by discussing the revenue/expense approach and then discuss the asset/liability approach.

---

[52]As discussed in further detail in the Addendum to Chapter 12, the overhaul of accounting for financial instruments being completed by the FASB and IASB includes removal of the fair value option.

Concept	Description
Recognition	General criteria: 1. Meets the definition of an element 2. Has a measurement attribute 3. Is relevant 4. Is reliable (representationally faithful) Examples of recognition timing: 1. Revenue realization 2. Expense matching
Measurement	Mixed attribute model in which the attribute used to measure an item is chosen to maximize relevance and representational faithfulness. These attributes include: 1. Historical cost 2. Net realizable value 3. Current cost 4. Present (or discounted) value of future cash flows 5. Fair value
Disclosure	Financial reports should include all information that could affect the decisions made by external users. Examples of disclosures: 1. Parenthetical amounts 2. Notes to the financial statements 3. Supplemental schedules and tables

Illustration 1–14

Summary of Recognition, Measurement, and Disclosure Concepts

Under the **revenue/expense approach**, we emphasize principles for recognizing revenues and expenses, with some assets and liabilities recognized as necessary to make the balance sheet reconcile with the income statement. For example, when accounting for a sales transaction our focus would be on whether revenue has been earned, and if we determine that to be the case, we would record an asset (usually cash or accounts receivable) that is associated with the revenue.[53] We would identify the expenses necessary to earn that revenue, and then would adjust assets and liabilities accordingly. Much of our accounting for revenues and expenses follows this revenue/expense approach. Key to the revenue/expense approach are the realization principle and the matching principle discussed previously in this chapter.

Under the **asset/liability approach**, on the other hand, we first recognize and measure the assets and liabilities that exist at a balance sheet date and, secondly, recognize and measure the revenues, expenses, gains and losses needed to account for the changes in these assets and liabilities from the previous measurement date. Proponents of this approach point out that, since revenues and expenses are defined in terms of inflows and outflows of assets and liabilities, the fundamental concepts underlying accounting are assets and liabilities. Therefore, we should try to recognize and measure assets and liabilities appropriately, and as a result will also capture their inflows and outflows in a manner that provides relevant and representationally faithful information about revenues and expenses.

For example, when accounting for a sales transaction, our focus would be on whether a potential accounts receivable meets the definition of an asset (a probable future economic benefit). We would consider such factors as whether the receivable is supported by an enforceable contract and whether the seller has performed its obligations enough to be able to expect receipt of cash flows. The key would be determining if the seller has an asset, and then recognizing whatever amount of revenue is implied by the inflow of that asset. Also, we would not attempt to match expenses to revenues. Rather, we would determine those net assets that had decreased as part of operations during the period, and

● LO1–10

With the *revenue/ expense approach,* recognition and measurement of revenues and expenses are emphasized.

With the *asset/liability approach,* recognition and measurement of assets and liabilities drives revenue and expense recognition.

---

[53]Some assets and liabilities aren't related to revenue or expense. For example, issuance of shares of stock increases cash as well as shareholders' equity. The treatment of these sorts of transactions is not affected by whether GAAP emphasizes revenues and expenses or assets and liabilities.

recognize those decreases as expenses. In subsequent chapters you will see that recent standards involving accounting for revenue, investments, and income taxes follow this asset/liability approach.

These changes are controversial. It may seem like it shouldn't matter whether standard setters use the revenue/expense or asset/liability approach, given that both approaches affect both the income statement and balance sheet, and it is true that these approaches often will result in the same accounting outcomes. For example, whether matching is a principle used to determine when expenses are recognized, or a result of recognizing that assets were consumed as part of the economic activity that occurred in a particular period in which revenue was also recognized, we typically still will see expenses recognized in the periods in which they are incurred to produce revenues. However, the particular approach used by a standard setter can affect recognition and measurement in important ways. In particular, the asset/liability approach encourages us to focus on accurately measuring assets and liabilities. It perhaps is not surprising, then, that a focus on assets and liabilities has led standard setters to lean more and more toward fair value measurement. The future changes to the conceptual framework discussed in the following Where We're Headed box are likely to continue this emphasis on the asset/liability approach.

Where We're Headed

The FASB and IASB are working together to develop a common and improved conceptual framework. The project has eight phases, and the Boards currently are working on the first four. Phase A, "Objective and Qualitative Characteristics," has been completed and resulted in the issuance of *SFAC 8*. That material is incorporated in this and subsequent chapters where applicable. There is no timetable for the completion of the remaining phases. However, the Boards have reached some tentative conclusions highlighted below.

Phase B: Elements and Recognition. The Boards have tentatively adopted working definitions for assets and liabilities that differ from those contained in *SFAC 6*.

	SFAC 6	Phase B
Assets	Probable future economic benefits obtained or controlled by a particular entity as a result of past transactions or events.	A present economic resource to which an entity has a right or other access that others do not have.
Liabilities	Probable future sacrifices of economic benefits arising from present obligations of a particular entity to transfer assets or provide services to other entities in the future as a result of past transactions or events.	A present economic obligation for which the entity is the obligor.

SFAC 6 identifies more elements than does the IASB's framework, and the two frameworks define common elements differently. The Boards are working toward a common set of elements and definitions.

Phase C: Measurement. The objective of Phase C is to provide guidance for selecting measurement bases that satisfy the objective and qualitative characteristics of financial reporting. No tentative conclusions have been reached on this issue.

Phase D: Reporting Entity. The objective of Phase D is to determine what constitutes a reporting entity for the purposes of financial reporting. The Board issued an exposure draft for this phase in March of 2010. The Board's preliminary view is that *control* is a key aspect in determining what constitutes a reporting entity. The Board defines "control" as the ability to direct the activities of the entity to generate benefits for (or limit losses to) itself.

Financial Reporting Case Solution

1. **What should you tell your friend about the presence of accounting standards in the United States? Who has the authority for standard setting? Who has the responsibility?** *(p. 8)* In the United States we have a set of standards known as generally accepted accounting principles (GAAP). GAAP is a dynamic set of both broad and specific guidelines that companies should follow when measuring and reporting the information in their financial statements and related notes. The Securities and Exchange Commission has the authority to set accounting standards for companies whose securities are publicly traded but always has delegated the primary responsibility to the accounting profession. At present, the Financial Accounting Standards Board is the private sector body responsible for standard setting.

2. **What is the economic and political environment in which standard setting occurs?** *(p. 13)* The setting of accounting and reporting standards often has been characterized as a *political process*. Standards, particularly changes in standards, can have significant differential effects on companies, investors and creditors, and other interest groups. A change in an accounting standard or the introduction of a new standard can result in a substantial redistribution of wealth within our economy. The FASB's due process is designed to obtain information from all interested parties to help determine the appropriate accounting approach, but standards are supposed to be neutral with respect to the interests of various parties. Nonetheless, both the FASB and IASB sometimes come under political pressure that sways the results of the standard-setting process.

3. **What is the relationship among management, auditors, investors, and creditors that tends to preclude the "What would you like it to be?" attitude?** *(p. 15)* It is the responsibility of management to apply accounting standards when communicating with investors and creditors through financial statements. Auditors serve as independent intermediaries to help ensure that the management-prepared statements are presented fairly in accordance with GAAP. In providing this assurance, the auditor precludes the "What would you like it to be?" attitude.

4. **In general, what is the conceptual framework that underlies accounting principles?** *(p. 19)* The conceptual framework is a coherent system of interrelated objectives and fundamentals that can lead to consistent standards and that prescribe the nature, function, and limits of financial accounting and reporting. The fundamentals are the underlying concepts of accounting, concepts that guide the selection of events to be accounted for, the measurement of those events, and the means of summarizing and communicating them to interested parties. ●

The Bottom Line

● **LO1–1** Financial accounting is concerned with providing relevant financial information to various external users. However, the primary focus is on the financial information provided by profit-oriented companies to their present and potential investors and creditors. *(p. 4)*

● **LO1–2** Cash basis accounting provides a measure of periodic performance called *net operating cash flow,* which is the difference between cash receipts and cash disbursements from transactions related to providing goods and services to customers. Accrual accounting provides a measure of performance called *net income,* which is the difference between revenues and expenses. Periodic net income is considered a better indicator of future operating cash flows than is current net operating cash flows. *(p. 6)*

● **LO1–3** Generally accepted accounting principles (GAAP) comprise a dynamic set of both broad and specific guidelines that companies follow when measuring and reporting the information in their financial statements and related notes. The Securities and Exchange Commission (SEC) has the authority to set accounting standards in the United States. However, the SEC has always delegated the task to a private sector body, at this time the Financial Accounting Standards Board (FASB). The International Accounting

Standards Board (IASB) sets global accounting standards and works with national accounting standard setters to achieve convergence in accounting standards around the world. (*p. 8*)

● **LO1–4** Accounting standards can have significant differential effects on companies, investors, creditors, and other interest groups. Various interested parties sometimes lobby standard setters for their preferred outcomes. For this reason, the setting of accounting standards often has been characterized as a political process. (*p. 13*)

● **LO1–5** Factors encouraging high-quality financial reporting include conceptually based financial accounting standards, external auditors, financial reporting reforms (such as the Sarbanes-Oxley Act), ethical management, and professional accounting organizations that prescribe ethical conduct and license practitioners. (*p. 15*)

● **LO1–6** The FASB's conceptual framework is a set of cohesive objectives and fundamental concepts on which financial accounting and reporting standards can be based. (*p. 19*)

● **LO1–7** The objective of financial reporting is to provide useful financial information to capital providers. The primary decision-specific qualities that make financial information useful are relevance and faithful representation. To be relevant, information must possess predictive value and/or confirmatory value, and all material information should be included. Completeness, neutrality, and freedom from error enhance faithful representation. The 10 elements of financial statements are assets, liabilities, equity, investments by owners, distributions to owners, revenues, expenses, gains, losses, and comprehensive income. (*p. 21*)

● **LO1–8** The four basic assumptions underlying GAAP are (1) the economic entity assumption, (2) the going concern assumption, (3) the periodicity assumption, and (4) the monetary unit assumption. (*p. 25*)

● **LO1–9** Recognition determines whether an item is reflected in the financial statements, and measurement determines the amount of the item. Measurement involves choice of a monetary unit and choice of a measurement attribute. In the United States, the monetary unit is the dollar. Various measurement attributes are used in GAAP, including historical cost, net realizable value, present value, and fair value. (*p. 27*)

● **LO1–10** A revenue/expense approach to financial reporting emphasizes recognition and measurement of revenues (typically using the realization principle) and expenses (typically applying the matching principle), while an asset/liability approach emphasizes recognition and measurement of assets and liabilities. (*p. 33*)

● **LO1–11** IFRS and U.S. GAAP are similar in the organizations that support standard setting and in the presence of ongoing political pressures on the standard-setting process. U.S. GAAP and IFRS also have similar conceptual frameworks, although the role of the conceptual framework in IFRS is to provide guidance to preparers as well as to standard setters, while the role of the conceptual framework in U.S. GAAP is more to provide guidance to standard setters. (*pp. 15* and *21*) ●

Questions For Review of Key Topics

Q 1–1 What is the function and primary focus of financial accounting?

Q 1–2 What is meant by the phrase *efficient allocation of resources?* What mechanism fosters the efficient allocation of resources in the United States?

Q 1–3 Identify two important variables to be considered when making an investment decision.

Q 1–4 What must a company do in the long run to be able to provide a return to investors and creditors?

Q 1–5 What is the primary objective of financial accounting?

Q 1–6 Define net operating cash flows. Briefly explain why periodic net operating cash flows may not be a good indicator of future operating cash flows.

Q 1–7 What is meant by GAAP? Why should all companies follow GAAP in reporting to external users?

Q 1–8 Explain the roles of the SEC and the FASB in the setting of accounting standards.

Q 1–9 Explain the role of the auditor in the financial reporting process.

Q 1–10 List three key provisions of the Sarbanes-Oxley Act of 2002. Order your list from most important to least important in terms of the likely long-term impact on the accounting profession and financial reporting.

Q 1–11 Explain what is meant by *adverse economic consequences* of new or changed accounting standards.

Q 1–12 Why does the FASB undertake a series of elaborate information-gathering steps before issuing a substantive accounting standard?

Q 1–13 What is the purpose of the FASB's conceptual framework project?

Q 1–14 Discuss the terms *relevance* and *faithful representation* as they relate to financial accounting information.

Q 1–15 What are the components of relevant information? What are the components of faithful representation?

Q 1–16 Explain what is meant by: The benefits of accounting information must exceed the costs.

Q 1–17 What is meant by the term *materiality* in financial reporting?

Q 1–18 Briefly define the financial accounting elements: (1) assets, (2) liabilities, (3) equity, (4) investments by owners, (5) distributions to owners, (6) revenues, (7) expenses, (8) gains, (9) losses, and (10) comprehensive income.

Q 1–19 What are the four basic assumptions underlying GAAP?

Q 1–20 What is the going concern assumption?

Q 1–21 Explain the periodicity assumption.

Q 1–22 What are four key accounting practices that often are referred to as principles in current GAAP?

Q 1–23 What are two important reasons to base the valuation of assets and liabilities on their historical cost?

Q 1–24 Describe the two criteria that must be satisfied before revenue can be recognized.

Q 1–25 What are the four different approaches to implementing the matching principle? Give an example of an expense that is recognized under each approach.

Q 1–26 In addition to the financial statement elements arrayed in the basic financial statements, what are some other ways to disclose financial information to external users?

Q 1–27 Briefly describe the inputs that companies should use when determining fair value. Organize your answer according to preference levels, from highest to lowest priority.

Q 1–28 What measurement attributes are commonly used in financial reporting?

Q 1–29 Distinguish between the revenue/expense and the asset/liability approaches to setting financial reporting standards.

● IFRS Q 1–30 What are the functions of the conceptual framework under IFRS?

● IFRS Q 1–31 What is the standard-setting body responsible for determining IFRS? How does it obtain its funding?

● IFRS Q 1–32 In late 2011, what further information did the SEC provide about its plans with respect to future convergence between U.S. GAAP and IFRS?

Brief Exercises

BE 1–1
Accrual accounting
● LO1–2

Cash flows during the first year of operations for the Harman-Kardon Consulting Company were as follows: Cash collected from customers, $340,000; Cash paid for rent, $40,000; Cash paid to employees for services rendered during the year, $120,000; Cash paid for utilities, $50,000.

In addition, you determine that customers owed the company $60,000 at the end of the year and no bad debts were anticipated. Also, the company owed the gas and electric company $2,000 at year-end, and the rent payment was for a two-year period. Calculate accrual net income for the year.

BE 1–2
Financial statement elements
● LO1–7

For each of the following items, identify the appropriate financial statement element or elements: (1) probable future sacrifices of economic benefits; (2) probable future economic benefits owned by the company; (3) inflows of assets from ongoing, major activities; (4) decrease in equity from peripheral or incidental transactions.

BE 1–3
Basic assumptions and principles
● LO1–7 through LO1–9

Listed below are several statements that relate to financial accounting and reporting. Identify the basic assumption, broad accounting principle, or pervasive constraint that applies to each statement.

1. Sirius Satellite Radio Inc. files its annual and quarterly financial statements with the SEC.
2. The president of Applebee's International, Inc., travels on the corporate jet for business purposes only and does not use the jet for personal use.
3. Jackson Manufacturing does not recognize revenue for unshipped merchandise even though the merchandise has been manufactured according to customer specifications.
4. Lady Jane Cosmetics depreciates the cost of equipment over their useful lives.

BE 1–4
Basic assumptions and principles
● LO1–7 through LO1–9

Identify the basic assumption or broad accounting principle that was violated in each of the following situations.

1. Astro Turf Company recognizes an expense, cost of goods sold, in the period the product is manufactured.
2. McCloud Drug Company owns a patent that it purchased three years ago for $2 million. The controller recently revalued the patent to its approximate market value of $8 million.
3. Philips Company pays the monthly mortgage on the home of its president, Larry Crosswhite, and charges the expenditure to miscellaneous expense.

BE 1–5
Basic assumptions and principles
● LO1–7 through LO1–9

For each of the following situations, (1) indicate whether you agree or disagree with the financial reporting practice employed and (2) state the basic assumption, pervasive constraint, or accounting principle that is applied (if you agree), or violated (if you disagree).

1. Winderl Corporation did not disclose that it was the defendant in a material lawsuit because the trial was still in progress.
2. Alliant Semiconductor Corporation files quarterly and annual financial statements with the SEC.

3. Reliant Pharmaceutical paid rent on its office building for the next two years and charged the entire expenditure to rent expense.

4. Rockville Engineering records revenue only after products have been shipped, even though customers pay Rockville 50% of the sales price in advance.

BE 1–6
IFRS
● **LO1–11**

⊙ **IFRS**

Indicate the organization related to IFRS that performs each of the following functions:

1. Obtains funding for the IFRS standard-setting process.
2. Determines IFRS.
3. Encourages cooperation among securities regulators to promote effective and efficient capital markets.
4. Provides input about the standard-setting agenda.
5. Provides implementation guidance about relatively narrow issues.

Exercises

An alternate exercise and problem set is available on the text website: www.mhhe.com/spiceland7e

E 1–1
Accrual
accounting
● **LO1–2**

Listed below are several transactions that took place during the first two years of operations for the law firm of Pete, Pete, and Roy.

	Year 1	Year 2
Amounts billed to customers for services rendered..................................	$170,000	$220,000
Cash collected from customers	160,000	190,000
Cash disbursements:..		
Salaries paid to employees for services rendered during the year	90,000	100,000
Utilities	30,000	40,000
Purchase of insurance policy	60,000	–0–

In addition, you learn that the company incurred utility costs of $35,000 in year 1, that there were no liabilities at the end of year 2, no anticipated bad debts on receivables, and that the insurance policy covers a three-year period.

Required:

1. Calculate the net operating cash flow for years 1 and 2.
2. Prepare an income statement for each year similar to Illustration 1–3 on page xxx according to the accrual accounting model.
3. Determine the amount of receivables from customers that the company would show in its year 1 and year 2 balance sheets prepared according to the accrual accounting model.

E 1–2
Accrual
accounting
● **LO1–2**

Listed below are several transactions that took place during the second two years of operations for RPG Consulting.

	Year 2	Year 3
Amounts billed to customers for services rendered	$350,000	$450,000
Cash collected from credit customers	260,000	400,000
Cash disbursements:		
Payment of rent	80,000	–0–
Salaries paid to employees for services rendered during the year	140,000	160,000
Travel and entertainment	30,000	40,000
Advertising	15,000	35,000

In addition, you learn that the company incurred advertising costs of $25,000 in year 2, owed the advertising agency $5,000 at the end of year 1, and there were no liabilities at the end of year 3. Also, there were no anticipated bad debts on receivables, and the rent payment was for a two-year period, year 2 and year 3.

Required:

1. Calculate accrual net income for both years.
2. Determine the amount due the advertising agency that would be shown as a liability on the RPG's balance sheet at the end of year 2.

E 1–3
FASB codification
research
● **LO1–3**

The *FASB Accounting Standards Codification* represents the single source of authoritative U.S. generally accepted accounting principles.

Required:

1. Obtain the relevant authoritative literature on fair value measurements using the FASB's Codification Research System at the FASB website (www.fasb.org). Identify the Codification topic number that provides guidance on fair value measurements.

2. What is the specific citation that lists the disclosures required in the notes to the financial statements for each major category of assets and liabilities measured at fair value?
3. List the disclosure requirements.

E 1–4
FASB codification research
● LO1–3

Access the FASB's Codification Research System at the FASB website (www.fasb.org). Determine the specific citation for each of the following items:
1. The topic number for business combinations.
2. The topic number for related party disclosures.
3. The topic, subtopic, and section number for the initial measurement of internal-use software.
4. The topic, subtopic, and section number for the subsequent measurement of asset retirement obligations.
5. The topic, subtopic, and section number for the recognition of stock compensation.

E 1–5
Participants in establishing GAAP
● LO1–3

Three groups that participate in the process of establishing GAAP are users, preparers, and auditors. These groups are represented by various organizations. For each organization listed below, indicate which of these groups it primarily represents.
1. Securities and Exchange Commission
2. Financial Executives International
3. American Institute of Certified Public Accountants
4. Institute of Management Accountants
5. Association of Investment Management and Research

E 1–6
Financial statement elements
● LO1–7

For each of the items listed below, identify the appropriate financial statement element or elements.
1. Obligation to transfer cash or other resources as a result of a past transaction.
2. Dividends paid by a corporation to its shareholders.
3. Inflow of an asset from providing a good or service.
4. The financial position of a company.
5. Increase in equity during a period from nonowner transactions.
6. Increase in equity from peripheral or incidental transaction.
7. Sale of an asset used in the operations of a business for less than the asset's book value.
8. The owners' residual interest in the assets of a company.
9. An item owned by the company representing probable future benefits.
10. Revenues plus gains less expenses and losses.
11. An owner's contribution of cash to a corporation in exchange for ownership shares of stock.
12. Outflow of an asset related to the production of revenue.

E 1–7
Concepts; terminology; conceptual framework
● LO1–7

Listed below are several terms and phrases associated with the FASB's conceptual framework. Pair each item from List A (by letter) with the item from List B that is most appropriately associated with it.

List A	List B
____ 1. Predictive value	a. Decreases in equity resulting from transfers to owners.
____ 2. Relevance	b. Requires consideration of the costs and value of information.
____ 3. Timeliness	c. Important for making interfirm comparisons.
____ 4. Distribution to owners	d. Applying the same accounting practices over time.
____ 5. Confirmatory value	e. Users understand the information in the context of the decision being made.
____ 6. Understandability	f. Agreement between a measure and the phenomenon it purports to represent.
____ 7. Gain	g. Information is available prior to the decision.
____ 8. Faithful representation	h. Pertinent to the decision at hand.
____ 9. Comprehensive income	i. Implies consensus among different measurers.
____10. Materiality	j. Information confirms expectations.
____11. Comparability	k. The change in equity from nonowner transactions.
____12. Neutrality	l. The process of admitting information into financial statements.
____13. Recognition	m. The absence of bias.
____14. Consistency	n. Results if an asset is sold for more than its book value.
____15. Cost effectiveness	o. Information is useful in predicting the future.
____16. Verifiability	p. Concerns the relative size of an item and its effect on decisions.

E 1–8
Qualitative
characteristics
● **LO1–7**

Phase A of the joint FASB and IASB conceptual framework project stipulates the desired fundamental and enhancing qualitative characteristics of accounting information. Several constraints impede achieving these desired characteristics. Answer each of the following questions related to these characteristics and constraints.

1. Which component would allow a company to record the purchase of a $120 printer as an expense rather than capitalizing the printer as an asset?
2. Donald Kirk, former chairman of the FASB, once noted that " . . . there must be public confidence that the standard-setting system is credible, that selection of board members is based on merit and not the influence of special interests . . ." Which characteristic is implicit in Mr. Kirk's statement?
3. Allied Appliances, Inc., changed its revenue recognition policies. Which characteristic is jeopardized by this change?
4. National Bancorp, a publicly traded company, files quarterly and annual financial statements with the SEC. Which characteristic is relevant to the timing of these periodic filings?
5. In general, relevant information possesses which qualities?
6. When there is agreement between a measure or description and the phenomenon it purports to represent, information possesses which characteristic?
7. Jeff Brown is evaluating two companies for future investment potential. Jeff's task is made easier because both companies use the same accounting methods when preparing their financial statements. Which characteristic does the information Jeff will be using possess?
8. A company should disclose information only if the perceived benefits of the disclosure exceed the costs of providing the information. Which constraint does this statement describe?

E 1–9
Basic assumptions,
principles, and
constraints
● **LO1–7 through
LO1–9**

Listed below are several terms and phrases associated with basic assumptions, broad accounting principles, and constraints. Pair each item from List A (by letter) with the item from List B that is most appropriately associated with it.

List A	List B
_____ 1. Matching principle	a. The enterprise is separate from its owners and other entities.
_____ 2. Periodicity	b. A common denominator is the dollar.
_____ 3. Historical cost principle	c. The entity will continue indefinitely.
_____ 4. Materiality	d. Record expenses in the period the related revenue is recognized.
_____ 5. Realization principle	e. The original transaction value upon acquisition.
_____ 6. Going concern assumption	f. All information that could affect decisions should be reported.
_____ 7. Monetary unit assumption	g. The life of an enterprise can be divided into artificial time periods.
_____ 8. Economic entity assumption	h. Criteria usually satisfied at point of sale.
_____ 9. Full-disclosure principle	i. Concerns the relative size of an item and its effect on decisions.

E 1–10
Basic assumptions
and principles
● **LO1–7 through
LO1–9**

Listed below are several statements that relate to financial accounting and reporting. Identify the basic assumption, broad accounting principle, or component that applies to each statement.

1. Jim Marley is the sole owner of Marley's Appliances. Jim borrowed $100,000 to buy a new home to be used as his personal residence. This liability was not recorded in the records of Marley's Appliances.
2. Apple Inc. distributes an annual report to its shareholders.
3. Hewlett-Packard Corporation depreciates machinery and equipment over their useful lives.
4. Crosby Company lists land on its balance sheet at $120,000, its original purchase price, even though the land has a current fair value of $200,000.
5. Honeywell Corporation records revenue when products are delivered to customers, even though the cash has not yet been received.
6. Liquidation values are not normally reported in financial statements even though many companies do go out of business.
7. IBM Corporation, a multibillion dollar company, purchased some small tools at a cost of $800. Even though the tools will be used for a number of years, the company recorded the purchase as an expense.

E 1–11
Basic assumptions
and principles
● **LO1–8, LO1–9**

Identify the basic assumption or broad accounting principle that was violated in each of the following situations.

1. Pastel Paint Company purchased land two years ago at a price of $250,000. Because the value of the land has appreciated to $400,000, the company has valued the land at $400,000 in its most recent balance sheet.
2. Atwell Corporation has not prepared financial statements for external users for over three years.
3. The Klingon Company sells farm machinery. Revenue from a large order of machinery from a new buyer was recorded the day the order was received.
4. Don Smith is the sole owner of a company called Hardware City. The company recently paid a $150 utility bill for Smith's personal residence and recorded a $150 expense.

5. Golden Book Company purchased a large printing machine for $1,000,000 (a material amount) and recorded the purchase as an expense.

6. Ace Appliance Company is involved in a major lawsuit involving injuries sustained by some of its employees in the manufacturing plant. The company is being sued for $2,000,000, a material amount, and is not insured. The suit was not disclosed in the most recent financial statements because no settlement had been reached.

E 1–12
Basic assumptions and principles
● **LO1–7 through LO1–9**

For each of the following situations, indicate whether you agree or disagree with the financial reporting practice employed and state the basic assumption, component, or accounting principle that is applied (if you agree) or violated (if you disagree).

1. Wagner Corporation adjusted the valuation of all assets and liabilities to reflect changes in the purchasing power of the dollar.

2. Spooner Oil Company changed its method of accounting for oil and gas exploration costs from successful efforts to full cost. No mention of the change was included in the financial statements. The change had a material effect on Spooner's financial statements.

3. Cypress Manufacturing Company purchased machinery having a five-year life. The cost of the machinery is being expensed over the life of the machinery.

4. Rudeen Corporation purchased equipment for $180,000 at a liquidation sale of a competitor. Because the equipment was worth $230,000, Rudeen valued the equipment in its subsequent balance sheet at $230,000.

5. Davis Bicycle Company received a large order for the sale of 1,000 bicycles at $100 each. The customer paid Davis the entire amount of $100,000 on March 15. However, Davis did not record any revenue until April 17, the date the bicycles were delivered to the customer.

6. Gigantic Corporation purchased two small calculators at a cost of $32.00. The cost of the calculators was expensed even though they had a three-year estimated useful life.

7. Esquire Company provides financial statements to external users every three years.

E 1–13
Basic assumptions and principles
● **LO1–7 through LO1–9**

For each of the following situations, state whether you agree or disagree with the financial reporting practice employed, and briefly explain the reason for your answer.

1. The controller of the Dumars Corporation increased the carrying value of land from its original cost of $2 million to its recently appraised value of $3.5 million.

2. The president of Vosburgh Industries asked the company controller to charge miscellaneous expense for the purchase of an automobile to be used solely for personal use.

3. At the end of its 2013 fiscal year, Dower, Inc., received an order from a customer for $45,350. The merchandise will ship early in 2014. Because the sale was made to a long-time customer, the controller recorded the sale in 2013.

4. At the beginning of its 2013 fiscal year, Rossi Imports paid $48,000 for a two-year lease on warehouse space. Rossi recorded the expenditure as an asset to be expensed equally over the two-year period of the lease.

5. The Reliable Tire Company included a note in its financial statements that described a pending lawsuit against the company.

6. The Hughes Corporation, a company whose securities are publicly traded, prepares monthly, quarterly, and annual financial statements for internal use but disseminates to external users only the annual financial statements.

E 1–14
Basic assumptions and principles
● **LO1–7 through LO1–9**

Listed below are the basic assumptions, broad accounting principles, and constraints discussed in this chapter.

a. Economic entity assumption
b. Going concern assumption
c. Periodicity assumption
d. Monetary unit assumption
e. Historical cost principle
f. Realization principle

g. Matching principle
h. Full-disclosure principle
i. Cost effectiveness
j. Materiality
k. Conservatism

Identify by letter the assumption, principle, or constraint that relates to each statement or phrase below.

_____ 1. Revenue is recognized only after certain criteria are satisfied.

_____ 2. Information that could affect decision making should be reported.

_____ 3. Cause-and-effect relationship between revenues and expenses.

_____ 4. The basis for measurement of many assets and liabilities.

_____ 5. Relates to the qualitative characteristic of timeliness.

_____ 6. All economic events can be identified with a particular entity.

_____ 7. The benefits of providing accounting information should exceed the cost of doing so.

_____ 8. A consequence is that GAAP need not be followed in all situations.

_____ 9. Not a qualitative characteristic, but a practical justification for some accounting choices.

_____10. Assumes the entity will continue indefinitely.

_____11. Inflation causes a violation of this assumption.

E 1–15
Multiple choice; concept statements, basic assumptions, principles
● **LO1–6 through LO1–9**

Determine the response that best completes the following statements or questions.

1. The primary objective of financial reporting is to provide information
   a. About a firm's management team.
   b. Useful to capital providers.
   c. Concerning the changes in financial position resulting from the income-producing efforts of the entity.
   d. About a firm's financing and investing activities.

2. *Statements of Financial Accounting Concepts* issued by the FASB
   a. Represent GAAP.
   b. Have been superseded by *SFAS*s.
   c. Are subject to approval of the SEC.
   d. Identify the conceptual framework within which accounting standards are developed.

3. In general, revenue is recognized as earned when the earning process is virtually complete and
   a. The sales price has been collected.
   b. A purchase order has been received.
   c. There is reasonable certainty as to the collectibility of the asset to be received.
   d. A contract has been signed.

4. In depreciating the cost of an asset, accountants are most concerned with
   a. Conservatism.
   b. The realization principle.
   c. Full disclosure.
   d. The matching principle.

5. The primary objective of the matching principle is to
   a. Provide full disclosure.
   b. Record expenses in the period that related revenues are recognized.
   c. Provide timely information to decision makers.
   d. Promote comparability between financial statements of different periods.

6. The separate entity assumption states that, in the absence of contrary evidence, all entities will survive indefinitely.
   a. True
   b. False

CPA and CMA Exam Questions

CPA Exam Questions

The following questions are adapted from a variety of sources including questions developed by the AICPA Board of Examiners and those used in the Kaplan CPA Review Course to study the environment and theoretical structure of financial accounting while preparing for the CPA examination. Determine the response that best completes the statements or questions.

● **LO1–7**

1. Which of the following is *not* a qualitative characteristic of accounting information according to the FASB's conceptual framework?
   a. Auditor independence.
   b. Neutrality.
   c. Timeliness.
   d. Predictive value.

● **LO1–7**

2. According to the conceptual framework, neutrality is a characteristic of
   a. Understandability.
   b. Faithful representation.
   c. Relevance.
   d. Both relevance and faithful representation.

● **LO1–3**

3. The Financial Accounting Standards Board (FASB)
   a. Is a division of the Securities and Exchange Commission (SEC).
   b. Is a private body that helps set accounting standards in the United States.

c. Is responsible for setting auditing standards that all auditors must follow.

d. Consists entirely of members of the American Institute of Certified Public Accountants.

LO1–7

4. Confirmatory value is an ingredient of the primary quality of

	Relevance	Faithful Representation
a.	Yes	No
b.	No	Yes
c.	Yes	Yes
d.	No	No

LO1–7

5. Predictive value is an ingredient of

	Faithful Representation	Relevance
a.	Yes	No
b.	No	No
c.	Yes	Yes
d.	No	Yes

LO1–7

6. Completeness is an ingredient of the primary quality of

a. Verifiability.

b. Faithful representation.

c. Relevance.

d. Understandability.

LO1–1

7. The objective of financial reporting for business enterprises is based on

a. Generally accepted accounting principles.

b. The needs of the users of the information.

c. The need for conservatism.

d. None of above.

LO1–7

8. According to the FASB's conceptual framework, comprehensive income includes which of the following?

	Operating Income	Investments by Owners
a.	No	Yes
b.	No	No
c.	Yes	Yes
d.	Yes	No

Beginning in 2011, International Financial Reporting Standards are tested on the CPA exam along with U.S. GAAP. The following questions deal with the application of IFRS.

LO1–11

IFRS

9. The equivalent to the FASB's Financial Accounting Standards Advisory Council (FASAC) for the IASB is:

a. International Financial Reporting Interpretations Committee (IFRIC).

b. International Organization of Securities Commissions (IOSCO).

c. International Financial Accounting Advisory Council (IFAAC).

d. Standards Advisory Council (SAC).

LO1–11

IFRS

10. Which of the following is not a function of the IASB's conceptual framework?

a. The conceptual framework provides guidance to standard setters to help them develop high quality standards.

b. The conceptual framework provides guidance to practitioners when individual standards to not apply.

c. The conceptual framework includes specific implementation guidance to enable consistent application of particular complex standards.

d. The conceptual framework emphasizes a "true and fair representation" of the company.

LO1–11

IFRS

11. Late in 2011, the SEC indicated what future direction concerning convergence of U.S. GAAP and IFRS?

a. The U.S. will continue to work with the IASB on convergence efforts, and the SEC will reassess whether adoption of IFRS is appropriate after several more years.

b. The U.S. will follow a "condorsement approach", whereby the U.S. endorses IFRS standards as they are issued and works to converge existing standards prior to adopting IFRS.

c. The U.S. will continue working on convergence projects with a goal to eventually adopt IFRS, and in the meantime large U.S. companies will be allowed to report under IFRS if they so choose.

d. None of the above.

CMA Exam Questions

The following questions dealing with the environment and theoretical structure of financial accounting are adapted from questions that previously appeared on Certified Management Accountant (CMA) examinations. The CMA designation sponsored by the Institute of Management Accountants (www.imanet.org) provides members with an objective measure of knowledge and competence in the field of management accounting. Determine the response that best completes the statements or questions.

● LO1–3

1. Accounting standard setting in the United States is
   a. Done primarily by the Securities and Exchange Commission.
   b. Done primarily by the private sector.
   c. The responsibility of the public sector.
   d. Done primarily by the International Accounting Standards Committee.

● LO1–7

2. Verifiability as used in accounting includes
   a. Determining the revenue first, then determining the costs incurred in earning that revenue.
   b. The entity's giving the same treatment to comparable transactions from period to period.
   c. Similar results being obtained by both the accountant and an independent party using the same measurement methods.
   d. The disclosure of all facts that may influence the judgment of an informed reader.

● LO1–7

3. Recognition is the process of formally recording and reporting an item in the financial statements. In order for a revenue item to be recognized, it must be all of the following except
   a. Measurable.
   b. Relevant.
   c. Material.
   d. Realized or realizable.

Broaden Your Perspective

Apply your critical-thinking ability to the knowledge you've gained. These cases will provide you an opportunity to develop your research, analysis, judgment, and communication skills. You will also work with other students, integrate what you've learned, apply it in real world situations, and consider its global and ethical ramifications. This practice will broaden your knowledge and further develop your decision-making abilities.

Judgment Case 1–1
The development of accounting standards
● LO1–3

In 1934, Congress created the Securities and Exchange Commission (SEC) and gave the commission both the power and responsibility for setting accounting and reporting standards in the United States.

Required:

1. Explain the relationship between the SEC and the various private sector standard-setting bodies that have, over time, been delegated the responsibility for setting accounting standards.
2. Can you think of any reasons why the SEC has delegated this responsibility rather than set standards directly?

Research Case 1–2
Accessing SEC information through the Internet
● LO1–3

Internet access to the World Wide Web has provided a wealth of information accessible with our personal computers. Many chapters in this text contain Real World Cases that require you to access the web to research an accounting issue. The purpose of this case is to introduce you to the Internet home page of the Securities and Exchange Commission (SEC) and its EDGAR database.

Required:

1. Access the SEC home page on the Internet. The web address is www.sec.gov.
2. Choose the subaddress "About the SEC." What are the two basic objectives of the 1933 Securities Act?
3. Return to the SEC home page and access EDGAR. Describe the contents of the database.

Research Case 1–3
Accessing FASB information through the Internet
● LO1–4

The purpose of this case is to introduce you to the information available on the website of the Financial Accounting Standards Board (FASB).

Required:

Access the FASB home page on the Internet. The web address is www.fasb.org. Answer the following questions.
1. Describe the mission of the FASB.
2. Who are the current Board members of the FASB? Briefly describe their backgrounds.
3. How are topics added to the FASB's technical agenda?

Research Case 1–4
Accessing IASB information through the Internet
● LO1–3

The purpose of this case is to introduce you to the information available on the website of the International Accounting Standards Board (IASB).

Required:

Access the IASB home page on the Internet. The web address is www.iasb.org. Answer the following questions.
1. Describe the mission of the IASB.
2. The IASB has how many board members?
3. Who is the current chairman of the IASB?
4. Where is the IASB located?

Research Case 1–5
Accounting standards in China
● LO1–3, LO1–4

Economic reforms in the People's Republic of China are moving that nation toward a market-driven economy. China's accounting practices must also change to accommodate the needs of potential investors. In an article entitled "Institutional Factors Influencing China's Accounting Reforms and Standards," Professor Bing Xiang analyzes the changes in the accounting environment of China during the recent economic reforms and their implications for the development of accounting reforms.

Required:

1. In your library or from some other source, locate the indicated article in *Accounting Horizons,* June 1998.
2. Briefly describe the economic reforms that led to the need for increased external financial reporting in China.
3. Conformity with International Accounting Standards was specified as an overriding objective in formulating China's accounting standards. What is the author's opinion of this objective?

Communication Case 1–6
Relevance and reliability
● LO1–7

Some theorists contend that companies that create pollution should report the social cost of that pollution in income statements. They argue that such companies are indirectly subsidized as the cost of pollution is borne by society while only production costs (and perhaps minimal pollution fines) are shown in the income statement. Thus, the product sells for less than would be necessary if all costs were included.

Assume that the FASB is considering a standard to include the social costs of pollution in the income statement. The process would require considering both relevance and faithful representation of the information produced by the new standard. Your instructor will divide the class into two to six groups depending on the size of the class. The mission of your group is to explain how the concepts of relevance and faithful representation relate to this issue.

Required:

Each group member should consider the question independently and draft a tentative answer prior to the class session for which the case is assigned.

In class, each group will meet for 10 to 15 minutes in different areas of the classroom. During that meeting, group members will take turns sharing their suggestions for the purpose of arriving at a single group treatment.

After the allotted time, a spokesperson for each group (selected during the group meetings) will share the group's solution with the class. The goal of the class is to incorporate the views of each group into a consensus answer to the question.

Communication Case 1–7
Accounting standard setting
● LO1–4

One of your friends is a financial analyst for a major stock brokerage firm. Recently she indicated to you that she had read an article in a weekly business magazine that alluded to the political process of establishing accounting standards. She had always assumed that accounting standards were established by determining the approach that conceptually best reflected the economics of a transaction.

Required:

Write a one to two-page article for a business journal explaining what is meant by the political process for establishing accounting standards. Be sure to include in your article a discussion of the need for the FASB to balance accounting considerations and economic consequences.

Ethics Case 1–8
The auditors' responsibility
● LO1–4

It is the responsibility of management to apply accounting standards when communicating with investors and creditors through financial statements. Another group, auditors, serves as an independent intermediary to help ensure that management has in fact appropriately applied GAAP in preparing the company's financial statements. Auditors examine (audit) financial statements to express a professional, independent opinion. The opinion reflects the auditors' assessment of the statements' fairness, which is determined by the extent to which they are prepared in compliance with GAAP.

Some feel that it is impossible for an auditor to give an independent opinion on a company's financial statements because the auditors' fees for performing the audit are paid by the company. In addition to the audit fee, quite often the auditor performs other services for the company such as preparing the company's income tax returns.

Required:

How might an auditor's ethics be challenged while performing an audit?

Judgment Case 1–9
Qualitative characteristics
● LO1–7

Generally accepted accounting principles do not require companies to disclose forecasts of any financial variables to external users. A friend, who is a finance major, is puzzled by this and asks you to explain why such relevant information is not provided to investors and creditors to help them predict future cash flows.

Required:
Explain to your friend why this information is not routinely provided to investors and creditors.

Judgment Case 1–10
GAAP, comparability, and the role of the auditor
● LO1–4, LO1–7

Mary McQuire is trying to decide how to invest her money. A friend recommended that she buy the stock of one of two corporations and suggested that she should compare the financial statements of the two companies before making a decision.

Required:
1. Do you agree that Mary will be able to compare the financial statements of the two companies?
2. What role does the auditor play in ensuring comparability of financial statements between companies?

Judgment Case 1–11
Cost effectiveness
● LO1–7

Phase A of the joint FASB and IASB conceptual framework project includes a discussion of the constraint cost effectiveness. Assume that the FASB is considering revising an important accounting standard.

Required:
1. What is the desired benefit from revising an accounting standard?
2. What are some of the possible costs that could result from a revision of an accounting standard?
3. What does the FASB do in order to assess possible benefits and costs of a proposed revision of an accounting standard?

Judgment Case 1–12
The realization principle
● LO1–9

A new client, the Wolf Company, asks your advice concerning the point in time that the company should recognize revenue from the rental of its office buildings. Renters usually pay rent on a quarterly basis at the beginning of the quarter. The owners contend that the critical event that motivates revenue recognition should be the date the cash is received from renters. After all, the money is in hand and is very seldom returned.

Required:
1. Describe the two criteria that must be satisfied before revenue can be recognized.
2. Do you agree or disagree with the position of the owners of Wolf Company? Support your answer.

Analysis Case 1–13
The matching principle
● LO1–9

Revenues measure the accomplishments of a company during the period. Expenses are then matched with revenues to produce a periodic measure of performance called *net income*.

Required:
1. Explain what is meant by the phrase *matched with revenues*.
2. Describe the four approaches used to implement the matching principle and label them 1 through 4.
3. For each of the following, identify which matching approach should be used to recognize the cost as expense.
    a. The cost of producing a product.
    b. The cost of advertising.
    c. The cost of monthly rent on the office building.
    d. The salary of an office employee.
    e. Depreciation on an office building.

Judgment Case 1–14
Capitalize or expense?
● LO1–9

When a company makes an expenditure that is neither a payment to a creditor nor a distribution to an owner, management must decide if the expenditure should be capitalized (recorded as an increase in an asset) or expensed (recorded as an expense thereby decreasing owners' equity).

Required:
1. Which factor or factors should the company consider when making this decision?
2. Which key accounting principle is involved?
3. Are there any constraints that could cause the company to alter its decision?

Real World Case 1–15
Elements; disclosures; The Gap Inc.
● LO1–7, LO1–9

Selected financial statements from a recent annual report of The Gap Inc. follow. Use these statements to answer the following questions.

Required:
1. What amounts did Gap report for the following items for the 2010 fiscal year ended January 29, 2011?
    a. Total net revenues
    b. Total operating expenses
    c. Net income (earnings)

    d. Total assets

    e. Total stockholders' equity

Real World Financials   2. How many shares of common stock did the company have issued on January 29, 2011?

    3. Why do you think Gap reports more than one year of data in its financial statements?

THE GAP INC.
Consolidated Balance Sheets

($ and shares in millions except par value)	January 29, 2011	January 30, 2010
Assets		
Current assets:		
Cash and cash equivalents	$ 1,561	$ 2,348
Short-term investments	100	225
Merchandise inventory	1,620	1,477
Other current assets	645	614
Total current assets	3,926	4,664
Property and equipment, net	2,563	2,628
Other long-term assets	576	693
Total assets	$ 7,065	$ 7,985
Liabilities and Stockholders' Equity		
Current liabilities:		
Accounts payable	$ 1,049	$ 1,027
Accrued expenses and other current liabilities	996	1,063
Income taxes payable	50	41
Total current liabilities	2,095	2,131
Lease incentives and other long-term liabilities	890	963
Commitments and contingencies (see Notes 9 and 13)		
Stockholders' equity:		
Common stock $0.05 par value		
Authorized 2,300 shares; Issued 1,106 for all periods		
presented; Outstanding 588 and 676 shares	55	55
Additional paid-in capital	2,939	2,935
Retained earnings	11,767	10,815
Accumulated other comprehensive earnings	185	155
Treasury stock, at cost (518 and 430 shares)	(10,866)	(9,069)
Total stockholders' equity	4,080	4,891
Total liabilities and stockholders' equity	$ 7,065	$ 7,985

THE GAP INC.
Consolidated Statements of Income

| ($ and shares in millions except per share amounts) | Fiscal Year | | |
	2010	2009	2008
Net sales	$14,664	$14,197	$14,526
Cost of goods sold and occupancy expenses	8,775	8,473	9,079
Gross profit	5,889	5,724	5,447
Operating expenses	3,921	3,909	3,899
Operating income	1,968	1,815	1,548
Interest expense (reversal)	(8)	6	1
Interest income	(6)	(7)	(37)
Income before income taxes	1,982	1,816	1,584
Income taxes	778	714	617
Net income	$ 1,204	$ 1,102	$ 967
Weighted-average number of shares—basic	636	694	716
Weighted-average number of shares—diluted	641	699	719
Earnings per share—basic	$1.89	$1.59	$1.35
Earnings per share—diluted	$1.88	$1.58	$1.34
Cash dividends declared and paid per share	$0.40	$0.34	$0.34

Judgment
Case 1–16
Convergence
● LO1–11

🌐 IFRS

Consider the question of whether the United States should converge accounting standards with IFRS.

Required:

1. Make a list of arguments that favor convergence.
2. Make a list of arguments that favor nonconvergence.
3. Indicate your own conclusion regarding whether the United States should converge with IFRS, and indicate the primary considerations that determined your conclusion.

Air France–KLM Case

AIRFRANCE   Air France–KLM (AF), a French company, prepares its financial statements according to International Financial Reporting Standards. AF's annual report for the year ended March 31, 2011, which includes financial statements and disclosure notes, is provided with all new textbooks. This material also is included in AF's "Registration Document 2010–11," dated June 15, 2011 and is available at www.airfranceklm.com.

● LO1–11

🌐 IFRS

Required:

1. What amounts did AF report for the following items for the 2011 fiscal year ended March 31, 2011?
   a. Total revenues
   b. Income from current operations
   c. Net income (AF equity holders)
   d. Total assets
   e. Total equity
2. What was AF's basic earnings per share for the 2011 fiscal year?
3. Examine Note 3.1.1 of AF's annual report. What accounting principles were used to prepare AF's financial statements? Under those accounting principles, could AF's financial information differ from that of a company that exactly followed IFRS as published by the IASB? Explain.

CHAPTER

3

The Balance Sheet and Financial Disclosures

OVERVIEW ——— Chapter 1 stressed the importance of the financial statements in helping investors and creditors predict future cash flows. The balance sheet, along with accompanying disclosures, provides relevant information useful in helping investors and creditors not only to predict future cash flows, but also to make the related assessments of liquidity and long-term solvency.

The purpose of this chapter is to provide an overview of the balance sheet and financial disclosures and to explore how this information is used by decision makers.

LEARNING ——— **After studying this chapter, you should be able to:**
OBJECTIVES

- **LO3–1** Describe the purpose of the balance sheet and understand its usefulness and limitations. (p. 115)
- **LO3–2** Identify and describe the various balance sheet asset classifications. (p. 117)
- **LO3–3** Identify and describe the two balance sheet liability classifications. (p. 120)
- **LO3–4** Explain the purpose of financial statement disclosures. (p. 124)
- **LO3–5** Explain the purpose of the management discussion and analysis disclosure. (p. 128)
- **LO3–6** Explain the purpose of an audit and describe the content of the audit report. (p. 130)
- **LO3–7** Describe the techniques used by financial analysts to transform financial information into forms more useful for analysis. (p. 132)
- **LO3–8** Identify and calculate the common liquidity and financing ratios used to assess risk. (p. 134)
- **LO3–9** Discuss the primary differences between U.S. GAAP and IFRS with respect to the balance sheet, financial disclosures, and segment reporting. (pp. 122 and 141)

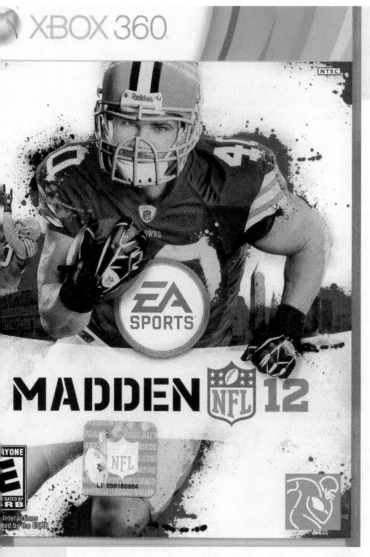

FINANCIAL REPORTING CASE

What's It Worth?

"I can't believe it. Why don't you accountants prepare financial statements that are relevant?" Your friend Jerry is a finance major and is constantly badgering you about what he perceives to be a lack of relevance of financial statements prepared according to generally accepted accounting principles. "For example, take a look at this balance sheet for Electronic Arts that I just downloaded off the Internet. Electronic Arts is the company in California that produces all those cool video games like Battlefield 2, NBA Live, and Madden NFL. Anyway, the shareholders' equity of the company according to the 2011 balance sheet is about $2.5 billion. But if you multiply the number of outstanding shares by the most recent stock price per share, the company's market value is three times that amount. I thought financial statements were supposed to help investors and creditors value a company." You decide to look at the company's balance sheet and try to set Jerry straight.

By the time you finish this chapter, you should be able to respond appropriately to the questions posed in this case. Compare your response to the solution provided at the end of the chapter.

— **QUESTIONS**

1. Respond to Jerry's criticism that shareholders' equity does not represent the market value of the company. What information does the balance sheet provide? (*p. 115*)

2. The usefulness of the balance sheet is enhanced by classifying assets and liabilities according to common characteristics. What are the classifications used in Electronic Arts' balance sheets and what elements do those categories include? (*p. 116*)

Real World Financials

ELECTRONIC ARTS INC.
AND SUBSIDIARIES
Consolidated Balance Sheets
(In millions, except par value data)

	March 31, 2011	March 31, 2010
Assets		
Current assets:		
Cash and cash equivalents	$1,579	$1,273
Short-term investments	497	432
Marketable equity securities	161	291
Receivables, net of allowances of $304 and $217, respectively	335	206
Inventories	77	100
Deferred income taxes, net	56	44
Other current assets	327	239
Total current assets	3,032	2,585
Property and equipment, net	513	537
Goodwill	1,110	1,093
Acquisition-related intangibles, net	144	204
Deferred income taxes, net	49	52
Other assets	80	175
Total Assets	$4,928	$4,646
Liabilities and Stockholders' Equity		
Current liabilities:		
Accounts payable	$ 228	$ 91
Accrued and other current liabilities	768	717
Deferred net revenue (packaged goods and digital content)	1,005	766
Total current liabilities	2,001	1,574
Income tax obligations	192	242
Deferred income taxes, net	37	2
Other liabilities	134	99
Total liabilities	2,364	1,917
Commitments and contingencies (See Note 10)		
Stockholders' equity:		
Preferred stock, $0.01 par value. 10 shares authorized	—	—
Common stock, $0.01 par value. 1,000 shares authorized; 333 and 330 shares issued and outstanding, respectively	3	3
Paid-in capital	2,495	2,375
Retained earnings (accumulated deficit)	(153)	123
Accumulated other comprehensive income	219	228
Total stockholders' equity	2,564	2,729
Total Liabilities and Stockholders' Equity	$4,928	$4,646

The balance sheet, along with accompanying disclosures, provides a wealth of information to external decision makers. The information provided is useful not only in the prediction of future cash flows but also in the related assessments of liquidity and long-term solvency.

This chapter begins our discussion of the financial statements by providing an overview of the balance sheet and the financial disclosures that accompany the financial statements. The first part of the chapter describes the usefulness and limitations of the balance sheet and illustrates the content of the statement. The second part illustrates financial statement disclosures presented to external users in addition to the basic financial statements. In the third part we discuss how this information can be used by decision makers to assess business risk. That discussion introduces some common financial ratios used to assess liquidity and long-term solvency.

Chapter 4 continues this discussion of the financial statements with its coverage of the income statement, statement of comprehensive income, and the statement of cash flows.

THE BALANCE SHEET

PART **A**

The purpose of the balance sheet, sometimes referred to as the statement of financial position, is to report a company's financial position on a particular date. Unlike the income statement, which is a change statement reporting events that occurred *during a period of time,* the balance sheet presents an organized array of assets, liabilities, and shareholders' equity *at a point in time.* It is a freeze frame or snapshot of financial position at the end of a particular day marking the end of an accounting period.

● LO3–1

Usefulness and Limitations

An important limitation of the balance sheet is that *it does not portray the market value of the entity* as a going concern, nor its liquidation value. Many assets, like land and buildings for example, are measured at their historical costs rather than their fair values. Relatedly, many company resources including its trained employees, its experienced management team, and its reputation are not recorded as assets at all. Also, many items and amounts reported in the balance sheet are heavily reliant on estimates rather than determinable amounts. For example, companies estimate the amount of receivables they will be able to actually collect and the amount of warranty costs they will eventually incur for products already sold. For these and other reasons, a company's book value, its assets minus its liabilities as shown in the balance sheet, usually will not directly measure the company's market value (number of shares of common stock outstanding multiplied by the price per share).

FINANCIAL Reporting Case

Q1, p. 113

Assets minus liabilities, measured according to GAAP, is not likely to be representative of the market value of the entity.

Consider for example that early in 2011, the 30 companies constituting the Dow Jones Industrial Average had an average ratio of market value to book value of approximately 3.5. The ratio for IBM, one of the world's largest technology companies, was almost 9.0. Can you think of a reason why IBM's market value would be nine times higher than its book value? A significant reason is the way we account for research and development costs. IBM invests considerable amounts, over $6 billion in 2010 alone, on research and development of new products. Quite a few of these products that the company has developed over the years have been market successes, and yet the costs to discover and develop them are not represented in the balance sheet. We expense research and development costs in the period incurred rather than capitalize them as assets for the balance sheet.

During the financial crisis of 2008–2009 we saw stock prices plummet resulting in historic declines in the market to book ratio for most companies. For example, in 2007 the average ratio of market to book for the 30 Dow Jones Industrial Average companies was 4.46, almost twice the early 2009 average. Particularly hard hit were financial services companies. Early in 2009, both Bank of America and Citigroup had market to book ratios significantly less than 1.0. Later in 2009, Citigroup was replaced and is no longer one of the Dow Jones Industrial 30 companies.

Despite these limitations, the balance sheet does have significant value. An important feature of the statement is that it describes many of the resources a company has available for generating future cash flows. Another way the statement's content is informative is in combination with income statement items. For example, the relation between net income and assets provides a measure of return that is useful in predicting future profitability. In fact, many of the amounts reported in either of the two statements are more informative when viewed relative to an amount from the other statement.[1]

The balance sheet provides information useful for assessing future cash flows, liquidity, and long-term solvency.

The balance sheet does not simply list assets and liabilities. Instead, assets and liabilities are classified (grouped) according to common characteristics. These classifications, which we explore in the next section, along with related disclosure notes, help the balance sheet to provide additional important information about liquidity and long-term solvency. Liquidity refers to the period of time before an asset is converted to cash or until a liability is paid. This information is useful in assessing a company's ability to pay its *current* obligations.

---

[1]We explore some of these relationships in Chapter 5.

Long-term solvency refers to the riskiness of a company with regard to the amount of liabilities in its capital structure. Other things being equal, the risk to an investor or creditor increases as the percentage of liabilities, relative to equity, increases.

Solvency also provides information about *financial flexibility*—the ability of a company to alter cash flows in order to take advantage of unexpected investment opportunities and needs. For example, the higher the percentage of a company's liabilities to its equity, the more difficult it typically will be to borrow additional funds either to take advantage of a promising investment opportunity or to meet obligations. In general, the less financial flexibility, the more risk there is that an enterprise will fail. In a subsequent section of this chapter, we introduce some common ratios used to assess liquidity and long-term solvency.

In summary, even though the balance sheet does not *directly measure* the market value of the entity, it provides valuable information that can be used to help *judge* market value.

Classifications

FINANCIAL Reporting Case

Q2, p. 113

The key classification of assets and liabilities in the balance sheet is the current versus noncurrent distinction.

The usefulness of the balance sheet is enhanced when assets and liabilities are grouped according to common characteristics. *The broad distinction made in the balance sheet is the current versus noncurrent classification of both assets and liabilities.* The remainder of Part A provides an overview of the balance sheet. We discuss each of the three primary elements of the balance sheet (assets, liabilities, and shareholders' equity) in the order they are reported in the statement as well as the classifications typically made within the elements. The balance sheet elements were defined in Chapter 1 as follows:

Assets are probable future economic benefits obtained or controlled by a particular entity as a result of past transactions or events.

Liabilities are probable future sacrifices of economic benefits arising from present obligations of a particular entity to transfer assets or provide services to other entities in the future as a result of past transactions or events.

Equity (or net assets), called **shareholders' equity** or **stockholders' equity** for a corporation, is the residual interest in the assets of an entity that remains after deducting liabilities.

Illustration 3–1 lists the balance sheet elements along with their subclassifications.

We intentionally avoid detailed discussion of the question of valuation in order to focus on an overview of the balance sheet. In later chapters we look closer at the nature and valuation of the specific assets and liabilities.

Illustration 3–1 Classification of Elements within a Balance Sheet

Assets
Current assets
Investments
Property, plant, and equipment
Intangible assets
Other assets
Liabilities
Current liabilities
Long-term liabilities
Shareholders' Equity
Paid-in capital
Retained earnings

Current assets include cash and all other assets expected to become cash or be consumed within one year or the *operating cycle,* whichever is longer.

Assets

CURRENT ASSETS.   Current assets include cash and other assets that are reasonably expected to be converted to cash or consumed within the coming year, or within the normal operating cycle of the business if that's longer than one year. The operating cycle for a typical manufacturing company refers to the period of time necessary to convert cash to raw materials, raw materials to a finished product, the finished product to receivables, and then finally receivables back to cash. This concept is illustrated in Illustration 3–2.

In some businesses, such as shipbuilding or distilleries, the operating cycle extends far beyond one year. For example, if it takes two years to build an oil-carrying supertanker, then the shipbuilder will classify as current those assets that will be converted to cash or consumed within two years. But for most businesses the operating cycle will be shorter than one year. In these situations the one-year convention is used to classify both assets and liabilities. Where a company has no clearly defined operating cycle, the one-year convention is used.

Illustration 3–3 presents the current asset sections of Dell Inc.'s 2011 and 2010 balance sheets (statements of financial position) that also can be located in the company's financial statements in Appendix B at the back of the text. In keeping with common practice, the individual current assets are listed in the order of their liquidity (nearness to cash).

Cash and Cash Equivalents. The most liquid asset, cash, is listed first. Cash includes cash on hand and in banks that is available for use in the operations of the business and such items as bank drafts, cashier's checks, and money orders. Cash equivalents frequently include certain negotiable items such as commercial paper, money market funds, and U.S. treasury bills. These are highly liquid investments that can be quickly converted into cash. Most companies draw a distinction between investments classified as cash equivalents and the next category of current assets, short-term investments, according to the scheduled maturity of the investment. It is common practice to classify investments that have a maturity date of three months or less from the date of purchase as cash equivalents. Dell Inc.'s policy follows this practice and is disclosed in the summary of significant accounting policies disclosure note. The portion of the note from the company's 2011 financial statements is shown in Illustration 3–4.

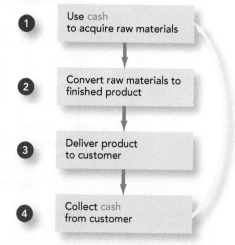

Illustration 3–2 Operating Cycle of a Typical Manufacturing Company

1. Use cash to acquire raw materials
2. Convert raw materials to finished product
3. Deliver product to customer
4. Collect cash from customer

● LO3–2

Illustration 3–3
Current Assets—Dell Inc.

Real World Financials

(In millions)	January 28, 2011	January 29, 2010
Assets		
Current assets:		
Cash and cash equivalents	$13,913	$10,635
Short-term investments	452	373
Accounts receivable, net	6,493	5,837
Financing receivables, net	3,643	2,706
Inventories, net	1,301	1,051
Other current assets	3,219	3,643
Total current assets	29,021	24,245

Note 1—Description of Business and Summary of Significant Accounting Policies
Cash and Cash Equivalents
All highly liquid investments, including credit card receivables, due from banks, with original maturities of three months or less at date of purchase are carried at cost and are considered to be cash equivalents. All other investments not considered to be cash equivalents are separately categorized as investments.

Illustration 3–4
Disclosure of Cash Equivalents—Dell Inc.

Real World Financials

Cash that is restricted for a special purpose and not available for current operations should not be classified as a current asset. For example, if cash is being accumulated to repay a debt due in five years, the cash is classified as investments, a noncurrent asset.[2]

Short-Term Investments. Liquid investments not classified as cash equivalents are reported as either short-term investments, sometimes called *temporary investments* or *short-term marketable securities*. Investments in stock and debt securities of other corporations are included as short-term investments *if* the company has the ability and intent to sell those securities within the next 12 months or operating cycle, whichever is longer. If, for example, a company owns 1,000 shares of IBM Corporation stock and intends to hold those shares for several years, the stock is a long-term investment and should be classified as a noncurrent asset, investments.

Investments **are classified as current if management has the ability and intent to liquidate the investment in the near term.**

---

[2]If the debt is due in the next year and classified as a current liability, then the cash also would be classified as current.

For reporting purposes, investments in debt and equity securities are classified in one of three categories: (1) held to maturity, (2) trading securities, or (3) securities available for sale. We discuss these different categories and their accounting treatment in Chapter 12.

Accounts Receivable.   Accounts receivable result from the sale of goods or services on credit. Notice in Illustration 3–3 that Dell's accounts receivable and financing receivables (discussed in Chapter 7) are valued net, that is, less an allowance for uncollectible accounts (the amount not expected to be collected). Accounts receivable often are referred to as *trade receivables* because they arise in the course of a company's normal trade. *Nontrade receivables* result from loans or advances by the company to individuals and other entities. When receivables are supported by a formal agreement or note that specifies payment terms they are called notes receivable.

Accounts receivable usually are due in 30 to 60 days, depending on the terms offered to customers and are, therefore, classified as current assets. Any receivable, regardless of the source, not expected to be collected within one year or the operating cycle, whichever is longer, is classified as a noncurrent asset, investments.

Inventories consist of assets that a retail or wholesale company acquires for resale or goods that manufacturers produce for sale.

Inventories.   Inventories include goods awaiting sale (finished goods), goods in the course of production (work in process), and goods to be consumed directly or indirectly in production (raw materials). Inventory for a wholesale or retail company consists only of finished goods, but the inventory of a manufacturer will include all three types of goods. Occasionally, a manufacturing company will report all three types of inventory directly in the balance sheet. More often, only the total amount of inventories is shown in the balance sheet and the balances of each type are shown in a disclosure note. For example, the note shown in Illustration 3–5 lists the components of inventory in the 2011 financial statements of Dell Inc.

Illustration 3–5

Inventories Disclosure—
Dell Inc.

Real World Financials

Note 12—Supplemental Consolidated Financial Information (in part)		
	January 28, 2011	**January 29, 2010**
Inventories, net:		
Production materials	$ 593	$ 487
Work-in-process	232	168
Finished goods	476	396
Total	$1,301	$1,051

Inventories are reported as current assets because they normally are sold within the operating cycle.

Prepaid Expenses.   Recall from Chapter 2 that a prepaid expense represents an asset recorded when an expense is paid in advance, creating benefits beyond the current period. Examples are prepaid rent and prepaid insurance. Even though these assets are not converted to cash, they would involve an outlay of cash if not prepaid.

Whether a prepaid expense is current or noncurrent depends on when its benefits will be realized. For example, if rent on an office building were prepaid for one year, then the entire prepayment is classified as a current asset. However, if rent were prepaid for a period extending beyond the coming year, a portion of the prepayment is classified as an other asset, a noncurrent asset.[3] Dell Inc. includes prepaid expenses in the other current assets category. Other current assets also include assets—such as nontrade receivables—that, because their amounts are not material, did not warrant separate disclosure.

When assets are expected to provide economic benefits beyond the next year, or operating cycle, they are reported as *noncurrent assets*. Typical classifications of noncurrent assets are (1) investments, (2) property, plant, and equipment, and (3) intangible assets.

---

[3]Companies often include prepayments for benefits extending beyond one year as current assets when the amounts are not material.

INVESTMENTS. Most companies occasionally acquire assets that are not used directly in the operations of the business. These assets include investments in equity and debt securities of other corporations, land held for speculation, noncurrent receivables, and cash set aside for special purposes (such as for future plant expansion). These assets are classified as noncurrent because management does not intend to convert the assets into cash in the next year (or the operating cycle if that's longer).

Investments are assets not used directly in operations.

PROPERTY, PLANT, AND EQUIPMENT. Virtually all companies own assets classified as property, plant, and equipment. The common characteristics these assets share are that they are *tangible, long-lived,* and *used in the operations of the business.* Property, plant, and equipment, along with intangible assets, often are the primary revenue-generating assets of the business.

Property, plant, and equipment includes land, buildings, equipment, machinery, and furniture, as well as natural resources, such as mineral mines, timber tracts, and oil wells. These various assets usually are reported as a single amount in the balance sheet, with details provided in a note. They are reported at original cost less accumulated depreciation (or depletion for natural resources) to date. Quite often, a company will present only the net amount of property, plant, and equipment in the balance sheet and provide details in a disclosure note. Land often is listed as a separate item in this classification because it has an unlimited useful life and thus is not depreciated.

Tangible, long-lived assets used in the operations of the business are classified as property, plant, and equipment.

INTANGIBLE ASSETS. Some assets used in the operations of a business have no physical substance. These are appropriately called intangible assets. Generally, these represent the ownership of an exclusive right to something such as a product, a process, or a name. This right can be a valuable resource in generating future revenues. Patents, copyrights, and franchises are examples. They are reported in the balance sheet net of accumulated amortization. Some companies include intangible assets as part of property, plant, and equipment, while others report them either in a separate intangible asset classification or as other noncurrent assets.

Quite often, much of the value of intangibles is not reported in the balance sheet. For example, it would not be unusual for the historical cost of a patent to be significantly lower than its market value. As we discuss in Chapter 10, for internally developed intangibles, the costs that are included as part of historical cost are limited. Specifically, none of the research and development costs incurred in developing the intangible asset are included in cost.

Intangible assets generally represent exclusive rights that a company can use to generate future revenues.

OTHER ASSETS. Balance sheets often include a catch-all classification of noncurrent assets called other assets. This classification includes long-term prepaid expenses, called *deferred charges,* and any noncurrent asset not falling in one of the other classifications. For instance, if a company's noncurrent investments are not material in amount, they might be reported in the other asset classification rather than in a separate investments category.

Illustration 3–6 reproduces the noncurrent asset section of Dell Inc.'s 2011 and 2010 balance sheets. For Dell, noncurrent assets include property, plant, and equipment, investments, long-term financing receivables, goodwill (an intangible asset), purchased intangible assets, and other noncurrent assets.

Illustration 3–6

Noncurrent Assets—
Dell Inc.

Real World Financials

	January 28, 2011	January 29, 2010
(In millions)		
Assets		
Property, plant, and equipment, net	1,953	2,181
Investments	704	781
Long-term financing receivables, net	799	332
Goodwill	4,365	4,074
Purchased intangible assets, net	1,495	1,694
Other noncurrent assets	262	345

We've seen how assets are grouped into current and noncurrent categories and that non-current assets always are subclassified further. Let's now turn our attention to liabilities. These, too, are separated into current and noncurrent (long-term) categories.

Liabilities

● LO3–3 Liabilities represent obligations to other entities. The information value of reporting these amounts is enhanced by classifying them as current liabilities and long-term liabilities. Illustration 3–7 shows the liability section of Dell Inc.'s 2011 and 2010 balance sheets.

Illustration 3–7
Liabilities—Dell Inc.

Real World Financials

(In millions)	January 28, 2011	January 29, 2010
Liabilities		
Current liabilities:		
Short-term debt	$ 851	$ 663
Accounts payable	11,293	11,373
Accrued and other	4,181	3,884
Short-term deferred services revenue	3,158	3,040
Total current liabilities	19,483	18,960
Long-term debt	5,146	3,417
Long-term deferred service revenue	3,518	3,029
Other noncurrent liabilities	2,686	2,605
Total liabilities	30,833	28,011

Current liabilities are expected to be satisfied within one year or the operating cycle, whichever is longer.

CURRENT LIABILITIES. Current liabilities are those obligations that are expected to be satisfied through the use of current assets or the creation of other current liabilities. So, this classification includes all liabilities that are expected to be satisfied within one year or the operating cycle, whichever is longer. An exception is a liability that management intends to refinance on a long-term basis. For example, if management intends to refinance a six-month note payable by substituting a two-year note payable and has the ability to do so, then the liability would not be classified as current even though it's due within the coming year. This exception is discussed in more detail in Chapter 13.

Current liabilities usually include *accounts* and *notes payable, unearned revenues, accrued liabilities,* and the *current maturities of long-term debt*.

The most common current liabilities are accounts payable, notes payable (short-term borrowings), unearned revenues, accrued liabilities, and the currently maturing portion of long-term debt. Accounts payable are obligations to suppliers of merchandise or of services purchased on open account, with payment usually due in 30 to 60 days. Notes payable are written promises to pay cash at some future date (I.O.U.s). Unlike accounts payable, notes usually require the payment of explicit interest in addition to the original obligation amount. Notes maturing in the next year or operating cycle, whichever is longer, will be classified as current liabilities. Unearned revenues, sometimes called deferred revenues as in Dell's balance sheet, represent cash received from a customer for goods or services to be provided in a future period.

Accrued liabilities represent obligations created when expenses have been incurred but will not be paid until a subsequent reporting period. Examples are accrued salaries payable, accrued interest payable, and accrued taxes payable. Dell Inc.'s accrued liabilities include accrued warranty liabilities, accrued income and other taxes, accrued compensation, and other.

Long-term notes, loans, mortgages, and bonds payable usually are reclassified and reported as current liabilities as they become payable within the next year (or operating cycle if that's longer).[4] Likewise, when long-term debt is payable in installments, the installment payable currently is reported as a current liability. For example, a $1,000,000 note payable requiring $100,000 in principal payments to be made in each of the next 10 years

---

[4]Payment can be with current assets or the creation of other current liabilities.

is classified as a $100,000 current liability—current maturities of long-term debt—and a $900,000 long-term liability.

Chapter 13 provides a more detailed analysis of current liabilities.

> Current liabilities include the *current maturities of long-term debt.*

LONG-TERM LIABILITIES. Long-term liabilities are obligations that will *not* be satisfied in the next year or operating cycle, whichever is longer. They do not require the use of current assets or the creation of current liabilities for payment. Examples are long-term notes, bonds, pension obligations, and lease obligations.

> Noncurrent, or long-term liabilities, usually are those payable beyond the current year.

But simply classifying a liability as long-term doesn't provide complete information to external users. For instance, long-term could mean anything from 2 to 20, 30, or 40 years. Payment terms, interest rates, and other details needed to assess the impact of these obligations on future cash flows and long-term solvency are reported in a disclosure note.

Dell Inc. reports long-term debt, long-term deferred services revenue, and other noncurrent liabilities at the end of its 2011 fiscal year. A disclosure note indicates that other noncurrent liabilities include warranty liabilities, income and other taxes payable, and other. Long-term liabilities are discussed in subsequent chapters.

Shareholders' Equity

Recall from our discussions in Chapters 1 and 2 that owners' equity is simply a residual amount derived by subtracting liabilities from assets. For that reason, it's sometimes referred to as net assets. Also recall that owners of a corporation are its shareholders, so owners' equity for a corporation is referred to as shareholders' equity or stockholders' equity. Shareholders' equity for a corporation arises primarily from two sources: (1) amounts *invested* by shareholders in the corporation, and (2) amounts *earned* by the corporation (on behalf of its shareholders). These are reported as (1) paid-in capital and (2) retained earnings. Retained earnings represents the accumulated net income earned since the inception of the corporation and not (yet) paid to shareholders as dividends.

> Shareholders' equity is composed of *paid-in capital* (invested capital) and *retained earnings* (earned capital).

Illustration 3–8 presents the shareholders' equity section of Dell Inc.'s 2011 and 2010 fiscal year-end balance sheets.

	January 28, 2011	January 29, 2010
(In millions)		
Stockholders' equity:		
Common stock and capital in excess of $.01 par value; shares authorized: 7,000; shares issued: 3,369 and 3,351, respectively; shares outstanding; 1,918 and 1,957, respectively	11,797	11,472
Treasury stock, at cost: 976 and 919 shares, respectively	(28,704)	(27,904)
Retained earnings	24,744	22,110
Accumulated other comprehensive loss	(71)	(37)
Total stockholders' equity	7,766	5,641

Illustration 3–8

Shareholders' Equity— Dell Inc.

Real World Financials

From the inception of the corporation through January 28, 2011, Dell has accumulated net income, less dividends, of $24,744 million which is reported as *retained earnings*. The company's *paid-in capital* is represented by common stock and additional paid-in capital less treasury stock, which collectively represent cash invested by shareholders in exchange for ownership interests. Information about the number of shares the company has authorized and how many shares have been issued and are outstanding also must be disclosed.

In addition to paid-in capital and retained earnings, shareholders' equity may include a few other equity components. For example, Dell reports accumulated other comprehensive loss. Accumulated other comprehensive income (loss) is discussed in Chapters 4, 12, and 18. Other equity components are addressed in later chapters, Chapter 18 in particular. We also discuss the concept of par value in Chapter 18.

International Financial Reporting Standards

● LO3–9

Balance Sheet Presentation. There are more similarities than differences in balance sheets prepared according to U.S. GAAP and those prepared applying IFRS. Some of the differences are:

- International standards specify a minimum list of items to be presented in the balance sheet. U.S. GAAP has no minimum requirements.
- *IAS No.1, revised,*[5] changed the title of the balance sheet to *statement of financial position,* although companies are not required to use that title. Some U.S. companies use the statement of financial position title as well.
- Under U.S. GAAP, we present current assets and liabilities before noncurrent assets and liabilities. *IAS No. 1* doesn't prescribe the format of the balance sheet, but balance sheets prepared using IFRS often report noncurrent items first. A recent survey of large companies that prepare their financial statements according to IFRS reports that in 2009, 73% of the surveyed companies list noncurrent items first.[6] For example, the balance sheet of Sanofi-Aventis, a French pharmaceutical company, included in a recent half-year report, presented assets, liabilities, and equity in the following order:

Real World Financials

Sanofi-Aventis
Balance Sheet (condensed)
At June 30

(€ in millions)	2011
Noncurrent assets (including property, plant, and equipment)	€76,958
Current assets	22,592
Assets held for sale or exchange	44
Total assets	€99,594
Shareholders' equity	€52,599
Noncurrent liabilities	30,943
Current liabilities	16,038
Liabilities related to assets held for sale or exchange	14
Total liabilities and equity	€99,594

Where We're Headed

● LO3–9

The FASB and IASB are working together on a standard that would have a dramatic impact on the format of financial statements.

Demonstrating the cohesiveness among the financial statements is a key objective of the Financial Statement Presentation project.

The FASB and IASB are working together on a project, Financial Statement Presentation, to establish a common standard for presenting information in the financial statements, including classifying and displaying line items and aggregating line items into subtotals and totals. This standard would have a dramatic impact on the format of financial statements. An important part of the proposal involves the organization of elements of the balance sheet (statement of financial position), statement of comprehensive income (including the income statement), and statement of cash flows into a common set of classifications.

Each of the financial statements would include classifications by operating, investing, and financing activities, providing a "cohesive" financial picture that stresses the relationships among the financial statements. Recall from your previous accounting education and from our brief discussion in Chapter 2, that this is the way we currently classify activities in the statement of cash flows.

(continued)

---

[5]"Financial Statement Presentation," *International Accounting Standard No. 1* (IASCF), as amended effective January 1, 2011.
[6]*IFRS Accounting Trends and Techniques*—2010 (New York, AICPA, 2010), p.133.

(concluded)

For each statement, though, operating and investing activities would be included within a new category, "business" activities. Each statement also would include three additional groupings: discontinued operations, income taxes, and equity (if needed). The new look for the balance sheet (statement of financial position) would be:

Statement of Financial Position

Business
- Operating assets and liabilities
- Investing assets and liabilities

Financing
- Debt
- Equity

Income Taxes

Discontinued Operations

The project has multiple phases and it is uncertain when it will be completed.

Concept Review Exercise

The following is a post-closing trial balance for the Sepia Paint Corporation at December 31, 2013, the end of the company's fiscal year:

BALANCE SHEET CLASSIFICATION

Account Title	Debits	Credits
Cash	80,000	
Accounts receivable	200,000	
Allowance for uncollectible accounts		20,000
Inventories	300,000	
Prepaid expenses	30,000	
Note receivable (due in one month)	60,000	
Investments	50,000	
Land	120,000	
Buildings	550,000	
Machinery	500,000	
Accumulated depreciation—buildings and machinery		450,000
Patent (net of amortization)	50,000	
Accounts payable		170,000
Salaries payable		40,000
Interest payable		10,000
Note payable		100,000
Bonds payable (due in 10 years)		500,000
Common stock, no par		400,000
Retained earnings		250,000
Totals	1,940,000	1,940,000

The $50,000 balance in the investment account consists of marketable equity securities of other corporations. The company's intention is to hold the securities for at least three years. The $100,000 note payable is an installment loan. $10,000 of the principal, plus interest, is due on each July 1 for the next 10 years. At the end of the year, 100,000 shares of common stock were issued and outstanding. The company has 500,000 shares of common stock authorized.

Required:
Prepare a classified balance sheet for the Sepia Paint Corporation at December 31, 2013.

Solution:

SEPIA PAINT CORPORATION
Balance Sheet
At December 31, 2013

Assets

Current assets:		
Cash		$ 80,000
Accounts receivable	$ 200,000	
Less: Allowance for uncollectible amounts	(20,000)	180,000
Note receivable		60,000
Inventories		300,000
Prepaid expenses		30,000
Total current assets		650,000
Investments		50,000
Property, plant, and equipment:		
Land	120,000	
Buildings	550,000	
Machinery	500,000	
	1,170,000	
Less: Accumulated depreciation	(450,000)	
Net property, plant, and equipment		720,000
Intangible assets:		
Patent		50,000
Total assets		$1,470,000

Liabilities and Shareholders' Equity

Current liabilities:		
Accounts payable		$ 170,000
Salaries payable		40,000
Interest payable		10,000
Current maturities of long-term debt		10,000
Total current liabilities		230,000
Long-term liabilities:		
Note payable	$ 90,000	
Bonds payable	500,000	
Total long-term liabilities		590,000
Shareholders' equity:		
Common stock, no par, 500,000 shares authorized, 100,000 shares issued and outstanding	400,000	
Retained earnings	250,000	
Total shareholders' equity		650,000
Total liabilities and shareholders' equity		$1,470,000

The usefulness of the balance sheet, as well as the other financial statements, is significantly enhanced by financial statement disclosures. We now turn our attention to these disclosures.

PART B

FINANCIAL DISCLOSURES

● LO3–4 Financial statements are included in the annual report a company mails to its shareholders. They are, though, only part of the information provided. Critical to understanding the financial statements and to evaluating a firm's performance and financial health are additional disclosures included as part of the financial statements.

Financial statement disclosures are provided (1) by including additional information, often parenthetically, on the face of the statement following a financial statement item and (2) in disclosure notes that often include supporting schedules. Common examples of disclosures included on the face of the balance sheet are the allowance for uncollectible accounts and information about common stock. Disclosure notes, discussed and illustrated in the next section, are the most common means of providing these additional disclosures. The specific format of disclosure is generally not important, only that the information is, in fact, disclosed.

> The full-disclosure principle requires that financial statements provide all material relevant information concerning the reporting entity.

Disclosure Notes

Disclosure notes typically span several pages and either explain or elaborate upon the data presented in the financial statements themselves, or provide information not directly related to any specific item in the statements. Throughout this text you will encounter examples of items that usually are disclosed this way. For instance, the fair values of financial instruments and "off-balance-sheet" risk associated with financial instruments are disclosed in notes. Information providing details of many financial statement items is provided using disclosure notes. Some examples include:

- Pension plans
- Leases
- Long-term debt
- Investments
- Income taxes
- Property, plant, and equipment
- Employee benefit plans

Disclosure notes must include certain specific notes such as a summary of significant accounting policies, descriptions of subsequent events, and related third-party transactions, but many notes are fashioned to suit the disclosure needs of the particular reporting enterprise. Actually, any explanation that contributes to investors' and creditors' understanding of the results of operations, financial position, and cash flows of the company should be included. Let's take a look at just a few disclosure notes.

Summary of Significant Accounting Policies

There are many areas where management chooses from among equally acceptable alternative accounting methods. For example, management chooses whether to use accelerated or straight-line depreciation, whether to use FIFO, LIFO, or average cost to measure inventories, and whether the completed contract or percentage-of-completion method best reflects the performance of construction operations. The company also defines which securities it considers to be cash equivalents and its policies regarding the timing of recognizing revenues. Typically, the first disclosure note consists of a summary of significant accounting policies that discloses the choices the company makes.[7] Illustration 3–9 shows you a portion of a typical summary note from a recent annual report of the Starbucks Corporation.

> The *summary of significant accounting policies* conveys valuable information about the company's choices from among various alternative accounting methods.

Studying this note is an essential step in analyzing financial statements. Obviously, knowing which methods were used to derive certain accounting numbers is critical to assessing the adequacy of those amounts.

Subsequent Events

When an event that has a material effect on the company's financial position occurs after the fiscal year-end but before the financial statements are issued or "available to be issued," the

---

[7]FASB ASC 235–10–50: Notes to Financial Statements—Overall—Disclosure (previously "Disclosure of Accounting Policies," *Accounting Principles Board Opinion No. 22* (New York: AICPA, 1972)).

Illustration 3–9 Summary of Significant Accounting Policies—Starbucks Corporation

Note 1: Summary of Accounting Policies (in part)

Principles of Consolidation

The consolidated financial statements reflect the financial position and operating results of Starbucks, which includes wholly owned subsidiaries and investees controlled by the Company.

Cash Equivalents

The Company considers all highly liquid instruments with a maturity of three months or less at the time of purchase to be cash equivalents.

Inventories

Inventories are stated at the lower of cost (primarily moving average cost) or market. The Company records inventory reserves for obsolete and slow-moving items and for estimated shrinkage between physical inventory counts.

Property, Plant, and Equipment

Property, plant, and equipment are carried at cost less accumulated depreciation. Depreciation of property, plant, and equipment which includes assets under leases, is provided on the straight-line method over estimated useful lives, generally ranging from two to seven years for equipment and 30 to 40 years for buildings. Leasehold improvements are amortized over the shorter of their estimated useful lives or the related lease life, generally 10 years.

Revenue Recognition

Company-operated retail store revenues are recognized when payment is tendered at the point of sale. Revenues from the Company's store value cards, such as the Starbucks Card, and gift certificates are recognized when tendered for payment, or upon redemption. Outstanding customer balances are included in Deferred revenue on the consolidated balance sheets.

Real World Financials

A *subsequent event* is a significant development that occurs after a company's fiscal year-end but before the financial statements are issued or available to be issued.

event is described in a subsequent event disclosure note.[8] Examples include the issuance of debt or equity securities, a business combination or the sale of a business, the sale of assets, an event that sheds light on the outcome of a loss contingency, or any other event having a material effect on operations. Illustration 3–10 illustrates the required disclosure by showing a note that Wal-Mart Stores, Inc., included in its January 31, 2011, financial statements, announcing both an increase in the company's annual dividend and the uncertainty of the damages to the company's business in Japan following the March 2011 earthquake.

We cover subsequent events in more depth in Chapter 13.

Illustration 3–10

Subsequent Event— Wal-Mart Stores, Inc.

Real World Financials

14 Subsequent Events (in part)

Dividends Declared

On March 3, 2011, our Board of Directors approved an increase in the annual dividend for fiscal 2012 to $1.46 per share, an increase of approximately 21% over the dividends paid in fiscal 2011. Dividends per share were $1.21 and $1.09 in fiscal 2011 and 2010, respectively. For the fiscal year ending January 31, 2012, the annual dividend will be paid in four quarterly installments.

Earthquake in Japan

On March 11, 2011, an earthquake of 9.0 magnitude occurred near the Northeastern coast of Japan, creating extremely destructive tsunami waves. The earthquake and tsunami waves caused extensive damage in Northeastern Japan and also affected other regions in Japan through a lack of electricity, water and transportation. We are currently unable to estimate the value of damages and the corresponding insurance recovery regarding our business in Japan, although we do not believe that any damages would be material to our financial position.

Noteworthy Events and Transactions

Some transactions and events occur only occasionally, but when they do occur are potentially important to evaluating a company's financial statements. In this category are related-party transactions, errors and irregularities, and illegal acts. The more frequent of these is related-party transactions.

---

[8]Financial statements are viewed as issued if they have been widely distributed to financial statement users in a format consistent with GAAP. Some entities (for example, private companies) don't widely distribute their financial statements to users. For those entities, the key date for subsequent events is not the date of issuance but rather the date upon which the financial statements are "available to be issued," which occurs when the financial statements are complete, in a format consistent with GAAP, and have obtained the necessary approvals for issuance. Companies must disclose the date through which subsequent events have been evaluated. (FASB ASC 855: Subsequent Events (previously "Subsequent Events," *Statement of Financial Accounting Standards No. 165* (Stamford, Conn.: FASB, 2009))).

Sometimes a company will engage in transactions with owners, management, families of owners or management, affiliated companies, and other parties that can significantly influence or be influenced by the company. The potential problem with related-party transactions is that their economic substance may differ from their legal form. For instance, borrowing or lending money at an interest rate that differs significantly from the market interest rate is an example of a transaction that could result from a related-party involvement. As a result of the potential for misrepresentation, financial statement users are particularly interested in more details about these transactions.

When related-party transactions occur, companies must disclose the nature of the relationship, provide a description of the transactions, and report the dollar amounts of transactions and any amounts due from or to related parties.[9] Illustration 3–11 shows a disclosure note from a recent annual report of Guess, Inc., the contemporary apparel and accessories company. The note describes the charter of aircraft from a trust organized for the benefit of executives of the company.

The economic substance of related-party transactions should be disclosed, including dollar amounts involved.

11. Related-Party Transactions (in part)

The Company and its subsidiaries periodically enter into transactions with other entities or individuals that are considered related parties, including certain transactions with entities affiliated with trusts for the respective benefit of Maurice and Paul Marciano, who are executives of the Company, Armand Marciano, their brother and former executive of the Company, and certain of their children (the "Marciano Trusts").

Aircraft Arrangements

The Company periodically charters aircraft owned by MPM Financial, LLC ("MPM Financial"), an entity affiliated with the Marciano Trusts, through independent third party management companies contracted by MPM Financial to manage its aircraft. Under an informal arrangement with MPM Financial and the third party management companies, the Company has chartered and may from time to time continue to charter aircraft owned by MPM Financial at a discount from the third party management companies' preferred customer hourly charter rates. The total fees paid under these arrangements for fiscal 2011, fiscal 2010 and fiscal 2009 were approximately $1.1 million, $0.4 million and $0.9 million, respectively.

Illustration 3–11

Related-Party Transactions Disclosure—Guess, Inc.

Real World Financials

More infrequent are errors, irregularities, and illegal acts; however, when they do occur, their disclosure is important. The distinction between errors and irregularities is that errors are unintentional while irregularities are *intentional* distortions of financial statements.[10] Obviously, management fraud might cause a user to approach financial analysis from an entirely different and more cautious viewpoint.

Closely related to irregularities are illegal acts such as bribes, kickbacks, illegal contributions to political candidates, and other violations of the law. Accounting for illegal practices has been influenced by the Foreign Corrupt Practices Act passed by Congress in 1977. The Act is intended to discourage illegal business practices through tighter controls and also encourage better disclosure of those practices when encountered. The nature of such disclosures should be influenced by the materiality of the impact of illegal acts on amounts disclosed in the financial statements.[11] However, the SEC issued guidance expressing its view that exclusive reliance on quantitative benchmarks to assess materiality in preparing financial statements is inappropriate.[12] A number of other factors, including whether the item in question involves an unlawful transaction, should also be considered when determining materiality.

As you might expect, any disclosures of related-party transactions, irregularities, and illegal acts can be quite sensitive. Although auditors must be considerate of the privacy of the parties involved, that consideration cannot be subordinate to users' needs for full disclosure.

---

[9]FASB ASC 850–10–50: Related Party Disclosures—Overall—Disclosure (previously "Related Party Disclosures," *Statement of Financial Accounting Standards No. 57* (Stamford, Conn.: FASB, 1982)).

[10]"The Auditor's Responsibility to Detect and Report Errors and Irregularities," *Statement on Auditing Standards No. 53* (New York: AICPA, 1988).

[11]"Illegal Acts by Clients," *Statement on Auditing Standards No. 54* (New York: AICPA, 1988).

[12]FASB ASC 250–10–S99–1, SAB Topic 1.M: Assessing Materiality (originally "Materiality," *Staff Accounting Bulletin No. 99* (Washington, D.C.: SEC, August 1999)).

Disclosure notes for some financial statement elements are required. Others are provided when required by specific situations in the interest of full disclosure.

We've discussed only a few of the disclosure notes most frequently included in annual reports. Other common disclosures include details concerning earnings per share calculations, income taxes, property and equipment, contingencies, long-term debt, leases, pensions, stock options, changes in accounting methods, fair values of financial instruments, and exposure to market risk and credit risk. We discuss and illustrate these in later chapters in the context of related financial statement elements.

Management Discussion and Analysis

● LO3-5

The management discussion and analysis provides a biased but informed perspective of a company's
(a) operations,
(b) liquidity, and
(c) capital resources.

In addition to the financial statements and accompanying disclosure notes, each annual report of a public company requires a fairly lengthy discussion and analysis provided by the company's management. In this section, management provides its views on significant events, trends, and uncertainties pertaining to the company's (a) operations, (b) liquidity, and (c) capital resources. Although the management discussion and analysis (MD&A) section may embody management's biased perspective, it can offer an informed insight that might not be available elsewhere. Illustration 3–12 contains part of the liquidity and capital resources portion of PetSmart, Inc.'s MDA that followed a discussion of operations in its annual report for the fiscal year ended January 30, 2011.

Illustration 3–12

Management Discussion and Analysis—PetSmart, Inc.

Real World Financials

Management Discussion and Analysis of Financial Condition and Results of Operations
(In part: Liquidity and Capital Resources only)

Cash Flow

We believe that our operating cash flow and cash on hand will be adequate to meet our operating, investing and financing needs in the foreseeable future. In addition, we also have access to our $350.0 million revolving credit facility, although there can be no assurance of our ability to access these markets on commercially acceptable terms in the future. We expect to continuously assess the economic environment and market conditions to guide our decisions regarding our uses of cash, including capital expenditures, investments, dividends and the purchase of our common stock.

Common Stock Purchase Program

In June 2010, the Board of Directors replaced the $350.0 million program with a new share purchase program authorizing the purchase of up to $400.0 million of our common stock through January 29, 2012. During the thirteen weeks ended January 30, 2011, we purchased 2.6 million shares of common stock for $99.9 million. Since the inception of the $400.0 million authorization in June 2010, we have purchased 4.2 million shares of common stock for $156.2 million. As of January 30, 2011, $243.8 million remained available under the $400.0 million program.

Common Stock Dividends

We presently believe our ability to generate cash allows us to invest in the growth of the business and, at the same time, distribute a quarterly dividend. Our credit facility and letter of credit facility permit us to pay dividends, so long as we are not in default and the payment of dividends would not result in default. During 2010, 2009, and 2008, we paid aggregate dividends of $0.45 per share, $0.26 per share, and $0.12 per share, respectively.

Operating Capital and Capital Expenditure Requirements

Substantially all our stores are leased facilities. We opened 46 new stores and closed 8 stores in 2010. Generally, each new store requires capital expenditures of approximately $1.0 million for fixtures, equipment and leasehold improvements, approximately $0.3 million for inventory and approximately $0.1 million for preopening costs. We expect total capital spending to be approximately $130.0 to $140.0 million for 2011, based on our plan to open 45 to 50 net new stores and 8 to 10 new PetsHotels, continuing our investment in the development of our information systems, adding to our services capacity with the expansion of certain grooming salons, remodeling or replacing certain store assets and continuing our store refresh program.

Management's Responsibilities

Management prepares and is responsible for the financial statements and other information in the annual report. To enhance the awareness of the users of financial statements concerning the relative roles of management and the auditor, annual reports of public companies include a management's responsibilities section that asserts the responsibility of management for the information contained in the annual report as well as an assessment of the company's internal control procedures.

Illustration 3–13 contains the statement of responsibility disclosure for Home Depot, Inc. included with the company's financial statements for the year ended January 30, 2011. Recall from our discussion of financial reporting reform in Chapter 1, that the *Sarbanes-Oxley Act of 2002* requires corporate executives to personally certify the financial statements. Submission of false statements carries a penalty of up to 20 years in jail. The illustration also contains Management's Report on Internal Control Over Financial Reporting. Francis S. Blake, Home Depot's chairman and chief executive officer, and Carol B. Tomé, the company's chief financial officer and executive vice president, signed the required certifications as well as these statements of responsibility.

Illustration 3–13

Management's Responsibilities—Home Depot, Inc.

Real World Financials

Management's Responsibility for Financial Statements

The financial statements presented in this Annual Report have been prepared with integrity and objectivity and are the responsibility of the management of The Home Depot, Inc. These financial statements have been prepared in conformity with U.S. generally accepted accounting principles and properly reflect certain estimates and judgments based upon the best available information.

The financial statements of the Company have been audited by KPMG LLP, an independent registered public accounting firm. Their accompanying report is based upon an audit conducted in accordance with the standards of the Public Company Accounting Oversight Board (United States).

The Audit Committee of the Board of Directors, consisting solely of outside directors, meets five times a year with the independent registered public accounting firm, the internal auditors and representatives of management to discuss auditing and financial reporting matters. In addition, a telephonic meeting is held prior to each quarterly earnings release. The Audit Committee retains the independent registered public accounting firm and regularly reviews the internal accounting controls, the activities of the independent registered public accounting firm and internal auditors and the financial condition of the Company. Both the Company's independent registered public accounting firm and the internal auditors have free access to the Audit Committee.

The *management's responsibilities* section avows the responsibility of management for the company's *financial* statements and internal control system.

Management's Report on Internal Control over Financial Reporting

Our management is responsible for establishing and maintaining adequate internal control over financial reporting, as such term is defined in Rules 13a–15(f) promulgated under the Securities Exchange Act of 1934, as amended (the "Exchange Act"). Under the supervision and with the participation of our management, including our Chief Executive Officer and Chief Financial Officer, we conducted an evaluation of the effectiveness of our internal control over financial reporting as of January 30, 2011 based on the framework in *Internal Control—Integrated Framework* issued by the Committee of Sponsoring Organizations of the Treadway Commission (COSO). Based on our evaluation, our management concluded that our internal control over financial reporting was effective as of January 30, 2011, in providing reasonable assurance regarding the reliability of financial reporting and the preparation of financial statements for external purposes in accordance with generally accepted accounting principles. The effectiveness of our internal control over financial reporting as of January 30, 2011, has been audited by KPMG LLP, an independent registered public accounting firm, as stated in their report which is included on page 30 in this Form 10-K.

Francis S. Blake   Carol B. Tomé
Chairman & Chief Executive Officer   Chief Financial Officer & Executive Vice President

Auditors' Report

● **LO3-6**

The auditors' report provides the analyst with an independent and professional opinion about the fairness of the representations in the financial statements and about the effectiveness of internal controls.

Illustration 3–14

Auditors' Report—
J. Crew Group, Inc.

Real World Financials

Auditors examine financial statements and the internal control procedures designed to support the content of those statements. Their role is to attest to the fairness of the financial statements based on that examination. The auditors' attest function results in an opinion stated in the auditors' report.

One step in financial analysis should be an examination of the auditors' report, which is issued by the CPAs who audit the financial statements and inform users of the audit findings. Every audit report of a public company looks similar to the one prepared by KPMG LLP for the financial statements of J. Crew Group, Inc., as shown in Illustration 3–14.

Report of Independent Registered Public Accounting Firm

The Board of Directors and Stockholders

J.Crew Group, Inc.:

We have audited the accompanying consolidated balance sheets of J.Crew Group, Inc. and subsidiaries ("Group") as of January 29, 2011 and January 30, 2010, and the related consolidated statements of operations, changes in stockholders' equity, and cash flows for each of the years in the three-year period ended January 29, 2011. In connection with our audits of the consolidated financial statements, we also have audited financial statement schedule II. These consolidated financial statements and the financial statement schedule are the responsibility of the Company's management. Our responsibility is to express an opinion on these consolidated financial statements and the financial statement schedule based on our audits.

We conducted our audits in accordance with the standards of the Public Company Accounting Oversight Board (United States). Those standards require that we plan and perform the audit to obtain reasonable assurance about whether the financial statements are free of material misstatement. An audit includes examining, on a test basis, evidence supporting the amounts and disclosures in the financial statements. An audit also includes assessing the accounting principles used and significant estimates made by management, as well as evaluating the overall financial statement presentation. We believe that our audits provide a reasonable basis for our opinion.

In our opinion, the consolidated financial statements referred to above present fairly, in all material respects, the financial position of Group as of January 29, 2011 and January 30, 2010 and the results of its operations and its cash flows for each of the years in the three-year period ended January 29, 2011, in conformity with U.S. generally accepted accounting principles. Also, in our opinion, the related financial statement schedule, when considered in relation to the consolidated financial statements taken as a whole, presents fairly, in all material respects, the information set forth therein.

We also have audited, in accordance with the standards of the Public Company Accounting Oversight Board (United States), Group's internal control over financial reporting as of January 29, 2011, based on the criteria established in Internal Control–Integrated Framework issued by the Committee of Sponsoring Organizations of the Treadway Commission (COSO), and our report dated March 21, 2011 expressed an unqualified opinion on the effectiveness of Group's internal control over financial reporting.

KPMG LLP
New York, New York
March 21, 2011

The reason for the similarities is that auditors' reports of public companies must be in compliance with the specifications of the PCAOB.[13] In most cases, including the report for J. Crew, the auditors will be satisfied that the financial statements "present fairly" the financial position, results of operations, and cash flows and are "in conformity with accounting principles generally accepted in the United States of America." These situations prompt an unqualified opinion. Notice that the last paragraph in J. Crew's report references the auditors' separate report on the effectiveness of the company's internal control over financial reporting.

---

[13]"An Audit of Internal Control over Financial Reporting That Is Integrated with An Audit of Financial Statements," *Auditing Standard No. 5* (Washington, D.C., PCAOB, 2007).

Sometimes circumstances cause the auditors' report to include an explanatory paragraph in addition to the standard wording, even though the report is unqualified. Most notably, these include:

- *Lack of consistency* due to a change in accounting principle such that comparability is affected even though the auditor concurs with the desirability of the change.
- *Uncertainty* as to the ultimate resolution of a contingency for which a loss is material in amount but not necessarily probable or probable but not estimable.
- *Emphasis* of a matter concerning the financial statements that does not affect the existence of an unqualified opinion but relates to a significant event such as a related-party transaction.

Some audits result in the need to issue other than an unqualified opinion due to exceptions such as (a) nonconformity with generally accepted accounting principles, (b) inadequate disclosures, and (c) a limitation or restriction of the scope of the examination. In these situations the auditor will issue a (an):

> The auditors' report calls attention to problems that might exist in the financial statements.

- *Qualified opinion* This contains an exception to the standard unqualified opinion but not of sufficient seriousness to invalidate the financial statements as a whole.
- *Adverse opinion* This is necessary when the exceptions (a) and (b) above are so serious that a qualified opinion is not justified. Adverse opinions are rare because auditors usually are able to persuade management to rectify problems to avoid this undesirable report.
- *Disclaimer* An auditor will disclaim an opinion for item (c) above such that insufficient information has been gathered to express an opinion.

During the course of each audit, the auditor is required to evaluate the company's ability to continue for a reasonable time as a going concern. If the auditor determines there is significant doubt, an explanation of the potential problem must be included in the auditors' report.[14]

> The auditor should assess the firm's ability to continue as a going concern.

Obviously, the auditors' report is most informative when any of these deviations from the standard unqualified opinion are present. These departures from the norm should raise a red flag to a financial analyst and prompt additional search for information.

As an example, a recent auditors' report of Blockbuster Inc. included a going concern paragraph shown in Illustration 3–15.

The accompanying consolidated financial statements have been prepared assuming that the Company will continue as a going concern. As discussed in Note 1 to the consolidated financial statements, the Company has incurred a net loss from operations for the year ended January 3, 2010 and has a stockholders' deficit as of January 3, 2010. In addition, the increasingly competitive industry conditions under which the Company operates have negatively impacted the Company's results of operations and cash flows and may continue to in the future. These factors raise substantial doubt about the Company's ability to continue as a going concern. Management's plans in regard to these matters are also described in Note 1. The financial statements do not include any adjustments that might result from the outcome of this uncertainty.

Illustration 3–15
Going Concern Paragraph—Blockbuster Inc.

Real World Financials

Compensation of Directors and Top Executives

In the early 1990s, the compensation large U.S. corporations paid their top executives became an issue of considerable public debate and controversy. Shareholders, employees, politicians, and the public in general began to question the huge pay packages received by company officials at the same time that more and more rank-and-file employees were being laid off as a result of company cutbacks. Contributing to the debate was the realization that the compensation gap between executives and lower-level employees was much wider than

[14]"The Auditor's Consideration of an Entity's Ability to Continue as a Going Concern," *Statement on Auditing Standards No. 59* (New York: AICPA, 1988).

in Japan and most other industrial countries. During this time, it also became apparent that discovering exactly how much compensation corporations paid their top people was nearly impossible.

Part of the problem stemmed from the fact that disclosures of these amounts were meager; but a large part of the problem was that a substantial portion of executive pay often is in the form of stock options. Executive stock options give their holders the right to buy stock at a specified price, usually equal to the market price when the options are granted. When stock prices rise, executives can exercise their options and realize a profit. In some cases, options have made executive compensation seem extremely high. Stock options are discussed in depth in Chapter 19.

The *proxy statement* contains disclosures on compensation to directors and executives.

To help shareholders and others sort out the content of executive pay packages and better understand the commitments of the company in this regard, SEC requirements provide for more disclosures on compensation to directors and executives, and in particular, concerning stock options. The proxy statement that must be sent each year to all shareholders, usually in the same mailing with the annual report, invites shareholders to the meeting to elect board members and to vote on issues before the shareholders or to vote using an enclosed proxy card. The proxy statement also includes compensation and stock option information for directors and top executives. Illustration 3–16 shows a portion of Best Buy Co. Inc.'s 2011 summary compensation table included in a recent proxy statement.

Illustration 3–16   Summary Compensation Table—Best Buy Co. Inc.

Summary Compensation Table (in part)

Name and Title	Fiscal Year	Salary and Bonus	Stock Awards	Option Awards	Non-Equity Incentive Plan Compensation	All Other Compensation	Total Compensation
Brian J. Dunn Chief Executive Officer	2011	$1,061,540	$ —	$3,206,125	$746,667	$15,168	$5,029,500
James L. Muehlbauer Executive VP Chief Financial Officer	2011	662,308	—	1,172,700	290,500	16,801	2,142,309
Shari L. Ballard Executive Vice President	2011	680,770	—	864,835	298,958	14,928	1,859,491
Michael A. Vitelli Executive Vice President	2011	661,540	—	864,835	291,667	18,110	1,836,152
Carol A. Surace Executive Vice President	2011	1,057,308	1,196,000	789,393	166,833	65,172	3,274,706

Real World Financials

PART C   RISK ANALYSIS
Using Financial Statement Information

● LO3–7

The overriding objective of financial reporting is providing information that investors and creditors can use to make decisions. Nevertheless, it's sometimes easy to lose sight of that objective while dealing with the intricacies that specific concepts and procedures can involve. In this part of the chapter we provide an overview of financial statement analysis and then demonstrate the use of ratios, a popular financial statement analysis technique, to analyze risk.

Investors, creditors, and others use information that companies provide in corporate financial reports to make decisions. Although the financial reports focus primarily on the past performance and the present financial condition of the reporting company, information users are most interested in the outlook for the future. Trying to gain a glimpse of the future from past and present data entails using various tools and techniques to formulate predictions. This is the goal of financial statement analysis.

Financial statements are not presented in isolation. Every financial statement issued is accompanied by the corresponding financial statement of the preceding year, and often the previous two years. These are called comparative financial statements. They enable investors, creditors, and other users to compare year-to-year financial position, results of operations, and cash flows. These comparative data help an analyst detect and predict trends. Because operations often expand and contract in a cyclical fashion, analysis of any one year's data may not provide an accurate picture of å company.

Comparative financial statements allow financial statement users to compare year-to-year financial position, results of operations, and cash flows.

Some analysts enhance their comparison by expressing each item as a percentage of that same item in the financial statements of another year (base amount) in order to more easily see year-to-year changes. This is referred to as horizontal analysis. Similarly, vertical analysis involves expressing each item in the financial statements as a percentage of an appropriate corresponding total, or base amount, but within the same year. For example, cash, inventory, and other assets can be restated as a percentage of total assets; net income and each expense can be restated as a percentage of revenues.

Regardless of the specific technique used, the essential point is that accounting numbers are virtually meaningless in isolation. Their value derives from comparison with other numbers. The most common way of comparing accounting numbers to evaluate the performance and risk of a firm is ratio analysis.

No accounting numbers are meaningful in and of themselves.

We use ratios every day. Batting averages indicate how well our favorite baseball players are performing. We evaluate basketball players by field goal percentage and rebounds per game. Speedometers measure the speed of our cars in terms of miles per hour. We compare grocery costs on the basis of price per pound or ounce. In each of these cases, the ratio is more meaningful than a single number by itself. Do 45 hits indicate satisfactory performance? It depends on the number of at-bats. Is $2 a good price for cheese? It depends on how many ounces the $2 buys. Ratios make these measurements meaningful.

Likewise, we can use ratios to help evaluate a firm's performance and financial position. Is net income of $4 million a cause for shareholders to celebrate? Probably not if shareholders' equity is $10 billion. But if shareholders equity is $10 million, that's a 40% return on equity! Although ratios provide more meaningful information than absolute numbers alone, the ratios are most useful when analyzed relative to some standard of comparison. That standard of comparison may be previous performance of the same company, the performance of a competitor company, or an industry average for the particular ratio.

Evaluating information in ratio form allows analysts to control for size differences over time and among firms.

Accountants should be conversant with ratio analysis for at least three reasons. First, when preparing financial statements, accountants should be familiar with the ways users will use the information provided to make better decisions concerning what and how to report. Second, when accountants participate in company decisions concerning operating and financing alternatives, they may find ratio analysis helpful in evaluating available choices. Third, during the planning stages of an audit, independent auditors often use ratio analysis. This analysis assists in identifying potential audit problems and determining the specific audit procedures that should be performed.

We introduce ratios related to risk analysis in this chapter and ratios related to profitability analysis in Chapter 5. You will also employ ratios in Decision Makers' Perspective sections of many of the chapters in this text. Analysis cases that benefit from ratio analysis are included in many of these chapters as well.

Investors and creditors use financial information to assess the future risk and return of their investments in business enterprises. The balance sheet provides information useful to this assessment. A key element of risk analysis is investigating a company's ability to pay

134   SECTION 1   The Role of Accounting as an Information System

its obligations when they come due. This type of risk often is referred to as default risk. Another aspect of risk is operational risk, which relates more to how adept a company is at withstanding various events and circumstances that might impair its ability to earn profits. Obviously, these two types of risk are not completely independent of one another. Inability to earn profits certainly increases a company's chances of defaulting on its obligations. Conversely, regardless of a company's long-run prospects for generating profits, if it can't meet its obligations, the company's operations are at risk.

Assessing risk necessarily involves consideration of a variety of economywide risk factors such as inflation, interest rates, and the general business climate. Industrywide influences including competition, labor conditions, and technological forces also affect a company's risk profile. Still other risk factors are specific to the company itself. Financial ratios often are used in risk analysis to investigate a company's liquidity and long-term solvency. As we discuss some of the more common ratios in the following paragraphs, keep in mind the inherent relationship between risk and return and thus between our risk analysis in this chapter and our profitability analysis in Chapter 5.

Liquidity Ratios

● LO3–8

Liquidity refers to the readiness of assets to be converted to cash. By comparing a company's liquid assets with its short-term obligations, we can obtain a general idea of the firm's ability to pay its short-term debts as they come due. Usually, current assets are thought of as the most liquid of a company's assets. Obviously, though, some are more liquid than others, so it's important also to evaluate the specific makeup of current assets. Two common measures of liquidity are (1) the current ratio and (2) the acid-test ratio (or quick ratio) calculated as follows:

$$\text{Current ratio} = \frac{\text{Current assets}}{\text{Current liabilities}}$$

$$\text{Acid-test ratio (or quick ratio)} = \frac{\text{Quick assets}}{\text{Current liabilities}}$$

Working capital, the difference between current assets and current liabilities, is a popular measure of a company's ability to satisfy its short-term obligations.

CURRENT RATIO.   Implicit in the definition of a current liability is the relationship between current assets and current liabilities. The difference between current assets and current liabilities is called working capital. By comparing a company's obligations that will shortly become due with the company's cash and other assets that, by definition, are expected to shortly be converted to cash, the analysis offers some indication as to ability to pay those debts. Although used in a variety of decisions, it is particularly useful to those considering whether to extend short-term credit. The current ratio is computed by dividing current assets by current liabilities. A current ratio of 2 indicates that the company has twice as many current assets available as current liabilities.

Dell Inc.'s working capital (in millions) at the end of its January 28, 2011, fiscal year is $9,538, consisting of current assets of $29,021 (Illustration 3–3 on page 117) minus current liabilities of $19,483 (Illustration 3–7 on page 120). The current ratio can be computed as follows:

$$\text{Current ratio} = \frac{\$29,021}{\$19,483} = 1.49$$

Working capital may not present an accurate or complete picture of a company's liquidity.

Care should be taken, however, in assessing liquidity based solely on working capital. Liabilities usually are paid with cash, not other components of working capital. A company could have difficulty paying its liabilities even with a current ratio significantly greater than 1.0. For example, if a significant portion of current assets consisted of inventories, and inventories usually are not converted to cash for several months, there could be a problem in paying accounts payable due in 30 days. On the other hand, a current ratio of less than 1.0 doesn't necessarily mean the company will have difficulty meeting its current obligations. A line of credit, for instance, which the company can use to borrow funds, provides financial flexibility. That also must be considered in assessing liquidity.

Ethical Dilemma ⚖

The Raintree Cosmetic Company has several loans outstanding with a local bank. The debt agreements all contain a covenant stipulating that Raintree must maintain a current ratio of at least .9. Jackson Phillips, company controller, estimates that the 2013 year-end current assets and current liabilities will be $2,100,000 and $2,400,000, respectively. These estimates provide a current ratio of only .875. Violation of the debt agreement will increase Raintree's borrowing costs as the loans are renegotiated at higher rates.

Jackson proposes to the company president that Raintree purchase inventory of $600,000 on credit before year-end. This will cause both current assets and current liabilities to increase by the same amount, but the current ratio will increase to .9. The extra $600,000 in inventory will be used over the later part of 2014. However, the purchase will cause warehousing costs and financing costs to increase.

Jackson is concerned about the ethics of his proposal. What do you think?

ACID-TEST RATIO (OR QUICK RATIO).   Some analysts like to modify the current ratio to consider only current assets that are readily available to pay current liabilities. One such variation in common use is the acid-test ratio. This ratio excludes inventories and prepaid items from current assets before dividing by current liabilities. The numerator, then, consists of cash, short-term investments, and accounts receivable, the "quick assets." By eliminating current assets less readily convertible into cash, the acid-test ratio provides a more rigorous indication of liquidity than does the current ratio.

The *acid-test ratio* provides a more stringent indication of a company's ability to pay its current obligations.

Dell Inc.'s quick assets at the end of its January 28, 2011, fiscal year (in millions) total $24,501 ($13,913 + 452 + 6,493 + 3,643). The acid-test ratio can be computed as follows:

$$\text{Acid-test ratio} = \frac{\$24,501}{\$19,483} = 1.26$$

Are these liquidity ratios adequate? It's generally difficult to say without some point of comparison. As indicated previously, common standards for such comparisons are industry averages for similar ratios or ratios of the same company in prior years. Industry averages for the above two ratios are as follows:

Industry Average
Current ratio = 1.39
Acid-test ratio = 1.04

Dell's ratios are higher than the industry average. What if the ratios were lower? Would that indicate a liquidity problem? Not necessarily, but it would raise a red flag that calls for caution in analyzing other areas. Remember that each ratio is but one piece of the entire puzzle. For instance, profitability is perhaps the best indication of liquidity in the long run. We discuss ratios that measure profitability in Chapter 5.

Also, management may be very efficient in managing current assets so that, let's say, receivables are collected faster than normal or inventory is sold faster than normal, making those assets more liquid than they otherwise would be. Higher turnover ratios, relative to those of a competitor or the industry, generally indicate a more liquid position for a given level of the current ratio. We discuss these turnover ratios in Chapter 5.

Liquidity ratios should be assessed in the context of both profitability and efficiency of managing assets.

Financing Ratios

Investors and creditors, particularly long-term creditors, are vitally interested in a company's long-term solvency and stability. Financing ratios provide some indication of the riskiness of a company with regard to its ability to pay its long-term debts. Two common financing ratios are (1) the debt to equity ratio and (2) the times interest earned ratio. These ratios are calculated as follows:

$$\text{Debt to equity ratio} = \frac{\text{Total liabilities}}{\text{Shareholders' equity}}$$

$$\text{Times interest earned ratio} = \frac{\text{Net income} + \text{Interest expense} + \text{Income taxes}}{\text{Interest expense}}$$

The debt to equity ratio indicates the extent of reliance on creditors, rather than owners, in providing resources.

DEBT TO EQUITY RATIO.   The debt to equity ratio compares resources provided by creditors with resources provided by owners. It is calculated by dividing total liabilities (current and noncurrent) by total shareholders' equity (including retained earnings).[15]

The ratio provides a measure of creditors' protection in the event of insolvency. Other things being equal, the higher the ratio, the higher the risk. The higher the ratio, the greater the creditor claims on assets, so the higher the likelihood an individual creditor would not be paid in full if the company is unable to meet its obligations. Relatedly, a high ratio indicates not only more fixed interest obligations, but probably a higher *rate* of interest as well because lenders tend to charge higher rates as the level of debt increases.

Dell Inc.'s liabilities at the end of its January 28, 2011, fiscal year (in millions) total $30,833 (Illustration 3–7 on page 120), and stockholders' equity totals $7,766 (Illustration 3–8 on page 121). The debt to equity ratio can be computed as follows:

$$\text{Debt to equity ratio} = \frac{\$30,833}{\$\ 7,766} = 3.97$$

As with all ratios, the debt to equity ratio is more meaningful if compared to some standard such as an industry average or a competitor. For example, the debt to equity ratio for Hewlett-Packard (HP), a major competitor, is 2.1, significantly lower than Dell's ratio, indicating that Dell has more liabilities in its capital structure than does HP. Does this mean that Dell's default risk is more than that of HP? Other things equal—yes. Is that good? Not necessarily. As discussed in the next section, it may be that debt is being underutilized by Hewlett-Packard. More debt might increase the potential for return to shareholders, but the price would be higher risk. This is a fundamental trade-off faced by virtually all firms when trying to settle on the optimal capital structure.

The makeup of liabilities also is important. For example, Dell's liabilities include $6,676 million of unearned (deferred) services revenue, representing 22% of total liabilities. Recall that unearned revenues are liabilities recorded when cash is received from customers in advance of providing a good or service. Dell will satisfy these liabilities not by paying cash, but by providing a service to its customers.

Relationship Between Risk and Profitability.   The proportion of debt in the capital structure also is of interest to shareholders. After all, shareholders receive no return on their investments until after all creditor claims are paid. Therefore, the higher the debt to equity ratio, the higher the risk to shareholders. On the other hand, by earning a return on borrowed funds that exceeds the cost of borrowing the funds, a company can provide its shareholders with a total return higher than it could achieve by employing equity funds alone. This is referred to as favorable financial leverage.

The debt to equity ratio indicates the extent of trading on the equity by using financial leverage.

For illustration, consider a newly formed corporation attempting to determine the appropriate mix of debt and equity. The initial capitalization goal is $50 million. The capitalization mix alternatives have been narrowed to two: (1) $10 million in debt and $40 million in equity and (2) $30 million in debt and $20 million in equity.

Also assume that regardless of the capitalization mix chosen, the corporation will be able to generate a 16% annual return, *before payment of interest and income taxes,* on the $50 million in assets acquired. In other words, income before interest and taxes will be $8 million (16% × $50 million). If the interest rate on debt is 8% and the income tax rate is 40%, comparative net income for the first year of operations for the two capitalization alternatives can be calculated as follows:

---

[15]A commonly used variation of the debt to equity ratio is found by dividing total liabilities by *total assets* (or total equities), rather than by shareholders' equity only. Of course, in this configuration the ratio measures precisely the same attribute of the firm's capital structure but can be interpreted as the percentage of a company's total assets provided by funds from creditors, rather than by owners.

	Alternative 1	Alternative 2
Income before interest and income taxes	$8,000,000	$8,000,000
Less: Interest expense	(800,000)[a]	(2,400,000)[b]
Income before income taxes	$7,200,000	$5,600,000
Less: Income tax expense (40%)	(2,880,000)	(2,240,000)
Net income	$4,320,000	$3,360,000

[a]8% × $10,000,000
[b]8% × $30,000,000

Choose Alternative 1? Probably not. Although alternative 1 provides a higher net income, the return on the shareholders' equity (net income divided by shareholders' equity) is higher for alternative 2. Here's why:

Favorable financial leverage means earning a return on borrowed funds that exceeds the cost of borrowing the funds.

	Alternative 1	Alternative 2
Return on shareholders' equity[16] =	$\dfrac{\$4,320,000}{\$40,000,000}$	$\dfrac{\$3,360,000}{\$20,000,000}$
=	10.8%	16.8%

Alternative 2 generated a higher return for each dollar invested by shareholders. This is because the company leveraged its $20 million equity investment with additional debt. Because the cost of the additional debt (8%) is less than the return on assets invested (16%), the return to shareholders is higher. This is the essence of favorable financial leverage.

Be aware, though, leverage is not always favorable; the cost of borrowing the funds might exceed the returns they provide. If the return on assets invested turned out to be less than expected, the additional debt could result in a lower return on equity for alternative 2. If, for example, the return on assets invested (before interest and income taxes) had been 6%, rather than 16%, alternative 1 would have provided the better return on equity:

	Alternative 1	Alternative 2
Income before interest and income taxes	$3,000,000	$3,000,000
Less: Interest expense	(800,000)[a]	(2,400,000)[b]
Income before income taxes	$2,200,000	$ 600,000
Less: Income tax expense (40%)	(880,000)	(240,000)
Net income	$1,320,000	$ 360,000

[a]8% × $10,000,000
[b]8% × $30,000,000

	Alternative 1	Alternative 2
Return on shareholders' equity[17] =	$\dfrac{\$1,320,000}{\$40,000,000}$	$\dfrac{\$360,000}{\$20,000,000}$
=	3.3%	1.8%

---

[16]If return is calculated on *average* shareholders' equity, we're technically assuming that all income is paid to shareholders in cash dividends, so that beginning, ending, and average shareholders' equity are the same. If we assume *no* dividends are paid, rates of return would be

	Alternative 1	Alternative 2
Return on shareholders' equity =	$\dfrac{\$4,320,000}{(\$44,320,000 + 40,000,000)/2}$	$\dfrac{\$3,360,000}{(\$20,000,000 + 23,360,000)/2}$
=	10.25%	15.50%

In any case our conclusions are the same.

[17]If we assume *no* dividends are paid, rates of return would be

	Alternative 1	Alternative 2
Return on shareholders' equity =	$\dfrac{\$1,320,000}{(\$41,320,000 + 40,000,000)/2}$	$\dfrac{\$360,000}{(\$20,000,000 + 20,360,000)/2}$
=	3.25%	1.78%

In any case our conclusions are the same.

So, shareholders typically are faced with a trade-off between the risk that high debt denotes and the potential for a higher return from having the higher debt. In any event, the debt to equity ratio offers a basis for making the choice.

The *times interest earned ratio* indicates the margin of safety provided to creditors.

TIMES INTEREST EARNED RATIO. Another way to gauge the ability of a company to satisfy its fixed debt obligations is by comparing interest charges with the income available to pay those charges. The times interest earned ratio is designed to do this. It is calculated by dividing income before subtracting interest expense and income taxes by interest expense.

Bondholders, noteholders, and other creditors can measure the margin of safety they are accorded by a company's earnings. If income is many times greater than interest expense, creditors' interests are more protected than if income just barely covers this expense. For this purpose, income should be the amount available to pay interest, which is income before subtracting interest and income taxes, calculated by adding back to net income the interest and income taxes that were deducted.

As an example, Dell Inc.'s financial statements for the fiscal year ended January 28, 2011, report the following:

	($ in millions)
Net income	$2,635
Interest expense	199
Income taxes	715
Income before interest and taxes	$3,549

The times interest earned ratio can be computed as follows:

$$\text{Times interest earned ratio} = \frac{\$3,549}{\$199} = 18$$

The ratio of 18 times indicates a considerable margin of safety for creditors. Income could decrease many times and the company would still be able to meet its interest payment obligations.[18] Dell is a highly profitable company with little interest-bearing debt. In comparison, the average times interest earned ratio for the S&P 500 companies is approximately 17 times, similar to Dell's ratio.

Especially when viewed alongside the debt-equity ratio, the coverage ratio seems to indicate a comfortable safety cushion for creditors. It also indicates a degree of financial mobility if the company were to decide to raise new debt funds to "trade on the equity" and attempt to increase the return to shareholders through favorable financial leverage.

Financial Reporting Case Solution

1. **Respond to Jerry's criticism that shareholders' equity does not represent the market value of the company. What information does the balance sheet provide?** *(p. 115)* Jerry is correct. The financial statements are supposed to help investors and creditors value a company. However, the balance sheet is not intended to portray the market value of the entity. The assets of a company minus its liabilities as shown in the balance sheet (shareholders' equity) usually will not equal the company's market value for several reasons. For example, many assets are measured at their historical costs rather than their fair values. Also, many company resources, including its trained employees, its experienced management team, and its reputation are not recorded as assets at all. The balance sheet must be used in conjunction with other financial statements, disclosure notes, and other publicly available information.

The balance sheet does, however, provide valuable information that can be used by investors and creditors to help determine market value. After all, it is the balance sheet that describes many of the resources a company has available for generating future cash

---

[18]Of course, interest is paid with cash, not with "income." The times interest earned ratio often is calculated by using cash flow from operations before subtracting either interest payments or tax payments as the numerator and interest payments as the denominator.

flows. The balance sheet also provides important information about liquidity and long-term solvency.

2. **The usefulness of the balance sheet is enhanced by classifying assets and liabilities according to common characteristics. What are the classifications used in Electronic Arts' balance sheets and what elements do those categories include?** *(p. 116)* Electronic Arts' balance sheets contain the following classifications:

Assets:

- *Current assets* include cash and several other assets that are reasonably expected to be converted to cash or consumed within the coming year, or within the normal operating cycle of the business if that's longer than one year.
- *Property and equipment* are the tangible long-lived assets used in the operations of the business. This category includes land, buildings, equipment, machinery, and furniture, as well as natural resources.
- *Goodwill* is a unique intangible asset in that its cost can't be directly associated with any specifically identifiable right and is not separable from the company as a whole. It represents the unique value of the company as a whole over and above all identifiable tangible and intangible assets.
- *Acquisition-related intangibles* are assets that represent exclusive rights to something such as a product, a process, or a name. Patents, copyrights, and franchises are examples. These intangible assets were acquired by purchasing other companies.
- *Deferred income taxes* result from temporary differences between taxable income and accounting income.
- *Other assets* is a "catch-all" classification of noncurrent assets and could include long-term prepaid expenses and any noncurrent asset not included in one of the other categories.

Liabilities:

- *Current liabilities* are those obligations that are expected to be satisfied through the use of current assets or the creation of other current liabilities. Usually, this means liabilities that are expected to be paid within one year, or the operating cycle if that's longer than one year.
- *Long-term liabilities* are payable further in the future and include bonds, deferred income taxes, and pension obligations. Electronic Arts lists *income tax obligations, deferred income taxes,* and *other liabilities* as its long-term liabilities.

Shareholders' equity:

- *Common stock* and *paid-in capital* collectively equal the amounts invested by shareholders in the corporation.
- *Retained earnings (accumulated deficit)* represents the accumulated net income earned or net loss incurred since inception of the corporation less dividends paid out to shareholders. If this amount is negative, as it is on March 31, 2011, it is called *accumulated deficit*.
- *Accumulated other comprehensive income* is the cumulative amount of other comprehensive income items. This topic is addressed in subsequent chapters. ●

The Bottom Line

● **LO3–1**   The balance sheet is a position statement that presents an organized array of assets, liabilities, and shareholders' equity at a particular point in time. The statement does not portray the market value of the entity. However, the information in the statement can be useful in assessing market value, as well as in providing important information about liquidity and long-term solvency. *(p. 115)*

● **LO3–2**   Current assets include cash and other assets that are reasonably expected to be converted to cash or consumed during one year or within the normal operating cycle of the business if the operating cycle is longer than one year. All other assets are classified as various types of noncurrent assets. In addition to cash and cash equivalents, current assets include short-term investments, accounts receivable, inventories, and pre-paid expenses. Other asset classifications include investments; property, plant, and equipment; intangible assets; and other assets. (*p. 117*)

● **LO3–3**   Current liabilities are those obligations that are expected to be satisfied through the use of current assets or the creation of other current liabilities. All other liabilities are classified as long term. Current liabilities include notes and accounts payable, unearned revenues, accrued liabilities, and the current maturities of long-term debt. Long-term liabilities include long-term notes, loans, mortgages, bonds, pension and lease obligations, as well as deferred income taxes. (*p. 120*)

● **LO3–4**   Financial statement disclosures are used to convey additional information about the account balances in the basic financial statements as well as to provide supplemental information. This information is dis-closed, often parenthetically in the basic financial statements, or in disclosure notes that often include supporting schedules. (*p. 124*)

● **LO3–5**   Annual reports of public companies will include management's discussion and analysis of key aspects of the company's business. The purpose of this disclosure is to provide external parties with management's insight into certain transactions, events, and circumstances that affect the enterprise, including their finan-cial impact. (*p. 128*)

● **LO3–6**   The purpose of an audit is to provide a professional, independent opinion as to whether or not the finan-cial statements are prepared in conformity with generally accepted accounting principles. The standard audit report of a public company contains four paragraphs; the first two deal with the scope of the audit and the third paragraph states the auditors' opinion regarding the financial statements. The fourth para-graph provides the auditors' opinion on the effectiveness of the company's internal control. (*p. 130*)

● **LO3–7**   Financial analysts use various techniques to transform financial information into forms more useful for analysis. Horizontal analysis and vertical analysis provide a useful way of analyzing year-to-year changes. Ratio analysis allows analysts to control for size differences over time and among firms while investigat-ing important relationships among financial variables. (*p. 132*)

● **LO3–8**   The balance sheet provides information that can be useful in assessing risk. A key element of risk analy-sis is investigating a company's ability to pay its obligations when they come due. Liquidity ratios and financing ratios provide information about a company's ability to pay its obligations. (*p. 134*)

● **LO3–9**   There are more similarities than differences in balance sheets and financial disclosures prepared accord-ing to U.S. GAAP and those prepared applying IFRS. Balance sheet presentation is one important differ-ence. Under U.S. GAAP, we present current assets and liabilities before noncurrent assets and liabilities. IFRS doesn't prescribe the format of the balance sheet, but balance sheets prepared using IFRS often report noncurrent items first. Reportable segment disclosures also are similar. However, IFRS requires an additional disclosure, the amount of segment liabilities (Appendix 3). (*pp. 122* and *141*) ●

APPENDIX 3   Reporting Segment Information

Many companies operate in several business segments as a strategy to achieve growth and to reduce operating risk through diversification.

Financial analysis of diversified companies is especially difficult. Consider, for example, a company that operates in several distinct business segments including computer peripher-als, home health care systems, textiles, and consumer food products. The results of these distinctly different activities will be aggregated into a single set of financial statements, making difficult an informed projection of future performance. It may well be that the five-year outlook differs greatly among the areas of the economy represented by the dif-ferent segments. To make matters worse for an analyst, the integrated financial statements do not reveal the relative investments in each of the business segments nor the success the company has had within each area. Given the fact that so many companies these days have chosen to balance their operating risks through diversification, aggregated financial statements pose a widespread problem for analysts, lending and credit officers, and other financial forecasters.

Segment reporting facilitates the financial statement analysis of diversified companies.

Reporting by Operating Segment

To address the problem, the accounting profession requires companies engaged in more than one significant business to provide supplemental information concerning individual operating segments. The supplemental disaggregated data do not include complete financial statements for each reportable segment, only certain specified items.

WHAT IS A REPORTABLE OPERATING SEGMENT?

According to U.S. GAAP guidelines, a *management approach* is used in determining which segments of a company are reportable. This approach is based on the way that management organizes the segments within the enterprise for making operating decisions and assessing performance. The segments are, therefore, evident from the structure of the enterprise's internal organization.

More formally, the following characteristics define an operating segment:[19]

An operating segment is a component of an enterprise:

- That engages in business activities from which it may earn revenues and incur expenses (including revenues and expenses relating to transactions with other components of the same enterprise).
- Whose operating results are regularly reviewed by the enterprise's chief operating decision maker to make decisions about resources to be allocated to the segment and assess its performance.
- For which discrete financial information is available.

The FASB hopes that this approach provides insights into the risk and opportunities management sees in the various areas of company operations. Also, reporting information based on the enterprise's internal organization should reduce the incremental cost to companies of providing the data. In addition, there are quantitative thresholds for the definition of an operating segment to limit the number of reportable segments. Only segments of certain size (10% or more of total company revenues, assets, or net income) must be disclosed. However, a company must account for at least 75% of consolidated revenue through segment disclosures.

WHAT AMOUNTS ARE REPORTED BY AN OPERATING SEGMENT?

For areas determined to be reportable operating segments, the following disclosures are required:

a. General information about the operating segment.

b. Information about reported segment profit or loss, including certain revenues and expenses included in reported segment profit or loss, segment assets, and the basis of measurement.

c. Reconciliations of the totals of segment revenues, reported profit or loss, assets, and other significant items to corresponding enterprise amounts.

d. Interim period information.[20]

Illustration 3A–1 shows the business segment information reported by 3M Co. in its 2010 annual report.

International Financial Reporting Standards

Segment Reporting. U.S. GAAP requires companies to report information about reported segment profit or loss, including certain revenues and expenses included in reported segment profit or loss, segment assets, and the basis of measurement. The international standard on segment reporting, *IFRS No. 8*,[21] requires that companies also disclose total *liabilities* of its reportable segments.

● LO3–9

---

[19]FASB ASC 280–10–50–1: Segment Reporting—Overall—Disclosure (previously "Disclosures about Segments of an Enterprise and Related Information," *Statement of Financial Accounting Standards No. 131* (Norwalk, Conn.: FASB, 1997), par. 10).

[20]FASB ASC 280–10–50–20 through 26 and 280–10–50–32: Segment Reporting—Overall—Disclosure (previously "Disclosures about Segments of an Enterprise and Related Information," *Statement of Financial Accounting Standards No. 131* (Norwalk, Conn.: FASB, 1997), par. 25).

[21]"Operating Segments," *International Financial Reporting Standard No. 8* (IASCF), as amended effective January 1, 2011.

142   SECTION 1   The Role of Accounting as an Information System

Illustration 3A–1
Business Segment
Information
Disclosure—3M Co.

Real World Financials

Business Segment Information
($ in millions)

		Net Sales	Operating Income	Assets	Depr. and Amort.	Capital Expendit.
Industrial and Transportation	2010	$ 8,581	$ 1,799	$ 6,813	$ 331	$ 343
	2009	7,232	1,259	6,441	333	235
	2008	8,294	1,568	6,373	288	355
Health Care	2010	4,521	1,364	4,190	131	78
	2009	4,294	1,350	3,218	143	125
	2008	4,303	1,175	3,096	146	169
Display and Graphics	2010	3,884	946	3,729	187	185
	2009	3,132	590	3,564	174	160
	2008	3,268	583	3,479	220	305
Consumer and Office	2010	3,853	840	2,149	100	69
	2009	3,471	748	1,819	88	43
	2008	3,578	683	1,815	79	87
Safety, Security and Protection Services	2010	3,308	707	3,995	168	130
	2009	3,064	724	3,206	169	93
	2008	3,330	689	3,127	147	107
Electro and Communications	2010	2,922	631	2,135	96	98
	2009	2,276	322	2,067	102	60
	2008	2,835	540	2,186	127	143
Corporate and Unallocated/Elimination of Dual Credit	2010	(407)	(369)	7,145	107	188
	2009	(346)	(179)	6,935	148	187
	2008	(339)	(20)	5,717	146	305
Total Company	2010	$26,662	$ 5,918	$30,156	$1,120	$1,091
	2009	23,123	4,814	27,250	1,157	903
	2008	25,269	5,218	25,793	1,153	1,471

REPORTING BY GEOGRAPHIC AREA

In today's global economy it is sometimes difficult to distinguish domestic and foreign companies. Most large U.S. firms conduct significant operations in other countries in addition to having substantial export sales from this country. Differing political and economic environments from country to country means risks and associated rewards sometimes vary greatly among the various operations of a single company. For instance, manufacturing facilities in a South American country embroiled in political unrest pose different risks from having a plant in Vermont, or even Canada. Without disaggregated financial information, these differences cause problems for analysts.

U.S. GAAP requires an enterprise to report certain geographic information unless it is impracticable to do so. This information includes:

a. Revenues from external customers (1) attributed to the enterprise's country of domicile and (2) attributed to all foreign countries in total from which the enterprise derives revenues, and

b. Long-lived assets other than financial instruments, long-term customer relationships of a financial institution, mortgage and other servicing rights, deferred policy acquisition costs, and deferred tax assets (1) located in the enterprise's country of domicile and (2) located in all foreign countries in total in which the enterprise holds assets.[22]

---

[22]FASB ASC 280–10–50–41: Segment Reporting—Overall—Disclosure (previously "Disclosures about Segments of an Enterprise and Related Information," *Statement of Financial Accounting Standards No. 131* (Norwalk, Conn.: FASB, 1997), par. 38).

3M reported its geographic area information separately in a table reproduced in Illustration 3A–2. Notice that both the business segment (Illustration 3A–1) and geographic information disclosures include a reconciliation to company totals. For example, in both illustrations, year 2010 net sales of both the segments and the geographic areas are reconciled to the company's total net sales of $26,662 ($ in millions).

Illustration 3A–2 Geographic Area Information Disclosure—3M Company

Geographic Areas
($ in millions)

		United States	Asia Pacific	Europe, Middle East, and Africa	Latin America and Canada	Other Unallocated	Total Company
Net sales	2010	$9,210	$8,259	$6,259	$2,950	$(16)	$26,662
	2009	8,509	6,120	5,972	2,516	6	23,123
	2008	9,179	6,423	6,941	2,723	3	25,269
Operating income	2010	1,636	2,400	1,112	797	(27)	5,918
	2009	1,640	1,528	1,003	631	12	4,814
	2008	1,578	1,662	1,294	693	(9)	5,218
Property, plant, and equipment	2010	3,888	1,605	1,239	547	—	7,279
	2009	3,809	1,366	1,318	507	—	7,000

Real World Financials

For another example of both business segment and geographic area disclosures, see the Dell Inc. segment information reported in the financial statements in Appendix B at the back of the text.

INFORMATION ABOUT MAJOR CUSTOMERS

Some companies in the defense industry derive substantial portions of their revenues from contracts with the Defense Department. When cutbacks occur in national defense or in specific defense systems, the impact on a company's operations can be considerable. Obviously, financial analysts are extremely interested in information concerning the extent to which a company's prosperity depends on one or more major customers such as in the situation described here. For this reason, if 10% or more of the revenue of an enterprise is derived from transactions with a single customer, the enterprise must disclose that fact, the total amount of revenue from each such customer, and the identity of the operating segment or segments earning the revenue. The identity of the major customer or customers need not be disclosed, although companies routinely provide that information. In its 2010 annual report, 3M did not report any major customer information. As an example of this type of disclosure, Procter & Gamble Company's business segment disclosure included information on its largest customer, Walmart, as shown in Illustration 3A–3 ●

Revenues from major customers must be disclosed.

Note 12. Segment Information (in part)
Our largest customer, Wal-Mart Stores, Inc. and its affiliates, accounted for 15% of consolidated net sales in 2011 and 16% in 2010 and 2009.

Illustration 3A–3

Major Customer Disclosure—Procter & Gamble Company

Real World Financials

Questions For Review of Key Topics

Q 3–1   Describe the purpose of the balance sheet.

Q 3–2   Explain why the balance sheet does not portray the market value of the entity.

Q 3–3   Define current assets and list the typical asset categories included in this classification.

Q 3–4   Define current liabilities and list the typical liability categories included in this classification.

Q 3–5   Describe what is meant by an operating cycle for a typical manufacturing company.

Q 3–6   Explain the difference(s) between investments in equity securities classified as current assets versus those classified as noncurrent assets.

Q 3–7   Describe the common characteristics of assets classified as property, plant, and equipment and identify some assets included in this classification.

Q 3–8   Distinguish between property, plant, and equipment and intangible assets.

Q 3–9   Explain how each of the following liabilities would be classified in the balance sheet:
- A note payable of $100,000 due in five years.
- A note payable of $100,000 payable in annual installments of $20,000 each, with the first installment due next year.

Q 3–10   Define the terms *paid-in-capital* and *retained earnings.*

Q 3–11   Disclosure notes are an integral part of the information provided in financial statements. In what ways are the notes critical to understanding the financial statements and to evaluating the firm's performance and financial health?

Q 3–12   A summary of the company's significant accounting policies is a required disclosure. Why is this disclosure important to external financial statement users?

Q 3–13   Define a subsequent event.

Q 3–14   Every annual report of a public company includes an extensive discussion and analysis provided by the company's management. Specifically, which aspects of the company must this discussion address? Isn't management's perspective too biased to be of use to investors and creditors?

Q 3–15   The auditors' report provides the analyst with an independent and professional opinion about the fairness of the representations in the financial statements. What are the four main types of opinion an auditor might issue? Describe each.

Q 3–16   What is a proxy statement? What information does it provide?

Q 3–17   Define the terms *working capital, current ratio,* and *acid-test ratio* (or *quick ratio*).

Q 3–18   Show the calculation of the following financing ratios: (1) the debt to equity ratio, and (2) the times interest earned ratio.

IFRS Q 3–19   Where can we find authoritative guidance for balance sheet presentation under IFRS?

IFRS Q 3–20   Describe at least two differences between U.S. GAAP and IFRS in balance sheet presentation.

Q 3–21   (Based on Appendix 3) Segment reporting facilitates the financial statement analysis of diversified companies. What determines whether an operating segment is a reportable segment for this purpose?

Q 3–22   (Based on Appendix 3) For segment reporting purposes, what amounts are reported by each operating segment?

IFRS Q 3–23   (Based on Appendix 3) Describe any differences in segment disclosure requirements between U.S. GAAP and IFRS.

Brief Exercises

BE 3–1
Current versus noncurrent classification
● LO3–2, LO3–3

Indicate whether each of the following assets and liabilities should be classified as current or noncurrent: (a) accounts receivable; (b) prepaid rent for the next six months; (c) note receivable due in two years; (d) note payable due in 90 days; (e) note payable due in five years; and (f) patent.

BE 3–2
Balance sheet classification
● LO3–2, LO3–3

The trial balance for K and J Nursery, Inc., listed the following account balances at December 31, 2013, the end of its fiscal year: cash, $16,000; accounts receivable, $11,000; inventories, $25,000; equipment (net), $80,000; accounts payable, $14,000; wages payable, $9,000; interest payable, $1,000; note payable (due in 18 months), $30,000; common stock, $50,000. Calculate total current assets and total current liabilities that would appear in the company's year-end balance sheet.

BE 3–3
Balance sheet classification
● LO3–2, LO3–3

Refer to the situation described in BE 3–2. Determine the year-end balance in retained earnings for K and J Nursery, Inc.

BE 3–4
Balance sheet classification
● LO3–2, LO3–3

Refer to the situation described in BE 3–2. Prepare a classified balance sheet for K and J Nursery, Inc. The equipment originally cost $140,000.

BE 3–5
Balance sheet
classification
● LO3–2, LO3–3

The following is a December 31, 2013, post-closing trial balance for Culver City Lighting, Inc. Prepare a classified balance sheet for the company.

Account Title	Debits	Credits
Cash	55,000	
Accounts receivable	39,000	
Inventories	45,000	
Prepaid insurance	15,000	
Equipment	100,000	
Accumulated depreciation—equipment		34,000
Patent, net	40,000	
Accounts payable		12,000
Interest payable		2,000
Note payable (due in 10, equal annual installments)		100,000
Common stock		70,000
Retained earnings		76,000
Totals	294,000	294,000

BE 3–6
Balance sheet
classification
● LO3–2, LO3–3

You have been asked to review the December 31, 2013, balance sheet for Champion Cleaning. After completing your review, you list the following three items for discussion with your superior:

1. An investment of $30,000 is included in current assets. Management has indicated that it has no intention of liquidating the investment in 2014.

2. A $100,000 note payable is listed as a long-term liability, but you have determined that the note is due in 10, equal annual installments with the first installment due on March 31, 2014.

3. Unearned revenue of $60,000 is included as a current liability even though only two-thirds will be earned in 2014.

Determine the appropriate classification of each of these items.

BE 3–7
Balance sheet
preparation;
missing elements
● LO3–2, LO3–3

The following information is taken from the balance sheet of Raineer Plumbing: cash and cash equivalents, $40,000; accounts receivable, $120,000; inventories, ?; total current assets, $235,000; property, plant, and equipment (net), ?; total assets, $400,000; accounts payable, $32,000; note payable (due in two years), $50,000; common stock; $100,000; and retained earnings, ?. Determine the missing amounts.

BE 3–8
Financial statement
disclosures
● LO3–4

For each of the following note disclosures, indicate whether the disclosure would likely appear in (A) the summary of significant accounts policies or (B) a separate note: (1) depreciation method; (2) contingency information; (3) significant issuance of common stock after the fiscal year-end; (4) cash equivalent designation; (5) long-term debt information; and (6) inventory costing method.

BE 3–9
Calculating ratios
● LO3–8

Refer to the trial balance information in BE 3–5. Calculate the (a) current ratio, (b) acid-test ratio, and (c) debt to equity ratio.

BE 3–10
Effect of decisions
on ratios
● LO3–8

At the end of 2013, Barker Corporation's preliminary trial balance indicated a current ratio of 1.2. Management is contemplating paying some of its accounts payable balance before the end of the fiscal year. Explain the effect this transaction would have on the current ratio. Would your answer be the same if the preliminary trial balance indicated a current ratio of .8?

BE 3–11
Calculating ratios;
solving for
unknowns
● LO3–8

The current asset section of Stibbe Pharmaceutical Company's balance sheet included cash of $20,000 and accounts receivable of $40,000. The only other current asset is inventories. The company's current ratio is 2.0 and its acid-test ratio is 1.5. Determine the ending balance in inventories and total current liabilities.

Exercises

An alternate exercise and problem set is available on the text website: www.mhhe.com/spiceland7e

E 3–1
Balance sheet;
missing elements
● LO3–2, LO3–3,
LO3–8

The following December 31, 2013, fiscal year-end account balance information is available for the Stonebridge Corporation:

Cash and cash equivalents	$ 5,000
Accounts receivable (net)	20,000
Inventories	60,000
Property, plant, and equipment (net)	120,000
Accounts payable	44,000
Wages payable	15,000
Paid-in-capital	100,000

The only asset not listed is short-term investments. The only liabilities not listed are a $30,000 note payable due in two years and related accrued interest of $1,000 due in four months. The current ratio at year-end is 1.5:1.

Required:
Determine the following at December 31, 2013:
1. Total current assets
2. Short-term investments
3. Retained earnings

E 3–2
Balance sheet classification
● **LO3–2, LO3–3**

The following are the typical classifications used in a balance sheet:

a. Current assets
b. Investments and funds
c. Property, plant, and equipment
d. Intangible assets
e. Other assets

f. Current liabilities
g. Long-term liabilities
h. Paid-in-capital
i. Retained earnings

Required:
For each of the following balance sheet items, use the letters above to indicate the appropriate classification category. If the item is a contra account, place a minus sign before the chosen letter.

1. _____ Equipment
2. _____ Accounts payable
3. _____ Allowance for uncollectible accounts
4. _____ Land, held for investment
5. _____ Note payable, due in 5 years
6. _____ Unearned rent revenue
7. _____ Note payable, due in 6 months
8. _____ Income less dividends, accumulated
9. _____ Investment in XYZ Corp., long-term

10. _____ Inventories
11. _____ Patent
12. _____ Land, in use
13. _____ Accrued liabilities
14. _____ Prepaid rent
15. _____ Common stock
16. _____ Building, in use
17. _____ Cash
18. _____ Taxes payable

E 3–3
Balance sheet classification
● **LO3–2, LO3–3**

The following are the typical classifications used in a balance sheet:

a. Current assets
b. Investments and funds
c. Property, plant, and equipment
d. Intangible assets
e. Other assets

f. Current liabilities
g. Long-term liabilities
h. Paid-in-capital
i. Retained earnings

Required:
For each of the following 2013 balance sheet items, use the letters above to indicate the appropriate classification category. If the item is a contra account, place a minus sign before the chosen letter.

1. _____ Accrued interest payable
2. _____ Franchise
3. _____ Accumulated depreciation
4. _____ Prepaid insurance, for 2014
5. _____ Bonds payable, due in 10 years
6. _____ Current maturities of long-term debt
7. _____ Note payable, due in three months
8. _____ Long-term receivables
9. _____ Bond sinking fund, will be used to retire bonds in 10 years

10. _____ Supplies
11. _____ Machinery
12. _____ Land, in use
13. _____ Unearned revenue
14. _____ Copyrights
15. _____ Preferred stock
16. _____ Land, held for speculation
17. _____ Cash equivalents
18. _____ Wages payable

E 3–4
Balance sheet preparation
● **LO3–2, LO3–3**

The following is a December 31, 2013, post-closing trial balance for the Jackson Corporation.

Account Title	Debits	Credits
Cash	40,000	
Accounts receivable	34,000	
Inventories	75,000	
Prepaid rent	16,000	
Marketable securities (short term)	10,000	
Machinery	145,000	
Accumulated depreciation—machinery		11,000
Patent (net of amortization)	83,000	
Accounts payable		8,000
Wages payable		4,000
Taxes payable		32,000

(continued)

(concluded)

Bonds payable (due in 10 years)		200,000
Common stock		100,000
Retained earnings		48,000
Totals	403,000	403,000

Required:
Prepare a classified balance sheet for Jackson Corporation at December 31, 2013.

E 3–5
Balance sheet
preparation
● LO3–2, LO3–3

The following is a December 31, 2013, post-closing trial balance for the Valley Pump Corporation.

Account Title	Debits	Credits
Cash	25,000	
Accounts receivable	56,000	
Inventories	81,000	
Interest payable		10,000
Marketable securities	44,000	
Land	120,000	
Buildings	300,000	
Accumulated depreciation—buildings		100,000
Equipment	75,000	
Accumulated depreciation—equipment		25,000
Copyright (net of amortization)	12,000	
Prepaid expenses	32,000	
Accounts payable		65,000
Unearned revenues		20,000
Notes payable		250,000
Allowance for uncollectible accounts		5,000
Common stock		200,000
Retained earnings		70,000
Totals	745,000	745,000

Additional Information:
1. The $120,000 balance in the land account consists of $100,000 for the cost of land where the plant and office buildings are located. The remaining $20,000 represents the cost of land being held for speculation.
2. The $44,000 in the marketable securities account represents an investment in the common stock of another corporation. Valley intends to sell one-half of the stock within the next year.
3. The notes payable account consists of a $100,000 note due in six months and a $150,000 note due in three annual installments of $50,000 each, with the first payment due in August of 2014.

Required:
Prepare a classified balance sheet for the Valley Pump Corporation at December 31, 2013.

E 3–6
Balance sheet;
Current versus
noncurrent
classification
● LO3–2, LO3–3

Presented below is a partial trial balance for the Kansas Instruments Corporation at December 31, 2013.

Account Title	Debits	Credits
Cash	20,000	
Accounts receivable	130,000	
Raw materials	24,000	
Note receivable	100,000	
Interest receivable	3,000	
Interest payable		5,000
Marketable securities	32,000	
Land	50,000	
Buildings	1,300,000	
Accumulated depreciation—buildings		620,000
Work in process	42,000	
Finished goods	89,000	
Equipment	300,000	
Accumulated depreciation—equipment		130,000
Patent (net of amortization)	120,000	
Prepaid rent (for the next two years)	60,000	
Unearned revenue		36,000
Accounts payable		180,000
Note payable		400,000
Cash restricted for payment of note payable	80,000	
Allowance for uncollectible accounts		13,000
Sales revenue		800,000
Cost of goods sold	450,000	
Rent expense	28,000	

Additional Information:

1. The note receivable, along with any accrued interest, is due on November 22, 2014.
2. The note payable is due in 2017. Interest is payable annually.
3. The marketable securities consist of treasury bills, all of which mature in the next year.
4. Unearned revenue will be earned equally over the next two years.

Required:
Determine the company's working capital (current assets minus current liabilities) at December 31, 2013.

E 3–7
Balance sheet
preparation;
errors
● LO3–2, LO3–3

The following balance sheet for the Los Gatos Corporation was prepared by a recently hired accountant. In reviewing the statement you notice several errors.

LOS GATOS CORPORATION
Balance Sheet
At December 31, 2013
Assets

Cash	$ 40,000
Accounts receivable	80,000
Inventories	55,000
Machinery (net)	120,000
Franchise (net)	30,000
Total assets	$325,000

Liabilities and Shareholders' Equity

Accounts payable	$ 50,000
Allowance for uncollectible accounts	5,000
Note payable	55,000
Bonds payable	110,000
Shareholders' equity	105,000
Total liabilities and shareholders' equity	$325,000

Additional Information:

1. Cash includes a $20,000 bond sinking fund to be used for repayment of the bonds payable in 2017.
2. The cost of the machinery is $190,000.
3. Accounts receivable includes a $20,000 note receivable from a customer due in 2016.
4. The note payable includes accrued interest of $5,000. Principal and interest are both due on February 1, 2014.
5. The company began operations in 2008. Income less dividends since inception of the company totals $35,000.
6. 50,000 shares of no par common stock were issued in 2008. 100,000 shares are authorized.

Required:
Prepare a corrected, classified balance sheet.

E 3–8
Balance sheet;
current versus
noncurrent
classification
● LO3–2, LO3–3

Cone Corporation is in the process of preparing its December 31, 2013, balance sheet. There are some questions as to the proper classification of the following items:

a. $50,000 in cash set aside in a savings account to pay bonds payable. The bonds mature in 2017.
b. Prepaid rent of $24,000, covering the period January 1, 2014, through December 31, 2015.
c. Note payable of $200,000. The note is payable in annual installments of $20,000 each, with the first installment payable on March 1, 2014.
d. Accrued interest payable of $12,000 related to the note payable.
e. Investment in marketable securities of other corporations, $80,000. Cone intends to sell one-half of the securities in 2014.

Required:
Prepare a partial classified balance sheet to show how each of the above items should be reported.

E 3–9
Balance sheet
preparation; cash
versus accrual
accounting;
Chapters 2 and 3
● LO3–2, LO3–3

The following is the balance sheet of Korver Supply Company at December 31, 2012.

KORVER SUPPLY COMPANY
Balance Sheet
At December 31, 2012
Assets

Cash	$120,000
Accounts receivable	300,000
Inventories	200,000
Furniture and fixtures, net	150,000
Total assets	$770,000

(continued)

(concluded)

Liabilities and Shareholders' Equity

Accounts payable (for merchandise)	$190,000
Note payable	200,000
Interest payable	6,000
Common stock	100,000
Retained earnings	274,000
Total liabilities and shareholders' equity	$770,000

Transactions during 2013 were as follows:

1.	Sales to customers on account	$800,000
2.	Cash collected from customers	780,000
3.	Purchase of merchandise on account	550,000
4.	Cash payment to suppliers	560,000
5.	Cost of merchandise sold	500,000
6.	Cash paid for operating expenses	160,000
7.	Cash paid for interest on note	12,000

The note payable is dated June 30, 2012 and is due on June 30, 2014. Interest at 6% is payable annually on June 30. Depreciation on the furniture and fixtures for the year is $20,000. The furniture and fixtures originally cost $300,000.

Required:
Prepare a classified balance sheet at December 21, 2013 (ignore income taxes).

E 3–10
Financial statement disclosures
● **LO3–4**

The following are typical disclosures that would appear in the notes accompanying financial statements. For each of the items listed, indicate where the disclosure would likely appear—either in (A) the significant accounting policies note or (B) a separate note.

1.	Inventory costing method	A
2.	Information on related party transactions	——
3.	Composition of property, plant, and equipment	——
4.	Depreciation method	——
5.	Subsequent event information	——
6.	Basis of revenue recognition on long-term contracts	——
7.	Important merger occurring after year-end	——
8.	Composition of receivables	——

E 3–11
Disclosure notes
● **LO3–4**

Hallergan Company produces car and truck batteries that it sells primarily to auto manufacturers. Dorothy Hawkins, the company's controller, is preparing the financial statements for the year ended December 31, 2013. Hawkins asks for your advice concerning the following information that has not yet been included in the statements. The statements will be issued on February 28, 2014.

1. Hallergan leases its facilities from the brother of the chief executive officer.
2. On January 8, 2014, Hallergan entered into an agreement to sell a tract of land that it had been holding as an investment. The sale, which resulted in a material gain, was completed on February 2, 2014.
3. Hallergan uses the straight-line method to determine depreciation on all of the company's depreciable assets.
4. On February 8, 2014, Hallergan completed negotiations with its bank for a $10,000,000 line of credit.
5. Hallergan uses the first-in, first-out (FIFO) method to value inventory.

Required:
For each of the above items, discuss any additional disclosures that Hawkins should include in Hallergan's financial statements.

E 3–12
Financial statement disclosures
● **LO3–4**

Parkman Sporting Goods is preparing its annual report for its 2013 fiscal year. The company's controller has asked for your help in determining how best to disclose information about the following items:

1. A related-party transaction.
2. Depreciation method.
3. Allowance for uncollectible accounts.
4. Composition of investments.
5. Composition of long-term debt.
6. Inventory costing method.
7. Number of shares of common stock authorized, issued, and outstanding.
8. Employee benefit plans.

Required:
Indicate whether the above items should be disclosed (A) in the summary of significant accounting policies note, (B) in a separate disclosure note, or (C) on the face of the balance sheet.

E 3–13
FASB codification research
● LO3–4

The *FASB Accounting Standards Codification* represents the single source of authoritative U.S. generally accepted accounting principles.

Required:
1. Obtain the relevant authoritative literature on the disclosure of accounting policies using the FASB's Codification Research System at the FASB website (www.fasb.org). Identify the topic number that provides guidance on information contained in the notes to the financial statements.
2. What is the specific citation that requires a company to identify and describe in the notes to the financial statements the accounting principles and methods used to prepare the financial statements?
3. Describe the disclosure requirements.

E 3–14
FASB codification research
● LO3–2, LO3–4

Access the FASB's Codification Research System at the FASB website (www.fasb.org). Determine the specific citation for each of the following items:
1. What is the balance sheet classification for a note payable due in six months that was used to purchase a building?
2. Which assets may be excluded from current assets?
3. Should a note receivable from a related party be included in the balance sheet with notes receivable or accounts receivable from customers?
4. What items are nonrecognized subsequent events that require a disclosure in the notes to the financial statements?

E 3–15
Concepts; terminology
● LO3–2 through LO3–4, LO3–6

Listed below are several terms and phrases associated with the balance sheet and financial disclosures. Pair each item from List A (by letter) with the item from List B that is most appropriately associated with it.

List A	List B
____ 1. Balance sheet	a. Will be satisfied through the use of current assets.
____ 2. Liquidity	b. Items expected to be converted to cash or consumed within one year or the operating cycle, whichever is longer.
____ 3. Current assets	c. The statements are presented fairly in conformity with GAAP.
____ 4. Operating cycle	d. An organized array of assets, liabilities, and equity.
____ 5. Current liabilities	e. Important to a user in comparing financial information across companies.
____ 6. Cash equivalent	f. Scope limitation or a departure from GAAP.
____ 7. Intangible asset	g. Recorded when an expense is incurred but not yet paid.
____ 8. Working capital	h. Relates to the amount of time before an asset is converted to cash or a liability is paid.
____ 9. Accrued liabilities	i. Occurs after the fiscal year-end but before the statements are issued.
____ 10. Summary of significant accounting policies	j. Cash to cash.
____ 11. Subsequent events	k. One-month U.S. Treasury bill.
____ 12. Unqualified opinion	l. Current assets minus current liabilities.
____ 13. Qualified opinion	m. Lacks physical substance.

E 3–16
Calculating ratios
● LO3–8

The 2013 balance sheet for Hallbrook Industries, Inc., is shown below.

HALLBROOK INDUSTRIES, INC.
Balance Sheet
December 31, 2013
($ in 000s)

Assets

Cash	$ 200
Short-term investments	150
Accounts receivable	200
Inventories	350
Property, plant, and equipment (net)	1,000
Total assets	$1,900

Liabilities and Shareholders' Equity

Current liabilities	$ 400
Long-term liabilities	350
Paid-in capital	750
Retained earnings	400
Total liabilities and shareholders' equity	$1,900

The company's 2013 income statement reported the following amounts ($ in 000s):

Net sales	$4,600
Interest expense	40
Income tax expense	100
Net income	160

Required:
Determine the following ratios for 2013:

1. Current ratio
2. Acid-test ratio
3. Debt to equity ratio
4. Times interest earned ratio

E 3–17
Calculating ratios;
Best Buy
● **LO3–8**

Real World Financials

Best Buy Co., Inc., is a leading retailer specializing in consumer electronics. A condensed income statement and balance sheet for the fiscal year ended February 26, 2011, are shown below.

Best Buy Co., Inc.
Balance Sheet
At February 26, 2011
($ in millions)
Assets

Current assets:	
Cash and cash equivalents	$ 1,103
Short-term investments	22
Accounts receivable, net	2,348
Merchandise inventories	5,897
Other current assets	1,103
Total current assets	10,473
Noncurrent assets	7,376
Total assets	$17,849

Liabilities and Shareholders' Equity

Current liabilities:	
Accounts payable	$ 4,894
Other current liabilities	3,769
Total current liabilities	8,663
Long-term liabilities	1,894
Shareholders' equity	7,292
Total liabilities and shareholders' equity	$17,849

Best Buy Co., Inc.
Income Statement
For the Year Ended February 26, 2011
($ in millions)

Revenues	$50,272
Costs and expenses	48,158
Operating income	2,114
Other income (expense)*	(34)
Income before income taxes	2,080
Income tax expense	714
Net income including noncontrolling interests	1,366
Net income attributable to noncontrolling interests	(89)
Net income	$ 1,277

*Includes $87 of interest expense.

Liquidity and financing ratios for the industry are as follows:

	Industry Average
Current ratio	1.25
Acid-test ratio	.63
Debt to equity	.63
Times interest earned	.89 times

Required:
1. Determine the following ratios for Best Buy for its fiscal year ended February, 26, 2011:
   a. Current ratio
   b. Acid-test ratio
   c. Debt to equity ratio
   d. Times interest earned ratio
2. Using the ratios from requirement 1, assess Best Buy's liquidity and solvency relative to its industry.

E 3–18
Calculating
ratios; solve for
unknowns
● LO3–8

The current asset section of the Excalibur Tire Company's balance sheet consists of cash, marketable securities, accounts receivable, and inventories. The December 31, 2013, balance sheet revealed the following:

Inventories	$ 840,000
Total assets	$2,800,000
Current ratio	2.25
Acid-test ratio	1.2
Debt to equity ratio	1.8

Required:
Determine the following 2013 balance sheet items:
1. Current assets
2. Shareholders' equity
3. Noncurrent assets
4. Long-term liabilities

E 3–19
Calculating
ratios; solve for
unknowns
● LO3–8

The current asset section of Guardian Consultant's balance sheet consists of cash, accounts receivable, and prepaid expenses. The 2013 balance sheet reported the following: cash, $1,300,000; prepaid expenses, $360,000; noncurrent assets, $2,400,000; and shareholders' equity, $2,500,000. The current ratio at the end of the year was 2.0 and the debt to equity ratio was 1.4.

Required:
Determine the following 2013 amounts and ratios:
1. Current liabilities.
2. Long-term liabilities.
3. Accounts receivable.
4. The acid-test ratio.

E 3–20
Effect of
management
decisions on
ratios
● LO3–8

Most decisions made by management impact the ratios analysts use to evaluate performance. Indicate (by letter) whether each of the actions listed below will immediately increase (I), decrease (D), or have no effect (N) on the ratios shown. Assume each ratio is less than 1.0 before the action is taken.

Action	Current Ratio	Acid-Test Ratio	Debt to Equity Ratio
1. Issuance of long-term bonds	——	——	——
2. Issuance of short-term notes	——	——	——
3. Payment of accounts payable	——	——	——
4. Purchase of inventory on account	——	——	——
5. Purchase of inventory for cash	——	——	——
6. Purchase of equipment with a 4-year note	——	——	——
7. Retirement of bonds	——	——	——
8. Sale of common stock	——	——	——
9. Write-off of obsolete inventory	——	——	——
10. Purchase of short-term investment for cash	——	——	——
11. Decision to refinance on a long-term basis some currently maturing debt	——	——	——

E 3–21
Segment
reporting
● Appendix 3

The Canton Corporation operates in four distinct business segments. The segments, along with 2013 information on revenues, assets and net income, are listed below ($ in millions):

Segment	Revenues	Assets	Net Income
Pharmaceuticals	$2,000	$1,000	$200
Plastics	3,000	1,500	270
Farm equipment	2,500	1,250	320
Electronics	500	250	40
Total company	$8,000	$4,000	$830

CHAPTER 3   The Balance Sheet and Financial Disclosures   **153**

Required:
1. For which segments must Canton report supplementary information according to U.S. GAAP?
2. What amounts must be reported for the segments you identified in requirement 1?

E 3–22
Segment reporting
● Appendix 3
LO3–9

 IFRS

Refer to Exercise 3–21.

Required:
How might your answers differ if Canton Corporation prepares its segment disclosure according to International Financial Reporting Standards?

CPA and CMA Review Questions

CPA Exam
Questions

The following questions are adapted from a variety of sources including questions developed by the AICPA Board of Examiners and those used in the Kaplan CPA Review Course to study balance sheet presentation, financial disclosures, and liquidity ratios while preparing for the CPA examination. Determine the response that best completes the statements or questions.

● LO3–2

1. In Merf's April 30, 2013, balance sheet, a note receivable was reported as a noncurrent asset and the related accrued interest for eight months was reported as a current asset. Which of the following descriptions would fit Merf's receivable classification?
   a. Both principal and interest amounts are due on August 31, 2013, and August 31, 2014.
   b. Principal is due August 31, 2014, and interest is due August 31, 2013, and August 31, 2014.
   c. Principal and interest are due December 31, 2013.
   d. Both principal and interest amounts are due on December 31, 2013, and December 31, 2014.

● LO3–3

2. Mill Co.'s trial balance included the following account balances at December 31, 2013:

Accounts payable	$15,000
Bond payable, due 2014	22,000
Dividends payable 1/31/14	8,000
Notes payable, due 2015	20,000

What amount should be included in the current liability section of Mill's December 31, 2013, balance sheet?
   a. $45,000
   b. $51,000
   c. $65,000
   d. $78,000

● LO3–4

3. Which of the following would be disclosed in the summary of significant accounting policies disclosure note?

	Composition of Plant Assets	Inventory Pricing
a.	No	Yes
b.	Yes	No
c.	Yes	Yes
d.	No	No

● LO3–6

4. How are management's responsibility and the auditor's report represented in the standard auditor's report?

	Management's Responsibility	Auditor's Responsibility
a.	Implicitly	Explicitly
b.	Implicitly	Implicitly
c.	Explicitly	Explicitly
d.	Explicitly	Implicitly

● LO3–8

5. At December 30, Vida Co. had cash of $200,000, a current ratio of 1.5:1, and a quick ratio of .5:1. On December 31, all the cash was used to reduce accounts payable. How did this cash payment affect the ratios?

	Current Ratio	Quick Ratio
a.	Increased	No effect
b.	Increased	Decreased
c.	Decreased	Increased
d.	Decreased	No effect

154   SECTION 1   The Role of Accounting as an Information System

● LO3–8   6. Zenk Co. wrote off obsolete inventory of $100,000 during 2013. What was the effect of this write-off on Zenk's ratio analysis?

a. Decrease in the current ratio but not the quick ratio.
b. Decrease in the quick ratio but not in the current ratio.
c. Increase in the current ratio but not in the quick ratio.
d. Increase in the quick ratio but not in the current ratio.

Beginning in 2011, International Financial Reporting Standards are tested on the CPA exam along with U.S. GAAP. The following questions deal with the application of IFRS.

● LO3–9   7. Noncurrent assets must be reported before current assets in a balance sheet reported by a company using:

 IFRS

a. IFRS.
b. U.S. GAAP.
c. Both U.S. GAAP and IFRS.
d. Neither U.S. GAAP nor IFRS.

● LO3–9   8. Total liabilities of a company's reportable segments must be reported when the company provides supple-
● Appendix 3   mental information on operating segments using:

IFRS

a. IFRS.
b. U.S. GAAP.
c. Both U.S. GAAP and IFRS.
d. Neither U.S. GAAP nor IFRS.

CMA Exam Questions   The following questions dealing with balance sheet presentation, financial disclosures, and liquidity ratios are adapted from questions that previously appeared on Certified Management Accountant (CMA) examinations. The CMA designation sponsored by the Institute of Management Accountants (www.imanet.org) provides members with an objective measure of knowledge and competence in the field of management accounting. Determine the response that best completes the statements or questions.

● LO3–4   1. The Financial Accounting Standards Board has provided guidance on disclosures of transactions between related parties, for example, transactions between subsidiaries of a common parent. GAAP regarding related-party transactions requires all of the following disclosures except

a. The nature of the relationship involved.
b. A description of the transactions for each period an income statement is presented.
c. The dollar amounts of transactions for each period an income statement is presented.
d. The effect on the cash flow statement for each period a cash flow statement is presented.

● LO3–5   2. The Management's Discussion and Analysis (MD&A) section of an annual report

a. Includes the company president's letter.
b. Covers three financial aspects of a firm's business: liquidity, capital resources, and results of operations.
c. Is a technical analysis of past results and a defense of those results by management.
d. Covers marketing and product line issues.

● LO3–8   3. Windham Company has current assets of $400,000 and current liabilities of $500,000. Windham Company's current ratio would be increased by

a. The purchase of $100,000 of inventory on account.
b. The payment of $100,000 of accounts payable.
c. The collection of $100,000 of accounts receivable.
d. Refinancing a $100,000 long-term loan with short-term debt.

Problems

An alternate exercise and problem set is available on the text website: www.mhhe.com/spiceland7e

P 3–1
Balance sheet preparation
● LO3–2, LO3–3

Presented below is a list of balance sheet accounts presented in alphabetical order.

Accounts payable	Cash
Accounts receivable	Common stock
Accumulated depreciation—buildings	Copyright
Accumulated depreciation—equipment	Equipment
Allowance for uncollectible accounts	Interest receivable (due in three months)
Bond sinking fund	Inventories
Bonds payable (due in 10 years)	Land (in use)
Buildings	Long-term investments (continued)

CHAPTER 3   The Balance Sheet and Financial Disclosures   **155**

(concluded)

Notes payable (due in 6 months)	Rent payable (current)
Notes receivable (due in 2 years)	Retained earnings
Patent	Short-term investments
Preferred stock	Taxes payable
Prepaid expenses	Wages payable

Required:
Prepare a classified balance sheet ignoring monetary amounts.

P 3–2
Balance sheet preparation; missing elements
● **LO3–2, LO3–3**

The data listed below are taken from a balance sheet of Trident Corporation. Some amounts, indicated by question marks, have been intentionally omitted.

	($ in 000s)
Cash and cash equivalents	$ 239,186
Short-term investments	353,700
Accounts receivable (net of allowance)	504,944
Inventories	?
Prepaid expenses (current)	83,259
Total current assets	1,594,927
Long-term receivables	110,800
Property and equipment (net)	?
Total assets	?
Notes payable and short-term debt	31,116
Accounts payable	?
Accrued liabilities	421,772
Other current liabilities	181,604
Total current liabilities	693,564
Long-term debt and deferred taxes	?
Total liabilities	956,140
Shareholders' equity	1,370,627

Required:
1. Determine the missing amounts.
2. Prepare Trident's classified balance sheet.

P 3–3
Balance sheet preparation
● **LO3–2, LO3–3**

The following is a December 31, 2013, post-closing trial balance for Almway Corporation.

Account Title	Debits	Credits
Cash	45,000	
Investments	110,000	
Accounts receivable	60,000	
Inventories	200,000	
Prepaid insurance	9,000	
Land	90,000	
Buildings	420,000	
Accumulated depreciation—buildings		100,000
Equipment	110,000	
Accumulated depreciation—equipment		60,000
Patents (net of amortization)	10,000	
Accounts payable		75,000
Notes payable		130,000
Interest payable		20,000
Bonds payable		240,000
Common stock		300,000
Retained earnings		129,000
Totals	1,054,000	1,054,000

Additional Information:

1. The investment account includes an investment in common stock of another corporation of $30,000 which management intends to hold for at least three years. The balance of these investments is intended to be sold in the coming year.
2. The land account includes land which cost $25,000 that the company has not used and is currently listed for sale.
3. The cash account includes $15,000 set aside in a fund to pay bonds payable that mature in 2016 and $23,000 set aside in a three-month Treasury bill.

4. The notes payable account consists of the following:
   a. a $30,000 note due in six months.
   b. a $50,000 note due in six years.
   c. a $50,000 note due in five annual installments of $10,000 each, with the next installment due February 15, 2014.
5. The $60,000 balance in accounts receivable is net of an allowance for uncollectible accounts of $8,000.
6. The common stock account represents 100,000 shares of no par value common stock issued and outstanding. The corporation has 500,000 shares authorized.

Required:
Prepare a classified balance sheet for the Almway Corporation at December 31, 2013.

P 3–4
Balance sheet preparation
● LO3–2, LO3–3

The following is a December 31, 2013, post-closing trial balance for the Weismuller Publishing Company.

Account Title	Debits	Credits
Cash	65,000	
Accounts receivable	160,000	
Inventories	285,000	
Prepaid expenses	148,000	
Machinery and equipment	320,000	
Accumulated depreciation—equipment		110,000
Investments	140,000	
Accounts payable		60,000
Interest payable		20,000
Unearned revenue		80,000
Taxes payable		30,000
Notes payable		200,000
Allowance for uncollectible accounts		16,000
Common stock		400,000
Retained earnings		202,000
Totals	1,118,000	1,118,000

Additional Information:

1. Prepaid expenses include $120,000 paid on December 31, 2013, for a two-year lease on the building that houses both the administrative offices and the manufacturing facility.
2. Investments include $30,000 in Treasury bills purchased on November 30, 2013. The bills mature on January 30, 2014. The remaining $110,000 includes investments in marketable equity securities that the company intends to sell in the next year.
3. Unearned revenue represents customer prepayments for magazine subscriptions. Subscriptions are for periods of one year or less.
4. The notes payable account consists of the following:
   a. a $40,000 note due in six months.
   b. a $100,000 note due in six years.
   c. a $60,000 note due in three annual installments of $20,000 each, with the next installment due August 31, 2014.
5. The common stock account represents 400,000 shares of no par value common stock issued and outstanding. The corporation has 800,000 shares authorized.

Required:
Prepare a classified balanced sheet for the Weismuller Publishing Company at December 31, 2013.

P 3–5
Balance sheet preparation
● LO3–2, LO3–3

The following is a June 30, 2013, post-closing trial balance for Excell Company.

Account Title	Debits	Credits
Cash	83,000	
Short-term investments	65,000	
Accounts receivable	280,000	
Prepaid expenses	32,000	
Land	75,000	
Buildings	320,000	
Accumulated depreciation—buildings		160,000
Equipment	265,000	
Accumulated depreciation—equipment		120,000
Accounts payable		173,000

(continued)

(concluded)

Accrued expenses		45,000
Notes payable		100,000
Mortgage payable		250,000
Common stock		100,000
Retained earnings		172,000
Totals	1,120,000	1,120,000

Additional Information:

1. The short-term investments account includes $18,000 in U.S. treasury bills purchased in May. The bills mature in July.

2. The accounts receivable account consists of the following:

a. Amounts owed by customers	$225,000
b. Allowance for uncollectible accounts—trade customers	(15,000)
c. Nontrade note receivable (due in three years)	65,000
d. Interest receivable on note (due in four months)	5,000
Total	$280,000

3. The notes payable account consists of two notes of $50,000 each. One note is due on September 30, 2013, and the other is due on November 30, 2014.

4. The mortgage payable is payable in *semiannual* installments of $5,000 each plus interest. The next payment is due on October 31, 2013. Interest has been properly accrued and is included in accrued expenses.

5. Five hundred thousand shares of no par common stock are authorized, of which 200,000 shares have been issued and are outstanding.

6. The land account includes $50,000 representing the cost of the land on which the company's office building resides. The remaining $25,000 is the cost of land that the company is holding for investment purposes.

Required:
Prepare a classified balance sheet for the Excell Company at June 30, 2013.

P 3–6
Balance sheet
preparation;
disclosures

● LO3–2 through
LO3–4

The following is a December 31, 2013, post-closing trial balance for the Vosburgh Electronics Corporation.

Account Title	Debits	Credits
Cash	67,000	
Short-term investments	182,000	
Accounts receivable	123,000	
Long-term investments	35,000	
Inventories	215,000	
Loans to employees	40,000	
Prepaid expenses (for 2014)	16,000	
Land	280,000	
Building	1,550,000	
Machinery and equipment	637,000	
Patent	152,000	
Franchise	40,000	
Note receivable	250,000	
Interest receivable	12,000	
Accumulated depreciation—building		620,000
Accumulated depreciation—equipment		210,000
Accounts payable		189,000
Dividends payable (payable on 1/16/14)		10,000
Interest payable		16,000
Taxes payable		40,000
Unearned revenue		60,000
Notes payable		300,000
Allowance for uncollectible accounts		8,000
Common stock		2,000,000
Retained earnings		146,000
Totals	3,599,000	3,599,000

Additional Information:

1. The common stock represents 1 million shares of no par stock authorized, 500,000 shares issued and outstanding.

2. The loans to employees are due on June 30, 2014.

3. The note receivable is due in installments of $50,000, payable on each September 30. Interest is payable annually.

4. Short-term investments consist of marketable equity securities that the company plans to sell in 2014 and $50,000 in treasury bills purchased on December 15 of the current year that mature on February 15, 2014. Long-term investments consist of marketable equity securities that the company does not plan to sell in the next year.

5. Unearned revenue represents customer payments for extended service contracts. Eighty percent of these contracts expire in 2014, the remainder in 2015.

6. Notes payable consists of two notes, one for $100,000 due on January 15, 2015, and another for $200,000 due on June 30, 2016.

Required:

1. Prepare a classified balance sheet for Vosburgh at December 31, 2013.

2. Identify the items that would require additional disclosure, either on the face of the balance sheet or in a disclosure note.

P 3–7
Balance sheet preparation; errors
● **LO3–2, LO3–3**

The following balance sheet for the Hubbard Corporation was prepared by the company:

HUBBARD CORPORATION
Balance Sheet
At December 31, 2013

Assets

Buildings	$ 750,000
Land	250,000
Cash	60,000
Accounts receivable (net)	120,000
Inventories	240,000
Machinery	280,000
Patent (net)	100,000
Investment in marketable equity securities	60,000
Total assets	$1,860,000

Liabilities and Shareholders' Equity

Accounts payable	$ 215,000
Accumulated depreciation	255,000
Notes payable	500,000
Appreciation of inventories	80,000
Common stock, authorized and issued 100,000 shares of no par stock	430,000
Retained earnings	380,000
Total liabilities and shareholders' equity	$1,860,000

Additional Information:

1. The buildings, land, and machinery are all stated at cost except for a parcel of land that the company is holding for future sale. The land originally cost $50,000 but, due to a significant increase in market value, is listed at $120,000. The increase in the land account was credited to retained earnings.

2. Marketable equity securities consist of stocks of other corporations and are recorded at cost, $20,000 of which will be sold in the coming year. The remainder will be held indefinitely.

3. Notes payable are all long-term. However, a $100,000 note requires an installment payment of $25,000 due in the coming year.

4. Inventories are recorded at current resale value. The original cost of the inventories is $160,000.

Required:

Prepare a corrected classified balance sheet for the Hubbard Corporation at December 31, 2013.

P 3–8
Balance sheet; errors; missing amounts
● **LO3–2, LO3–3**

The following incomplete balance sheet for the Sanderson Manufacturing Company was prepared by the company's controller. As accounting manager for Sanderson, you are attempting to reconstruct and revise the balance sheet.

Sanderson Manufacturing Company
Balance Sheet
At December 31, 2013
($ in 000s)

Assets

Current assets:	
Cash	$ 1,250
Accounts receivable	3,500
Allowance for uncollectible accounts	(400)
Finished goods inventory	6,000
Prepaid expenses	1,200
Total current assets	11,550
Noncurrent assets:	
Investments	3,000
Raw materials and work in process inventory	2,250
Equipment	15,000
Accumulated depreciation—equipment	(4,200)
Patent	?
Total assets	$?

Liabilities and Shareholders' Equity

Current liabilities:		
Accounts payable		$ 5,200
Note payable		4,000
Interest payable—note		100
Unearned revenue		3,000
Total current liabilities		12,300
Long-term liabilities:		
Bonds payable		5,500
Interest payable—bonds		200
Shareholders' equity:		
Common stock	$?	
Retained earnings	?	?
Total liabilities and shareholders' equity		?

Additional Information ($ in 000s):

1. Certain records that included the account balances for the patent and shareholders' equity items were lost. However, the controller told you that a complete, preliminary balance sheet prepared before the records were lost showed a debt to equity ratio of 1.2. That is, total liabilities are 120% of total shareholders' equity. Retained earnings at the beginning of the year was $4,000. Net income for 2013 was $1,560 and $560 in cash dividends were declared and paid to shareholders.

2. Management intends to sell the investments in the next six months.

3. Interest on both the note and the bonds is payable annually.

4. The note payable is due in annual installments of $1,000 each.

5. Unearned revenue will be earned equally over the next two fiscal years.

6. The common stock represents 400,000 shares of no par stock authorized, 250,000 shares issued and outstanding.

Required:
Prepare a complete, corrected, classified balance sheet.

P 3–9
Balance sheet
preparation
● LO3–2, LO3–3

Presented below is the balance sheet for HHD, Inc., at December 31, 2013.

Current assets	$ 600,000	Current liabilities	$ 400,000
Investments	500,000	Long-term liabilities	1,100,000
Property, plant, and equipment	2,000,000	Shareholders' equity	1,800,000
Intangible assets	200,000		
Total assets	$3,300,000	Total liabilities and shareholders' equity	$3,300,000

The captions shown in the summarized statement above include the following:

a. Current assets: cash, $150,000; accounts receivable, $200,000; inventories, $225,000; and prepaid insurance, $25,000.

b. Investments: investments in common stock, short term, $90,000, and long term, $160,000; and bond sinking fund, $250,000.

c. Property, plant, and equipment: buildings, $1,500,000 less accumulated depreciation, $600,000; equipment, $500,000 less accumulated depreciation, $200,000; and land, $800,000.

d. Intangible assets: patent, $110,000; and copyright, $90,000.

e. Current liabilities: accounts payable, $100,000; notes payable, short term, $150,000, and long term, $90,000; and taxes payable, $60,000.

f. Long-term liabilities: bonds payable due 2018.

g. Shareholders' equity: common stock, $1,000,000; retained earnings, $800,000. Five hundred thousand shares of no par common stock are authorized, of which 200,000 shares were issued and are outstanding.

Required:
Prepare a corrected classified balance sheet for HHD, Inc., at December 31, 2013.

P 3–10
Balance sheet
preparation
● **LO3–2, LO3–3**

Melody Lane Music Company was started by John Ross early in 2013. Initial capital was acquired by issuing shares of common stock to various investors and by obtaining a bank loan. The company operates a retail store that sells records, tapes, and compact discs. Business was so good during the first year of operations that John is considering opening a second store on the other side of town. The funds necessary for expansion will come from a new bank loan. In order to approve the loan, the bank requires financial statements.

John asks for your help in preparing the balance sheet and presents you with the following information for the year ending December 31, 2013:

a. Cash receipts consisted of the following:

From customers	$360,000
From issue of common stock	100,000
From bank loan	100,000

b. Cash disbursements were as follows:

Purchase of inventory	$300,000
Rent	15,000
Salaries	30,000
Utilities	5,000
Insurance	3,000
Purchase of equipment and furniture	40,000

c. The bank loan was made on March 31, 2013. A note was signed requiring payment of interest and principal on March 31, 2014. The interest rate is 12%.

d. The equipment and furniture were purchased on January 3, 2013, and have an estimated useful life of 10 years with no anticipated salvage value. Depreciation per year is $4,000.

e. Inventories on hand at the end of the year cost $100,000.

f. Amounts owed at December 31, 2013, were as follows:

To suppliers of inventory	$20,000
To the utility company	1,000

g. Rent on the store building is $1,000 per month. On December 1, 2013, four months' rent was paid in advance.

h. Net income for the year was $76,000. Assume that the company is not subject to federal, state, or local income tax.

i. One hundred thousand shares of no par common stock are authorized, of which 20,000 shares were issued and are outstanding.

Required:
Prepare a balance sheet at December 31, 2013.

Broaden Your Perspective

Apply your critical-thinking ability to the knowledge you've gained. These cases will provide you an opportunity to develop your research, analysis, judgment, and communication skills. You also will work with other students, integrate what you've learned, apply it in real world situations, and consider its global and ethical ramifications. This practice will broaden your knowledge and further develop your decision-making abilities.

Communication Case 3–1
Current versus noncurrent classification
● LO3–2

A first-year accounting student is confused by a statement made in a recent class. Her instructor stated that the assets listed in the balance sheet of the IBM Corporation include computers that are classified as current assets as well as computers that are classified as noncurrent assets. In addition, the instructor stated that investments in marketable securities of other corporations could be classified in the balance sheet as either current or noncurrent assets.

Required:

Explain to the student the distinction between current and noncurrent assets pertaining to the IBM computers and the investments in marketable securities.

Analysis Case 3–2
Current versus noncurrent classification
● LO3–2, LO3–3

The usefulness of the balance sheet is enhanced when assets and liabilities are grouped according to common characteristics. The broad distinction made in the balance sheet is the current versus noncurrent classification of both assets and liabilities.

Required:

1. Discuss the factors that determine whether an asset or liability should be classified as current or noncurrent in a balance sheet.
2. Identify six items that under different circumstances could be classified as either current or noncurrent. Indicate the factors that would determine the correct classification.

Communication Case 3–3
FASB codification research; inventory or property, plant, and equipment
● LO3–2

The Red Hen Company produces, processes, and sells fresh eggs. The company is in the process of preparing financial statements at the end of its first year of operations and has asked for your help in determining the appropriate treatment of the cost of its egg-laying flock. The estimated life of a laying hen is approximately two years, after which they are sold to soup companies.

The controller considers the company's operating cycle to be two years and wants to present the cost of the egg-producing flock as inventory in the current asset section of the balance sheet. He feels that the hens are "goods awaiting sale." The chief financial officer does not agree with this treatment. He thinks that the cost of the flock should be classified as property, plant, and equipment because the hens are used in the production of product—the eggs.

The focus of this case is the balance sheet presentation of the cost of the egg-producing flock. Your instructor will divide the class into two to six groups depending on the size of the class. The mission of your group is to reach consensus on the appropriate presentation.

Required:

1. Each group member should deliberate the situation independently and draft a tentative argument prior to the class session for which the case is assigned.
2. In class, each group will meet for 10 to 15 minutes in different areas of the classroom. During that meeting, group members will take turns sharing their suggestions for the purpose of arriving at a single group treatment.
3. After the allotted time, a spokesperson for each group (selected during the group meetings) will share the group's solution with the class. The goal of the class is to incorporate the views of each group into a consensus approach to the situation.

IFRS Case 3–4
Balance sheet presentation; Vodafone Group, Plc.
● LO3–2, LO3–3, LO3–9

🌐 IFRS

Real World Financials

Vodafone Group, Plc., a U.K. company, is the largest mobile telecommunications network company in the world. The company prepares its financial statements in accordance with International Financial Reporting Standards. Below are partial company balance sheets (statements of financial position) included in a recent annual report:

Vodafone Group, Plc. Consolidated Statements of Financial Position At March 31		
	2011	**2010**
	£m	£m
Noncurrent assets		
Goodwill	45,236	51,838
Other intangible assets	23,322	22,420
Property, plant, and equipment	20,181	20,642
Investments in associates	38,105	36,377
Other investments	1,381	7,591
Deferred tax assets	2,018	1,033
Post employment benefits	97	34
Trade and other receivables	3,877	2,831
	134,217	142,766

(continued)

(concluded)	2011	2010
	£m	£m
Current assets		
Inventory	537	433
Taxation recoverable	281	191
Trade and other receivables	9,259	8,784
Other investments	674	388
Cash and cash equivalents	6,252	4,423
	17,003	14,219
Total assets	151,220	156,985
Equity (details provided in complete statement)	87,561	90,810
Noncurrent liabilities		
Long-term borrowings	28,375	28,632
Taxation liabilities	350	—
Deferred tax liabilities	6,486	7,377
Postemployment benefits	87	237
Provisions	482	497
Trade and other payables	804	816
	36,584	37,559
Current liabilities		
Short-term borrowings	9,906	11,163
Taxation liabilities	1,912	2,874
Provisions	559	497
Trade and other payables	14,698	14,082
	27,075	28,616
Total equity and liabilities	151,220	156,985

Required:

1. Describe the differences between Vodafone's balance sheets and a typical U.S. company balance sheet.
2. What type of liabilities do you think are included in the *provisions* category in Vodafone's balance sheets?

Judgment Case 3–5
Balance sheet; errors
● LO3–2 through LO3–4

You recently joined the internal auditing department of Marcus Clothing Corporation. As one of your first assignments, you are examining a balance sheet prepared by a staff accountant.

MARCUS CLOTHING CORPORATION
Balance Sheet
At December 31, 2013

Assets

Current assets:		
Cash		$ 137,000
Accounts receivable, net		80,000
Note receivable		53,000
Inventories		240,000
Investments		66,000
Total current assets		576,000
Other assets:		
Land	$200,000	
Equipment, net	320,000	
Prepaid expenses	27,000	
Patent	22,000	
Total other assets		569,000
Total assets		$1,145,000

Liabilities and Shareholders' Equity

Current liabilities:		
Accounts payable		$ 125,000
Salaries payable		32,000
Total current liabilities		157,000
		(continued)

(concluded)	Long-term liabilities:		
	Note payable	$100,000	
	Bonds payable	300,000	
	Interest payable	20,000	
	Total long-term liabilities		420,000
	Shareholders' equity:		
	Common stock	500,000	
	Retained earnings	68,000	
	Total shareholders' equity		568,000
	Total liabilities and shareholders' equity		$1,145,000

In the course of your examination you uncover the following information pertaining to the balance sheet:

1. The company rents its facilities. The land that appears in the statement is being held for future sale.
2. The note receivable is due in 2015. The balance of $53,000 includes $3,000 of accrued interest. The next interest payment is due in July 2014.
3. The note payable is due in installments of $20,000 per year. Interest on both the notes and bonds is payable annually.
4. The company's investments consist of marketable equity securities of other corporations. Management does not intend to liquidate any investments in the coming year.

Required:
Identify and explain the deficiencies in the statement prepared by the company's accountant. Include in your answer items that require additional disclosure, either on the face of the statement or in a note.

Judgment Case 3–6
Financial disclosures
● LO3–4

You recently joined the auditing staff of Best, Best, and Krug, CPAs. You have been assigned to the audit of Clearview, Inc., and have been asked by the audit senior to examine the balance sheet prepared by Clearview's accountant.

CLEARVIEW, INC.
Balance Sheet
At December 31, 2013
($ in millions)

Assets

Current assets:		
Cash		$ 10.5
Accounts receivable		112.1
Inventories		220.6
Prepaid expenses		5.5
Total current assets		348.7
Investments		22.0
Property, plant, and equipment, net		486.9
Total assets		$857.6

Liabilities and Shareholders' Equity

Current liabilities:		
Accounts payable		$ 83.5
Accrued taxes and interest		25.5
Current maturities of long-term debt		20.0
Total current liabilities		129.0
Long-term liabilities:		420.0
Total liabilities		549.0
Shareholders' equity:		
Common stock	$100.0	
Retained earnings	208.6	
Total shareholders' equity		308.6
Total liabilities and shareholders' equity		$857.6

Required:

Identify the items in the statement that most likely would require further disclosure either on the face of the statement or in a note. Further identify those items that would require disclosure in the significant accounting policies note.

Real World Case 3–7
Balance sheet and significant accounting policies disclosure; Walmart
● **LO3–2 through LO3–4, LO3–8**

Real World Financials

The balance sheet and disclosure of significant accounting policies taken from the 2011 annual report of Wal-Mart Stores, Inc., appear below. Use this information to answer the following questions:

1. What are the asset classifications contained in Walmart's balance sheet?
2. What amounts did Walmart report for the following items for 2011:
   a. Total assets
   b. Current assets
   c. Current liabilities
   d. Total shareholders' equity
   e. Retained earnings
   f. Inventories
3. What is the par value of Walmart's common stock? How many shares of common stock are authorized, issued, and outstanding at the end of 2011?
4. Compute Walmart's current ratio for 2011.
5. Identify the following items:
   a. The company's inventory valuation method.
   b. The definition of cash equivalents.

WAL-MART STORES, INC.
Consolidated Balance Sheets
(Amounts in millions except per share data)

As of January 31,	2011	2010 As Adjusted
Assets		
Current assets:		
Cash and cash equivalents	$ 7,395	$ 7,907
Receivables, net	5,089	4,144
Inventories	36,318	32,713
Prepaid expenses and other	2,960	3,128
Current assets of discontinued operations	131	140
Total current assets	51,893	48,032
Property and equipment:		
Land	24,386	22,591
Buildings and improvements	79,051	73,657
Fixtures and equipment	38,290	34,035
Transportation equipment	2,595	2,355
Construction in process	4,262	5,210
Property and equipment	148,584	137,848
Less accumulated depreciation	(43,486)	(38,304)
Property and equipment, net	105,098	99,544
Property under leases:		
Property under leases	5,905	5,669
Less accumulated amortization	(3,125)	(2,906)
Property under leases, net	2,780	2,763
Goodwill	16,763	16,126
Other assets and deferred charges	4,129	3,942
Total assets	$180,663	$170,407
Liabilities and Shareholders' Equity		
Current liabilities:		
Short-term borrowings	$ 1,031	$ 523
Accounts payable	33,557	30,451
Accrued liabilities	18,701	18,734
Accrued income taxes	157	1,347

(continued)

(concluded)

Long-term debt due within one year	4,655	4,050
Obligations under capital due within one year	336	346
Current liabilities of discontinued operations	47	92
Total current liabilities	58,484	55,543
Long-term debt	40,692	33,231
Long-term obligations under leases	3,150	3,170
Deferred income taxes and other	6,682	5,508
Redeemable noncontrolling interest	408	307
Commitments and contingencies		
Shareholders' equity:		
Preferred stock ($0.10 par value; 100 shares authorized, none issued)	—	—
Common stock ($0.10 par value; 11,000 shares authorized, 3,516 and 3,786 issued and outstanding at January 31, 2011 and 2010, respectively)	352	378
Capital in excess of par value	3,577	3,803
Retained earnings	63,967	66,357
Accumulated other comprehensive income (loss)	646	(70)
Total Walmart shareholders' equity	68,542	70,468
Noncontrolling interest	2,705	2,180
Total equity	71,247	72,648
Total liabilities and shareholders' equity	$180,663	$170,407

NOTES TO CONSOLIDATED FINANCIAL STATEMENTS
WAL-MART STORES, INC.

1 Summary of Significant Accounting Policies (in part)

Cash and Cash Equivalents

The Company considers investments with a maturity of three months or less when purchased to be cash equivalents.

Inventories

The Company values inventories at the lower of cost or market as determined primarily by the retail method of accounting, using the last-in, first-out ("LIFO") method for substantially all of the Walmart U.S. segment's merchandise inventories. Inventories for the Walmart International operations are primarily valued by the retail method of accounting, using the first-in, first-out ("FIFO") method. At January 31, 2011 and 2010, our inventories valued at LIFO approximate those inventories as if they were valued at FIFO.

Revenue Recognition

The Company recognizes sales revenue net of sales taxes and estimated sales returns at the time it sells merchandise to the customer. Customer purchases of shopping cards are not recognized as revenue until the card is redeemed and the customer purchases merchandise by using the shopping card. The Company also recognizes revenue from service transactions at the time the service is performed. Generally, revenue from services is classified as a component of net sales on our consolidated statements of income.

Judgment
Case 3–8
Post fiscal year-
end events
● LO3–4

The fiscal year-end for the Northwest Distribution Corporation is December 31. The company's 2013 financial statements were issued on March 15, 2014. The following events occurred between December 31, 2013, and March 15, 2014.

1. On January 22, 2014, the company negotiated a major merger with Blandon Industries. The merger will be completed by the middle of 2014.

2. On February 3, 2014, Northwest negotiated a $10 million long-term note with the Credit Bank of Ohio. The amount of the note is material.

3. On February 25, 2014, a flood destroyed one of the company's manufacturing plants causing $600,000 of uninsured damage.

Required:

Determine the appropriate treatment of each of these events in the 2013 financial statements of Northwest Distribution Corporation.

Research Case 3–9
FASB codification; locate and extract relevant information and cite authoritative support for a financial reporting issue; related-party disclosures; Enron Corporation

● LO3–4

Real World Financials

Enron Corporation was a darling in the energy-provider arena, and in January 2001 its stock price rose above $100 per share. A collapse of investor confidence in 2001 and revelations of accounting irregularities led to one of the largest bankruptcies in U.S. history. By the end of the year, Enron's stock price had plummeted to less than $1 per share. Investigations and lawsuits followed. One problem area concerned transactions with related parties that were not adequately disclosed in the company's financial statements. Critics stated that the lack of information about these transactions made it difficult for analysts following Enron to identify problems the company was experiencing.

Required:

1. Obtain the relevant authoritative literature on related-party transactions using the FASB's Codification Research System. You might gain access at the FASB website (www.fasb.org). What is the specific citation that outlines the required information on related-party disclosures that must be included in the notes to the financial statements?
2. Describe the disclosures required for related-party transactions.
3. Use EDGAR (www.sec.gov) or another method to locate the December 31, 2000, financial statements of Enron. Search for the related-party disclosure. Briefly describe the relationship central to the various transactions described.
4. Why is it important that companies disclose related-party transactions? Use the Enron disclosure of the sale of dark fiber inventory in your answer.

Real World Case 3–10
Disclosures; proxy statement; Nordstrom

● LO3–4, LO3–6

Real World Financials

EDGAR, the Electronic Data Gathering, Analysis, and Retrieval system, performs automated collection, validation, indexing, and forwarding of submissions by companies and others who are required by law to file forms with the SEC. All publicly traded domestic companies use EDGAR to make the majority of their filings. (Some foreign companies file voluntarily.) Form 10-K, which includes the annual report, is required to be filed on EDGAR. The SEC makes this information available on the Internet.

Required:

1. Access EDGAR on the Internet. The web address is www.sec.gov.
2. Search for Nordstrom, Inc., a leading clothing department store chain. Access the 10-K for the fiscal year ended January 29, 2011. Search or scroll to find the disclosure notes and audit report.
3. Answer the following questions:
   a. Describe the subsequent events disclosed by the company.
   b. Which firm is the company's auditor? What type of audit opinion did the auditor render?
4. Access the proxy statement filed with the SEC on March 31, 2011 (the proxy statement designation is Def 14A), locate the executive officers summary compensation table and answer the following questions:
   a. What is the principal position of Michael G. Koppel?
   b. What was the salary paid to Mr. Koppel during the year ended January 29, 2011?

Judgment Case 3–11
Debt versus equity

● LO3–7

A common problem facing any business entity is the debt versus equity decision. When funds are required to obtain assets, should debt or equity financing be used? This decision also is faced when a company is initially formed. What will be the mix of debt versus equity in the initial capital structure? The characteristics of debt are very different from those of equity as are the financial implications of using one method of financing as opposed to the other.

Cherokee Plastics Corporation is formed by a group of investors to manufacture household plastic products. Their initial capitalization goal is $50,000,000. That is, the incorporators have decided to raise $50,000,000 to acquire the initial assets of the company. They have narrowed down the financing mix alternatives to two:
1. All equity financing.
2. $20,000,000 in debt financing and $30,000,000 in equity financing.

No matter which financing alternative is chosen, the corporation expects to be able to generate a 10% annual return, before payment of interest and income taxes, on the $50,000,000 in assets acquired. The interest rate on debt would be 8%. The effective income tax rate will be approximately 50%.

Alternative 2 will require specified interest and principal payments to be made to the creditors at specific dates. The interest portion of these payments (interest expense) will reduce the taxable income of the corporation and hence the amount of income tax the corporation will pay. The all-equity alternative requires no specified payments to be made to suppliers of capital. The corporation is not legally liable to make distributions to its owners. If the board of directors does decide to make a distribution, it is not an expense of the corporation and does not reduce taxable income and hence the taxes the corporation pays.

Required:

1. Prepare abbreviated income statements that compare first-year profitability for each of the two alternatives.
2. Which alternative would be expected to achieve the highest first-year profits? Why?

3. Which alternative would provide the highest rate of return on shareholders' equity? Why?

4. What other related implications of the decision should be considered?

**Analysis
Case 3–12**
Obtain and
critically evaluate
an actual annual
report
● **LO3–4, LO3–6
through LO3–8**

Real World Financials

Financial reports are the primary means by which corporations report their performance and financial condition. Financial statements are one component of the annual report mailed to their shareholders and to interested others.

Required:

Obtain an annual report from a corporation with which you are familiar. Using techniques you learned in this chapter and any analysis you consider useful, respond to the following questions:

1. Do the firm's auditors provide a clean opinion on the financial statements?

2. Has the company made changes in any accounting methods it uses?

3. Have there been any subsequent events, errors and irregularities, illegal acts, or related-party transactions that have a material effect on the company's financial position?

4. What are two trends in the company's operations or capital resources that management considers significant to the company's future?

5. Is the company engaged in more than one significant line of business? If so, compare the relative profitability of the different segments.

6. How stable are the company's operations?

7. Has the company's situation deteriorated or improved with respect to liquidity, solvency, asset management, and profitability?

Note: You can obtain a copy of an annual report from a local company, from a friend who is a shareholder, from the investor relations department of the corporation, from a friendly stockbroker, or from EDGAR (Electronic Data Gathering, Analysis, and Retrieval) on the Internet (www.sec.gov).

**Analysis
Case 3–13**
Obtain and
compare annual
reports from
companies in the
same industry
● **LO3–4, LO3–7,
LO3–8**

Real World Financials

Insight concerning the performance and financial condition of a company often comes from evaluating its financial data in comparison with other firms in the same industry.

Required:

Obtain annual reports from three corporations in the same primary industry. Using techniques you learned in this chapter and any analysis you consider useful, respond to the following questions:

1. Are there differences in accounting methods that should be taken into account when making comparisons?

2. How do earnings trends compare in terms of both the direction and stability of income?

3. Which of the three firms had the greatest earnings relative to resources available?

4. Which corporation has made most effective use of financial leverage?

5. Of the three firms, which seems riskiest in terms of its ability to pay short-term obligations? Long-term obligations?

Note: You can obtain copies of annual reports from friends who are shareholders, from the investor relations department of the corporations, from a friendly stockbroker, or from EDGAR (Electronic Data Gathering, Analysis, and Retrieval) on the Internet (www.sec.gov).

**Analysis
Case 3–14**
Balance sheet
information
● **LO3–2 through
LO3–4**

Refer to the financial statements and related disclosure notes of Dell Inc. in Appendix B located at the back of the text.

Required:

1. What categories does the company use to classify its assets? Its liabilities?

2. Why are investments shown as a current asset?

3. Explain the current liability "deferred services revenue."

4. What purpose do the disclosure notes serve?

5. What method does the company use to depreciate its property and equipment?

6. Does the company report any subsequent events or related party transactions in its disclosure notes?

**Analysis
Case 3–15**
Segment
reporting
concepts
● **Appendix 3
LO3–9**

 IFRS

Levens Co. operates in several distinct business segments. The company does not have any reportable foreign operations or major customers.

Required:

1. What is the purpose of operating segment disclosures?

2. Define an operating segment.

3. List the amounts to be reported by operating segment.

4. How would your answer to requirement 3 differ if Levens Co. prepares its segment disclosure according to International Financial Reporting Standards?

Ethics Case 3–16
Segment
reporting
● **Appendix 3**

You are in your third year as an accountant with McCarver-Lynn Industries, a multidivisional company involved in the manufacturing, marketing, and sales of surgical prosthetic devices. After the fiscal year-end, you are working with the controller of the firm to prepare supplemental business segment disclosures. Yesterday you presented her with the following summary information:

	($ in millions)					
	Domestic	Union of South Africa	Egypt	France	Denmark	Total
Revenues	$ 845	$222	$265	$343	$311	$1,986
Capital expenditures	145	76	88	21	42	372
Assets	1,005	301	290	38	285	1,919

Upon returning to your office after lunch, you find the following memo:

Nice work. Let's combine the data this way:

	($ in millions)			
	Domestic	Africa	Europe	Total
Revenues	$ 845	$487	$654	$1,986
Capital expenditures	145	164	63	372
Assets	1,005	591	323	1,919

Some of our shareholders might react unfavorably to our recent focus on South African operations.

Required:
Do you perceive an ethical dilemma? What would be the likely impact of following the controller's suggestions? Who would benefit? Who would be injured?

Air France–KLM Case

AIRFRANCE

● **LO3-9**

🌐 **IFRS**

Air France–KLM (AF), a French company, prepares its financial statements according to International Financial Reporting Standards. AF's annual report for the year ended March 31, 2011, which includes financial statements and disclosure notes, is provided with all new textbooks. This material also is included in AF's "Registration Document 2010–11," dated June 15, 2011 and is available at www.airfranceklm.com.

Required:
Describe the apparent differences in the order of presentation of the components of the balance sheet between IFRS as applied by Air France–KLM (AF) and a typical balance sheet prepared in accordance with U.S. GAAP.

CHAPTER

4

The Income Statement, Comprehensive Income, and the Statement of Cash Flows

OVERVIEW ——— The purpose of the income statement is to summarize the profit-generating activities that occurred during a particular reporting period. Comprehensive income includes net income as well as a few gains and losses that are not part of net income and are considered other comprehensive income items instead.

The purpose of the statement of cash flows is to provide information about the cash receipts and cash disbursements of an enterprise that occurred during the period.

This chapter has a twofold purpose: (1) to consider important issues dealing with the content, presentation, and disclosure of net income and other components of comprehensive income and (2) to provide an *overview* of the statement of cash flows, which is covered in depth in Chapter 21.

LEARNING ——— **After studying this chapter, you should be able to:**
OBJECTIVES

● **LO4–1** Discuss the importance of income from continuing operations and describe its components. (*p. 172*)

● **LO4–2** Describe earnings quality and how it is impacted by management practices to manipulate earnings. (*p. 177*)

● **LO4–3** Discuss the components of operating and nonoperating income and their relationship to earnings quality. (*p. 178*)

● **LO4–4** Define what constitutes discontinued operations and describe the appropriate income statement presentation for these transactions. (*p. 184*)

● **LO4–5** Define extraordinary items and describe the appropriate income statement presentation for these transactions. (*p. 188*)

● **LO4–6** Define earnings per share (EPS) and explain required disclosures of EPS for certain income statement components. (*p. 192*)

● **LO4–7** Explain the difference between net income and comprehensive income and how we report components of the difference. (*p. 192*)

● **LO4–8** Describe the purpose of the statement of cash flows. (*p. 198*)

● **LO4–9** Identify and describe the various classifications of cash flows presented in a statement of cash flows. (*p. 198*)

● **LO4–10** Discuss the primary differences between U.S. GAAP and IFRS with respect to the income statement, statement of comprehensive income, and statement of cash flows. (*pp. 177, 184, 189, 194, 199,* and *204*)

FINANCIAL REPORTING CASE

Alberto-Culver Company

Your friend, Becky Morgan, just received a generous gift from her grandfather. Accompanying a warm letter were 200 shares of stock of the Alberto-Culver Company, a global manufacturer of beauty and health care products, along with the most recent quarterly financial statements of the company. Becky knows that you are an accounting major and pleads with you to explain some items in the company's income statement. "I remember studying the income statement in my introductory accounting course," says Becky, "but I am still confused. What is this item *discontinued operations?* How about *restructuring costs?* These don't sound good. Are they something I should worry about? We studied earnings per share briefly, but what does *diluted earnings per share* mean?" You agree to try to help.

ALBERTO-CULVER COMPANY & SUBSIDIARIES
Income Statements
Year Ended September 30
($ in thousands, except per share data)

	2010	2009
Sales	$1,597,233	$1,433,980
Cost of products sold	762,557	698,778
Gross profit	834,676	735,202
Marketing, selling and administrative expenses	609,407	545,261
Restructuring costs	5,101	6,776
Operating income	220,168	183,165
Interest expense (income) net	2,324	(2,673)
Income from continuing operations before income taxes	217,844	185,838
Provision for income taxes	62,708	68,005
Income from continuing operations	155,136	117,833
Income from discontinued operations, net of income taxes	174	1,541
Net income	$ 155,310	$ 119,374
Basic earnings per share:		
Continuing operations	$ 1.58	$ 1.21
Discontinued operations	.01	.01
Net income	$ 1.59	$ 1.22
Diluted earnings per share:		
Continuing operations	$ 1.55	$ 1.19
Discontinued operations	.01	.01
Net income	$ 1.56	$ 1.20

By the time you finish this chapter, you should be able to respond appropriately to the questions posed in this case. Compare your response to the solution provided at the end of the chapter.

———QUESTIONS

1. How would you explain restructuring costs to Becky? Are restructuring costs something Becky should worry about? (*p. 179*)

2. Explain to Becky what is meant by discontinued operations and describe to her how that item is reported in an income statement. (*p. 184*)

3. In addition to discontinued operations, what other events sometimes are reported separately in the income statement that you might tell Becky about? Why are these items reported separately? (*p. 188*)

4. Describe to Becky the difference between basic and diluted earnings per share. (*p. 192*)

In Chapter 1 we discussed the critical role of financial accounting information in allocating resources within our economy. Ideally, resources should be allocated to private enterprises that will (1) provide the goods and services our society desires and (2) at the same time provide a fair rate of return to those who supply the resources. A company will be able to achieve these goals only if it can use the resources society provides to generate revenues from selling products and services that exceed the expenses necessary to provide those products and services (that is, generate a profit).

> The income statement displays a company's operating performance, that is, its net profit or loss, during the reporting period.

The purpose of the income statement, sometimes called the statement of operations or statement of earnings, is to summarize the profit-generating activities that occurred during a particular reporting period. Many investors and creditors perceive it as the statement most useful for predicting future profitability (future cash-generating ability).

A few types of gains and losses are excluded from the determination of net income and the income statement but are included in the broader concept of comprehensive income. We refer to these as items of other comprehensive income (OCI) or loss. Comprehensive income can be reported in one of two ways: (1) in a single, continuous statement of comprehensive income or (2) in two separate but consecutive statements—an income statement and a statement of comprehensive income that begins with net income and then reports OCI items to combine for comprehensive income.

The purpose of the statement of cash flows is to provide information about the cash receipts and cash disbursements of an enterprise that occurred during a period. In describing cash flows, the statement provides valuable information about the operating, investing, and financing activities that occurred during the period.

> The *income statement* and *statement of cash flows* report changes that occurred during a particular reporting period.

Unlike the balance sheet, which is a position statement, the income statement and statement of cash flows are *change* statements. The income statement reports the changes in shareholders' equity (retained earnings) that occurred during the reporting period as a result of revenues, expenses, gains, and losses. The statement of cash flows also is a change statement, disclosing the events that caused cash to change during the period.

This chapter is divided into two parts. The first part describes the content and presentation of the income statement and comprehensive income as well as related disclosure issues. The second part provides an overview of the statement of cash flows.

PART A — THE INCOME STATEMENT AND COMPREHENSIVE INCOME

Before we discuss the specific components of an income statement in much depth, let's take a quick look at the general makeup of the statement. Illustration 4–1 offers a statement for a hypothetical manufacturing company that you can refer to as we proceed through the chapter. At this point, our objective is only to gain a general perspective on the items reported and classifications contained in corporate income statements.

Let's first look closer at the components of net income. At the end of this part, we'll see how net income fits within the concept of comprehensive income and how comprehensive income is reported.

● LO4–1 | Income from Continuing Operations

> Income from continuing operations includes the revenues, expenses, gains and losses that will probably continue in future periods.

The need to provide information to help analysts predict future cash flows emphasizes the importance of properly reporting the amount of income from the entity's continuing operations. Clearly, it is the operating transactions that probably will continue into the future that are the best predictors of future cash flows. The components of income from continuing operations are revenues, expenses (including income taxes), gains, and losses, excluding those related to discontinued operations and extraordinary items.[1]

---
[1] These two separately reported items are addressed in a subsequent section.

Income Statements
(In millions, except earnings per share)

Illustration 4–1
Income Statement

		Years Ended June 30	
		2013	**2012**
Income from Continuing Operations	Sales revenue	$1,450.6	$1,380.0
	Cost of goods sold	832.6	800.4
	Gross profit	618.0	579.6
	Operating expenses:		
	Selling	123.5	110.5
	General and administrative	147.8	139.1
	Research and development	55.0	65.0
	Restructuring costs	125.0	—
	Total operating expenses	451.3	314.6
	Operating income	166.7	265.0
	Other income (expense):		
	Interest income	12.4	11.1
	Interest expense	(25.9)	(24.8)
	Gain on sale of investments	18.0	19.0
	Income from continuing operations before income taxes and extraordinary item	171.2	270.3
	Income tax expense	59.9	94.6
	Income from continuing operations before extraordinary item	111.3	175.7
Separately Reported Items	Discontinued operations:		
	Loss from operations of discontinued component (including gain on disposal in 2013 of $47)	(7.6)	(45.7)
	Income tax benefit	2.0	13.0
	Loss on discontinued operations	(5.6)	(32.7)
	Income before extraordinary item	105.7	143.0
	Extraordinary gain, net of $11 in income tax expense	—	22.0
	Net income	$ 105.7	$ 165.0
Earnings per Share	**Earnings per common share—basic:**		
	Income from continuing operations before extraordinary item	$ 2.14	$ 3.38
	Discontinued operations	(.11)	(.62)
	Extraordinary gain	—	.42
	Net income	$ 2.03	$ 3.18
	Earnings per common share—diluted:		
	Income from continuing operations before extraordinary item	$ 2.06	$ 3.25
	Discontinued operations	(.11)	(.62)
	Extraordinary gain	—	.42
	Net income	$ 1.95	$ 3.05

Revenues, Expenses, Gains, and Losses

Revenues are inflows of resources resulting from providing goods or services to customers. For merchandising companies like Walmart, the main source of revenue is sales revenue derived from selling merchandise. Service firms such as FedEx and State Farm Insurance generate revenue by providing services.

Expenses are outflows of resources incurred while generating revenue. They represent the costs of providing goods and services. The *matching principle* is a key player in the way we measure expenses. We attempt to establish a causal relationship between revenues and expenses. If causality can be determined, expenses are reported in the same period that the related revenue is recognized. If a causal relationship cannot be established, we relate the expense to a particular period, allocate it over several periods, or expense it as incurred.

Gains and losses are increases or decreases in equity from peripheral or incidental transactions of an entity. In general, these gains and losses result from changes in equity that do not result directly from operations but nonetheless are related to those activities. For example, gains and losses from the routine sale of equipment, buildings, or other operating assets and from the sale of investment assets normally would be included in income from continuing operations. Later in the chapter we discuss certain gains and losses that are excluded from continuing operations.

Income Tax Expense

Income tax expense is shown as a separate expense in the income statement.

Income taxes represent a major expense to a corporation, and accordingly, income tax expense is given special treatment in the income statement. Income taxes are levied on taxpayers in proportion to the amount of taxable income that is reported to taxing authorities. Like individuals, corporations are income-tax-paying entities.[2] Because of the importance and size of income tax expense (sometimes called *provision for income taxes*), it always is reported as a separate expense in corporate income statements.

Federal, state, and sometimes local taxes are assessed annually and usually are determined by first applying a designated percentage (or percentages), the tax rate (or rates), to taxable income. Taxable income comprises revenues, expenses, gains, and losses as measured according to the regulations of the appropriate taxing authority.

Many of the components of taxable income and income reported in the income statement coincide. But sometimes tax rules and GAAP differ with respect to when and even whether a particular revenue or expense is included in income. When tax rules and GAAP differ regarding the timing of revenue or expense recognition, the actual payment of taxes may occur in a period different from when income tax expense is reported in the income statement. A common example is when a corporation takes advantage of tax laws by legally deducting more depreciation in the early years of an asset's life on its federal income tax return than it reports in its income statement. The amount of tax actually paid in the early years is less than the amount that is found by applying the tax rate to the reported GAAP income before taxes. We discuss this and other issues related to accounting for income taxes in Chapter 16. At this point, consider income tax expense to be simply a percentage of income before taxes.

While the actual measurement of income tax expense can be complex, at this point we can consider income tax expense to be a simple percentage of income before taxes.

Operating versus Nonoperating Income

A distinction often is made between operating and nonoperating income.

Many corporate income statements distinguish between operating income and nonoperating income. Operating income includes revenues and expenses directly related to the primary revenue-generating activities of the company. For example, operating income for a manufacturing company includes sales revenues from selling the products it manufactures as well as all expenses related to this activity. Similarly, operating income might also include gains and losses from selling equipment and other assets used in the manufacturing process.[3]

Nonoperating income relates to peripheral or incidental activities of the company. For example, a manufacturer would include interest and dividend revenue, gains and losses from selling investments, and interest expense in nonoperating income. *Other income (expense)* often is the classification heading companies use in the income statement for nonoperating items. On the other hand, a financial institution like a bank would consider those items to be a part of operating income because they relate to the principal revenue-generating activities for that type of business.

---

[2]Partnerships are not tax-paying entities. Their taxable income or loss is included in the taxable income of the individual partners.
[3]FASB ASC 360–10–45–5: Property, plant, and equipment—Overall—Other Presentation Matters (previously "Accounting for the Impairment of Long-Lived Assets and for Long-Lived Assets to Be Disposed Of," *Statement of Financial Accounting Standards No. 144* (Norwalk, Conn.: FASB, 2001)).

Illustration 4–2 presents the 2011, 2010, and 2009 income statements for Dell Inc. Notice that Dell distinguishes between operating income and nonoperating income (labeled Interest and other, net). Nonoperating revenues, expenses, gains and losses, and income tax expense (called Income tax provision) are added to or subtracted from operating income to arrive at net income. As Dell has no separately reported items, *income from continuing operations equals net income.*[4]

Consolidated Statements of Income

(In millions, except per share amounts)

	Fiscal Year Ended		
	January 28, 2011	**January 29, 2010**	**January 30, 2009**
Net revenue:			
Products	$50,002	$43,697	$52,337
Services, including software related	11,492	9,205	8,764
Total net revenue	61,494	52,902	61,101
Cost of net revenue:			
Products	42,068	37,534	44,670
Services, including software related	8,030	6,107	5,474
Total cost of net revenue	50,098	43,641	50,144
Gross margin	11,396	9,261	10,957
Operating expenses:			
Selling, general, and administrative	7,302	6,465	7,102
Research, development, and engineering	661	624	665
Total operating expenses	7,963	7,089	7,767
Operating income	3,433	2,172	3,190
Interest and other, net	(83)	(148)	134
Income before income taxes	3,350	2,024	3,324
Income tax provision	715	591	846
Net income	$ 2,635	$ 1,433	$ 2,478
Earnings per common share:			
Basic	$ 1.36	$ .73	$ 1.25
Diluted	$ 1.35	$ .73	$ 1.25

Illustration 4–2

Income Statement—
Dell Inc.

Real World Financials

Now let's consider the formats used to report the components of net income.

Income Statement Formats

No specific standards dictate how income from continuing operations must be displayed, so companies have considerable latitude in how they present the components of income from continuing operations. This flexibility has resulted in a variety of income statement presentations. However, we can identify two general approaches, the single-step and the multiple-step formats, that might be considered the two extremes, with the income statements of most companies falling somewhere in between.

The single-step format first lists all the revenues and gains included in income from continuing operations. Then, expenses and losses are grouped, subtotaled, and subtracted—in a single step—from revenues and gains to derive income from continuing operations. In a departure from that, though, companies usually report income tax expense as a separate last item in the statement. Operating and nonoperating items are not separately classified. Illustration 4–3 shows an example of a single-step income statement for a hypothetical manufacturing company, Maxwell Gear Corporation.

A *single-step* income statement format groups all revenues and gains together and all expenses and losses together.

---
[4]In a later section we discuss items that are reported separately from continuing operations.

Illustration 4–3

Single-Step Income
Statement

MAXWELL GEAR CORPORATION		
Income Statement		
For the Year Ended December 31, 2013		
Revenues and gains:		
Sales		$573,522
Interest and dividends		26,400
Gain on sale of investments		5,500
Total revenues and gains		605,422
Expenses and losses:		
Cost of goods sold	$302,371	
Selling	47,341	
General and administrative	24,888	
Research and development	16,300	
Interest	14,522	
Total expenses and losses		405,422
Income before income taxes		200,000
Income tax expense		80,000
Net income		$120,000

A *multiple-step* income
statement format
includes a number of
intermediate subtotals
before arriving at
income from continuing
operations.

The multiple-step format reports a series of intermediate subtotals such as gross profit, operating income, and income before taxes. The overview income statements presented in Illustration 4–1 and the Dell Inc. income statements in Illustration 4–2 are variations of the multiple-step format. Illustration 4–4 presents a multiple-step income statement for the Maxwell Gear Corporation.

Illustration 4–4

Multiple-Step Income
Statement

MAXWELL GEAR CORPORATION		
Income Statement		
For the Year Ended December 31, 2013		
Sales revenue		$573,522
Cost of goods sold		302,371
Gross profit		271,151
Operating expenses:		
Selling	$47,341	
General and administrative	24,888	
Research and development	16,300	
Total operating expenses		88,529
Operating income		182,622
Other income (expense):		
Interest and dividend revenue	26,400	
Gain on sale of investments	5,500	
Interest expense	(14,522)	
Total other income, net		17,378
Income before income taxes		200,000
Income tax expense		80,000
Net income		$120,000

An advantage of the single-step format is its simplicity. Revenues and expenses are not classified or prioritized. A primary advantage of the multiple-step format is that, by separately classifying operating and nonoperating items, it provides information that might be useful in analyzing trends. Similarly, the classification of expenses by function also provides useful information. For example, reporting gross profit for merchandising companies highlights the important relationship between sales revenue and cost of goods sold. It is important to note that this issue is one of presentation. The bottom line, net income, is the same regardless of the format used. A recent survey of income statements of 500 large public companies indicates that the multiple-step format is used more than five times as often as the single-step format[5] We use the multiple-step format for illustration purposes throughout the remainder of this chapter.

International Financial Reporting Standards

● LO4–10

Income Statement Presentation. There are more similarities than differences between income statements prepared according to U.S. GAAP and those prepared applying international standards. Some of the differences are:

- International standards require certain minimum information to be reported on the face of the income statement. U.S. GAAP has no minimum requirements.
- International standards allow expenses to be classified either by function (e.g., cost of goods sold, general and administrative, etc.), or by natural description (e.g., salaries, rent, etc.). SEC regulations require that expenses be classified by function.
- In the United States, the "bottom line" of the income statement usually is called either *net income* or *net loss*. The descriptive term for the bottom line of the income statement prepared according to international standards is either *profit* or *loss*.
- As we discuss later in the chapter, we report "extraordinary items" separately in an income statement prepared according to U.S. GAAP. International standards prohibit reporting "extraordinary items."

Before we investigate separately reported items, let's take a closer look at the components of both operating and nonoperating income and their relationship to earnings quality.

Earnings Quality

● LO4–2

Financial analysts are concerned with more than just the bottom line of the income statement—net income. The presentation of the components of net income and the related supplemental disclosures provide clues to the user of the statement in an assessment of *earnings quality*. Earnings quality is used as a framework for more in-depth discussions of operating and nonoperating income.

The term **earnings quality** refers to the ability of reported earnings (income) to predict a company's future earnings. After all, an income statement simply reports on events that already have occurred. The relevance of any historical-based financial statement hinges on its predictive value. To enhance predictive value, analysts try to separate a company's *transitory earnings* effects from its *permanent earnings*. Transitory earnings effects result from transactions or events that are not likely to occur again in the foreseeable future or that are likely to have a different impact on earnings in the future. Later in the chapter we address two items that, because of their transitory nature, are required to be reported separately at the bottom of the income statement. Analysts begin their assessment of permanent earnings with income before these two items, that is, income from continuing operations.

> Earnings quality refers to the ability of reported earnings (income) to predict a company's future earnings.

It would be a mistake, though, to assume income from continuing operations reflects permanent earnings entirely. In other words, there may be transitory earnings effects included in income from continuing operations. In a sense, the phrase *continuing* may be misleading.

Manipulating Income and Income Smoothing

An often-debated contention is that, within GAAP, managers have the power, to a limited degree, to manipulate reported company income. And the manipulation is not always in the

---

[5]*Accounting Trends and Techniques—2011* (New York: AICPA, 2011), p. 305.

direction of higher income. One author states that "Most executives prefer to report earnings that follow a smooth, regular, upward path. They hate to report declines, but they also want to avoid increases that vary wildly from year to year; it's better to have two years of 15% earnings increases than a 30% gain one year and none the next. As a result, some companies 'bank' earnings by understating them in particularly good years and use the banked profits to polish results in bad years."[6]

Many believe that corporate earnings management practices reduce the quality of reported earnings.

Arthur Levitt, Jr.
While the problem of earnings management is not new, it has swelled in a market that is unforgiving of companies that miss their estimates. I recently read of one major U.S. company that failed to meet its so-called numbers by one penny and lost more than six percent of its stock value in one day.[7]

Many believe that manipulating income reduces earnings quality because it can mask permanent earnings. A 1998 *BusinessWeek* issue was devoted entirely to the topic of earnings management. The issue, entitled "Corporate Earnings: Who Can You Trust," contains articles that are highly critical of corporate America's earnings manipulation practices. Arthur Levitt, Jr., former Chairman of the Securities and Exchange Commission, has been outspoken in his criticism of corporate earnings management practices and their effect on earnings quality. In an article appearing in the *CPA Journal,* he states,

Increasingly, I have become concerned that the motivation to meet Wall Street earnings expectations may be overriding commonsense business practices. Too many corporate managers, auditors, and analysts are participants in a game of nods and winks. In the zeal to satisfy consensus earnings estimates and project a smooth earnings path, wishful thinking may be winning the day over faithful representation. As a result, I fear that we are witnessing an erosion in the *quality of earnings,* and therefore, the quality of financial reporting. Managing may be giving way to manipulation; integrity may be losing out to illusion. (emphasis added)[8]

How do managers manipulate income? Two major methods are (1) income shifting and (2) income statement classification. Income shifting is achieved by accelerating or delaying the recognition of revenues or expenses. For example, a practice called "channel stuffing" accelerates revenue recognition by persuading distributors to purchase more of your product than necessary near the end of a reporting period. The most common income statement classification manipulation involves the inclusion of recurring operating expenses in "special charge" categories such as restructuring costs (discussed below). This practice sometimes is referred to as "big bath" accounting, a reference to cleaning up company balance sheets. Asset reductions, or the incurrence of liabilities, for these restructuring costs result in large reductions in income that might otherwise appear as normal operating expenses either in the current or future years.

Mr. Levitt called for changes by standard setters to improve the transparency of financial statements. He did not want to eliminate necessary flexibility in financial reporting, but wanted to make it easier for financial statement users to "see through the numbers" to the future. A key to a meaningful assessment of a company's future profitability is to understand the events reported in the income statement and their relationship with future earnings. Let's now revisit the components of operating income.

Operating Income and Earnings Quality

● LO4–3   Should all items of revenue and expense included in operating income be considered indicative of a company's permanent earnings? No, not necessarily. Sometimes, for example, operating expenses include some unusual items that may or may not continue in the future. Look closely at the 2010 and 2009 partial income statements of JDS Uniphase Corporation, a leading provider of optical products for telecommunications service providers, presented in Illustration 4–5. What items appear unusual? Certainly "Impairment of goodwill," "Impairment of long-lived assets" and "Restructuring costs" require further investigation. We discuss restructuring costs first.

---

[6]Ford S. Worthy, "Manipulating Profits: How It's Done," *Fortune,* June 25, 1984, p. 50.
[7]Arthur Levitt, Jr., "The Numbers Game," *The CPA Journal,* December 1998, p. 16.
[8]Ibid., p. 14.

Income Statements (in part)

($ in millions)	Years Ended	
	July 3, 2010	June 27, 2009
Net revenue	$1,363.9	$1,283.3
Cost of sales	816.8	796.7
Gross profit	547.1	486.6
Operating expenses:		
Research and development	174.9	167.1
Selling, general and administrative	380.9	399.0
Amortization of intangibles	27.8	27.0
Impairment of goodwill	—	741.7
Impairment of long-lived assets	—	13.2
Restructuring costs	17.7	38.5
Total operating expenses	601.3	1,386.5
Operating loss	(54.2)	(899.9)

Illustration 4–5

Partial Income Statement— JDS Uniphase Corporation

Real World Financials

RESTRUCTURING COSTS.   It's not unusual for a company to reorganize its operations to attain greater efficiency. When this happens, the company often incurs significant associated restructuring costs. Facility closings and related employee layoffs translate into costs incurred for severance pay and relocation costs. Restructuring costs are incurred in connection with:

FINANCIAL Reporting Case

Q1, p. 171

Restructuring costs include costs associated with shutdown or relocation of facilities or downsizing of operations.

A program that is planned and controlled by management, and materially changes either the scope of a business undertaken by an entity, or the manner in which that business is conducted.[9]

Restructuring costs appear frequently in corporate income statements. In fact, a recent survey reports that in 2010, of the 500 companies surveyed, 41% included restructuring costs in their income statements.[10] For instance, consider again our JDS Uniphase Corporation example. A disclosure note accompanying the company's financial statements indicates workforce reductions as well as manufacturing transfer costs resulting from plant closures and consolidation of operations. Illustration 4–6 reports a portion of the disclosure note related to the restructuring costs.

Restructuring Costs (in part)
During fiscal 2010, the Company reported $17.7 million in restructuring related charges. The charges were primarily a result of (i) $7.1 million for severance and benefits primarily in the Communications Test and measurement segment . . .; (ii) $8.5 million for manufacturing transfer costs primarily in the Communications and Commercial Optical Products segments, which were the result of a production site closure in California, the consolidation of Lasers manufacturing operations at a contract manufacturer in Asia, the transfer of certain production processes into existing sites in California, and the reduction in force of the Company's manufacturing support organization across all sites.

Illustration 4–6

Disclosure of Restructuring Costs— JDS Uniphase Corporation

Real World Financials

Restructuring costs are recognized in the period the exit or disposal cost obligation actually is incurred. As an example, suppose terminated employees are to receive termination benefits, but only after they remain with the employer beyond a minimum retention

GAAP requires that restructuring costs be recognized only in the period incurred.

[9]FASB ASC 420–10–20: Exit or Disposal Cost Obligations—Overall—Glossary (previously "Accounting for Costs Associated with Exit or Disposal Activities," *Statement of Financial Accounting Standards No. 146* (Norwalk, Conn.: FASB, 2002)).
[10]*Accounting Trends and Techniques—2011* (New York: AICPA, 2011), p. 326.

period. In that case, a liability for termination benefits, and corresponding expense, should be accrued in the period(s) the employees render their service. On the other hand, if future service beyond a minimum retention period is not required, the liability and corresponding expense for benefits are recognized at the time the company communicates the arrangement to employees. In both cases, the liability and expense are recorded at the point they are deemed incurred. Similarly, costs associated with closing facilities and relocating employees are recognized when goods or services associated with those activities are received.

Fair value is the objective for the initial measurement of a liability associated with restructuring costs.

GAAP also establishes that fair value is the objective for initial measurement of the liability, and that a liability's fair value often will be measured by determining the present value of future estimated cash outflows. We discuss such present value calculations at length in later chapters, particularly in Chapters 6 and 14. Because some restructuring costs require estimation, actual costs could differ. Also, the costs might not occur until a subsequent reporting period. As we discuss later in this chapter and throughout the text, when an estimate is changed, the company should record the effect of the change in the period the estimate is changed rather than by restating prior years' financial statements to correct the estimate. On occasion, this process has resulted in a negative expense amount for restructuring costs due to the overestimation of costs in a prior reporting period.

Should restructuring costs be considered part of a company's permanent earnings stream?

Now that we understand the nature of restructuring costs, we can address the important question: Should investors attempting to forecast future earnings consider these costs to be part of a company's permanent earnings stream, or are they transitory in nature? There is no easy answer. For example, JDS Uniphase incurred restructuring costs in both 2010 and 2009. Will the company incur these costs again in the near future? Consider the following facts. During the 10-year period from 2001 through 2010, the Dow Jones Industrial 30 companies reported 114 restructuring charges in their collective income statements. That's an average of 3.8 per company. But the average is deceiving. Five of the 30 companies reported no restructuring charges during that period, while three of the 30 companies reported restructuring charges in each of the 10 years. The inference: an analyst must interpret restructuring charges in light of a company's past history. In general, the more frequently these sorts of unusual charges occur, the more appropriate it is that analysts include them in the company's permanent earnings stream. Information in disclosure notes describing the restructuring and management plans related to the business involved also can be helpful.

Arthur Levitt, Jr.
When a company decides to restructure, management and employees, investors and creditors, customers and suppliers all want to understand the expected effects. We need, of course, to ensure that financial reporting provides this information. But this should not lead to flushing all the associated costs—and maybe a little extra—through the financial statements.[11]

Two other expenses in JDS Uniphase's income statements that warrant additional scrutiny are *impairment of goodwill* and *impairment of long-lived assets*. These expenses involve what is referred to as asset impairment losses or charges. Any long-lived asset, whether tangible or intangible, should have its balance reduced if there has been a significant impairment of value. We explore property, plant, and equipment and intangible assets in Chapters 10 and 11. After discussing this topic in more depth in those chapters, we revisit the concept of earnings quality as it relates to asset impairment.

Is it possible that financial analysts might look favorably at a company in the year it incurs a substantial restructuring charge or other unusual expense such as an asset impairment loss? Perhaps so, if they view management as creating higher profits in future years through operating efficiencies. Would analysts then reward that company again in future years when those operating efficiencies materialize? Certainly this double halo effect might provide an attractive temptation to the management of some companies.

Unusual or infrequent items included in operating income require investigation to determine their permanent or transitory nature.

These aren't the only components of operating expenses that call into question this issue of earnings quality. For example, in Chapter 9 we discuss the write-down of inventory to comply with the lower-of-cost-or-market rule. Earnings quality also is influenced by the way a company records income from investments (Chapter 12) and accounts for its pension plans (Chapter 17).

---

[11]Arthur Levitt, Jr. "The Numbers Game," *The CPA Journal,* December 1998, p. 16.

Earnings quality is affected by revenue issues as well. As an example, suppose that toward the end of its fiscal year, a company loses a major customer that can't be replaced. That would mean the current year's revenue numbers include a transitory component equal to the revenue generated from sales to the lost customer. Of course, in addition to its effect on revenues, losing the customer would have implications for the transitory/permanent nature of expenses and net income.

Another revenue issue affecting earnings quality is the timing of revenue recognition. Companies face continual pressure to meet their earnings expectations. That pressure often has led to premature revenue recognition, reducing the quality of reported earnings.

Accelerating revenue recognition has caused problems for many companies. For example, in 2008, International Rectifier Corporation, a manufacturer of power management products, was named defendant in a federal class action suit related to numerous irregularities including premature revenue recognition. The company admitted shipping products and recording sales with no obligation by customers to receive and pay for the products.

Real World Financials

We explore these issues in Chapter 5, when we discuss revenue recognition in considerable depth, and in Chapter 13, when we discuss liabilities that companies must record when they receive payment prior to having actually earned the related revenue. Now, though, let's discuss earnings quality issues related to *nonoperating* items.

Nonoperating Income and Earnings Quality

Most of the components of earnings in an income statement relate directly to the ordinary, continuing operations of the company. Some, though, such as interest and gains or losses are only tangentially related to normal operations. These we refer to as nonoperating items. Some nonoperating items have generated considerable discussion with respect to earnings quality, notably gains and losses generated from the sale of investments. For example, as the stock market boom reached its height late in the year 2000, many companies recorded large gains from sale of investments that had appreciated significantly in value. How should those gains be interpreted in terms of their relationship to future earnings? Are they transitory or permanent? Let's consider an example.

Gains and losses from the sale of investments often can significantly inflate or deflate current earnings.

Intel Corporation is the world's largest manufacturer of semiconductors. Illustration 4–7 shows the nonoperating section of Intel's income statements for the 2000 and 1999 fiscal years. In 2000, income before taxes increased by approximately 35% from the prior year. But notice that the *gains on investments, net* (net means net of losses) increased from $883 million to over $3.7 billion, accounting for a large portion of the increase in income. Some analysts questioned the quality of Intel's 2000 earnings because of these large gains.

Illustration 4–7

Income Statements (in part)—Intel Corporation

Real World Financials

Income Statements (in part)
(in millions)

	Years Ended December 30	
	2000	**1999**
Operating income	10,395	9,767
Gains on investments, net	3,759	883
Interest and other, net	987	578
Income before taxes	15,141	11,228

Consider Hecla Mining, a precious metals company. In one fiscal year, the company reported income before income taxes of $61.8 million. Included in this amount was a $36.4 million gain on the sale of investments, representing 59% of total before-tax income. Can Hecla sustain these gains? Should they be considered part of permanent earnings or are they transitory? There are no easy answers to these questions. It's interesting to note that in the prior two years Hecla reported no investment gains.

Many companies voluntarily provide *pro forma earnings*— management's assessment of permanent earnings.

Companies often voluntarily provide a pro forma earnings number when they announce annual or quarterly earnings. Supposedly, these pro forma earnings numbers are management's view of "permanent earnings," in the sense of being a better long-run performance measure. For example, in January 2011, Google Inc. announced that its income for the fourth quarter of 2010 was $2.54 billion or $7.95 per share. At the same time, the company announced that its *pro forma net income* (for which Google excluded stock-based compensation expense) for the quarter was $2.85 billion or $8.75 per share. These pro forma earnings numbers are controversial because determining which items to exclude is at the discretion of management. Therefore, management could mislead investors. Nevertheless, these disclosures do represent management's perception of what its permanent earnings are and provides additional information to the financial community.

The Sarbanes-Oxley Act addressed pro forma earnings in its Section 401. One of the act's important provisions requires that if pro forma earnings are included in any periodic or other report filed with the SEC or in any public disclosure or press release, the company also must provide a reconciliation with earnings determined according to generally accepted accounting principles.[12]

We now turn our attention to two income statement items—discontinued operations and extraordinary items—that, because of their nature, are more obviously not part of a company's permanent earnings and, appropriately, are excluded from continuing operations.

> **Real World Financials**

> **The Sarbanes-Oxley Act requires reconciliation between pro forma earnings and earnings determined according to GAAP.**

Separately Reported Items

The information in the income statement is useful if it can help users predict the future. Toward this end, users should be made aware of events reported in the income statement that are not likely to occur again in the foreseeable future.

There are two types of events that, if they have a material effect[13] on the income statement, require separate reporting below income from continuing operations as well as separate disclosure: (1) discontinued operations, and (2) extraordinary items.[14] Although a company has considerable flexibility in reporting income from *continuing operations,* the presentation order of these items is mandated as follows:[15]

> **GAAP requires that certain transactions be reported separately in the income statement, below income from continuing operations.**

Income from continuing operations before income taxes and extraordinary items	$xxx
Income tax expense	xx
Income from continuing operations before extraordinary items	xxx
Discontinued operations, net of $xx in tax	xx
Extraordinary items, net of $xx in tax[16]	xx
Net income	**$xxx**

The objective is to separately report all of the income effects of these items. That's why we include the income tax effect of each item in this separate presentation rather than report them as part of income tax expense. The process of associating income tax effects with the income statement components that create them is referred to as *intraperiod tax allocation.* We address this process in the next section.

Intraperiod Income Tax Allocation

Intraperiod tax allocation associates (allocates) income tax expense (or income tax benefit if there is a loss) with each major component of income that causes it.[17] More specifically,

---

[12]The Congress of the United States of America, *The Sarbanes-Oxley Act of 2002,* Section 401 (b) (2), Washington, D.C., 2004.

[13]We discussed the concept of materiality in Chapter 1. If the effect on the income statement is not material, these items are included in income from continuing operations.

[14]FASB ASC 225–20–45: Income Statement—Extraordinary Items—Other Presentation Matters, and FASB ASC 205–20–45: Presentation of Financial Statement—Discontinued Operations—Other Presentation Matters (previously "Reporting Results of Operations," *Accounting Principles Board Opinion No. 30* (New York: AICPA, 1973)).

[15]The presentation of these separately reported items is the same for single-step and multiple-step income statement formats. The single-step versus multiple-step distinction applies to items included in income from continuing operations.

[16]Companies that report discontinued operations and extraordinary items sometimes show a subtotal after discontinued operations. This is not required.

[17]*Intraperiod* tax allocation refers to the association of income tax with various components of net income within the income statement. *Interperiod* tax allocation, covered in Chapter 16, refers to allocating income taxes between two or more reporting periods by recognizing deferred tax assets and liabilities.

income tax is allocated to income from continuing operations and each of the two separately reported items. For example, assume a company experienced an extraordinary gain during the year.[18] The amount of income tax expense deducted to arrive at income from continuing operations is the amount of income tax expense that the company would have incurred *if there were no extraordinary gain.* The effect on income taxes caused by the extraordinary item is deducted directly from the extraordinary gain in the income statement. Illustration 4–8 demonstrates this concept.

> The Maxwell Gear Corporation had income from continuing operations before income tax expense of $200,000 and an extraordinary gain of $60,000 in 2013. The income tax rate is 40% on all items of income or loss. Therefore, the company's total income tax expense is $104,000 (40% × $260,000).

Illustration 4–8
Intraperiod Tax Allocation

How should the company allocate the tax expense between income from continuing operations and the extraordinary gain? A partial income statement, beginning with income from continuing operations before income tax expense, *ignoring* intraperiod tax allocation, is shown in Illustration 4–8A.

Incorrect Presentation	
Income before income taxes and extraordinary item	$200,000
Income tax expense	(104,000)
Income before extraordinary item	96,000
Extraordinary gain (gross)	60,000
Net income	$156,000

Illustration 4–8A
Income Statement
Presented *Incorrectly—*
No Intraperiod Tax
Allocation (extraordinary gain)

The deficiency of this presentation is that the apparent contribution to net income of (a) income before the extraordinary gain (that is, income from continuing operations) and (b) the extraordinary gain is misleading. If the extraordinary gain had not occurred, income tax expense would not have been $104,000 but rather $80,000 (40% × $200,000). Similarly, the net benefit of the extraordinary gain is not $60,000, but rather $36,000 ($60,000 minus 40% × $60,000). The total tax expense of $104,000 must be *allocated,* $80,000 to continuing operations and $24,000 (40% × $60,000) to the extraordinary gain. The appropriate income statement presentation appears in Illustration 4–8B.

Correct Presentation	
Income before income taxes and extraordinary item	$200,000
Income tax expense	(80,000)
Income before extraordinary item	120,000
Extraordinary gain, net of $24,000 tax expense	36,000
Net income	$156,000

Illustration 4–8B
Income Statement
Presented *Correctly—*
Intraperiod Tax Allocation
(extraordinary gain)

Net income is $156,000 either way. Intraperiod tax allocation is not an issue of measurement but an issue of presentation. The $120,000 income before extraordinary gain properly reflects income from continuing operations *including* the appropriate tax effects. Also, notice that income tax expense represents taxes that relate to the total of all of the revenue, expense, gain, and loss items included in continuing operations. Each of the items following continuing operations (discontinued operations and extraordinary items) are presented *net of their tax effect.* No individual items included in the computation of income from continuing operations are reported net of tax.

The two items reported separately below income from continuing operations are presented net of the related income tax effect.

---

[18]The criteria for classifying gains and losses as extraordinary are discussed in a later section of this chapter.

In the illustration, the extraordinary gain caused additional income tax expense to be incurred. What if the company had experienced an extraordinary loss of $60,000 instead of an extraordinary gain? In that case, rather than creating additional tax, the loss actually decreases tax due to its reducing taxable income by $60,000. The company's total income tax expense would be $56,000 [40% × ($200,000 − 60,000)].

The extraordinary loss *decreased* the amount of tax the company otherwise would have had to pay by $24,000. This is commonly referred to as a *tax benefit*. A partial income statement, beginning with income from continuing operations before income tax expense, *ignoring* intraperiod tax allocation is shown in Illustration 4–8C.

Illustration 4–8C

Income Statement Presented *Incorrectly*— No Intraperiod Tax Allocation (extraordinary loss)

Incorrect Presentation	
Income before income taxes and extraordinary item	$200,000
Income tax expense	(56,000)
Income before extraordinary item	144,000
Extraordinary loss (gross)	(60,000)
Net income	$ 84,000

Once again, income before the extraordinary loss (that is, income from continuing operations) is misleading. If the extraordinary loss had not occurred, income tax expense would not have been $56,000 but rather $80,000 (40% × $200,000). The total tax expense of $56,000 must be *allocated,* $80,000 tax expense to continuing operations and $24,000 tax benefit to the extraordinary loss. The appropriate income statement presentation appears in Illustration 4–8D.

Illustration 4–8D

Income Statement Presented *Correctly*— Intraperiod Tax Allocation (extraordinary loss)

Correct Presentation	
Income before income taxes and extraordinary item	$200,000
Income tax expense	(80,000)
Income before extraordinary item	120,000
Extraordinary loss, net of $24,000 tax benefit	(36,000)
Net income	$ 84,000

Now that we have seen how to report items net of their related tax effects, let's look closer at the two items reported net of tax below income from continuing operations: discontinued operations and extraordinary items.

Discontinued Operations

● LO4–4

FINANCIAL Reporting Case

Q2, p. 171

Time Warner, Inc., is a leading media and entertainment company. Prior to 2009, the company operated the following business segments: AOL, cable, filmed entertainment, networks, and publishing. In 2009, the company sold its cable business. The Procter & Gamble Company is perhaps best known for providing a wide variety of consumer packaged goods to consumers. Prior to 2010, the company also operated a global pharmaceuticals business. But the company sold the pharmaceuticals business during its 2010 fiscal year. Time Warner's sale of its cable business and Proctor & Gamble's sale of its pharmaceutical business are examples of discontinued operations.

WHAT CONSTITUTES AN OPERATION?   For purposes of reporting discontinued operations, in 2001 the FASB issued a standard that defined an operation as a *component of an entity* whose operations and cash flows can be clearly distinguished, operationally and for financial reporting purposes, from the rest of the entity. International standards also defined a discontinued operation as a discontinued component of an entity. However, what constitutes a "component" of an entity differed significantly between U.S. GAAP and *IFRS No. 5*.[19]

As part of the continuing process to converge U.S. GAAP and international standards, the FASB and IASB have been working together to develop a common definition and a common set of disclosures for discontinued operations. At the time this text was published, a final Accounting Standards Update had not been issued, but the two Boards had expressed a new direction in an Exposure Draft of a new ASU.

The proposed ASU defines a discontinued operation as a "component" that either (a) has been disposed of or (b) is classified as held for sale, and represents one of the following:

1. a separate major line of business or major geographical area of operations,
2. part of a single coordinated plan to dispose of a separate major line of business or geographical area of operations, or
3. a business that meets the criteria to be classified as held for sale on acquisition.[20]

Many were critical of prior guidance, feeling its definition of a component of the entity was too broad. In addition to achieving convergence with international standards, the new guidance is expected to reduce the number of business segments that require separate income statement presentation as a discontinued operation.

REPORTING DISCONTINUED OPERATIONS.   By definition, the income or loss stream from a discontinued operation no longer will continue. An analyst concerned with Time Warner's and Procter & Gamble's future profitability is more interested in the results of their operations that will continue. It is informative, then, for companies to separate the effects of the discontinued operations from the results of operations that will continue. This information might have a significant impact on the analyst's assessment of future profitability.

For this reason, the revenues, expenses, gains, losses, and income tax related to a *discontinued* operation must be removed from *continuing* operations and reported separately for all years presented.[21] A key for assessing profitability is comparing the company's performance from *continuing* operations from year to year and from company to company.

Sometimes a discontinued component actually has been sold by the end of a reporting period. Often, though, the component is being held for sale, but the disposal transaction has not yet been completed as of the end of the reporting period. We consider these two possibilities next.

> The net-of-tax income effects of a discontinued operation are reported separately in the income statement, below income from continuing operations.

When the component has been sold.   When the discontinued component is sold before the end of the reporting period, the reported income effects of a discontinued operation will include two elements:

1. Income or loss from operations (revenues, expenses, gains, and losses) of the component from the beginning of the reporting period to the disposal date.
2. Gain or loss on disposal of the component's assets.

These two elements can be combined or reported separately, net of their tax effects. If combined, the gain or loss component must be indicated. In our illustrations to follow, we combine the income effects. Illustration 4–9 describes a situation in which the discontinued component is sold before the end of the reporting period.

Notice that a tax *benefit* occurs because a *loss* reduces taxable income, saving the company $880,000. On the other hand, had there been *income* from operations of $2,200,000, the $880,000 income tax effect would have represented additional income tax expense.

For comparison purposes, the net of tax income or loss from operations of the discontinued component for any prior years included in the comparative income statements also are separately reported as discontinued operations.

---

[19]"Non-current Assets Held for Sale and Discontinued Operations," *International Financial Reporting Standard No. 5* (IASCF), as amended effective January 1, 2011.

[20]"FAS 144—Reporting Discontinued Operations—Joint Project of the IASB and FASB," *Project Update* (Norwalk, Conn.: FASB, July 29, 2010).

[21]For example, even though Time Warner did not sell its cable business until 2009, it's important for comparative purposes to separate the effects for any prior years presented. This allows an apples-to-apples comparison of income from *continuing* operations. So, in its 2009 three-year comparative income statements, the 2008 and 2007 income statements were reclassified and the income from discontinued operations presented as a separately reported item. In addition, there was a disclosure note to inform readers that prior years were reclassified.

Illustration 4–9
Discontinued
Operations—
Gain on Disposal

The Duluth Holding Company has several operating divisions. In October 2013, management decided to sell one of its divisions that qualifies as a separate component according to generally accepted accounting principles. The division was sold on December 18, 2013, for a net selling price of $14,000,000. On that date, the assets of the division had a book value of $12,000,000. For the period January 1 through disposal, the division reported a pretax loss from operations of $4,200,000. The company's income tax rate is 40% on all items of income or loss. Duluth generated after-tax profits of $22,350,000 from its continuing operations.

Duluth's income statement for the year 2013, beginning with income from continuing operations, would be reported as follows:

Income from continuing operations		$22,350,000
Discontinued operations:		
Loss from operations of discontinued component (including gain on disposal of $2,000,000*)	$(2,200,000)[†]	
Income tax benefit	880,000[‡]	
Loss on discontinued operations		(1,320,000)
Net income		$21,030,000

* Net selling price of $14 million less book value of $12 million
[†] Loss from operations of $4.2 million less gain on disposal of $2 million
[‡] $2,200,000 × 40%

If a component to be discontinued has not yet been sold, its income effects, including any impairment loss, usually still are reported separately as discontinued operations.

When the component is considered held for sale.   What if a company has decided to discontinue a component but, when the reporting period ends, the component has not yet been sold? If the situation indicates that the component is likely to be sold within a year, the component is considered "held for sale."[22] In that case, the income effects of the discontinued operation still are reported, but the two components of the reported amount are modified as follows:

1. Income or loss from operations (revenues, expenses, gains and losses) of the component from the beginning of the reporting period *to the end of the reporting period.*
2. An "impairment loss" if the carrying value (book value) of the assets of the component is more than fair value minus cost to sell.

The two income elements can be combined or reported separately, net of their tax effects. In addition, if the amounts are combined and there is an impairment loss, the loss must be disclosed, either parenthetically on the face of the statement or in a disclosure note. Consider the example in Illustration 4–10.

A disclosure note would provide additional details about the discontinued component, including the identity of the component, the major classes of assets and liabilities of the component, the reason for the discontinuance, and the expected manner of disposition. Also, the net-of-tax income or loss from operations of the component being discontinued is also reported separate from continuing operations for any prior year that is presented for comparison purposes along with the 2013 income statement.

In Illustration 4–10, if the fair value of the division's assets minus cost to sell exceeded the book value of $12,000,000, there is no impairment loss and the income effects of the discontinued operation would include only the loss from operations of $4,200,000, less the income tax benefit.[23]

The balance sheet is affected, too. The assets and liabilities of the component considered held for sale are reported at the lower of their carrying amount (book value) or fair value minus cost to sell. And, because it's not in use, an asset classified as held for sale is no longer reported as part of property, plant, and equipment or intangible assets and is not depreciated or amortized.

---

[22]Six criteria are used to determine whether the component is likely to be sold and therefore considered "held for sale." You can find these criteria in FASB ASC 360–10–45–9: Property, Plant, and Equipment—Overall—Other Presentation Matters—Long-Lived Assets Classified as Held for Sale (previously "Accounting for the Impairment or Disposal of Long-Lived Assets," *Statement of Financial Accounting Standards No. 144* (Norwalk, Conn.: FASB, 2001), par. 30).

[23]In the following year when the component is sold, the income effects also must be reported as a discontinued operation.

The Duluth Holding Company has several operating divisions. In October 2013, management decided to sell one of its divisions that qualifies as a separate component according to generally accepted accounting principles. On December 31, 2013, the end of the company's fiscal year, the division had not yet been sold. On that date, the assets of the division had a book value of $12,000,000 and a fair value, minus anticipated cost to sell, of $9,000,000. For the year, the division reported a pre-tax loss from operations of $4,200,000. The company's income tax rate is 40% on all items of income or loss. Duluth generated after-tax profits of $22,350,000 from its continuing operations.

Duluth's income statement for 2013, beginning with income from continuing operations, would be reported as follows:

Income from continuing operations		$22,350,000
Discontinued operations:		
Loss from operations of discontinued component (including impairment loss of $3,000,000*)	$(7,200,000)†	
Income tax benefit	2,880,000‡	
Loss on discontinued operations		(4,320,000)
Net income		$18,030,000

*Book value of $12 million less fair value net of cost to sell of $9 million
†Loss from operations of $4.2 million plus impairment loss of $3 million
‡$7,200,000 × 40%

Illustration 4–10

Discontinued Operations— Impairment Loss

As an example, Phoenix Footwear Group specializes in quality comfort women's and men's footwear. Late in its fiscal year ended January 1, 2011, the company adopted a plan to cease operating PGX Canada, its Canadian distribution company, and at year-end this business was considered held for sale. This was one of three businesses considered held for sale at year-end. The current asset and current liability sections of the year-end balance sheet reported $404 thousand in "Current assets of discontinued operations," and $412 thousand in "Current liabilities of discontinued operations," respectively. Information about these assets was included in the disclosure note shown in Illustration 4–11.

4. Discontinued Operations (in part)
Assets and liabilities of Tommy Bahama, Chambers, and PXG Canada businesses included in the Consolidated Balance Sheet are summarized as follows:

($ in thousands)	January 1, 2011
Assets:	
Accounts receivable	$ 139
Inventories, net	213
Other current assets	52
Total current assets	$ 404
Liabilities:	
Accounts payable	$ 179
Accrued liabilities	233
Total current liabilities	$ 412

Illustration 4–11

Discontinued Operations Disclosure—Phoenix Footwear Group

Real World Financials

Notice that the assets and liabilities held for sale are classified as *current* because the company expects to sell or liquidate the businesses within one year.

Interim reporting. Remember that companies whose ownership shares are publicly traded in the United States must file quarterly reports with the Securities and Exchange Commission. If a component of an entity is considered held for sale at the end of a quarter, the income effects of the discontinued component must be separately reported in the quarterly income statement. These effects would include the income or loss from operations for the quarter as well as an impairment loss if the component's assets have a book value more than fair value minus cost to sell. If the assets are impaired and written down, any gain or loss on disposal in a subsequent quarter is determined relative to the new, written-down book value.

Let's now turn our attention to the second separately reported item, extraordinary gains and losses.

Extraordinary Items

● LO4–5

FINANCIAL Reporting Case

Q3, p. 172

Extraordinary items are material gains and losses that are both *unusual in nature* and *infrequent in occurrence.*

Occasionally, an unusual event may occur that materially affects the current year's income but is highly unlikely to occur again in the foreseeable future. If such an item is allowed to simply alter net income without pointing out its extraordinary nature, earnings quality is seriously compromised and investors and creditors may be misled into basing predictions of future income on current income that includes the nonrecurring event. For that reason, extraordinary items are "red flagged" in an income statement by being reported separately, net of tax, and appropriately labeled. Extraordinary items are material events and transactions that are both:

1. Unusual in nature
2. Infrequent in occurrence[24]

These criteria must be considered in light of the environment in which the entity operates. There obviously is a considerable degree of subjectivity involved in the determination. The concepts of unusual and infrequent require judgment. In making these judgments, an accountant should keep in mind the overall objective of the income statement. The key question is how the event relates to a firm's future profitability. If it is judged that the event, because of its unusual nature and infrequency of occurrence, *is not likely to occur again,* separate reporting is warranted.

Companies often experience *unexpected* events that are not considered extraordinary items. The loss of a major customer and the death of the company president are unexpected events that likely will affect a company's future but are both normal risks of operating a business that could recur in the future. Other gains and losses from unexpected events that are *not* considered extraordinary include the effects of a strike, including those against competitors and major suppliers, and the adjustment of accruals on long-term contracts.[25]

The determination of whether an item is unusual and infrequent should consider the environment in which the company operates.

A key point in the definition of an extraordinary item is that determining whether an event satisfies *both* criteria depends on the environment in which the firm operates. The environment includes factors such as the type of products or services sold and the geographical location of the firm's operations. What is extraordinary for one firm may not be extraordinary for another firm. For example, a loss caused by a tornado in Missouri may not be judged to be extraordinary. However, tornado damage in another state may indeed be unusual and infrequent.

Companies frequently sell subsidiary companies or their partial ownership interest in companies. Generally, the gain or loss is reported as a nonoperating item in the income statement or as a discontinued operation if the subsidiary is considered a component of the entity according to generally accepted accounting principles. In contrast, though, consider the disclosure note from a quarterly financial statement of Verizon Communications, Inc., shown in Illustration 4–12.

Why was the loss on sale of the company's 28.5% interest in a Venezuelan company considered an extraordinary item? The unusual nature of the forced sale, the nationalization (expropriation) of CANTV by a foreign government, resulted in the conclusion by Verizon that such a loss was unlikely to occur again in the foreseeable future.

Logic and reasoning must be applied to the determination of whether or not an event is extraordinary. Keep in mind that the income statement should be a guide to predicting the

---

[24]FASB ASC 225–20–45–2: Income Statement—Extraordinary and Unusual Items—Other Presentation Matters (previously "Reporting Results of Operations," *Accounting Principles Board Opinion No. 30* (New York: AICPA, 1973), par. 20).

[25]FASB ASC 225–20–45–4: Income Statement—Extraordinary and Unusual Items—Other Presentation Matters (previously "Reporting Results of Operations," *Accounting Principles Board Opinion No. 30* (New York: AICPA, 1973), par. 23).

Extraordinary Item (in part)
In January of the current year, the Bolivarian Republic of Venezuela declared its intent to nationalize certain companies, including CANTV. In February, we entered into a Memorandum of Understanding (MOU) with the Republic. The MOU provides that the Republic will offer to purchase all of the equity securities of CANTV, including our 28.5% interest . . . at a price equivalent to $17.85 . . . Based upon the terms of the MOU and our current investment balance in CANTV, we recorded an extraordinary loss on our investment of $131 million, net of tax, or $.05 per diluted shares, in the first quarter.

Illustration 4–12
Extraordinary Loss Disclosure—Verizon Communications, Inc.

Real World Financials

future. If it is extremely unlikely that a material gain or loss will occur again in the future, the quality of earnings is improved and the usefulness of the income statement in predicting the future is enhanced if the income effects of that gain or loss are reported separately.

As shown previously on page 182, the net-of-tax effects of extraordinary gains and losses are presented in the income statement below discontinued operations. In addition, a disclosure note is necessary to describe the nature of the event and the tax effects, if they are not indicated on the face of the income statement.

Extraordinary gains and losses are presented, net of tax, in the income statement below discontinued operations.

International Financial Reporting Standards

Extraordinary Items. U.S. GAAP provides for the separate reporting, as an extraordinary item, of a material gain or loss that is unusual in nature and infrequent in occurrence. In 2003, the IASB revised *IAS No. 1.*[26] The revision states that neither the income statement nor any notes may contain any items called "extraordinary."

● LO4–10

A recent survey of 500 large public companies reported that only 24 of the companies disclosed an extraordinary gain or loss in their 2010 income statements.[27] Losses from two 21st century "extraordinary" events, the September 11, 2001, terrorist attacks and Hurricane Katrina in 2005, were not reported as extraordinary items. The treatment of these two events, the scarcity of extraordinary gains and losses reported in corporate income statements, and the desire to converge U.S. and international accounting standards could guide the FASB to the elimination of the extraordinary item classification.[28]

Very few extraordinary gains and losses are reported in corporate income statements.

The extraordinary item classification could soon be eliminated.

Unusual or Infrequent Items

If the income effect of an event is material and the event is either unusual or infrequent— but not both—the item should be *included in continuing operations* but reported as a separate income statement component. Recall the JDS Uniphase Corporation example in Illustration 4–5 on page 179. Restructuring costs and the impairment of goodwill and long-lived assets included in that company's continuing operations are examples of this type of event. The events may be unusual or infrequent, but, by their nature, they could occur again in the foreseeable future. However, rather than include these items with other gains and losses or with other expenses, they are reported as a separate line item in the income statement.[29] This method of reporting, including note disclosure, enhances earnings quality by providing information to the statement user to help assess the events' relationship with future profitability.

In the next section, we briefly discuss the way various types of accounting changes are reported.

The income effect of an event that is either unusual or infrequent should be reported as a separate component of continuing operations.

---

[26]"Financial Statement Presentation," *International Accounting Standard No. 1* (IASCF), as amended effective January 1, 2011.
[27]*Accounting Trends and Techniques—2011* (New York: AICPA, 2011), p. 418.
[28]For a thorough discussion of this topic, see Massoud, Raiborn and Humphrey, "Extraordinary Items: Time to Eliminate the Classification," *The CPA Journal* (February 2007).
[29]These items are *not* reported net of tax. Only the two separately reported items—discontinued operations and extraordinary items—are reported net of tax.

Accounting Changes

Accounting changes fall into one of three categories: (1) a change in an accounting principle, (2) a change in estimate, or (3) a change in reporting entity. The correction of an error is another adjustment that is accounted for in the same way as certain accounting changes. A brief overview of a change in accounting principle, a change in estimate, and correction of errors is provided here. We cover accounting changes in detail, including changes in reporting entities, in subsequent chapters, principally in Chapter 20.

Change in Accounting Principle

A change in accounting principle refers to a change from one acceptable accounting method to another. There are many situations that allow alternative treatments for similar transactions. Common examples of these situations include the choice among FIFO, LIFO, and average cost for the measurement of inventory and among alternative revenue recognition methods. New accounting standard updates issued by the FASB also may require companies to change their accounting methods.

VOLUNTARY CHANGES IN ACCOUNTING PRINCIPLES.   Occasionally, a company will change from one generally accepted treatment to another. When these changes in accounting principles occur, information lacks consistency, hampering the ability of external users to compare financial information among reporting periods. If, for example, inventory and cost of goods sold are measured in one reporting period using the LIFO method, but are measured using the FIFO method in a subsequent period, inventory, cost of goods sold, and hence net income for the two periods are not comparable. Difficulties created by inconsistency and lack of comparability are alleviated by the way we report voluntary accounting changes.

GAAP requires that voluntary accounting changes be accounted for retrospectively.[30] That is, we recast prior years' financial statements when we report those statements again (in comparative statements, for example) to appear as if the new accounting method had been used in those periods. For each year in the comparative statements reported, we revise the balance of each account affected to make those statements appear as if the newly adopted accounting method had been applied all along. Then, a journal entry is created to adjust all account balances affected to what those amounts would have been. An adjustment is made to the beginning balance of retained earnings for the earliest period reported in the comparative statements of shareholders' equity to account for the cumulative income effect of changing to the new principle in periods prior to those reported.[31]

We will see these aspects of accounting for the change in accounting principle demonstrated in Chapter 9 in the context of our discussion of inventory methods. We'll also discuss changes in accounting principles in depth in Chapter 20.

> Voluntary changes in accounting principles are accounted for retrospectively by revising prior years' financial statements.

MANDATED CHANGES IN ACCOUNTING PRINCIPLES.   When a new FASB accounting standard update mandates a change in accounting principle, the board often allows companies to choose among multiple ways of accounting for the changes. One approach generally allowed is to account for the change retrospectively, exactly as we account for voluntary changes in principles. The FASB may also allow companies to report the cumulative effect on the income of previous years from having used the old method rather than the new method in the income statement of the year of change as a separately reported item below extraordinary items. Other approaches might also be allowed. Therefore, when a mandated change in accounting principle occurs, it is important to check the accounting standards update to determine how companies might account for the change.

---

[30]FASB ASC 250–10–45–5: Accounting Changes and Error Corrections—Overall—Other Presentation Matters (previously "Accounting Changes and Error Corrections—a replacement of APB Opinion No. 20 and FASB Statement No. 3," *Statement of Financial Accounting Standard No. 154* (Norwalk, Conn.: FASB, 2005)).

[31]Sometimes a lack of information makes it impracticable to report a change retrospectively so the new method is simply applied prospectively, that is, we simply use the new method from now on. Also, if a new standard specifically requires prospective accounting, that requirement is followed.

Change in Depreciation, Amortization, or Depletion Method

A change in depreciation, amortization, or depletion method is considered to be a change in accounting estimate that is achieved by a change in accounting principle. We account for this change prospectively, almost exactly as we would any other change in estimate. One difference is that most changes in estimate don't require a company to justify the change. However, this change in estimate is a result of changing an accounting principle and therefore requires a clear justification as to why the new method is preferable. Chapter 11 provides an illustration of a change in depreciation method.

> Changes in depreciation, amortization, or depletion methods are accounted for the same way as a change in an accounting estimate.

Change in Accounting Estimate

Estimates are a necessary aspect of accounting. A few of the more common accounting estimates are the amount of future bad debts on existing accounts receivable, the useful life and residual value of a depreciable asset, and future warranty expenses.

> A *change in accounting estimate* is reflected in the financial statements of the current period and future periods.

Because estimates require the prediction of future events, it's not unusual for them to turn out to be wrong. When an estimate is modified as new information comes to light, accounting for the change in estimate is quite straightforward. We do not revise prior years' financial statements to reflect the new estimate. Instead, we merely incorporate the new estimate in any related accounting determinations from that point on, that is, we account for a change in accounting estimate prospectively.[32] If the effect of the change is material, a disclosure note is needed to describe the change and its effect on both net income and earnings per share. Chapters 11 and 20 provide illustrations of changes in accounting estimates.

Correction of Accounting Errors

Errors occur when transactions are either recorded incorrectly or not recorded at all. We briefly discuss the correction of errors here as an overview and in later chapters in the context of the effect of errors on specific chapter topics. In addition, Chapter 20 provides comprehensive coverage of the correction of errors.

Accountants employ various control mechanisms to ensure that transactions are accounted for correctly. In spite of this, errors occur. When errors do occur, they can affect any one or several of the financial statement elements on any of the financial statements a company prepares. In fact, many kinds of errors simultaneously affect more than one financial statement. When errors are discovered, they should be corrected.

Most errors are discovered in the same year that they are made. These errors are simple to correct. The original erroneous journal entry is reversed and the appropriate entry is recorded. If an error is discovered in a year subsequent to the year the error is made, the accounting treatment depends on whether or not the error is material with respect to its effect on the financial statements. In practice, the vast majority of errors are not material and are, therefore, simply corrected in the year discovered. However, material errors that are discovered in subsequent periods require a prior period adjustment.

Prior Period Adjustments

Assume that after its financial statements are published and distributed to shareholders, Roush Distribution Company discovers a material error in the statements. What does it do? Roush must make a prior period adjustment.[33] Roush would record a journal entry that adjusts any balance sheet accounts to their appropriate levels and would account for the income effects of the error by increasing or decreasing the beginning retained earnings balance in a statement of shareholders' equity. Remember, net income in prior periods was closed to retained earnings so, by adjusting retained earnings, the prior period adjustment accounts for the error's effect on prior periods' net income.

---

[32]If the original estimate had been based on erroneous information or calculations or had not been made in good faith, the revision of that estimate would constitute the correction of an error.

[33]FASB ASC 250–10–45–23: Accounting Changes and Error Corrections—Overall—Other Presentation Matters (previously "Prior Period Adjustments," *Statement of Financial Accounting Standards No. 16* (Norwalk, Conn.: FASB, 1977)).

Simply reporting a corrected retained earnings amount might cause misunderstanding for someone familiar with the previously reported amount. Explicitly reporting a prior period adjustment in the statement of shareholders' equity (or statement of retained earnings if that's presented instead) highlights the adjustment and avoids this confusion.

In addition to reporting the prior period adjustment to retained earnings, previous years' financial statements that are incorrect as a result of the error are retrospectively restated to reflect the correction. Also, a disclosure note communicates the impact of the error on prior periods' net income.

Earnings per Share Disclosures

● LO4-6

FINANCIAL Reporting Case

Q4, p. 172

All corporations whose common stock is publicly traded must disclose EPS.

As we discussed in Chapter 3, financial statement users often use summary indicators, called *ratios,* to more efficiently make comparisons among different companies and over time for the same company. Besides highlighting important relationships among financial statement variables, ratios also accommodate differences in company size.

One of the most widely used ratios is earnings per share (EPS), which shows the amount of income earned by a company expressed on a per share basis. Public companies report basic EPS and, if there are certain potentially dilutive securities, diluted EPS, on the face of the income statement. Basic EPS is computed by dividing income available to common shareholders (net income less any preferred stock dividends) by the weighted-average number of common shares outstanding (weighted by time outstanding) for the period. For example, suppose the Fetzer Corporation reported net income of $600,000 for its fiscal year ended December 31, 2013. Preferred stock dividends of $75,000 were declared during the year. Fetzer had one million shares of common stock outstanding at the beginning of the year and issued an additional one million shares on March 31, 2013. Basic EPS of $.30 per share for 2013 is computed as follows:

$$\frac{\$600,000 - 75,000}{\underbrace{1,000,000}_{\substack{\text{Shares} \\ \text{at Jan. 1}}} + \underbrace{1,000,000\ (^9\!/_{12})}_{\text{New shares}}} = \frac{\$525,000}{1,750,000} = \$0.30$$

DELL

Diluted EPS reflects the potential dilution that could occur for companies that have certain securities outstanding that are convertible into common shares or stock options that could create additional common shares if the options were exercised. These items could cause EPS to decrease (become diluted). Because of the complexity of the calculation and the importance of EPS to investors, we devote a substantial portion of Chapter 19 to this topic. At this point, we focus on the financial statement presentation of EPS. In Illustration 4–2 on page 175, Dell Inc. discloses both basic and diluted EPS in its income statements for all years presented.

Companies must disclose per share amounts for (1) income before any separately reported items, (2) each separately reported item, and (3) net income (loss).

When the income statement includes one or more of the separately reported items, we report per-share amounts for both income (loss) from continuing operations and net income (loss), as well as for each separately reported item. We see this demonstrated in income statements of Charming Shoppes, Inc., a specialty retailer of plus-size women's apparel that includes the Lane Bryant brand, partially reproduced in Illustration 4–13.

Comprehensive Income

● LO4-7

Accounting professionals have engaged in an ongoing debate concerning which transactions should be included as components of periodic income. For instance, some argue that certain changes in shareholders' equity besides those attributable to traditional net income should be included in the determination of income. In what might be viewed as a compromise, the FASB decided to maintain the traditional view of net income, but to require companies also to report an expanded version of income called comprehensive income to include four types of gains and losses that traditionally hadn't been included in income statements. Let's consider what that means.

CHARMING SHOPPES, INC.
Consolidated Statements of Operations (in part)

($ in thousands, except per share data)	Year Ended		
	January 30, 2010	January 31, 2009	February 2, 2008
Loss from continuing operations before extraordinary item	$(77,962)	$(180,351)	$ (4,163)
Loss from discontinued operations, net of tax		(74,922)	(85,039)
Extraordinary item, net of tax	—	—	912
Net loss	$(77,962)	$(255,273)	$(88,290)
Basic earnings (loss) per share:			
Loss from continuing operations before extraordinary item	$ (.67)	$ (1.57)	$ (.03)
Loss from discontinued operations	—	(.65)	(.70)
Extraordinary item	—	—	.01
Net loss	$ (.67)	$ (2.23)	$ (.73)
Diluted earnings (loss) per share:			
Loss from continuing operations before extraordinary item	$ (.67)	$ (1.57)	$ (.03)
Loss from discontinued operations	—	(.65)	(.70)
Extraordinary gain	—	—	.01
Net loss	$ (.67)	$ (2.22)	$ (.72)

Illustration 4–13

EPS Disclosures—
Charming Shoppes, Inc

Real World Financials

Other Comprehensive Income

The calculation of net income omits certain types of gains and losses that are included in comprehensive income. As one example, in Chapter 12 you will learn that certain investments are reported in the balance sheet at their fair values, but that the gains and losses resulting from adjusting those investments to fair value might not be included in net income. Instead, they are reported as a separate component of shareholders' equity, other comprehensive income (OCI) (loss).

Comprehensive income is the total change in equity for a reporting period other than from transactions with owners.

Companies must report both net income and comprehensive income and reconcile the difference between the two.[34] Be sure to remember that net income actually is a part of comprehensive income. The reconciliation simply extends net income to include other comprehensive income items, reported net of tax, as shown in Illustration 4–14.

The actual terminology used by companies for the four other comprehensive income items varies considerably. For instance, deferred gains (losses) from derivatives are sometimes called *derivative mark-to-market adjustments* or *changes in fair value of derivatives,* and gains (losses) from foreign currency translation are often identified as *foreign currency translation adjustments.*

Flexibility in Reporting

The information in the income statement and other comprehensive income items shown in Illustration 4–14 can be presented either (1) in a single, continuous statement of comprehensive income or (2) in two separate, but consecutive statements, an income statement and a statement of comprehensive income. Each component of other comprehensive income can be displayed net of tax, as in Illustration 4–14, or alternatively, before tax with one amount shown for the aggregate income tax expense (or benefit).[35]

Reporting comprehensive income can be accomplished with a single, continuous statement or in two separate, but consecutive statements.

---

[34]FASB ASC 220-10-45-1A and 1B: Comprehensive Income–Overall–Other Presentation Matters (previously "Reporting Comprehensive Income," *Statement of Financial Accounting Standards No. 130* (Norwalk, Conn.: FASB, 1997)).

[35]GAAP does not require the reporting of comprehensive earnings per share.

Illustration 4–14
Comprehensive Income

Comprehensive income includes net income as well as other gains and losses that change shareholders' equity but are not included in traditional net income.

	($ in millions)
Net income	$xxx
Other comprehensive income:	
Net unrealized holding gains (losses) on investments (net of tax)*	$x
Gains (losses) from and amendments to postretirement benefit plans (net of tax)†	(x)
Deferred gains (losses) from derivatives (net of tax)‡	(x)
Gains (losses) from foreign currency translation (net of tax)§	x xx
Comprehensive income	$xxx

*Changes in the market value of certain investments (described in Chapter 12).
†Gains and losses due to revising assumptions or market returns differing from expectations and prior service cost from amending the plan (described in Chapter 17).
‡When a derivative designated as a cash flow hedge is adjusted to fair value, the gain or loss is deferred as a component of comprehensive income and included in earnings later, at the same time as earnings are affected by the hedged transaction (described in the Derivatives Appendix to the text).
§Gains or losses from changes in foreign currency exchange rates. The amount could be an addition to or reduction in shareholders' equity. (This item is discussed elsewhere in your accounting curriculum.)

Companies such as McAfee, Inc., and The Standard Register Company, choose to present comprehensive income in a single statement. On the other hand, in its 2011 financial statements, Astro-Med Inc., a manufacturer of a broad range of specialty technology products, chose to use the separate statement approach, as shown in Illustration 4–15.

Illustration 4–15
Comprehensive Income Presented as a Separate Statement—Astro-Med Inc.

Real World Financials

ASTRO-MED INC.
Consolidated Statements of Comprehensive Income
For the Year Ended January 31,

($ in thousands)	2011	2010	2009
Net income	$2,062	$2,766	$2,964
Other comprehensive income (loss):			
Foreign currency translation adjustments, net of tax	(66)	328	(627)
Unrealized gain (loss) on securities, net of tax	15	(12)	(21)
Other comprehensive income (loss)	(51)	316	(648)
Comprehensive income	$2,011	$3,082	$2,316

International Financial Reporting Standards

● LO4–10

Comprehensive Income. Both U.S. GAAP and IFRS allow companies to report comprehensive income in either a single statement of comprehensive income or in two separate statements.

Other comprehensive income items are similar under the two sets of standards. However, an additional OCI item, *changes in revaluation surplus*, is possible under IFRS. In Chapter 10 you will learn that *IAS No. 16*[36] permits companies to value property, plant, and equipment at (1) cost less accumulated depreciation or (2) fair value (revaluation). *IAS No. 38*[37] provides a similar option for the valuation of intangible assets. U.S. GAAP prohibits revaluation.

If the revaluation option is chosen and fair value is higher than book value, the difference, changes in revaluation surplus, is reported as *other comprehensive income* and then accumulates in a revaluation surplus account in equity.

---

[36]"Property, Plant and Equipment," *International Accounting Standard No. 16* (IASCF), as amended effective January 1, 2011.
[37]"Intangible Assets," *International Accounting Standard No. 38* (IASCF), as amended effective January 1, 2011.

Accumulated Other Comprehensive Income

In addition to reporting OCI that occurs in the current reporting period, we must also report these amounts on a cumulative basis in the balance sheet. This is consistent with the way we report net income that occurs in the current reporting period in the income statement and also report accumulated net income (that hasn't been distributed as dividends) in the balance sheet as retained earnings. Similarly, we report OCI as it occurs in the current reporting period and also report accumulated other comprehensive income (AOCI) in the balance sheet. This is demonstrated in Illustration 4–16 for Astro-Med Inc.

> The cumulative total of OCI (or comprehensive loss) is reported as accumulated other comprehensive income (AOCI), an additional component of shareholders' equity that is displayed separately.

ASTRO-MED INC.
Consolidated Balance Sheets (in part)
Years Ended January 31

($ in thousands)	2011	2010
Shareholders' equity:		
Common stock	433	416
Additional paid-in capital	36,586	34,713
Retained earnings	26,843	26,817
Accumulated other comprehensive income	266	317
Treasury stock	(9,840)	(8,030)
Total shareholders' equity	$54,288	$54,233

Illustration 4–16
Shareholders' Equity—
Astro-Med Inc.

Real World Financials

Referring to the numbers reported in Illustration 4–15, we can reconcile the changes in both retained earnings and AOCI:

($ in thousands)	Retained Earnings	Accumulated Other Comprehensive Income
Balance, 1/31/10	$26,817	$317
Add: Net income	2,062	
Deduct: Dividends	(2,036)	
Other comprehensive loss		(51)
Balance, 1/31/11	$26,843	$266

> AOCI decreased by $51 thousand, from $317 thousand to $266 thousand.

   To further understand the relationship between net income and other comprehensive income, consider another example. Suppose Philips Corporation began 2013 with retained earnings of $600 million and accumulated other comprehensive income of $34 million. Let's also assume that net income for 2013, before considering the gain discussed below, is $100 million, of which $40 million was distributed to shareholders as dividends. Now assume that Philips purchased shares of IBM stock for $90 million during the year and sold them at year-end for $100 million. In that case, Philips would include the realized gain of $10 million in determining net income. If the income tax rate is 40%, net income includes a $6 million net-of-tax gain from the sale. This means that shareholders' equity, specifically retained earnings, also will include the $6 million.

($ in millions)	Retained Earnings	Accumulated Other Comprehensive Income
Balance, 12/31/12	$600	$34
Net income ($100 + 6)	106	
Dividends	(40)	
Other comprehensive income		–0–
Balance, 12/31/13	$666	$34

If the shares are not sold, the unrealized gain is part of other comprehensive income.

On the other hand, what if the shares are not sold before the end of the fiscal year but the year-end fair value is $100 million and Philips accounts for the shares as an other comprehensive income item? In that case, the *unrealized* gain of $10 million is not included in net income. Instead, $6 million net-of-tax gain is considered a component of *other comprehensive income (loss)* for 2013 and results in an increase in *accumulated other comprehensive income (loss),* rather than retained earnings, in the 2013 balance sheet. The total of retained earnings and accumulated other comprehensive income is $700 million either way, as demonstrated below.

($ in millions)	Retained Earnings	Accumulated Other Comprehensive Income
Balance, 12/31/12	$600	$34
Net income	100	
Dividends	(40)	
Other comprehensive income		6
Balance, 12/31/13	$660	$40

Net income and comprehensive income are identical for an enterprise that has no other comprehensive income items. When this occurs for all years presented, a statement of comprehensive income is not required. Components of other comprehensive income are described in subsequent chapters.

Concept Review Exercise

INCOME STATEMENT PRESENTATION; COMPREHENSIVE INCOME

The Barrington Construction Company builds office buildings. It also owns and operates a chain of motels throughout the Northwest. On September 30, 2013, the company decided to sell the entire motel business for $40 million. The sale was completed on December 15, 2013. Income statement information for 2013 is provided below for the two components of the company.

	($ in millions)	
	Construction Component	Motel Component
Sales revenue	$450.0	$200.0
Operating expenses	226.0	210.0
Other income (loss)*	16.0	(30.0)
Income (loss) before income taxes	$240.0	$ (40.0)
Income tax expense (benefit)†	96.0	(16.0)
Net income (loss)	$144.0	$ (24.0)

*For the motel component, the entire Other income (loss) amount represents the loss on sale of assets of the component for $40 million when their book value was $70 million.
†A 40% tax rate applies to all items of income or loss.

In addition to the revenues and expenses of the construction and motel components, Barrington experienced a before-tax loss of $20 million to its construction business from damage to buildings and equipment caused by volcanic activity at Mount St. Helens. The event was considered unusual and infrequent. Also, in 2013 the company had pretax net unrealized holding gains on investment securities of $3 million and a foreign currency translation adjustment gain of $1 million.

Required:
1. Prepare a single, continuous 2013 statement of comprehensive income for the Barrington Construction Company including EPS disclosures. There were 100 million shares of common stock outstanding throughout 2013. The company had no potential

common shares outstanding. Use the multiple-step approach for the income statement portion of the statement.

2. Prepare a separate 2013 statement of comprehensive income.

Solution:

1. Prepare a single, continuous 2013 statement of comprehensive income.

BARRINGTON CONSTRUCTION COMPANY
Statement of Comprehensive Income
For the Year Ended December 31, 2013
($ in millions, except per share amounts)

Sales revenue		$450.0
Operating expenses		226.0
Operating income		224.0
Other income		16.0
Income from continuing operations before income taxes and extraordinary item		240.0
Income tax expense		96.0
Income from continuing operations before extraordinary item		144.0
Discontinued operations:		
Loss from operations of discontinued motel component (including loss on disposal of $30)	$(40)	
Income tax benefit	16	
Loss on discontinued operations		(24.0)
Income before extraordinary item		120.0
Extraordinary loss from volcano damage, net of $8.0 tax benefit		(12.0)
Net income		$108.0
Other comprehensive income:		
Unrealized gains on investment securities, net of tax	1.8	
Foreign currency translation gain, net of tax	.6	
Total other comprehensive income		2.4
Comprehensive income		$110.4
Earnings per share:		
Income from continuing operations before extraordinary item		$ 1.44
Discontinued operations		(.24)
Extraordinary loss		(.12)
Net income		$ 1.08

2. Prepare a separate 2013 statement of comprehensive income.

BARRINGTON CONSTRUCTION COMPANY
Statement of Comprehensive Income
For the Year Ended December 31, 2013
($ in millions)

Net income		$108.0
Other comprehensive income:		
Unrealized gains on investment securities, net of tax	1.8	
Foreign currency translation gain, net of tax	.6	
Total other comprehensive income		2.4
Comprehensive income		$110.4

Now that we have discussed the presentation and content of the income statement, we turn our attention to the statement of cash flows.

<table>
<tr><td>

PART B

</td><td></td></tr>
</table>

THE STATEMENT OF CASH FLOWS

● LO4–8

> A *statement of cash flows* is presented for each period for which results of operations are provided.

In addition to the income statement and the balance sheet, a statement of cash flows (SCF) is an essential component within the set of basic financial statements.[38] Specifically, when a balance sheet and an income statement are presented, a statement of cash flows is required for each income statement period. The purpose of the SCF is to provide information about the cash receipts and cash disbursements of an enterprise that occurred during a period. Similar to the income statement, it is a *change* statement, summarizing the transactions that caused cash to change during a reporting period. The term *cash* refers to *cash plus cash equivalents*. Cash equivalents, discussed in Chapter 3, include highly liquid (easily converted to cash) investments such as Treasury bills. Chapter 21 is devoted exclusively to the SCF. A brief overview is provided here.

Usefulness of the Statement of Cash Flows

We discussed the difference between cash and accrual accounting in Chapter 1. It was pointed out and illustrated that over short periods of time, operating cash flows may not be indicative of the company's long-run cash-generating ability, and that accrual-based net income provides a more accurate prediction of future operating cash flows. Nevertheless, information about cash flows from operating activities, when combined with information about cash flows from other activities, can provide information helpful in assessing future profitability, liquidity, and long-term solvency. After all, a company must pay its debts with cash, not with income.

Of particular importance is the amount of cash generated from operating activities. In the long run, a company must be able to generate positive cash flow from activities related to selling its product or service. These activities must provide the necessary cash to pay debts, provide dividends to shareholders, and provide for future growth.

Classifying Cash Flows

● LO4–9

A list of cash flows is more meaningful to investors and creditors if they can determine the type of transaction that gave rise to each cash flow. Toward this end, the statement of cash flows classifies all transactions affecting cash into one of three categories: (1) operating activities, (2) investing activities, and (3) financing activities.

Operating Activities

> *Operating activities* are inflows and outflows of cash related to the transactions entering into the determination of net operating income.

The inflows and outflows of cash that result from activities reported in the income statement are classified as cash flows from operating activities. In other words, this classification of cash flows includes the elements of net income reported on a cash basis rather than an accrual basis.[39]

Cash inflows include cash received from:

1. Customers from the sale of goods or services.
2. Interest and dividends from investments.

These amounts may differ from sales and investment income reported in the income statement. For example, sales revenue measured on the accrual basis reflects revenue earned during the period, not necessarily the cash actually collected. Revenue will not equal cash collected from customers if receivables from customers or unearned revenue changed during the period.

Cash outflows include cash paid for:

1. The purchase of inventory.
2. Salaries, wages, and other operating expenses.
3. Interest on debt.
4. Income taxes.

---

[38]FASB ASC 230–10–45: Statement of Cash Flows—Overall—Other Presentation Matters (previously "Statement of Cash Flows," *Statement of Financial Accounting Standards No. 95* (Norwalk, Conn.: FASB, 1987)).

[39]Cash flows related to gains and losses from the sale of assets shown in the income statement are reported as investing activities in the SCF.

CHAPTER 4   The Income Statement, Comprehensive Income, and the Statement of Cash Flows   **199**

Likewise, these amounts may differ from the corresponding accrual expenses reported in the income statement. Expenses are reported when incurred, not necessarily when cash is actually paid for those expenses. Also, some revenues and expenses, like depreciation expense, don't affect cash at all and aren't included as cash outflows from operating activities.

The difference between the inflows and outflows is called *net cash flows from operating activities.* This is equivalent to net income if the income statement had been prepared on a cash basis rather than an accrual basis.

International Financial Reporting Standards

Classification of Cash Flows. Like U.S. GAAP, international standards also require a statement of cash flows. Consistent with U.S. GAAP, cash flows are classified as operating, investing, or financing. However, the U.S. standard designates cash outflows for interest payments and cash inflows from interest and dividends received as operating cash flows. Dividends paid to shareholders are classified as financing cash flows.

● LO4–10

IAS No. 7,[40] on the other hand, allows more flexibility. Companies can report interest and dividends paid as either operating or financing cash flows and interest and dividends received as either operating or investing cash flows. Interest and dividend payments usually are reported as financing activities. Interest and dividends received normally are classified as investing activities.

Typical Classification of Cash Flows from Interest and Dividends

U.S. GAAP	IFRS
Operating Activities	*Operating Activities*
Dividends received	
Interest received	
Interest paid	
Investing Activities	*Investing Activities*
	Dividends received
	Interest received
Financing Activities	*Financing Activities*
Dividends paid	Dividends paid
	Interest paid

Siemens AG, a German company, prepares its financial statements according to IFRS. In the statement of cash flows for quarter ended March 31, 2011, the company reported interest and dividends received as operating cash flows, as would a U.S. company. However, Siemens classified interest paid as a financing cash flow.

Real World Financials

SIEMENS AG
Statement of Cash Flows (partial)
For the Three Months Ended March 31, 2011

(€ in millions)

Cash flows from financing activities:	
Proceeds from re-issuance of treasury stock	109
Repayment of long-term debt	(13)
Change in short-term debt and other	85
Interest paid	(72)
Dividends paid	(2,356)
Dividends paid to minority shareholders	(81)
Financing discontinued operations	(401)
Net cash used in financing activities—continuing operations	(2,729)

---

[40]"Statement of Cash Flows," *International Accounting Standard No. 7* (IASCF), as amended effective January 1, 2011.

By the *direct method,* the cash effect of each operating activity is reported directly in the SCF.

DIRECT AND INDIRECT METHODS OF REPORTING.   Two generally accepted formats can be used to report operating activities, the direct method and the indirect method. Under the direct method, the cash effect of each operating activity is reported directly in the statement. For example, *cash received from customers* is reported as the cash effect of sales activities. Income statement transactions that have no cash flow effect, such as depreciation, are simply not reported.

By the *indirect method,* cash flow from operating activities is derived indirectly by starting with reported net income and adding or subtracting items to convert that amount to a cash basis.

By the indirect method, on the other hand, we arrive at net cash flow from operating activities indirectly by starting with reported net income and working backwards to convert that amount to a cash basis. Two types of adjustments to net income are needed. First, components of net income that do not affect cash are reversed. That means that noncash revenues and gains are subtracted, while noncash expenses and losses are added. For example, depreciation expense does not reduce cash, but it is subtracted in the income statement. To reverse this, then, we add back depreciation expense to net income to arrive at the amount that we would have had if depreciation had not been subtracted.

Second, we make adjustments for changes in operating assets and liabilities during the period that indicate that amounts included as components of net income are not the same as cash flows for those components. For instance, suppose accounts receivable increases during the period because cash collected from customers is less than sales revenue. This increase in accounts receivable would then be subtracted from net income to arrive at *cash flow from operating activities.* In the indirect method, positive adjustments to net income are made for decreases in related assets and increases in related liabilities, while negative adjustments are made for increases in those assets and decreases in those liabilities.

To contrast the direct and indirect methods further, consider the example in Illustration 4–17.

Illustration 4–17

Contrasting the Direct and Indirect Methods of Presenting Cash Flows from Operating Activities

Net income is $35,000, but cash flow from these same activities is not necessarily the same amount.

Arlington Lawn Care (ALC) began operations at the beginning of 2013. ALC's 2013 income statement and its year-end balance sheet are shown below ($ in thousands).

ARLINGTON LAWN CARE
Income Statement
For the Year Ended December 31, 2013

Service revenue		$90
Operating expenses:		
General and administrative	$32*	
Depreciation	8	
Total operating expenses		40
Income before income taxes		50
Income tax expense		15
Net income		$35

*Includes $6 in insurance expense

ARLINGTON LAWN CARE
Balance Sheet
At December 31, 2013

Changes in assets and liabilities can indicate that cash inflows are different from revenues and cash outflows are different from expenses.

Assets		Liabilities and Shareholders' Equity	
Current assets:		Current liabilities:	
Cash	$ 54	Accounts payable**	$ 7
Accounts receivable	12	Income taxes payable	15
Prepaid insurance	4	Total current liabilities	22
Total current assets	70	Shareholders' equity:	
Equipment	40	Common stock	50
Less: Accumulated depreciation	(8)	Retained earnings	30***
Total assets	$102	Total liabilities and shareholders' equity	$102

**For general and administrative expenses
***Net income of $35 less $5 in cash dividends paid

DIRECT METHOD.   Let's begin with the direct method of presentation. We illustrated this method previously in Chapter 2. In that chapter, specific cash transactions were provided and we simply included them in the appropriate cash flow category in the SCF. Here, we start with account balances, so the direct method requires a bit more reasoning.

From the income statement, we see that ALC's net income has four components. Three of those—service revenue, general and administrative expenses, and income tax expense—affect cash flows, but not by the accrual amounts reported in the income statement. One component—depreciation—reduces net income but not cash; it's simply an allocation over time of a prior year's expenditure for a depreciable asset. So, to report these operating activities on a cash basis, rather than an accrual basis, we take the three items that affect cash and adjust the amounts to reflect cash inflow rather than revenue earned and cash outflows rather than expenses incurred. Let's start with service revenue.

Service revenue is $90,000, but ALC did not collect that much cash from its customers. We know that because accounts receivable increased from $0 to $12,000, ALC must have collected to date only $78,000 of the amount earned.

Similarly, general and administrative expenses of $32,000 were incurred, but $7,000 of that hasn't yet been paid. We know that because accounts payable increased by $7,000. Also, prepaid insurance increased by $4,000 so ALC must have paid $4,000 more cash for insurance coverage than the amount that expired and was reported as insurance expense. That means cash paid thus far for general and administrative expenses was only $29,000 ($32,000 less the $7,000 increase in accounts payable plus the $4,000 increase in prepaid insurance). The other expense, income tax, was $15,000, but that's the amount by which income taxes payable increased so no cash has yet been paid for income taxes.

We can report ALC's cash flows from operating activities using the direct method as shown in Illustration 4–17A.

Accounts receivable			
Beg. bal.	0		
Revenue	90		
		78	Cash
End bal.	12		

ARLINGTON LAWN CARE
Statement of Cash Flows
For the Year Ended December 31, 2013

($ in thousands)

Cash Flows from Operating Activities	
Cash received from customers*	$78
Cash paid for general and administrative expenses**	(29)
Net cash flows from operating activities	$49

*Service revenue of $90 thousand, less increase of $12 thousand in accounts receivable.

**General and administrative expenses of $32 thousand, less increase of $7 thousand in accounts payable, plus increase of $4 thousand in prepaid insurance.

Illustration 4–17A

Direct Method of Presenting Cash Flows from Operating Activities

By the direct method, we report the components of net income on a cash basis.

INDIRECT METHOD.   To report operating cash flows using the indirect method, we take a different approach. We start with ALC's net income but realize that the $35,000 includes both cash and noncash components. We need to adjust net income, then, to eliminate the noncash effects so that we're left with only the cash flows. We start by eliminating the only noncash component of net income in our illustration—depreciation expense. Depreciation of $8,000 was subtracted in the income statement, so we simply add it back in to eliminate it.

That leaves us with the three components that do affect cash but not by the amounts reported. For those, we need to make adjustments to net income to cause it to reflect cash flows rather than accrual amounts. For instance, we saw earlier that only $78,000 cash was received from customers even though $90,000 in revenue is reflected in net income. That means we need to include an adjustment to reduce net income by $12,000, the increase in accounts receivable. In a similar manner, we include adjustments for the changes in accounts payable, income taxes payable, and prepaid insurance to cause net income to reflect cash payments rather than expenses incurred. For accounts payable and taxes payable, because more was subtracted in the income statement than cash paid for the expenses related to these two liabilities, we need to add back the differences. Note that if these liabilities had

Depreciation expense does not reduce cash, but is subtracted in the income statement. So, we add back depreciation expense to net income to eliminate it.

We make adjustments for changes in assets and liabilities that indicate that components of net income are not the same as cash flows.

decreased, we would have subtracted, rather than added, the changes. For prepaid insurance, because less was subtracted in the income statement than cash paid, we need to subtract the difference—the increase in prepaid insurance. If this asset had decreased, we would have added, rather than subtracted, the change.

Cash flows from operating activities using the indirect method are shown in Illustration 4–17B.

Illustration 4–17B

Indirect Method of Presenting Cash Flows from Operating Activities

By the indirect method, we start with net income and work backwards to convert that amount to a cash basis.

ARLINGTON LAWN CARE
Statement of Cash Flows
For the Year Ended December 31, 2013

($ in thousands)

Cash Flows from Operating Activities		
Net income		$35
Adjustments for noncash effects:		
Depreciation expense	$ 8	
Changes in operating assets and liabilities:		
Increase in prepaid insurance	(4)	
Increase in accounts receivable	(12)	
Increase in accounts payable	7	
Increase in income taxes payable	15	14
Net cash flows from operating activities		$49

Both the direct and the indirect methods produce the same net cash flows from operating activities ($49 thousand in our illustration); they are merely alternative approaches to reporting the cash flows. The FASB, in promulgating GAAP for the statement of cash flows, stated its preference for the direct method. However, while both methods are used in practice, the direct method is infrequently used.

The choice of presentation method for cash flow from operating activities has no effect on how investing activities and financing activities are reported. We now look at how cash flows are classified into those two categories.

Investing Activities

Investing activities involve the acquisition and sale of (1) long-term assets used in the business and (2) nonoperating investment assets.

Cash flows from investing activities include inflows and outflows of cash related to the acquisition and disposition of long-lived assets used in the operations of the business (such as property, plant, and equipment) and investment assets (except those classified as cash equivalents and trading securities). The purchase and sale of inventories are not considered investing activities. Inventories are purchased for the purpose of being sold as part of the company's operations, so their purchase and sale are included with operating activities rather than investing activities.

Cash outflows from investing activities include cash paid for:

1. The purchase of long-lived assets used in the business.
2. The purchase of investment securities like stocks and bonds of other entities (other than those classified as cash equivalents and trading securities).
3. Loans to other entities.

Later, when the assets are disposed of, cash inflow from the sale of the assets (or collection of loans and notes) also is reported as cash flows from investing activities. As a result, cash inflows from these transactions are considered investing activities:

1. The sale of long-lived assets used in the business.
2. The sale of investment securities (other than cash equivalents and trading securities).
3. The collection of a nontrade receivable (excluding the collection of interest, which is an operating activity).

Net cash flows from investing activities represents the difference between the inflows and outflows. The only investing activity indicated in Illustration 4–17 is ALC's investment of $40,000 cash for equipment.

Financing Activities

Financing activities relate to the external financing of the company. Cash inflows occur when cash is borrowed from creditors or invested by owners. Cash outflows occur when cash is paid back to creditors or distributed to owners. The payment of interest to a creditor, however, is classified as an operating activity.

> *Financing activities involve cash inflows and outflows from transactions with creditors (excluding trade creditors) and owners.*

Cash inflows include cash received from:

1. Owners when shares are sold to them.
2. Creditors when cash is borrowed through notes, loans, mortgages, and bonds.

Cash outflows include cash paid to:

1. Owners in the form of dividends or other distributions.
2. Owners for the reacquisition of shares previously sold.
3. Creditors as repayment of the principal amounts of debt (excluding trade payables that relate to operating activities).

Net cash flows from financing activities is the difference between the inflows and outflows. The only financing activities indicated in Illustration 4–17 are ALC's receipt of $50,000 cash from issuing common stock and the payment of $5,000 in cash dividends.

Noncash Investing and Financing Activities

As we just discussed, the statement of cash flows provides useful information about the investing and financing activities in which a company is engaged. Even though these primarily result in cash inflows and cash outflows, there may be significant investing and financing activities occurring during the period that do not involve cash flows at all. In order to provide complete information about these activities, any significant *noncash* investing and financing activities (that is, noncash exchanges) are reported either on the face of the SCF or in a disclosure note. An example of a significant noncash investing and financing activity is the acquisition of equipment (an investing activity) by issuing either a long-term note payable or equity securities (a financing activity).

> *Significant investing and financing transactions not involving cash also are reported.*

The 2013 statement of cash flows for ALC, beginning with net cash flows from operating activities, is shown in Illustration 4–18.

ARLINGTON LAWN CARE Statement of Cash Flows (in part) For the Year Ended December 31, 2013		
		($ in thousands)
Net cash flows from operating activities		$49
Cash flows from investing activities:		
Purchase of equipment		(40)
Cash flows from financing activities:		
Sale of common stock	$50	
Payment of cash dividends	(5)	
Net cash flows from financing activities		45
Net increase in cash		54
Cash balance, January 1		0
Cash balance, December 31		$54

Illustration 4–18

Statement of Cash Flows (beginning with net cash flows from operating activities)

We know $40 thousand was paid to buy equipment because that balance sheet account increased from no balance to $40 thousand. Likewise, because common stock increased from zero to $50 thousand, we include that amount as a cash inflow from financing activities. Finally, Illustration 4–17 told us that $5 thousand was paid as a cash dividend, also a financing activity.

Where We're Headed

● LO4–10

The FASB and IASB are working together on a standard that would have a dramatic impact on the format of financial statements.

Demonstrating the cohesiveness among the financial statements is a key objective of the Financial Statement Presentation project.

The FASB and IASB are working together on a project, Financial Statement Presentation, to establish a common standard for presenting information in the financial statements, including classifying and displaying line items and aggregating line items into subtotals and totals. This standard would have a dramatic impact on the format of financial statements. An important part of the proposal involves the organization of elements of the balance sheet (statement of financial position), statement of comprehensive income (including the income statement), and statement of cash flows (SCF) into a common set of classifications.

The income statement (statement of comprehensive income) and the statement of cash flows are slated to change in several ways. First, though, we should note that the SCF would retain the three major classifications of cash flows. The income statement (and balance sheet as well) also would include classifications by operating, investing, and financing activities, providing a "cohesive" financial picture that stresses the relationships among the financial statements.

For each statement, though, operating and investing activities would be included within a new category, "business" activities. Each statement also would include three additional groupings: discontinued operations, income taxes, and equity (if needed). The new look for the statement of comprehensive income and the statement of cash flows would be:

Statement of Comprehensive Income	Statement of Cash Flows
Business • Operating income and expenses • Investing income and expenses	**Business** • Operating cash flows • Investing cash flows
Financing • Debt expense	**Financing** • Debt cash flows • Equity cash flows
Multi-category transactions **Income Taxes**	**Multi-category transactions** **Income Taxes**
Discontinued Operations (net of tax)	**Discontinued Operations**
Other Comprehensive Income (net of tax)	

The proposed new standard would require the direct method.

One change planned for the statement of cash flows is to no longer permit a choice between the direct method and the indirect method, but to require the direct method, reasoning that it provides more useful information to investors. Another change is to eliminate the concept of cash equivalents in favor of cash only. Also, while we still will have operating, investing, and financing activities, some cash flows will switch categories. Under the new "management approach," cash flows will be classified based on how related assets and liabilities are used by management. For instance, expenditures for property, plant, and equipment likely would be classified as operating, because those assets are used in the "core" business. Investing activities would be limited primarily to investments in stock, bonds, and other securities. The multicategory sections primarily encompass the acquisition and sale of other companies since they include assets and liabilities in different categories.

Concept Review Exercise

STATEMENT OF CASH FLOWS

Dublin Enterprises, Inc. (DEI), owns a chain of retail electronics stores located in shopping malls. The following are the company's 2013 income statement and comparative balance sheets ($ in millions):

Income Statement
For the Year Ended December 31, 2013

Revenue		$2,100
Cost of goods sold		1,400
Gross profit		700
Operating expenses:		
Selling and administrative	$ 355	
Depreciation	85	
Total operating expenses		440
Income before income taxes		260
Income tax expense		78
Net income		$ 182

Comparative Balance Sheets	12/31/13	12/31/12
Assets:		
Cash	$ 300	$ 220
Accounts receivable (net)	227	240
Inventory	160	120
Property, plant & equipment	960	800
Less: Accumulated depreciation	(405)	(320)
Total assets	$1,242	$1,060
Liabilities and shareholders' equity:		
Accounts payable	$ 145	$ 130
Payables for selling and admin. expenses	147	170
Income taxes payable	95	50
Long-term debt	–0–	100
Common stock	463	400
Retained earnings	392	210
Total liabilities and shareholders' equity	$1,242	$1,060

Required:
1. Prepare DEI's 2013 statement of cash flows using the direct method.
2. Prepare the cash flows from operating activities section of DEI's 2013 statement of cash flows using the indirect method.

Solution
1. Prepare DEI's 2013 statement of cash flows using the direct method.

DUBLIN ENTERPRISES, INC.
Statement of Cash Flows
For the Year Ended December 31, 2013
($ in millions)

Cash Flows from Operating Activities	
Collections from customers[1]	$2,113
Purchase of inventory[2]	(1,425)
Payment of selling and administrative expenses[3]	(378)
Payment of income taxes[4]	(33)
Net cash flows from operating activities	$277

[1]Sales revenue of $2,100 million, plus $13 million decrease in accounts receivable (net).
[2]Cost of goods sold of $1,400 million, plus $40 million increase in inventory, less $15 million increase in accounts payable.
[3]Selling and administrative expenses of $355 million, plus $23 million decrease in payables for selling and administrative expenses.
[4]Income tax expense of $78 million, less $45 million increase in income taxes payable.

(continued)

206   SECTION 1   The Role of Accounting as an Information System

(concluded)

Cash Flows from Investing Activities		
Purchase of property, plant, and equipment		(160)
Cash Flows from Financing Activities		
Issuance of common stock	63	
Payment on long-term debt	(100)	
Net cash flows from financing activities		(37)
Net increase in cash		80
Cash, January 1		220
Cash, December 31		$300

2. Prepare the cash flows from operating activities section of DEI's 2013 statement of cash flows using the indirect method.

DUBLIN ENTERPRISES, INC.
Statement of Cash Flows
For the Year Ended December 31, 2013
($ in millions)

Cash Flows from Operating Activities	
Net Income	$182
Adjustments for noncash effects:	
Depreciation expense	85
Changes in operating assets and liabilities:	
Decrease in accounts receivable (net)	13
Increase in inventory	(40)
Increase in accounts payable	15
Increase in income taxes payable	45
Decrease in payables for selling and administrative expenses	(23)
Net cash flows from operating activities	$277

Financial Reporting Case Solution

1. **How would you explain restructuring costs to Becky? Are restructuring costs something Becky should worry about?** *(p. 179)* Restructuring costs include employee severance and termination benefits plus other costs associated with the shutdown or relocation of facilities or downsizing of operations. Restructuring costs are not necessarily bad. In fact, the objective is to make operations more efficient. The costs are incurred now in hopes of better earnings later.

2. **Explain to Becky what is meant by discontinued operations and describe to her how that item is reported in an income statement.** *(p. 184)* A discontinued operation occurs when a company decides to discontinue a separate component. The net-of-tax effect of discontinued operations is separately reported below income from continuing operations. If the component has been disposed of by the end of the reporting period, the income effects include: (1) income or loss from operations of the discontinued component from the beginning of the reporting period through the disposal date and (2) gain or loss on disposal of the component's assets. If the component has not been disposed of by the end of the reporting period, the income effects include: (1) income or loss from operations of the discontinued component from the beginning of the reporting period through the end of the reporting period, and (2) an impairment loss if the fair value minus cost to sell of the component's assets is less than their carrying amount (book value).

3. **In addition to discontinued operations, what other events sometimes are reported separately in the income statement that you might tell Becky about? Why are these items reported separately?** *(p. 188)*   In addition to discontinued operations, extraordinary items also are reported separately in the income statement when they are present. The predictive ability of an income statement is significantly enhanced if normal and recurrent transactions are separated from unusual and nonrecurrent items. The income statement is a historical report, summarizing the most recent profit-generating activities of a company. The information in the statement is useful if it can help users predict the future. Toward this end, users should be made aware of events reported in the income statement that are not likely to occur again in the foreseeable future.

4. **Describe to Becky the difference between basic and diluted earnings per share.** *(p. 192)*   Basic earnings per share is computed by dividing income available to common shareholders (net income less any preferred stock dividends) by the weighted-average number of common shares outstanding for the period. Diluted earnings per share reflects the potential dilution that could occur for companies that have certain securities outstanding that are convertible into common shares or stock options that could create additional common shares if the options were exercised. These items could cause earnings per share to decrease (become diluted). Because of the complexity of the calculation and the importance of earnings per share to investors, the text devotes a substantial portion of Chapter 19 to this topic. ●

The Bottom Line

● **LO4–1**   The components of income from continuing operations are revenues, expenses (including income taxes), gains, and losses, excluding those related to discontinued operations and extraordinary items. Companies often distinguish between operating and nonoperating income within continuing operations. *(p. 172)*

● **LO4–2**   The term *earnings quality* refers to the ability of reported earnings (income) to predict a company's future earnings. The relevance of any historical-based financial statement hinges on its predictive value. To enhance predictive value, analysts try to separate a company's *transitory earnings* effects from its *permanent earnings.* Many believe that manipulating income reduces earnings quality because it can mask permanent earnings. Two major methods used by managers to manipulate earnings are (1) income shifting and (2) income statement classification. *(p. 177)*

● **LO4–3**   Analysts begin their assessment of permanent earnings with income from continuing operations. It would be a mistake to assume income from continuing operations reflects permanent earnings entirely. In other words, there may be transitory earnings effects included in both operating and nonoperating income. *(p. 178)*

● **LO4–4**   A discontinued operation refers to the disposal or planned disposal of a component of the entity. The net-of-tax effect of discontinued operations is separately reported below income from continuing operations. *(p. 184)*

● **LO4–5**   Extraordinary items are material gains and losses that are both unusual in nature and infrequent in occurrence. The net-of-tax effects of extraordinary items are presented in the income statement below discontinued operations, if any. *(p. 188)*

● **LO4–6**   Earnings per share (EPS) is the amount of income achieved during a period expressed per share of common stock outstanding. The EPS must be disclosed for income from continuing operations and for each item below continuing operations. *(p. 192)*

● **LO4–7**   The FASB's Concept Statement 6 defines the term *comprehensive income* as the change in equity from nonowner transactions. The calculation of net income, however, excludes certain transactions that are included in comprehensive income. To convey the relationship between the two measures, companies must report both net income and comprehensive income and reconcile the difference between the two. The presentation can be (1) in a single, continuous statement of comprehensive income, or (2) in two separate, but consecutive statements—an income statement and a statement of comprehensive income. *(p. 192)*

208   SECTION 1   The Role of Accounting as an Information System

● **LO4–8**   When a company provides a set of financial statements that reports both financial position and results of operations, a statement of cash flows is reported for each period for which results of operations are provided. The purpose of the statement is to provide information about the cash receipts and cash disbursements that occurred during the period. (*p. 198*)

● **LO4–9**   To enhance the usefulness of the information, the statement of cash flows classifies all transactions affecting cash into one of three categories: (1) operating activities, (2) investing activities, or (3) financing activities. (*p. 198*)

● **LO4–10**   There are more similarities than differences between income statements and statements of cash flows prepared according to U.S. GAAP and those prepared applying international standards. However, we report extraordinary items separately in an income statement prepared according to U.S. GAAP, but international standards prohibit reporting extraordinary items. In a statement of cash flows, some differences are possible in the classifications of interest and divided revenue, interest expense, and dividends paid. (*pp. 177, 184, 189, 194, 199, and 204*) ●

Questions For Review of Key Topics

Q 4–1   The income statement is a change statement. Explain what is meant by this.

Q 4–2   What transactions are included in income from continuing operations? Briefly explain why it is important to segregate income from continuing operations from other transactions affecting net income.

Q 4–3   Distinguish between operating and nonoperating income in relation to the income statement.

Q 4–4   Briefly explain the difference between the single-step and multiple-step income statement formats.

Q 4–5   Explain what is meant by the term *earnings quality*.

Q 4–6   What are restructuring costs and where are they reported in the income statement?

Q 4–7   Define intraperiod tax allocation. Why is the process necessary?

Q 4–8   How are discontinued operations reported in the income statement?

Q 4–9   Define extraordinary items.

Q 4–10   How should extraordinary gains and losses be reported in the income statement?

Q 4–11   What is meant by a change in accounting principle? Describe the accounting treatment for a voluntary change in accounting principle.

Q 4–12   Accountants very often are required to make estimates, and very often those estimates prove incorrect. In what period(s) is the effect of a change in an accounting estimate reported?

Q 4–13   The correction of a material error discovered in a year subsequent to the year the error was made is considered a prior period adjustment. Briefly describe the accounting treatment for prior period adjustments.

Q 4–14   Define earnings per share (EPS). For which income statement items must EPS be disclosed?

Q 4–15   Define comprehensive income. What are the two ways companies can present comprehensive income?

Q 4–16   Describe the purpose of the statement of cash flows.

Q 4–17   Identify and briefly describe the three categories of cash flows reported in the statement of cash flows.

Q 4–18   Explain what is meant by noncash investing and financing activities pertaining to the statement of cash flows. Give an example of one of these activities.

Q 4–19   Distinguish between the direct method and the indirect method for reporting the results of operating activities in the statement of cash flows.

IFRS   Q 4–20   Identify any differences between U.S. GAAP and International Financial Reporting Standards (IFRS) in the number of possible separately reported items that could appear in income statements.

IFRS   Q 4–21   Describe the potential statement of cash flows classification differences between U.S. GAAP and IFRS.

Brief Exercises

BE 4–1
Single-step
income
statement
● LO4–1

The adjusted trial balance of Pacific Scientific Corporation on December 31, 2013, the end of the company's fiscal year, contained the following income statement items ($ in millions): sales revenue, $2,106; cost of goods sold, $1,240; selling expenses, $126; general and administrative expenses, $105; interest expense, $35; and gain on sale of investments, $45. Income tax expense has not yet been accrued. The income tax rate is 40%. Prepare a single-step income statement for 2013. Ignore EPS disclosures.

CHAPTER 4   The Income Statement, Comprehensive Income, and the Statement of Cash Flows   **209**

BE 4–2
Multiple-step income statement
● LO4–1, LO4–3

Refer to the situation described in BE 4–1. If the company's accountant prepared a multiple-step income statement, what amount would appear in that statement for (a) operating income and (b) nonoperating income?

BE 4–3
Multiple-step income statement
● LO4–1, LO4–3

Refer to the situation described in BE 4–1. Prepare a multiple-step income statement for 2013. Ignore EPS disclosures.

BE 4–4
Multiple-step income statement
● LO4–1, LO4–3

The following is a partial year-end adjusted trial balance.

Account Title	Debits	Credits
Sales revenue		300,000
Loss on sale of investments	22,000	
Interest revenue		4,000
Loss from flood damage (unusual and infrequent)	50,000	
Cost of goods sold	160,000	
General and administrative expenses	40,000	
Restructuring costs	50,000	
Selling expenses	25,000	
Income tax expense	0	

Income tax expense has not yet been accrued. The income tax rate is 40%. Determine the following: (a) operating income (loss), (b) income (loss) before any separately reported items, and (c) net income (loss).

BE 4–5
Extraordinary item
● LO4–5

Memorax Company earned before-tax income of $790,000 for its 2013 fiscal year. During the year the company experienced a $520,000 loss from earthquake damage that it considered to be an extraordinary item. This loss is not included in the $790,000 before-tax income figure. The company's income tax rate is 40%. Prepare the lower portion of the 2013 income statement beginning with $790,000.

BE 4–6
Separately reported items
● LO4–3, LO4–5, LO4–6

The following are partial income statement account balances taken from the December 31, 2013, year-end trial balance of White and Sons, Inc.: restructuring costs, $300,000; interest revenue, $40,000; loss from earthquake (unusual and infrequent), $400,000; and loss on sale of investments, $50,000. Income tax expense has not yet been accrued. The income tax rate is 40%. Prepare the lower portion of the 2013 income statement beginning with $850,000 income before income taxes and extraordinary item. Include appropriate basic EPS disclosures. The company had 100,000 shares of common stock outstanding throughout the year.

BE 4–7
Discontinued operations
● LO4–4

On December 31, 2013, the end of the fiscal year, California Microtech Corporation completed the sale of its semiconductor business for $10 million. The business segment qualifies as a component of the entity according to GAAP. The book value of the assets of the segment was $8 million. The loss from operations of the segment during 2013 was $3.6 million. Pretax income from continuing operations for the year totaled $5.8 million. The income tax rate is 30%. Prepare the lower portion of the 2013 income statement beginning with pretax income from continuing operations. Ignore EPS disclosures.

BE 4–8
Discontinued operations
● LO4–4

Refer to the situation described in BE 4–7. Assume that the semiconductor segment was not sold during 2013 but was held for sale at year-end. The estimated fair value of the segment's assets, less costs to sell, on December 31 was $10 million. Prepare the lower portion of the 2013 income statement beginning with pretax income from continuing operations. Ignore EPS disclosures.

BE 4–9
Discontinued operations
● LO4–4

Refer to the situation described in BE 4–8. Assume instead that the estimated fair value of the segment's assets, less costs to sell, on December 31 was $7 million rather than $10 million. Prepare the lower portion of the 2013 income statement beginning with pretax income from continuing operations. Ignore EPS disclosures.

BE 4–10
Comprehensive income
● LO4–7

O'Reilly Beverage Company reported net income of $650,000 for 2013. In addition, the company deferred a $60,000 pretax loss on derivatives and had pretax net unrealized holding gains on investment securities of $40,000. Prepare a separate statement of comprehensive income for 2013. The company's income tax rate is 40%.

BE 4–11
Statement of
cash flows; direct
method
● LO4–9

The following are summary cash transactions that occurred during the year for Hilliard Healthcare Co. (HHC):

Cash received from:	
Customers	$660,000
Interest on note receivable	12,000
Collection of note receivable	100,000
Sale of land	40,000
Issuance of common stock	200,000
Cash paid for:	
Interest on note payable	18,000
Purchase of equipment	120,000
Operating expenses	440,000
Dividends to shareholders	30,000

Prepare the cash flows from operating activities section of HHC's statement of cash flows using the direct method.

BE 4–12
Statement of cash
flows; investing
and financing
activities
● LO4–9

Refer to the situation described in BE 4–11. Prepare the cash flows from investing and financing activities sections of HHC's statement of cash flows.

BE 4–13
Statement of
cash flows;
indirect method
● LO4–9

Net income of Mansfield Company was $45,000. The accounting records reveal depreciation expense of $80,000 as well as increases in prepaid rent, salaries payable, and income taxes payable of $60,000, $15,000, and $12,000, respectively. Prepare the cash flows from operating activities section of Mansfield's statement of cash flows using the indirect method.

BE 4–14
IFRS; Statement
of cash flows
● LO4–9, LO4–10

Refer to the situation described in BE 4–11 and BE 4–12. How might your solution to those brief exercises differ if Hilliard Healthcare Co. prepares its statement of cash flows according to International Financial Reporting Standards?

 IFRS

Exercises

An alternate exercise and problem set is available on the text website: www.mhhe.com/spiceland7e

E 4–1
Income
statement format;
single step and
multiple step
● LO4–1, LO4–6

The following is a partial trial balance for the Green Star Corporation as of December 31, 2013:

Account Title	Debits	Credits
Sales revenue		1,300,000
Interest revenue		30,000
Gain on sale of investments		50,000
Cost of goods sold	720,000	
Selling expenses	160,000	
General and administrative expenses	75,000	
Interest expense	40,000	
Income tax expense	130,000	

100,000 shares of common stock were outstanding throughout 2013.

Required:
1. Prepare a single-step income statement for 2013, including EPS disclosures.
2. Prepare a multiple-step income statement for 2013, including EPS disclosures.

CHAPTER 4   The Income Statement, Comprehensive Income, and the Statement of Cash Flows   **211**

E 4–2
Income statement format; single step and multiple step
● **LO4–1, LO4–3, LO4–5, LO4–6**

The following is a partial trial balance for General Lighting Corporation as of December 31, 2013:

Account Title	Debits	Credits
Sales revenue		2,350,000
Rental revenue		80,000
Loss on sale of investments	22,500	
Loss from flood damage (event is both unusual and infrequent)	120,000	
Cost of goods sold	1,200,300	
Loss from write-down of inventory due to obsolescence	200,000	
Selling expenses	300,000	
General and administrative expenses	150,000	
Interest expense	90,000	

300,000 shares of common stock were outstanding throughout 2013. Income tax expense has not yet been accrued. The income tax rate is 40%.

Required:
1. Prepare a single-step income statement for 2013, including EPS disclosures.
2. Prepare a multiple-step income statement for 2013, including EPS disclosures.

E 4–3
Multiple-step continuous statement of comprehensive income
● **LO4–1, LO4–5, LO4–6, LO4–7**

The trial balance for Lindor Corporation, a manufacturing company, for the year ended December 31, 2013, included the following income accounts:

Account Title	Debits	Credits
Sales revenue		2,300,000
Gain on litigation settlement (unusual and infrequent)		400,000
Cost of goods sold	1,400,000	
Selling and administrative expenses	420,000	
Interest expense	40,000	
Unrealized holding gains on investment securities		80,000

The trial balance does not include the accrual for income taxes. Lindor's income tax rate is 30%. One million shares of common stock were outstanding throughout 2013.

Required:
Prepare a single, continuous multiple-step statement of comprehensive income for 2013, including appropriate EPS disclosures.

E 4–4
Income statement presentation; intraperiod tax allocation
● **LO4–1, LO4–5, LO4–6**

The following *incorrect* income statement was prepared by the accountant of the Axel Corporation:

AXEL CORPORATION
Income Statement
For the Year Ended December 31, 2013

Revenues and gains:		
Sales		$592,000
Interest and dividends		32,000
Gain from litigation settlement		86,000
Total revenues and gains		710,000
Expenses and losses:		
Cost of goods sold	$325,000	
Selling expenses	67,000	
Administrative expenses	87,000	
Interest	26,000	
Restructuring costs	55,000	
Income taxes	60,000	
Total expenses and losses		620,000
Net Income		$ 90,000
Earnings per share		$ 0.90

Required:
Prepare a multiple-step income statement for 2013 applying generally accepted accounting principles. The income tax rate is 40%. The gain from litigation settlement is considered an unusual and infrequent event and the amount is material.

E 4–5
Discontinued operations
● LO4–4, LO4–6

Chance Company had two operating divisions, one manufacturing farm equipment and the other office supplies. Both divisions are considered separate components as defined by generally accepted accounting principles. The farm equipment component had been unprofitable, and on September 1, 2013, the company adopted a plan to sell the assets of the division. The actual sale was completed on December 15, 2013, at a price of $600,000. The book value of the division's assets was $1,000,000, resulting in a before-tax loss of $400,000 on the sale.

The division incurred a before-tax operating loss from operations of $130,000 from the beginning of the year through December 15. The income tax rate is 40%. Chance's after-tax income from its continuing operations is $350,000.

Required:
Prepare an income statement for 2013 beginning with income from continuing operations. Include appropriate EPS disclosures assuming that 100,000 shares of common stock were outstanding throughout the year.

E 4–6
Income statement presentation; discontinued operations; restructuring charges
● LO4–1, LO4–3, LO4–4

Esquire Comic Book Company had income before tax of $1,000,000 in 2013 *before* considering the following material items:
1. Esquire sold one of its operating divisions, which qualified as a separate component according to generally accepted accounting principles. The before-tax loss on disposal was $350,000. The division generated before-tax income from operations from the beginning of the year through disposal of $500,000. Neither the loss on disposal nor the operating income is included in the $1,000,000 before-tax income the company generated from its other divisions.
2. The company incurred restructuring costs of $80,000 during the year.

Required:
Prepare a 2013 income statement for Esquire beginning with income from continuing operations. Assume an income tax rate of 40%. Ignore EPS disclosures.

E 4–7
Discontinued operations; disposal in subsequent year
● LO4–4

Kandon Enterprises, Inc., has two operating divisions; one manufactures machinery and the other breeds and sells horses. Both divisions are considered separate components as defined by generally accepted accounting principles. The horse division has been unprofitable, and on November 15, 2013, Kandon adopted a formal plan to sell the division. The sale was completed on April 30, 2014. At December 31, 2013, the component was considered held for sale.

On December 31, 2013, the company's fiscal year-end, the book value of the assets of the horse division was $250,000. On that date, the fair value of the assets, less costs to sell, was $200,000. The before-tax loss from operations of the division for the year was $140,000. The company's effective tax rate is 40%. The after-tax income from continuing operations for 2013 was $400,000.

Required:
1. Prepare a partial income statement for 2013 beginning with income from continuing operations. Ignore EPS disclosures.
2. Repeat requirement 1 assuming that the estimated net fair value of the horse division's assets was $400,000, instead of $200,000.

E 4–8
Discontinued operations; disposal in subsequent year; solving for unknown
● LO4–4

On September 17, 2013, Ziltech, Inc. entered into an agreement to sell one of its divisions that qualifies as a component of the entity according to generally accepted accounting principles. By December 31, 2013, the company's fiscal year-end, the division had not yet been sold, but was considered held for sale. The net fair value (fair value minus costs to sell) of the division's assets at the end of the year was $11 million. The pretax income from operations of the division during 2013 was $4 million. Pretax income from continuing operations for the year totaled $14 million. The income tax rate is 40%. Ziltech reported net income for the year of $7.2 million.

Required:
Determine the book value of the division's assets on December 31, 2013.

E 4–9
Earnings per share
● LO4–6

The Esposito Import Company had 1 million shares of common stock outstanding during 2013. Its income statement reported the following items: income from continuing operations, $5 million; loss from discontinued operations, $1.6 million; extraordinary gain, $2.2 million. All of these amounts are net of tax.

Required:
Prepare the 2013 EPS presentation for the Esposito Import Company.

E 4–10
Comprehensive income
● LO4–7

The Massoud Consulting Group reported net income of $1,354,000 for its fiscal year ended December 31, 2013. In addition, during the year the company experienced a foreign currency translation adjustment gain of $240,000 and had unrealized losses on investment securities of $80,000. The company's effective tax rate on all items affecting comprehensive income is 30%. Each component of other comprehensive income is displayed net of tax.

CHAPTER 4   The Income Statement, Comprehensive Income, and the Statement of Cash Flows   **213**

Required:
Prepare a separate statement of comprehensive income for 2013.

E 4–11
Statement of cash flows; classifications
● **LO4–9**

The statement of cash flows classifies all cash inflows and outflows into one of the three categories shown below and lettered from a through c. In addition, certain transactions that do not involve cash are reported in the statement as noncash investing and financing activities, labeled d.
a. Operating activities
b. Investing activities
c. Financing activities
d. Noncash investing and financing activities

Required:
For each of the following transactions, use the letters above to indicate the appropriate classification category.
1. _____Purchase of equipment for cash.
2. _____Payment of employee salaries.
3. _____Collection of cash from customers.
4. _____Cash proceeds from a note payable.
5. _____Purchase of common stock of another corporation for cash.
6. _____Issuance of common stock for cash.
7. _____Sale of machinery for cash.
8. _____Payment of interest on note payable.
9. _____Issuance of bonds payable in exchange for land and building.
10. _____Payment of cash dividends to shareholders.
11. _____Payment of principal on note payable.

E 4–12
Statement of cash flows preparation
● **LO4–9**

The following summary transactions occurred during 2013 for Bluebonnet Bakers:

Cash Received from:	
Customers	$380,000
Interest on note receivable	6,000
Principal on note receivable	50,000
Sale of investments	30,000
Proceeds from note payable	100,000
Cash Paid for:	
Purchase of inventory	160,000
Interest on note payable	5,000
Purchase of equipment	85,000
Salaries to employees	90,000
Principal on note payable	25,000
Payment of dividends to shareholders	20,000

The balance of cash and cash equivalents at the beginning of 2013 was $17,000.

Required:
Prepare a statement of cash flows for 2013 for Bluebonnet Bakers. Use the direct method for reporting operating activities.

E 4–13
IFRS; statement of cash flows
● **LO4–9, LO4–10**

 IFRS

Refer to the situation described in Exercise 4–12.

Required:
How might your solution differ if Bluebonnet Bakers prepares the statement of cash flows according to International Financial Reporting Standards?

E 4–14
Indirect method; reconciliation of net income to net cash flows from operating activities
● **LO4–9**

The accounting records of Hampton Company provided the data below ($ in 000s).

Net income	$17,300
Depreciation expense	7,800
Increase in accounts receivable	4,000
Decrease in inventory	5,500
Decrease in prepaid insurance	1,200
Decrease in salaries payable	2,700
Increase in interest payable	800

Required:

Prepare a reconciliation of net income to net cash flows from operating activities.

E 4–15
Statement of cash flows; directly from transactions
● **LO4–9**

The following transactions occurred during March 2013 for the Wainwright Corporation. The company owns and operates a wholesale warehouse. [These are the same transactions analyzed in Exercise 2–1, when we determined their effect on elements of the accounting equation.]

1. Issued 30,000 shares of capital stock in exchange for $300,000 in cash.
2. Purchased equipment at a cost of $40,000. $10,000 cash was paid and a note payable was signed for the balance owed.
3. Purchased inventory on account at a cost of $90,000. The company uses the perpetual inventory system.
4. Credit sales for the month totaled $120,000. The cost of the goods sold was $70,000.
5. Paid $5,000 in rent on the warehouse building for the month of March.
6. Paid $6,000 to an insurance company for fire and liability insurance for a one-year period beginning April 1, 2013.
7. Paid $70,000 on account for the merchandise purchased in 3.
8. Collected $55,000 from customers on account.
9. Recorded depreciation expense of $1,000 for the month on the equipment.

Required:

1. Analyze each transaction and classify each as a financing, investing, and/or operating activity (a transaction can represent more than one type of activity). In doing so, also indicate the cash effect of each, if any. If there is no cash effect, simply place a check mark (√) in the appropriate column(s).

    Example:

Financing	Investing	Operating
1. $300,000		

2. Prepare a statement of cash flows, using the direct method to present cash flows from operating activities. Assume the cash balance at the beginning of the month was $40,000.

E 4–16
Statement of cash flows; indirect method
● **LO4–9**

Cemptex Corporation prepares its statement of cash flows using the indirect method to report operating activities. Net income for the 2013 fiscal year was $624,000. Depreciation and amortization expense of $87,000 was included with operating expenses in the income statement. The following information describes the changes in current assets and liabilities other than cash:

Decrease in accounts receivable	$22,000
Increase in inventories	9,200
Increase prepaid expenses	8,500
Increase in salaries payable	10,000
Decrease in income taxes payable	14,000

Required:

Prepare the operating activities section of the 2013 statement of cash flows.

E 4–17
IFRS; statement of cash flows
● **LO4–9, LO4–10**

🌐 **IFRS**

The statement of cash flows for the year ended December 31, 2013, for Bronco Metals is presented below.

BRONCO METALS
Statement of Cash Flows
For the Year Ended December 31, 2013

Cash flows from operating activities:		
Collections from customers	$ 353,000	
Interest on note receivable	4,000	
Dividends received from investments	2,400	
Purchase of inventory	(186,000)	
Payment of operating expenses	(67,000)	
Payment of interest on note payable	(8,000)	
Net cash flows from operating activities		$ 98,400
Cash flows from investing activities:		
Collection of note receivable	100,000	
Purchase of equipment	(154,000)	
Net cash flows from investing activities		(54,000)

(continued)

CHAPTER 4 The Income Statement, Comprehensive Income, and the Statement of Cash Flows **215**

(concluded)

Cash flows from financing activities:

Proceeds from issuance of common stock	200,000	
Dividends paid	(40,000)	
Net cash flows from financing activities		160,000
Net increase in cash		204,400
Cash and cash equivalents, January 1		28,600
Cash and cash equivalents, December 31		$233,000

Required:
Prepare the statement of cash flows assuming that Bronco prepares its financial statements according to International Financial Reporting Standards. Where IFRS allows flexibility, use the classification used most often in IFRS financial statements.

E 4–18
Statement of cash flows; indirect method
● LO4–9

Presented below is the 2013 income statement and comparative balance sheet information for Tiger Enterprises.

TIGER ENTERPRISES
Income Statement
For the Year Ended December 31, 2013

($ in thousands)		
Sales revenue		$7,000
Operating expenses:		
Cost of goods sold	$3,360	
Depreciation	240	
Insurance	100	
Administrative and other	1,800	
Total operating expenses		5,500
Income before income taxes		1,500
Income tax expense		600
Net income		$ 900

Balance Sheet Information ($ in thousands)	Dec. 31, 2013	Dec. 31, 2012
Assets:		
Cash	$ 300	$ 200
Accounts receivable	750	830
Inventory	640	600
Prepaid insurance	50	20
Plant and equipment	2,100	1,800
Less: Accumulated depreciation	(840)	(600)
Total assets	$3,000	$2,850
Liabilities and Shareholders' Equity:		
Accounts payable	$ 300	$ 360
Payables for administrative and other expenses	300	400
Income taxes payable	200	150
Note payable (due 12/31/2014)	800	600
Common stock	900	800
Retained earnings	500	540
Total liabilities and shareholders' equity	$3,000	$2,850

Required:
Prepare Tiger's statement of cash flows, using the indirect method to present cash flows from operating activities. (Hint: You will have to calculate dividend payments.)

E 4–19
Statement of cash flows; direct method
● LO4–9

Refer to the situation described in Exercise 4–18.

Required:
Prepare the cash flows from operating activities section of Tiger's 2013 statement of cash flows using the direct method. Assume that all purchases and sales of inventory are on account, and that there are no anticipated bad debts for accounts receivable. (Hint: Use T-accounts for the pertinent items to isolate the information needed for the statement.)

E 4–20
FASB codification research
● LO4–6

The *FASB Accounting Standards Codification* represents the single source of authoritative U.S. generally accepted accounting principles.

Required:
1. Obtain the relevant authoritative literature on earnings per share using the FASB's Codification Research System at the FASB website (www.fasb.org). Identify the Codification topic number that provides the accounting for earnings per share.
2. What is the specific citation that describes the additional information for earnings per share that must be included in the notes to the financial statements?
3. Describe the required disclosures.

E 4–21
FASB codification research
● LO4–5, LO4–6, LO4–7, LO4–9

Access the FASB's Codification Research System at the FASB website (www.fasb.org). Determine the specific citation for each of the following items:
1. The criteria for determining if a gain or loss should be reported as an extraordinary item.
2. The calculation of the weighted average number of shares for basic earnings per share purposes.
3. The alternative formats permissible for reporting comprehensive income.
4. The classifications of cash flows required in the statement of cash flows.

E 4–22
Concepts; terminology
● LO4–1 through LO4–9

Listed below are several terms and phrases associated with income statement presentation and the statement of cash flows. Pair each item from List A (by letter) with the item from List B that is most appropriately associated with it.

List A	List B
_____ 1. Intraperiod tax allocation	a. Unusual, infrequent, and material gains and losses.
_____ 2. Comprehensive income	b. Starts with net income and works backwards to convert to cash.
_____ 3. Extraordinary items	c. Reports the cash effects of each operating activity directly on the statement.
_____ 4. Operating income	d. Correction of a material error of a prior period.
_____ 5. A discontinued operation	e. Related to the external financing of the company.
_____ 6. Earnings per share	f. Associates tax with income statement item.
_____ 7. Prior period adjustment	g. Total nonowner change in equity.
_____ 8. Financing activities	h. Related to the transactions entering into the determination of net income.
_____ 9. Operating activities (SCF)	i. Related to the acquisition and disposition of long-term assets.
_____ 10. Investing activities	j. Required disclosure for publicly traded corporation.
_____ 11. Direct method	k. A component of an entity.
_____ 12. Indirect method	l. Directly related to principal revenue-generating activities.

CPA and CMA Review Questions

CPA Exam Questions

● LO4–4

The following questions are adapted from a variety of sources including questions developed by the AICPA Board of Examiners and those used in the Kaplan CPA Review Course to study the income statement and statement of cash flows while preparing for the CPA examination. Determine the response that best completes the statements or questions.

1. Roco Company manufactures both industrial and consumer electronics. Due to a change in its strategic focus, the company decided to exit the consumer electronics business, and in 2013 sold the division to Sunny Corporation. The consumer electronics division qualifies as a component of the entity according to GAAP. How should Roco report the sale in its 2013 income statement?
   a. Include in income from continuing operations as a nonoperating gain or loss.
   b. As an extraordinary item.
   c. As a discontinued operation, reported below income from continuing operations.
   d. None of the above.

● LO4–3, LO4–4, LO4–5

2. Bridge Company's results for the year ended December 31, 2013, include the following material items:

Sales revenue	$5,000,000
Cost of goods sold	3,000,000
Administrative expenses	1,000,000
Gain on sale of equipment	200,000
Loss on discontinued operations	400,000
Loss from earthquake damage (unusual and infrequent event)	500,000
Understatement of depreciation expense in 2012 caused by mathematical error	250,000

CHAPTER 4   The Income Statement, Comprehensive Income, and the Statement of Cash Flows   **217**

Bridge Company's income from continuing operations before income taxes for 2013 is:
a. $700,000
b. $950,000
c. $1,000,000
d. $1,200,000

● LO4–4, LO4–5   3. In Baer Food Co.'s 2013 single-step income statement, the section titled "Revenues" consisted of the following:

Net sales revenue	$187,000
Income on discontinued operations including gain on	
disposal of $21,000 and net taxes of $6,000	12,000
Interest revenue	10,200
Gain on sale of equipment	4,700
Extraordinary gain net of $750 tax effect	1,500
Total revenues	$215,400

In the revenues section of the 2013 income statement, Baer Food should have reported total revenues of
a. $201,900
b. $203,700
c. $215,400
d. $216,300

● LO4–4   4. On November 30, 2013, Pearman Company committed to a plan to sell a division that qualified as a component of the entity according to GAAP, and was properly classified as held for sale on December 31, 2013, the end of the company's fiscal year. The division was tested for impairment and a $400,000 loss was indicated. The division's loss from operations for 2013 was $1,000,000. The final sale was expected to occur on February 15, 2014. What before-tax amount(s) should Pearman report as loss on discontinued operations in its 2013 income statement?

a. $1,400,000 loss.
b. $400,000 loss.
c. None.
d. $400,000 impairment loss included in continuing operations and a $1,000,000 loss from discontinued operations.

● LO4–9   5. Which of the following items is *not* considered an operating cash flow in the statement of cash flows?
a. Dividends paid to stockholders.
b. Cash received from customers.
c. Interest paid to creditors.
d. Cash paid for salaries.

● LO4–9   6. Which of the following items is *not* considered an investing cash flow in the statement of cash flows?
a. Purchase of equipment.
b. Purchase of securities.
c. Issuing common stock for cash.
d. Sale of land.

Beginning in 2011, International Financial Reporting Standards are tested on the CPA exam along with U.S. GAAP. The following questions deal with the application of IFRS.

● LO4–10

● IFRS

7. Under *both* U.S. GAAP and IFRS, which one of the following items is reported separately in the income statement, net of tax?
a. Restructuring costs.
b. Discontinued operations.
c. Extraordinary gains and losses.
d. None of the above.

● LO4–10

● IFRS

8. In a statement of cash flows prepared under IFRS, interest paid
a. Must be classified as an operating cash flow.
b. Can be classified as either an operating cash flow or an investing cash flow.
c. Can be classified as either an operating cash flow or a financing cash flow.
d. Can be classified as either an investing cash flow or a financing cash flow.

CMA Exam Questions

The following questions dealing with the income statement are adapted from questions that previously appeared on Certified Management Accountant (CMA) examinations. The CMA designation sponsored by the Institute of Management Accountants (www.imanet.org) provides members with an objective measure of knowledge and competence in the field of management accounting. Determine the response that best completes the statements or questions.

● LO4–1

1. Which one of the following items is included in the determination of income from continuing operations?
    a. Discontinued operations.
    b. Extraordinary loss.
    c. Cumulative effect of a change in an accounting principle.
    d. Unusual loss from a write-down of inventory.

● LO4–3

2. In a multiple-step income statement for a retail company, all of the following are included in the operating section except
    a. Sales.
    b. Cost of goods sold.
    c. Dividend revenue.
    d. Administrative and selling expenses.

● LO4–5

3. When reporting extraordinary items,
    a. Each item (net of tax) is presented on the face of the income statement separately as a component of net income for the period.
    b. Each item is presented exclusive of any related income tax.
    c. Each item is presented as an unusual item within income from continuing operations.
    d. All extraordinary gains or losses that occur in a period are summarized as total gains and total losses and then offset to present the net extraordinary gain or loss.

Problems

An alternate exercise and problem set is available on the text website: www.mhhe.com/spiceland7e

P 4–1
Comparative income statements; multiple-step format

● LO4–1, LO4–3 through LO4–5, LO4–6

Selected information about income statement accounts for the Reed Company is presented below (the company's fiscal year ends on December 31):

	2013	2012
Sales	$4,400,000	$3,500,000
Cost of goods sold	2,860,000	2,000,000
Administrative expenses	800,000	675,000
Selling expenses	360,000	312,000
Interest revenue	150,000	140,000
Interest expense	200,000	200,000
Loss on sale of assets of discontinued component	50,000	—

On July 1, 2013, the company adopted a plan to discontinue a division that qualifies as a component of an entity as defined by GAAP. The assets of the component were sold on September 30, 2013, for $50,000 less than their book value. Results of operations for the component (*included* in the above account balances) were as follows:

	1/1/13–9/30/13	2012
Sales	$400,000	$500,000
Cost of goods sold	(290,000)	(320,000)
Administrative expenses	(50,000)	(40,000)
Selling expenses	(20,000)	(30,000)
Operating income before taxes	$ 40,000	$110,000

In addition to the account balances above, several events occurred during 2013 that have *not* yet been reflected in the above accounts:

1. A fire caused $50,000 in uninsured damages to the main office building. The fire was considered to be an infrequent but not unusual event.

2. An earthquake caused $100,000 in property damage to one of Reed's factories. The amount of the loss is material and the event is considered unusual and infrequent.

3. Inventory that had cost $40,000 had become obsolete because a competitor introduced a better product. The inventory was sold as scrap for $5,000.

4. Income taxes have not yet been accrued.

Required:
Prepare a multiple-step income statement for the Reed Company for 2013, showing 2012 information in comparative format, including income taxes computed at 40% and EPS disclosures assuming 300,000 shares of common stock.

CHAPTER 4   The Income Statement, Comprehensive Income, and the Statement of Cash Flows   **219**

P 4–2
Discontinued
operations
● **LO4–4**

The following condensed income statements of the Jackson Holding Company are presented for the two years ended December 31, 2013 and 2012:

	2013	2012
Sales	$15,000,000	$9,600,000
Cost of goods sold	9,200,000	6,000,000
Gross profit	5,800,000	3,600,000
Operating expenses	3,200,000	2,600,000
Operating income	2,600,000	1,000,000
Gain on sale of division	600,000	—
	3,200,000	1,000,000
Income tax expense	1,280,000	400,000
Net income	$ 1,920,000	$ 600,000

On October 15, 2013, Jackson entered into a tentative agreement to sell the assets of one of its divisions. The division qualifies as a component of an entity as defined by GAAP. The division was sold on December 31, 2013, for $5,000,000. Book value of the division's assets was $4,400,000. The division's contribution to Jackson's operating income before-tax for each year was as follows:

2013	$400,000 loss
2012	$300,000 loss

Assume an income tax rate of 40%.

Required:

1. Prepare revised income statements according to generally accepted accounting principles, beginning with income from continuing operations before income taxes. Ignore EPS disclosures.

2. Assume that by December 31, 2013, the division had not yet been sold but was considered held for sale. The fair value of the division's assets on December 31 was $5,000,000. How would the presentation of discontinued operations be different from your answer to requirement 1?

3. Assume that by December 31, 2013, the division had not yet been sold but was considered held for sale. The fair value of the division's assets on December 31 was $3,900,000. How would the presentation of discontinued operations be different from your answer to requirement 1?

P 4–3
Income
statement
presentation
● **LO4–4, LO4–5**

For the year ending December 31, 2013, Micron Corporation had income from continuing operations before taxes of $1,200,000 before considering the following transactions and events. All of the items described below are before taxes and the amounts should be considered material.

1. During 2013, one of Micron's factories was damaged in an earthquake. As a result, the firm recognized a loss of $800,000. The event is considered unusual and infrequent.

2. In November 2013, Micron sold its Waffle House restaurant chain that qualified as a component of an entity. The company had adopted a plan to sell the chain in May 2013. The income from operations of the chain from January 1, 2013, through November was $160,000 and the loss on sale of the chain's assets was $300,000.

3. In 2013, Micron sold one of its six factories for $1,200,000. At the time of the sale, the factory had a carrying value of $1,100,000. The factory was not considered a component of the entity.

4. In 2011, Micron's accountant omitted the annual adjustment for patent amortization expense of $120,000. The error was not discovered until December 2013.

Required:

1. Prepare Micron's income statement, beginning with income from continuing operations before taxes, for the year ended December 31, 2013. Assume an income tax rate of 30%. Ignore EPS disclosures.

2. Briefly explain the motivation for segregating certain income statement events from income from continuing operations.

P 4–4
Income
statement
presentation;
unusual items
● **LO4–3, LO4–5**

The preliminary 2013 income statement of Alexian Systems, Inc., is presented below:

ALEXIAN SYSTEMS, INC.
Income Statement
For the Year Ended December 31, 2013
($ in millions, except earnings per share)

Revenues and gains:	
Net sales	$ 425
Interest	3
Other income	126
Total revenues and gains	554

(continued)

220 SECTION 1 The Role of Accounting as an Information System

(concluded)

Expenses:	
Cost of goods sold	270
Selling and administrative	154
Income taxes	52
Total expenses	476
Net Income	$ 78
Earnings per share	$3.90

Additional Information:

1. Selling and administrative expenses include $26 million in restructuring costs.

2. Included in other income is an extraordinary gain of $120 million. The remaining $6 million is from the gain on sale of investments.

3. Cost of goods sold was increased by $5 million to correct an error in the calculation of 2012's ending inventory. The amount is material.

Required:
For each of the three additional facts listed above, discuss the appropriate presentation of the item described. Do not prepare a revised statement.

P 4–5
Income statement presentation; unusual items
● LO4–1, LO4–3, LO4–5, LO4–6

[This is a variation of the previous problem focusing on income statement presentation.]

Required:
Refer to the information presented in Problem 4–4. Prepare a revised income statement for 2013 reflecting the additional facts. Use a multiple-step format. Assume that an income tax rate of 40% applies to all income statement items, and that 20 million shares of common stock were outstanding throughout the year.

P 4–6
Income statement presentation
● LO4–1, LO4–3 through LO4–5, LO4–6

Rembrandt Paint Company had the following income statement items for the year ended December 31, 2013 ($ in 000s):

Net sales	$18,000	Cost of goods sold	$10,500
Interest income	200	Selling and administrative expenses	2,500
Interest expense	350	Restructuring costs	800
Extraordinary gain	3,000		

In addition, during the year the company completed the disposal of its plastics business and incurred a loss from operations of $1.6 million and a gain on disposal of the component's assets of $2 million. 500,000 shares of common stock were outstanding throughout 2013. Income tax expense has not yet been accrued. The income tax rate is 30% on all items of income (loss).

Required:
Prepare a multiple-step income statement for 2013, including EPS disclosures.

P 4–7
Income statement presentation; statement of comprehensive income; unusual items
● LO4–1, LO4–3, LO4–4, LO4–5, LO4–6, LO4–7

The following income statement items appeared on the adjusted trial balance of Schembri Manufacturing Corporation for the year ended December 31, 2013 ($ in 000s): sales revenue, $15,300; cost of goods sold, $6,200; selling expenses, $1,300; general and administrative expenses, $800; interest revenue, $85; interest expense, $180. Income taxes have not yet been accrued. The company's income tax rate is 40% on all items of income or loss. These revenue and expense items appear in the company's income statement every year. The company's controller, however, has asked for your help in determining the appropriate treatment of the following nonrecurring transactions that also occurred during 2013 ($ in 000s). All transactions are material in amount.

1. Investments were sold during the year at a loss of $220. Schembri also had unrealized gains of $320 for the year on investments.

2. One of the company's factories was closed during the year. Restructuring costs incurred were $1,200.

3. An earthquake destroyed a warehouse causing $2,000 in damages. The event is considered to be unusual and infrequent.

4. During the year, Schembri completed the sale of one of its operating divisions that qualifies as a component of the entity according to GAAP. The division had incurred a loss from operations of $560 in 2013 prior to the sale, and its assets were sold at a gain of $1,400.

5. In 2013, the company's accountant discovered that depreciation expense in 2012 for the office building was understated by $200.

6. Foreign currency translation losses for the year totaled $240.

CHAPTER 4   The Income Statement, Comprehensive Income, and the Statement of Cash Flows   **221**

Required:
1. Prepare Schembri's single, continuous multiple-step statement of comprehensive income for 2013, including basic earnings per share disclosures. One million shares of common stock were outstanding at the beginning of the year and an additional 400,000 shares were issued on July 1, 2013.
2. Prepare a separate statement of comprehensive income for 2013.

P 4–8
Multiple-step
statement of
income and
comprehensive
income
● LO4–1, LO4–3,
LO4–5, LO4–7

e**X**cel

Duke Company's records show the following account balances at December 31, 2013:

Sales	$15,000,000
Cost of goods sold	9,000,000
General and administrative expenses	1,000,000
Selling expenses	500,000
Interest expense	700,000

Income tax expense has not yet been determined. The following events also occurred during 2013. All transactions are material in amount.
1. $300,000 in restructuring costs were incurred in connection with plant closings.
2. The company operates a factory in South America. During the year, the foreign government took over (expropriated) the factory and paid Duke $1,000,000, which was one-fourth of the book value of the assets involved. The factory is not a component of the entity and the event is considered to be unusual and infrequent.
3. Inventory costing $400,000 was written off as obsolete. Material losses of this type are not considered to be unusual.
4. It was discovered that depreciation expense for 2012 was understated by $50,000 due to a mathematical error.
5. The company experienced a foreign currency translation adjustment loss of $200,000 and had unrealized gains on investments of $180,000.

Required:
Prepare a single, continuous multiple-step statement of comprehensive income for 2013. The company's effective tax rate on all items affecting comprehensive income is 40%. Each component of other comprehensive income should be displayed net of tax. Ignore EPS disclosures.

P 4–9
Statement of
cash flows
● LO4–9

The Diversified Portfolio Corporation provides investment advice to customers. A condensed income statement for the year ended December 31, 2013, appears below:

Service revenue	$900,000
Operating expenses	700,000
Income before income taxes	200,000
Income tax expense	80,000
Net income	$120,000

The following balance sheet information also is available:

	12/31/13	12/31/12
Cash	$275,000	$ 70,000
Accounts receivable	120,000	100,000
Accounts payable (operating expenses)	70,000	60,000
Income taxes payable	10,000	15,000

In addition, the following transactions took place during the year:
1. Common stock was issued for $100,000 in cash.
2. Long-term investments were sold for $50,000 in cash. The original cost of the investments also was $50,000.
3. $80,000 in cash dividends was paid to shareholders.
4. The company has no outstanding debt, other than those payables listed above.
5. Operating expenses include $30,000 in depreciation expense.

Required:
1. Prepare a statement of cash flows for 2013 for the Diversified Portfolio Corporation. Use the direct method for reporting operating activities.
2. Prepare the cash flows from operating activities section of Diversified's 2013 statement of cash flows using the indirect method.

P 4–10
Integration
of financial
statements;
Chapters 3 and 4
● LO4–9

The chief accountant for Grandview Corporation provides you with the company's 2013 statement of cash flows and income statement. The accountant has asked for your help with some missing figures in the company's comparative balance sheets. These financial statements are shown next ($ in millions).

GRANDVIEW CORPORATION
Statement of Cash Flows
For the Year Ended December 31, 2013

Cash Flows from Operating Activities:		
Collections from customers	$71	
Payment to suppliers	(30)	
Payment of general & administrative expenses	(18)	
Payment of income taxes	(9)	
Net cash flows from operating activities		$14
Cash Flows from Investing Activities:		
Sale of investments		65
Cash Flows from Financing Activities:		
Issuance of common stock	10	
Payment of dividends	(3)	
Net cash flows from financing activities		7
Net increase in cash		$86

GRANDVIEW CORPORATION
Income Statement
For the Year Ended December 31, 2013

Sales revenue		$80
Cost of goods sold		32
Gross profit		48
Operating expenses:		
General and administrative	$18	
Depreciation	10	
Total operating expenses		28
Operating income		20
Other income:		
Gain on sale of investments		15
Income before income taxes		35
Income tax expense		7
Net income		$28

GRANDVIEW CORPORATION
Balance Sheets
At December 31

	2013	2012
Assets:		
Cash	$145	$?
Accounts receivable	?	84
Investments	—	50
Inventory	60	?
Property, plant & equipment	150	150
Less: Accumulated depreciation	(65)	?
Total assets	?	?
Liabilities and Shareholders' Equity:		
Accounts payable to suppliers	$ 40	$ 30
Payables for selling & admin. expenses	9	9
Income taxes payable	22	?
Common stock	240	230
Retained earnings	?	47
Total liabilities and shareholders' equity	?	?

CHAPTER 4   The Income Statement, Comprehensive Income, and the Statement of Cash Flows   **223**

Required:
1. Calculate the missing amounts.
2. Prepare the operating activities section of Grandview's 2013 statement of cash flows using the indirect method.

P 4–11
Statement of
cash flows;
indirect method
● LO4–9

Presented below are the 2013 income statement and comparative balance sheets for Santana Industries.

SANTANA INDUSTRIES
Income Statement
For the Year Ended December 31, 2013
($ in thousands)

Sales revenue	$14,250	
Service revenue	3,400	
Total revenue		$17,650
Operating expenses:		
Cost of goods sold	7,200	
Selling	2,400	
General and administrative	1,500	
Total operating expenses		11,100
Operating income		6,550
Interest expense		200
Income before income taxes		6,350
Income tax expense		2,500
Net income		$ 3,850

Balance Sheet Information ($ in thousands)	Dec. 31, 2013	Dec. 31, 2012
Assets:		
Cash	$ 7,350	$ 2,200
Accounts receivable	2,500	2,200
Inventory	4,000	3,000
Prepaid rent	150	300
Plant and equipment	14,500	12,000
Less: Accumulated depreciation	(5,100)	(4,500)
Total assets	$23,400	$15,200
Liabilities and Shareholders' Equity:		
Accounts payable	$ 1,400	$ 1,100
Interest payable	100	0
Unearned service revenue	800	600
Income taxes payable	550	800
Loan payable (due 12/31/2012)	5,000	0
Common stock	10,000	10,000
Retained earnings	5,550	2,700
Total liabilities and shareholders' equity	$23,400	$15,200

Additional information for the 2013 fiscal year ($ in thousands):
1. Cash dividends of $1,000 were declared and paid.
2. Equipment costing $4,000 was purchased with cash.
3. Equipment with a book value of $500 (cost of $1,500 less accumulated depreciation of $1,000) was sold for $500.
4. Depreciation of $1,600 is included in operating expenses.

Required:
Prepare Santana Industries' 2013 statement of cash flows, using the indirect method to present cash flows from operating activities.

Broaden Your Perspective

Apply your critical-thinking ability to the knowledge you've gained. These cases will provide you an opportunity to develop your research, analysis, judgment, and communication skills. You also will work with other students, integrate what you've learned, apply it in real world situations, and consider its global and ethical ramifications. This practice will broaden your knowledge and further develop your decision-making abilities.

Judgment Case 4–1
Earnings quality
● LO4–2, LO4–3

The financial community in the United States has become increasingly concerned with the quality of reported company earnings.

Required:

1. Define the term *earnings quality*.
2. Explain the distinction between permanent and transitory earnings as it relates to the concept of earnings quality.
3. How do earnings management practices affect the quality of earnings?
4. Assume that a manufacturing company's annual income statement included a large gain from the sale of investment securities. What factors would you consider in determining whether or not this gain should be included in an assessment of the company's permanent earnings?

Judgment Case 4–2
Restructuring costs
● LO4–3

The appearance of restructuring costs in corporate income statements increased significantly in the 1980s and 1990s and continues to be relevant today.

Required:

1. What types of costs are included in restructuring costs?
2. When are restructuring costs recognized?
3. How would you classify restructuring costs in a multi-step income statement?
4. What factors would you consider in determining whether or not restructuring costs should be included in an assessment of a company's permanent earnings?

Judgment Case 4–3
Earnings management
● LO4–2, LO4–3

Companies often are under pressure to meet or beat Wall Street earnings projections in order to increase stock prices and also to increase the value of stock options. Some resort to earnings management practices to artificially create desired results.

Required:

Is *earnings management* always intended to produce higher income? Explain.

Real World Case 4–4
Earnings quality and pro forma earnings
● LO4–3

Companies often voluntarily provide a pro forma earnings number when they announce annual or quarterly earnings.

Required:

1. What is meant by the term *pro forma earnings* in this context?
2. How do pro forma earnings relate to the concept of earnings quality?

Communication Case 4–5
Income statement presentation of gain
● LO4–5

McMinville Corporation manufactures paper products. In 2009, the company purchased several large tracts of timber for $22 million with the intention of harvesting the timber rather than buying this critical raw material from outside suppliers. However, in 2013, McMinville abandoned the idea and all of the timber tracts were sold for $31 million. Net income for 2013, before considering this event, is $17.5 million and the company's effective tax rate is 30%.

The focus of this case is the income statement presentation of the gain on the sale of the timber tracts. Your instructor will divide the class into two to six groups depending on the size of the class. The mission of your group is to reach consensus on the appropriate income statement presentation of the gain.

Required:

Each group member should deliberate the situation independently and draft a tentative argument prior to the class session for which the case is assigned.

In class, each group will meet for 10 to 15 minutes in different areas of the classroom. During that meeting, group members will take turns sharing their suggestions for the purpose of arriving at a single group treatment.

After the allotted time, a spokesperson for each group (selected during the group meetings) will share the group's solution with the class. The goal of the class is to incorporate the views of each group into a consensus approach to the situation.

Communication Case 4–6
Income statement presentation
● LO4–5

Real World Financials

Carter Hawley Hale Stores (CHHS), Inc., was one of the largest department store retailers in the United States. At the end of fiscal 1989, the company operated 113 stores in the Sunbelt regions of the country. The company's divisions included The Broadway, with 43 stores in Southern California and 11 stores in the southwest, and Emporium, with 22 stores in the greater San Francisco Bay Area.

On October 17, 1989, a 7.1 Richter scale earthquake caused significant amounts of monetary damage to the San Francisco Bay Area. This was the largest earthquake to hit the Bay Area since the quake of 1906 destroyed much of San Francisco. California is lined with many active earthquake faults. Hundreds of small earthquakes occur each year throughout the state.

CHAPTER 4   The Income Statement, Comprehensive Income, and the Statement of Cash Flows   **225**

The Emporium division of CHHS suffered extensive damage as a result of the October 17 earthquake. Twelve of the twenty-two stores were closed for varying periods of time, with the Oakland store hardest hit. In total, uninsured damage was $27.5 million ($16.5 million after tax benefits).

For the fiscal year ending August 4, 1990, CHHS reported an after-tax loss of $9.47 million *before* considering the earthquake loss. Total revenues for the year were $2.857 billion.

Required:

Assume that you are the CHHS controller. The chief financial officer of CHHS has asked you to prepare a short report (1–2 pages) in memo form giving your recommendation as to the proper reporting of the earthquake damage costs in the income statement for the year ending August 4, 1990. Explain why your recommendation is appropriate. Be sure to include in your report any references to authoritative pronouncements that support your recommendation.

Ethics Case 4–7
Income statement presentation of unusual loss
● LO4–3, LO4–5

After a decade of consistent income growth, the Cranor Corporation sustained a before-tax loss of $8.4 million in 2013. The loss was primarily due to $10 million in expenses related to a product recall. Cranor manufactures medical equipment, including x-ray machines. The recall was attributable to a design flaw in the manufacture of the company's new line of machines.

The company controller, Jim Dietz, has suggested that the loss should be included in the 2013 income statement as an extraordinary item. "If we report it as an extraordinary item, our income from continuing operations will actually show an increase from the prior year. The stock market will appreciate the continued growth in ongoing profitability and will discount the one-time loss. And our bonuses are tied to income from continuing operations, not net income."

The chief executive officer asked Jim to justify this treatment. "I know we have had product recalls before and, of course, they do occur in our industry," Jim replied, "but we have never had a recall of this magnitude, and we fixed the design flaw and upgraded our quality control procedures."

Required:

Discuss the ethical dilemma faced by Jim Dietz and the company's chief executive officer.

Research Case 4–8
FASB codification; locate and extract relevant information and cite authoritative support for a financial reporting issue; restructuring costs; exit or disposal cost obligations
● LO4–2, LO4–3

The accrual of restructuring costs creates obligations (liabilities) referred to as *exit or disposal cost obligations*.

Required:

1. Obtain the relevant authoritative literature on exit or disposal cost obligations using the FASB's Codification Research System. You might gain access at the FASB website (www.fasb.org). What is the Codification topic number that addresses this issue?
2. What is the specific citation that addresses the initial measurement of these obligations?
3. How are these obligations and related costs to be measured?
4. What is the specific citation that describes the disclosure requirements in the notes to the financial statements for exit or disposal obligations?
5. List the required disclosures.

Judgment Case 4–9
Income statement presentation
● LO4–3 through LO4–5

Each of the following situations occurred during 2013 for one of your audit clients:
1. The write-off of inventory due to obsolescence.
2. Discovery that depreciation expenses were omitted by accident from 2012's income statement.
3. The useful lives of all machinery were changed from eight to five years.
4. The depreciation method used for all equipment was changed from the declining-balance to the straight-line method.
5. Ten million dollars face value of bonds payable were repurchased (paid off) prior to maturity resulting in a material loss of $500,000. The company considers the event unusual and infrequent.
6. Restructuring costs were incurred.
7. The Stridewell Company, a manufacturer of shoes, sold all of its retail outlets. It will continue to manufacture and sell its shoes to other retailers. A loss was incurred in the disposition of the retail stores. The retail stores are considered a component of the entity.
8. The inventory costing method was changed from FIFO to average cost.

Required:

1. For each situation, identify the appropriate reporting treatment from the list below (consider each event to be material):

    a. As an extraordinary item.

    b. As an unusual or infrequent gain or loss.

    c. As a prior period adjustment.

    d. As a change in accounting principle.

    e. As a discontinued operation.

    f. As a change in accounting estimate.

    g. As a change in accounting estimate achieved by a change in accounting principle.

2. Indicate whether each situation would be included in the income statement in continuing operations (CO) or below continuing operations (BC), or if it would appear as an adjustment to retained earnings (RE). Use the format shown below to answer requirements 1 and 2.

Situation	Treatment (a–g)	Financial Statement Presentation (CO, BC, or RE)
1.		
2.		
3.		
4.		
5.		
6.		
7.		
8.		

Judgment Case 4–10
Income statement presentation
● LO4–3 through LO4–5

The following events occurred during 2013 for various audit clients of your firm. Consider each event to be independent and the effect of each event to be material.

1. A manufacturing company recognized a loss on the sale of investments.

2. An automobile manufacturer sold all of the assets related to its financing component. The operations of the financing business is considered a component of the entity.

3. A company changed its depreciation method from the double-declining-balance method to the straight-line method.

4. Due to obsolescence, a company engaged in the manufacture of high-technology products incurred a loss on the write-down of inventory.

5. One of your clients discovered that 2012's depreciation expense was overstated. The error occurred because of a miscalculation of depreciation for the office building.

6. A cosmetics company decided to discontinue the manufacture of a line of women's lipstick. Other cosmetic lines will be continued. A loss was incurred on the sale of assets related to the lipstick product line. The operations of the discontinued line is not considered a component of the entity.

Required:

Discuss the 2013 financial statement presentation of each of the above events. Do not consider earnings per share disclosures.

IFRS Case 4–11
Statement of cash flows; GlaxoSmithKline Plc.
● LO4–9, LO4–10

 IFRS

GlaxoSmithKline Plc. (GSK) is a global pharmaceutical and consumer health-related products company located in the United Kingdom. The company prepares its financial statements in accordance with International Financial Reporting Standards. Below is a portion of the company's statements of cash flows included in recent financial statements:

Real World Financials

		GLAXOSMITHKLINE PLC. Consolidated Statements of Cash Flows (in part) For the Years Ended December 31		
	Notes	2010 £m	2009 £m	2008 £m
Cash flow from investing activities				
Purchase of property, plant and equipment		(1,014)	(1,418)	(1,437)
Proceeds from sale of property, plant and equipment		92	48	20
Purchase of intangible assets		(621)	(455)	(632)
Proceeds from sale of intangible assets		126	356	171

(continued)

CHAPTER 4   The Income Statement, Comprehensive Income, and the Statement of Cash Flows   **227**

(concluded)

Purchase of equity investments			(279)	(154)	(87)
Proceeds from sale of equity investments		27	59	42
Share transactions with minority shareholders				
Purchase of businesses, net of cash acquired	38	(354)	(2,792)	(454)
Disposal of businesses and interest in associates		—	178	—
Investments in associates and joint ventures	38	(61)	(29)	(9)
Decrease/(increase) in liquid investments		91	87	905
Interest received		107	90	320
Dividends from associates and joint ventures		18	17	12
Net cash outflow from investing activities		(1,868)	(4,013)	(1,149)
Cash flow from financing activities				
Proceeds from own shares for employee share options		17	13	9
Shares acquired by ESOP Trusts		(16)	(57)	(19)
Issue of share capital	33	62	43	62
Purchase of own shares for cancellation		—	—	(3,706)
Purchase of Treasury shares				
Increase in long-term loans		—	1,358	5,523
Repayment of long-term loans				
Net (repayment of)/increase in short-term loans				
Net repayment of obligations under finance leases		(45)	(48)	(48)
Interest paid		(775)	(780)	(730)
Dividends paid to shareholders		(3,205)	(3,003)	(2,929)
Dividends paid to minority interests				
Other financing cash flows		(201)	(109)	68
Net cash outflow from financing activities		(5,571)	(2,774)	(4,908)
Increase/(decrease) in cash and bank overdrafts	37	(642)	1,054	1,148

Required:

Identify the items in the above statements that would be reported differently if GlaxoSmithKline prepared its financial statements according to U.S. GAAP rather than IFRS.

Judgment Case 4–12
Income statement presentation; unusual items; comprehensive income

● LO4–3 through LO4–5, LO4–7

Norse Manufacturing Inc. prepares an annual single, continuous statement of income and comprehensive income. The following situations occurred during the company's 2013 fiscal year:

1. Restructuring costs were incurred due to the closing of a factory.
2. Investments were sold, and a loss was recognized.
3. Gains from foreign currency translation were recognized.
4. Interest expense was incurred.
5. A division was sold that qualifies as a separate component of the entity according to GAAP.
6. Obsolete inventory was written off.
7. The controller discovered an error in the calculation of 2012's patent amortization expense.
8. A volcano destroyed a storage facility on a South Sea island. The event is considered to be unusual and infrequent in occurrence.

Required:

1. For each situation, identify the appropriate reporting treatment from the list below (consider each event to be material).
    a. As a component of operating income.
    b. As a nonoperating income item (other income or expense).
    c. As a separately reported item.
    d. As an other comprehensive income item.
    e. As an adjustment to retained earnings.
2. Identify the situations that would be reported net-of-tax.

Judgment Case 4–13
Management incentives for change

● LO4–2

It has been suggested that not all accounting choices are made by management in the best interest of fair and consistent financial reporting.

Required:

What motivations can you think of for management's choice of accounting methods?

Research Case 4–14
Pro forma earnings
● **LO4–3**

Companies often voluntarily provide a pro forma earnings number when they announce annual or quarterly earnings. These pro forma earnings numbers are controversial as they represent management's view of permanent earnings. The Sarbanes-Oxley Act (SOX), issued in 2002, requires that if pro forma earnings are included in any periodic or other report filed with the SEC or in any public disclosure or press release, the company also must provide a reconciliation with earnings determined according to GAAP.

Professors Entwistle, Feltham, and Mbagwu, in "Financial Reporting Regulation and the Reporting of Pro Forma Earnings," examine whether firms changed their reporting practice in response to the pro forma regulations included in SOX.

Required:

1. In your library or from some other source, locate the indicated article in *Accounting Horizons*, March 2006.
2. What sample of firms did the authors use in their examination?
3. What percent of firms reported pro forma earnings in 2001? In 2003?
4. What percent of firms had pro forma earnings greater than GAAP earnings in 2001? In 2003?
5. What was the most frequently reported adjusting item in 2001? In 2003?
6. What are the authors' main conclusions of the impact of SOX on pro forma reporting?

Integrating Case 4–15
Balance sheet and income statement; Chapters 3 and 4
● **LO4–3, LO4–5**

Rice Corporation is negotiating a loan for expansion purposes and the bank requires financial statements. Before closing the accounting records for the year ended December 31, 2013, Rice's controller prepared the following financial statements:

RICE CORPORATION
Balance Sheet
At December 31, 2013
($ in 000s)

Assets	
Cash	$ 275
Marketable securities	78
Accounts receivable	487
Inventories	425
Allowance for uncollectible accounts	(50)
Property and equipment, net	160
Total assets	$1,375

Liabilities and Shareholders' Equity	
Accounts payable and accrued liabilities	$ 420
Notes payable	200
Common stock	260
Retained earnings	495
Total liabilities and shareholders' equity	$1,375

RICE CORPORATION
Income Statement
For the Year Ended December 31, 2013
($ in 000s)

Net sales		$1,580
Expenses:		
Cost of goods sold	$755	
Selling and administrative	385	
Miscellaneous	129	
Income taxes	100	
Total expenses		1,369
Net income		$ 211

Additional Information:

1. The company's common stock is traded on an organized stock exchange.
2. The investment portfolio consists of short-term investments valued at $57,000. The remaining investments will not be sold until the year 2015.
3. Miscellaneous expense represents the before-tax loss from damages caused by an earthquake. The event is considered to be both unusual and infrequent.
4. Notes payable consist of two notes:

   Note 1: $80,000 face value dated September 30, 2013. Principal and interest at 10% are due on September 30, 2014.

CHAPTER 4   The Income Statement, Comprehensive Income, and the Statement of Cash Flows   **229**

Note 2: $120,000 face value dated April 30, 2013. Principal is due in two equal installments of $60,000 plus interest on the unpaid balance. The two payments are scheduled for April 30, 2014, and April 30, 2015.

Interest on both loans has been correctly accrued and is included in accrued liabilities on the balance sheet and selling and administrative expenses on the income statement.

5. Selling and administrative expenses include a $90,000 charge incurred by the company in restructuring some of its operations. The amount of the charge is material.

Required:

Identify and explain the deficiencies in the presentation of the statements prepared by the company's controller. Do not prepare corrected statements. Include in your answer a list of items which require additional disclosure, either on the face of the statement or in a note.

**Analysis
Case 4–16**
Income statement information
● LO4–1

Refer to the income statements of Dell Inc. included in the company's financial statements in Appendix B at the back of the text.

Required:

1. What was the percentage increase or decrease in the company's net income from 2010 to 2011? From 2009 to 2010?
2. Using 2011 data, what is the company's approximate income tax rate?
3. Using 2011 data, what is the percentage of net income relative to revenue dollars?

**Real World
Case 4–17**
Income statement information
● LO4–1, LO4–3 through LO4–5

Real World Financials

EDGAR, the Electronic Data Gathering, Analysis, and Retrieval system, performs automated collection, validation, indexing, and forwarding of submissions by companies and others who are required by law to file forms with the U.S. Securities and Exchange Commission (SEC). All publicly traded domestic companies use EDGAR to make the majority of their filings. (Some foreign companies file voluntarily.) Form 10-K, which includes the annual report, is required to be filed on EDGAR. The SEC makes this information available on the Internet.

Required:

1. Access EDGAR on the Internet. The web address is www.sec.gov.
2. Search for a public company with which you are familiar. Access the most recent 10-K filing. Search or scroll to find the financial statements and related notes.
3. Answer the following questions related to the company's income statement:
    a. Does the company use the single-step or multiple-step format, or a variation?
    b. Does the income statement contain any separately reported items in any year presented (discontinued operation or extraordinary item)? If it does, describe the event that caused the item. (Hint: there should be a related disclosure note.)
    c. Describe the trend in net income over the years presented.
4. Repeat requirements 2 and 3 for two additional companies.

Air France–KLM Case

AIRFRANCE ✈

● LO4–10

Air France–KLM (AF), a French company, prepares its financial statements according to International Financial Reporting Standards. AF's annual report for the year ended March 31, 2011, which includes financial statements and disclosure notes, is provided with all new textbooks. This material also is included in AF's "Registration Document 2010–11," dated June 15, 2011 and is available at www.airfranceklm.com.

Required:

1. How does AF classify operating expenses in its income statement? How are these expenses typically classified in a U.S. company income statement?
2. How does AF classify interest paid, interest received, and dividends received in its statement of cash flows? What other alternatives, if any, does the company have for the classification of these items? How are these items classified under U.S. GAAP?

CPA Simulation 4–1

Bart Company
Income statement presentation

CPA Review

Test your knowledge of the concepts discussed in this chapter, practice critical professional skills necessary for career success, and prepare for the computer-based CPA exam by accessing our CPA simulations at the text website: www.mhhe.com/spiceland7e.

The Bart Company simulation tests your knowledge of the contents and presentation of the income statement.

CHAPTER

5 Income Measurement and Profitability Analysis

OVERVIEW — The focus of this chapter is revenue recognition. We first discuss the general circumstance in which revenue is recognized when a good or service is delivered. Then we discuss circumstances in which revenue should be deferred until after delivery or should be recognized prior to delivery. The chapter also includes an Appendix describing requirements for interim financial reporting and a Where We're Headed Supplement explaining in detail a proposed Accounting Standards Update (hereafter, "the proposed ASU") that the FASB and IASB plan to issue in 2012 that substantially changes how we account for revenue recognition.

LEARNING OBJECTIVES — **After studying this chapter, you should be able to:**

- **LO5–1** Discuss the timing of revenue recognition, list the two general criteria that must be satisfied before revenue can be recognized, and explain why these criteria usually are satisfied when products or services are delivered. (p. 232)

- **LO5–2** Discuss the principal/agent distinction that determines the amount of revenue to record. (p. 237)

- **LO5–3** Describe the installment sales and cost recovery methods of recognizing revenue and explain the unusual conditions under which these methods might be used. (p. 239)

- **LO5–4** Discuss the implications for revenue recognition of allowing customers the right of return. (p. 243)

- **LO5–5** Identify situations requiring recognition of revenue over time and demonstrate the percentage-of-completion and completed contract methods of recognizing revenue for long-term contracts. (p. 244)

- **LO5–6** Discuss the revenue recognition issues involving multiple-deliverable contracts, software, and franchise sales. (pp. 258 and 260)

- **LO5–7** Identify and calculate the common ratios used to assess profitability. (p. 263)

- **LO5–8** Discuss the primary differences between U.S. GAAP and IFRS with respect to revenue recognition. (pp. 235, 255, 260, 262 and 272)

FINANCIAL REPORTING CASE

You Don't Have to Be a Rocket Scientist

"Good news! I got the job," she said, closing the door behind her.

Your sister, an aerospace engineer, goes on to explain that she accepted a position at Lockheed Martin Corporation, a world leader in the design, development, manufacture, and servicing of aircraft, spacecraft and launch vehicles, missiles, electronics, and information and telecommunication systems. She will supervise a long-term government contract beginning Tuesday.

"I got the salary I was asking for too," she continued. "Mr. Watson, my supervisor, also said I'll be getting a bonus tied to the gross profit on the project. It didn't hit me until I left his office, though, that this project will take two and a half years to complete. I hope I don't have to wait that long to get my bonus." Pointing to a page where she's circled part of a disclosure note, your sister hands you Lockheed's annual report. "I can't believe they wait that long to record income on all these multiyear projects. You're the accountant in the family; is that what this note is telling us?"

Sales and earnings (in part)
We record net sales and estimated profits on a percentage-of-completion (POC) basis for cost reimbursable and fixed-price design, development, and production (DD&P) contracts. . . .

By the time you finish this chapter, you should be able to respond appropriately to the questions posed in this case. Compare your response to the solution provided at the end of the chapter.

— **QUESTIONS**

1. Does your sister have to wait two and a half years to get her bonus? Explain. *(p. 238)*
2. How are gross profits recognized using the percentage-of-completion method? *(p. 245)*
3. Are there other situations in which revenue is recognized at times other than when a product is delivered? *(p. 248)*

| PART **A** | # REVENUE RECOGNITION |

In Chapter 4 we discussed the *nature of income* and its presentation in the income statement. In this chapter we turn our attention to the *measurement* of periodic accounting income. Of primary interest here is the timing of revenue recognition.

What is revenue? According to the FASB, "Revenues are inflows or other enhancements of assets of an entity or settlements of its liabilities (or a combination of both) from delivering or producing goods, rendering services, or other activities that constitute the entity's ongoing major or central operations."[1] In other words, revenue tracks the inflow of net assets that occurs when a business provides goods or services to its customers.

Why is the timing of revenue recognition so important? An income statement should report the results of operations only for the time period specified in the report. That is, a one-year income statement should report the company's accomplishments and sacrifices (revenues and expenses) only for that one-year period.[2] Revenue recognition criteria help ensure that a proper cutoff is made each period and that no more than one year's activity is reported in the annual income statement. Revenues reflect positive inflows from activities that eventually generate cash flows. By comparing these activity levels period to period, a user can better assess future activities and thus future cash flows.

Our objective, then, is to recognize revenue in the period or periods that the revenue-generating activities of the company are performed. But we also must consider that recognizing revenue presumes that an asset (usually cash) has been received or will be received in exchange for the goods or services sold. Our judgment as to the collectibility of the cash from the sale of a product or service will, therefore, affect the timing of revenue recognition. These two concepts of performance and collectibility are captured by the general guidelines for revenue recognition in the realization principle.

> Revenue recognition criteria help ensure that an income statement reflects the actual accomplishments of a company for the period.

● LO5–1   The **realization principle** requires that two criteria be satisfied before revenue can be recognized (recorded):[3]

1. The earnings process is judged to be complete or virtually complete (the earnings process refers to the activity or activities performed by the company to generate revenue).

2. There is reasonable certainty as to the collectibility of the asset to be received (usually cash).

Even with these guidelines, revenue recognition continues to be a controversial issue. Premature revenue recognition reduces the quality of reported earnings, particularly if those revenues never materialize. Many sad stories have surfaced involving companies forced to revise earnings numbers downward due to a restatement of revenues. The case of Krispy Kreme Doughnuts offers a prime example. In January 2005, the company announced that it would be restating its earnings for the last three quarters of fiscal 2004. Investors were already alarmed by the recent filing of a lawsuit that alleged the company routinely padded sales by doubling shipments to wholesale customers at the end of the quarter. In the two-day period following the announced restatement, the company's stock price dropped over 20% in value!

> **Arthur Levitt, Jr.**
> Lastly, companies try to boost earnings by manipulating the recognition of revenue. Think about a bottle of fine wine. You wouldn't pop the cork on that bottle before it was ready. But some companies are doing this with their revenue . . .[4]

---

[1]"Elements of Financial Statements," *Statement of Financial Concepts No. 6* (Stamford, Conn.: FASB, 1985, par. 78).

[2]In addition to reporting on an annual basis, companies often provide information quarterly and, on occasion, monthly. The SEC requires its registrants to provide information on a quarterly and annual basis. This information, referred to as *interim financial statements*, pertains to any financial report covering a period of less than one year. The key accounting issues related to the presentation of interim statements are discussed in Appendix 5.

[3]These criteria are addressed in SFAC 5, "Recognition and Measurement in Financial Statements," *Statement of Financial Accounting Concepts No. 5* (Stamford, Conn.: FASB, 1984).

[4]Arthur Levitt, Jr., "The Numbers Game," *The CPA Journal*, December 1998, p. 18.

As part of its crackdown on earnings management, the SEC issued additional guidance, summarized in *Staff Accounting Bulletin (SAB) No. 101* and later in *SAB No. 104,*[5] indicating the SEC's views on revenue. The *SABs* provide additional criteria for judging whether or not the realization principle is satisfied:

1. Persuasive evidence of an arrangement exists.
2. Delivery has occurred or services have been rendered.
3. The seller's price to the buyer is fixed or determinable.
4. Collectibility is reasonably assured.

In addition to these four criteria, the *SABs* also pose a number of revenue recognition questions relating to each of the criteria. The questions provide the facts of the scenario and then the SEC offers its interpretive response. These responses and supporting explanations provide guidance to companies with similar revenue recognition issues. For example, the following question relates to the delivery and performance criteria necessary to recognize revenue on a transaction commonly referred to as a "Bill and Hold" sale:

Facts: Company A receives purchase orders for products it manufactures. At the end of its fiscal quarters, customers may not yet be ready to take delivery of the products for various reasons. These reasons may include, but are not limited to, a lack of available space for inventory, having more than sufficient inventory in their distribution channel, or delays in customers' production schedules.

Questions: May Company A recognize revenue for the sale of its products once it has completed manufacturing if it segregates the inventory of the products in its own warehouse from its own products? May Company A recognize revenue for the sale if it ships the products to a third-party warehouse but (1) Company A retains title to the product and (2) payment by the customer is dependent upon ultimate delivery to a customer-specified site?

How would you answer these questions? The SEC's response is that, generally, revenue should not be recognized upon shipment to a third-party warehouse. Delivery generally is not considered to have occurred unless the end customer takes title and assumes the risk and rewards of ownership of the specific products in the customer's purchase order or sales agreement. Typically this occurs when a product is delivered to the customer's delivery site and accepted by the customer.[6]

Soon after *SAB No. 101* was issued, many companies changed their revenue recognition methods. In most cases, the changes resulted in a deferral of revenue recognition. As a case in point, consider the change made by Brown & Sharpe Manufacturing Company, a multinational manufacturer of metrology products, described in a disclosure note, displayed in Illustration 5–1.

2. Accounting Change (in part)
In 2000, the Company adopted *SEC Staff Accounting Bulletin No. 101 (SAB 101)*. As a result of adopting *SAB 101*, the Company changed the way it recognizes revenue for machines sold to customers. Prior to the adoption of *SAB 101*, the Company recognized revenue when the machines were shipped and title passed to the customer. Effective as of January 1, 2001, the Company recognizes revenue for machines sold to customers once the performance of machines is accepted by the customers.

Illustration 5–1

Disclosure of Change in Revenue Recognition Policy—Brown & Sharpe Manufacturing Company

Real World Financials

Although this example relates to product delivery, much of *SAB 101* and *104* are related to service revenue. We discuss some of these issues later in the chapter.

---

[5]FASB ASC 605–10–S99: Revenue Recognition–Overall–SEC Materials (originally "Revenue Recognition in Financial Statements," *Staff Accounting Bulletin No. 101* (Washington, D.C.: SEC, December 1999) and *Staff Accounting Bulletin No. 104* (Washington, D.C.: SEC, December 2003)).
[6]Ibid., p. 5.

Ethical Dilemma

The Precision Parts Corporation manufactures automobile parts. The company has reported a profit every year since the company's inception in 1980. Management prides itself on this accomplishment and believes one important contributing factor is the company's incentive plan that rewards top management a bonus equal to a percentage of operating income *if the operating income goal for the year is achieved*. However, 2013 has been a tough year, and prospects for attaining the income goal for the year are bleak.

Tony Smith, the company's chief financial officer, has determined a way to increase December sales by an amount sufficient to boost operating income over the goal for the year and earn bonuses for all top management. A reputable customer ordered $120,000 of parts to be shipped on January 15, 2014. Tony told the rest of top management "I know we can get that order ready by December 31 even though it will require some production line overtime. We can then just leave the order on the loading dock until shipment. I see nothing wrong with recognizing the sale in 2013, since the parts will have been manufactured and we do have a firm order from a reputable customer." The company's normal procedure is to ship goods f.o.b. destination and to recognize sales revenue when the customer receives the parts.

Illustration 5–2 relates various revenue-recognition methods to critical steps in the earnings process, and Illustration 5–3 provides a more detailed overview of the methods used in current practice. As noted in the chapter supplement, some of these methods change with new FASB guidance, but adoption of the new revenue recognition standard is not likely to be required before 2015 at the earliest, so it is important to understand current practice.

Recall that the realization principle indicates that the central issues for recognizing revenue are (a) judging when the earnings process is substantially complete and (b) whether there is reasonable certainty as to the collectibility of the cash to be received. Often this decision is straightforward and tied to delivery of the product from the seller to the buyer. At delivery, the earnings process is virtually complete and the seller receives either cash or a receivable. At other times, though, recognizing revenue upon delivery may be inappropriate. It may be that revenue should be deferred to a point *after* delivery because the seller is unable to estimate whether the buyer will return the product or pay the receivable. Or, sometimes revenue should be recognized at a point *prior* to delivery because the earnings process occurs over multiple reporting periods and the company can better inform financial statement users by making reliable estimates of revenue and cost prior to delivery.

Now let's consider specific revenue recognition methods in more detail. We start with revenue recognition at delivery, then discuss circumstances where revenue recognition must be postponed until after delivery, and then discuss circumstances that allow revenue recognition prior to delivery.

Illustration 5–2

Relation between Earnings Process and Revenue Recognition Methods

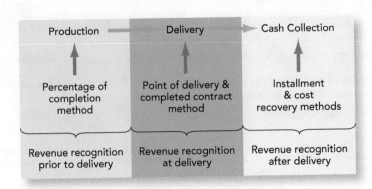

Nature of the Revenue	Usually Recognize Revenue for:	
	Sale of a Product	Sale of a Service
Revenue Recognition Prior to Delivery		
Dependable estimates of progress are available.	Each period during the earnings process (e.g., long-term construction contract) in proportion to its percentage of completion (percentage-of-completion method)	Not applicable
Dependable estimates of progress are not available.	At the completion of the project (completed contract method)	Not applicable
Revenue Recognition at Delivery	When product is delivered and title transfers	As the service is provided or the key activity is performed
Revenue Recognition After Delivery, Because:		
• Payments are significantly uncertain	When cash is collected (installment sales or cost recovery method)	When cash is collected
• Reliable estimates of product returns are unavailable	When critical event occurs that reduces product return uncertainty	Not applicable
• The product sold is out on consignment	When the consignee sells the product to the ultimate consumer	Not applicable

Illustration 5–3

Revenue Recognition Methods

When revenue is being earned in a multi-period contract, sometimes it is more meaningful to recognize revenue over time in proportion to the percentage of work completed.

We usually recognize revenue at or near the completion of the earnings process.

If collectibility is an issue, we defer revenue recognition until we can reasonably estimate the amount to be received.

International Financial Reporting Standards

Revenue Recognition Concepts. *IAS No. 18* governs most revenue recognition under IFRS. Similar to U.S. GAAP, it defines revenue as "the gross inflow of economic benefits during the period arising in the course of the ordinary activities of an entity when those inflows result in increases in equity, other than increases relating to contributions from equity participants."[7] IFRS allows revenue to be recognized when the following conditions have been satisfied:

(a) The amount of revenue and costs associated with the transaction can be measured reliably,

(b) It is probable that the economic benefits associated with the transaction will flow to the seller,

(c) (for sales of goods) the seller has transferred to the buyer the risks and rewards of ownership, and doesn't effectively manage or control the goods,

(d) (for sales of services) the stage of completion can be measured reliably.

These general conditions typically will lead to revenue recognition at the same time and in the same amount as would occur under U.S. GAAP, but there are exceptions. For example, later in this chapter we discuss differences between IFRS and U.S. GAAP that may affect the timing of revenue recognition with respect to multiple-deliverable contracts. More generally, IFRS has much less industry-specific guidance than does U.S. GAAP, leading to fewer exceptions to applying these revenue recognition conditions.

● LO5–8

---

[7]"Revenue," *International Accounting Standard No. 18* (IASCF), as amended effective January 1, 2011, par. 7.

Revenue Recognition at Delivery

Product Revenue

While revenue usually is earned during a period of time, it often is recognized at one specific point in time when both revenue recognition criteria are satisfied.

Consider the timing of revenue recognition for a typical manufacturing company that sells its products on credit. Illustration 5–2 shows three alternative points in time during the earnings process that could be considered the critical event for revenue recognition. It should be pointed out that revenue actually is earned *throughout* the earnings process. The critical event is the point in time when the realization principle is satisfied.[8]

Let's first consider the date production ends. At that point, it might be said that the earnings process is virtually complete. After all, the majority of the costs that must be expended to generate revenue have been incurred. The product has been produced and the remaining tasks are to sell the product and collect the asset to be exchanged for the product, which is usually cash.

Revenue from the sale of products usually is recognized at the point of product delivery.

However, at this point there usually exist significant uncertainties. We don't know if the product will be sold, the selling price, the buyer, or the collectibility of the asset to be received. Because of these uncertainties, revenue recognition usually is delayed until the point of sale, at product delivery. The product delivery date occurs when legal title to the goods passes from seller to buyer, which depends on the terms of the sales agreement. If the goods are shipped *f.o.b. (free on board) shipping point,* then legal title to the goods changes hands at the point of shipment, when the seller delivers the goods to the common carrier (for example, a trucking company), and the purchaser is responsible for shipping costs and transit insurance. On the other hand, if the goods are shipped *f.o.b. destination,* the seller is responsible for shipping, and legal title does not pass until the goods arrive at the customer's location.[9]

The point of delivery refers to the date legal title to the product passes from seller to buyer.

The basic journal entries to record revenue upon delivery should look familiar. As an example, assume that Taft Company sells a supercomputer for $5,000,000 that cost $4,100,000 to produce. The journal entries to record the sale, assuming that Taft uses the perpetual inventory method, would be

Accounts receivable	5,000,000	
Revenue		5,000,000
Cost of goods sold	4,100,000	
Inventory		4,100,000

This sale yields gross profit of $900,000 ($5,000,000 − 4,100,000).

At the product delivery date we know the product has been sold, the price, and the buyer. However, usually the buyer is given a length of time, say 30 days, to pay for the goods after they have been delivered. Therefore, the only remaining uncertainty at the time of delivery involves the ultimate cash collection, which usually can be accounted for by estimating and recording allowances for possible return of the product and for uncollectibility of the cash, that is, bad debts. Both of these estimates are discussed in Chapter 7. As we discuss later in this chapter, significant uncertainty at point of product delivery related to either collectibility or product return causes a delay in revenue recognition.

Service Revenue

Service revenue, too, often is recognized at a point in time if there is one final activity that is deemed critical to the earnings process. In this case, all revenue is deferred until this final activity has been performed. For example, a moving company will pack, load, transport, and deliver household goods for a fixed fee. Although packing, loading, and transporting all are important to the earning process, delivery is the culminating event of the earnings

---

[8]As you will learn later in this chapter when we discuss the percentage-of-completion method, revenue can be recognized during the earnings process rather than at one particular point in time as long as particular criteria have been met.
[9]We discuss this aspect of title transfer further in Chapter 7.

process. So, the entire service fee is recognized as revenue after the goods have been delivered. FedEx recognizes revenue in this manner. The Company's Summary of Significant Accounting Policies disclosure note indicates that "Revenue is recognized upon delivery of shipments." As with the sale of product, estimates of uncollectible amounts must be made for service revenue provided to customers on a credit basis.

However, in many instances, service revenue activities occur over extended periods, so recognizing revenue at any single date within one period would be inappropriate. Instead, it's more meaningful to recognize revenue over time as the service is performed.

> Service revenue often is recognized over time, in proportion to the amount of service performed.

As an example, consider the revenue a property owner earns when renting office space. If a landlord charges a tenant $12,000 in rent for the upcoming year, it would seem logical to recognize $1,000 of rent revenue each month over the one-year period (i.e., straight-line method) since similar services are performed throughout the period. The landlord recognizes rent revenue in proportion to the passage of time. Likewise, Gold's Gym will recognize revenue from a two-year membership ratably over the 24-month membership period. If the customer pays in advance in such cases, the seller debits cash and credits a liability (unearned revenue) because the seller is holding the customer's cash and has the obligation to provide the service. The seller only reduces that liability when the service has been provided and therefore revenue has been earned. We discuss unearned revenue liabilities and customer advances more in Chapter 13.

A similar situation occurs if you buy a season pass to Disney World. When would Walt Disney Co. recognize revenue for the cash it collects for the sale of a 365-day pass? Rationalizing that a pass can be used any number of times during the season, thus making it difficult to determine when service is provided, many companies once recognized all revenue from the sale of season passes on the date of sale. However, the SEC's *Staff Accounting Bulletins No. 101* and *104,* discussed earlier in the chapter, motivated most of these companies to change to recognizing revenue throughout the service period. For example, Illustration 5–4 provides a disclosure note Walt Disney Co. included in a recent annual report. Notice that the company recognizes revenue *over time*, based on the anticipated usage of the season pass over the operating season.

Revenue Recognition (in part)
Revenues from advance theme park ticket sales are recognized when the tickets are used. For non-expiring, multi-day tickets, revenues are recognized over a three-year time period based on estimated usage, which is derived from historical usage patterns.

Illustration 5–4

Disclosure of Revenue Recognition Policy—Walt Disney Co.

Real World Financials

Is the Seller a Principal or an Agent?

Regardless of whether we are dealing with a product or a service, an important consideration is whether the seller is acting as a "principal" or as an "agent." Here's the difference. A principal has primary responsibility for delivering a product or service, and typically is vulnerable to risks associated with delivering the product or service and collecting payment from the customer. In contrast, an agent doesn't primarily deliver goods or services, but acts as a facilitator that earns a commission for helping sellers transact with buyers.

● LO5–2

> An *agent* doesn't control goods or services, but rather facilitates transfers between sellers and buyers.

If the company is a principal, the company should recognize as revenue the gross (total) amount received from a customer. If instead the company is an agent, it recognizes as revenue only the *net* commission it receives for facilitating the sale.

There are many examples of agents in business. One you're familiar with is a real estate agent. Real estate agents don't own the houses they sell, but rather charge a commission to help home owners transact with home buyers. Similarly, online auction houses like eBay, travel facilitators like Expedia, Inc. and priceline.com, and broad web-based retailers like Amazon.com act as agents for a variety of sellers. Complicating matters, these same companies also act as *principals* on some other arrangements, selling their own products and services directly to customers. For example, eBay acts as an agent by linking sellers with buyers, but acts as a principal when selling its PayPal transaction-processing service.

Companies use a number of indicators to help determine if they are principals or agents with respect to a particular transaction. Indicators that the company is a principal include the following:

- The company is primarily responsible for providing the product or service to the customer.
- The company owns inventory prior to a customer ordering it and after a customer returns it.
- The company has discretion in setting prices and identifying suppliers.[10]

An agent only records its commission as revenue.

The reason the principal versus agent distinction is important is because, if the company is a principal, it records (a) the sales price to customers as revenue and (b) the cost of the item sold as cost of goods sold. On the other hand, if the company is an agent, it records as revenue only the commission it earns on the transaction. In Illustration 5–5 we see the difference in accounting by principals and agents.

Illustration 5–5

Comparison of Revenue Recognition by Principals and Agents

Ima Buyer purchases a television from an online retailer for $375. Let's consider accounting for that sale by two retailers: PrinCo and AgenCo:

- PrinCo obtains TVs directly from a supplier for $250, has the TVs shipped to its distribution center in Kansas, and then ships individual TVs to buyers when a sale is made. PrinCo offers occasional price discounts according to its marketing strategy. Because PrinCo is responsible for fulfilling the contract, bears the risk of holding inventory, and has latitude in setting sales prices, the evidence suggests that PrinCo is a principal in this transaction.
- AgenCo serves as a web portal by which multiple TV manufacturers can offer their products for sale. The manufacturers ship directly to buyers when a sale is made. AgenCo earns a flat 50% of the wholesale price set by the manufacturers as a commission. Given that AgenCo is not primarily responsible for fulfilling the contract, bears no inventory risk, has no latitude in setting sales prices, and is paid on commission, the evidence suggests AgenCo is an agent in this transaction.

The first part of the income statement for each retailer is shown below. Notice that the same amount of gross profit, $125, is recognized by the principal and the agent. What differs are the amounts of revenue and expense that are recognized and reported.

A Principal Records Gross Revenue (PrinCo)		An Agent Records Net Revenue (AgenCo)	
Revenue	$375		
Less: Cost of goods sold	250		
Gross profit	$125	Revenue	$125

We see from Illustration 5–5 that reporting revenue gross versus net can have a significant effect on a company's revenue. Particularly for start-up or growth-oriented companies that may be valued more on growth in revenue, rather than on growth in net income, determining whether a company should be considered a principal or an agent is critical.

Revenue Recognition after Delivery

FINANCIAL Reporting Case

Q3, p. 231

Recognizing revenue when goods and services are delivered as described in the previous section assumes we are able to make reasonable estimates of amounts due from customers that potentially might be uncollectible. For product sales, this also includes amounts not collectible due to customers returning the products they purchased. Otherwise, we would violate one of the requirements of the revenue realization principle we discussed earlier— that there must be reasonable certainty as to the collectibility of cash from the customer. In this section we address a few situations in which uncertainties are so severe that they could cause a delay in recognizing revenue from a sale of a product or service. For each of these

---

[10]FASB ASC 605–45–45: Revenue Recognition–Principal Agent Considerations–Other Presentation Matters (originally *EITF 99-19: Reporting Revenue Gross as a Principal versus Net as an Agent* (Stamford, Conn.: FASB, 2000)).

situations, notice that the accounting is essentially the same—*deferring* recognition of the gross profit arising from a sale of a product or service until uncertainties have been resolved.

Installment Sales

Customers sometimes are allowed to pay for purchases in installments over a long period of time. Many large retail stores, such as Sears and J.C. Penney, sell products on an installment plan. Increasing the length of time allowed for payment usually increases the uncertainty about whether the store actually will collect a receivable. Is the uncertainty sufficient in an installment sale to cause these companies to delay recognizing revenue and related expenses beyond the point of sale? Usually, it's not.

● LO5–3

In most situations, the increased uncertainty concerning the collection of cash from installment sales can be accommodated satisfactorily by estimating uncollectible amounts. If, however, the installment sale creates significant uncertainty concerning cash collection, making impossible a reasonable assessment of future bad debts, then revenue and expense recognition should be delayed. For example, real estate sales often are made on an installment basis with relatively small down payments and long payment periods, perhaps 25 years or more. These payment characteristics, combined with the general speculative nature of many of these transactions, may translate into extreme uncertainty concerning the collectibility of the installment receivable.[11] In fact, GAAP requires that the installment sales method (discussed below) be applied to a retail land sale that meets certain criteria.[12]

At times, revenue recognition is delayed due to a high degree of uncertainty related to ultimate cash collection.

When extreme uncertainty exists regarding the ultimate collectibility of cash, we delay recognizing revenue and related expenses using one of two accounting techniques, the installment sales method or the cost recovery method. *We emphasize that these methods should be used only in situations involving exceptional uncertainty.* As an example, consider Nathan's Famous, Inc., which operates company-owned stores and franchise stores specializing in selling hot dogs. Illustration 5–6 shows part of the revenue recognition disclosure note included with Nathan's 2011 financial statements.

The *installment sales* and *cost recovery* methods are only used in unusual circumstances.

Sales of Restaurants (in part)
The Company recognizes profit on sales of restaurants or real estate under the full accrual method, the installment method and the deposit method (deferring revenue when a deposit is made until the earnings process is complete), depending on the specific terms of each sale. Profit recognition by the full accrual method is appropriate provided (a) the profit is determinable, that is, the collectibility of the sales price is reasonably assured or the amount that will not be collectible can be estimated, and (b) the earnings process is virtually complete, that is, the seller is not obliged to perform significant activities after the sale to earn the profit. Unless both conditions exist, recognition of all or part of the profit shall be postponed and other methods of profit recognition shall be followed.

Illustration 5–6

Disclosure of Revenue Recognition Policy— Nathan's Famous, Inc.

Real World Financials

INSTALLMENT SALES METHOD. To deal with the uncertainty of collection, the installment sales method recognizes revenue and costs only when cash payments are received. Each payment is assumed to be composed of two components: (1) a partial recovery of the cost of the item sold and (2) a gross profit component. These components are determined by the gross profit percentage applicable to the sale. For example, if the gross profit percentage (gross profit ÷ sales price) is 40%, then 60% of each dollar collected represents cost recovery and the remaining 40% is gross profit. Consider the example in Illustration 5–7.

On November 1, 2013, the Belmont Corporation, a real estate developer, sold a tract of land for $800,000. The sales agreement requires the customer to make four equal annual payments of $200,000 plus interest on each November 1, beginning November 1, 2013. The land cost $560,000 to develop. The company's fiscal year ends on December 31.

Illustration 5–7

Installment Sales Method

---

[11]For income tax purposes, the installment sales method applies only to gains from the sale of certain types of properties. The tax law requires the use of the installment sales method for these transactions unless a taxpayer elects not to use the method.
[12]FASB ASC 360–20: Property, Plant, and Equipment—Real Estate Sales (previously "Accounting for Sales of Real Estate," *Statement of Financial Accounting Standards No. 66* (Stamford, Conn.: FASB, 1982)).

The *installment sales method* recognizes the gross profit by applying the gross profit percentage on the sale to the amount of cash actually received.

The gross profit of $240,000 ($800,000 − 560,000) represents 30% of the sales price ($240,000 ÷ $800,000). The collection of cash and the recognition of gross profit under the installment method are summarized below. In this example, we ignore the collection of interest charges and the recognition of interest revenue to concentrate on the collection of the $800,000 sales price and the recognition of gross profit on the sale.

| Date | Cash Collected | Amount Allocated to: | |
		Cost (70%)	Gross Profit (30%)
Nov. 1, 2013	$200,000	$140,000	$ 60,000
Nov. 1, 2014	200,000	140,000	60,000
Nov. 1, 2015	200,000	140,000	60,000
Nov. 1, 2016	200,000	140,000	60,000
Totals	$800,000	$560,000	$240,000

The gross profit recognized in a period will be equal to the gross profit percentage multiplied by the period's cash collection. The following journal entries are recorded (interest charges ignored):

Inventory is credited for the portion of the receivable that represents the cost of the land sold. The difference is deferred gross profit.

Make Installment Sale:
November 1, 2013

Installment receivables	800,000	
Inventory		560,000
Deferred gross profit		240,000
To record installment sale.		

The first entry records the installment receivable and the reduction of inventory. The difference between the $800,000 selling price and the $560,000 cost of sales represents the gross profit on the sale of $240,000. As gross profit will be recognized in net income only as collections are received, it is recorded initially in an account called *deferred gross profit*. This is a contra account to the installment receivable. The deferred gross profit account will be reduced to zero as collections are received.[13]

When payments are received, gross profit is recognized, calculated by applying the gross profit percentage to the cash collected (30% × $200,000).

Collect Cash:
November 1, 2013

Cash	200,000	
Installment receivables		200,000
To record cash collection from installment sale.		
Deferred gross profit	60,000	
Realized gross profit		60,000
To recognize gross profit from installment sale.		

The second set of entries records the collection of the first installment and recognizes the gross profit component of the payment, $60,000. Realized gross profit gets closed to income summary as part of the normal year-end closing process and is included in net income in the income statement. Journal entries to record the remaining three payments on November 1, 2014, 2015, and 2016, are identical.

---

[13] Accountants sometimes record installment sales in the following manner:

Installment receivables	800,000	
Installment sales		800,000
To record installment sales.		

Cost of installment sales	560,000	
Inventory		560,000
To record the cost of installment sales.		

Then at the end of the period, the following adjusting/closing entry is recorded:

Installment sales	800,000	
Cost of installment sales		560,000
Deferred gross profit on installment sales		240,000

The text entries concentrate on the effect of the transactions and avoid this unnecessary procedural complexity.

At the end of 2013, the balance sheet would report the following:

Installment receivables ($800,000 − 200,000)	$600,000
Less: Deferred gross profit ($240,000 − 60,000)	(180,000)
Installment receivables (net)	$420,000

The net amount of the receivable reflects the portion of the remaining payments to be received that represents cost recovery (70% × $600,000). The installment receivables are classified as current assets if they will be collected within one year (or within the company's operating cycle, if longer); otherwise, they are classified as noncurrent assets.

The income statement for 2013 would report gross profit from installment sales of $60,000. Sales and cost of goods sold associated with installment sales usually are not reported in the income statement under the installment method, just the resulting gross profit. However, if those amounts aren't included in the income statement in the period in which the installment sale is made, they need to be included in the notes to the financial statements, along with the amount of gross profit that has not yet been recognized.

Additional Consideration

We discuss in significant depth in Chapter 7 the problem of accounting for bad debts. However, bad debts related to receivables on sales accounted for using the installment method create a unique problem. A company uses the installment method because it can't reliably estimate bad debts. Therefore, the company doesn't explicitly recognize bad debts or create an allowance for uncollectible accounts in the installment method. Rather, bad debts are dealt with implicitly by deferring gross profit until cash is collected. If the cash never is collected, the related deferred gross profit never gets included in net income. To illustrate, assume that in the example described in Illustration 5–7, the Belmont Corporation collected the first payment but the customer was unable to make the remaining payments. Typically, the seller would repossess the item sold and make the following journal entry:

Repossessed inventory..	420,000	
Deferred gross profit...	180,000	
Installment receivable..		600,000

This entry removes the receivable and the remaining deferred gross profit and records the repossessed land in an inventory account. This example assumes that the repossessed land's current fair value is equal to the net receivable of $420,000. If the land's fair value at the date of repossession is less than $420,000, a loss on repossession is recorded (debited).

COST RECOVERY METHOD. In situations where there is an extremely high degree of uncertainty regarding the ultimate cash collection on an installment sale, an even more conservative approach, the cost recovery method, can be used. This method defers all gross profit recognition until the cost of the item sold has been recovered. The gross profit recognition pattern applying the cost recovery method to the Belmont Corporation situation used in Illustration 5–7 is shown below.

The *cost recovery method* defers all gross profit recognition until cash equal to the cost of the item sold has been received.

Date	Cash Collected	Cost Recovery	Gross Profit Recognized
Nov. 1, 2013	$200,000	$200,000	$ –0–
Nov. 1, 2014	200,000	200,000	–0–
Nov. 1, 2015	200,000	160,000	40,000
Nov. 1, 2016	200,000	–0–	200,000
Totals	$800,000	$560,000	$240,000

The journal entries using this method are similar to those for the installment sales method except that $40,000 in gross profit is recognized in 2015 and $200,000 in 2016.

The cost recovery method's initial journal entry is identical to the installment sales method.

Make Installment Sale:		
November 1, 2013		
Installment receivables...	800,000	
Inventory..		560,000
Deferred gross profit		240,000
To record installment sale.		
Collect Cash:		
November 1, 2013, 2014, 2015, and 2016		
Cash...	200,000	
Installment receivables.......................................		200,000
To record cash collection from installment sale.		
November 1, 2013 and 2014		
No entry for gross profit.		

When payments are received, gross profit is recognized only after cost has been fully recovered.

November 1, 2015		
Deferred gross profit	40,000	
Realized gross profit		40,000
To recognize gross profit from installment sale.		
November 1, 2016		
Deferred gross profit	200,000	
Realized gross profit		200,000
To recognize gross profit from installment sale.		

Why not use the installment sales method or cost recovery method for all installment sales? Because doing so would violate the realization principle and be inconsistent with accrual accounting. If bad debts can be reasonably estimated, there is no reason to delay revenue recognition.

Concept Review Exercise

INSTALLMENT SALES

Boatwright Implements, Inc., manufactures and sells farm machinery. For most of its sales, revenue and cost of sales are recognized at the delivery date. In 2013 Boatwright sold a cotton baler to a new customer for $100,000. The cost of the machinery was $60,000. Payment will be made in five annual installments of $20,000 each, with the first payment due in 2013. Boatwright usually does not allow its customers to pay in installments. Due to the unusual nature of the payment terms and the uncertainty of collection of the installment payments, Boatwright is considering alternative methods of recognizing profit on this sale.

Required:
Ignoring interest charges, prepare a table showing the gross profit to be recognized from 2013 through 2017 on the cotton-baler sale using the following three methods:

1. Point of delivery revenue recognition.
2. The installment sales method.
3. The cost recovery method.

Solution:

	Point of Delivery	Installment Sales Method (40% × cash collection)	Cost Recovery Method
2013	$40,000	$ 8,000	$ –0–
2014	–0–	8,000	–0–
2015	–0–	8,000	–0–
2016	–0–	8,000	20,000
2017	–0–	8,000	20,000
Totals	$40,000	$40,000	$40,000

Right of Return

Retailers usually give their customers the right to return merchandise if they are not satisfied. In most situations, even though the right to return merchandise exists, revenues and expenses can be appropriately recognized at point of delivery. Based on past experience, a company usually can estimate the returns that will result for a given volume of sales. These estimates are used to reduce both sales and cost of goods sold in anticipation of returns. The purpose of the estimates is to avoid overstating gross profit in the period of sale and understating gross profit in the period of return. The specific accounting treatment for sales returns is illustrated in Chapter 7 in conjunction with discussing the valuation of accounts receivable.

Because the return of merchandise can negate the benefits of having made a sale, the seller must meet specific criteria before revenue is recognized in situations when the right of return exists. The most critical of these criteria is that the seller must be able to make reliable estimates of future returns.[14] In some situations, these criteria are not satisfied at the point of delivery of the product. For example, manufacturers of semiconductors like Intel Corporation and Motorola Corporation usually sell their products through independent distributor companies. Economic factors, competition among manufacturers, and rapid obsolescence of the product motivate these manufacturers to grant the distributors the right of return if they are unable to sell the semiconductors. So, revenue recognition often is deferred beyond the delivery point to the date the products actually are sold by the distributor to an end user. The disclosure note shown in Illustration 5–8 appeared in a recent annual report of Intel Corporation.

● LO5–4

Revenue Recognition

We recognize net product revenue when the earnings process is complete, as evidenced by an agreement with the customer, transfer of title, and acceptance, if applicable, as well as fixed pricing and probable collectability. . . . Because of frequent sales price reductions and rapid technology obsolescence in the industry, we defer product revenue and related costs of sales from sales made to distributors under agreements allowing price protection or right of return until the distributors sell the merchandise.

Illustration 5–8

Disclosure of Revenue Recognition Policy—Intel Corporation

Real World Financials

For Intel, the event critical to revenue recognition is *not* the delivery of the product to a distributor but the ultimate sale of the product by the distributor to an end user.

Alternatively, the right of return could be specified contractually as expiring on some future date, and revenue recognition could be deferred to that date. Regardless, the accounting treatment in these situations would be similar to that used for the installment sales and cost recovery methods. The difference is that the journal entries we use to move deferred gross profit to realized gross profit would be recorded in whatever period that returns can be estimated reliably or the right of return no longer exists.

Similarly, sometimes, a sales agreement requires additional, important performance steps to be performed by the seller. In this case, the earnings process is not virtually complete until those steps are performed, but as in the case of significant uncertainty about cash collection, revenue recognition must be deferred. Illustration 5–1 on page 233 illustrates a situation where the seller, Brown & Sharpe, delays revenue recognition beyond delivery of machines until the performance of the machines has been accepted by the buyer. Customer acceptance is an important part of the agreement between buyer and seller.

Any time a company recognizes revenue at a point other than the point of delivery, the revenue recognition method used is disclosed in the summary of significant accounting policies. Intel's disclosure note is an example. As another example, Illustration 5–9 shows a disclosure note included with the 2011 first quarter financial statements of Helicos Biosciences Corporation, a producer of genetic analysis instrumentation for research, pharmaceutical, and medical applications.

---

[14]Other, less critical criteria are listed in FASB ASC 605–15–25: Revenue Recognition–Products–Recognition (previously "Revenue Recognition When Right of Return Exists," *Statement of Financial Accounting Standards No. 48* (Stamford, Conn.: FASB, 1981)).

Illustration 5–9

Disclosure of Revenue
Recognition Policy—
Helicos Biosciences
Corporation

Real World Financials

2. Summary of Significant Accounting Policies: Revenue Recognition (in part)
The Company recognizes revenue in accordance with accounting guidance on revenue recognition in financial statements. . . . This guidance requires that persuasive evidence of a sales arrangement exists, delivery of goods occurs through transfer of title and risk and rewards of ownership, the selling price is fixed or determinable and collectability is reasonably assured. . . . In instances where the Company sells an instrument with specified acceptance criteria, the Company will defer revenue recognition until such acceptance has been obtained.

As the note indicates, some of Helicos's revenue is delayed beyond the point of product delivery. Until the product has been installed and meets customer acceptance criteria, there is a high degree of uncertainty concerning the possibility the product might be returned, so Helicos has not completed its obligation to its customer until acceptance has occurred.

Consignment Sales

Consigned inventory
stays in the balance
sheet of the consignor
until an arms-length
transaction transfers title
to a buyer.

Sometimes a company arranges for another company to sell its product under consignment. The "consignor" physically transfers the goods to the other company (the consignee), but the consignor retains legal title. If the consignee can't find a buyer within an agreed-upon time, the consignee returns the goods to the consignor. However, if a buyer is found, the consignee remits the selling price (less commission and approved expenses) to the consignor.

Because the consignor retains the risks and rewards of ownership of the product and title does not pass to the consignee, the consignor does not record a sale (revenue and related expenses) until the consignee sells the goods and title passes to the eventual customer. Of course, that means goods on consignment still are part of the consignor's inventory. As an example, Boston Scientific Corporation earns revenue from selling single-use medical devices. Some of the company's product is sold using consignment arrangements. Illustration 5–10 shows a portion of the revenue recognition disclosure note that Boston Scientific included in a recent annual report.

Illustration 5–10

Disclosure of Revenue
Recognition Policy—
Boston Scientific
Corporation

Real World Financials

Note 1: Business and Summary of Significant Accounting Policies: *Revenue Recognition* **(in part)**
We consider revenue to be realized or realizable and earned when all of the following criteria are met: persuasive evidence of a sales arrangement exists; delivery has occurred or services have been rendered; the price is fixed or determinable; and collectibility is reasonably assured. We generally meet these criteria at the time of shipment, unless a consignment arrangement exists or we are required to provide additional services. We recognize revenue from consignment arrangements based on product usage, or implant, which indicates that the sale is complete.

Up until now, we've focused on revenue-generating activities in which some specific event (e.g., delivery, collection, product performance, and resale) indicates that the earnings process is substantially completed and significant uncertainties have been alleviated, prompting us to recognize revenue and related expenses. We now turn our attention to situations in which it's desirable to recognize revenue over more than one reporting period—before a specific event indicates the earnings process is substantially completed.

Revenue Recognition Prior to Delivery

● LO5–5

The types of companies that make use of long-term contracts are many and varied. A recent survey of reporting practices of 500 large public companies indicates that approximately one in every six companies engages in long-term contracts.[15] And they are not just construction

---

[15]*Accounting Trends and Techniques—2011* (New York: AICPA, 2011), p. 410.

companies. In fact, even services such as research, installation, and consulting often are contracted for on a long-term basis. Illustration 5–11 lists just a sampling of companies that use long-term contracts, many of which you might recognize.

Company	Type of Industry or Product
Oracle Corp.	Computer software, license and consulting fees
Lockheed Martin Corporation	Aircraft, missiles, and spacecraft
Hewlett-Packard	Information technology
Northrop Grumman Newport News	Shipbuilding
Nortel Networks Corp.	Networking solutions and services to support the Internet
SBA Communications Corp.	Telecommunications
Layne Christensen Company	Water supply services and geotechnical construction
Kaufman & Broad Home Corp.	Commercial and residential construction
Raytheon Company	Defense electronics
Foster Wheeler Corp.	Construction, petroleum and chemical facilities
Halliburton	Construction, energy services
Allied Construction Products Corp.	Large metal stamping presses

Illustration 5–11

Companies Engaged in Long-Term Contracts

The general revenue recognition criteria described in the realization principle suggest that revenue should be recognized when a long-term project is finished (that is, when the earnings process is virtually complete). This is known as the completed contract method of revenue recognition. The problem with this method is that all revenues, expenses, and resulting income from the project are recognized in the period in which the project is completed; no revenues or expenses are reported in the income statements of earlier reporting periods in which much of the work may have been performed. Net income should provide a measure of periodic accomplishment to help predict future accomplishments. Clearly, income statements prepared using the completed contract method do not fairly report each period's accomplishments when a project spans more than one reporting period. Much of the earnings process is far removed from the point of delivery.

The percentage-of-completion method of revenue recognition for long-term construction and other projects is designed to help address this problem. By this approach, we recognize revenues (and expenses) over time by allocating a share of the project's expected revenues and expenses to each period in which the earnings process occurs, that is, the contract period. Although the contract usually specifies total revenues, the project's expenses are not known until completion. Consequently, it's necessary for a company to estimate the project's future costs at the end of each reporting period in order to estimate total gross profit to be earned on the project.

Because the percentage-of-completion method does a better job of recognizing revenue in the periods in which revenue is earned, U.S. and international GAAP require the use of that method unless it's not possible to make reliable estimates of revenues, expenses, and progress toward completion.[16] Companies prefer the percentage-of-completion method as well because it allows earlier revenue and profit recognition than does the completed contract method. For both reasons, the percentage-of-completion method is more prevalent in practice. However, much of the accounting is the same under either method, so we start by discussing the similarities between the two methods, and then the differences. You'll see that we recognize the same total amounts or revenue and profit over the life of the contract under either method. Only the timing of recognition differs.

The *completed contract method* recognizes revenue at a point in time when the earnings process is complete.

FINANCIAL Reporting Case

Q1, p. 231

The *percentage-of-completion method* allocates a share of a project's revenues and expenses to each reporting period as construction occurs.

---

[16]Specifically, U.S. GAAP requires that the percentage-of-completion method be used whenever (1) reasonable estimates can be made of revenues and costs; (2) the contract specifies the parties' rights, consideration to be paid, and payment terms; and (3) both the purchaser and seller have the ability and expectation to fulfill their obligations under the contract [FASB ASC 605–35-25: Revenue Recognition–Construction-Type and Production-Type Contracts–Recognition (previously "Accounting for Performance of Construction-Type and Certain Production-Type Contracts," *Statement of Position 81-1* (New York: AICPA, 1981))]. Similar criteria are included in IAS No. 11, "Construction Contracts" (IASCF, as amended, effective January 1, 2011, paragraph 23).

Illustration 5–12 provides information to compare accounting for long-term contracts using the completed contract and percentage-of-completion methods.

Illustration 5–12

Completed Contract and Percentage-of-Completion Methods Compared

At the beginning of 2013, the Harding Construction Company received a contract to build an office building for $5 million. The project is estimated to take three years to complete. According to the contract, Harding will bill the buyer in installments over the construction period according to a prearranged schedule. Information related to the contract is as follows:

	2013	2014	2015
Construction costs incurred during the year	$1,500,000	$1,000,000	$1,600,000
Construction costs incurred in prior years	–0–	1,500,000	2,500,000
Cumulative construction costs	1,500,000	2,500,000	4,100,000
Estimated costs to complete at end of year	2,250,000	1,500,000	–0–
Total estimated and actual construction costs	$3,750,000	$4,000,000	$4,100,000
Billings made during the year	$1,200,000	$2,000,000	$1,800,000
Cash collections during year	1,000,000	1,400,000	2,600,000

Construction costs include the labor, materials, and overhead costs directly related to the construction of the building. Notice how the total of estimated and actual construction costs changes from period to period. Cost revisions are typical in long-term contracts in which costs are estimated over long periods of time.

ACCOUNTING FOR THE COST OF CONSTRUCTION AND ACCOUNTS RECEIVABLE. Summary journal entries for both the percentage-of-completion and completed contract methods are shown in Illustration 5–12A for construction costs, billings, and cash receipts.

Illustration 5–12A Journal Entries—Costs, Billings, and Cash Receipts

	2013		2014		2015	
Construction in progress	1,500,000		1,000,000		1,600,000	
Cash, materials, etc.		1,500,000		1,000,000		1,600,000
To record construction costs.						
Accounts receivable..............................	1,200,000		2,000,000		1,800,000	
Billings on construction contract		1,200,000		2,000,000		1,800,000
To record progress billings.						
Cash...	1,000,000		1,400,000		2,600,000	
Accounts receivable		1,000,000		1,400,000		2,600,000
To record cash collections.						

Accounting for costs, billings, and cash receipts are the same for both the percentage-of-completion and completed contract methods.

With both the completed contract and percentage-of-completion methods, all costs incurred in the construction process are initially recorded in an asset account called construction in progress. This asset account is equivalent to work-in-process inventory in a manufacturing company. This is logical since the construction project is essentially an inventory item in process for the contractor.

Notice that periodic billings are credited to billings on construction contract. This account is a contra account to the construction in progress asset. At the end of each period, the balances in these two accounts are compared. If the net amount is a debit, it is reported in the balance sheet as an asset. Conversely, if the net amount is a credit, it is reported as a liability.[17]

---

[17]If the company is engaged in more than one long-term contract, all contracts for which construction in progress exceeds billings are grouped together and all contracts for which billings exceed construction in progress also are grouped together. This would result in the presentation of both an asset and a liability in the balance sheet.

To understand why we use the billings on construction contract account (or *billings* for short), consider a key difference between accounting for a long-term contract and accounting for a typical sale in which revenue is recognized upon delivery. Recall our earlier example in which Taft Company gives up its physical asset (inventory; in this instance a supercomputer) and recognizes cost of goods sold at the same time it gets a financial asset (an account receivable) and recognizes revenue. So, first a physical asset is in the balance sheet, and then a financial asset, but the two are not in the balance sheet at the same time.

> *Construction in progress is the contractor's work-in-process inventory.*

Now consider our Harding Construction example. Harding is creating a physical asset (construction in progress) in the same periods it recognizes a financial asset (first recognizing accounts receivable when the customer is billed and then recognizing cash when the receivable is collected). Having both the physical asset and the financial asset in the balance sheet at the same time constitutes double counting the same arrangement. The billings account solves this problem. Whenever an account receivable is recognized, the other side of the journal entry increases the billings account, which is contra to (and thus reduces) construction in progress. As a result, the financial asset (accounts receivable) increases and the physical asset (the net amount of construction in progress and billings) decreases, and no double counting occurs.

> *The billings on construction contract account prevents "double counting" assets by reducing construction in progress whenever an accounts receivable is recognized.*

GROSS PROFIT RECOGNITION—GENERAL APPROACH.   Now let's consider recognition of gross profit. The top portion of Illustration 5–12B shows the journal entry to recognize revenue, cost of construction (think of this as cost of goods sold), and gross profit under the completed contract method, while the bottom portion shows the journal entries that achieve this for the percentage-of-completion method. At this point focus on the structure of the journal entries (what is debited and credited). We'll discuss how to calculate the specific amounts later in the chapter.

Illustration 5–12B Journal Entries—Profit Recognition

	2013	2014	2015
Completed Contract			
Construction in progress (gross profit)			900,000
Cost of construction			4,100,000
Revenue from long-term contracts			5,000,000
To record gross profit.			
Percentage-of-Completion			
Construction in progress (gross profit)	500,000	125,000	275,000
Cost of construction	1,500,000	1,000,000	1,600,000
Revenue from long-term contracts	2,000,000	1,125,000	1,875,000
To record gross profit.			

It's important to understand two key aspects of Illustration 5–12B. First, the same amounts of revenue, cost, and gross profit are recognized under both the completed contract and percentage-of-completion methods. The only difference is timing. To check this, sum all of the revenue recognized for both methods over the three years:

> *The same total amount of revenue is recognized under both the completed contract and the percentage-of-completion methods, but the timing of recognition differs.*

	Percentage-of-Completion	Completed Contract
Revenue recognized:		
2013	$2,000,000	–0–
2014	1,125,000	–0–
2015	1,875,000	$5,000,000
Total revenue	$5,000,000	$5,000,000

Second, notice that in both methods we add gross profit (the difference between revenue and cost) to the construction in progress asset. That seems odd—why add *profit* to what is essentially an *inventory* account? The key here is that, when Harding recognizes gross profit, Harding is acting like it has sold some portion of the asset to the customer, but Harding keeps the asset in Harding's own balance sheet (in the construction in progress account)

Construction in progress includes profits and losses on the contract that have been recognized to date.

until delivery to the customer. Putting recognized gross profit into the construction in progress account just updates that account to reflect the total value (cost + gross profit = sales price) of the customer's asset. However, don't forget that the billings account is contra to the construction in progress account. Over the life of the construction project, Harding will bill the customer for the entire sales price of the asset. Therefore, at the end of the contract, the construction in progress account (containing total cost and gross profit) and the billings account (containing all amounts billed to the customer) will have equal balances that exactly offset to create a net value of zero.

The same journal entry is recorded to close out the billings and construction in progress accounts under the completed contract and percentage-of-completion methods.

The only task remaining is for Harding to officially transfer title to the finished asset to the customer. At that time, Harding will prepare a journal entry that removes the contract from its balance sheet by debiting billings and crediting construction in progress for the entire value of the contract. As shown in Illustration 5–12C, the same journal entry is recorded to close out the billings on construction contract and construction in progress accounts under the completed contract and percentage-of-completion methods.

Illustration 5–12C

Journal Entry to Close Billings and Construction in Progress Accounts

	2013	2014	2015
Billings on construction contract			5,000,000
Construction in progress			5,000,000
To close accounts.			

Now that we've seen how gross profit is recognized for long-term contracts, let's consider how the timing of that recognition differs between the completed contract and percentage-of-completion methods.

Under the completed contract method, profit is not recognized until the project is completed.

TIMING OF GROSS PROFIT RECOGNITION UNDER THE COMPLETED CONTRACT METHOD. The timing of gross profit recognition under the completed contract method is simple. As the name implies, all revenues and expenses related to the project are recognized when the contract is completed. As shown in Illustration 5–12B and in the T-accounts below, completion occurs in 2015 for our Harding example. Prior to then, construction in progress includes only costs, showing a balance of $1,500,000 and $2,500,000 of cost at the end of 2013 and 2014, respectively, and including $4,100,000 of cost when the project is completed in 2015. Harding includes an additional $900,000 of gross profit in construction in progress when the project is completed in 2015 because the asset is viewed as "sold" on that date. The company records revenue of $5,000,000, cost of construction (similar to cost of goods sold) of $4,100,000, and the resulting $900,000 gross profit on that date.

FINANCIAL Reporting Case

Q3, p. 231

Completed Contract

	Construction in Progress		Billings on Construction Contract	
2013 construction costs	1,500,000		1,200,000	2013 billings
End balance, 2013	1,500,000		2,000,000	2014 billings
2014 construction costs	1,000,000		1,800,000	2015 billings
End balance, 2014	2,500,000		5,000,000	Balance, before closing
2015 construction costs	1,600,000			
2015 gross profit	900,000			
Balance, before closing	5,000,000			

Under the completed contract method, construction in progress is updated to include gross profit at the end of the life of the contract.

Under the percentage-of-completion method, profit is recognized over the life of the project as the project is completed.

TIMING OF GROSS PROFIT RECOGNITION UNDER THE PERCENTAGE-OF-COMPLETION METHOD. Using the percentage-of-completion method we recognize a portion of the estimated gross profit each period based on progress to date. How should progress to date be estimated?

One approach is to use *output* measures like units of production. For example, with a multi-year contract to deliver airplanes we might recognize progress according to the number of planes delivered. Another example of an output measure is recognizing portions of revenue associated with achieving particular milestones specified in a sales contract. Accounting guidance[18] states a preference for output measures when they can be established, arguing that they are more directly and reliably related to assessing progress than are input measures.

Progress to date can be estimated using input and output measures.

Another approach is to use an *input* measure like the "cost-to-cost ratio," by which progress to date is estimated by calculating the percentage of estimated total cost that has been incurred to date. Similar input measures might be used instead, like the number of labor hours incurred to date compared to estimated total hours. One advantage of input measures is that they capture progress on long-term contracts that may not translate easily into simple output measures. For example, a natural output measure for highway construction might be finished miles of road, but that measure could be deceptive if not all miles of road require the same effort. A highway contract for the state of Arizona would likely pay the contractor more for miles of road blasted through the mountains than for miles paved across flat dessert, and a cost-to-cost approach reflects that difference. Research suggests that the cost-to-cost input measure is most common in practice.[19]

A common input measure is a *cost-to-cost ratio*.

Regardless of the specific approach used to estimate progress to date, under the percentage-of-completion method we determine the amount of gross profit recognized in each period using the following logic:

$$\begin{pmatrix} \text{Gross profit} \\ \text{recognized this} \\ \text{period} \end{pmatrix} = \begin{pmatrix} \text{Total estimated} \\ \text{gross profit} \end{pmatrix} \times \begin{pmatrix} \text{Percentage completed} \\ \text{to date} \end{pmatrix} - \begin{pmatrix} \text{Gross profit} \\ \text{recognized in} \\ \text{prior periods} \end{pmatrix}$$

where total estimated gross profit = total estimated revenue − total estimated cost.

Illustration 5–12D shows the calculation of gross profit for each of the years for our Harding Construction Company example, with progress to date estimated using the cost-to-cost ratio. Refer to the bottom part of Illustration 5–12B to see the journal entries used to recognize gross profit in each period, and the T-accounts on the next page to see that the gross profit recognized in each period is added to the construction in progress account.

	2013	2014	2015
Contract price (A)	$5,000,000	$5,000,000	$5,000,000
Construction costs:			
Construction costs incurred during the year	$1,500,000	$1,000,000	$1,600,000
Construction costs incurred in prior years	–0–	1,500,000	2,500,000
Actual costs to date	$1,500,000	$2,500,000	$4,100,000
Estimated remaining costs to complete	2,250,000	1,500,000	–0–
Total cost (estimated + actual) (B)	$3,750,000	$4,000,000	$4,100,000
Total gross profit (A − B)	$1,250,000	$1,000,000	$ 900,000
Multiplied by:	×	×	×
Percentage of completion:	$\left(\dfrac{\$1,500,000}{\$3,750,000}\right.$	$\left(\dfrac{\$2,500,000}{\$4,000,000}\right.$	$\left(\dfrac{\$4,100,000}{\$4,100,000}\right.$
$\dfrac{\text{Actual costs to date}}{\text{Total cost (est. + actual)}}$	$\left. = 40\%\right)$	$\left. = 62.5\%\right)$	$\left. = 100\%\right)$
Equals:			
Gross profit earned to date	$ 500,000	$ 625,000	$ 900,000
Less:			
Gross profit recognized in prior periods	–0–	(500,000)	(625,000)
Equals:			
Gross profit recognized currently	$ 500,000	$ 125,000	$ 275,000

Illustration 5–12D

Percentage-of-Completion Method— Allocation of Gross Profit to Each Period

---

[18]FASB ASC 605–35–25–71: Revenue Recognition–Construction–Type and Production-Type Contracts–Recognition–Input and Output Measures (previously "Accounting for Performance of Construction-Type and Certain Production-Type Contracts," *Statement of Position No. 81-1* (New York: AICPA, 1981)).

[19]R. K. Larson and K. L. Brown, 2004, "Where Are We with Long-Term Contract Accounting?" *Accounting Horizons,* September, pp. 207–219.

250   SECTION 1   The Role of Accounting as an Information System

	Percentage-of-Completion				
	Construction in Progress		Billings on Construction Contract		
2013 construction costs	1,500,000			1,200,000	2013 billings
2013 gross profit	500,000			2,000,000	2014 billings
End balance, 2013	2,000,000			1,800,000	2015 billings
2014 construction costs	1,000,000			5,000,000	Balance, before closing
2014 gross profit	125,000				
End balance, 2014	3,125,000				
2015 construction costs	1,600,000				
2015 gross profit	275,000				
Balance, before closing	5,000,000				

Under the percentage-of-completion method, construction in progress is updated each period to include gross profit.

Income statements are more informative if the sales revenue and cost components of gross profit are reported rather than the net figure alone. So, the income statement for each year will report the appropriate revenue and cost of construction amounts. For example, in 2013, the gross profit of $500,000 consists of revenue of $2,000,000 (40% of the $5,000,000 contract price) less the $1,500,000 cost of construction. In subsequent periods, we calculate revenue by multiplying the percentage of completion by the contract price and then subtracting revenue recognized in prior periods, similar to the way we calculate gross profit each period. The cost of construction, then, is the difference between revenue and gross profit. In most cases, cost of construction also equals the construction costs incurred during the period.[20] The table in Illustration 5–12E shows the revenue and cost of construction recognized in each of the three years of our example. Of course, as you can see in this illustration, we could have initially determined the gross profit by first calculating revenue and then subtracting cost of construction.[21]

In the income statement, we separate the gross profit into its two components: revenue and cost of construction.

Illustration 5–12E
Percentage-of-Completion Method— Allocation of Revenue and Cost of Construction to Each Period

2013

Revenue recognized ($5,000,000 × 40%)		$2,000,000
Cost of construction		(1,500,000)
Gross profit		$ 500,000

2014

Revenue recognized to date ($5,000,000 × 62.5%)	$3,125,000	
Less: revenue recognized in 2013	2,000,000	
Revenue recognized		$1,125,000
Cost of construction		(1,000,000)
Gross profit		$ 125,000

2015

Revenue recognized to date ($5,000,000 × 100%)	$5,000,000	
Less: revenue recognized in 2013 and 2014	3,125,000	
Revenue recognized		$1,875,000
Cost of construction		(1,600,000)
Gross profit		$ 275,000

---

[20]Cost of construction does not equal the construction costs incurred during the year when a loss is projected on the entire project. This situation is illustrated later in the chapter.

[21]As a practical matter, if the percentage of completion figure is rounded we may calculate different amounts of revenue by (a) directly calculating revenue using the percentage of completion, and (b) indirectly calculating revenue by first calculating gross profit using the percentage of completion and then calculating revenue by adding gross profit to cost of construction. In that case, given that gross profit is defined as revenue minus cost, it is best to use approach (a) and first calculate revenue directly, solving for gross profit by subtracting cost of construction from revenue.

A Comparison of the Completed Contract and Percentage-of-Completion Methods

INCOME RECOGNITION.   Illustration 5–12B shows journal entries that would determine the amount of revenue, cost, and therefore gross profit that would appear in the income statement under the percentage-of-completion and completed contract methods. Comparing the gross profit patterns produced by each method of revenue recognition demonstrates the essential difference between them:

	Percentage-of-Completion	Completed Contract
Gross profit recognized:		
2013	$500,000	–0–
2014	125,000	–0–
2015	275,000	$900,000
Total gross profit	$900,000	$900,000

> The same total amount of profit or loss is recognized under both the completed contract and the percentage-of-completion methods, but the timing of recognition differs.

Although both methods yield identical gross profit of $900,000 for the entire 3-year period, the timing differs. The completed contract method defers all gross profit to 2015, when the project is completed. Obviously, the percentage-of-completion method provides a better measure of the company's economic activity and progress over the three-year period. That's why the percentage-of-completion method is preferred, and, as mentioned previously, the completed contract method should be used only when the company is unable to make dependable estimates of future revenue and costs necessary to apply the percentage-of-completion method.[22]

BALANCE SHEET RECOGNITION.   The balance sheet presentation for the construction-related accounts by both methods is shown in Illustration 5–12F. The balance in the construction in progress account differs between methods because of the earlier gross profit recognition that occurs under the percentage-of-completion method.

Balance Sheet (End of Year)	2013	2014
Percentage-of-Completion:		
Current assets:		
Accounts receivable	$200,000	$800,000
Costs and profit ($2,000,000) in excess of billings ($1,200,000)	800,000	
Current liabilities:		
Billings ($3,200,000) in excess of costs and profit ($3,125,000)		$ 75,000
Completed Contract:		
Current assets:		
Accounts receivable	$200,000	$800,000
Costs ($1,500,000) in excess of billings ($1,200,000)	300,000	
Current liabilities:		
Billings ($3,200,000) in excess of costs ($2,500,000)		$700,000

Illustration 5–12F
Balance Sheet Presentation

In the balance sheet, the construction in progress (CIP) account (containing costs and profit) is offset against the billings on construction contract account, with CIP > Billings shown as an asset and Billings > CIP shown as a liability. Because a company may have some contracts that have a net asset position and others that have a net liability position, we usually will see both net assets and net liabilities shown in a balance sheet at the same time.

Construction in progress in excess of billings essentially represents an unbilled receivable. Companies include it in their balance sheets as a component of accounts receivable, as part of

> Billings on construction contracts are subtracted from construction in progress to determine balance sheet presentation.

---

[22]For income tax purposes, the completed contract method may be used for home construction contracts and certain other real estate construction contracts. All other contracts must use the percentage-of-completion method.

inventory, or on its own line. The construction company is incurring construction costs (and recognizing gross profit using the percentage-of-completion method) for which it will be paid by the buyer. If the construction company bills the buyer an amount exactly equal to these costs (and profits recognized) then the accounts receivable balance properly reflects the claims of the construction company. If, however, the amount billed is less than the costs incurred (plus profits recognized) the difference represents the remaining claim to cash—an asset.

On the other hand, *Billings in excess of construction in progress* essentially indicates that the overbilled accounts receivable overstates the amount of the claim to cash earned to that date and must be reported as a liability. This is similar to the unearned revenue liability that is recorded when a customer pays for a product or service in advance. The advance is properly shown as a liability representing the obligation to provide the good or service in the future.

Disclosure of the method used to account for long-term contracts will appear in the summary of significant accounting policies.

LONG-TERM CONTRACT LOSSES.
The Harding Construction Company example above involves a situation in which a profit was realized on the construction contract. Unfortunately, losses sometimes occur on long-term contracts.

Periodic loss occurs for profitable project.
When using the percentage-of-completion method, a loss sometimes must be recognized in at least one period over the life of the project even though the project as a whole is expected to be profitable. We determine the loss in precisely the same way we determined the profit in profitable years. For example, assume the same $5 million contract for Harding Construction Company described in Illustration 5–12 but with the following cost information:

	2013	2014	2015
Construction costs incurred during the year	$1,500,000	$1,260,000	$1,840,000
Construction costs incurred in prior years	–0–	1,500,000	2,760,000
Cumulative construction costs	1,500,000	2,760,000	4,600,000
Estimated costs to complete at end of year	2,250,000	1,840,000	–0–
Total estimated and actual construction costs	$3,750,000	$4,600,000	$4,600,000

At the end of 2013, gross profit of $500,000 (revenue of $2,000,000 less cost of construction of $1,500,000) is recognized as previously determined.

At the end of 2014, the company now forecasts a total profit of $400,000 ($5,000,000 − 4,600,000) on the project and, at that time, the project is estimated to be 60% complete ($2,760,000 ÷ 4,600,000). Applying this percentage to the anticipated gross profit of $400,000 results in a gross profit *to date* of $240,000. But remember, a gross profit of $500,000 was recognized in 2013.

This situation is treated as a *change in accounting estimate* because it resulted from a change in the estimation of costs to complete at the end of 2013. Actual total costs to complete—$4,600,000—were much higher than the 2013 year-end estimate of $3,750,000. Recall from our discussion of changes in accounting estimates in Chapter 4 that we don't go back and restate the prior year's gross profit. Instead, the 2014 income statement would report *a loss of $260,000* ($500,000 − 240,000) so that the cumulative amount recognized to date totals $240,000 of gross profit. The loss consists of 2014 revenue of $1,000,000 (computed as $5,000,000 × 60% = $3,000,000 revenue to be recognized by end of 2014 less 2013 revenue of $2,000,000) less cost of construction of $1,260,000 (cost incurred in 2014). The following journal entry records the loss in 2014:

Recognized losses on long-term contracts reduce the construction in progress account.

Cost of construction	1,260,000	
Revenue from long-term contracts (below)		1,000,000
Construction in progress (loss)		260,000

The 2015 gross profit comprises $2,000,000 in revenue ($5,000,000 less revenue of $3,000,000 recognized in 2013 and 2014) and $1,840,000 in cost of construction (cost incurred in 2015). The 2015 income statement would report a gross profit of $160,000:

Revenue	$2,000,000
Less: Cost of construction	(1,840,000)
Gross profit	$ 160,000

Of course, when using the completed contract method, no profit or loss is recorded in 2013 or 2014. Instead, a $400,000 gross profit (revenue of $5,000,000 and cost of construction of $4,600,000) is recognized in 2015.

Loss is projected on the entire project.   If an overall loss is projected on the entire contract, the total loss must be recognized in the period in which that projection occurs, regardless of whether the percentage-of-completion or completed contract method is being used. Again consider the Harding Construction Company example but with the following cost information:

	2013	2014	2015
Construction costs incurred during the year	$1,500,000	$1,260,000	$2,440,000
Construction costs incurred in prior years	–0–	1,500,000	2,760,000
Cumulative construction costs	1,500,000	2,760,000	5,200,000
Estimated costs to complete at end of year	2,250,000	2,340,000	–0–
Total estimated and actual construction costs	$3,750,000	$5,100,000	$5,200,000

At the end of 2014, revised costs indicate a loss of $100,000 for the entire project ($5,000,000 − 5,100,000). In this situation, the *total* anticipated loss must be recognized in 2014 for both the percentage-of-completion method and the completed contract method. As a gross profit of $500,000 was recognized in 2013 using the percentage-of-completion method, *a $600,000 loss is recognized in 2014* so that the cumulative amount recognized to date totals a $100,000 loss. Once again, this situation is treated as a change in accounting estimate, with no restatement of 2013 income. If the completed contract method is used, because no gross profit is recognized in 2013, the $100,000 loss for the project is recognized in 2014 by debiting loss from long-term contracts and crediting construction in progress for $100,000.

> An estimated loss on a long-term contract is fully recognized in the first period the loss is anticipated, regardless of the revenue recognition method used.

Why recognize the estimated overall loss of $100,000 in 2014, rather than at the end of the contract? If the loss was not recognized in 2014, construction in progress would be valued at an amount greater than the company expects to realize from the contract. To avoid that problem, the construction in progress account is reduced to $2,660,000 ($2,760,000 in costs to date less $100,000 estimated total loss). This amount combined with the estimated costs to complete of $2,340,000 equals the realizable contract price of $5,000,000. Recognizing losses on long-term projects in the period the losses become known is equivalent to measuring inventory at the lower of cost or market.

The pattern of gross profit (loss) over the contract period for the two methods is summarized in the following table. Notice that an unanticipated increase in costs of $100,000 causes a further loss of $100,000 to be recognized in 2015.

	Percentage-of-Completion	Completed Contract
Gross profit (loss) recognized:		
2013	$ 500,000	–0–
2014	(600,000)	$(100,000)
2015	(100,000)	(100,000)
Total project loss	$(200,000)	$(200,000)

The table in Illustration 5–12G shows the revenue and cost of construction recognized in each of the three years using the percentage-of-completion method.

Revenue is recognized in the usual way by multiplying a percentage of completion by the total contract price. In situations where a loss is expected on the entire project, cost of construction for the period will no longer be equal to cost incurred during the period. The easiest way to compute cost of construction is to add the amount of the recognized loss to

Illustration 5–12G

Percentage-of-Completion Method: Allocation of Revenue and Cost of Construction to Each Period—Loss on Entire Project

2013		
Revenue recognized ($5,000,000 × 40%)		$2,000,000
Costs of construction		(1,500,000)
Gross profit		$ 500,000
2014		
Revenue recognized to date ($5,000,000 × 54.12%)*	$2,706,000	
Less: Revenue recognized in 2013	(2,000,000)	
Revenue recognized		$ 706,000
Cost of construction†		(1,306,000)
Loss		$ (600,000)
2015		
Revenue recognized to date ($5,000,000 × 100%)	$5,000,000	
Less: Revenue recognized in 2013 and 2014	(2,706,000)	
Revenue recognized		$2,294,000
Cost of construction†		(2,394,000)
Loss		$ (100,000)

*$2,760,000 ÷ $5,100,000 = 54.12%
†The difference between revenue and loss

the amount of revenue recognized. For example, in 2014 revenue recognized of $706,000 is added to the loss of $600,000 to arrive at the cost of construction of $1,306,000.[23]

The journal entries to record the losses in 2014 and 2015 are as follows:

2014		
Cost of construction	1,306,000	
Revenue from long-term contracts		706,000
Construction in progress (loss)		600,000
2015		
Cost of construction	2,394,000	
Revenue from long-term contracts		2,294,000
Construction in progress (loss)		100,000

Recognized losses on long-term contracts reduce the construction in progress account.

Using the completed contract method, no revenue or cost of construction is recognized until the contract is complete. In 2014, a loss on long-term contracts (an income statement account) of $100,000 is recognized. In 2015, the income statement will report revenue of $5,000,000 and cost of construction of $5,100,000, thus reporting the additional loss of $100,000. The journal entries to record the losses in 2014 and 2015 are as follows:

2014		
Loss on long-term contracts	100,000	
Construction in progress (loss)		100,000
2015		
Cost of construction	5,100,000	
Revenue from long-term contracts		5,000,000
Construction in progress (loss)		100,000

---

[23]The cost of construction also can be determined as follows:

Loss to date (100% recognized)		$ 100,000
Add:		
Remaining total project cost, not including the loss		
($5,100,000 − 100,000)	$5,000,000	
Multiplied by the percentage of completion	× .5412*	2,706,000
Total		2,806,000
Less: Cost of construction recognized in 2011		(1,500,000)
Cost of construction recognized in 2012		$1,306,000

*$2,760,000 ÷ 5,100,000

You can see from this example that use of the percentage-of-completion method in this case produces a large overstatement of income in 2013 and a large understatement in 2014 caused by a change in the estimation of future costs. These estimate revisions happen occasionally. However, recall that if management believes they are unable to make dependable forecasts of future costs, the completed contract method should be used.

International Financial Reporting Standards

Long-Term Construction Contracts. *IAS No. 11* governs revenue recognition for long-term construction contracts.[24] Like U.S. GAAP, that standard requires the use of the percentage-of-completion method when reliable estimates can be made. However, unlike U.S. GAAP, *IAS No. 11* requires the use of the cost recovery method rather than the completed contract method when reliable estimates can't be made.[25] Under the cost recovery method, contract costs are expensed as incurred, and an offsetting amount of contract revenue is recognized to the extent that it is probable that costs will be recoverable from the customer. No gross profit is recognized until all costs have been recovered, which is why this method is also sometimes called the "zero-profit method." Note that under both the completed contract and cost recovery methods no gross profit is recognized until the contract is essentially completed, but revenue and construction costs will be recognized earlier under the cost recovery method than under the completed contract method. Also, under both methods an expected loss is recognized immediately.

● LO5–8

To see this difference between the completed contract and cost recovery methods, here is a version of Illustration 5–12B that compares revenue, cost, and gross profit recognition under the two methods:

IFRS ILLUSTRATION

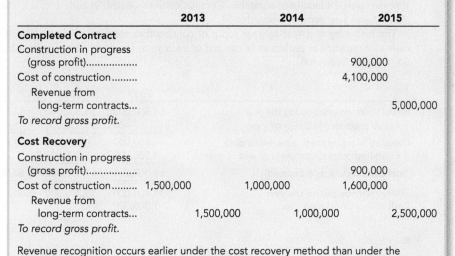

	2013	2014	2015
Completed Contract			
Construction in progress (gross profit).................			900,000
Cost of construction.........			4,100,000
Revenue from long-term contracts...			5,000,000
To record gross profit.			
Cost Recovery			
Construction in progress (gross profit).................			900,000
Cost of construction.........	1,500,000	1,000,000	1,600,000
Revenue from long-term contracts...	1,500,000	1,000,000	2,500,000
To record gross profit.			

Revenue recognition occurs earlier under the cost recovery method than under the completed contract method, but gross profit recognition occurs at the end of the contract for both methods. As a result, gross profit as a percentage of revenue differs between the two methods at various points in the life of the contract.

---

[24]"Construction Contracts," *International Accounting Standard No. 11* (IASCF), as amended, effective January 1, 2011.

[25]Earlier in this chapter we referred to the "cost recovery method" in a different circumstance—when a company had already delivered a product to a customer but had to delay gross profit recognition until a point after delivery because of an inability to make reliable estimates of uncollectible accounts. In that case, gross profit only could be recognized after costs had been recovered (and cash collections exceeded cost of goods sold). IFRS' use of "cost recovery method" is similar, in that gross profit recognition is delayed until after cost has been recovered, but note that in this case the product is being constructed for the customer and therefore has not yet been delivered.

The first disclosure note to any set of financial statements usually is a summary of significant accounting policies. This note discloses the method the company uses to account for its long-term contracts. As an example of this, Illustration 5–13 shows the disclosure note that appeared in a recent annual report of Fluor Corporation.

Illustration 5–13

Disclosure of Revenue Recognition Policy for Construction Contracts—Fluor Corporation

Real World Financials

> **Notes: Engineering and Construction Contracts (in part)**
>
> The company recognizes engineering and construction contract revenue using the percentage-of-completion method, based primarily on contract cost incurred to date compared to total estimated contract cost. . . . Contracts are generally segmented between types of services, such as engineering and construction, and accordingly, gross margin related to each activity is recognized as those separate services are rendered. Changes to total estimated contract cost or losses, if any, are recognized in the period in which they are determined. Pre-contract costs are expensed as incurred. Revenue recognized in excess of amounts billed is classified as a current asset under contract work in progress. Amounts billed to clients in excess of revenue recognized to date are classified as a current liability under advance billings on contracts.

Concept Review Exercise

LONG-TERM CONSTRUCTION CONTRACTS

During 2013, the Samuelson Construction Company began construction on an office building for the City of Gernon. The contract price is $8,000,000 and the building will take approximately 18 months to complete. Completion is scheduled for early in 2015. The company's fiscal year ends on December 31.

The following is a year-by-year recap of construction costs incurred and the estimated costs to complete the project as of the end of each year. Progress billings and cash collections also are indicated.

	2013	2014	2015
Actual costs incurred during the year	$1,500,000	$4,500,000	$1,550,000
Actual costs incurred in prior years	–0–	1,500,000	6,000,000
Cumulative actual costs incurred to date	1,500,000	6,000,000	7,550,000
Estimated costs to complete at end of year	4,500,000	1,500,000	–0–
Total costs (actual + estimated)	$6,000,000	$7,500,000	$7,550,000
Billings made during the year	$1,400,000	$5,200,000	$1,400,000
Cash collections during year	1,000,000	4,000,000	3,000,000

Required:

1. Determine the amount of gross profit or loss to be recognized in each of the three years applying both the percentage-of-completion and completed contract methods.
2. Prepare the necessary summary journal entries for each of the three years to account for construction costs incurred, recognized revenue and cost of construction, contract billings, and cash collections and to close the construction accounts in 2015 using the percentage-of-completion method only.
3. Prepare a partial balance sheet for 2013 and 2014 to include all construction-related accounts using the percentage-of-completion method.

Solution:

1. Determine the amount of gross profit or loss to be recognized in each of the three years applying both the percentage-of-completion and completed contract methods.

Percentage-of-Completion Method

	2013	2014	2015
Contract price	$8,000,000	$8,000,000	$8,000,000
Less: total cost*	6,000,000	$7,500,000	7,550,000
Total estimated gross profit to date	2,000,000	500,000	450,000
Multiplied by % of completion**	25%	80%	100%
Gross profit recognized to date	500,000	400,000	450,000
Less gross profit recognized in prior years	–0–	(500,000)	(400,000)
Gross profit (loss) recognized	$ 500,000	$ (100,000)	$ 50,000

*Estimated in 2013 & 2014; Actual in 2015.
**Estimated percentage of completion:

2013	2014	2015
$\frac{1,500,000}{6,000,000} = 25\%$	$\frac{6,000,000}{7,500,000} = 80\%$	Project complete

Completed Contract Method

	2013	2014	2015
Gross profit recognized	–0–	–0–	$450,000

2. Prepare the necessary summary journal entries for each of the three years to account for construction costs incurred, recognized revenue and cost of construction, contract billings, and cash collections and to close the construction accounts in 2015 using the percentage-of-completion method only.

	2013		2014		2015	
Construction in progress	1,500,000		4,500,000		1,550,000	
Cash, materials, etc.		1,500,000		4,500,000		1,550,000
To record construction costs.						
Construction in progress (gross profit) ...	500,000				50,000	
Cost of construction	1,500,000				1,550,000	
Revenue from long-term						
contracts (below)		2,000,000				1,600,000
To record gross profit.						
Cost of construction			4,500,000			
Revenue from long-term						
contracts (below)				4,400,000		
Construction in progress (loss)				100,000		
To record loss.						
Accounts receivable	1,400,000		5,200,000		1,400,000	
Billings on construction contract		1,400,000		5,200,000		1,400,000
To record progress billings.						
Cash	1,000,000		4,000,000		3,000,000	
Accounts receivable		1,000,000		4,000,000		3,000,000
To record cash collections.						
Billings on construction contract					8,000,000	
Construction in progress						8,000,000
To close accounts.						

Revenue recognized:		
2013:	$8,000,000 × 25% =	$2,000,000
2014:	$8,000,000 × 80% =	$6,400,000
	Less: Revenue recognized in 2013	(2,000,000)
	Revenue recognized in 2014	$4,400,000
2015:	$8,000,000 × 100% =	$8,000,000
	Less: Revenue recognized in 2013 and 2014	(6,400,000)
	Revenue recognized in 2015	$1,600,000

3. Prepare a partial balance sheet for 2013 and 2014 to include all construction-related accounts using the percentage-of-completion method.

Balance Sheet
(End of Year)

	2013	2014
Current assets:		
Accounts receivable	$400,000	$1,600,000
Costs and profit ($2,000,000) in excess of billings ($1,400,000)	600,000	
Current liabilities:		
Billings ($6,600,000) in excess of costs and profit ($6,400,000)		200,000

Industry-Specific Revenue Issues

The previous sections addressed situations when revenue is recognized either at a point in time after the earnings process is virtually complete or over time during the earnings process. We now look at situations that require revenue recognition using a combination of the two approaches.

● LO5–6

Software and Other Multiple-Element Arrangements

The software industry is a key economic component of our economy. Microsoft alone reported revenues of almost $70 billion for its 2011 fiscal year. Yet, the recognition of software revenues has been a controversial accounting issue. The controversy stems from the way software vendors typically package their products. It is not unusual for these companies to sell multiple software element in a bundle for a lump-sum contract price. The bundle often includes product, upgrades, postcontract customer support, and other services. The critical accounting question concerns the timing of revenue recognition.

GAAP indicates that if a software arrangement includes multiple elements, the revenue from the arrangement should be allocated to the various elements based on "vendor-specific objective evidence" ("VSOE") of fair values of the individual elements. It doesn't matter what separate prices are indicated in the multiple-element contract. Rather, the VSOE of fair values are the sales prices of the elements when sold separately by that vendor. If VSOE doesn't exist, revenue recognition is deferred until VSOE is available or until all elements of the arrangement are delivered.[26]

Generally, a portion of the proceeds received from the sale of software is deferred and recognized as revenue in future periods.

For example, suppose that a vendor sold software to a customer for $90,000. As part of the contract, the vendor promises to provide "free" technical support over the next six months. However, the vendor sells the same software without technical support for $80,000, and the vendor sells a stand-alone six-month technical support contract for $20,000, so those products would sell for $100,000 if sold separately. Based on that VSOE, the software comprises 80% of the total fair values, and the technical support 20%. Prior to the AICPA guidance, some vendors were recognizing the entire $90,000 as revenue when the initial software was delivered. Now, the $90,000 contract price must be allocated based on VSOE. Therefore, the seller would recognize $72,000 ($90,000 × 80%) in revenue up front when the software is delivered, and defer the remaining $18,000 ($90,000 × 20%) and recognize it ratably over the next six

---

[26]FASB ASC 985–605–25: Software–Revenue Recognition–Recognition (previously "Software Revenue Recognition," *Statement of Position 97-2* (New York: AICPA, 1997), p. 14).

months as the technical support service is provided. If VSOE was not available, the vendor couldn't recognize any revenue initially, and instead would recognize the entire $90,000 ratably over the six-month period.

These revenue deferrals can be material. For example, in its 2011 balance sheet, Microsoft reported a liability for unearned (deferred) software revenue of over $17 billion.

In 2009, the FASB's Emerging Issues Task Force (EITF) issued guidance to broaden the application of this basic perspective to other arrangements that involve "multiple deliverables."[27] Examples of such arrangements are sales of appliances with maintenance contracts, cellular phone contracts that come with a "free phone," and even painting services that include sales of paint as well as labor. Other examples are products that contain both hardware and software essential to the functioning of the product, such as computers and smart phones that are always sold with an operating system. Now, as with software-only contracts, sellers allocate total revenue to the various parts of a multiple-deliverable arrangement on the basis of the relative stand-alone selling prices of the parts. Sellers must defer revenue recognition for parts that don't have stand-alone value, or whose value is contingent upon other undelivered parts. However, unlike software-only arrangements, sellers offering other multiple-deliverable contracts now are allowed to *estimate* selling prices when they lack VSOE from stand-alone sales prices. Using estimated selling prices allows earlier revenue recognition than would be allowed if sellers had to have VSOE in order to recognize revenue.

For some sellers this change had a huge effect. As an example, consider Apple Inc. and the highly successful iPhone. Prior to the change, Apple deferred revenue on iPhones and other products because it didn't have VSOE of the sales price of future software upgrades included with the phones. This practice resulted in over $12 billion of deferred (unearned) revenue as of the end of fiscal 2009. The excerpt from Apple's 2009 amended 10-K shown in Illustration 5–14 highlights that being able to use estimated selling prices to allocate revenue amongst multiple deliverables had a big effect on Apple's financial statements.

Explanatory Note (in part)
The new accounting principles generally require the Company to account for the sale of both iPhone and Apple TV as two deliverables. The first deliverable is the hardware and software delivered at the time of sale, and the second deliverable is the right included with the purchase of iPhone and Apple TV to receive on a when-and-if-available basis future unspecified software upgrades and features relating to the product's software. The new accounting principles result in the recognition of substantially all of the revenue and product costs from sales of iPhone and Apple TV at the time of sale. Additionally, the Company is required to estimate a standalone selling price for the unspecified software upgrade right included with the sale of iPhone and Apple TV and recognizes that amount ratably over the 24-month estimated life of the related hardware device. For all periods presented, the Company's estimated selling price for the software upgrade right included with each iPhone and Apple TV sold is $25 and $10, respectively. The adoption of the new accounting principles increased the Company's net sales by $6.4 billion, $5.0 billion and $572 million for 2009, 2008 and 2007, respectively. As of September 26, 2009, the revised total accumulated deferred revenue associated with iPhone and Apple TV sales to date was $483 million. . . .

Illustration 5–14

Disclosure of Revenue Recognition Policy for Multiple Deliverables—Apple, Inc.

Real World Financials

After this accounting change, Apple recognizes almost all of the revenue associated with an iPhone at the time of sale. The only amount deferred is the small amount of revenue estimated for future software upgrade rights.

---

[27]FASB ASC 605–25–25: Revenue Recognition–Multiple-Element Arrangements–Recognition (originally *EITF 08-1: Revenue Arrangements with Multiple Deliverables* (Stamford, Conn.: FASB, 2009)), and *EITF 09-3: Applicability of AICPA Statement of Position 97-2 to Certain Arrangements That Include Software Elements* (Stamford, Conn.: FASB, 2009)).

International Financial Reporting Standards

● LO5–8

Multiple-Deliverable Arrangements. IFRS contains very little guidance about multiple-deliverable arrangements. *IAS No. 18* simply states that: ". . . in certain circumstances, it is necessary to apply the recognition criteria to the separately identifiable components of a single transaction in order to reflect the substance of the transaction" and gives a couple of examples.[28] Allocations of total revenue to individual components are based on fair value, with no requirements to focus on VSOE. Also, IFRS tends to encourage focus on the underlying economics of revenue transactions, so particular contractual characteristics like contingencies may matter less under IFRS than they do under U.S. GAAP.

Franchise Sales

The use of franchise arrangements has become increasingly popular in the United States over the past 30 years. Many retail outlets for fast food, restaurants, motels, and auto rental agencies are operated as franchises. In the franchise arrangements, the franchisor, for example McDonald's Corporation, grants to the franchisee, quite often an individual, the right to sell the franchisor's products and use its name for a specified period of time. The restaurant where you ate your last Big Mac was probably owned and operated by an individual under a franchise agreement, not by McDonald's Corporation.

The fees to be paid by the franchisee to the franchisor usually comprise (1) the *initial franchise fee* and (2) *continuing franchise fees*. The services to be performed by the franchisor in exchange for the initial franchise fee, in addition to the right to use its name and sell its products, might include assistance in finding a location, constructing the facilities, and training employees. The initial franchise fee usually is a fixed amount, but it may be payable in installments.

> **FASB**
> Franchise fee revenue from an individual franchise sale ordinarily shall be recognized, with an appropriate provision for estimated uncollectible amounts, when all material services or conditions relating to the sale have been substantially performed or satisfied by the franchisor.[29]

The continuing franchise fees are paid to the franchisor for continuing rights as well as for advertising and promotion and other services provided over the life of the franchise agreement. These fees sometimes are a fixed annual or monthly amount, a percentage of the volume of business done by the franchise, or a combination of both.

The continuing franchise fees usually do not present any accounting difficulty and are recognized by the franchisor as revenue *over time* in the periods the services are performed by the franchisor, which generally corresponds to the periods they are received. The challenging revenue recognition issue pertains to the initial franchise fee. In the early 1960s and 1970s, many franchisors recognized the entire initial franchise fee as revenue in the period in which the contract was signed. In many cases, there were significant services to be performed and the fee was collectible in installments over an extended period of time creating uncertainty as to cash collection.

Specific guidelines for revenue recognition of the initial franchise fee are provided by GAAP. You should notice the similarity of these specific guidelines with those of the general revenue recognition guidelines we've discussed previously. A key to these conditions is the concept of *substantial performance*. It requires that substantially all of the initial services of the franchisor required by the franchise agreement be performed before the initial franchise fee can be recognized as revenue. The term *substantial* requires professional judgment on the part of the accountant. In situations when the initial franchise fee is collectible in installments, even after substantial performance has occurred, the installment sales or cost recovery methods should be used for profit recognition, if a reasonable estimate of uncollectibility cannot be made.

Consider the example in Illustration 5–15.

---

[28]"Revenue," *International Accounting Standard No. 18* (IASCF), as amended effective January 1, 2011, par. 13.
[29]FASB ASC 952–605–25: Franchisors–Revenue Recognition–Recognition (previously "Accounting for Franchise Fee Revenue," *Statement of Financial Accounting Standards No. 45* (Stamford, Conn.: FASB, 1981)).

> On March 31, 2013, the Red Hot Chicken Wing Corporation entered into a franchise agreement with Thomas Keller. In exchange for an initial franchise fee of $50,000, Red Hot will provide initial services to include the selection of a location, construction of the building, training of employees, and consulting services over several years. $10,000 is payable on March 31, 2013, with the remaining $40,000 payable in annual installments which include interest at an appropriate rate. In addition, the franchisee will pay continuing franchise fees of $1,000 per month for advertising and promotion provided by Red Hot, beginning immediately after the franchise begins operations. Thomas Keller opened his Red Hot franchise for business on September 30, 2013.

Illustration 5–15
Franchise Sales

INITIAL FRANCHISE FEE.   Assuming that the initial services to be performed by Red Hot subsequent to the contract signing are substantial but that collectibility of the installment receivable is reasonably certain, the following journal entry is recorded:

March 31, 2013

Cash	10,000	
Note receivable	40,000	
Unearned franchise fee revenue		50,000
To record franchise agreement and down payment.		

Unearned franchise fee revenue is a liability. It would be reduced to zero and revenue would be recognized when the initial services have been performed. This could occur in increments or at one point in time, depending on the circumstances.[30] For example, in our illustration, if substantial performance was deemed to have occurred when the franchise began operations, the following entry would be recorded:

Sept. 30, 2013

Unearned franchise fee revenue	50,000	
Franchise fee revenue		50,000
To recognize franchise fee revenue.		

If collectibility of the installment receivable is uncertain and there is no basis for estimating uncollectible amounts, the initial entry would record a credit to deferred franchise fee revenue, which is then recognized as being earned using either the installment sales or cost recovery methods.

CONTINUING FRANCHISE FEES.   Continuing franchise fee revenue is recognized on a monthly basis as follows:

Cash (or accounts receivable)	1,000	
Service revenue		1,000
To recognize continuing franchise fee revenue.		

Expenses incurred by the franchisor in providing these continuing franchise services should be recognized in the same periods as the service revenue.

Other unique industry-specific revenue recognition situations exist besides those we have discussed. The FASB and AICPA have issued detailed revenue recognition guidance for such industries as insurance, record and music, cable television, and motion pictures.[31]

---

[30]Franchise agreements sometimes require that any payments made to the franchisor will be refunded if the franchise fails to open. If this condition is present, it would be an important factor in deciding whether to recognize revenue before the franchise opens.

[31]FASB ASC 944: Financial Services–Insurance (previously "Accounting and Reporting by Insurance Enterprises," *Statement of Financial Accounting Standards No. 60* (Stamford, Conn.: FASB, 1982)); FASB ASC 928—Entertainment–Music (previously "Financial Reporting in the Record and Music Industry," *Statement of Financial Accounting Standards No. 50* (Stamford, Conn.: FASB, 1981)); FASB ASC 922: Entertainment—Cable Television (previously "Financial Reporting by Cable Television Companies," *Statement of Financial Accounting Standards No. 51* (Stamford, Conn.: FASB, 1981)); FASB ASC 928: Entertainment–Films (previously "Accounting by Producers or Distributors of Films," *Statement of Position 00-2* (New York: AICPA, 2000)).

These industry standards are beyond the scope of this text. However, in each case, the objective is the same: to recognize revenue in the period or periods that the revenue-generating activities of the company are performed.

Additional Consideration

In certain circumstances, revenue is recognized at the completion of the production process (before delivery). This approach generally is used by companies that deal in precious metals, and ". . . agricultural, mineral, and other products, units of which are interchangeable and have an immediate marketability at quoted prices. . . ."[32] This is called the *production basis* of recognizing revenue and is accomplished by writing inventory up from cost to market value.

Recall that in a typical manufacturing situation, revenue is not recognized at the completion of the production process due to significant uncertainty as to the collectibility of the asset to be received. We don't know if the product will be sold, nor the selling price, nor the buyer if eventually sold. These uncertainties are not significant when there is immediate marketability at quoted market prices for products like precious metals.

In cases when the production basis of recognizing revenue is used, full disclosure of the fact is required.

Where We're Headed

The FASB and IASB are working together on a comprehensive revenue-recognition standard.

● LO5–8

The FASB and IASB are in the process of finalizing an Accounting Standards Update (ASU) that provides a new, comprehensive approach to revenue recognition. Why? Currently, the FASB has over 100 revenue-related standards that sometimes contradict each other and that treat similar economic events differently. The IASB has two primary standards (*IAS No. 11* and *IAS No. 18*) that also sometimes contradict each other and that don't offer guidance in some important areas (like multiple deliverables).[33] And, although both the FASB and IASB define revenue in terms of flows of assets and liabilities, the FASB guidance typically bases revenue recognition on the earnings process, while the IASB standards base it on the transfer of the risks and rewards of ownership, which can lead to different outcomes. So, the accounting guidance on revenue recognition could use some improvement.

The Boards' new approach is similar in many ways to the current U.S. guidance for recognizing revenue on multiple-deliverable contracts. The focus is on contracts between a seller and a buyer. A seller identifies all of its distinct performance obligations under a contract, determines the transaction price of the contract, and then allocates that price to the various performance obligations according to the estimated stand-alone selling prices of those obligations. The seller then recognizes revenue as each of those performance obligations is satisfied.

For many types of sales arrangements, adopting the proposed ASU will not change current practice. However, it will create consistency in revenue recognition across industries, and in some areas it will change practice considerably. For example, estimates of variable future payments will be included in revenue to a greater extent than exists currently, affecting revenue recognition on many contracts that peg future payments to future outcomes. Also, while companies still will estimate bad debts, an inability to estimate bad debts will not prevent revenue recognition, so the installment and cost-recovery methods will not exist.

The proposed ASU is being finalized at the time this text is being written. It is slated for issuance in late 2012, and adoption by companies will be required no sooner than 2015. We provide a detailed discussion of the proposed ASU in the chapter supplement.

---

[32]FASB ASC 330–10–35–16 : Inventory–Overall–Subsequent Measurement–Stating Inventories Above Cost (previously "Restatement and Revision of Accounting Research Bulletins," *Accounting Research Bulletin No. 43* (New York: AICPA, 1953), Chapter 4, par. 16).
[33]"Construction Contracts," *International Accounting Standard No. 11* (IASCF), as amended effective January 1, 2011, and "Revenue," *International Accounting Standard No. 18* (IASCF), as amended effective January 1, 2011.

PROFITABILITY ANALYSIS

Chapter 3 provided an overview of financial statement analysis and introduced some of the common ratios used in risk analysis to investigate a company's liquidity and long-term solvency. We now introduce ratios related to profitability analysis.

● LO5–7

Activity Ratios

One key to profitability is how well a company manages and utilizes its assets. Some ratios are designed to evaluate a company's effectiveness in managing assets. Of particular interest are the activity, or turnover ratios, of certain assets. The greater the number of times an asset turns over—the higher the ratio—the fewer assets are required to maintain a given level of activity (revenue). Given that a company incurs costs to finance its assets with debt (paying interest) or equity (paying dividends), high turnovers are usually attractive.

Activity ratios measure a company's efficiency in managing its assets.

Although, in concept, the activity or turnover can be measured for any asset, activity ratios are most frequently calculated for total assets, accounts receivable, and inventory. These ratios are calculated as follows:

$$\text{Asset turnover ratio} = \frac{\text{Net sales}}{\text{Average total assets}}$$

$$\text{Receivables turnover ratio} = \frac{\text{Net sales}}{\text{Average accounts receivable (net)}}$$

$$\text{Inventory turnover ratio} = \frac{\text{Cost of goods sold}}{\text{Average inventory}}$$

ASSET TURNOVER. A broad measure of asset efficiency is the asset turnover ratio. The ratio is computed by dividing a company's net sales or revenues by the average total assets available for use during a period. The denominator, average assets, is determined by adding beginning and ending total assets and dividing by two. The asset turnover ratio provides an indication of how efficiently a company utilizes all of its assets to generate revenue.

The *asset turnover ratio* measures a company's efficiency in using assets to generate revenue.

RECEIVABLES TURNOVER. The receivables turnover ratio is calculated by dividing a period's net credit sales by the average net accounts receivable. Because income statements seldom distinguish between cash sales and credit sales, this ratio usually is computed using total net sales as the numerator. The denominator, average accounts receivable, is determined by adding beginning and ending net accounts receivable (gross accounts receivable less allowance for uncollectible accounts) and dividing by two.[34]

The *receivables turnover ratio* offers an indication of how quickly a company is able to collect its accounts receivable.

The receivables turnover ratio provides an indication of a company's efficiency in collecting receivables. The ratio shows the number of times during a period that the average accounts receivable balance is collected. The higher the ratio, the shorter the average time between credit sales and cash collection.

A convenient extension is the average collection period. This measure is computed simply by dividing 365 days by the receivables turnover ratio. The result is an approximation of the number of days the average accounts receivable balance is outstanding.

$$\text{Average collection period} = \frac{365}{\text{Receivables turnover ratio}}$$

The *average collection period* indicates the average age of accounts receivable.

Monitoring the receivables turnover ratio (and average collection period) over time can provide useful information about a company's future prospects. For example, a decline in the receivables turnover ratio (an increase in the average collection period) could be an indication that sales are declining because of customer dissatisfaction with the company's products. Another possible explanation is that the company has changed its credit policy and is granting extended credit terms in order to maintain customers. Either explanation could

---

[34]Although *net* accounts receivable typically is used in practice for the denominator of receivables turnover, some prefer to use *gross* accounts receivable. Why? As the allowance for bad debts increases, net accounts receivable decreases, so if net accounts receivable is in the denominator, more bad debts have the effect of decreasing the denominator and therefore increasing receivables turnover. All else equal, an analyst would rather see receivables turnover improve because of more sales or less gross receivables, and not because of an increase in the allowance for bad debts.

signal a future increase in bad debts. Ratio analysis does not explain what is wrong. It does provide information that highlights areas for further investigation.

INVENTORY TURNOVER. An important activity measure for a merchandising company (a retail, wholesale, or manufacturing company) is the inventory turnover ratio. The ratio shows the number of times the average inventory balance is sold during a reporting period. It indicates how quickly inventory is sold. The more frequently a business is able to sell, or turn over, its inventory, the lower its investment in inventory must be for a given level of sales. The ratio is computed by dividing the period's cost of goods sold by the average inventory balance. The denominator, average inventory, is determined by adding beginning and ending inventory and dividing by two.[35]

The *inventory turnover ratio* measures a company's efficiency in managing its investment in inventory.

A relatively high ratio, say compared to a competitor, usually is desirable. A high ratio indicates comparative strength, perhaps caused by a company's superior sales force or maybe a successful advertising campaign. However, it might also be caused by a relatively low inventory level, which could mean either very efficient inventory management or stockouts and lost sales in the future.

On the other hand, a relatively low ratio, or a decrease in the ratio over time, usually is perceived to be unfavorable. Too much capital may be tied up in inventory. A relatively low ratio may result from overstocking, the presence of obsolete items, or poor marketing and sales efforts.

Similar to the receivables turnover, we can divide the inventory turnover ratio into 365 days to compute the average days in inventory. This measure indicates the number of days it normally takes to sell inventory.

$$\text{Average days in inventory} = \frac{365}{\text{Inventory turnover ratio}}$$

Profitability Ratios

A fundamental element of an analyst's task is to develop an understanding of a firm's profitability. Profitability ratios attempt to measure a company's ability to earn an adequate return relative to sales or resources devoted to operations. Resources devoted to operations can be defined as total assets or only those assets provided by owners, depending on the evaluation objective.

Profitability ratios assist in evaluating various aspects of a company's profit-making activities.

Three common profitability measures are (1) the profit margin on sales, (2) the return on assets, and (3) the return on shareholders' equity. These ratios are calculated as follows:

$$\text{Profit margin on sales} = \frac{\text{Net income}}{\text{Net sales}}$$

$$\text{Return on assets} = \frac{\text{Net income}}{\text{Average total assets}}$$

$$\text{Return on shareholder's equity} = \frac{\text{Net income}}{\text{Average shareholders' equity}}$$

Notice that for all of the profitability ratios, our numerator is net income. Recall our discussion in Chapter 4 on earnings quality. The relevance of any historical-based financial statement hinges on its predictive value. To enhance predictive value, analysts often adjust net income in these ratios to separate a company's *transitory earnings* effects from its *permanent earnings*. Analysts begin their assessment of permanent earnings with income from continuing operations. Then, adjustments are made for any unusual, one-time gains or losses included in income from continuing operations. It is this adjusted number that they use as the numerator in these ratios.

When calculating profitability ratios, analysts often adjust net income for any transitory income effects.

PROFIT MARGIN ON SALES. The profit margin on sales is simply net income divided by net sales. The ratio measures an important dimension of a company's profitability. It indicates the portion of each dollar of revenue that is available after all expenses have been covered. It offers a measure of the company's ability to withstand either higher expenses or lower revenues.

The *profit margin on sales* measures the amount of net income achieved per sales dollar.

What is considered to be a desirable profit margin is highly sensitive to the nature of the business activity. For instance, you would expect a specialty shop to have a higher profit

---

[35]Notice the consistency in the measure used for the numerator and denominator of the two turnover ratios. For the receivables turnover ratio, both numerator and denominator are based on sales dollars, whereas they are both based on cost for the inventory turnover ratio.

margin than, say, Walmart. A low profit margin can be compensated for by a high asset turnover rate, and vice versa, which brings us to considering the trade-offs inherent in generating return on assets.

RETURN ON ASSETS. The return on assets (ROA) ratio expresses income as a percentage of the average total assets available to generate that income. Because total assets are partially financed with debt and partially by equity funds, this is an inclusive way of measuring earning power that ignores specific sources of financing.

A company's return on assets is related to both profit margin and asset turnover. Specifically, profitability can be achieved by either a high profit margin, high turnover, or a combination of the two. In fact, the return on assets can be calculated by multiplying the profit margin and the asset turnover.

$$\text{Return on assets} = \text{Profit margin} \times \text{Asset turnover}$$

$$\frac{\text{Net income}}{\text{Average total assets}} = \frac{\text{Net income}}{\text{Net sales}} \times \frac{\text{Net sales}}{\text{Average total assets}}$$

Profit margin and asset turnover combine to yield return on assets, which measures the return generated by a company's assets.

Industry standards are particularly important when evaluating asset turnover and profit margin. Some industries are characterized by low turnover but typically make up for it with higher profit margins. Others have low profit margins but compensate with high turnover. Grocery stores typically have relatively low profit margins but relatively high asset turnover. In comparison, a manufacturer of specialized equipment will have a higher profit margin but a lower asset turnover ratio.

RETURN ON SHAREHOLDERS' EQUITY. Equity investors typically are concerned about the amount of profit that management can generate from the resources that owners provide. A closely watched measure that captures this concern is return on equity (ROE), calculated by dividing net income by average shareholders' equity.

The return on shareholders' equity measures the return to suppliers of equity capital.

Additional Consideration

The return on assets ratio often is computed as follows:

$$\text{Return on assets} = \frac{\text{Net income} + \text{Interest expense } (1 - \text{Tax rate})}{\text{Average total assets}}$$

The reason for adding back interest expense (net of tax) is that interest represents a return to suppliers of debt capital and should not be deducted in the computation of net income when computing the return on total assets. In other words, the numerator is the total amount of income available to both debt and equity capital.

In addition to monitoring return on equity, investors want to understand how that return can be improved. The DuPont framework provides a convenient basis for analysis that breaks return on equity into three key components:[36]

The DuPont framework shows that return on equity depends on profitability, activity, and financial leverage.

- **Profitability,** measured by the profit margin (Net income ÷ Sales). As discussed already, a higher profit margin indicates that a company is generating more profit from each dollar of sales.
- **Activity,** measured by asset turnover (Sales ÷ Average total assets). As discussed already, higher asset turnover indicates that a company is using its assets efficiently to generate more sales from each dollar of assets.
- **Financial Leverage,** measured by the equity multiplier (Average total assets ÷ Average total equity). A high equity multiplier indicates that relatively more of the company's assets have been financed with debt. As indicated in Chapter 3, leverage can provide additional return to the company's equity holders.

---

[36]DuPont analysis is so named because the basic model was developed by F. Donaldson Brown, an electrical engineer who worked for DuPont in the early part of the 20th century.

In equation form, the DuPont framework looks like this:

$$\textbf{Return on equity} = \textbf{Profit margin} \times \textbf{Asset turnover} \times \textbf{Equity multiplier}$$

$$\frac{\text{Net income}}{\text{Avg. total equity}} = \frac{\text{Net income}}{\text{Total sales}} \times \frac{\text{Total sales}}{\text{Avg. total assets}} \times \frac{\text{Avg. total assets}}{\text{Avg. total equity}}$$

Notice that total sales and average total assets appear in the numerator of one ratio and the denominator of another, so they cancel to yield net income ÷ average total equity, or ROE.

We have already seen that ROA is determined by profit margin and asset turnover, so another way to compute ROE is by multiplying ROA by the equity multiplier:

$$\textbf{Return on equity} = \textbf{Return on assets} \times \textbf{Equity multiplier}$$

$$\frac{\text{Net income}}{\text{Avg. total equity}} = \frac{\text{Net income}}{\text{Avg. total assets}} \times \frac{\text{Avg. total assets}}{\text{Avg. total equity}}$$

We can see from this equation that an equity multiplier of greater than 1 will produce a return on equity that is higher than the return on assets. However, as with all ratio analysis, there are trade-offs. If leverage is too high, creditors become concerned about the potential for default on the company's debt and require higher interest rates. Because interest is recognized as an expense, net income is reduced, so at some point the benefits of a higher equity multiplier are offset by a lower profit margin. Part of the challenge of managing a company is to identify the combination of profitability, activity, and leverage that produces the highest return for equity holders.

> **Because profit margin and asset turnover combine to create return on assets, the DuPont framework can also be viewed as indicating that return on equity depends on return on assets and financial leverage.**

Additional Consideration

> Sometimes when return on equity is calculated, shareholders' equity is viewed more narrowly to include only common shareholders. In that case, preferred stock is excluded from the denominator, and preferred dividends are deducted from net income in the numerator. The resulting rate of return on common shareholders' equity focuses on profits generated on resources provided by common shareholders.

Illustration 5–16 provides a recap of the ratios we have discussed.

Illustration 5–16

Summary of Profitability Analysis Ratios

Activity ratios		
Asset turnover	=	$\dfrac{\text{Net sales}}{\text{Average total assets}}$
Receivables turnover	=	$\dfrac{\text{Net sales}}{\text{Average accounts receivable (net)}}$
Average collection period	=	$\dfrac{365}{\text{Receivables turnover ratio}}$
Inventory turnover	=	$\dfrac{\text{Cost of goods sold}}{\text{Average inventory}}$
Average days in inventory	=	$\dfrac{365}{\text{Inventory turnover ratio}}$
Profitability ratios		
Profit margin on sales	=	$\dfrac{\text{Net income}}{\text{Net sales}}$
Return on assets	=	$\dfrac{\text{Net income}}{\text{Average total assets}}$
Return on shareholders' equity	=	$\dfrac{\text{Net income}}{\text{Average shareholders' equity}}$
Leverage ratio		
Equity multiplier	=	$\dfrac{\text{Average total assets}}{\text{Average total equity}}$

Profitability Analysis—An Illustration

To illustrate the application of the DuPont framework and the computation of the activity and profitability ratios, we analyze the 2011 financial statements of two well-known retailers, **Target Corporation** and **Wal-Mart Stores, Inc.**[37] The operations of these two companies are similar in terms of their focus on operating large general merchandising and food discount stores. Illustration 5–17A presents selected financial statement information for the two companies.

	Target		Walmart	
	2011	**2010**	**2011**	**2010**
Accounts receivable (net)	$ 6,153	$ 6,966	$ 5,089	$ 4,144
Inventories	$ 7,596	$ 7,179	$ 36,318	$ 32,713
Total assets	$43,705	$44,533	$180,663	$170,407
Total liabilities	$28,218	$29,186	$109,008	$ 97,452
Total shareholders' equity	$15,487	$15,347	$ 71,655	$ 72,955
Two-year averages:				
Accounts receivable (net)		$ 6,560		$ 4,617
Inventories		$ 7,388		$ 34,516
Total assets		$44,119		$175,535
Total shareholders' equity		$15,417		$ 72,305
Income Statement—2011				
Net sales		$65,786		$421,849
Cost of goods sold		$46,451		$315,287
Net Income (income from continuing operations for Walmart)		$ 2,920		$ 16,389

Illustration 5–17A

Selected Financial Information for Target Corporation and Wal-Mart Stores, Inc.

Real World Financials

On the surface it appears that Walmart is far more profitable than Target. As shown in Illustration 5–17A, Walmart's 2011 net income was $16.389 billion, compared to Target's $2.920 billion. But that's not the whole story. Even though both are very large companies, Walmart is more than four times the size of Target in terms of total assets, so how can they be compared? Focusing on financial ratios helps adjust for size differences, and the DuPont framework helps identify the determinants of profitability from the perspective of shareholders.

Illustration 5–17B includes the DuPont analysis for Walmart and Target, as well as some additional activity ratios we've discussed. Walmart's return on assets (ROA) is higher than Target's (9.34% for Walmart compared to 6.62% for Target). Why? Remember that both profitability and activity combine to determine return on assets. Target's profit margin actually is a bit higher than Walmart's (4.44% compared to 3.89%), but Walmart's asset turnover is much higher than Target's (2.40 compared to 1.49). So, even though Target makes more profit on each sale, Walmart makes significantly more sales with its assets, and Walmart ends up coming out ahead on return on assets, both compared to Target and compared to the industry average.

The average days in inventory provides insight into Walmart's higher asset turnover. Inventory takes only 40 days on average before being sold by Walmart, compared with 47 for the industry average and 58 days for Target. Walmart also turns over its accounts receivable faster than Target does, but accounts receivable are small and don't matter much

[37]Walmart's financial statements are for the fiscal year ended January 31, 2011. Walmart refers to this as its 2011 fiscal year. Target's financial statements are for the fiscal year ended January 29, 2011. Target refers to this as its 2010 fiscal year, but for consistency with Walmart we refer to it as 2011.

Illustration 5–17B

DuPont Framework and Activity Ratios—Target Corporation and Wal-Mart Stores, Inc.

	Target		Walmart		Industry Average*
DuPont analysis:					
Profit margin on sales	$= \dfrac{\$2{,}920}{\$65{,}786} =$	4.44%	$\dfrac{\$16{,}389}{\$421{,}849} =$	3.89%	3.43%
×		×		×	
Asset turnover	$= \dfrac{\$65{,}786}{\$44{,}119} =$	1.49	$\dfrac{\$421{,}849}{\$175{,}535} =$	2.40	2.19
=		=		=	
Return on assets	$= \dfrac{\$2{,}920}{\$44{,}119} =$	6.62%	$\dfrac{\$16{,}389}{\$175{,}535} =$	9.34%	7.51%
×		×		×	
Equity Multiplier	$= \dfrac{\$44{,}119}{\$15{,}417} =$	2.86	$\dfrac{\$175{,}535}{\$72{,}305} =$	2.43	2.23
=		=		=	
Return on shareholders' equity	$= \dfrac{\$2{,}920}{\$15{,}417} =$	18.94%	$\dfrac{\$16{,}389}{\$72{,}305} =$	22.67%	16.76%
Other activity ratios:					
Receivables turnover	$= \dfrac{\$65{,}786}{\$6{,}560} =$	10.03	$\dfrac{\$421{,}849}{\$4{,}617} =$	91.37	44.11
Average collection period	$= \dfrac{365}{10.03} =$	36.39 days	$\dfrac{365}{91.37} =$	3.99 days	8.28 days
Inventory turnover	$= \dfrac{\$46{,}451}{\$7{,}388} =$	6.29	$\dfrac{\$315{,}287}{\$34{,}516} =$	9.13	7.73
Average days in inventory	$= \dfrac{365}{6.29} =$	58.03 days	$\dfrac{365}{9.13} =$	39.98 days	47.24 days

*Industry average based on sample of eleven discount retail companies.

for Walmart (Target offers a charge card and so maintains a higher receivable balance, on which it earns interest revenue).

What matters most to the shareholders of these companies is not return on assets, but the return on equity (ROE). Both beat the industry average, but Walmart also wins on this measure, with an ROE of 22.67% compared to Target's 18.94%. Target's equity multiplier is higher than Walmart's (2.86 for Target compared to 2.43 for Walmart), but that difference in leverage is not enough to make up for Walmart's much higher ROA.

A Target shareholder looking at these numbers might wonder how best to increase ROE. Should Target attempt to increase operational efficiency in hopes of approaching Walmart on the asset turnover dimension? Or, should Target attempt to increase profit margin? Given competitive pressures on retail pricing, can Target earn a much higher profit margin with its current product mix by including more upscale items in its inventory? Or, should Target attempt to increase leverage, such that debtholders are financing a greater percentage of assets?

The essential point of our discussion here, and in Part C of Chapter 3, is that raw accounting numbers alone mean little to decision makers. The numbers gain value when viewed in relation to other numbers. Similarly, the financial ratios formed by those relationships provide even greater perspective when compared with similar ratios of other companies, or relatedly, with averages for several companies in the same industry. Accounting information is useful in making decisions. Financial analysis that includes comparisons of financial ratios enhances the value of that information.

Financial Reporting Case Solution

1. **Does your sister have to wait two and a half years to get her bonus? Explain.**
   (p. 238)   No. The *general* revenue recognition criteria would suggest that revenue and costs should be recognized when a project is finished. The difficulty this would create is that all revenues, expenses, and resulting profit from the project are recognized when the project is completed; no revenues or expenses would be reported in the income statements of earlier reporting periods in which much of the work may have been performed. The percentage-of-completion method of revenue recognition for long-term projects addresses this problem. A share of the project's profit is allocated to each period in which the earnings process occurs. This is two and a half years in this instance.

2. **How are gross profits recognized using the percentage-of-completion method?**
   (p. 245)   The percentage-of-completion method recognizes part of the estimated gross profit each period. The amount recognized is based on progress to date, which is estimated as the fraction of the project's cost incurred to date divided by total estimated costs. The estimated percentage of completion is multiplied by the revised project gross profit estimate. This yields the estimated gross profit earned from the beginning of the project. The gross profit recognized is calculated by subtracting from this amount the gross profit recognized in previous periods.

3. **Are there other situations in which revenue is recognized at times other than when a product is delivered?** *(p. 248)*   Yes, revenue recognition sometimes is delayed until after the product is delivered. These situations involve either the possibility of product returns or bad debts. In most cases, product returns and bad debt are estimated and revenues are recognized when a product is delivered. However, in situations involving an abnormal degree of uncertainty about cash collection caused by potential returns or bad debts, revenue recognition *after* delivery sometimes is appropriate. ●

The Bottom Line

● **LO5–1**   The objective of revenue recognition is to recognize revenue in the period or periods that the revenue-generating activities of the company are performed. Also, judgment as to the collectibility of the cash from the sale of a product or service will impact the timing of revenue recognition. These two concepts of performance and collectibility are captured by the general guidelines for revenue recognition in the realization principle, which requires that revenue should be recognized only after (1) the earnings process is virtually complete and (2) there is reasonable certainty of collecting the asset to be received (usually cash) from the customer. For the sale of product, these criteria usually are satisfied at the point of product delivery. At that point, the majority of the productive activities have taken place and any remaining uncertainty concerning asset collection can be accounted for by estimating possible returns and bad debts. Also, service revenue often is recognized at a point in time if there is one final activity that is deemed critical to the earnings process. *(p. 232)*

● **LO5–2**   A *principal* has primary responsibility for delivering a product or service and recognizes as revenue the gross amount received from a customer. An *agent* doesn't primarily deliver goods or services, but acts as a facilitator that earns a commission for helping sellers transact with buyers and recognizes as revenue only the commission it receives for facilitating the sale. Various indicators can be used to determine which treatment is appropriate for a particular transaction. *(p. 237)*

● **LO5–3**   The installment sales method recognizes gross profit in collection periods by applying the gross profit percentage on the sale to the amount of cash actually received. The cost recovery method defers all gross profit recognition until cash has been received equal to the cost of the item sold. These methods of recognizing revenue should only be used in situations where there is an unusually high degree of uncertainty regarding the ultimate cash collection on an installment sale. *(p. 239)*

● **LO5–4**   In most situations, even though the right to return merchandise exists, revenues and expenses can be appropriately recognized at point of delivery. Based on past experience, a company usually can estimate the returns that will result for a given volume of sales. These estimates reduce both sales and cost of goods sold in anticipation of returns. Revenue cannot be recognized at the point of delivery unless the seller is able to make reliable estimates of future returns. Otherwise, revenue recognition is deferred beyond the delivery point. (*p. 243*)

● **LO5–5** Revenue recognition at a single point in time when the earnings process is virtually complete is inappropriate for certain types of service revenue activities and also, usually, for long-term contracts. The completed contract method recognizes revenues and expenses on long-term construction and other long-term contracts at a point in time when the project is complete. This method is only used in unusual situations. The preferable method for recognizing revenues and expenses for long-term contracts is the percentage-of-completion method, which recognizes revenues over time by assigning a share of the project's revenues and costs to each reporting period during the project. (*p. 244*)

● **LO5–6** Industry guidelines require that the lump-sum contract price for software be allocated to the various elements of the package based on the relative fair values of the individual elements. Generally, this results in a deferral of a portion of the proceeds that are then recognized as revenue in future periods. Other multiple-deliverable arrangements are accounted for in a similar manner. The use of franchise arrangements has become increasingly popular. The fees to be paid by the franchisee to the franchisor usually are composed of (1) the initial franchise fee and (2) continuing franchise fees. GAAP requires that the franchisor has substantially performed the services promised in the franchise agreement and that the collectibility of the initial franchise fee is reasonably assured before the initial fee can be recognized as revenue. The continuing franchise fees are recognized by the franchisor as revenue over time in the periods the services are performed by the franchisor. (*pp. 258* and *260*)

● **LO5–7** Activity and profitability ratios provide information about a company's profitability. Activity ratios include the receivables turnover ratio, the inventory turnover ratio, and the asset turnover ratio. Profitability ratios include the profit margin on sales, the return on assets, and the return on shareholders' equity. DuPont analysis explains return on stockholders' equity as determined by profit margin, asset turnover, and the extent to which assets are financed with equity versus debt. (*p. 263*)

● **LO5–8** For the most part, revenue recognition requirements are similar under U.S. GAAP and IFRS. U.S. GAAP is much more detailed, though, especially with respect to industry-specific guidance and multi-deliverable arrangements. In addition, when the percentage-of-completion method is not used to account for a long-term contract, U.S. GAAP requires the use of the completed contract method (in which revenue, cost, and gross profit are all typically recognized at the end of the contract), while IFRS requires the cost recovery method (in which revenue and cost are recognized over the life of the contract, but gross profit is recognized only after all costs have been recovered, which is typically at the end of the contract). As indicated in Appendix 5, IFRS views interim reports on a stand-alone basis rather than as an integral part of the annual report, as done in U.S. GAAP. As a result, interim period income under IFRS may be more volatile than under U.S. GAAP (*pp. 235, 255, 260, 262* and *272*) ●

APPENDIX 5   Interim Reporting

Interim reports are issued for periods of less than a year, typically as quarterly financial statements.

Financial statements covering periods of less than a year are called *interim reports.* Companies registered with the SEC, which includes most public companies, must submit quarterly reports, and you will see excerpts from these reports throughout this book.[38] Though there is no requirement to do so, most also send quarterly reports to their shareholders and typically include abbreviated, unaudited interim reports as supplemental information within their annual reports. For instance, Illustration 5A-1 shows the quarterly information disclosed in the 2011 annual report of **Dell Inc.**

For accounting information to be useful to decision makers, it must be available on a timely basis. One of the objectives of interim reporting is to enhance the timeliness of financial information. In addition, quarterly reports provide investors and creditors with additional insight on the seasonality of business operations that might otherwise get lost in annual reports.

The fundamental debate regarding interim reporting centers on the choice between the *discrete* and *integral part* approaches.

However, the downside to these benefits is the relative unreliability of interim reporting. With a shorter reporting period, questions associated with estimation and allocation are magnified. For example, certain expenses often benefit an entire year's operations and yet

---

[38]Quarterly reports are filed with the SEC on form 10-Q. Annual reports to the SEC are on form 10-K.

Illustration 5A-1 Interim Data in Annual Report—Dell Inc.

	Fiscal Year 2011			
	First Quarter	Second Quarter	Third Quarter	Fourth Quarter
	(in millions, except per share data)			
Net revenue	$14,874	$15,534	$15,394	$15,692
Gross margin	2,516	2,586	3,003	3,291
Net income	341	545	822	927
Earnings per common share:				
Basic	0.17	0.28	0.42	0.48
Diluted	0.17	0.28	0.42	0.48
Weighted-average shares outstanding:				
Basic	1,961	1,952	1,939	1,924
Diluted	1,973	1,960	1,949	1,938
Stock sales price per share:				
High	17.52	16.46	14.89	14.70
Low	12.92	11.72	11.34	13.06

Real World Financials

are incurred primarily within a single interim period. Similarly, should smaller companies use lower tax rates in the earlier quarters and higher rates in later quarters as higher tax brackets are reached? Another result of shorter reporting periods is the intensified effect of major events such as discontinued operations or extraordinary items. A second quarter casualty loss, for instance, that would reduce annual profits by 10% might reduce second quarter profits by 40% or more. Is it more realistic to allocate such a loss over the entire year? These and similar questions tend to hinge on the way we view an interim period in relation to the fiscal year. More specifically, should each interim period be viewed as a *discrete* reporting period or as an *integral part* of the annual period?

Reporting Revenues and Expenses

Existing practice and current reporting requirements for interim reporting generally follow the viewpoint that interim reports are an integral part of annual statements, although the discrete approach is applied to some items. Most revenues and expenses are recognized using the same accounting principles applicable to annual reporting. Some modifications are necessary to help cause interim statements to relate better to annual statements. This is most evident in the way costs and expenses are recognized. Most are recognized in interim periods as incurred. But when an expenditure clearly benefits more than just the period in which it is incurred, the expense should be allocated among the periods benefited on an allocation basis consistent with the company's annual allocation procedures. For example, annual repair expenses, property tax expense, and advertising expenses incurred in the first quarter that clearly benefit later quarters are assigned to each quarter through the use of accruals and deferrals. Costs and expenses subject to year-end adjustments, such as depreciation expense, are estimated and allocated to interim periods in a systematic way. Similarly, income tax expense at each interim date should be based on estimates of the effective tax rate for the whole year. This would mean, for example, that if the estimated effective rate has changed since the previous interim period(s), the tax expense period would be determined as the new rate times the cumulative pretax income to date, less the total tax expense reported in previous interim periods.

With only a few exceptions, the same accounting principles applicable to annual reporting are used for interim reporting.

Reporting Unusual Items

On the other hand, major events such as discontinued operations or extraordinary items should be reported separately in the interim period in which they occur. That is, these amounts should not be allocated among individual quarters within the fiscal year. The same is true for items that are unusual or infrequent but not both. Treatment of these items is more consistent with the discrete view than the integral part view.

Discontinued operations, extraordinary items, and unusual items are reported entirely within the interim period in which they occur.

International Financial Reporting Standards

● LO5–8

Interim Reporting. *IAS No. 34* requires that a company apply the same accounting policies in its interim financial statements as it applies in its annual financial statements. Therefore, IFRS takes much more of a discrete-period approach than does U.S. GAAP. For example, costs for repairs, property taxes, and advertising that do not meet the definition of an asset at the end of an interim period are expensed entirely in the period in which they occur under IFRS, but are accrued or deferred and then charged to each of the periods they benefit under U.S. GAAP. This difference would tend to make interim period income more volatile under IFRS than under U.S. GAAP. However, as in U.S. GAAP, income taxes are accounted for based on an estimate of the tax rate expected to apply for the entire year.[39]

Earnings Per Share

Quarterly EPS calculations follow the same procedures as annual calculations.

A second item that is treated in a manner consistent with the discrete view is earnings per share. EPS calculations for interim reports follow the same procedures as annual calculations that you will study in Chapter 19. The calculations are based on conditions actually existing during the particular interim period rather than on conditions estimated to exist at the end of the fiscal year.

Reporting Accounting Changes

Accounting changes made in an interim period are reported by retrospectively applying the changes to prior financial statements.

Recall from Chapter 4 that we account for a change in accounting principle retrospectively, meaning we recast prior years' financial statements when we report those statements again in comparative form. In other words, we make those statements appear as if the newly adopted accounting method had been used in those prior years. It's the same with interim reporting. We retrospectively report a change made during an interim period in similar fashion. Then in financial reports of subsequent interim periods of the same fiscal year, we disclose how that change affected (a) income from continuing operations, (b) net income, and (c) related per share amounts for the postchange interim period.

Minimum Disclosures

Complete financial statements are not required for interim period reporting, but certain minimum disclosures are required as follows:[40]

- Sales, income taxes, extraordinary items, and net income.
- Earnings per share.
- Seasonal revenues, costs, and expenses.
- Significant changes in estimates for income taxes.
- Discontinued operations, extraordinary items, and unusual or infrequent items.
- Contingencies.
- Changes in accounting principles or estimates.
- Information about fair value of financial instruments and the methods and assumptions used to estimate fair values.
- Significant changes in financial position.

When fourth quarter results are not separately reported, material fourth quarter events, including year-end adjustments, should be reported in disclosure notes to annual statements. ●

---

[39]"Interim Financial Reporting," *International Accounting Standard No. 34* (IASCF), as amended effective January 1, 2011, par. 28–30.
[40]FASB ASC 270–10–50: Interim Reporting–Overall–Disclosure (previously "Interim Financial Reporting," *Accounting Principles Board Opinion No 28* (New York: AICPA, 1973)).

Questions For Review of Key Topics

Q 5–1   What are the two general criteria that must be satisfied before a company can recognize revenue?

Q 5–2   Explain why, in most cases, a seller recognizes revenue when it delivers its product rather than when it produces the product.

Q 5–3   What is the difference between a principal and an agent for purposes of determining whether a company should report revenue on a gross or net basis?

Q 5–4   Revenue recognition for most installment sales occurs at the point of delivery of the product or service. Under what circumstances would a seller delay revenue recognition for installment sales beyond the delivery date?

Q 5–5   Distinguish between the installment sales method and the cost recovery method of accounting for installment sales.

Q 5–6   How does a company report deferred gross profit resulting from the use of the installment sales method in its balance sheet?

Q 5–7   Revenue recognition for most product sales that allow the right of return occurs at the point of product delivery. Under what circumstances would revenue recognition be delayed?

Q 5–8   Describe a consignment sale. When does a consignor recognize revenue for a consignment sale?

Q 5–9   Service revenue is recognized either at one point in time or over extended periods. Explain the rationale for recognizing revenue using these two approaches.

Q 5–10   Distinguish between the percentage-of-completion and completed contract methods of accounting for long-term contracts with respect to income recognition. Under what circumstances should a company use the completed contract method?

IFRS Q 5–11   When percentage-of-completion accounting is not appropriate, U.S. GAAP requires the use of the completed contract method, while IFRS requires the use of the cost recovery method. Explain how the two methods affect recognition of revenue, cost of construction, and gross profit over the life of a profitable contract.

Q 5–12   Periodic billings to the customer for a long-term construction contract are recorded as billings on construction contract. How is this account reported in the balance sheet?

Q 5–13   When is an estimated loss on a long-term contract recognized using the percentage-of-completion method? The completed contract method?

Q 5–14   Briefly describe the guidelines for recognizing revenue from the sale of software and other multiple-deliverable arrangements.

IFRS Q 5–15   Briefly describe how IFRS guidelines for recognizing revenue from multiple-deliverable arrangements differ from U.S. GAAP guidelines.

Q 5–16   Briefly describe the guidelines provided by GAAP for the recognition of revenue by a franchisor for an initial franchise fee.

Q 5–17   Show the calculation of the following activity ratios: (1) the receivables turnover ratio, (2) the inventory turnover ratio, and (3) the asset turnover ratio. What information about a company do these ratios offer?

Q 5–18   Show the calculation of the following profitability ratios: (1) the profit margin on sales, (2) the return on assets, and (3) the return on shareholders' equity. What information about a company do these ratios offer?

Q 5–19   Show the DuPont framework's calculation of the three components of return on shareholders' equity. What information about a company do these ratios offer?

Q 5–20   [Based on Appendix 5] Interim reports are issued for periods of less than a year, typically as quarterly financial statements. Should these interim periods be viewed as separate periods or integral parts of the annual period?

IFRS Q 5–21   [Based on Appendix 5] What is the primary difference between interim reports under IFRS and U.S. GAAP?

Brief Exercises

BE 5–1
Point of delivery
recognition
● LO5–1

On July 1, 2013, Apache Company sold a parcel of undeveloped land to a construction company for $3,000,000. The book value of the land on Apache's books was $1,200,000. Terms of the sale required a down payment of $150,000 and 19 annual payments of $150,000 plus interest at an appropriate interest rate due on each July 1 beginning in 2014. Apache has no significant obligations to perform services after the sale. How much gross profit will Apache recognize in both 2013 and 2014 assuming point of delivery profit recognition?

274   SECTION 1   The Role of Accounting as an Information System

BE 5–2
Principal or agent
● LO5–2

Assume that Amazon.com sells the MacBook Pro, a computer brand produced by Apple. Amazon arranges its operations such that customers receive products from Apple Stores rather than Amazon. Customers purchase from Amazon using credit cards, and Amazon forwards cash to Apple less a fixed commission that Amazon keeps above the normal wholesale MacBook Pro price. In this arrangement, is Amazon a principal or an agent? Why? Given that answer, would Amazon recognize revenue for the entire sales price of the MacBook Pro or only the amount of the commission received in exchange for arranging sales for Apple Stores?

BE 5–3
Installment sales method
● LO5–3

Refer to the situation described in BE 5–1. How much gross profit will Apache recognize in both 2013 and 2014 applying the installment sales method?

BE 5–4
Cost recovery method
● LO5–3

Refer to the situation described in BE 5–1. How much gross profit will Apache recognize in both 2013 and 2014 applying the cost recovery method?

BE 5–5
Installment sales method
● LO5–3

Refer to the situation described in BE 5–1. What should be the balance in the deferred gross profit account at the end of 2014 applying the installment sales method?

BE 5–6
Right of return
● LO5–4

Meyer Furniture sells office furniture mainly to corporate clients. Customers who return merchandise within 90 days for any reason receive a full refund. Discuss the issues Meyer must consider in determining its revenue recognition policy.

BE 5–7
Percentage-of-completion method; profit recognition
● LO5–5

A construction company entered into a fixed-price contract to build an office building for $20 million. Construction costs incurred during the first year were $6 million and estimated costs to complete at the end of the year were $9 million. How much gross profit will the company recognize in the first year using the percentage-of-completion method? How much revenue will appear in the company's income statement?

BE 5–8
Percentage-of-completion method; balance sheet
● LO5–5

Refer to the situation described in BE 5–7. During the first year the company billed its customer $7 million, of which $5 million was collected before year-end. What would appear in the year-end balance sheet related to this contract?

BE 5–9
Completed contract method
● LO5–5

Refer to the situation described in BE 5–7. The building was completed during the second year. Construction costs incurred during the second year were $10 million. How much gross profit will the company recognize in the first year and in the second year applying the completed contract method?

BE 5–10
IFRS; cost recovery method
● LO5–5, LO5–8

● IFRS

Refer to the situation described in BE 5–9. How much revenue, cost, and gross profit will the company recognize in the first and second year of the contract applying the cost recovery method that is required by IFRS?

BE 5–11
Percentage-of-completion and completed contract methods; loss on entire project
● LO5–5

Franklin Construction entered into a fixed-price contract to build a freeway-connecting ramp for $30 million. Construction costs incurred in the first year were $16 million and estimated remaining costs to complete at the end of the year were $17 million. How much gross profit or loss will Franklin recognize the first year applying the percentage-of-completion method? Applying the completed contract method?

BE 5–12 Revenue recognition; software contracts ● LO5–6	Orange, Inc., sells a LearnIt-Plus software package that consists of their normal LearnIt math tutorial program along with a one-year subscription to the online LearnIt Office Hours virtual classroom. LearnIt-Plus retails for $200. When sold separately, the LearnIt math tutorial sells for $150, and access to the LearnIt Office Hours sells for $100 per year. When should Orange recognize revenue for the parts of this arrangement? Would your answer change if Orange did not sell the LearnIt Office Hours separately, but believed it would price it at $100 per year if they ever decided to do so?
BE 5–13 Revenue recognition; software contracts under IFRS ● LO5–6, LO5–8 IFRS	Refer to the situation described in BE 5–12. How would your answer change if Orange reported under IFRS?
BE 5–14 Revenue recognition; franchise sales ● LO5–6	Collins, Inc., entered into a 10-year franchise agreement with an individual. For an initial franchise fee of $40,000, Collins agrees to assist in design and construction of the franchise location and in all other necessary start-up activities. Also, in exchange for advertising and promotional services, the franchisee agrees to pay continuing franchise fees equal to 5% of revenue generated by the franchise. When should Collins recognize revenue for the initial and continuing franchise fees?
BE 5–15 Receivables and inventory turnover ratios ● LO5–7	Universal Calendar Company began the year with accounts receivable and inventory balances of $100,000 and $80,000, respectively. Year-end balances for these accounts were $120,000 and $60,000, respectively. Sales for the year of $600,000 generated a gross profit of $200,000. Calculate the receivables and inventory turnover ratios for the year.
BE 5–16 Profitability ratios ● LO5–7	The 2013 income statement for Anderson TV and Appliance reported sales revenue of $420,000 and net income of $65,000. Average total assets for 2013 was $800,000. Shareholders' equity at the beginning of the year was $500,000 and $20,000 was paid to shareholders as dividends. There were no other shareholders' equity transactions that occurred during the year. Calculate the profit margin on sales, return on assets, and return on shareholders' equity for 2013.
BE 5–17 Profitability ratios ● LO5–7	Refer to the facts described in BE 5–16. Show the DuPont framework's calculation of the three components of the 2013 return on shareholders' equity for Anderson TV and Appliance.
BE 5–18 Inventory turnover ratio ● LO5–7	During 2013, Rogue Corporation reported sales revenue of $600,000. Inventory at both the beginning and end of the year totaled $75,000. The inventory turnover ratio for the year was 6.0. What amount of gross profit did the company report in its income statement for 2013?

Exercises

An alternate exercise and problem set is available on the text website: www.mhhe.com/spiceland7e

E 5–1 Service revenue ● LO5–1	Alpine West, Inc., operates a downhill ski area near Lake Tahoe, California. An all-day, adult ticket can be purchased for $55. Adult customers also can purchase a season pass that entitles the pass holder to ski any day during the season, which typically runs from December 1 through April 30. The season pass is nontransferable, and the $450 price is nonrefundable. Alpine expects its season pass holders to use their passes equally throughout the season. The company's fiscal year ends on December 31. On November 6, 2013, Jake Lawson purchased a season ticket. **Required:** 1. When should Alpine West recognize revenue from the sale of its season passes? 2. Prepare the appropriate journal entries that Alpine would record on November 6 and December 31. 3. What will be included in the 2013 income statement and 2013 balance sheet related to the sale of the season pass to Jake Lawson?

E 5–2
Principal or agent
● LO5–2

AuctionCo.com sells used products collected from different suppliers. Assume a customer ordered a used bicycle through AuctionCo.com for $30. The cost of this bicycle is $20 to AuctionCo.com. The bicycle will be shipped to the customer by the original bicycle owner.

Required:

1. Assume AuctionCo.com takes control of this used bicycle before sale. Under this assumption, how much revenue would the company recognize?
2. Assume AuctionCo.com never takes control of this used bicycle before sale. Under this assumption, how much revenue would the company recognize?
3. Which assumption do you think is more appropriate for the AuctionCo.com case? Explain.

E 5–3
Installment sales method
● LO5–3

Charter Corporation, which began business in 2013, appropriately uses the installment sales method of accounting for its installment sales. The following data were obtained for sales made during 2013 and 2014:

	2013	2014
Installment sales	$360,000	$350,000
Cost of installment sales	234,000	245,000
Cash collections on installment sales during:		
2013	150,000	100,000
2014	—	120,000

Required:

1. How much gross profit should Charter recognize in 2013 and 2014 from installment sales?
2. What should be the balance in the deferred gross profit account at the end of 2013 and 2014?

E 5–4
Installment sales method; journal entries
● LO5–3

[This is a variation of Exercise 5–3 focusing on journal entries.]

Charter Corporation, which began business in 2013, appropriately uses the installment sales method of accounting for its installment sales. The following data were obtained for sales during 2013 and 2014:

	2013	2014
Installment sales	$360,000	$350,000
Cost of installment sales	234,000	245,000
Cash collections on installment sales during:		
2013	150,000	100,000
2014	—	120,000

Required:

Prepare summary journal entries for 2013 and 2014 to account for the installment sales and cash collections. The company uses the perpetual inventory system.

E 5–5
Installment sales; alternative recognition methods
● LO5–3

On July 1, 2013, the Foster Company sold inventory to the Slate Corporation for $300,000. Terms of the sale called for a down payment of $75,000 and three annual installments of $75,000 due on each July 1, beginning July 1, 2014. Each installment also will include interest on the unpaid balance applying an appropriate interest rate. The inventory cost Foster $120,000. The company uses the perpetual inventory system.

Required:

1. Compute the amount of gross profit to be recognized from the installment sale in 2013, 2014, 2015, and 2016 using point of delivery revenue recognition. Ignore interest charges.
2. Repeat requirement 1 applying the installment sales method.
3. Repeat requirement 1 applying the cost recovery method.

E 5–6
Journal entries; point of delivery, installment sales, and cost recovery methods
● LO5–1, LO5–3

[This is a variation of Exercise 5–5 focusing on journal entries.]

On July 1, 2013, the Foster Company sold inventory to the Slate Corporation for $300,000. Terms of the sale called for a down payment of $75,000 and three annual installments of $75,000 due on each July 1, beginning July 1, 2014. Each installment also will include interest on the unpaid balance applying an appropriate interest rate. The inventory cost Foster $120,000. The company uses the perpetual inventory system.

Required:

1. Prepare the necessary journal entries for 2013 and 2014 using point of delivery revenue recognition. Ignore interest charges.
2. Repeat requirement 1 applying the installment sales method.
3. Repeat requirement 1 applying the cost recovery method.

E 5–7
Installment sales and cost recovery methods; solve for unknowns
● LO5–3

Wolf Computer Company began operations in 2013. The company allows customers to pay in installments for many of its products. Installment sales for 2013 were $1,000,000. If revenue is recognized at the point of delivery, $600,000 in gross profit would be recognized in 2013. If the company instead uses the cost recovery method, $100,000 in gross profit would be recognized in 2013.

Required:
1. What was the amount of cash collected on installment sales in 2013?
2. What amount of gross profit would be recognized if the company uses the installment sales method?

E 5–8
Installment sales; default and repossession
● LO5–3

Sanchez Development Company uses the installment sales method to account for some of its installment sales. On October 1, 2013, Sanchez sold a parcel of land to the Kreuze Corporation for $4 million. This amount was not considered significant relative to Sanchez's other sales during 2013. The land had cost Sanchez $1.8 million to acquire and develop. Terms of the sale required a down payment of $800,000 and four annual payments of $800,000 plus interest at an appropriate interest rate, with payments due on each October 1 beginning in 2014. Kreuze paid the down payment, but on October 1, 2014, defaulted on the remainder of the contract. Sanchez repossessed the land. On the date of repossession the land had a fair value of $1.3 million.

Required:
Prepare the necessary entries for Sanchez to record the sale, receipt of the down payment, and the default and repossession applying the installment sales method. Ignore interest charges.

E 5–9
Real estate sales; gain recognition
● LO5–1, LO5–3

On April 1, 2013, the Apex Corporation sold a parcel of underdeveloped land to the Applegate Construction Company for $2,400,000. The book value of the land on Apex's books was $480,000. Terms of the sale required a down payment of $120,000 and 19 annual payments of $120,000 plus interest at an appropriate interest rate due on each April 1 beginning in 2014. Apex has no significant obligations to perform services after the sale.

Required:
1. Prepare the necessary entries for Apex to record the sale, receipt of the down payment, and receipt of the first installment assuming that Apex is able to make a reliable estimate of possible uncollectible amounts (that is, point of delivery profit recognition is used). Ignore interest charges.
2. Repeat requirement 1 assuming that Apex cannot make a reliable estimate of possible uncollectible amounts and decides to use the installment sales method for profit recognition.

E 5–10
FASB codification research
● LO5–3, LO5–4, LO5–5

CODE

Access the *FASB's Codification Research System* at the FASB website (www.fasb.org).

Required:
Determine the specific citation for accounting for each of the following items:
1. When a provision for loss is recognized for a percentage-of-completion contract.
2. Circumstances indicating when the installment method or cost recovery method is appropriate for revenue recognition.
3. Criteria determining when a seller can recognize revenue at the time of sale from a sales transaction in which the buyer has the right to return the product.

E 5–11
Long-term contract; percentage-of-completion and completed contract methods
● LO5–5

Assume Nortel Networks contracted to provide a customer with Internet infrastructure for $2,000,000. The project began in 2013 and was completed in 2014. Data relating to the contract are summarized below:

	2013	2014
Costs incurred during the year	$ 300,000	$1,575,000
Estimated costs to complete as of 12/31	1,200,000	–0–
Billings during the year	380,000	1,620,000
Cash collections during the year	250,000	1,750,000

Required:
1. Compute the amount of gross profit or loss to be recognized in 2013 and 2014 using the percentage-of-completion method.
2. Compute the amount of gross profit or loss to be recognized in 2013 and 2014 using the completed contract method.
3. Prepare a partial balance sheet to show how the information related to this contract would be presented at the end of 2013 using the percentage-of-completion method.
4. Prepare a partial balance sheet to show how the information related to this contract would be presented at the end of 2013 using the completed contract method.

E 5–12
Long-term
contract;
percentage of
completion,
completed
contract and
cost recovery
methods
● LO5–5, LO5–8

On June 15, 2013, Sanderson Construction entered into a long-term construction contract to build a baseball sta-
dium in Washington D.C. for $220 million. The expected completion date is April 1 of 2015, just in time for the
2015 baseball season. Costs incurred and estimated costs to complete at year-end for the life of the contract are
as follows ($ in millions):

	2013	2014	2015
Costs incurred during the year	$ 40	$80	$50
Estimated costs to complete as of 12/31	120	60	—

Required:
1. Determine the amount of gross profit or loss to be recognized in each of the three years using the percentage-of-
   completion method.
2. How much revenue will Sanderson report in its 2013 and 2014 income statements related to this contract
   using the percentage-of-completion method?
3. Determine the amount of gross profit or loss to be recognized in each of the three years using the completed
   contract method.

● IFRS

4. Determine the amount of revenue, cost, and gross profit or loss to be recognized in each of the three years
   under IFRS, assuming that using the percentage-of-completion method is not appropriate.
5. Suppose the estimated costs to complete at the end of 2014 are $80 million instead of $60 million. Determine
   the amount of gross profit or loss to be recognized in 2014 using the percentage-of-completion method.

E 5–13
Percentage-of-
completion
method; loss
projected on
entire project
● LO5–5

On February 1, 2013, Arrow Construction Company entered into a three-year construction contract to build
a bridge for a price of $8,000,000. During 2013, costs of $2,000,000 were incurred with estimated costs of
$4,000,000 yet to be incurred. Billings of $2,500,000 were sent and cash collected was $2,250,000.
    In 2014, costs incurred were $2,500,000 with remaining costs estimated to be $3,600,000. 2014 billings
were $2,750,000 and $2,475,000 cash was collected. The project was completed in 2015 after additional costs
of $3,800,000 were incurred. The company's fiscal year-end is December 31. Arrow uses the *percentage-of-
completion* method.

Required:
1. Calculate the amount of gross profit or loss to be recognized in each of the three years.
2. Prepare journal entries for 2013 and 2014 to record the transactions described (credit various accounts for
   construction costs incurred).
3. Prepare a partial balance sheet to show the presentation of the project as of December 31, 2013 and 2014.

E 5–14
Completed
contract method;
loss projected on
entire project
● LO5–5

[This is a variation of Exercise 5–13 focusing on the completed contract method.]
    On February 1, 2013, Arrow Construction Company entered into a three-year construction contract to build
a bridge for a price of $8,000,000. During 2013, costs of $2,000,000 were incurred with estimated costs of
$4,000,000 yet to be incurred. Billings of $2,500,000 were sent and cash collected was $2,250,000.
    In 2014, costs incurred were $2,500,000 with remaining costs estimated to be $3,600,000. 2014 billings were
$2,750,000 and $2,475,000 cash was collected. The project was completed in 2015 after additional costs of
$3,800,000 were incurred. The company's fiscal year-end is December 31. Arrow uses the *completed contract*
method.

Required:
1. Calculate the amount of gross profit or loss to be recognized in each of the three years.
2. Prepare journal entries for 2013 and 2014 to record the transactions described (credit various accounts for
   construction costs incurred).
3. Prepare a partial balance sheet to show the presentation of the project as of December 31, 2013 and 2014.

E 5–15
Income (loss)
recognition;
percentage-of-
completion
and completed
contract methods
compared
● LO5–5

Brady Construction Company contracted to build an apartment complex for a price of $5,000,000. Construction
began in 2013 and was completed in 2015. The following are a series of independent situations, numbered
1 through 6, involving differing costs for the project. All costs are stated in thousands of dollars.

	Costs Incurred During Year			Estimated Costs to Complete (As of the End of the Year)		
Situation	2013	2014	2015	2013	2014	2015
1	1,500	2,100	900	3,000	900	—
2	1,500	900	2,400	3,000	2,400	—
3	1,500	2,100	1,600	3,000	1,500	—
4	500	3,000	1,000	3,500	875	—
5	500	3,000	1,300	3,500	1,500	—
6	500	3,000	1,800	4,600	1,700	—

Required:
Copy and complete the following table.

| | | Gross Profit (Loss) Recognized | | | | | |
| | | Percentage-of-Completion | | | Completed Contract | | |
Situation		2013	2014	2015	2013	2014	2015
1							
2							
3							
4							
5							
6							

E 5–16
Percentage-of-completion method; solve for unknowns
● LO5–5

In 2013, Long Construction Corporation began construction work under a three-year contract. The contract price is $1,600,000. Long uses the percentage-of-completion method for financial reporting purposes. The financial statement presentation relating to this contract at December 31, 2013, is as follows:

Balance Sheet

Accounts receivable (from construction progress billings)		$30,000
Construction in progress	$100,000	
Less: Billings on construction contract	(94,000)	
Cost of uncompleted contracts in excess of billings		6,000

Income Statement

Income (before tax) on the contract recognized in 2013	$20,000

Required:
1. What was the cost of construction actually incurred in 2013?
2. How much cash was collected in 2013 on this contract?
3. What was the estimated cost to complete as of the end of 2013?
4. What was the estimated percentage of completion used to calculate income in 2013?

(AICPA adapted)

E 5–17
FASB codification research
● LO5–5

The *FASB Accounting Standards Codification* represents the single source of authoritative U.S. generally accepted accounting principles.

Required:
1. Obtain the relevant authoritative literature on the percentage-of-completion method using the FASB's Codification Research System at the FASB website (www.fasb.org). What is the specific citation that describes the circumstances and conditions under which it is preferable to use the percentage-of-completion method?
2. List the circumstances and conditions.

E 5–18
Revenue recognition; software
● LO5–6

Easywrite Software Company shipped software to a customer on July 1, 2013. The arrangement with the customer also requires the company to provide technical support over the next 12 months and to ship an expected software upgrade on January 1, 2014. The total contract price is $243,000, and Easywrite estimates that the individual fair values of the components of the arrangement if sold separately would be:

Software	$210,000
Technical support	30,000
Upgrade	30,000

Required:
1. Determine the timing of revenue recognition for the $243,000.
2. Assume that the $243,000 contract price was paid on July 1, 2013. Prepare a journal entry to record the cash receipt. Do not worry about the cost of the items sold.

E 5–19
Multiple-deliverable arrangements
● LO5–6

Richardson Systems sells integrated bottling manufacturing systems that involve a conveyer, a labeler, a filler, and a capper. All of this equipment is sold separately by other vendors, and the fair values of the separate equipment are as follows:

Conveyer	$20,000
Labeler	10,000
Filler	15,000
Capper	5,000
Total	$50,000

Richardson sells the integrated system for $45,000. Each of the components is shipped separately to the customer for the customer to install.

Required:
1. Assume that each of the components can be used independently, even though Richardson sells them as an integrated system. How much revenue should be allocated to each component?
2. Now assume that the labeler, filler, and capper can't be used in production without the conveyer, and that the conveyer is the last component installed. How much revenue should be recognized at the time the conveyer is installed?

E 5–20
Multiple-deliverable arrangements under IFRS
● LO5–6, LO5–8

 IFRS

Assume the same facts as in E5–19, but that Richardson Systems reports under IFRS. How would your answers change? (Assume for requirement 2 that separate shipment is part of the normal course of Richardson's operations, and successful customer installation is highly probable.)

E 5–21
Revenue recognition; franchise sales
● LO5–6

On October 1, 2013, the Submarine Sandwich Company entered into a franchise agreement with an individual. In exchange for an initial franchise fee of $300,000, Submarine will provide initial services to the franchisee to include assistance in design and construction of the building, help in training employees, and help in obtaining financing. 10% of the initial franchise fee is payable on October 1, 2013, with the remaining $270,000 payable in nine equal annual installments beginning on October 1, 2014. These installments will include interest at an appropriate rate. The franchise opened for business on January 15, 2014.

Required:
Assume that the initial services to be performed by Submarine Sandwich subsequent to October 1, 2013, are substantial and that collectibility of the installment receivable is reasonably certain. Substantial performance of the initial services is deemed to have occurred when the franchise opened. Prepare the necessary journal entries for the following dates (ignoring interest charges):
1. October 1, 2013
2. January 15, 2014

E 5–22
Concepts; terminology
● LO5–3 through LO5–7

Listed below are several terms and phrases associated with revenue recognition and profitability analysis. Pair each item from List A (by letter) with the item from List B that is most appropriately associated with it.

List A	List B
_____ 1. Inventory turnover	a. Net income divided by net sales.
_____ 2. Return on assets	b. Defers recognition until cash collected equals cost.
_____ 3. Return on shareholders' equity	c. Defers recognition until project is complete.
_____ 4. Profit margin on sales	d. Net income divided by assets.
_____ 5. Cost recovery method	e. Risks and rewards of ownership retained by seller.
_____ 6. Percentage-of-completion method	f. Contra account to construction in progress.
_____ 7. Completed contract method	g. Net income divided by shareholders' equity.
_____ 8. Asset turnover	h. Cost of goods sold divided by inventory.
_____ 9. Receivables turnover	i. Recognition is in proportion to work completed.
_____ 10. Right of return	j. Recognition is in proportion to cash received.
_____ 11. Billings on construction contract	k. Net sales divided by assets.
_____ 12. Installment sales method	l. Net sales divided by accounts receivable.
_____ 13. Consignment sales	m. Could cause the deferral of revenue recognition beyond delivery point.

E 5–23
Inventory turnover; calculation and evaluation
● LO5–7

The following is a portion of the condensed income statement for Rowan, Inc., a manufacturer of plastic containers:

Net sales		$2,460,000
Less: Cost of goods sold:		
Inventory, January 1	$ 630,000	
Net purchases	1,900,000	
Inventory, December 31	(690,000)	1,840,000
Gross profit		$ 620,000

Required:
1. Determine Rowan's inventory turnover.
2. What information does this ratio provide?

E 5–24
Evaluating
efficiency of asset
management
● LO5–7

The 2013 income statement of Anderson Medical Supply Company reported net sales of $8 million, cost of goods sold of $4.8 million, and net income of $800,000. The following table shows the company's comparative balance sheets for 2013 and 2012:

	($ in 000s)	
	2013	**2012**
Assets		
Cash	$ 300	$ 380
Accounts receivable	700	500
Inventory	900	700
Property, plant, and equipment (net)	2,400	2,120
Total assets	$4,300	$3,700
Liabilities and Shareholders' Equity		
Current liabilities	$ 960	$ 830
Bonds payable	1,200	1,200
Paid-in capital	1,000	1,000
Retained earnings	1,140	670
Total liabilities and shareholders' equity	$4,300	$3,700

Some industry averages for Anderson's line of business are

Inventory turnover	5 times
Average collection period	25 days
Asset turnover	1.8 times

Required:
Assess Anderson's asset management relative to its industry.

E 5–25
Profitability ratios
● LO5–7

The following condensed information was reported by Peabody Toys, Inc., for 2013 and 2012:

	($ in 000s)	
	2013	**2012**
Income statement information		
Net sales	$5,200	$4,200
Net income	180	124
Balance sheet information		
Current assets	$ 800	$ 750
Property, plant, and equipment (net)	1,100	950
Total assets	$1,900	$1,700
Current liabilities	$ 600	$ 450
Long-term liabilities	750	750
Paid-in capital	400	400
Retained earnings	150	100
Liabilities and shareholders' equity	$1,900	$1,700

Required:
1. Determine the following ratios for 2013:
    a. Profit margin on sales.
    b. Return on assets.
    c. Return on shareholders' equity.
2. Determine the amount of dividends paid to shareholders during 2013.

E 5–26
DuPont analysis
● LO5–7

This exercise is based on the Peabody Toys, Inc., data from Exercise 5–25.

Required:
1. Determine the following components of the DuPont framework for 2013:
    a. Profit margin on sales.
    b. Asset turnover.
    c. Equity multiplier.
    d. Return on shareholders' equity.
2. Write an equation that relates these components in calculating ROE. Use the Peabody Toys data to show that the equation is correct.

E 5–27
Interim financial
statements;
income tax
expense
● Appendix 5

Joplin Laminating Corporation reported income before income taxes during the first three quarters and management's estimates of the annual effective tax rate at the end of each quarter as shown below:

	Quarter		
	First	**Second**	**Third**
Income before income taxes	$50,000	$40,000	$100,000
Estimated annual effective tax rate	34%	30%	36%

Required:
Determine the income tax expense to be reported in the income statement in each of the three quarterly reports.

E 5–28
Interim reporting;
recognizing
expenses
● Appendix 5

Security-Rand Corporation determines executive incentive compensation at the end of its fiscal year. At the end of the first quarter, management estimated that the amount will be $300 million. Depreciation expense for the year is expected to be $60 million. Also during the quarter, the company realized a gain of $23 million from selling two of its manufacturing plants.

Required:
What amounts for these items should be reported in the first quarter's income statement?

E 5–29
Interim financial
statements;
reporting
expenses
● Appendix 5

Shields Company is preparing its interim report for the second quarter ending June 30. The following payments were made during the first two quarters:

Required:

Expenditure	Date	Amount
Annual advertising	January	$800,000
Property tax for the fiscal year	February	350,000
Annual equipment repairs	March	260,000
Extraordinary casualty loss	April	185,000
One-time research and development fee to consultant	May	96,000

For each expenditure indicate the amount that would be reported in the quarterly income statements for the periods ending March 31, June 30, September 30, and December 31.

E 5–30
Interim financial
statements
● Appendix 5

IFRS

Assume the same facts as in E 5–29, but that Shields Company reports under IFRS. For each expenditure indicate the amount that would be reported in the quarterly income statements for the periods ending March 31, June 30, September 30, and December 31.

CPA and CMA Review Questions

CPA Exam
Questions

The following questions are adapted from a variety of sources including questions developed by the AICPA Board of Examiners and those used in the Kaplan CPA Review Course to study revenue recognition while preparing for the CPA examination. Determine the response that best completes the statements or questions.

● LO5–1

1. On October 1, 2013, Acme Fuel Co. sold 100,000 gallons of heating oil to Karn Co. at $3 per gallon. Fifty thousand gallons were delivered on December 15, 2013, and the remaining 50,000 gallons were delivered on January 15, 2014. Payment terms were 50% due on October 1, 2013, 25% due on first delivery, and the remaining 25% due on second delivery. What amount of revenue should Acme recognize from this sale during 2014?

   a. $ 75,000
   b. $150,000
   c. $225,000
   d. $300,000

● LO5–3

2. Since there is no reasonable basis for estimating the degree of collectibility, Astor Co. uses the installment sales method of revenue recognition for the following sales:

	2013	2014
Sales	$600,000	$900,000
Collections from:		
2013 sales	200,000	100,000
2014 sales	—	300,000
Accounts written off:		
2013 sales	50,000	150,000
2014 sales	—	50,000
Gross profit percentage	30%	40%

What amount should Astor report as deferred gross profit in its December 31, 2014, balance sheet for the 2013 and 2014 sales?

a. $225,000
b. $150,000
c. $160,000
d. $250,000

● LO5–3

3. Dolce Co., which began operations on January 1, 2013, appropriately uses the installment sales method of accounting to record revenues. The following information is available for the years ended December 31, 2013 and 2014:

	2013	2014
Sales	$1,000,000	$2,000,000
Gross profit realized on sales made in:		
2013	150,000	90,000
2014	—	200,000
Gross profit percentages	30%	40%

What amount of installment accounts receivable should Dolce report in its December 31, 2014, balance sheet?

a. $1,700,000
b. $1,225,000
c. $1,300,000
d. $1,775,000

● LO5–5

4. Which of the following statements regarding the percentage-of-completion method of accounting is FALSE? The construction-in-progress account:

a. is shown net of advance billings as a liability if the amount is less than the amount of advance billings.
b. is an asset.
c. is shown net of advance billings on the balance sheet.
d. does not include the cumulative effect of gross profit recognition.

● LO5–5

5. The following data relates to a construction job started by Syl Co. during 2013:

Total contract price	$100,000
Actual costs during 2013	20,000
Estimated remaining costs	40,000
Billed to customer during 2013	30,000
Received from customer during 2013	10,000

Under the percentage-of-completion method, how much should Syl recognize as gross profit for 2013?

a. $26,667
b. $0
c. $13,333
d. $33,333

● LO5–5

6. Hansen Construction Inc. has consistently used the percentage-of-completion method of recognizing income. During 2013, Hansen started work on a $3,000,000 fixed-price construction contract. The accounting records disclosed the following data for the year ended December 31, 2013:

Costs incurred	$ 930,000
Estimated cost to complete	2,170,000
Progress billings	1,100,000
Collections	700,000

How much loss should Hansen have recognized in 2013?

a. $180,000
b. $230,000
c. $30,000
d. $100,000

Beginning in 2011, International Financial Reporting Standards are tested on the CPA exam along with U.S. GAAP. The following questions deal with the application of IFRS.

● LO5–8

🌐 IFRS

7. Which of the following is NOT a condition that must be satisfied under IFRS before revenue for a service can be recognized?

a. The stage of completion can be measured reliably.
b. It is probable that the economic benefits associated with the transaction will flow to the seller.
c. Cash collection is at least reasonably possible.
d. The amount of revenue and costs associated with the transaction can be measured reliably.

● LO5–8

🌐 IFRS

8. O'Hara Company recognizes revenue on long-term construction contracts under IFRS. It cannot estimate progress toward completion accurately, and so uses the cost recovery method (also called the "zero profit method") to estimate revenue. O'Hara writes a contract to deliver an automated assembly line to Easley Motors. Easley will pay $2,000,000 to O'Hara, and O'Hara estimates the line will cost $1,500,000 to construct. The job is estimated to take three years to complete. In the first year of its contract with Easley Motors, O'Hara incurs $1,000,000 of cost, which O'Hara believes will eventually be recovered in the contract. How much revenue will O'Hara recognize in the first year of the contract?

a. $1,000,000
b. $0
c. $1,333,333
d. $666,667

● LO5–8

🌐 IFRS

9. Which of the following is NOT true about revenue recognition for multiple deliverable contracts under IFRS?

a. *IAS No. 18* provides extensive guidance determining how contracts are to be separated into components for purposes of revenue recognition.
b. IFRS encourages focus on the economic substance of transactions, so some arrangements are likely to be accounted for differently than under U.S. GAAP.
c. Unlike U.S. GAAP, IFRS does not require VSOE for software contracts in order to separate contracts into multiple deliverables.
d. IFRS focuses on fair values to allocate total revenue to components.

● LO5–8
Appendix 5

🌐 IFRS

10. Barrett Inc. paid $50,000 of property taxes in January that constitute the entire property tax bill for the year. Which of the following is true concerning how Barrett would account for those taxes in interim periods?

a. Under IFRS, Barrett would expense the entire $50,000 in the last quarter of the year.
b. Under U.S. GAAP, Barrett would expense the entire $50,000 of property taxes when the tax was paid in the first quarter of the year.
c. Under U.S. GAAP, Barrett would finish the first quarter of the year with a prepaid property taxes asset of $30,000.
d. Unlike IFRS, Barrett would start the third quarter of the year with a prepaid property tax asset of $0.

CMA Exam
Questions

The following questions dealing with income measurement are adapted from questions that previously appeared on Certified Management Accountant (CMA) examinations. The CMA designation sponsored by the Institute of Management Accountants (www.imanet.org) provides members with an objective measure of knowledge and competence in the field of management accounting. Determine the response that best completes the statements or questions.

● LO5–1

1. On May 28, Markal Company purchased a tooling machine from Arens and Associates for $1,000,000 payable as follows: 50 percent at the transaction closing date and 50 percent due June 28. The cost of the machine to Arens is $800,000. Markal paid Arens $500,000 at the transaction closing date and took possession of the machine. On June 10, Arens determined that a change in the business environment has created a great deal of uncertainty regarding the collection of the balance due from Markal, and the amount is probably uncollectible. Arens and Markal have a fiscal year-end of May 31. The revenue recognized by Arens and Associates on May 28 is

a. $200,000
b. $800,000
c. $1,000,000
d. $0

● LO5–5   2. The percentage-of-completion method of accounting for long-term construction contracts is an exception to the
   a. Matching principle.
   b. Going-concern assumption.
   c. Economic-entity assumption.
   d. Point-of-sale recognition practice.

● LO5–5   3. Roebling Construction signed a $24 million contract on August 1, 2012, with the city of Candu to construct a
   bridge over the Vine River. Roebling's estimated cost of the bridge on that date was $18 million. The bridge was
   to be completed by April 2015. Roebling uses the percentage-of-completion method for income recognition. Roebling's fiscal year ends May 31. Data regarding the bridge contract are presented in the schedule below.

	At May 31 ($000 omitted)	
	2013	**2014**
Actual costs to date	$ 6,000	$15,000
Estimated costs to complete	12,000	5,000
Progress billings to date	5,000	14,000
Cash collected to date	4,000	12,000

The gross profit or loss recognized in the fiscal year ended May 31, 2013, from this bridge contract is
   a. $6,000,000 gross profit.
   b. $2,000,000 gross profit.
   c. $3,000,000 gross profit.
   d. $1,000,000 gross profit.

Problems

An alternate exercise and problem set is available on the text website: www.mhhe.com/spiceland7e

P 5–1
Income
statement
presentation;
installment
sales method
(Chapters 4 and 5)
● LO5–3

Reagan Corporation computed income from continuing operations before income taxes of $4,200,000 for 2013.
The following material items have not yet been considered in the computation of income:
1. The company sold equipment and recognized a gain of $50,000. The equipment had been used in the manu-
   facturing process and was replaced by new equipment.
2. In December, the company received a settlement of $1,000,000 for a lawsuit it had filed based on antitrust
   violations of a competitor. The settlement was considered to be an unusual and infrequent event.
3. Inventory costing $400,000 was written off as obsolete. Material losses of this type were incurred twice in
   the last eight years.
4. It was discovered that depreciation expense on the office building of $50,000 per year was not recorded in
   either 2012 or 2013.

   In addition, you learn that *included* in revenues is $400,000 from installment sales made during the year. The
cost of these sales is $240,000. At year-end, $100,000 in cash had been collected on the related installment receivables. Because of considerable uncertainty regarding the collectibility of receivables from these sales, the company's accountant should have used the installment sales method to recognize revenue and gross profit on these sales.
   Also, the company's income tax rate is 40% and there were 1 million shares of common stock outstanding
throughout the year.

Required:
Prepare an income statement for 2013 beginning with income from continuing operations before income taxes.
Include appropriate EPS disclosures.

P 5–2
Installment sales
and cost recovery
methods
● LO5–3

eXcel

Ajax Company appropriately accounts for certain sales using the installment sales method. The perpetual inventory system is used. Information related to installment sales for 2013 and 2014 is as follows:

	2013	2014
Sales	$300,000	$400,000
Cost of sales	180,000	280,000
Customer collections on:		
2013 sales	120,000	100,000
2014 sales	—	150,000

Required:
1. Calculate the amount of gross profit that would be recognized each year from installment sales.
2. Prepare all necessary journal entries for each year.
3. Repeat requirements 1 and 2 assuming that Ajax uses the cost recovery method to account for its installment sales.

P 5–3
Installment sales; alternative recognition methods
● LO5–3

On August 31, 2013, the Silva Company sold merchandise to the Bendix Corporation for $500,000. Terms of the sale called for a down payment of $100,000 and four annual installments of $100,000 due on each August 31, beginning August 31, 2014. Each installment also will include interest on the unpaid balance applying an appropriate interest rate. The book value of the merchandise on Silva's books on the date of sale was $300,000. The perpetual inventory system is used. The company's fiscal year-end is December 31.

Required:
1. Prepare a table showing the amount of gross profit to be recognized in each of the five years of the installment sale applying each of the following methods:
   a. Point of delivery revenue recognition.
   b. Installment sales method.
   c. Cost recovery method.
2. Prepare journal entries for each of the five years applying the three revenue recognition methods listed in requirement 1. Ignore interest charges.
3. Prepare a partial balance sheet as of the end of 2013 and 2014 listing the items related to the installment sale applying each of the three methods listed in requirement 1.

P 5–4
Installment sales and cost recovery methods
● LO5–3

Mulcahey Builders (MB) remodels office buildings in low-income urban areas that are undergoing economic revitalization. MB typically accepts a 25% down payment when they complete a job and a note which requires that the remainder be paid in three equal installments over the next three years, plus interest. Because of the inherent uncertainty associated with receiving these payments, MB has historically used the cost recovery method to recognize revenue.

As of January 1, 2013, MB's outstanding gross installment accounts receivable (not net of deferred gross profit) consist of the following:
1. $400,000 due from the Bluebird Motel. MB completed the Bluebird job in 2011, and estimated gross profit on that job is 25%.
2. $150,000 due from the PitStop Gas and MiniMart. MB completed the PitStop job in 2010, and estimated gross profit on that job is 35%.

Dan Mulcahey has been considering switching from the cost recovery method to the installment sales method, because he wants to show the highest possible gross profit in 2013 and he understands that the installment sales method recognizes gross profit sooner than does the cost recovery method.

Required:
1. Calculate how much gross profit is expected to be earned on these jobs in 2013 under the cost recovery method, and how much would be earned if MB instead used the installment sales method. Ignore interest.
2. If Dan is primarily concerned about 2013, do you think he would be happy with a switch to the installment sales method? Explain.

P 5–5
Percentage-of-completion method
● LO5–5

In 2013, the Westgate Construction Company entered into a contract to construct a road for Santa Clara County for $10,000,000. The road was completed in 2015. Information related to the contract is as follows:

	2013	2014	2015
Cost incurred during the year	$2,400,000	$3,600,000	$2,200,000
Estimated costs to complete as of year-end	5,600,000	2,000,000	–0–
Billings during the year	2,000,000	4,000,000	4,000,000
Cash collections during the year	1,800,000	3,600,000	4,600,000

Westgate uses the percentage-of-completion method of accounting for long-term construction contracts.

Required:
1. Calculate the amount of gross profit to be recognized in each of the three years.
2. Prepare all necessary journal entries for each of the years (credit *various accounts* for construction costs incurred).
3. Prepare a partial balance sheet for 2013 and 2014 showing any items related to the contract.
4. Calculate the amount of gross profit to be recognized in each of the three years assuming the following costs incurred and costs to complete information:

	2013	2014	2015
Costs incurred during the year	$2,400,000	$3,800,000	$3,200,000
Estimated costs to complete as of year-end	5,600,000	3,100,000	–0–

5. Calculate the amount of gross profit to be recognized in each of the three years assuming the following costs incurred and costs to complete information:

	2013	2014	2015
Costs incurred during the year	$2,400,000	$3,800,000	$3,900,000
Estimated costs to complete as of year-end	5,600,000	4,100,000	–0–

P 5–6
Completed
contract method
● LO5–5

[This is a variation of Problem 5–5 modified to focus on the completed contract method.]

Required:
Complete the requirements of Problem 5–5 assuming that Westgate Construction uses the completed contract method.

P 5–7
Construction
accounting under
IFRS
● LO5–5, LO5–8

 IFRS

[This is a variation of the Problem 5–5 modified to focus on IFRS.]

Required:
Complete the requirements of Problem 5–5 assuming that Westgate Construction reports under IFRS and concludes that the percentage-of-completion method is not appropriate.

P 5–8
Construction
accounting; loss
projected on
entire project
● LO5–5

Curtiss Construction Company, Inc., entered into a fixed-price contract with Axelrod Associates on July 1, 2013, to construct a four-story office building. At that time, Curtiss estimated that it would take between two and three years to complete the project. The total contract price for construction of the building is $4,000,000. Curtiss appropriately accounts for this contract under the completed contract method in its financial statements. The building was completed on December 31, 2015. Estimated percentage of completion, *accumulated* contract costs incurred, estimated costs to complete the contract, and *accumulated* billings to Axelrod under the contract were as follows:

	At 12-31-2013	At 12-31-2014	At 12-31-2015
Percentage of completion	10%	60%	100%
Costs incurred to date	$ 350,000	$2,500,000	$4,250,000
Estimated costs to complete	3,150,000	1,700,000	–0–
Billings to Axelrod, to date	720,000	2,170,000	3,600,000

Required:
1. Prepare schedules to compute gross profit or loss to be recognized as a result of this contract for each of the three years.
2. Assuming Curtiss uses the percentage-of-completion method of accounting for long-term construction contracts, compute gross profit or loss to be recognized in each of the three years.
3. Assuming the percentage-of-completion method, compute the amount to be shown in the balance sheet at the end of 2013 and 2014 as either cost in excess of billings or billings in excess of costs.

(AICPA adapted)

P 5–9
Long-term
contract;
percentage-of-
completion
and completed
contract methods
● LO5–1, LO5–5

Citation Builders, Inc., builds office buildings and single-family homes. The office buildings are constructed under contract with reputable buyers. The homes are constructed in developments ranging from 10–20 homes and are typically sold during construction or soon after. To secure the home upon completion, buyers must pay a deposit of 10% of the price of the home with the remaining balance due upon completion of the house and transfer of title. Failure to pay the full amount results in forfeiture of the down payment. Occasionally, homes remain unsold for as long as three months after construction. In these situations, sales price reductions are used to promote the sale.

During 2013, Citation began construction of an office building for Altamont Corporation. The total contract price is $20 million. Costs incurred, estimated costs to complete at year-end, billings, and cash collections for the life of the contract are as follows:

	2013	2014	2015
Costs incurred during the year	$ 4,000,000	$ 9,500,000	$4,500,000
Estimated costs to complete as of year-end	12,000,000	4,500,000	—
Billings during the year	2,000,000	10,000,000	8,000,000
Cash collections during the year	1,800,000	8,600,000	9,600,000

Also during 2013, Citation began a development consisting of 12 identical homes. Citation estimated that each home will sell for $600,000, but individual sales prices are negotiated with buyers. Deposits were received for eight of the homes, three of which were completed during 2013 and paid for in full for $600,000 each by the buyers. The completed homes cost $450,000 each to construct. The construction costs incurred during 2013 for the nine uncompleted homes totaled $2,700,000.

Required:

1. Briefly explain the difference between the percentage-of-completion and the completed contract methods of accounting for long-term construction contracts.

2. Answer the following questions assuming that Citation uses the completed contract method for its office building contracts:

    a. What is the amount of gross profit or loss to be recognized for the Altamont contract during 2013 and 2014?

    b. How much revenue related to this contract will Citation report in its 2013 and 2014 income statements?

    c. What will Citation report in its December 31, 2013, balance sheet related to this contract (ignore cash)?

3. Answer requirements 2a through 2c assuming that Citation uses the percentage-of-completion method for its office building contracts.

4. Assume that as of year-end 2014 the estimated cost to complete the office building is $9,000,000 and that Citation uses the percentage-of-completion method.

    a. What is the amount of gross profit or loss to be recognized for the Altamont contract during 2014?

    b. How much revenue related to this contract will Citation report in the 2014 income statement?

    c. What will Citation report in its 2014 balance sheet related to this contract (ignore cash)?

5. When should Citation recognize revenue for the sale of its single-family homes?

6. What will Citation report in its 2013 income statement and 2013 balance sheet related to the single-family home business (ignore cash in the balance sheet)?

P 5–10
Franchise sales; installment sales method
● **LO5–3, LO5–6**

Olive Branch Restaurant Corporation sells franchises throughout the western states. On January 30, 2013, the company entered into the following franchise agreement with Jim and Tammy Masters:

1. The initial franchise fee is $1.2 million. $200,000 is payable immediately and the remainder is due in 10, $100,000 installments plus 10% interest on the unpaid balance each January 30, beginning January 30, 2014. The 10% interest rate is an appropriate market rate.

2. In addition to allowing the franchisee to use the franchise name for the 10-year term of the agreement, in exchange for the initial fee Olive Branch agrees to assist the franchisee in selecting a location, obtaining financing, designing and constructing the restaurant building, and training employees.

3. All of the initial down payment of $200,000 is to be refunded by Olive Branch and the remaining obligation canceled if, for any reason, the franchisee fails to open the franchise.

4. In addition to the initial franchise fee, the franchisee is required to pay a monthly fee of 3% of franchise sales for advertising, promotion, menu planning, and other continuing services to be provided by Olive Branch over the life of the agreement. This fee is payable on the 10th of the following month.

Substantial performance of the initial services provided by Olive Branch, which are significant, is deemed to have occurred when the franchise opened on September 1, 2013. Franchise sales for the month of September 2013 were $40,000.

Required:

1. Assuming that collectibility of the installment receivable is reasonably certain, prepare the necessary journal entries for Olive Branch on the following dates (ignore interest charges on the installment receivable and the costs of providing franchise services):

    a. January 30, 2013

    b. September 1, 2013

    c. September 30, 2013

    d. January 30, 2014

2. Assume that significant uncertainty exists as to the collection of the installment receivable and that Olive Branch elects to recognize initial franchise fee revenue using the installment sales method. Prepare the necessary journal entries for the dates listed in requirement 1 (ignore interest charges on the installment receivable and the costs of providing franchise services).

3. Examine your answer to requirement 1a of this problem (the January 30, 2013, journal entry under the installment sales method). What is the effect of that journal entry on Olive Branch's balance sheet? (Ignore cash.) Briefly explain your answer.

P 5–11
Calculating
activity and
profitability ratios
● LO5–7

Financial statements for Askew Industries for 2013 are shown below:

2013 Income Statement

	($ in 000s)
Sales	$ 9,000
Cost of goods sold	(6,300)
Gross profit	2,700
Operating expenses	(2,000)
Interest expense	(200)
Tax expense	(200)
Net income	$ 300

Comparative Balance Sheets

	Dec. 31	
	2013	2012
Assets		
Cash	$ 600	$ 500
Accounts receivable	600	400
Inventory	800	600
Property, plant, and equipment (net)	2,000	2,100
	$4,000	$3,600
Liabilities and Shareholders' Equity		
Current liabilities	$1,100	$ 850
Bonds payable	1,400	1,400
Paid-in capital	600	600
Retained earnings	900	750
	$4,000	$3,600

Required:
Calculate the following ratios for 2013.
1. Inventory turnover ratio
2. Average days in inventory
3. Receivables turnover ratio
4. Average collection period
5. Asset turnover ratio
6. Profit margin on sales
7. Return on assets
8. Return on shareholders' equity
9. Equity multiplier
10. Return on shareholders' equity (using the DuPont framework)

P 5–12
Use of ratios to
compare two
companies in the
same industry
● LO5–7

Presented below are condensed financial statements adapted from those of two actual companies competing in the pharmaceutical industry—Johnson and Johnson (J&J) and Pfizer, Inc. ($ in millions, except per share amounts).

Required:
Evaluate and compare the two companies by responding to the following questions.
   Note: Because two-year comparative statements are not provided, you should use year-end balances in place of average balances as appropriate.
1. Which of the two companies appears more efficient in collecting its accounts receivable and managing its inventory?
2. Which of the two firms had greater earnings relative to resources available?
3. Have the two companies achieved their respective rates of return on assets with similar combinations of profit margin and turnover?
4. From the perspective of a common shareholder, which of the two firms provided a greater rate of return?
5. From the perspective of a common shareholder, which of the two firms appears to be using leverage more effectively to provide a return to shareholders above the rate of return on assets?

Balance Sheets
($ in millions, except per share data)

	J&J	Pfizer
Assets:		
Cash	$ 5,377	$ 1,520
Short-term investments	4,146	10,432
Accounts receivable (net)	6,574	8,775
Inventories	3,588	5,837
Other current assets	3,310	3,177
Current assets	22,995	29,741
Property, plant, and equipment (net)	9,846	18,287
Intangibles and other assets	15,422	68,747
Total assets	$48,263	$116,775
Liabilities and Shareholders' Equity:		
Accounts payable	$ 4,966	$ 2,601
Short-term notes	1,139	8,818
Other current liabilities	7,343	12,238
Current liabilities	13,448	23,657
Long-term debt	2,955	5,755
Other long-term liabilities	4,991	21,986
Total liabilities	21,394	51,398
Capital stock (par and additional paid-in capital)	3,120	67,050
Retained earnings	30,503	29,382
Accumulated other comprehensive income (loss)	(590)	195
Less: treasury stock and other equity adjustments	(6,164)	(31,250)
Total shareholders' equity	26,869	65,377
Total liabilities and shareholders' equity	$48,263	$116,775

Income Statements

	J&J	Pfizer
Net sales	$41,862	$ 45,188
Cost of goods sold	12,176	9,832
Gross profit	29,686	35,356
Operating expenses	19,763	28,486
Other (income) expense—net	(385)	3,610
Income before taxes	10,308	3,260
Tax expense	3,111	1,621
Net income	$ 7,197	$ 1,639*
Basic net income per share	$ 2.42	$ .22

* This is before income from discontinued operations.

P 5–13
Creating a balance sheet from ratios;
Chapters 3 and 5
● **LO5–7**

Cadux Candy Company's income statement for the year ended December 31, 2013, reported interest expense of $2 million and income tax expense of $12 million. Current assets listed in its balance sheet include cash, accounts receivable, and inventories. Property, plant, and equipment is the company's only noncurrent asset. Financial ratios for 2013 are listed below. Profitability and turnover ratios with balance sheet items in the denominator were calculated using year-end balances rather than averages.

Debt to equity ratio	1.0
Current ratio	2.0
Acid-test ratio	1.0
Times interest earned ratio	17 times
Return on assets	10%
Return on shareholders' equity	20%
Profit margin on sales	5%
Gross profit margin (gross profit divided by net sales)	40%
Inventory turnover	8 times
Receivables turnover	20 times

Required:
Prepare a December 31, 2013, balance sheet for the Cadux Candy Company.

CHAPTER 5   Income Measurement and Profitability Analysis   **291**

P 5–14
Compare two companies in the same industry; Chapters 3 and 5
● LO5–7

Presented below are condensed financial statements adapted from those of two actual companies competing as the primary players in a specialty area of the food manufacturing and distribution industry. ($ in millions, except per share amounts.)

Balance Sheets

Assets	Metropolitan	Republic
Cash	$ 179.3	$ 37.1
Accounts receivable (net)	422.7	325.0
Short-term investments	—	4.7
Inventories	466.4	635.2
Prepaid expenses and other current assets	134.6	476.7
Current assets	$1,203.0	$1,478.7
Property, plant, and equipment (net)	2,608.2	2,064.6
Intangibles and other assets	210.3	464.7
Total assets	$4,021.5	$4,008.0
Liabilities and Shareholders' Equity		
Accounts payable	$ 467.9	$ 691.2
Short-term notes	227.1	557.4
Accruals and other current liabilities	585.2	538.5
Current liabilities	$1,280.2	$1,787.1
Long-term debt	535.6	542.3
Deferred tax liability	384.6	610.7
Other long-term liabilities	104.0	95.1
Total liabilities	$2,304.4	$3,035.2
Common stock (par and additional paid-in capital)	144.9	335.0
Retained earnings	2,476.9	1,601.9
Less: treasury stock	(904.7)	(964.1)
Total liabilities and shareholders' equity	$4,021.5	$4,008.0

Income Statements

	Metropolitan	Republic
Net sales	$5,698.0	$7,768.2
Cost of goods sold	(2,909.0)	(4,481.7)
Gross profit	$2,789.0	$3,286.5
Operating expenses	(1,743.7)	(2,539.2)
Interest expense	(56.8)	(46.6)
Income before taxes	$ 988.5	$ 700.7
Tax expense	(394.7)	(276.1)
Net income	$ 593.8	$ 424.6
Net income per share	$ 2.40	$ 6.50

Required:
Evaluate and compare the two companies by responding to the following questions.

Note: Because comparative statements are not provided you should use year-end balances in place of average balances as appropriate.

1. Which of the two firms had greater earnings relative to resources available?
2. Have the two companies achieved their respective rates of return on assets with similar combinations of profit margin and turnover?
3. From the perspective of a common shareholder, which of the two firms provided a greater rate of return?
4. Which company is most highly leveraged and which has made most effective use of financial leverage?
5. Of the two companies, which appears riskier in terms of its ability to pay short-term obligations?
6. How efficiently are current assets managed?
7. From the perspective of a creditor, which company offers the most comfortable margin of safety in terms of its ability to pay fixed interest charges?

P 5–15
Interim financial reporting
● **Appendix 5**

Branson Electronics Company is a small, publicly traded company preparing its first quarter interim report to be mailed to shareholders. The following information for the quarter has been compiled:

Revenues		$180,000
Cost of goods sold		35,000
Operating expenses:		
Fixed	$59,000	
Variable	48,000	107,000

Fixed operating expenses include payments of $50,000 to an advertising firm to promote the firm through various media throughout the year. The income tax rate for the firm's level of operations in the first quarter is 30%, but management estimates the effective rate for the entire year will be 36%.

Required:
Prepare the income statement to be included in Branson's first quarter interim report.

Broaden Your Perspective

Apply your critical-thinking ability to the knowledge you've gained. These cases will provide you an opportunity to develop your research, analysis, judgment, and communication skills. You also will work with other students, integrate what you've learned, apply it in real world situations, and consider its global and ethical ramifications. This practice will broaden your knowledge and further develop your decision-making abilities.

Real World Case 5–1
Chainsaw Al; revenue recognition and earnings management
● **LO5–1**

In May 2001, the Securities and Exchange Commission sued the former top executives at Sunbeam, charging the group with financial reporting fraud that allegedly cost investors billions in losses. Sunbeam Corporation is a recognized designer, manufacturer, and marketer of household and leisure products, including Coleman, Eastpak, First Alert, Grillmaster, Mixmaster, Mr. Coffee, Oster, Powermate, and Campingaz. In the mid-1990s, Sunbeam needed help: its profits had declined by over 80% percent, and in 1996, its stock price was down over 50% from its high. To the rescue: Albert Dunlap, also known as "Chainsaw Al" based on his reputation as a ruthless executive known for his ability to restructure and turn around troubled companies, largely by eliminating jobs.

The strategy appeared to work. In 1997, Sunbeam's revenues had risen by 18 percent. However, in April 1998, the brokerage firm of Paine Webber downgraded Sunbeam's stock recommendation. Why the downgrade? Paine Webber had noticed unusually high accounts receivable, massive increases in sales of electric blankets in the third quarter 1997, which usually sell best in the fourth quarter, as well as unusually high sales of barbeque grills for the fourth quarter. Soon after, Sunbeam announced a first quarter loss of $44.6 million, and Sunbeam's stock price fell 25 percent.

It eventually came to light that Dunlap and Sunbeam had been using a "bill and hold" strategy with retail buyers. This involved selling products at large discounts to retailers before they normally would buy and then holding the products in third-party warehouses, with delivery at a later date.

Many felt Sunbeam had deceived shareholders by artificially inflating earnings and the company's stock price. A class-action lawsuit followed, alleging that Sunbeam and Dunlap violated federal securities laws, suggesting the motivation to inflate the earnings and stock price was to allow Sunbeam to complete hundreds of millions of dollars of debt financing in order to complete some ongoing mergers. Shareholders alleged damages when Sunbeam's subsequent earnings decline caused a huge drop in the stock price.

Required:
1. How might Sunbeam's 1997 "bill and hold" strategy have contributed to artificially high earnings in 1997?
2. How would the strategy have led to the unusually high accounts receivable Paine Webber noticed?
3. How might Sunbeam's 1997 "bill and hold" strategy have contributed to a 1998 earnings decline?
4. How does earnings management of this type affect earnings quality?

Judgment Case 5–2
Revenue recognition
● **LO5–1**

Revenue earned by a business enterprise is recognized for accounting purposes at different times, according to the circumstances. In some situations revenue is recognized approximately as it is earned in the economic sense. In other situations revenue is recognized at point of delivery.

Required:
1. Explain and justify why revenue often is recognized as earned at point of delivery.
2. Explain in what situations it would be useful to recognize revenue as the productive activity takes place.
3. At what times, other than those included in (1) and (2) above, may it be appropriate to recognize revenue?

Judgment Case 5–3
Service revenue
● **LO5–1**

Mega Fitness, Inc., operates fitness centers throughout the Western states. Members pay a nonrefundable, initial fee of $100, as well as a monthly fee of $40. As an option, a member could reduce the monthly fee to $30 by increasing the initial fee to $300. The monthly fee is billed to the member near the end of each month and is due by the 15th of the following month. The only cost incurred by Mega when a new member joins a center is the cost of issuing a laminated identification card with the member's picture. The card costs $3 to produce.

Required:

When should Mega Fitness recognize revenue for the initial fee and for the monthly fee?

Judgment Case 5–4
Revenue recognition; trade-ins
● LO5–1

Apex Computer Company manufactures and sells large mainframe computers. The computers range in price from $1 to $3 million and gross profit averages 40% of sales price. The company has a liberal trade-in policy. Customers are allowed to trade in their computers for a new generation machine anytime within three years of sale. The trade-in allowance granted will vary depending on the number of years between original sale and trade-in. However, in all cases, the allowance is expected to be approximately 25% higher than the prevailing market price of the computer.

As an example, in 2013 a customer who purchased a computer in 2011 for $2 million (the computer cost Apex $1,200,000 to manufacture) decided to trade it in for a new computer. The sales price of the new computer was $2.5 million and a trade-in allowance of $600,000 was granted on the old machine. As a result of the trade-in allowance, the customer had to pay only $1.9 million ($2.5 million less $600,000) for the new computer. The old computer taken back by Apex had a resale value of $480,000. The new computer cost $1.5 million to manufacture. The company accounted for the trade-in by recognizing revenue of $2,380,000 ($1.9 million received in cash + $480,000 value of old computer).

Required:

Does the company's revenue recognition policy for trade-ins seem appropriate? If not, describe the problem created by the liberal trade-in policy.

Communication Case 5–5
Revenue recognition
● LO5–1

Jerry's Ice Cream Parlor is considering a marketing plan to increase sales of ice cream cones. The plan will give customers a free ice cream cone if they buy 10 ice cream cones at regular prices. Customers will be issued a card that will be punched each time an ice cream cone is purchased. After 10 punches, the card can be turned in for a free cone.

Jerry Donovan, the company's owner, is not sure how the new plan will affect accounting procedures. He realizes that the company will be incurring costs each time a free ice cream cone is awarded, but there will be no corresponding revenue or cash inflow.

The focus of this case is the matching of revenues and expenses related to the free ice cream cones that will be awarded if the new plan is adopted. Your instructor will divide the class into two to six groups depending on the size of the class. The mission of your group is to reach consensus on the appropriate accounting treatment for the new plan.

Required:

1. Each group member should deliberate the situation independently and draft a tentative argument prior to the class session for which the case is assigned.
2. In class, each group will meet for 10–15 minutes in different areas of the classroom. During that meeting, group members will take turns sharing their suggestions for the purpose of arriving at a single group treatment.
3. After the allotted time, a spokesperson for each group (selected during the group meetings) will share the group's solution with the class. The goal of the class is to incorporate the views of each group into a consensus approach to the situation.

Research Case 5–6
Long-term contract accounting
● LO5–5

An article published in *Accounting Horizons* describes the current accounting practices and disclosures for long-term contracts for the Fortune 500 companies.

Required:

In your library or from some other source, locate the indicated article in *Accounting Horizons,* September 2004, and answer the following questions:
1. How many firms reported the use of one of the two long-term contract accounting methods?
2. Approximately half of the firms are in which industry?
3. How many firms reported the use of the percentage-of-completion method? The completed contract method?
4. What is the most frequently used approach to estimating a percentage-of-completion?

Research Case 5–7
Earnings management with respect to revenues
● LO5–1

An article published in *Accounting Horizons* describes various techniques that companies use to manage their earnings.

Required:

In your library or from some other source, locate the article "How Are Earnings Managed? Evidence from Auditors" in *Accounting Horizons,* 2003 (Supplement), and answer the following questions:
1. What are the four most common revenue-recognition abuses identified by auditors in that article? From the examples provided in the article, briefly explain each abuse.
2. What is the revenue-recognition abuse identified in the article related to the percentage-of-completion method?

294   SECTION 1   The Role of Accounting as an Information System

3. Did revenue-recognition abuses tend to increase or decrease net income in the year they occurred?

4. Did auditors tend to require their clients to make adjustments that reduced the revenue-recognition abuses they detected?

Ethics Case 5–8
Revenue
recognition
● LO5–1

Horizon Corporation manufactures personal computers. The company began operations in 2004 and reported profits for the years 2008 through 2011. Due primarily to increased competition and price slashing in the industry, 2012's income statement reported a loss of $20 million. Just before the end of the 2013 fiscal year, a memo from the company's chief financial officer to Jim Fielding, the company controller, included the following comments:

If we don't do something about the large amount of unsold computers already manufactured, our auditors will require us to write them off. The resulting loss for 2013 will cause a violation of our debt covenants and force the company into bankruptcy. I suggest that you ship half of our inventory to J.B. Sales, Inc., in Oklahoma City. I know the company's president and he will accept the merchandise and acknowledge the shipment as a purchase. We can record the sale in 2013 which will boost profits to an acceptable level. Then J.B. Sales will simply return the merchandise in 2014 after the financial statements have been issued.

Required:
Discuss the ethical dilemma faced by Jim Fielding.

**Judgment
Case 5–9**
Revenue
recognition;
installment sale
● LO5–1, LO5–3

On October 1, 2013, the Marshall Company sold a large piece of machinery to the Hammond Construction Company for $80,000. The cost of the machine was $40,000. Hammond made a down payment of $10,000 and agreed to pay the remaining balance in seven equal monthly installments of $10,000, plus interest at 12% on the unpaid balance, beginning November 1.

Required:

1. Identify three alternative methods for recognizing revenue and costs for the situation described and compute the amount of gross profit that would be recognized in 2013 using each method.

2. Discuss the circumstances under which each of the three methods would be used.

**Judgment
Case 5–10**
Revenue
recognition;
SAB 101
questions; FASB
codification
● LO5–1

As part of its crackdown on earnings management, the SEC issued *Staff Accounting Bulletins No.s 101 and 104* to provide additional guidance on when revenue should be recognized. Consider the following situations posed by the SEC and, for each, discuss whether or not you believe it is appropriate to recognize revenue. You might gain access to this literature through the FASB Codification Research System via the FASB website (www.fasb.org), the SEC (www.sec.gov), your school library, or some other source.

1. **Facts:** Company M is a discount retailer. It generates revenue from annual membership fees it charges customers to shop at its stores and from the sale of products at a discount price to those customers. The membership arrangements with retail customers require the customer to pay the entire membership fee (e.g., $35) at the outset of the arrangement. However, the customer has the unilateral right to cancel the arrangement at any time during its term and receive a full refund of the initial fee. Based on historical data collected over time for a large number of homogeneous transactions, Company M estimates that approximately 40% of the customers will request a refund before the end of the membership contract term. Company M's data for the past five years indicates that significant variations between actual and estimated cancellations have not occurred, and Company M does not expect significant variations to occur in the foreseeable future.

   Question: May Company M recognize revenue for the membership fees and accrue the costs to provide membership services at the outset of the arrangement?

2. **Facts:** Company Z enters into an arrangement with Customer A to deliver Company Z's products to Customer A on a consignment basis. Pursuant to the terms of the arrangement, Customer A is a consignee, and title to the products does not pass from Company Z to Customer A until Customer A consumes the products in its operations. Company Z delivers product to Customer A under the terms of their arrangement.

   Question: May Company Z recognize revenue upon delivery of its product to Customer A?

3. **Facts:** Company R is a retailer that offers "layaway" sales to its customers. Company R retains the merchandise, sets it aside in its inventory, and collects a cash deposit from the customer. Although Company R may set a time period within which the customer must finalize the purchase, Company R does not require the customer to enter into an installment note or other fixed payment commitment or agreement when the initial deposit is received. The merchandise generally is not released to the customer until the customer pays the full purchase price. In the event that the customer fails to pay the remaining purchase price, the customer forfeits its cash deposit. In the event the merchandise is lost, damaged, or destroyed, Company R either must refund the cash deposit to the customer or provide replacement merchandise.

   Question: When may Company R recognize revenue for merchandise sold under its layaway program?

Research Case 5–11
Locate and extract relevant information and authoritative support for a financial reporting issue; revenue recognition; right of return; FASB codification
● **LO5–4**

Many companies sell products allowing their customers the right to return merchandise if they are not satisfied. Because the return of merchandise can retroactively negate the benefits of having made a sale, the seller must meet certain criteria before revenue is recognized in situations when the right of return exists. Generally accepted accounting principles list the criteria, the most critical of which is that the seller must be able to make reliable estimates of future returns.

Required:

1. Obtain the relevant authoritative literature on accounting for the right to return merchandise using the FASB's Codification Research System. You might gain access at the FASB (www.fasb.org), from your school library, or some other source.

2. What factors do generally accepted accounting principles discuss that may impair the ability to make a reasonable estimate of returns? Cite the reference location regarding these factors.

3. List the criteria that must be met before revenue can be recognized when the right of return exists.

4. Using EDGAR (www.sec.gov) access the 10-K reports for the most recent fiscal year for Hewlett-Packard Company and for Advanced Micro Devices, Inc. Search for the revenue recognition policy to determine when these two companies recognize revenue for product sales allowing customers the right of return.

5. Using your answers to requirements 2 and 3, speculate as to why the two revenue recognition policies differ.

Research Case 5–12
FASB codification; locate and extract relevant information and authoritative support for a financial reporting issue; reporting revenue as a principal or as an agent
● **LO5–1, LO5–2**

The birth of the Internet in the 1990s led to the creation of a new industry of online retailers such as Amazon, Overstock.com, and PC Mall, Inc. Many of these companies often act as intermediaries between the manufacturer and the customer without ever taking possession of the merchandise sold. Revenue recognition for this type of transaction has been controversial.

Assume that Overstock.com sold you a product for $200 that cost $150. The company's profit on the transaction clearly is $50. Should Overstock recognize $200 in revenue and $150 in cost of goods sold (the gross method), or should it recognize only the $50 in gross profit (the net method) as commission revenue?

Required:

1. Obtain the relevant authoritative literature on reporting revenue at gross versus net using the FASB's Codification Research System. You might gain access at the FASB website (www.fasb.org), from your school library, or some other source. *Hint:* this guidance was originally issued in the Emerging Issues Task Force document EITF 99-19, and you can use the codification's "Cross Reference" function to identify where that EITF appears in the codification.

2. What factors does the authoritative literature discuss that will influence the choice of reporting method used by these companies? Cite the reference location and the specific titles pertaining to this reference location.

3. Using EDGAR (www.sec.gov), access Google, Inc.'s 2010 10-K. Locate the disclosure note that discusses the company's revenue recognition policy.

4. Does Google discuss determining whether they should report revenue on a gross versus net basis with respect to any of their products or services? What is the reason Google provides for its choices? Do you agree with Google's reasoning?

Judgment Case 5–13
Revenue recognition; service sales
● **LO5–1, LO5–5**

Each of the following situations concerns revenue recognition for services.

1. Delta Airlines books a reservation for a roundtrip flight to Orlando for Ming Tsai on April 12. Delta charges the $425 to Tsai's Visa card on April 13 and receives the cash from Visa on May 1. The roundtrip flight commences on May 15. The ticket is nonrefundable.

2. Highlife Ski Resort in Colorado sells a season pass to Larry Werner on October 15. Highlife usually opens its season just after Thanksgiving and stays open until approximately April 30.

3. Dixon Management requires tenants to sign a three-year lease and charges $5,000 per month for one floor in its midtown high-rise. In addition to the monthly fee, payable at the beginning of each month, tenants pay a nonrefundable fee of $12,000 to secure the lease.

4. Janora Hawkins, attorney, agrees to accept an accident victim's case. Hawkins will be paid on a contingency basis. That is, if she wins the case, she will receive 30% of the total settlement. The case commences on July 15 and is settled successfully on August 28. On September 15, Hawkins receives her contingency payment of $60,000.

Required:

For each of the above situations, determine the appropriate timing of revenue recognition.

296 SECTION 1 The Role of Accounting as an Information System

Judgment Case 5–14
Revenue recognition; long-term construction contracts
● LO5–5

Two accounting students were discussing the alternative methods of accounting for long-term construction contracts. The discussion focused on which method was most like the typical revenue recognition method of recognizing revenue at point of product delivery. Bill argued that the completed contract method was preferable because it was analogous to recognizing revenue at the point of delivery. John disagreed and supported the percentage-of-completion method, stating that it was analogous to accruing revenue during the earnings process, that is, as the work was performed.

Required:
Discuss the arguments made by both students. Which argument do you support? Why?

Communication Case 5–15
Percentage-of-completion and completed contract methods
● LO5–5

Willingham Construction is in the business of building high-priced, custom, single-family homes. The company, headquartered in Anaheim, California, operates throughout the Southern California area. The construction period for the average home built by Willingham is six months, although some homes have taken as long as nine months.

You have just been hired by Willingham as the assistant controller and one of your first tasks is to evaluate the company's revenue recognition policy. The company presently uses the completed contract method for all of its projects and management is now considering a switch to the percentage-of-completion method.

Required:
Write a 1- to 2-page memo to Virginia Reynolds, company controller, describing the differences between the percentage-of-completion and completed contract methods. Be sure to include references to GAAP as they pertain to the choice of method. Do not address the differential effects on income taxes nor the effect on the financial statements of switching between methods.

IFRS Case 5–16
Comparison of revenue recognition in Sweden and the United States
● LO5–1, LO5–8

 IFRS

Vodafone Group, Plc, headquartered in the United Kingdom, is one of the world's largest telecommunications companies. Excerpts from the revenue recognition disclosure included in its 2011 annual report are reproduced below.

Note 2: Significant accounting policies

Revenue

Revenue is recognised to the extent the Group has delivered goods or rendered services under an agreement, the amount of revenue can be measured reliably and it is probable that the economic benefits associated with the transaction will flow to the Group. Revenue is measured at the fair value of the consideration received, exclusive of sales taxes and discounts.

The Group principally obtains revenue from providing the following telecommunication services: access charges, airtime usage, messaging, interconnect fees, data services and information provision, connection fees and equipment sales. Products and services may be sold separately or in bundled packages.

Revenue for access charges, airtime usage and messaging by contract customers is recognised as services are performed, with unbilled revenue resulting from services already provided accrued at the end of each period and unearned revenue from services to be provided in future periods deferred. Revenue from the sale of prepaid credit is deferred until such time as the customer uses the airtime, or the credit expires.

Revenue from interconnect fees is recognised at the time the services are performed.

Revenue from data services and information provision is recognised when the Group has performed the related service and, depending on the nature of the service, is recognised either at the gross amount billed to the customer or the amount receivable by the Group as commission for facilitating the service. . .

Revenue for device sales is recognised when the device is delivered to the end customer and the sale is considered complete. For device sales made to intermediaries, revenue is recognised if the significant risks associated with the device are transferred to the intermediary and the intermediary has no general right of return. If the significant risks are not transferred, revenue recognition is deferred until sale of the device to an end customer by the intermediary or the expiry of the right of return.

Required:
On the basis of the information the disclosures provide, compare revenue recognition under IFRS (as applied by Vodafone) with that in the United States.

IFRS Case 5–17
Comparison of revenue recognition for construction contracts
● LO5–5, LO5–8

 IFRS

ThyssenKrupp AG, headquartered in Germany, is one of the world's largest technology companies, with 177,346 employees worldwide and primary segments in steel, technology, and capital goods and services.

Required:
1. Access ThyssenKrupp's most recent annual report using the Internet. Find the footnote describing significant accounting policies. Indicate the methods that ThyssenKrupp uses to account for long-term construction contracts when they can and cannot make an accurate estimate of the income on a construction contract.

2. If ThyssenKrupp was a U.S. company, how would you expect its accounting for these contracts to differ?

Trueblood Accounting Case 5–18
Revenue recognition for multiple-deliverable contracts involving software
● LO5–6

The following Trueblood case is recommended for use with this chapter. The case provides an excellent opportunity for class discussion, group projects, and writing assignments. The case, along with Professor's Discussion Material, can be obtained from the Deloitte Foundation at its website www.deloitte.com/us/truebloodcases.

Case 10-11: *Eye Vision*

This case concerns the appropriate timing of revenue recognition for a bundled product and service.

Trueblood Accounting Case 5–19
Revenue recognition for multiple-deliverable contracts
● LO5–6

The following Trueblood case is recommended for use with this chapter. The case provides an excellent opportunity for class discussion, group projects, and writing assignments. The case, along with Professor's Discussion Material, can be obtained from the Deloitte Foundation at its website www.deloitte.com/us/truebloodcases.

Case 07-3 Part 1: *Columbia On-Line Networks*

This case concerns recognizing revenue of arrangements that have multiple elements.

Real World Case 5–20
Revenue recognition; franchise sales
● LO5–6

EDGAR, the Electronic Data Gathering, Analysis, and Retrieval system, performs automated collection, validation, indexing, and forwarding of submissions by companies and others who are required by law to file forms with the U.S. Securities and Exchange Commission (SEC). All publicly traded domestic companies use EDGAR to make the majority of their filings. (Some foreign companies file voluntarily.) Form 10-K which includes the annual report, is required to be filed on EDGAR. The SEC makes this information available on the Internet.

Required:

1. Access EDGAR on the Internet. The web address is www.sec.gov.
2. Search for Jack in the Box, Inc. Access the most recent 10-K filing. Search or scroll to find the financial statements and related notes.
3. Answer the following questions related to the company's revenue recognition policies:
   a. When does the company recognize initial franchise license fee revenue?
   b. How are continuing fees determined?
4. Repeat requirements 2 and 3 for two additional companies that you suspect also earn revenues through the sale of franchise rights. Compare their revenue recognition policies with the policies of Jack in the Box.

Real World Case 5–21
Principal agent considerations
● LO5–2

EDGAR, the Electronic Data Gathering, Analysis, and Retrieval system, performs automated collection, validation, indexing, and forwarding of submissions by companies and others who are required by law to file forms with the U.S. Securities and Exchange Commission (SEC). All publicly traded domestic companies use EDGAR to make the majority of their filings. (Some foreign companies file voluntarily.) Form 10-K which includes the annual report, is required to be filed on EDGAR. The SEC makes this information available on the Internet.

Required:

1. Access EDGAR on the Internet. The web address is www.sec.gov.
2. Search for the most recent 10-K's of Orbitz and priceline.com. Search or scroll to find the revenue recognition note in the financial statements.
3. For each of the following types of revenue, indicate whether the amount shown on the income statement is "net" or "gross" as those terms have been used with respect to revenue recognition in our course, and briefly explain your answer.
   a. Orbitz's "merchant model" revenues.
   b. Orbitz's "retail model" revenues.
   c. priceline.com's "merchant revenues for 'Name Your Own Price'® services."
   d. priceline.com's "merchant revenues for 'Price-Disclosed Hotel' services."
   e. priceline.com's agency revenues.
4. Consider your responses to 3a through 3e. Does it look like there is the potential for noncomparability when readers consider Orbitz and priceline.com? Indicate "yes" or "no," and briefly explain your answer.

Analysis
Case 5–22
Evaluating profitability and asset management; obtain and compare annual reports from companies in the same industry
● LO5–7

Performance and profitability of a company often are evaluated using the financial information provided by a firm's annual report in comparison with other firms in the same industry. Ratios are useful in this assessment.

Required:

Obtain annual reports from two corporations in the same primary industry. Using techniques you learned in this chapter and any analysis you consider useful, respond to the following questions:

1. How do earnings trends compare in terms of both the direction and stability of income?
2. Which of the two firms had greater earnings relative to resources available?
3. How efficiently are current assets managed?
4. Has each of the companies achieved its respective rate of return on assets with similar combinations of profit margin and turnover?
5. Are there differences in accounting methods that should be taken into account when making comparisons?

Note: You can obtain copies of annual reports from friends who are shareholders, the investor relations department of the corporations, from a friendly stockbroker, or from EDGAR (Electronic Data Gathering, Analysis, and Retrieval) on the Internet (www.sec.gov).

Judgment
Case 5–23
Relationships among ratios; Chapters 3 and 5
● LO5–7

You are a part-time financial advisor. A client is considering an investment in common stock of a waste recycling firm. One motivation is a rumor the client heard that the company made huge investments in a new fuel creation process. Unable to confirm the rumor, your client asks you to determine whether the firm's assets had recently increased significantly.

Because the firm is small, information is sparse. Last quarter's interim report showed total assets of $324 million, approximately the same as last year's annual report. The only information more current than that is a press release last week in which the company's management reported "record net income for the year of $21 million, representing a 14.0% return on shareholders' equity. Performance was enhanced by the Company's judicious use of financial leverage on a debt/equity ratio of 2 to 1."

Required:

Use the information available to provide your client with an opinion as to whether the waste recycling firm invested in the new fuel creation process during the last quarter of the year.

Integrating
Case 5–24
Using ratios to test reasonableness of data; Chapters 3 and 5
● LO5–7

You are a new staff accountant with a large regional CPA firm, participating in your first audit. You recall from your auditing class that CPAs often use ratios to test the reasonableness of accounting numbers provided by the client. Since ratios reflect the relationships among various account balances, if it is assumed that prior relationships still hold, prior years' ratios can be used to estimate what current balances should approximate. However, you never actually performed this kind of analysis until now. The CPA in charge of the audit of Covington Pike Corporation brings you the list of ratios shown below and tells you these reflect the relationships maintained by Covington Pike in recent years.

> Profit margin on sales = 5%
> Return on assets = 7.5%
> Gross profit margin = 40%
> Inventory turnover ratio = 6 times
> Receivables turnover ratio = 25 times
> Acid-test ratio = .9 to one
> Current ratio = 2 to 1
> Return on shareholders' equity = 10%
> Debt to equity ratio = $1/3$
> Times interest earned ratio = 12 times

Jotted in the margins are the following notes:

● Net income $15,000
● Only one short-term note ($5,000); all other current liabilities are trade accounts
● Property, plant, and equipment are the only noncurrent assets
● Bonds payable are the only noncurrent liabilities
● The effective interest rate on short-term notes and bonds is 8%
● No investment securities
● Cash balance totals $15,000

Required:

You are requested to approximate the current year's balances in the form of a balance sheet and income statement, to the extent the information allows. Accompany those financial statements with the calculations you use to estimate each amount reported.

Air France–KLM Case

AIRFRANCE

● LO5–8

◉ IFRS

Air France–KLM (AF), a French company, prepares its financial statements according to International Financial Reporting Standards. AF's annual report for the year ended March 31, 2011, which includes financial statements and disclosure notes, is provided with all new textbooks. This material also is included in AF's "Registration Document 2010–11," dated June 15, 2011 and is available at www.airfranceklm.com.

Required:

1. In note 3.6, AF indicates that "Upon issuance, both passenger and cargo tickets are recorded as "Deferred revenue on ticket sales" and that "Sales related to air transportation are recognized when the transportation service is provided."

   a. Examine AF's balance sheet. What is the total amount of deferred revenue on ticket sales as of March 31, 2011?

   b. When transportation services are provided with respect to the deferred revenue on ticket sales, what journal entry would AF make to reduce deferred revenue?

   c. Does AF's treatment of deferred revenue under IFRS appear consistent with how these transactions would be handled under U.S. GAAP? Explain.

2. AF has a frequent flyer program, "Flying Blue," which allows members to acquire "miles" as they fly on Air France or partner airlines that are redeemable for free flights or other benefits.

   a. How does AF account for these miles?

   b. Does AF report any liability associated with these miles as of March 31, 2011?

   c. Is AF's accounting approach under IFRS consistent with how U.S. GAAP accounts for multiple-deliverable contracts? Explain.

REVENUE RECOGNITION

Where We're Headed

PREFACE — The FASB and the IASB are collaborating on several major new standards designed in part to move U.S. GAAP and IFRS closer together (convergence). This reading is based on their joint Exposure Draft of a new revenue recognition Accounting Standards Update (ASU) and "tentative decisions" of the Boards after receiving feedback from the Exposure Draft as of the date this text went to press.[41]

Even after the proposed ASU is issued, previous GAAP will be relevant until the ASU becomes effective, and students taking the CPA or CMA exams will be responsible for the previous GAAP until six months after that effective date. Conversely, prior to the effective date of the proposed ASU it is useful for students to have an understanding of the new guidance on the horizon.

In June 2010 the FASB and IASB issued identical Exposure Drafts (ED) for a new ASU entitled "Revenue from Contracts with Customers," and followed up with another Exposure Draft in November of 2011.[42] The purpose of the proposed ASU is to improve revenue recognition guidance and in the process to eliminate current revenue recognition differences among industries and between U.S. GAAP and IFRS. It appears likely that the final ASU will become effective for fiscal years starting no sooner than 2015. This chapter supplement covers the main points of the proposed ASU. We focus in particular on important changes from current GAAP, identified with a *GAAP Change* note in the margin of the supplement.

The core revenue recognition principle and key application steps of the proposed ASU are shown in Illustration 5–18.

Illustration 5–18

Core Revenue
Recognition Principle
and Key Steps in
Applying the Principle

GAAP Change

Core Revenue Recognition Principle[43]

A company must recognize revenue when goods or services are transferred to customers in an amount that reflects the consideration the company expects to be entitled to receive in exchange for those goods or services.

Key Steps in Applying The Principle

1. Identify a contract with a customer.
2. Identify the separate performance obligation(s) in the contract.
3. Determine the transaction price.
4. Allocate the transaction price to the separate performance obligations.
5. Recognize revenue when (or as) each performance obligation is satisfied.

---

[41]Because the proposed ASU had not been finalized as of the date this text went to press, it is possible that some aspects of the final ASU are different from what we show in this Supplement. Check the FASB Updates page (http://lsb.scu.edu/jsepe/fasb-update-7e.htm) to see if any changes have occurred.
[42]*Proposed Accounting Standards Update (Revised): Revenue Recognition (Topic 605)*, "Revenue from Contracts with Customers" (Norwalk, Conn: FASB, November 14, 2011).
[43]Ibid.

This approach may seem familiar—it is similar to what we use for "multiple-element contracts" in current U.S. GAAP. For many contracts, applying this approach is very straightforward and results in accounting that is very similar to what is required under current GAAP. As a simple example, assume Macy's sells a skirt to a woman named Susan for $75 that Macy's previously purchased from a wholesaler for $40. Given that the skirt is on sale, Macy's has a "no returns" policy. How would Macy's account for the sale?

1. **Identify the contract with a customer:** In this case, the contract is implicit but clear—Macy's delivers the skirt and Susan pays cash of $75.
2. **Identify the separate performance obligation(s) in the contract:** Macy's has only a single performance obligation—deliver the skirt.
3. **Determine the transaction price:** The price is $75.
4. **Allocate the transaction price to the separate performance obligations:** With only one performance obligation, no allocation is necessary.
5. **Recognize revenue when (or as) each performance obligation is satisfied:** Macy's satisfies its performance obligation when it delivers the skirt to Susan, and makes the following journal entries:

Cash	75	
Revenue		75
Cost of goods sold	40	
Inventory		40

Unfortunately, applying this revenue recognition approach in practice often is much more complicated, because different kinds of businesses use different arrangements to sell various combinations of goods and services. Let's walk through each of the five key steps in more detail.

Step 1: Identify the Contract

Under the proposed ASU we recognize revenue associated with contracts that are legally enforceable. We normally think of a contract as being specified in a written document, but that doesn't have to be the case for revenue recognition to occur. Contracts can be oral rather than written. They can be explicit, but they also can be implicit based on the typical business practices that a company uses to sell products or services.

Enforceable contracts can be explicit or implicit.

When does an enforceable contract exist for purposes of revenue recognition?[44] As shown in Illustration 5–19, the contract must meet five criteria.

For purposes of applying revenue recognition criteria, a contract needs to have the following characteristics:

1. **Commercial substance.** The contract is expected to affect the seller's future cash flows.
2. **Approval.** Each party to the contract has approved the contract and is committed to satisfying their respective obligations.
3. **Rights.** Each party's rights are specified with regard to the goods or services to be transferred.
4. **Payment terms.** The terms and manner of payment are specified.
5. **Performance.** A contract does not exist if each party can terminate the contract without penalty before any obligations are performed.

Illustration 5–19

Criteria for Determining Whether a Contract Exists for Purposes of Revenue Recognition

If an unperformed contract can be cancelled without penalty, a contract does not exist for purposes of revenue recognition.

Illustration 5–20 shows these criteria applied to a TrueTech example that we will use throughout the remainder of this supplement.

---

[44]Our focus will be on accounting for a single contract. The proposed ASU requires sellers with multiple contracts to account for them as a single contract if (1) the contracts are negotiated as a package with a single commercial objective, (2) the transaction price of one contract depends on the price of the other contract, or (3) some or all of the goods or services promised in the contracts are a single performance obligation.

Illustration 5–20

Determining Whether a Contract Exists for Revenue Recognition Purposes

TrueTech Industries manufactures the Tri-Box System, a multiplayer gaming system allowing players to compete with each other over the Internet.

- The Tri-Box System has a wholesale price of $270 that includes the physical Tri-Box module as well as a one-year subscription to the Tri-Net of Internet-based games and other applications.
- TrueTech sells one-year subscriptions to the Tri-Net separately for $50 to owners of Tri-Box modules as well as owners of other gaming systems.
- TrueTech does not sell a Tri-Box module without the initial one-year Tri-Net subscription, but estimates that it would charge $250 per module if modules were sold alone.

CompStores orders 1,000 Tri-Box Systems at the normal wholesale price of $270.

- CompStores places its order on May 10, 2013, promising payment within 30 days after delivery. TrueTech or CompStores can cancel the order at any time prior to delivery without penalty.
- TrueTech delivers the Tri-Boxes to CompStores on May 20, 2013.

Is the TrueTech arrangement with CompStores a contract for purposes of revenue recognition? Yes, but only as of May 20, the date TrueTech delivers the systems to CompStores.

1. **Commercial substance.** The contract will affect TrueTech's cash flows.
2. **Approval.** TrueTech and CompStores both approved the contract.
3. **Rights.** Each party's rights are specified–TrueTech will deliver the Tri-Boxes and one-year subscriptions to Tri-Net; CompStores will pay $270 per unit.
4. **Payment terms.** The terms and manner of payment are specified—CompStores will pay the full balance within 30 days of delivery.
5. **Performance.** Prior to delivery, both parties can cancel the order without penalty, so the arrangement doesn't qualify as a contract for purposes of revenue recognition. Once TrueTech makes delivery, one party has performed a part of the contract, so the contract exists as of that date for purposes of revenue recognition.

Current GAAP requires persuasive evidence of an arrangement, which is similar to the idea of an enforceable contract in the proposed ASU, so for most arrangements this step will not change existing revenue recognition practice.

Step 2: Identify the Performance Obligation(s)

Performance obligations are promises to transfer goods and services to the buyer.

Once a contract is identified, the next step is to determine what separate **performance obligation(s)** the seller must satisfy to fulfill the contract. A contract could obligate a seller to provide multiple goods and services. For example, when **Verizon** signs up a new cell phone customer, the sales contract could require delivery of a smart phone, delivery of the related software, and provision of a warranty on the phone, ongoing network access, and optional future upgrades.

Sellers account for performance obligations separately if the performance obligations are **distinct**. A performance obligation is distinct if either:

1. the seller regularly sells the good or service separately, or
2. a buyer could use the good or service on its own or in combination with goods or services the buyer could obtain elsewhere.

Performance obligations are accounted for separately if they are distinct.

In Illustration 5–21 we apply these criteria in determining the separate performance obligations for our TrueTech example.

If performance obligations are distinct, we account for them separately. The idea is to identify parts of contracts that can be viewed on a stand-alone basis, so that the financial statements can capture the transfer of separate goods and services and the profit margin that is attributable to each one.

> Assume the same facts as in Illustration 5–20. What distinct performance obligations exist in the TrueTech contract with CompStores?
>
> Although TrueTech does not sell the module separately, the module would have a function to the buyer in combination with games and subscription services the buyer could obtain elsewhere. The Tri-Net subscription is sold separately. Therefore, the module and subscription are distinct, and the contract has two separate performance obligations: (1) delivery of Tri-Box modules, and (2) fulfillment of Tri-Net subscriptions via access to the Tri-Net network over a one-year period.

Illustration 5–21
Determining If Performance Obligations Are Distinct

Sometimes, though, a *bundle* of goods and services is treated as a single performance obligation. That occurs if both of the following two criteria are met:

1. The goods or services in the bundle are highly interrelated and the seller provides a significant service of integrating the goods or services into the combined item(s) delivered to a customer.
2. The bundle of goods or services is significantly modified or customized to fulfill the contract.

A bundle of goods and services is viewed as a single performance obligation if the seller provides a significant integration service and significantly modifies the bundle to fulfill the contract.

For example, when a construction company integrates many goods and services to provide a finished building, we view the construction company as providing an integration service that is a single performance obligation.

Also, if multiple distinct goods or services have the same pattern of transfer to the customer, the seller can treat them as a single performance obligation. The proposed ASU provides this alternative to sellers as a practical way to simplify accounting for these arrangements.

Several common aspects of contracts make it difficult to identify separate performance obligations: prepayments, right of return, warranties, and options. We discuss each in turn.

PREPAYMENTS

Some contracts may require up front payments associated with particular initial activities (for example, registration fees to join health clubs and activation fees for cell phone service). Prepayments are *not* separate performance obligations because they aren't a promise to transfer a product or service to a customer. Instead, the upfront fee is an advance payment for future products or services and should be included in the transaction price, allocated to the various performance obligations in the contract and recognized as revenue when each performance obligation is satisfied.

A prepayment is not a separate performance obligation.

RIGHT OF RETURN

In some industries it's common for a seller to give customers the right to return merchandise. A right of return is not a separate performance obligation. Instead, it represents a failure to satisfy the performance obligation to deliver satisfactory goods. As a result, sellers need to estimate the amount of product that will be returned and account for those returns as a reduction in revenue and as a refund liability. We discuss accounting for returns further in Chapter 7.

A right of return is not a separate performance obligation.

WARRANTIES

Most products are sold with a quality assurance warranty that obligates the seller for some period of time after the sale to make repairs or replace products that are later demonstrated to be defective. Quality assurance warranties can be stated explicitly, or can be implicit because of normal business practice. Quality assurance warranties are not separate performance obligations. Rather, they are viewed as a cost of satisfying the performance obligation to deliver products of acceptable quality. Therefore, the seller recognizes in the period of sale an expense and related contingent liability for these warranties. For example, Dell reports a quality assurance warranty liability of $895 million as of the end of fiscal 2011. We discuss accounting for warranties further in Chapter 13.

A quality assurance warranty is not a separate performance obligation.

An *extended warranty* is a separate performance obligation.

Other warranties are offered as an additional, extended service that covers new problems arising after the buyer takes control of the product. You probably have been offered extended warranties for an additional charge when you purchased electronics, appliances, automobiles, or other products. Unlike quality-assurance warranties, extended warranties *do* qualify as separate performance obligations because they represent additional services that could be (and often are) sold separately. Like other separate performance obligations, extended warranties are allocated a portion of the transaction price at the start of the contract, and then that portion of the transaction price is recognized as revenue over the extended warranty period. Dell reports a liability for deferred extended warranty revenue of $6,416 million as of the end of fiscal 2011.

It can be difficult to determine whether a warranty is only providing assurance that the product was delivered free from defects (and so is a quality assurance warranty and only accrued as a cost) or provides an additional service much like insurance (and so is an extended warranty that is treated as a separate performance obligation). The proposed ASU indicates that a warranty qualifies as a separate performance obligation if either (a) the buyer has the option to purchase the warranty separately from the seller or (b) the warranty provides a service to the customer beyond only assuring that the seller delivered a product or service that was free from defects.

CUSTOMER OPTIONS FOR ADDITIONAL GOODS OR SERVICES

An *option* for additional goods and services is a separate performance obligation if it confers a material right to the buyer.

Some contracts involve the seller granting to the buyer an option to receive additional goods or services at no cost or at a discount. These options include software upgrades, customer loyalty programs (frequent flier miles, points), and contract renewal options. These sorts of options are separate performance obligations if they provide a material right to the buyer that the buyer would not receive otherwise.

GAAP Change

Depending on the industry, we treat customer options very differently under the proposed ASU than under current GAAP. For example, when you purchase a plane ticket, you might also have some number of miles added to a frequent flier plan that you have with the airline. Under current GAAP most airlines don't recognize frequent flier plans as creating separate performance obligations, and so don't allocate any revenue to them. Rather, airlines typically recognize all of the ticket revenue when customers take their flights, and only accrue an expense and liability for the estimated incremental cost of redeeming frequent flier miles. Under the proposed ASU, frequent flier miles create a separate performance obligation for the airline, because customers can redeem them for free airfare or discounts on other products or services that they could not obtain for the same price otherwise. Therefore, some of the price of the airline ticket is allocated to the miles and only recognized as revenue when the airline satisfies the performance obligation associated with the miles (for example, by the passenger redeeming the miles or the miles expiring).

On the other hand, as indicated earlier in Chapter 5, customer options for software upgrades are already treated as separate performance obligations by Apple and other smartphone venders, which is consistent with the proposed ASU. One goal of the ASU is to remove such between-industry differences in revenue recognition practice.

More generally, the proposed ASU may identify multiple performance obligations in arrangements that current GAAP treats as a single product or service. Complex contracts in telecommunications, pharmaceutical research, media distribution, and other industries will need to be reevaluated to determine which performance obligations are distinct under the ASU.

Step 3: Determine the Transaction Price

The *transaction price* is the amount the seller expects to be entitled to receive from the buyer in exchange for providing goods and services.

Determining the transaction price is simple if the buyer pays a fixed amount immediately or in the near future (remember Macy's' sale of a skirt to Susan?). However, in some contracts this determination is more difficult. Specific complications we discuss are variable consideration, time value of money, and collectibility of the transaction price.

VARIABLE CONSIDERATION

Sometimes a transaction price is uncertain because some of the price is to be paid to the seller depending on future events. Such variable consideration occurs in many industries, including construction (incentive payments), entertainment and media (royalties), health care (Medicare and Medicaid reimbursements), manufacturing (volume discounts), and telecommunications (rebates).

The seller should include variable consideration in the transaction price by estimating it as either the probability-weighted amount or the most likely amount, depending on which better predicts the amount that the seller will receive.[45] If there are many possible outcomes, a probability-weighted amount will be more appropriate. On the other hand, if there are only two outcomes, the most likely amount might be the best indication of the amount the seller will likely receive. Illustration 5–22 provides an example.

Variable consideration is estimated as either the probability-weighted amount or the most likely amount.

Illustration 5–22
Accounting for Variable Consideration

TrueTech enters into a contract with ProSport Gaming to add ProSport's online games to the Tri-Net network. ProSport will pay TrueTech an up front $300,000 fixed fee for six months of featured access, as well as a $200,000 bonus if Tri-Net users access ProSport products for at least 15,000 hours during the six-month period. TrueTech estimates a 75% chance that it will achieve the usage target and earn the $200,000 bonus.

TrueTech would make the following entry at contract inception to record receipt of the cash:

Cash	300,000	
Unearned Revenue		300,000

Probability-Weighted Amount

A probability-weighted transaction price would be calculated as follows:

Possible Amounts	Probabilities		Expected Amounts
$500,000 ($300,000 + 200,000)	× 75%	=	$375,000
$300,000 ($300,000 + 0)	× 25%	=	75,000
Expected contract price at inception			$450,000

Most Likely Amount

The most likely amount of bonus is $200,000, so a transaction price based on the most likely amount would be $300,000 + 200,000, or $500,000.

In this case, it is likely that TrueTech would use the estimate based on the most likely amount, $500,000, because only two outcomes are possible, and it is likely that the bonus will be received. In each successive month, TrueTech would recognize one month's revenue based on a total transaction price of $500,000, reducing unearned revenue and recognizing bonus receivable:

Unearned revenue ($300,000 ÷ 6 months)........	50,000	
Bonus receivable (to balance)	33,333	
Revenue ($500,000 ÷ 6 months)[46]..............		83,333

After six months, TrueTech's Unearned revenue account would be reduced to a zero balance, and the Bonus receivable would have a balance of $200,000 ($33,333 × 6). At that point TrueTech would know if the usage of ProSport products had reached the bonus threshold and would make one of the following two journal entries:

If TrueTech receives the bonus:		If TrueTech does not receive bonus:	
Cash........................... 200,000		Revenue...................... 200,000	
Bonus receivable.....	200,000	Bonus receivable......	200,000

This treatment of variable consideration is a significant departure from current GAAP, by which we typically only recognize revenue associated with variable consideration when the

GAAP Change

---

[45]Normally, sellers receive cash consideration, but sometimes sellers receive noncash consideration instead, like property or other assets. In those circumstances, the seller measures the noncash consideration at fair value.

[46]If TrueTech instead used the probability-weighted transaction price, the journal entries would be the same except that the amount of revenue recognized each month would be $75,000 ($450,000 ÷ 6 months) and the amount of bonus receivable accrued each month would be $25,000 (to balance).

uncertainty associated with the consideration has been resolved. Under the proposed ASU sellers might recognize revenue earlier and in different amounts than under current guidance.

THE TIME VALUE OF MONEY

It's common for contracts to specify that payment occurs before or after delivery. A sale of a product on account, for instance, calls for the customer to pay for the product *after* it's been delivered. In that case, the seller can be viewed as loaning money to the buyer for the period in which the receivable is outstanding. On the other hand, when payment occurs significantly *before* delivery, the buyer can be viewed as loaning money to the seller in addition to buying goods or services from the seller.

If delivery and payment occur relatively near each other, the time value of money is not significant and it can be ignored. However, if the time value of money is significant, a sales transaction is viewed as including two parts: a delivery component (for goods or services) and a financing component (either interest paid to the buyer in the case of a prepayment or to the seller in the case of a receivable). Illustration 5–23 shows the accounting for the prepayment and receivable cases.

> The time value of money is not considered *significant* if delivery and payment occur within one year of each other.

An obvious question is *when* a financing component is considered *significant*. Certainly, it's a matter of professional judgment, but there are indicators that might suggest

Illustration 5–23   Accounting for the Time Value of Money

On January 1, 2013, TrueTech enters into a contract with GameStop Stores to deliver four Tri-Box modules that have a fair value of $1,000.

- **Prepayment Case:** GameStop pays TrueTech $907 on January 1, 2013, and TrueTech agrees to deliver the modules on December 31, 2014. GameStop pays significantly in advance of delivery, such that TrueTech is viewed as borrowing money from GameStop and TrueTech incurs interest *expense*.
- **Receivable Case:** TrueTech delivers the modules on January 1, 2013, and GameStop agrees to pay TrueTech $1,000 on December 31, 2014. TrueTech delivers the modules significantly in advance of payment, such that TrueTech is viewed as loaning money to GameStop and TrueTech earns interest *revenue*.

The fiscal year-end for both companies is December 31. The time value of money in both cases is 5%. The following table compares TrueTech's accounting for the contract between the two cases (ignoring the entry for cost of goods sold):

Prepayment (payment *before* delivery)			Receivable (payment *after* delivery)		
January 1, 2013			**January 1, 2013**		
When prepayment occurs:			*When delivery occurs:*		
Cash..	907*		Accounts receivable	1,000	
Unearned revenue...........................		907	Revenue		1,000
December 31, 2013			**December 31, 2013**		
Accrual of year 1 interest expense:			*Accrual of year 1 interest revenue:*		
Interest expense ($907 × 5%).................	45		Accounts receivable	50	
Unearned revenue...........................		45	Interest revenue ($1000 × 5%)		50
December 31, 2014			**December 31, 2014**		
When subsequent delivery occurs:			*When subsequent payment occurs:*		
Interest expense ($952 × 5%)	48		Cash..	1,103**	
Unearned revenue.................................	952		Interest revenue ($1050 × 5%)		53
Revenue		1,000	Accounts receivable........................		1,050

*$907 = $1000 × .90703 (present value of $1, n = 2, I = 5%; from Table 2)
**Note that in the prepayment case TrueTech receives less cash from GameStop than it receives in the receivables case. That is because TrueTech is paying interest to GameStop in the prepayment case, but is receiving interest from GameStop in the receivables case.

significance. If the customer would pay a substantially different amount if it paid cash at the time the good or service was delivered, the financing component is likely significant. Also, the financing component is more likely to be significant as the time between delivery and payment increases, or if the interest rate implicit in the contract is large. As a practical matter, sellers can assume the financing component is not significant if the period between delivery and payment is less than a year.

Current GAAP typically accounts for the time value of money for long-term receivables, but not for customer prepayments. For example, if the prepayment case in Illustration 5–23 were handled under current GAAP, the journal entry at delivery would not recognize any interest expense, and instead would simply debit unearned revenue and credit revenue for $907. Under the proposed ASU, the seller recognizes more revenue but also more interest expense than it does currently.

GAAP Change

We discuss the time value of money concept further in Chapter 6.

COLLECTIBILITY OF THE TRANSACTION PRICE

Whenever sales are made on credit, there is some potential for bad debts. Under the proposed ASU, an estimate is made of the amount of bad debts, and that amount is treated as a contra-revenue, similar to how sales returns are treated in current GAAP. The estimated amount of bad debts is presented in the income statement as a separate line item immediately below gross revenue that reduces gross revenue to a net amount.

This treatment of collectibility of the transaction price differs from current GAAP in two important ways. First, under the proposed ASU, collectibility does not affect *whether* revenue is recognized. Current GAAP requires that there be reasonable certainty as to the collectibility of the asset to be received before revenue can be recognized. Otherwise, revenue is deferred and recognized under the installment method, cost recovery method, or when collectibility becomes reasonably assured. The ASU eliminates this criterion for revenue recognition, and as a consequence eliminates the installment and cost recovery methods.

GAAP Change

Second, under the proposed ASU, bad debts are shown as a contra-revenue, rather than as an expense. This change does not affect how bad debts are estimated, but does affect how they appear in the income statement. Under current GAAP bad debt expense is typically shown as part of selling, general, and administrative expenses ("SG&A"), below the gross profit line.[47] Under the proposed ASU, bad debts are deducted from gross revenue, similar to how sales returns are treated currently, before showing net revenue and before calculating gross profit.

We discuss accounting for bad debts further in Chapter 7.

Step 4: Allocate the Transaction Price to the Performance Obligations

If an arrangement has more than one separate performance obligation, the seller allocates the transaction price to the separate performance obligations in proportion to the **stand-alone selling price** of the goods or services underlying those performance obligations.[48] If the seller can't observe actual stand-alone selling prices, the seller should estimate them. Illustration 5–24 provides an example.

The transaction price is allocated to separate performance obligations in proportion to their *relative stand-alone selling prices.*

Sometimes the stand-alone selling price of a good or service underlying a performance obligation is uncertain. In that case, a seller might estimate the stand-alone selling price of that performance obligation using the residual technique, by subtracting the stand-alone selling prices of the other performance obligations from the total contract price. Illustration 5–25 provides an example.

The *residual* technique is used to estimate a stand-alone selling price that is very uncertain.

[47]An exception is that recently GAAP changed to require some health care providers to display bad debts as a reduction of gross revenues, similar to how the proposed ASU would require bad debts to be displayed for all companies. This change is discussed more fully in "Presentation and Disclosure of Patient Service Revenue, Provision for Bad Debts, and the Allowance for Doubtful Accounts for Certain Health Care Entities" *Accounting Standards Update 2011-7* (Norwalk, Conn: FASB, 2011).

[48]A contractually stated "list price" doesn't necessarily represent a stand-alone selling price. The seller has to reference stand-alone selling prices, or estimate those prices.

Illustration 5–24

Allocating Transaction Price to Performance Obligations Based on Relative Selling Prices

Recall the initial data for the TrueTech example from Illustration 5–20:

- The Tri-Box System has a wholesale price of $270, which includes the physical Tri-Box console as well as a one-year subscription to the Tri-Net of Internet-based games and other applications.
- Owners of Tri-Box modules as well as other game consoles can purchase one-year subscriptions to the Tri-Net from TrueTech for $50.
- TrueTech does not sell a Tri-Box module without the initial one-year Tri-Net subscription, but estimates that it would charge $250 per unit if it chose to do so.

CompStores orders 1,000 Tri-Boxes at the normal wholesale price of $270. Because the standalone price of the Tri-Box module ($250) represents $5/6$ of the total fair values ($250 ÷ [$250 + 50]), and the Tri-Net subscription comprises $1/6$ of the total ($50 ÷ [$250 + 50]), we allocate $5/6$ of the transaction price to the Tri-Boxes and $1/6$ of the transaction price to the Tri-Net subscriptions. Accordingly, TrueTech would recognize the following journal entry (ignoring any entry to record the reduction in inventory and the corresponding cost of goods sold):

Accounts receivable	270,000	
Revenue ($270,000 × $5/6$)		225,000
Unearned revenue ($270,000 × $1/6$)......................		45,000

TrueTech then converts the unearned revenue to revenue over the one-year term of the Tri-Net subscription as that revenue is earned.

Illustration 5–25

Allocating Transaction Price to Performance Obligations Using the Residual Technique

Assume the same facts as Illustration 5–24, except that there is no basis on which to estimate the value of the one-year Tri-Net subscription. In that case, the value of the subscription would be estimated as follows:

Total price of Tri-Box with Tri-Net subscription	$270,000
Estimated price of Tri-Box sold without subscription ($250 × 1,000)	250,000
Estimated price of Tri-Net subscription	$ 20,000

Based on these relative stand-alone selling prices, if CompStores orders 1,000 Tri-Boxes at the normal wholesale price of $270, TrueTech would recognize the following journal entry (ignoring any entry to record the reduction in inventory and corresponding cost of goods sold):

Accounts receivable...	270,000	
Revenue ($270,000 × 250/270)............................		250,000
Unearned revenue ($270,000 × 20/250)..............		20,000

TrueTech would convert the unearned revenue to revenue over the one-year term of the Tri-Net subscription.

A contract might include a provision that specifies that the transaction price will change depending on some aspect of future performance. For example, the total price of a consulting service might depend on how successful that service is. Or, the contract price might be changed by mutual agreement. In general, the seller allocates resulting price changes to all the performance obligations in the contract in the same proportions that were used at the beginning of the contract. However, if the price change relates specifically to the seller's efforts to satisfy one particular performance obligation, the entire price change is allocated to that particular performance obligation only.[49]

Similarly, a contract might be modified by mutual agreement between the buyer and seller to add or change performance obligations. If goods and services yet to be transferred are distinct from previously satisfied performance obligations in the contract, the seller

---

[49]If an amount is allocated to a performance obligation that has already been completed, the amount is recognized by increasing or decreasing revenue.

allocates any remaining transaction price to the remaining performance obligations as if the prior contract was terminated and a new contract created. On the other hand, if remaining goods and services are not distinct, and instead are part of a single, partially satisfied performance obligation, the seller simply updates the transaction price and recognizes whatever amount of revenue is necessary to reflect the revised progress toward completion.

Overall, the allocation of transaction price to performance obligations required by the proposed ASU is very similar to what is used for multiple-element arrangements in current GAAP. However, important differences will occur in particular industries that currently have specialized revenue recognition approaches. For example, as discussed earlier in Chapter 5, current GAAP for software contracts requires vendor-specific objective evidence (VSOE) of stand-alone selling prices in order to allocate the transaction price to multiple deliverables. The proposed ASU would allow the use of estimated selling prices for these arrangements. Also, the proposed ASU would once again allow the residual technique for allocating revenue. GAAP disallowed that technique in 2009.[50]

GAAP Change

Step 5: Recognize Revenue When (Or As) Each Performance Obligation Is Satisfied

In general, a seller recognizes revenue allocated to each performance obligation when it satisfies the performance obligation. We first discuss performance obligations that are satisfied over time, and then discuss performance obligations that are satisfied at a point in time. After that, we discuss an important limitation on the amount of revenue that can be recognized for goods and services during a long-term contract.

PERFORMANCE OBLIGATIONS SATISFIED OVER TIME

Services such as lending money, performing audits, and providing consulting advice all are performed over a period of time. Also, many construction contracts are long-term in nature. So when can a seller recognize revenue over time, as such activities are performed, rather than waiting until performance has been completed?

Performance obligations of services can be satisfied at one time or continuously.

Determining whether a performance obligation is satisfied over time.   As shown in Illustration 5–26, the proposed ASU specifies criteria for determining whether a seller is satisfying a performance obligation over time.

A performance obligation is satisfied *over time* if at least one of the following two criteria is met:

1. **The seller is creating or enhancing an asset that the buyer controls as the service is performed.** This criterion captures many types of long-term construction arrangements in which the buyer owns the work-in-process as it is constructed by the seller.

OR

2. **The seller is not creating an asset that the buyer controls or that has alternative use to the seller, and at *least one* of the following conditions hold:**

    a. **The buyer simultaneously receives and consumes a benefit as the seller performs.** For example, this condition would be met by a technical support service that provides answers as questions are received.

    b. **Another seller would not need to reperform the tasks performed to date if that other seller were to fulfill the remaining obligation.** For example, a transportation company that ships goods across the country would qualify under this condition.

    c. **The seller has the right to payment for performance even if the buyer could cancel the contract, and it expects to fulfill the contract.** Many service contracts include this provision.

Illustration 5–26
Determining Whether a Performance Obligation Is Satisfied Over Time

When a performance obligation is satisfied over time, service revenue is recognized in proportion to the amount of service performed.

If a performance obligation meets at least one of the criteria listed in Illustration 5–26, we recognize revenue over time, in proportion to the amount of the performance obligation that

---

[50]The residual method is not currently permitted under GAAP as per *Accounting Standards Update 2009-13* codified in ASC 605-25-30-3

has been satisfied. For instance, if, say, one-third of a service has been performed, one-third of the performance obligation has been satisfied, so one-third of the revenue should be recognized. If none of the criteria in Illustration 5–26 is met, we recognize revenue at the point in time when the performance obligation has been completely satisfied.

The criteria in Illustration 5–26 seem broad enough to include many service contracts. So, what doesn't qualify? As an example, consider a market research firm that develops a market analysis for a consumer electronics company. The market research firm receives payment when the report is delivered to the customer, but other companies in the industry could purchase the market research. This case doesn't satisfy the first criterion in Illustration 5–26, because the buyer does not control the market research as it is being produced. It doesn't satisfy the second criterion in Illustration 5–26, because the seller has an alternate use for the report (the seller can sell it to other companies in the industry). Therefore, the performance obligation is not being satisfied over time, and the market research firm will wait until the report is delivered before recognizing revenue.

Long-term construction contracts typically are viewed as services that are provided continuously to the buyer.

Most long-term construction contracts qualify for revenue recognition over time under these criteria. Many contracts are structured such that the buyer owns the work-in-process (WIP) as it is constructed, which satisfies the first criterion. Also, even if the buyer doesn't own the WIP during construction, the second criterion is satisfied if the asset the seller is creating has no alternate use to the seller and another seller would not have to reperform the work done to date if that other seller were to finish the contract. If the construction contract qualifies for revenue recognition over time, the 'percentage-of-completion' method described in the chapter can be used to account simultaneously for the asset as it is being constructed and the accounts receivable due from the customer. If instead, revenue must be deferred until construction is completed, the completed contract method is used.

GAAP Change

The criteria for satisfying a performance obligation over time differ from current GAAP in important ways. For example, as discussed earlier in Chapter 5, under current GAAP a long-term construction contract is always accounted for under the percentage-of-completion method (which recognizes revenue over time) unless the seller can't make accurate estimates of revenues, costs, and progress toward completion. Under the proposed ASU, revenue recognition over time depends on various characteristics of the sales contract. So, the proposed ASU might allow revenue recognition over time when current GAAP would not. The reverse also could be true, with current GAAP allowing revenue recognition over time that the proposed ASU does not permit.

Also, the proposed ASU may encourage sellers to view as integration services some transactions that current GAAP typically views as product sales. For example, a manufacturing contract in which the manufacturer produces goods to a customer's specifications could be viewed as a manufacturing service. Depending on the specifics of the contract, the manufacturer could recognize revenue over time as the product is manufactured. Under current GAAP such manufacturers typically recognize revenue upon delivery.

Determining progress toward completion. The seller can recognize revenue over time only if it can reasonably measure progress toward completion. The seller needs to adopt a method for estimating how much transfer has occurred to determine how much revenue to recognize. As under current GAAP with respect to the percentage-of-completion method, sellers should choose a method that accurately depicts the transfer of goods or services while also being cost-effective to implement. As discussed in chapter 5, either output or input methods can be used for this purpose.

Input and output methods are used to estimate progress toward completion when performance obligations are satisfied over time.

Illustration 5–27 continues our TrueTech example from Illustration 5–24, showing how TrueTech recognizes revenue as its Tri-Net service obligation is satisfied over time.

Two other aspects of determining progress towards completion are emphasized in the proposed ASU. First, sometimes a contract involves a seller buying goods from another company and transferring them to a customer significantly prior to actually providing services to the customer. For example, a construction contractor might acquire materials and ship them to the job site well in advance of actually providing construction services. Second, sometimes a seller lacks the ability to make a reasonable estimate of its the progress towards completion, but expects to be able to at least recover its the costs on the contract. In each of those cases, the proposed ASU indicates that the seller should only recognize an amount of revenue equal to the cost of the goods. This approach is basically the "cost recovery" or "zero profit" method described in Chapter 5.

Recall that TrueTech recorded the following journal entry to recognize the sale of 1,000 Tri-Box systems:

Accounts receivable ($270 × 1,000).............................	270,000	
Revenue ($270,000 × 5/6)..		225,000
Unearned revenue ($270,000 × 1/6).......................		45,000

TrueTech recognized $225,000 of revenue immediately because it had fulfilled the performance obligation to transfer 1,000 Tri-Box modules, but recognized an unearned revenue liability for $45,000 associated with the performance obligation to provide those customers access to the Tri-Net for a one-year period. The Tri-Net subscriptions qualify for revenue recognition over time under Illustration 5–26's criterion 2a *("The customer simultaneously receives and consumes a benefit as the seller performs")*, because Tri-Net subscribers receive benefit each day by having access to the Tri-Net network. Therefore, in each of the 12 months following sale, TrueTech would make the following entry to recognize Tri-Net subscription revenue:

Unearned revenue ($45,000 × 1/12).............................	3,750	
Revenue		3,750

After 12 months TrueTech will have recognized all of the Tri-Net subscription revenue associated with this contract and the unearned revenue liability would be reduced to zero.

Illustration 5–27

Satisfying a Performance Obligation Over Time

PERFORMANCE OBLIGATIONS SATISFIED AT A POINT IN TIME

If a performance obligation is not satisfied over time, it is satisfied at a single point in time, when the seller **transfers control** of goods to the buyer. Often transfer of control is obvious and coincides with delivery, as in our Macy's example when Susan leaves the store with her purchased skirt. In other circumstances, though, transfer of control is not as clear. Illustration 5–28 lists five key indicators that should be considered when judging whether control of a good has passed from the seller to the buyer, but sellers also should consider whether other indicators are appropriate.

Performance obligations of goods are satisfied when the seller transfers control *of goods to the buyer.*

Key indicators that control of a good has passed from the seller to the buyer:

1. **Buyer has an unconditional obligation to pay.** An obligation to pay is unconditional if its only requirement is the passage of time.
2. **Buyer has legal title.** Legal title typically indicates which party has the ability to direct the use of, and receive the benefit from, a good.[51]
3. **Buyer has physical possession.** Buyers typically control the goods they possess.
4. **Buyer assumes risks and rewards of ownership.** Risks include suffering loss if the good is stolen or damaged; rewards include benefiting from increase in the value of the good.
5. **The buyer has accepted the asset.** Acceptance indicates the buyer has obtained the benefits of owning the asset.

Illustration 5–28

Key Indicators of Transfer of Control

Two common situations in which transfer of control is not the same as transfer of the physical goods are (1) bill-and-hold arrangements and (2) consignment sales. Bill-and-hold arrangements, in which a seller bills the buyer but does not ship the product until a later date, typically won't satisfy these indicators until shipment to the buyer actually occurs. Consignment sales, in which a seller ships inventory that it still owns to an intermediary for resale, typically won't satisfy these indicators until sale by the intermediary to a buyer occurs.

Some contractual arrangements involve one business paying a licensing fee for the right to use another business's intellectual property. These arrangements are common in the software, technology, media and entertainment (including motion pictures and music) industries. The performance obligation associated with a license or other rights of use is satisfied at the point in time that the buyer has the use of the rights. Therefore, the beginning of a license agreement is the point in time when revenue is recognized.

---

[51]In some circumstances sellers retain title in case the buyer does not follow through on some aspect of the contract. In those circumstances, retaining title is a "protective right" and doesn't necessarily indicate control.

KEY LIMITATION ON CUMULATIVE AMOUNT OF REVENUE THAT CAN BE RECOGNIZED

GAAP Change

When a contract includes uncertain consideration to be received from a customer, you learned earlier in this supplement that the transaction price is measured as either (a) the most likely amount or (b) a probability-weighted estimate of the amount that eventually should be received. Consequently, the transaction price includes uncertain amounts that are allocated to performance obligations and then recognized as revenue when the performance obligations are satisfied. However, the proposed ASU limits the cumulative amount of revenue that may be recognized under a contract to the amount to which the seller is *reasonably assured to be entitled*. Reasonable assurance exists only if the seller has experience or other evidence with similar types of performance obligations that can predict the amount of consideration to which the seller will be entitled when it satisfies the performance obligations. The word "entitled" is important, because it highlights that the uncertainty here is with the amounts the seller is owed, not uncertainty about whether the account will prove uncollectible. Circumstances in which a seller would *not* be reasonably assured to be entitled to an amount include:

The cumulative amount of revenue that can be recognized is limited to the amount to which the seller is *reasonably assured to be entitled.*

- The customer could avoid paying an amount without breaching the contract (for example, not pay a sales-based royalty by not making sales).
- The seller lacks experience selling similar products and doesn't have evidence with which to estimate uncertain amounts.
- The uncertain amounts are very hard to estimate due to susceptibility to factors outside the seller's control, the uncertainty resolving only far in the future, or there being a high number of possible outcomes.

Illustration 5–29 demonstrates how this cumulative limitation would be applied.

Illustration 5–29

Applying the Cumulative Limitation on Revenue Recognition

ChemCo sells Juniper Inc. a piece of specialized manufacturing equipment. The sales agreement specifies that Juniper will pay ChemCo a $50,000 fixed payment upon delivery of the equipment plus a 5% royalty on sales of products made using the equipment. ChemCo's probability-weighted estimate of royalties is $150,000, so the transaction price is estimated to be $200,000 ($50,000 + 150,000).

   Upon delivery of the equipment, ChemCo recognizes revenue of only $50,000, because it is not reasonably assured of receiving the other $150,000. ChemCo would recognize the remaining revenue as Juniper records sales and ChemCo becomes reasonably assured of being entitled to its 5% royalty on sold items.

This cumulative limitation actually reduces the difference between current GAAP and the proposed ASU. Current GAAP typically does not allow recognition of revenue associated with variable consideration until all relevant uncertainty has been resolved. The proposed ASU includes variable consideration in the transaction price and so includes it in revenue recognition. The cumulative limitation means that we would defer revenue recognition if an uncertain amount is very difficult to estimate or if the customer potentially could avoid owing it, similar to how we account for that circumstance under current GAAP.

Additional Considerations

CONTRACT ACQUISITION AND FULFILLMENT COSTS

Incremental costs of obtaining a contract are capitalized as an asset and subsequently amortized or impaired.

For contracts lasting over one year, sellers are allowed to capitalize (record as an asset) incremental costs of obtaining a contract, such as sales commissions, that the company would not have incurred if it had not obtained the contract. Sellers also can capitalize other costs that relate directly to satisfying performance obligations under the contract in the future, so long as the seller expects those costs to be recovered. The resulting asset is amortized over the period the goods and services are transferred to the customer. Like other intangible assets, this one also is tested for impairment. We briefly discuss this intangible asset in Chapter 10 and its amortization and impairment testing in Chapter 11.

ONEROUS PERFORMANCE OBLIGATIONS

Sometimes a seller anticipates losing money on a performance obligation. The proposed ASU may require the seller to recognize a liability and expense for such an *onerous* performance obligation under some circumstances. Specifically, if the onerous performance obligation is to be settled over a period of greater than one year, a liability and expense are recorded for an amount equal to the lowest cost of settling the performance obligation minus the amount of the transaction price that has been allocated to it. In subsequent periods the seller increases or decreases the liability (with an offsetting entry to expense) until the performance obligation eventually is satisfied. We also discuss accounting for onerous performance obligations in Chapter 13.

Onerous performance obligations satisfied over a period of time greater than one year produce a liability and expense.

DISCLOSURE

The proposed ASU significantly expands the disclosure requirements associated with revenue recognition. For example, sellers must describe the significant judgments they use to (a) allocate transaction prices to performance obligations and (b) determine when performance obligations have been satisfied. Sellers also must disaggregate their revenue into categories, maybe product lines of goods or services, geographic regions, types of customers, or types of contracts. The choice of category should be the one that best indicates how the amount, timing, and uncertainty of the revenues and cash flows are affected by economic factors.

GAAP Change

A significant provision of the new guidance is the requirement for plentiful disclosures regarding a company's revenues.

Sellers should describe their outstanding performance obligations, discuss how performance obligations typically are satisfied, and describe important contractual terms like payment terms and policies for refunds, returns, and warranties. Sellers also must reconcile the beginning and ending balances of contract assets, contract liabilities, and liabilities for onerous performance obligations.

The objective of these disclosures is to help users of financial statements understand the amount, timing, and uncertainty of revenue and cash flows arising from contracts with customers. Of course, the downside of these disclosures is that sellers also are providing information to key competitors, suppliers, and customers.

Concept Review Exercise

Four Flags Fitness sold 100 memberships with the following characteristics:

- Members pay a $150 annual fee to cover the administrative costs of registering them in the Four Flags system.
- Members then pay an additional $400 in four equal quarterly installments of $100. The first installment is due at membership signing, and the other installments are due in 3, 6, and 9 months, paid by automatic withdrawal from bank accounts (so historically bad debts have been immaterial).
- Members have unlimited use of fitness equipment, spa and locker-rooms.
- Members also have access to Four Flags' health-oriented snack bar, but have the same access as and pay the same prices there that are paid by nonmembers.
- Each annual membership also includes a coupon for a complimentary session with a personal fitness trainer. Those sessions normally cost $50 per hour. On average 50 percent of members make use of a session.
- Each annual membership also includes access to the "Fit Buddies" website, featuring online content and social networking. Annual subscriptions to Fit Buddies cost $100 for nonmembers.
- Comparable gym memberships that lack complimentary fitness sessions or access to websites have an annual fee of $500.

ACCOUNTING FOR REVENUE IN SINGLE-PERIOD CONTRACTS

Required:

1. Determine whether a gym membership constitutes a contract for purposes of applying revenue recognition criteria.

2. Identify the separate performance obligations in the contract.

3. Determine the transaction price.

4. Allocate the transaction price to the separate performance obligations, and prepare a journal entry to record the initial sale of 100 memberships.

5. Assume 14 members use their coupon for a complimentary session of fitness training. Prepare a journal entry to record the revenue earned at the end of one month.

Solution:

1. Determine whether each gym membership constitutes a contract for purposes of applying revenue recognition criteria.

   Applying the criteria in Illustration 2, each gym membership is a contract for purposes of applying revenue recognition criteria. Specifically:

   a. The contract will affect Four Flags' cash flows, so has commercial substance.

   b. Members and Four Flags both indicate contract approval.

   c. The contract clearly specifies contractual rights and obligations.

   d. The contract clearly specifies payment terms.

   e. Member prepayment constitutes performance by the member, so the contract is not wholly unperformed.

2. Identify the separate performance obligations in the contract.

   - Access to gym facilities, provision of a session of fitness training, and access to the Fit Buddies website all are separate performance obligations, as those services are sold separately.

   - Registering members in Four Flags' administrative system is not a performance obligation, as it does not transfer a service to a customer.

   - Access to the snack bar is not a performance obligation, as the access is not a material right beyond the rights of a nonmember.

3. Determine the transaction price.

   The transaction price is the probability-weighted expected consideration of $550 (the $150 up-front fee plus $400 to be paid in quarterly installments).

4. Allocate the transaction price to the separate performance obligations, and prepare a journal entry to record the initial sale of 100 memberships.

   The stand-alone selling price of access to gym facilities is $500. The probability-weighted stand-alone selling price of the training session is $25 ($50 × 50%). The stand-alone selling price of the website is $100. So, the total of the stand-alone selling prices is $625 ($500 + $25 + $100). Therefore, the total transaction price of $550 would be allocated as follows:

   Gym access: $550 × ($500 ÷ $625) = $440.
   Training coupon: $550 × ($25 ÷ $625) = $22.
   Fit Buddies access: $550 × ($100 ÷ $625) = $88.

Cash ([$150 initial fee + $100 Q1 fee] × 100)	25,000	
Accounts receivable ($100 × 3 payments × 100 members)	30,000	
Unearned revenue, gym ($440 × 100 members)		44,000
Unearned revenue, Fit Buds ($88 × 100 members)		8,800
Unearned revenue, training ($22 × 100 members)		2,200

5. Assume 14 members use their coupon for a complimentary session of fitness training. Prepare a journal entry to record the revenue earned at the end of one month.

   The journal entry recognizes revenue for one month of gym access, one month of training access, and an appropriate proportion of training revenue (With 50% usage, we would anticipate 100 members × 50% = 50 coupons to be exercised, yielding proportion of 14 ÷ 50 = 28% of anticipated training coupons used to date).

Unearned revenue, gym ($44,000 ÷ 12)	3,667
Unearned revenue, Fit Buds ($8,800 ÷ 12)	733
Unearned revenue, training ($2,200 × 28%)	616
Revenue (to balance)	5,016

Respond to the questions, brief exercises, exercises, and problems in this Supplement with the presumption that the guidance provided by the proposed Accounting Standards Update is being applied.

Questions For Review of Key Topics

Q 5–22   What are the five key steps to recognizing revenue?

Q 5–23   What characteristics make a good or service a separate performance obligation?

Q 5–24   When does an option granted with the sale of a good or service give rise to a separate performance obligation in the contract?

Q 5–25   On what basis is the transaction price of a contract allocated to the contract's separate performance obligations?

Q 5–26   What indicators suggest that a performance obligation has been satisfied with respect to a good (merchandise)?

Q 5–27   What determines whether a company can recognize revenue over time when constructing an asset for a customer?

Brief Exercises

BE 5–19
Definition of a contract

Richter Landscaping writes an agreement with a customer indicating that it will provide future landscaping services at a date and price to be determined. Does this agreement meet the definition of a contract? Briefly explain your answer.

BE 5–20
Separate performance obligation

A car dealer sells a particular brand of luxury sedan to individual affluent customers. Is each sedan a separate performance obligation? Briefly explain your answer.

BE 5–21
Separate performance obligation

McAfee sells a subscription to its anti-virus software along with a subscription renewal option that allows renewal at half the prevailing price for a new subscription. Are the software and subscription renewal option separate performance obligations? Briefly explain your answer.

BE 5–22
Variable consideration

Leo Consulting writes a contract with Highgate University to restructure Highgate's processes for purchasing goods and services from suppliers. The contract promises that Leo will earn a fixed fee of $25,000, and earn an additional $10,000 if Highgate achieves $100,000 of cost savings. Leo estimates that there is a 50% chance that Highgate will achieve $100,000 of cost savings. Assuming Leo determines transaction price as the probability-weighted amount of expected consideration, what transaction price would Leo estimate for this contract?

BE 5–23
Allocating transaction price

Sarjit Systems sold software to a customer for $90,000. As part of the contract, Sarjit promises to provide "free" technical support over the following six months. Sarjit sells the same software without technical support for $80,000 and a stand-alone six-month technical support contract for $20,000, so these products would sell for $100,000 if sold separately. Prepare Sarjit's journal entry to record the sale of the software (ignore any potential entry to revenue or cost of sales).

BE 5–24
Long-term contracts

Assume Estate Construction is constructing a building for CyberB, an online retailing company. Under the construction agreement, if for some reason Estate could not complete construction, CyberB would own the partially completed building and could retain another construction company to complete the job. When should Estate recognize revenue, as the building is constructed or after construction is completed? Explain your answer.

BE 5–25
Time value of money

Patterson, Inc. receives a $10,000 payment two years in advance of delivering a completed novel. A five percent interest rate applies. How much revenue would Patterson recognize associated with delivery of the novel, assuming delivery occurs on time?

Exercises

E 5–31
Options

Clarks Inc., a shoe retailer, sells boots in different styles. In early November the company starts selling "SunBoots" to customers for $70 per pair. Clarks obtains the boots from wholesalers for $40 per pair. As part of the sales contract, Clarks gives customers who participate in an online survey a 30 percent discount voucher for any additional purchases in the next 30 days. Clarks anticipates that approximately 20 percent of customers will complete the survey and utilize the coupon, purchasing an average of $100 of goods. Clarks intends to offer a 10 percent discount on all sales during the next 30 days as part of a seasonal promotion during the Thanksgiving holidays.

Required:
1. Determine whether the discount voucher by Clarks is a separate performance obligation.
2. Prepare a journal entry to record the sale of 1,000 pairs of SunBoots.

E 5–32
Separate performance obligation, option, upfront fee

A New York City daily newspaper called "Manhattan Today" charges an annual subscription fee of $150. Customers prepay their subscriptions, and receive 260 issues for an annual subscription. To attract more subscribers, the company offered new subscribers a coupon to receive a 40 percent discount on a ride through Central Park on a horse-drawn carriage. The list price of a carriage ride is $130 per hour. The company estimates that approximately 30% of the vouchers will be redeemed.

Required:
1. Can Manhattan Today recognize any of the $150 subscription fee as revenue upon receipt? Explain.
2. When will Manhattan Today recognize revenue associated with the $150 subscription price?
3. What separate performance obligations exist in this contract?
4. Prepare the journal entry to recognize sale of one new subscription, clearly identifying the revenue or unearned revenue associated with each distinct performance obligation.

E 5–33
Separate performance obligation, licensing

Pfizer, a large research-based pharmaceutical company, enters into a contract with a start-up biotechnology company called HealthPro and promises:
1. To grant HealthPro the exclusive rights to use Pfizer's Technology A for the life of its patent. The license gives HealthPro the exclusive right to market, distribute, and manufacture Drug B as developed using Technology A.
2. To assign four full-time equivalent employees to perform research and development services for HealthPro in a specially designated Pfizer lab facility. The primary objective of these services is to receive regulatory approval to market and distribute Drug B using Technology A.

HealthPro is required to use Pfizer's lab to perform the research and development services necessary to develop Drug B using Technology A, because the know how and expertise related to Technology A are proprietary to Pfizer and not available elsewhere.

Required:
Determine which parts of this contract are separate performance obligations. Explain your reasoning for each obligation.

E 5–34
Variable consideration

Thomas Consultants provided Bran Construction with assistance with implementing various cost-savings initiatives. Thomas' contract specifies that it will receive a flat rate of $50,000 and an additional $20,000 if Bran reaches a prespecified target amount of cost savings. Thomas estimates that there is a 20% chance that Bran will achieve the cost-savings target.

Required:
1. Assuming Thomas uses a probability-weighted transaction price, calculate the amount of the transaction price.
2. Assuming Thomas uses the most likely value as the transaction price, calculate the amount of the transaction price.
3. Assuming Thomas is trying to apply the revenue recognition rules most appropriately, do you think the company is more likely to use the probability-weighted amount or the most likely value? Briefly explain your answer.
4. Assume that Thomas provides a plan for Bran, but Bran is responsible for implementing it. Also assume that Thomas delivers the plan in the first quarter of the year, but Bran will be implementing the plan and determining total cost savings over the entire year. Should Thomas recognize the entire transaction price when it delivers the plan? Briefly explain your reasoning.

E 5–35
Variable consideration

On January 1, Seneca Asset Management enters into a contract with a client to provide fund management services for one year. The client is required to pay a fixed amount of $100,000 at the end of each quarter, plus 10 percent of the increase in the fund's value relative to an observable index at the end of the year. Assume the fund increased by $800,000 over the course of the year.

Required:
1. Prepare the journal entry to record the first fixed payment.
2. Prepare the journal entry to record any additional revenue beyond the $100,000 fixed payment at the end of the fourth quarter

E 5–36
Satisfaction of performance obligation

McDonald's enters into a contract to sell Billy Bear dolls for Toys4U Stores. Based on the contract, McDonald's displays the dolls in selected stores. Toys4U is not paid until the dolls have been sold by McDonald's, and unsold dolls are returned to Toys4U.

Required:
Determine whether Toys4U has satisfied its performance obligation when it delivers the dolls to McDonald's. Explain your answer.

E 5–37
Satisfaction of performance obligation

Cutler Education Corporation developed a software product to help children under age 12 to learn mathematics. The software contains two separate parts: Basic Level (Level I) and Intermediate Level (Level II). The list price of the software contains the access code only for Level I. Parents are eligible to purchase the access code for a higher level only if their children pass an exam created by software. The accounting period ends December 31.

Kerry purchases the software at a price of $50 for his child, Tom, on December 1, 2012. Suppose Tom passed the Level I test on December 31, 2012, and Kerry immediately purchased the access code for Level II part for Tom for an additional $10. Cutler licensed Level II to Kerry on the same day, December 31, but provides him the access code to Level II on January 10, 2013.

Required:
When would Cutler recognize revenue for the sale of Level I and II software?

E 5–38
Time value of money

Stewart receives a $20,000 payment three years in advance of a scheduled appearance as a graduation speaker at a major state university. A four percent interest rate applies.

Required:
1. Prepare the journal entry to record Stewart's initial receipt of the $20,000 payment.
2. Prepare journal entries to record any interest revenue or expense recognized by Stewart for years one, two and three of the contract.
3. Prepare a journal entry to record revenue when Stewart delivers his graduation speech.

Problems

P 5–16
Upfront fees, separate performance obligations

Fit & Slim is a health club that offers members various gym services. F&S accounts reports.

Required:
1. Assume F&S offers a deal whereby enrolling in a new membership also entitles the member to receive a voucher redeemable for 25 percent off a year's worth of premium yoga classes. A new membership costs $800, and a year's worth of premium yoga costs an additional $600. F&S estimates that approximately 40 percent of the vouchers will be redeemed. F&S offers a 10 percent discount on all courses as part of its seasonal promotion strategy.
   a. Identify the separate performance obligations in the new member deal.
   b. Allocate the contract price to the separate performance obligations.
   c. Prepare the journal entry to recognize revenue for the sale of a new membership. Clearly identify revenue or unearned revenue associated with each distinct performance obligation.
2. Assume F&S offers a "Fit 50" coupon book with 50 prepaid visits over the next year. F&S has learned that Fit 50 purchasers make an average of 40 visits before the coupon book expires. A customer purchases a Fit 50 book by paying $500 in advance, and for any additional visit over 50 during the year after the book is purchased, the customer can pay a $15 visitation fee. Depending on the season, F&S typically charges between $12 and $18 to nonmembers who wish to work out on a single day.
   a. Identify the separate performance obligations in the Fit 50 member deal.
   b. Allocate the contract price to the separate performance obligations.
   c. Prepare the journal entry to recognize revenue for the sale of a new Fit 50 book. When will F&S recognize revenue associated with people using its Fit 50 plans?

P 5–17
Satisfying performance obligations

Consider each of the following scenarios separately, assuming the company accounts for the arrangement:
Scenario 1: Crown Construction Company enters into a contract with Star Hotel for building a highly sophisticated, customized conference room to be completed for a fixed price of $400,000. Nonrefundable progress payments are made on a monthly basis for work completed during the month. Legal title to the conference room

equipment is held by Crown until the end of the construction project, but if the contract is terminated before the conference room is finished, the Hotel retains the partially completed job and must pay for any work completed to date.

Scenario 2: Crown Company enters into a contract with Star Hotel for constructing and installing a standard designed gym for a fixed price of $400,000. Nonrefundable progress payments are made on a monthly basis for work completed during the month. Legal title to the gym passes to Star upon completion of the building process. If Star cancels the contract before the gym construction is completed, Crown removes all the installed equipment and Star must compensate Crown for any loss of profit on sale of the gym to another customer.

Scenario 3: On January 1, the CostDriver Company, a consulting firm, enters into a three-month contract with Coco Seafood Restaurant to analyze its cost structure in order to find a way to reduce operating costs and increase profits. CostDriver promises to share findings with the restaurant every two weeks and to provide the restaurant with a final analytical report at the end of the contract. This service is customized to Coco, and CostDriver would need to start from scratch if it provided a similar service to another client. Coco promises to pay $5,000 per month. If Coco chooses to terminate the contract, it is entitled to receive a summary report detailing analyses to that stage.

Scenario 4: Assume Trump International Tower (Phase II) is developing luxury residential real estate and begins to market individual apartments during their construction. The Tower enters into a contract with Edwards for the sale of a specific apartment. Edwards pays a deposit that is refundable only if the Tower fails to deliver the completed apartment in accordance with the contract. The remainder of the purchase price is paid on completion of the contract when Edwards obtains possession of the apartment.

Required:
For each of the scenarios, determine whether the seller should recognize revenue over time or when the product or service is completed. Explain your answer.

P 5–18
Variable
transaction price

On January 1 Revis Consulting enters into a contract to complete a cost reduction program for Green Financial over a six-month period. Green will pay Revis $20,000 at the end of each month. If total cost savings reach a specific target, Green will pay an additional $10,000 to Revis at the end of the contract, but if total cost savings fall short, Revis will refund $10,000 to Green. Revis estimates an 80% chance that cost savings will reach the target and calculates the contract price based on the probability-weighted amounts of future payments to be received. Revis accounts for this arrangement.

Required:
Prepare the following journal entries for Revis:
1. The journal entry on January 31 to record the first month of revenue under the contract.
2. Assuming total cost savings exceed target, the journal entry on June 30 to record receipt of the bonus.
3. Assuming total cost savings fall short of target, the journal entry on June 30 to record payment of the penalty.

P 5–19
Variable
transaction price

Velocity consulting firm enters into a contract to help Burger Boy, a fast-food restaurant, design a marketing strategy to compete with Burger King. The contract spans eight months. Burger Boy promises to pay $60,000 at the beginning of each month. At the end of the contract, Velocity either will give Burger Boy a refund of $20,000 or will be entitled to an additional $20,000 bonus, depending on whether sales at Burger Boy at the year-end has increased to a target level. At the inception of the contract, Velocity estimates an 80% chance that it will earn the $20,000 bonus. After four months, circumstances change and Velocity revises to 60% its estimate of the chance that it will earn the bonus. At the end of the contract, Velocity receives the additional consideration of $20,000. Velocity accounts for this arrangement.

Required:
1. Prepare a journal entry to record the revenue Velocity would recognize each month for the first four months.
2. Prepare a journal entry that the Velocity Company would make after four months to record the change in estimate associated with the likelihood that additional $20,000 would be received.
3. Prepare a journal entry to record the revenue that Velocity Company would recognize each month for the second four months.
4. Prepare a journal entry after eight months to record resolution of the uncertainty associated with receipt of the additional consideration of $20,000.

A Derivatives

"... derivatives are financial weapons of mass destruction ..."
— Warren Buffett, Berkshire Hathaway CEO

"... the growing use of complex financial instruments known as derivatives does not pose a threat to the country's financial system ..."
— Alan Greenspan, Federal Reserve Chairman

"Total world derivatives are $1000 trillion or 19 times the total world GDP of $54 trillion."
— Chuck Burr, *Culture Change*

In today's global economy and evolving financial markets, businesses are increasingly exposed to a variety of risks, which, unmanaged, can have major impacts on earnings or even threaten a company's very existence. Risk management, then, has become critical. Derivative financial instruments have become the key tools of risk management.[1]

Derivatives are financial instruments that "derive" their values from some other security or *index*.

Derivatives are financial instruments that "derive" their values or contractually required cash flows from some other security or index. For instance, a contract allowing a company to buy a particular asset (say steel, gold, or flour) at a designated future date at a predetermined price is a financial instrument that derives its value from expected and actual changes in the price of the underlying asset. Financial futures, forward contracts, options, and interest rate swaps are the most frequently used derivatives. Derivatives are valued as tools to manage or hedge companies' increasing exposures to risk, including interest rate risk, price risk, and foreign exchange risk. The variety, complexity, and magnitude of derivatives have grown rapidly in recent years. Accounting standard-setters have scrambled to keep pace.

Derivatives serve as a form of "insurance" against risk.

A persistent stream of headline stories has alerted us to multimillion-dollar losses by many companies and the financial collapse of Bear Stearns and AIG. Focusing on these headlines, it would be tempting to conclude that derivatives are risky business indeed. Certainly they can be quite risky, if misused, but the fact is, these financial instruments exist to lessen, not increase, risk. Properly used, they serve as a form of "insurance" against risk. In fact, if a company is exposed to a substantial risk and does not hedge that risk, it is taking a gamble. On the other hand, if a derivative is used improperly, it can be a huge gamble itself. Total world derivatives are $1,000 trillion or 19 times the total world GDP of $54 trillion.

Derivatives Used to Hedge Risk

Hedging means taking a risk position that is opposite to an actual position that is exposed to risk.

Hedging means taking an action that is expected to produce exposure to a particular type of risk that is precisely the *opposite* of an actual risk to which the company already is exposed. For instance, the volatility of interest rates creates exposure to interest-rate risk for companies that issue debt—which, of course, includes most companies. So, a company that frequently arranges short-term loans from its bank under a floating (variable) interest rate agreement is exposed to the risk that interest rates might increase and adversely affect borrowing costs. Similarly, a company that regularly reissues commercial paper as it matures faces the possibility that new rates will be higher and cut into forecasted income. When borrowings are large, the potential cost can be substantial. So, the firm might choose to hedge its position by entering into a transaction that would produce a *gain* of roughly the same amount as the potential loss if interest rates do, in fact, increase.

Hedging is used to deal with three areas of risk exposure: fair value risk, cash flow risk, and foreign currency risk. Let's look at some of the more common derivatives.

---

[1]Almost all financial institutions and over half of all nonfinancial companies use derivatives.

FINANCIAL FUTURES A futures contract is an agreement between a seller and a buyer that requires the seller to deliver a particular commodity (say corn, gold, or pork bellies) at a designated future date, at a *predetermined* price. These contracts are actively traded on regulated futures exchanges. When the "commodity" is a *financial instrument,* such as a Treasury bond, Treasury bill, commercial paper, or a certificate of deposit, the agreement is referred to as a *financial futures contract.*[2]

> A *futures contract* allows a firm to sell (or buy) a financial instrument at a designated future date, at today's price.

To appreciate the way these hedges work, you need to remember that when interest rates rise, the market price of interest-bearing securities goes down. For instance, if you have an investment in a 10% bond and market interest rates go up to, say, 12%, your 10% bond is less valuable relative to other bonds paying the higher rate. Conversely, when interest rates decline, the market price of interest-bearing securities goes up. This risk that the investment's value might change is referred to as *fair value risk.* The company that issued the securities is faced with fair value risk also. If interest rates decline, the fair value of that company's debt would rise, a risk the borrower may want to hedge against. Later in this section, we'll look at an illustration of how the borrower would account for and report such a hedge.

Now let's look at the effect on a contract to sell or buy securities (or any asset for that matter) at preset prices. One who is contracted to *sell* securities at a *preset* price after their market price has fallen benefits from the rise in interest rates. Consequently, the value of the *contract* that gives one the right to sell securities at a preset price goes up as the market price declines. The seller in a futures contract derives a gain (loss) when interest rates rise (decline).[3] Conversely, the one obligated to *buy* securities at a preset price experiences a loss. This risk of having to pay more cash or receive less cash is referred to as *cash flow risk.*

> The seller in a financial futures contract realizes a gain (loss) when interest rates rise (decline).

Another example of cash flow risk would be borrowing money by issuing a variable (floating) rate note. If market interest rates rise, the borrower would have to pay more interest. Similarly, the lender (investor) in the variable (floating) rate note transaction would face cash flow risk that interest rates would decline, resulting in lower cash interest receipts.

Let's look closer at how a futures contract can mitigate cash flow risk. Consider a company in April that will replace its $10 million of 8.5% bank notes when they mature in June. The company is exposed to the risk that interest rates in June will have risen, increasing borrowing costs. To counteract that possibility, the firm might enter a contract in April to deliver (sell) bonds in June at their *current* price. Since there are no corporate bond futures contracts, the company buys Treasury bond futures, which will accomplish essentially the same purpose. In essence, the firm agrees to sell Treasury bonds in June at a price established now (April). Let's say it's April 6 and the price of Treasury bond futures on the International Monetary Market of the Chicago Mercantile Exchange is quoted as 95.24.[4] Since the trading unit of Treasury bond futures is a 15-year, $100,000, 8% Treasury bond, the company might sell 105 Treasury bond futures to hedge the June issuance of debt. This would effectively provide a hedge of 105 × $100,000 × 95.24% = $10,000,200.[5]

Here's what happens then. If interest rates rise, borrowing costs will go up for our example company because it will have to sell debt securities at a higher interest cost (or lower price). But that loss will be offset (approximately) by the gain produced by being in the opposite position on Treasury bond futures. Take note, though, this works both ways. If interest rates go down causing debt security prices to rise, the potential benefit of being able to issue debt at that lower interest rate (higher price) will be offset by a loss on the futures position.

A very important point about futures contracts is that the seller does not need to have actual possession of the commodity (the Treasury bonds, in this case), nor is the purchaser of the contract required to take possession of the commodity. In fact, virtually all financial futures contracts are "netted out" before the actual transaction is to take place. This is

---

[2]Note that a financial futures contract meets the definition of a financial instrument because it entails the exchange of financial instruments (cash for Treasury bonds, for instance). But, a futures contract for the sale or purchase of a nonfinancial commodity like corn or gold does not meet the definition because one of the items to be exchanged is not a financial instrument.
[3]The seller of a futures contract is obligated to sell the bonds at a future date. The buyer of a futures contract is obligated to buy the bonds at a future date. The company in our example, then, is the seller of the futures contract.
[4]Price quotes are expressed as a percentage of par.
[5]This is a simplification of the more sophisticated way financial managers determine the optimal number of futures.

simply a matter of reversing the original position. A seller closes out his transaction with a purchase. Likewise, a purchaser would close out her transaction with a sale. After all, the objective is not to actually buy or sell Treasury bonds (or whatever the commodity might be), but to incur the financial impact of movements in interest rates as reflected in changes in Treasury bond prices. Specifically, it will buy at the lower price (to reverse the original seller position) at the same time it's selling its new bond issue at that same lower price. The financial futures market is an "artificial" exchange in that its reason for existing is to provide a mechanism to transfer risk from those exposed to it to those willing to accept the risk, not to actually buy and sell the underlying financial instruments.

> The effectiveness of a hedge is influenced by the closeness of the match between the item being hedged and the financial instrument chosen as a hedge.

If the impending debt issue being hedged is a short-term issue, the company may attain a more effective hedge by selling Treasury *bill* futures since Treasury bills are 90-day securities, or maybe certificate of deposit (CD) futures that also are traded in futures markets. The object is to get the closest association between the financial effects of interest rate movements on the actual transaction and the effects on the financial instrument used as a hedge.

FINANCIAL FORWARD CONTRACTS   A forward contract is similar to a futures contract but differs in three ways:

1. A forward contract calls for delivery on a specific date, whereas a futures contract permits the seller to decide later which specific day within the specified month will be the delivery date (if it gets as far as actual delivery before it is closed out).
2. Unlike a futures contract, a forward contract usually is not traded on a market exchange.
3. Unlike a futures contract, a forward contract does not call for a daily cash settlement for price changes in the underlying contract. Gains and losses on forward contracts are paid only when they are closed out.

OPTIONS   Options frequently are purchased to hedge exposure to the effects of changing interest rates. Options serve the same purpose as futures in that respect but are fundamentally different. An option on a financial instrument—say a Treasury bill—gives its holder the right either to buy or to sell the Treasury bill at a specified price and within a given time period. Importantly, though, the option holder has no obligation to exercise the option. On the other hand, the holder of a futures contract must buy or sell within a specified period unless the contract is closed out before delivery comes due.

FOREIGN CURRENCY FUTURES   Foreign loans frequently are denominated in the currency of the lender (Japanese yen, Swiss franc, Euro, and so on). When loans must be repaid in foreign currencies, a new element of risk is introduced. This is because if exchange rates change, the dollar equivalent of the foreign currency that must be repaid differs from the dollar equivalent of the foreign currency borrowed.

> Foreign exchange risk often is hedged in the same manner as interest rate risk.

To hedge against "foreign exchange risk" exposure, some firms buy or sell foreign currency futures contracts. These are similar to financial futures except specific foreign currencies are specified in the futures contracts rather than specific debt instruments. They work the same way to protect against foreign exchange risk as financial futures protect against fair value or cash flow risk.

> *Interest rate swaps* exchange fixed interest payments for floating rate payments, or vice versa, without exchanging the underlying notional amounts.

INTEREST RATE SWAPS   Over 65% of derivatives are interest rate swaps. These contracts exchange fixed interest payments for floating rate payments, or vice versa, without exchanging the underlying principal amounts. For example, suppose you owe $100,000 on a 10% fixed rate home loan. You envy your neighbor who also is paying 10% on her $100,000 mortgage, but hers is a floating rate loan, so if market rates fall, so will her loan rate. To the contrary, she is envious of your fixed rate, fearful that rates will rise, increasing her payments. A solution would be for the two of you to effectively swap interest payments using an interest rate swap agreement. The way a swap works, you both would continue to actually make your own interest payments, but would exchange the net cash difference between payments at specified intervals. So, in this case, if market rates (and thus floating payments) increase, you would pay your neighbor; if rates fall, she pays you. The net effect is to exchange the consequences of rate changes. In other words, you have effectively converted your fixed-rate debt to floating-rate debt; your neighbor has done the opposite.

Of course, this technique is not dependent on happening into such a fortuitous pairing of two borrowers with opposite philosophies on interest rate risk. Instead, banks or other intermediaries offer, for a fee, one-sided swap agreements to companies desiring to be either fixed-rate payers or variable-rate payers. Intermediaries usually strive to maintain a balanced portfolio of matched, offsetting swap agreements.

Theoretically, the two parties to such a transaction exchange principal amounts, say the $100,000 amount above, in addition to the interest on those amounts. It makes no practical sense, though, for the companies to send each other $100,000. So, instead, the principal amount is not actually exchanged, but serves merely as the computational base for interest calculations and is called the *notional amount.* Similarly, the fixed-rate payer doesn't usually send the entire fixed interest amount (say $10\% \times \$100,000 = \$10,000$) and receive the entire variable interest amount (say $9\% \times \$100,000 = \$9,000$). Generally, only the net amount ($1,000 in this case) is exchanged. This is illustrated in Illustration A–1.

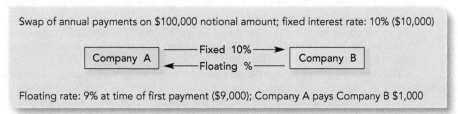

Swap of annual payments on $100,000 notional amount; fixed interest rate: 10% ($10,000)

Company A —— Fixed 10% ——▶ Company B
Company A ◀—— Floating % —— Company B

Floating rate: 9% at time of first payment ($9,000); Company A pays Company B $1,000

Illustration A–1
Interest Rate Swap—
Shortcut Method

From an accounting standpoint, the central issue is not the operational differences among various hedge instruments, but their similarities in functioning as hedges against risk.

Accounting for Derivatives

A key to accounting for derivatives is knowing the purpose for which a company holds them and whether the company is effective in serving that purpose. Derivatives, for instance, may be held for risk management (hedging activities). The desired effect, and often the real effect, is a reduction in risk. On the other hand, derivatives sometimes are held for speculative position taking, hoping for large profits. The effect of this activity usually is to *increase* risk. Perhaps more important, derivatives acquired as hedges and intended to reduce risk may, in fact, unintentionally increase risk instead.

It's important to understand that, serving as investments rather than as hedges, derivatives are extremely speculative. This is due to the high leverage inherent in derivatives. Here's why. The investment outlay usually is negligible, but, the potential gain or loss on the investment usually is quite high. A small change in interest rates or another underlying event can trigger a large change in the fair value of the derivative. Because the initial investment was minimal, the change in value relative to the investment itself represents a huge percentage gain or loss. Their extraordinarily risky nature prompted Warren Buffett, one of the country's most celebrated financiers, to refer to derivatives as "financial weapons of mass destruction." Accounting for derivatives is designed to treat differently (a) derivatives designated as hedges and those not designated as hedges as well as (b) the effective portion and the ineffective portion of gains and losses from intended hedges.

The basic approach to accounting for derivatives is fairly straightforward, although implementation can be quite cumbersome. All derivatives, no exceptions, are carried on the

> Derivatives not serving as hedges are extremely speculative due to the high leverage inherent in such investments.

Each derivative contract has a "fair value," which is an amount that one side owes the other at a particular moment.

balance sheet as either assets or liabilities at fair (or market) value.[6] The reasoning is that (a) derivatives create either rights or obligations that meet the definition of assets or liabilities, and (b) fair value is the most meaningful measurement.

Accounting for the gain or loss on a derivative depends on how it is used. Specifically, if the derivative is not designated as a hedging instrument, or doesn't qualify as one, any gain or loss from fair value changes is recognized immediately in earnings. On the other hand, if a derivative is used to hedge against exposure to risk, any gain or loss from fair value changes is either (a) recognized immediately in earnings along with an offsetting loss or gain on the item being hedged or (b) deferred in comprehensive income until it can be recognized in earnings at the same time as earnings are affected by a hedged transaction. Which way depends on whether the derivative is designated as a (a) fair value hedge, (b) cash flow hedge, or (c) foreign currency hedge. Let's look now at each of the three hedge designations.

A gain or loss from a *fair value hedge* is recognized immediately in earnings along with the loss or gain from the item being hedged.

FAIR VALUE HEDGES A company can be adversely affected when a change in either prices or interest rates causes a change in the fair value of one of its assets, its liabilities, or a commitment to buy or sell assets or liabilities. If a derivative is used to hedge against the exposure to changes in the fair value of an asset or liability or a firm commitment, it can be designated as a fair value hedge. In that case, when the derivative is adjusted to reflect changes in fair value, the other side of the entry recognizes a gain or loss to be included *currently* in earnings. At the same time, though, the loss or gain from changes in the fair value (due to the risk being hedged)[7] of the item being hedged also is included currently in earnings. This means that, to the extent the hedge is effective in serving its purpose, the gain or loss on the derivative will be offset by the loss or gain on the item being hedged. In fact, this is precisely the concept behind the procedure.

The income effects of the hedge instrument and the income effects of the item being hedged should affect earnings at the same time.

The reasoning is that as interest rates or other underlying events change, a hedge instrument will produce a gain approximately equal to a loss on the item being hedged (or vice versa). These income effects are interrelated and offsetting, so it would be improper to report the income effects in different periods. More critically, the intent and effect of having the hedge instrument is to *lessen* risk. And yet, recognizing gains in one period and counterbalancing losses in another period would tend to cause fluctuations in income that convey an *increase* in risk. However, to the extent that a hedge is ineffective and produces gains or losses different from the losses or gains being hedged, the ineffective portion is recognized in earnings immediately.

Some of the more common fair value hedges use:

- An interest rate swap to synthetically convert fixed-rate debt (for which interest rate changes could change the fair value of the debt) into floating-rate debt.
- A futures contract to hedge changes in the fair value (due to price changes) of aluminum, sugar, or some other type of inventory.
- A futures contract to hedge the fair value (due to price changes) of a firm commitment to sell natural gas or some other asset.

ILLUSTRATION Because interest rate swaps comprise over 65% of derivatives in use, we will use swaps to illustrate accounting for derivatives. Let's look at the example in Illustration A–2 on the next page.

When the floating rate declined from 10% to 9%, the fair values of both the derivative (swap) and the note increased. This created an offsetting gain on the derivative and holding loss on the note. Both are recognized in earnings at the same time (at June 30, 2013).

---

[6]FASB ASC 815–10: Derivatives and Hedging–Overall (previously "Accounting for Derivative Instruments and Hedging Activities," *Statement of Financial Accounting Standards No. 133* (Norwalk, Conn.: FASB, 1998)).

[7]The fair value of a hedged item might also change for reasons other than from effects of the risk being hedged. For instance, the hedged risk may be that a change in interest rates will cause the fair value of a bond to change. The bond price might also change, though, if the market perceives that the bond's default risk has changed.

Illustration A–2
Interest Rate Swap—
Shortcut Method

Wintel Semiconductors issued $1 million of 18-month, 10% bank notes on January 1, 2013. Wintel is exposed to the risk that general interest rates will decline, causing the fair value of its debt to rise. (If the fair value of Wintel's debt increases, its effective borrowing cost is higher relative to the market.) To hedge against this fair value risk, the firm entered into an 18-month interest rate swap agreement on January 1 and designated the swap as a hedge against changes in the fair value of the note. The swap calls for the company to *receive payment* based on a 10% fixed interest rate on a notional amount of $1 million and to *make payment* based on a floating interest rate tied to changes in general rates.[8] As the Illustration will show, this effectively converts Wintel's fixed-rate debt to floating-rate debt. Cash settlement of the net interest amount is made semiannually at June 30 and December 31 of each year with the net interest being the difference between the $50,000 fixed interest [$1 million × (10% × ½)] and the floating interest rate times $1 million at those dates.

Floating (market) settlement rates were 9% at June 30, 2013, 8% at December 31, 2013, and 9% at June 30, 2014. Net interest receipts can be calculated as shown below. Fair values of both the derivative and the note resulting from those market rate changes are assumed to be quotes obtained from securities dealers.

	1/1/13	6/30/13	12/31/13	6/30/14
Fixed rate	10%	10%	10%	10%
Floating rate	10%	9%	8%	9%
Fixed payments ($1 million × [10% × ½])		$ 50,000	$ 50,000	$ 50,000
Floating payments ($1 million × ½ floating rate)		45,000	40,000	45,000
Net interest receipts		$ 5,000	$ 10,000	$ 5,000
Fair value of interest rate swap	0	$ 9,363	$ 9,615	0
Fair value of note payable	$1,000,000	$1,009,363	$1,009,615	$1,000,000

January 1, 2013
Cash	1,000,000	
Notes payable		1,000,000

To record the issuance of the note.

The interest rate swap is designated as a fair value hedge on this note at issuance.

June 30, 2013
Interest expense (10% × ½ × $1 million)	50,000	
Cash		50,000

To record interest.

Cash ($50,000 – [9% × ½ × $1 million])	5,000	
Interest expense		5,000

To record the net cash settlement.

The swap settlement is the difference between the fixed interest (5%) and variable interest (4.5%).

Interest rate swap[9] ($9,363 – 0)	9,363	
Holding gain—interest rate swap		9,363

To record change in fair value of the derivative.

The fair value of derivatives is recognized in the balance sheet.

Holding loss—hedged note	9,363	
Note payable ($1,009,363 – 1,000,000)		9,363

To record change in fair value of the note due to interest rate changes.

The hedged liability (or asset) is adjusted to fair value as well.

The net interest settlement on June 30, 2013, is $5,000 because the fixed rate is 5% (half of the 10% annual rate) and the floating rate is 4.5% (half of the 9% annual rate).

---

[8]A common measure for benchmarking variable interest rates is LIBOR, the London Interbank Offered Rate, a base rate at which large international banks lend funds to each other.
[9]This would be a liability rather than an investment (asset) if the fair value had declined.

A-6   APPENDIX A   Derivatives

As with any debt, interest expense is the effective rate times the outstanding balance.

December 31, 2013		
Interest expense	50,000	
Cash (10% × ½ × $1,000,000)		50,000
To record interest.		

The settlement is the difference between the fixed interest (5%) and variable interest (4%).

Cash ($50,000 – [8% × ½ × $1 million])	10,000	
Interest expense		10,000
To record the net cash settlement.		

The derivative is increased by the change in fair value. The note is increased by the change in fair value.

Interest rate swap ($9,615 – 9,363)	252	
Holding gain—interest rate swap		252
To record the change in fair value of the derivative.		
Holding loss—hedged note	252	
Note payable ($1,009,615 – 1,009,363)		252
To record the change in fair value of the note due to interest rate changes.		

The fair value of the swap increased by $252 (from $9,363 to $9,615). Similarly, we adjust the note's carrying value by the amount necessary to increase it to fair value. This produces a holding loss on the note that exactly offsets the gain on the swap. This result is the hedging effect that motivated Wintel to enter the fair value hedging arrangement in the first place.

At June 30, 2014, Wintel repeats the process of adjusting to fair value both the derivative investment and the note being hedged.

The net interest received is the difference between the fixed interest (5%) and floating interest (4.5%).

June 30, 2014		
Interest expense	50,000	
Cash (10% × ½ × $1,000,000)		50,000
To record interest.		
Cash [$50,000 – (9% × ½ × $1 million)]	5,000	
Interest expense		5,000
To record the net cash settlement.		

The swap's fair value now is zero.

Holding loss—interest rate swap	9,615	
Interest rate swap ($0 – 9,615)		9,615
To record the change in fair value of the derivative.		
Note payable ($1,000,000 – 1,009,615)	9,615	
Holding gain—hedged note		9,615
To record the change in fair value of the note due to interest rate changes.		
Note payable	1,000,000	
Cash		1,000,000
To repay the loan.		

The net interest received is the difference between the fixed rate (5%) and floating rate (4.5%) times $1 million. The fair value of the swap decreased by $9,615 (from $9,615 to zero).[10] That decline represents a holding *loss* that we recognize in earnings. Similarly, we record an offsetting holding *gain* on the note for the change in its fair value.

Now let's see how the carrying values changed for the swap account and the note:

	Swap			Note	
Jan. 1, 2013					1,000,000
June 30, 2013	9,363				9,363
Dec. 31, 2013	252				252
June 30, 2014		9,615		9,615	
				1,000,000	
		0			0

---

[10]Because there are no future cash receipts from the swap arrangement at this point, the fair value of the swap is zero.

The income statement is affected as follows:

Income Statement + (−)		
June 30, 2013	(50,000)	Interest expense—fixed payment
	5,000	Interest expense—net cash settlement
	9,363	Holding gain—interest rate swap
	(9,363)	Holding loss—hedged note
	(45,000)	Net effect—same as floating interest payment
Dec. 31, 2013	(50,000)	Interest expense—fixed payment
	10,000	Interest expense—net cash settlement
	252	Holding gain—interest rate swap
	(252)	Holding loss—hedged note
	(40,000)	Net effect—same as floating interest payment
June 30, 2014	(50,000)	Interest expense—fixed payment
	5,000	Interest expense—net cash settlement
	9,615	Holding gain—interest rate swap
	(9,615)	Holding loss—hedged note
	(45,000)	Net effect—same as floating interest payment

As this demonstrates, the swap effectively converts fixed-interest debt to floating-interest debt.

Additional Consideration

Fair Value of the Swap

The fair value of a derivative typically is based on a quote obtained from a derivatives dealer. That fair value will approximate the present value of the expected net interest settlement receipts for the remaining term of the swap. In fact, we can actually calculate the fair value of the swap that we accepted as given in our illustration.

Since the June 30, 2013, floating rate of 9% caused the cash settlement on that date to be $5,000, it's reasonable to look at 9% as the best estimate of future floating rates and therefore assume the remaining two cash settlements also will be $5,000 each. We can then calculate at June 30, 2013, the present value of those expected net interest settlement receipts for the remaining term of the swap:

Fixed interest	10% × ½ × $1 million	$ 50,000
Expected floating interest	9% × ½ × $1 million	45,000
Expected cash receipts for both Dec. 31, 2013 and June 30, 2014		$ 5,000
		× 1.87267*
Present value		$ 9,363

*Present value of an ordinary annuity of $1: $n = 2$, $i = 4.5\%$ (½ of 9%) (from Table 4)

Fair Value of the Notes

The fair value of the note payable will be the present value of principal and remaining interest payments discounted at the *market rate*. The market rate will vary with the designated floating rate but might differ due to changes in default (credit) risk and the term structure of interest rates. Assuming it's 9% at June 30, 2013, we can calculate the fair value (present value) of the notes:

Interest	$50,000* × 1.87267† =	$ 93,633
Principal	$1,000,000 × .91573‡ =	915,730
		$1,009,363

*½ of 10% × $1,000,000
†Present value of an ordinary annuity of $1: $n = 2$, $i = 4.5\%$ (from Table 4)
‡Present value of $1: $n = 2$, $i = 4.5\%$ (from Table 2)

(continued)

A-8   APPENDIX A   Derivatives

(concluded)

Note: Often the cash settlement rate is "reset" as of each cash settlement date (thus the floating rate actually used at the end of each period to determine the payment is the floating market rate as of the *beginning* of the same period). In our illustration, for instance, there would have been no cash settlement at June 30, 2013, since we would use the beginning floating rate of 10% to determine payment. Similarly, we would have used the 9% floating rate at June 30, 2013, to determine the cash settlement six months later at December 31. In effect, each cash settlement would be delayed six months. Had this arrangement been in effect in the current illustration, there would have been one fewer cash settlement payments (two rather than three), but would not have affected the fair value calculations above because, either way, our expectation would be cash receipts of $5,000 for both Dec. 31, 2013, and June 30, 2014.

CASH FLOW HEDGES The risk in some transactions or events is the risk of a change in cash flows, rather than a change in fair values. We noted earlier, for instance, that *fixed-rate* debt subjects a company to the risk that interest rate changes could change the fair value of the debt. On the other hand, if the obligation is *floating-rate* debt, the fair value of the debt will not change when interest rates do, but cash flows will. If a derivative is used to hedge against the exposure to changes in cash inflows or cash outflows of an asset or liability or a forecasted transaction (like a future purchase or sale), it can be designated as a cash flow hedge. In that case, when the derivative is adjusted to reflect changes in fair value, the other side of the entry is a gain or loss to be deferred as a component of other comprehensive income and included in earnings later, at the same time as earnings are affected by the hedged transaction. Once again, the effect is matching the earnings effect of the derivative with the earnings effect of the item being hedged, precisely the concept behind hedge accounting.

> A gain or loss from a *cash flow hedge* is deferred as other comprehensive income until it can be recognized in earnings along with the earnings effect of the item being hedged.

To understand the deferral of the gain or loss, we need to revisit the concept of comprehensive income. Comprehensive income, as you may recall from Chapters 4, 12, 17, and 18, is a more expansive view of the change in shareholders' equity than traditional net income. In fact, it encompasses all changes in equity other than from transactions with owners.[11] So, in addition to net income itself, comprehensive income includes up to four other changes in equity that don't (yet) belong in net income, namely, net holding gains (losses) on investments (Chapter 12), gains (losses) from and amendments to postretirement benefit plans (Chapter 17), gains (losses) from foreign currency translation, and deferred gains (losses) from derivatives designated as cash flow hedges.[12]

Some of the more commonly used cash flow hedges are:

- An interest rate swap to synthetically convert floating rate debt (for which interest rate changes could change the cash interest payments) into fixed rate debt.
- A futures contract to hedge a forecasted sale (for which price changes could change the cash receipts) of natural gas, crude oil, or some other asset.

FOREIGN CURRENCY HEDGES Today's economy is increasingly a global one. The majority of large "U.S." companies are, in truth, multinational companies that may receive only a fraction of their revenues from U.S. operations. Many operations of those companies are located abroad. Foreign operations often are denominated in the currency of the foreign country (the Euro, Japanese yen, Russian rubles, and so on). Even companies without foreign operations sometimes hold investments, issue debt, or conduct other transactions denominated in foreign currencies. As exchange rates change, the dollar equivalent of the

> The possibility that foreign currency exchange rates might change exposes many companies to foreign currency risk.

---

[11]Transactions with owners primarily include dividends and the sale or purchase of shares of the company's stock.
[12]FASB ASC 220–10–55–2: Comprehensive Income–Overall–Implementation Guidance and Illustrations (previously "Reporting Comprehensive Income," *Statement of Financial Accounting Standards No. 130* (Norwalk, Conn.: FASB, 1997)).

foreign currency changes. The possibility of currency rate changes exposes these companies to the risk that some transactions require settlement in a currency other than the entities' functional currency or that foreign operations will require translation adjustments to reported amounts.

A foreign currency hedge can be a hedge of foreign currency exposure of:

- A firm commitment—treated as a fair value hedge.
- An available-for-sale security—treated as a fair value hedge.
- A forecasted transaction—treated as a cash flow hedge.
- A company's net investment in a foreign operation—the gain or loss is reported in *other comprehensive income* as part of unrealized gains and losses from foreign currency translation.[13]

HEDGE EFFECTIVENESS When a company elects to apply hedge accounting, it must establish at the inception of the hedge the method it will use to assess the effectiveness of the hedging derivative as well as the measurement approach it will use to determine the ineffective portion of the hedge.[14] The key criterion for qualifying as a hedge is that the hedging relationship must be "highly effective" in achieving offsetting changes in fair values or cash flows based on the hedging company's specified risk management objective and strategy.

> To qualify as a hedge, the hedging relationship must be highly effective in achieving offsetting changes in fair values or cash flows.

An assessment of this effectiveness must be made at least every three months and whenever financial statements are issued. There are no precise guidelines for assessing effectiveness, but it generally means a high correlation between changes in the fair value or cash flows of the derivative and of the item being hedged, not necessarily a specific reduction in risk. Hedge accounting must be terminated for hedging relationships that no longer are highly effective.

HEDGE INEFFECTIVENESS In Illustration A–2, the loss on the hedged note exactly offset the gain on the swap. This is because the swap in this instance was highly effective in hedging the risk due to interest rate changes. However, the loss and gain would not have exactly offset each other if the hedging arrangement had been ineffective. For instance, suppose the swap's term had been different from that of the note (say a three-year swap term compared with the 18-month term of the note) or if the notional amount of the swap differed from that of the note (say $500,000 rather than $1 million). In that case, changes in the fair value of the swap and changes in the fair value of the note would not be the same. The result would be a greater (or lesser) amount recognized in earnings for the swap than for the note. Because there would not be an exact offset, earnings would be affected, an effect resulting from hedge ineffectiveness. That is a desired effect of hedge accounting; to the extent that a hedge is effective, the earnings effect of a derivative cancels out the earnings effect of the item being hedged. However, even if a hedge is highly effective, all ineffectiveness is recognized currently in earnings.

> Imperfect hedges result in part of the derivative gain or loss being included in current earnings.

FAIR VALUE CHANGES UNRELATED TO THE RISK BEING HEDGED In Illustration A–2, the fair value of the hedged note and the fair value of the swap changed by the same amounts each year because we assumed the fair values changed only due to interest rate changes. It's also possible, though, that the note's fair value would change by an amount different from that of the swap for reasons unrelated to interest rates. Remember from our earlier discussion that the market's perception of a company's creditworthiness, and thus its ability to pay interest and principal when due, also can affect the value of debt, whether interest rates change or not. In hedge accounting, we ignore those changes. We recognize

---

[13]This is the same treatment previously prescribed for these translation adjustments by *Statement of Financial Accounting Standards No. 52* [FASB ASC 830: Foreign Currency Matters].

[14]Remember, if a derivative is not designated as a hedge, any gains or losses from changes in its fair value are recognized immediately in earnings.

only the fair value changes in the hedged item that we can attribute to the risk being hedged (interest rate risk in this case). For example, if a changing perception of default risk had caused the note's fair value to increase by an additional, say $5,000, our journal entries in Illustration A–2 would have been unaffected. Notice, then, that although we always mark a *derivative* to fair value, the reported amount of the *item being hedged* may not be its fair value. We mark a hedged item to fair value only to the extent that its fair value changed due to the risk being hedged.

Fair value changes unrelated to the risk being hedged are ignored.

Disclosure of Derivatives and Risk

To be adequately informed about the effectiveness of a company's risk management, investors and creditors need information about strategies for holding derivatives and specific hedging activities. Toward that end, extensive disclosure requirements provide information that includes:

- Objectives and strategies for holding and issuing derivatives.
- A description of the items for which risks are being hedged.
- For forecasted transactions: a description, time before the transaction is expected to occur, the gains and losses accumulated in other comprehensive income, and the events that will trigger their recognition in earnings.
- Beginning balance of, changes in, and ending balance of the derivative component of other comprehensive income.
- The net amount of gain or loss reported in earnings (representing aggregate hedge ineffectiveness).
- Qualitative and quantitative information about failed hedges: canceled commitments or previously hedged forecasted transactions no longer expected to occur.

The intent is to provide information about the company's success in reducing risks and consequently about risks not managed successfully. Remember, too, that when derivatives are employed ineffectively, risks can escalate. Ample disclosures about derivatives are essential to maintain awareness of potential opportunities and problems with risk management.

In addition, newly issued GAAP requires companies to provide enhanced disclosures indicating (a) how and why the company uses derivative instruments, (b) how the company accounts for derivative instruments and related hedged items, and (c) how derivative instruments and related hedged items affect the company's balance sheet, income statement, and cash flows.[15] The required disclosures includes two tables, one that highlights the location and fair values of derivative instruments in the balance sheet, and another that indicates the location and amounts of gains and losses on derivative instruments in the income statement. The two tables distinguish between derivative instruments that are designated as hedging instruments and those that are not. The tables also categorize derivative instruments by each major type—interest rate contracts, foreign exchange contracts, equity contracts, commodity contracts, credit contracts and other types of contracts.

Even for some traditional liabilities, the amounts reported on the face of the financial statements provide inadequate disclosure about the degree to which a company is exposed to risk of loss. To provide adequate disclosure about a company's exposure to risk, additional information must be provided about (a) concentrations of credit risk and (b) the fair value of all financial instruments.[16]

---

[15]FASB ASC 815: Derivatives and Hedging (previously "Disclosures about Derivative Instruments and Hedging Activities—an amendment of FASB Statement No. 133," *Statement of Financial Accounting Standards No. 161* (Stamford, Conn.: FASB, 2008)).
[16]FASB ASC 825-10-50-1: Financial Instruments–Overall–Disclosure (previously "Disclosures About Fair Values of Financial Instruments," *Statement of Financial Accounting Standards No. 107* (Norwalk, Conn.: FASB, 1991), as amended by *Statement of Financial Accounting Standards No. 133,* "Accounting for Derivative Instruments and Hedging Activities" (Norwalk, Conn.: FASB, 1998)).

Extended Method for Interest Rate Swap Accounting

A shortcut method for accounting for an interest rate swap is permitted when a hedge meets certain criteria. In general, the criteria are designed to see if the hedge supports the assumption of "no ineffectiveness." Illustration A–2 of a fair value hedge met those criteria, in particular, (a) the swap's notional amount matches the note's principal amount, (b) the swap's expiration date matches the note's maturity date, (c) the fair value of the swap is zero at inception, and (d) the floating payment is at the market rate.[17] Because Wintel can conclude that the swap will be highly effective in offsetting changes in the fair value of the debt, it can use the changes in the fair value of the swap to measure the offsetting changes in the fair value of the debt. That's the essence of the shortcut method used in Illustration A–2. The extended method required when the criteria are *not* met for the short-cut method is described in this section (Illustration A–3). It produces the same effect on earnings and in the balance sheet as does the procedure shown in Illustration A–2.

Illustration A–3
Interest Rate Swap—Extended Method

Wintel Semiconductors issued $1 million of 18-month, 10% bank notes on January 1, 2013. Wintel is exposed to the risk that general interest rates will decline, causing the fair value of its debt to rise. (If the fair value of Wintel's debt increases, its effective borrowing cost is higher relative to the market.) To hedge against this fair value risk, the firm entered into an 18-month interest rate swap agreement on January 1 and designated the swap as a hedge against changes in the fair value of the note. The swap calls for the company to *receive payment* based on a 10% fixed interest rate on a notional amount of $1 million and to *make payment* based on a floating interest rate tied to changes in general rates. Cash settlement of the net interest amount is made semiannually at June 30 and December 31 of each year with the net interest being the difference between the $50,000 fixed interest [$1 million × (10% × ½)] and the floating interest rate times $1 million at those dates.

Floating (market) settlement rates were 9% at June 30, 2013, 8% at December 31, 2013, and 8% at June 30, 2014. Net interest receipts can be calculated as shown below. Fair values of both the derivative and the note resulting from those market rate changes are assumed to be quotes obtained from securities dealers.

	1/1/13	6/30/13	12/31/13	6/30/14
Fixed rate	10%	10%	10%	10%
Floating rate	10%	9%	8%	9%
Fixed payments				
[$1 million × (10% × ½)]		$ 50,000	$ 50,000	$ 50,000
Floating payments				
($1 million × ½ floating rate)		45,000	40,000	45,000
Net interest receipts		$ 5,000	$ 10,000	$ 5,000
Fair value of interest rate swap	0	$ 9,363	$ 9,615	0
Fair value of note payable	$1,000,000	$1,009,363	$1,009,615	$1,000,000

When the floating rate declined in Illustration A–3 from 10% to 9%, the fair values of both the derivative (swap) and the note increased. This created an offsetting gain on the derivative and holding loss on the note. Both are recognized in earnings the same period (June 30, 2013).

January 1, 2013

Cash	1,000,000	
Notes payable		1,000,000
To record the issuance of the note.		

The interest rate swap is designated as a fair value hedge on this note at issuance.

---

[17]There is no precise minimum interval, though it generally is three to six months or less. Other criteria are specified by previously FASB ASC 815–20–25–104: Derivatives and Hedging–Hedging-General–Recognition–Shortcut Method, *SFAS No. 133* (para. 68) in addition to the key conditions listed here.

A-12   APPENDIX A   Derivatives

The swap settlement is the difference between the fixed interest (5%) and variable interest (4.5%).

The fair value of derivatives is recognized in the balance sheet.

The hedged liability (or asset) is adjusted to fair value as well.

June 30, 2013

Interest expense (10% × ½ × $1 million)	50,000	
Cash		50,000
To record interest.		
Cash ($50,000 – [9% × ½ × $1 million])	5,000	
Interest rate swap ($9,363 – 0)	9,363	
Interest revenue (10% × ½ × $0)		0
Holding gain—interest rate swap (to balance)		14,363
To record the net cash settlement, accrued interest on the swap,		
and change in the fair value of the derivative.		
Holding loss—hedged note	9,363	
Notes payable ($1,009,363 – 1,000,000)		9,363
To record change in fair value of the note due to interest rate changes.		

The net interest settlement on June 30, 2013, is $5,000 because the fixed rate is 5% (half of the 10% annual rate) and the floating rate is 4.5% (half of the 9% annual rate). A holding gain ($14,363) is produced by holding the derivative security during a time when an interest rate decline caused an increase in the value of that asset. A portion ($5,000) of the gain was received in cash and another portion ($9,363) is reflected as an increase in the value of the asset.

We also have holding loss of the same amount. This is because we also held a liability during the same time period, and the interest rate change caused its fair value to increase as well.

As with any debt, interest expense is the effective rate times the outstanding balance.

The cash settlement is the difference between the fixed interest (5%) and variable interest (4%).

Interest ($421) accrues on the asset.

The note is increased by the change in fair value.

December 31, 2013

Interest expense (9% × ½ × $1,009,363)	45,421	
Notes payable (difference)*	4,579	
Cash (10% × ½ × $1,000,000)		50,000
To record interest.		
Cash [$50,000 – (8% × ½ × $1 million)]	10,000	
Interest rate swap ($9,615 – 9,363)	252	
Interest revenue (9% × ½ × $9,363)		421
Holding gain—interest rate swap (to balance)		9,831
To record the net cash settlement, accrued interest on the swap,		
and change in the fair value of the derivative.		
Holding loss—hedged note	4,831	
Notes payable ($1,009,615 – 1,009,363 + 4,579)		4,831
To record the change in fair value of the note due to interest rate changes.		

*We could use a premium on the note to adjust its carrying amount.

We determine interest on the note the same way we do for any liability, as you learned earlier—at the effective rate (9% × ½) times the outstanding balance ($1,009,363). This results in reducing the note's carrying amount for the cash interest paid in excess of the interest expense.

The fair value of the swap increased due to the interest rate decline by $252 (from $9,363 to $9,615). The holding gain we recognize in earnings consists of that increase (a) plus the $10,000 cash settlement also created by the interest rate decline and (b) minus the $421 increase that results not from the interest rate decline, but from interest accruing on the asset.[18] Similarly, we adjust the note's carrying value by the amount necessary to increase it to fair value, allowing for the $4,579 reduction in the note in the earlier entry to record interest.

At June 30, 2014, Wintel repeats the process of adjusting to fair value both the derivative investment and the note being hedged.

---

[18]The investment in the interest rate swap represents the present value of expected future net interest receipts. As with other such assets, interest accrues at the effective rate times the outstanding balance. You also can think of the accrued interest mathematically as the increase in present value of the future cash flows as we get one period nearer to the dates when the cash will be received.

June 30, 2014

Interest expense (8% × ½ × $1,009,615)	40,385	
Notes payable (difference)	9,615	
Cash (10% × ½ × $1,000,000)		50,000

To record interest.

Cash [$50,000 − (9% × ½ × $1 million)]	5,000	
Holding loss—interest rate swap (to balance)	5,000	
Interest rate swap ($0 − $9,615)		9,615
Interest revenue (8% × ½ × $9,615)		385

To record the net cash settlement, accrued interest on the swap, and change in the fair value of the derivative.

Notes payable ($1,000,000 − 1,009,615 + 9,615)	0	
Holding gain—hedged note		0

To record the change in fair value of the note due to interest rate changes.

Note payable	1,000,000	
Cash		1,000,000

To repay the loan

> Interest expense is the effective rate times the outstanding balance.

> The net interest received is the difference between the fixed interest (5%) and floating interest (4.5%).

> The swap's fair value now is zero.

The net interest received is the difference between the fixed rate (5%) and floating rate (4.5%) times $1 million. The fair value of the swap decreased by $9,615 (from $9,615 to zero).[19] The holding loss we recognize in earnings consists of that decline (a) minus the $5,000 portion of the decline resulting from it being realized in cash settlement and (b) plus the $385 increase that results not from the interest rate change, but from interest accruing on the asset.

Now let's see how the carrying values changed for the swap account and the note:

	Swap		Note	
Jan. 1, 2013				1,000,000
June 30, 2013	9,363			9,363
Dec. 31, 2013	252		4,579	4,831
June 30, 2014		9,615	9,615	
			1,000,000	
	0			0

The income statement is affected as follows:

	Income Statement + (−)	
June 30, 2013	(50,000)	Interest expense
	0	Interest revenue (no time has passed)
	14,363	Holding gain interest rate swap
	(9,363)	Holding loss—hedged note
	(45,000)	Net effect—same as floating interest payment
Dec. 31, 2013	(45,421)	Interest expense
	421	Interest revenue
	9,831	Holding gain—interest rate swap
	(4,831)	Holding loss—hedged note
	(40,000)	Net effect—same as floating interest payment
June 30, 2014	(40,385)	Interest expense
	385	Interest revenue
	(5,000)	Holding gain—interest rate swap
	0	Holding loss—hedged note
	(45,000)	Net effect—same as floating interest payment

[19]Because there are no future cash receipts or payments from the swap arrangement at this point, the fair value of the swap is zero.

As this demonstrates, the swap effectively converts Wintel's fixed-interest debt to floating-interest debt.

International Financial Reporting Standards

Accounting for Derivatives.

"With IAS 39, if you understand it, you haven't read it properly," said International Accounting Standards Board Chairman, Sir David Tweedie.[20]

As with U.S. GAAP, accounting for derivatives under IFRS is quite complex. In fact, *IAS No. 39* provides an example of international accounting that defies the usual characterization of IFRS as being "principles-based accounting" in comparison with "rules-based" U.S. GAAP. Like U.S. GAAP, all freestanding derivatives are recognized in the balance sheet and measured at fair value under IFRS. And, unless they qualify as hedging instruments in a cash flow hedge or net investment in a foreign operation, all changes in fair value are recognized immediately in net income, as under U.S. GAAP. Although the hedging models under U.S. GAAP and IFRS are similar, several differences exist. Here are a few significant ones:

- The short-cut method for interest rate swaps described in this Appendix is not permitted under IFRS.
- The key criterion for qualifying as a hedge is that the hedging relationship must be "highly effective" in achieving offsetting changes in fair values or cash flows, which under U.S. GAAP generally means a high correlation between changes in the fair value or cash flows of the derivative and the item being hedged. Highly effective is more precisely defined under IFRS: the hedge must be within the range of 80–120 percent effective.
- U.S. GAAP does not permit a single hedging instrument to hedge more than one risk in two or more hedged items. However, IFRS allows a single hedging instrument to be designated as a hedge of more than one type of risk if the risks being hedged can be clearly identified, the hedge effectiveness can be demonstrated, and specific designation to different risk positions can be ensured.

Where We're Headed

The Financial Accounting Standards Board and the International Accounting Standards Board, after working jointly on new guidance for when companies would be allowed to offset financial assets and financial liabilities in the balance sheet, a practice also known as "netting," issued an Exposure Draft of a new Accounting Standards Update in January 2011. The new ASU would have drawn U.S. GAAP closer to IFRS with regard to presenting a single net amount in the balance sheet only when it (a) has an unconditional and legally enforceable right to set off the financial asset and liability and (b) intends to settle on a net basis (or to realize the financial asset and liability simultaneously). And, because master netting agreements usually include only a conditional right of offset, many more derivatives would have been reported gross (rather than net) in the balance sheet.

In June 2011, the FASB, under pressure from constituents, had a change of mind. The U.S. Board decided to support an approach for derivatives very close to what is permitted currently under U.S. GAAP. Financial institutions in particular lobbied the FASB to continue to allow companies to net derivatives that are subject to master netting agreements, a practice critical to leverage and other key measures that affect debt covenants and other contractual agreements.

The following month, the IASB decided that although they would not be issuing a joint ASU, the two boards agreed to at least fill the gap with additional disclosure requirements to enable users to sort out the differences.

---

[20]Michael Cohn, "Tweedie Says FASB Will Always Play a Role," WebCPA, December 11, 2008.

The Bottom Line

● **LOA–1**   All derivatives are reported in the balance sheet at fair value.

● **LOA–2**   *Hedging* means taking a risk position that is opposite to an actual position that is exposed to risk. For a derivative used to hedge against exposure to risk, treatment of any gain or loss from fair value changes depends on whether the derivative is designated as (a) a fair value hedge, (b) a cash flow hedge, or (c) a foreign currency hedge.

● **LOA–3**   We recognize a gain or loss from a *fair value hedge* immediately in earnings along with the loss or gain from the item being hedged. This is so the income effects of the hedge instrument and the income effects of the item being hedged will affect earnings at the same time.

● **LOA–4**   We defer a gain or loss from a *cash flow hedge* as part of other comprehensive income until it can be recognized in earnings along with the earnings effect of the item being hedged.

● **LOA–5**   Imperfect hedges result in part of the derivative gain or loss being included in current earnings. We ignore market value changes unrelated to the risk being hedged.

● **LOA–6**   Extensive disclosure requirements about derivatives are designed to provide investors and creditors information about the adequacy of a company's risk management and the company's success in reducing risks, including risks not managed successfully. ●

Questions For Review of Key Topics

Q A–1   Some financial instruments are called derivatives. Why?

Q A–2   Should gains and losses on a fair value hedge be recorded as they occur, or should they be recorded to coincide with losses and gains on the item being hedged?

Q A–3   Hines Moving Company held a fixed-rate debt of $2 million. The company wanted to hedge its fair value exposure with an interest rate swap. However, the only notional available at the time, on the type of swap it desired, was $2.5 million. What will be the effect of any gain or loss on the $500,000 notional difference?

Q A–4   What is a futures contract?

Q A–5   What is the effect on interest of an interest rate swap?

Q A–6   How are derivatives reported on the balance sheet? Why?

Q A–7   When is a gain or a loss from a cash flow hedge reported in earnings?

Exercises

E A–1
Derivatives-hedge classification

Indicate (by abbreviation) the type of hedge each activity described below would represent.

Hedge Type

FV   Fair value hedge
CF   Cash flow hedge
FC   Foreign currency hedge
N   Would not qualify as a hedge

Activity

_____ 1. An options contract to hedge possible future price changes of inventory.
_____ 2. A futures contract to hedge exposure to interest rate changes prior to replacing bank notes when they mature.
_____ 3. An interest rate swap to synthetically convert floating rate debt into fixed rate debt.
_____ 4. An interest rate swap to synthetically convert fixed rate debt into floating rate debt.
_____ 5. A futures contract to hedge possible future price changes of timber covered by a firm commitment to sell.
_____ 6. A futures contract to hedge possible future price changes of a forecasted sale of tin.
_____ 7. ExxonMobil's net investment in a Kuwait oil field.
_____ 8. An interest rate swap to synthetically convert floating rate interest on a stock investment into fixed rate interest.
_____ 9. An interest rate swap to synthetically convert fixed rate interest on a held-to-maturity debt investment into floating rate interest.
_____ 10. An interest rate swap to synthetically convert floating rate interest on a held-to-maturity debt investment into fixed rate interest.
_____ 11. An interest rate swap to synthetically convert fixed rate interest on a stock investment into floating rate interest.

A-16 APPENDIX A Derivatives

E A–2
Derivatives;
interest rate
swap; fixed rate
debt

On January 1, 2013, LLB Industries borrowed $200,000 from Trust Bank by issuing a two-year, 10% note, with interest payable quarterly. LLB entered into a two-year interest rate swap agreement on January 1, 2013, and designated the swap as a fair value hedge. Its intent was to hedge the risk that general interest rates will decline, causing the fair value of its debt to increase. The agreement called for the company to receive payment based on a 10% fixed interest rate on a notional amount of $200,000 and to pay interest based on a floating interest rate. The contract called for cash settlement of the net interest amount quarterly.

Floating (LIBOR) settlement rates were 10% at January 1, 8% at March 31, and 6% June 30, 2013. The fair values of the swap are quotes obtained from a derivatives dealer. Those quotes and the fair values of the note are as indicated below.

	January 1	March 31	June 30
Fair value of interest rate swap	0	$ 6,472	$ 11,394
Fair value of note payable	$200,000	$206,472	$211,394

Required:

1. Calculate the net cash settlement at March 31 and June 30, 2013.
2. Prepare the journal entries through June 30, 2013, to record the issuance of the note, interest, and necessary adjustments for changes in fair value.

E A–3
Derivatives;
interest rate
swap; fixed rate
investment

(This is a variation of Exercise A–2, modified to consider an investment in debt securities.)
On January 1, 2013, S&S Corporation invested in LLB Industries' negotiable two-year, 10% notes, with interest receivable quarterly. The company classified the investment as available-for-sale. S&S entered into a two-year interest rate swap agreement on January 1, 2013, and designated the swap as a fair value hedge. Its intent was to hedge the risk that general interest rates will decline, causing the fair value of its investment to increase. The agreement called for the company to make payment based on a 10% fixed interest rate on a notional amount of $200,000 and to receive interest based on a floating interest rate. The contract called for cash settlement of the net interest amount quarterly.

Floating (LIBOR) settlement rates were 10% at January 1, 8% at March 31, and 6% June 30, 2013. The fair values of the swap are quotes obtained from a derivatives dealer. Those quotes and the fair values of the investment in notes are as follows:

	January 1	March 31	June 30
Fair value of interest rate swap	0	$ 6,472	$ 11,394
Fair value of the investment in notes	$200,000	$206,472	$211,394

Required:

1. Calculate the net cash settlement at March 31 and June 30, 2013.
2. Prepare the journal entries through June 30, 2013, to record the investment in notes, interest, and necessary adjustments for changes in fair value.

E A–4
Derivatives;
interest rate
swap; fixed rate
debt; fair value
change unrelated
to hedged risk

(This is a variation of Exercise A–2, modified to consider fair value change unrelated to hedged risk.)
LLB Industries borrowed $200,000 from Trust Bank by issuing a two-year, 10% note, with interest payable quarterly. LLB entered into a two-year interest rate swap agreement on January 1, 2013 and designated the swap as a fair value hedge. Its intent was to hedge the risk that general interest rates will decline, causing the fair value of its debt to increase. The agreement called for the company to receive payment based on a 10% fixed interest rate on a notional amount of $200,000 and to pay interest based on a floating interest rate.

Floating (LIBOR) settlement rates were 10% at January 1, 8% at March 31, and 6% at June 30, 2013. The fair values of the swap are quotes obtained from a derivatives dealer. Those quotes and the fair values of the note are as indicated below. The additional rise in the fair value of the note (higher than that of the swap) on June 30 was due to investors' perceptions that the creditworthiness of LLB was improving.

	January 1	March 31	June 30
Fair value of interest rate swap	0	$ 6,472	$ 11,394
Fair value of note payable	$200,000	$206,472	$220,000

Required:

1. Calculate the net cash settlement at June 30, 2013.
2. Prepare the journal entries on June 30, 2013, to record the interest and necessary adjustments for changes in fair value.

E A–5
Derivatives;
interest rate swap;
fixed rate debt;
extended method

(This is a variation of Exercise A–2, modified to consider the extended method.)
On January 1, 2013, LLB Industries borrowed $200,000 from Trust Bank by issuing a two-year, 10% note, with interest payable quarterly. LLB entered into a two-year interest rate swap agreement on January 1, 2013, and designated the swap as a fair value hedge. Its intent was to hedge the risk that general interest rates will decline,

causing the fair value of its debt to increase. The agreement called for the company to receive payment based on a 10% fixed interest rate on a notional amount of $200,000 and to pay interest based on a floating interest rate. The contract called for cash settlement of the net interest amount quarterly.

Floating (LIBOR) settlement rates were 10% at January 1, 8% at March 31, and 6% at June 30, 2013. The fair values of the swap are quotes obtained from a derivatives dealer. Those quotes and the fair values of the note are as follows:

	January 1	March 31	June 30
Fair value of interest rate swap	0	$ 6,472	$ 11,394
Fair value of note payable	$200,000	$206,472	$211,394

Required:

Prepare the journal entries through June 30, 2013, to record the issuance of the note, interest, and necessary adjustments for changes in fair value. Use the extended method demonstrated in Illustration A–3.

E A–6
Derivatives;
interest rate
swap; fixed-rate
debt; fair value
change unrelated
to hedged
risk; extended
method

(Note: This is a variation of Exercise A–5, modified to consider fair value change unrelated to hedged risk.)
On January 1, 2013, LLB Industries borrowed $200,000 from trust Bank by issuing a two-year, 10% note, with interest payable quarterly. LLB entered into a two-year interest rate swap agreement on January 1, 2013, and designated the swap as a fair value hedge. Its intent was to hedge the risk that general interest rates will decline, causing the fair value of its debt to increase. The agreement called for the company to receive payment based on a 10% fixed interest rate on a notional amount of $200,000 and to pay interest based on a floating interest rate. The contract called for cash settlement of the net interest amount quarterly.

Floating (LIBOR) settlement rates were 10% at January 1, 8% at March 31, and 6% June 30, 2013. The fair values of the swap are quotes obtained from a derivatives dealer. Those quotes and the fair values of the note are as indicated below. The additional rise in the fair value of the note (higher than that of the swap) on June 30 was due to investors' perceptions that the creditworthiness of LLB was improving.

	January 1	March 31	June 30
Fair value of interest rate swap	0	$ 6,472	$ 11,394
Fair value of note payable	$200,000	206,472	220,000

Required:

1. Calculate the net cash settlement at June 30, 2013.
2. Prepare the journal entries on June 30, 2013, to record the interest and necessary adjustments for changes in fair value. Use the extended method demonstrated in Illustration A–3.

Problems

P A–1
Derivatives—
interest rate swap

On January 1, 2013, Labtech Circuits borrowed $100,000 from First Bank by issuing a three-year, 8% note, payable on December 31, 2015. Labtech wanted to hedge the risk that general interest rates will decline, causing the fair value of its debt to increase. Therefore, Labtech entered into a three-year interest rate swap agreement on January 1, 2013, and designated the swap as a fair value hedge. The agreement called for the company to receive payment based on an 8% fixed interest rate on a notional amount of $100,000 and to pay interest based on a floating interest rate tied to LIBOR. The contract called for cash settlement of the net interest amount on December 31 of each year.

Floating (LIBOR) settlement rates were 8% at inception and 9%, 7%, and 7% at the end of 2013, 2014, and 2015, respectively. The fair values of the swap are quotes obtained from a derivatives dealer. These quotes and the fair values of the note are as follows:

	January 1	December 31		
	2013	2013	2014	2015
Fair value of interest rate swap	0	$ (1,759)	$ 935	0
Fair value of note payable	$100,000	$98,241	$100,935	$100,000

Required:

1. Calculate the net cash settlement at the end of 2013, 2014, and 2015.
2. Prepare the journal entries during 2013 to record the issuance of the note, interest, and necessary adjustments for changes in fair value.
3. Prepare the journal entries during 2014 to record interest, net cash interest settlement for the interest rate swap, and necessary adjustments for changes in fair value.

4. Prepare the journal entries during 2015 to record interest, net cash interest settlement for the interest rate swap, necessary adjustments for changes in fair value, and repayment of the debt.

5. Calculate the carrying values of both the swap account and the note in each of the three years.

6. Calculate the net effect on earnings of the hedging arrangement in each of the three years. (Ignore income taxes.)

7. Suppose the fair value of the note at December 31, 2013, had been $97,000 rather than $98,241 with the additional decline in fair value due to investors' perceptions that the creditworthiness of Labtech was worsening. How would that affect your entries to record changes in the fair values?

P A–2
Derivatives;
interest
rate swap;
comprehensive

CMOS Chips is hedging a 20-year, $10 million, 7% bond payable with a 20-year interest rate swap and has designated the swap as a fair value hedge. The agreement called for CMOS to receive payment based on a 7% fixed interest rate on a notional amount of $10 million and to pay interest based on a floating interest rate tied to LIBOR. The contract calls for cash settlement of the net interest amount on December 31 of each year.

    At December 31, 2013, the fair value of the derivative and of the hedged bonds has increased by $100,000 because interest rates declined during the reporting period.

Required:

1. Does CMOS have an unrealized gain or loss on the derivative for the period? On the bonds? Will earnings increase or decrease due to the hedging arrangement? Why?

2. Suppose interest rates increased, rather than decreased, causing the fair value of both the derivative and of the hedged bonds to decrease by $100,000. Would CMOS have an unrealized gain or loss on the derivative for the period? On the bonds? Would earnings increase or decrease due to the hedging arrangement? Why?

3. Suppose the fair value of the bonds at December 31, 2013, had increased by $110,000 rather than $100,000, with the additional increase in fair value due to investors' perceptions that the creditworthiness of CMOS was improving. Would CMOS have an unrealized gain or loss on the derivative for the period? On the bonds? Would earnings increase or decrease due to the hedging arrangement? Why?

4. Suppose the notional amount of the swap had been $12 million, rather than the $10 million principal amount of the bonds. As a result, at December 31, 2013, the swap's fair value had increased by $120,000 rather than $100,000. Would CMOS have an unrealized gain or loss on the derivative for the period? On the bonds? Would earnings increase or decrease due to the hedging arrangement? Why?

5. Suppose BIOS Corporation is an investor having purchased all $10 million of the bonds issued by CMOS as described in the original situation above. BIOS is hedging its investment, classified as available-for-sale, with a 20-year interest rate swap and has designated the swap as a fair value hedge. The agreement called for BIOS to make *payment* based on a 7% fixed interest rate on a notional amount of $10 million and to *receive* interest based on a floating interest rate tied to LIBOR. Would BIOS have an unrealized gain or loss on the derivative for the period due to interest rates having declined? On the bonds? Would earnings increase or decrease due to the hedging arrangement? Why?

P A–3
Derivatives;
interest rate
swap; fixed rate
debt; extended
method

(Note: This is a variation of Problem A–1, modified to consider the extended method demonstrated in Illustration A–3.)

On January 1, 2013, Labtech Circuits borrowed $100,000 from First Bank by issuing a three-year, 8% note, payable on December 31, 2015. Labtech wanted to hedge the risk that general interest rates will decline, causing the fair value of its debt to increase. Therefore, Labtech entered into a three-year interest rate swap agreement on January 1, 2013, and designated the swap as a fair value hedge. The agreement called for the company to receive payment based on an 8% fixed interest rate on a notional amount of $100,000 and to pay interest based on a floating interest rate tied to LIBOR. The contract called for cash settlement of the net interest amount on December 31 of each year.

    Floating (LIBOR) settlement rates were 8% at inception and 9%, 7%, and 7% at the end of 2013, 2014, and 2015, respectively. The fair values of the swap are quotes obtained from a derivatives dealer. Those quotes and the fair values of the note are as follows:

	January 1	December 31		
	2013	2013	2014	2015
Fair value of interest rate swap	0	$ (1,759)	$ 935	0
Fair value of note payable	$100,000	$ 98,241	100,935	$100,000

Required:

Use the extended method demonstrated in Illustration A–3.

1. Calculate the net cash settlement at the end of 2013, 2014, and 2015.

2. Prepare the journal entries during 2013 to record the issuance of the note, interest, and necessary adjustments for changes in fair value.

3. Prepare the journal entries during 2014 to record interest, net cash interest settlement for the interest rate swap, and necessary adjustments for changes in fair value.

4. Prepare the journal entries during 2015 to record interest, net cash interest settlement for the interest rate swap, necessary adjustments for changes in fair value, and repayment of the debt.

5. Calculate the carrying values of both the swap account and the note in each of the three years.

6. Calculate the net effect on earnings of the hedging arrangement in each of the three years. (Ignore income taxes.)

7. Suppose the fair value of the note at December 31, 2013, had been $97,000 rather than $98,241 with the additional decline in fair value due to investors' perceptions that the creditworthiness of Labtech was worsening. How would that affect your entries to record changes in the fair values?

Broaden Your Perspective

Apply your critical-thinking ability to the knowledge you've gained. These cases will provide you an opportunity to develop your research, analysis, judgment, and communication skills. You also will work with other students, integrate what you've learned, apply it in real world situations, and consider its global and ethical ramifications. This practice will broaden your knowledge and further develop your decision-making abilities.

Real World Case A–1
Derivative losses; recognition in earnings

The following is an excerpt from a disclosure note of Johnson & Johnson:

15. Financial Instruments (in part)
As of December 28, 2008, the balance of deferred net gains on derivatives included in accumulated other comprehensive income was $121 million after-tax. The Company expects that substantially all of this amount will be reclassified into earnings over the next 12 months as a result of transactions that are expected to occur over that period.

Required:

1. Johnson & Johnson indicates that it expects that substantially all of the balance of deferred net gains on derivatives will be reclassified into earnings over the next 12 months as a result of transactions that are expected to occur over that period. What is meant by "reclassified into earnings"?

2. What type(s) of hedging transaction might be accounted for in this way?

Communication Case A–2
Derivatives; hedge accounting

A conceptual question in accounting for derivatives is: Should gains and losses on a hedge instrument be recorded as they occur, or should they be recorded to coincide (match) with income effects of the item being hedged?

ABI Wholesalers plans to issue long-term notes in May that will replace its $20 million of 9.5% bonds when they mature in July. ABI is exposed to the risk that interest rates in July will have risen, increasing borrowing costs (reducing the selling price of its notes). To hedge that possibility, ABI entered a (Treasury bond) futures contract in May to deliver (sell) bonds in July at their *current* price.

As a result, if interest rates rise, borrowing costs will go up for ABI because it will sell notes at a higher interest cost (or lower price). But that loss will be offset (approximately) by the gain produced by being in the opposite position on Treasury bond futures.

Two opposing viewpoints are:

View 1: Gains and losses on instruments designed to hedge anticipated transactions should be recorded as they occur.

View 2: Gains and losses on instruments designed to hedge anticipated transactions should be recorded to coincide (match) with income effects of the item being hedged.

In considering this question, focus on conceptual issues regarding the practicable and theoretically appropriate treatment, unconstrained by GAAP. Your instructor will divide the class into two to six groups depending on the size of the class. The mission of your group is to reach consensus on the appropriate accounting for the gains and losses on instruments designed to hedge anticipated transactions.

Required:

1. Each group member should deliberate the situation independently and draft a tentative argument prior to the class session for which the case is assigned.

2. In class, each group will meet for 10 to 15 minutes in different areas of the classroom. During that meeting, group members will take turns sharing their suggestions for the purpose of arriving at a single group treatment.

3. After the allotted time, a spokesperson for each group (selected during the group meetings) will share the group's solution with the class. The goal of the class is to incorporate the views of each group into a consensus approach to the situation.

A-20   APPENDIX A   Derivatives

Real World Case A–3
Researching the way interest rate futures prices are quoted on the Chicago Mercantile Exchange; retrieving information from the Internet

The Chicago Mercantile Exchange, or Merc, at 30 S. Wacker Drive in Chicago, is the world's largest financial exchange, an international marketplace enabling institutions and businesses to trade futures and options contracts including currencies, interest rates, stock indices, and agricultural commodities.

Required:

1. Access the Merc on the Internet. The web address is www.cme.com.
2. Access the daily settlement prices within the site. Scroll to find "Interest products" and, within that, the 13-week Treasury bill futures.
3. What are the settlement prices for September futures contracts?

Research Case A–4
Issue related to the derivatives standard; research an article

In an effort to keep up with the rapidly changing global financial markets, the FASB issued standards on accounting for and disclosure of derivative financial instruments. A *Journal of Accountancy* article that discusses this standard is "The Decision on Derivatives," by Arlette C. Wilson, Gary Waters, and Barry J. Bryan, November 1998.

Required:

On the Internet, go to the AICPA site at www.aicpa.org and find the article mentioned.

1. What are the primary problems or issues the FASB attempts to address regarding accounting for derivative financial instruments?
2. In considering the issues, the FASB made four fundamental decisions that became the cornerstones of the statement issued in 1998. What are those fundamental decisions? Which do you think is most critical to fair financial reporting?

Chapter **Three**

International Convergence of Financial Reporting

Learning Objectives

After reading this chapter, you should be able to

- Explain the meaning of convergence.
- Identify the arguments for and against international convergence of financial reporting standards.
- Discuss major harmonization efforts under the IASC.
- Explain the principles-based approach used by the IASB in setting accounting standards.
- Describe the proposed changes to the IASB's *Framework*.
- Discuss the IASB's Standards related to the first-time adoption of International Financial Reporting Standards (IFRS) and the presentation of financial statements.
- Describe the support for, and the use of, IFRS across countries.
- Examine the issues related to international convergence of financial reporting standards.
- Describe the progress made with regard to the IASB/FASB convergence project.
- Explain the meaning of "Anglo-Saxon" accounting.

INTRODUCTION

In Chapter 2, we discussed worldwide diversity in accounting practices and some of the problems caused by such diversity. Sir Bryan Carsberg, former secretary-general of the International Accounting Standards Committee (IASC), explained how accounting diversity affects international capital markets:

> Imagine the case of an international business, with operations in many different countries. It is likely to be required to prepare accounts for its operations in each country, in compliance with the rules of that country. It will then have to convert those accounts to conform to the rules of the country in which the holding company is resident, for the preparation of group accounts. If the company has listings on stock exchanges outside its home country, these exchanges or their

regulators may require the accounts to be filed under some other basis. The extra cost could be enormous. Heavy costs also fall on investors in trying to compare the results of companies based in different countries and they may just be unable to make such comparisons.... But the biggest cost may be in limiting the effectiveness of the international capital markets. Cross border investment is likely to be inhibited.[1]

The accounting profession and standard-setters have been under pressure from multinational companies, stock exchanges, securities regulators, international lending institutions such as the World Bank, and other international bodies such as G20 to reduce diversity and harmonize accounting standards and practices internationally. This chapter focuses on the activities of the International Accounting Standards Board (IASB), which replaced the IASC in 2001. The chapter also includes a discussion of the major harmonization efforts under the IASC. We identify the arguments for and against convergence, and discuss the adoption of International Financial Reporting Standards (IFRS), including national efforts to converge with those standards.

INTERNATIONAL ACCOUNTING STANDARD-SETTING

The evolution of the International Accounting Standards Committee and the International Accounting Standards Board shows international accounting standard-setting in the private sector with the support of the accounting bodies, standard-setters, capital market regulators, and government authorities in various countries, as well as the preparers and users of financial statements around the world.

Before the formation of the IASC in 1973, even within the Anglo-American countries, there were important differences in financial reporting; for example, in the United Kingdom, Australia, and New Zealand, companies could revalue their fixed assets, whereas in the United States and Canada, this was not allowed. Even greater differences existed between the GAAP in the Anglo-American countries and those in the Continental European countries and in Japan. For example, unlike in the Anglo-American countries, in countries on the European continent and in Japan, income taxation drove accounting practice. In most developing countries, financial disclosure was minimal. There was a rapid expansion of international trade, foreign direct investment, and engagement in international transactions by companies during the 1950s and 1960s. This situation fueled the clamor for harmonization of financial reporting standards by various interested groups, the main argument being that it would assist companies to compare financial statements prepared by companies in different countries for investment and other purposes.

The word *harmonization* appears to have had its day. It means different things to different people. Some view harmonization as the same as standardization. However, whereas standardization implies the elimination of alternatives in accounting for economic transactions and other events, harmonization refers to the reduction of alternatives while retaining a high degree of flexibility in accounting practices. Harmonization allows different countries to have different standards as long as

---

[1] Excerpt from Sir Bryan Carsberg, "Global Issues and Implementing Core International Accounting Standards: Where Lies IASC's Final Goal?" Remarks made at the 50th Anniversary Dinner, Japanese Institute of CPAs, Tokyo, October 23, 1998.

the standards do not conflict. For example, prior to 2005, within the European Union harmonization program, if appropriate disclosures were made, companies were permitted to use different measurement methods: German companies could use historical cost for valuing assets, while Dutch companies could use replacement cost without violating the harmonization requirements.

Harmonization is a process that takes place over time. Accounting harmonization can be considered in two ways, namely, harmonization of accounting regulations or standards (also known as formal or de jure harmonization), and harmonization of accounting practices (also known as material or de facto harmonization). Harmonization of accounting practices is the ultimate goal of international harmonization efforts. Harmonization of standards may not necessarily lead to harmonization of accounting practices adopted by companies. For example, a study in China in 2002 found that despite the Chinese government's efforts through legislation to ensure harmonization between Chinese GAAP and IASC GAAP, there was no evidence that such efforts eliminated or significantly reduced the differences that exist between earnings calculated under Chinese and IASC GAAP.[2] Other factors such as differences in the quality of audits, enforcement mechanisms, culture, legal requirements, and socioeconomic and political systems may lead to noncomparable accounting numbers despite similar accounting standards. An empirical study conducted in 1996 to assess the impact of the IASC's harmonization efforts, focusing on the accounting practices of major companies based in France, Germany, Japan, the United Kingdom, and the United States, concluded that the impact had been quite modest. The study considered 26 major accounting measurement issues and found that in 14 cases harmonization had increased, but in 12 cases harmonization had decreased.[3]

The phrase "international convergence of accounting standards" refers to both a goal and the process adopted to achieve it. The goal of "convergence" in accounting standards can be interpreted differently. From a strict viewpoint, it refers to the enforcement of a single set of accepted standards by several regulatory bodies, for example, the convergence project of the IASB and the FASB. From a soft viewpoint, it refers to diminishing differences among accounting standards issued by several regulators. According to a third viewpoint, it refers to a situation where two or more jurisdictions agree on a core set of common standards, allowing varying interpretations regarding non-core issues. Similarly, in implementing the international "convergence" process, three fundamental approaches can be adopted. First, the aim could be to merge all standard-setting bodies into a unified "global" body. From a theoretical point of view, it is often argued that the unified solution of a single international standard-setting body is optimal. Second, the aim could be to recognize each of the existing standard-setting bodies as the sole authority in its respective jurisdiction. Accordingly, it can also be argued that discretion and flexibility in accounting standards through mutual recognition is theoretically more desirable than uniformity and rigidity, and when the incentive consequences and the investment effects of accounting standards are taken into consideration, then discretion can be superior to uniformity. Third, the aim could also be to recognize

---

[2] S. Chen, Z. Sun, and Y. Wang, "Evidence from China on Whether Harmonized Accounting Standards Harmonize Accounting Practices," *Accounting Horizons* 16, no. 3 (2002), pp. 183–97.

[3] Emmanuel N. Emenyonu and Sidney J. Gray, "International Accounting Harmonization and the Major Developed Stock Market Countries: An Empirical Study," *International Journal of Accounting* 31, no. 3 (1996), pp. 269–79.

that a national standard-setting body can coexist with international coordination bodies. The IASB's main objective is to achieve international convergence with its standards. In other words, the efforts of the IASB are directed toward developing a high-quality set of standards for use internationally for financial reporting purposes (global standard-setting).[4]

HARMONIZATION EFFORTS

Several international organizations were involved in harmonization efforts either regionally (such as the Association of Southeast Asian Nations) or worldwide (such as the United Nations). The two most important players in this effort were the European Union (regionally) and the International Accounting Standards Committee (globally). The International Organization of Securities Commissions, the International Federation of Accountants, and the International Forum of Accountancy Development also have contributed to the harmonization efforts at the global level.

International Organization of Securities Commissions

Established in 1974, the International Organization of Securities Commissions (IOSCO) was initially limited to providing a *framework* in which securities regulatory agencies in the Americas could exchange information, and providing advice and assistance to those agencies supervising emerging markets. In 1986, IOSCO opened its membership to regulatory agencies in other parts of the world, thus giving it the potential to become a truly international organization. Today, IOSCO is the leading organization for securities regulators around the world, with about 177 ordinary, associate, and affiliate members (including the U.S. Securities and Exchange Commission) from about 100 countries.

IOSCO aims, among other things, to ensure a better regulation of the markets on both the domestic and international levels. It provides assistance to ensure the integrity of the markets by a rigorous application of the standards and by effective enforcement.

As one of its objectives, IOSCO works to facilitate cross-border securities offerings and listings by multinational issuers. It has consistently advocated the adoption of a set of high-quality accounting standards for cross-border listings. For example, a 1989 IOSCO report entitled "International Equity Offers" noted that cross-border offerings would be greatly facilitated by the development of internationally accepted accounting standards.[5] To this end, IOSCO supported the efforts of the International Accounting Standards Committee (IASC) in developing international accounting standards that foreign issuers could use in lieu of local accounting standards when entering capital markets outside of their home country. As one observer notes: "This could mean, for example, that if a French company had a simultaneous stock offering in the United States, Canada, and Japan, financial statements prepared in accordance with international standards could be used in all three nations."[6]

[4] G. Whittington, "The Adoption of International Accounting Standards in the European Union," *European Accounting Review* 14, no.1 (2005), pp. 127–53.

[5] This report is available from IOSCO's Web site, www.iosco.org.

[6] Stephen H. Collins, "The SEC on Full and Fair Disclosure," *Journal of Accountancy*, January 1989, p. 84.

International Federation of Accountants

The International Federation of Accountants (IFAC) was established in October 1977 at the 11th World Congress of Accountants in Munich, with 63 founding members representing 51 countries. It is now a global organization of 158 member bodies and associates in 123 countries, representing over 2.5 million accountants employed in public practice, industry and commerce, government, and academia. Its mission is to serve the public interest and to strengthen the worldwide accountancy profession and contribute to the development of strong international economies by establishing and promoting adherence to high-quality professional standards on auditing, ethics, education, and training.

In June 1999, IFAC launched the International Forum on Accountancy Development (IFAD) in response to a criticism from the World Bank (following the Asian financial crisis) that the accounting profession was not doing enough to enhance the accounting capacity and capabilities in developing and emerging nations. IFAD's membership includes the international financial institutions (such as the World Bank, International Monetary Fund, and Asian Development Bank); other key international organizations (such as IOSCO, IASB, and SEC); and the large accountancy firms.[7] The primary aim of this forum is to promote transparent financial reporting, duly audited to high standards by a strong accounting and auditing profession.

In May 2000, IFAC and the large international accounting firms established the Forum of Firms, also aimed at raising standards of financial reporting and auditing globally in order to protect the interests of cross-border investors and promote international flows of capital. The forum works alongside IFAD in achieving common objectives.

European Union

The European Union (EU) was founded in March 1957 with the signing of the Treaty of Rome by six European nations: Belgium, France, Germany, Italy, Luxembourg, and the Netherlands.[8] Between 1973 and 1995, nine other countries joined the common market (Denmark, Ireland, and the United Kingdom in 1973; Greece in 1981; Portugal and Spain in 1986; and Austria, Finland, and Sweden in January 1995), creating a 15-nation trading bloc. Another 10 new members (namely, Latvia, Estonia, Lithuania, Poland, Hungary, Czech Republic, Slovakia, Slovenia, and the Mediterranean islands of Cyprus and Malta) joined the EU in May 2004. In addition, Bulgaria and Romania joined in 2007, and Croatia in 2013, for a total of 28 countries. Until May 2004 all EU countries possessed similar traits in many respects. They all were wealthy industrial nations with similar political goals, comparable standards of living, high volumes of trade within the union, and good transportation links. The 2004 additions to EU membership are likely to change the dynamics of the group, especially considering that 8 of the 10 new entrants were members of the former Soviet bloc.

The European Commission is responsible for administering the EU. From the beginning, the EU's aim has been to create a unified business environment. Accordingly, the harmonization of company laws and taxation, the promotion of full freedom in the movement of goods and labor between member countries, and the

---

[7] Details at www.ifad.org.

[8] The original European Economic Community (EEC) became the European Union (EU) on January 1, 1994.

creation of a community capital market have been high on its agenda. In July 2002, most EU members adopted a single currency, the euro, as envisaged in the Treaty of Maastricht signed in 1991.[9]

The EU attempted to harmonize financial reporting practices within the community by issuing directives that member nations had to incorporate into their laws. EU directives possess the force of law.[10] They were binding on EU members with respect to the results to be achieved, but the manner in which the desired results were achieved was left to the discretion of the individual countries.

Two directives aimed at harmonizing accounting: the Fourth Directive (issued in 1978) dealt with valuation rules, disclosure requirements, and the format of financial statements, and the Seventh Directive (issued in 1983) dealt with consolidated financial statements. The latter required companies to prepare consolidated financial statements and outlined the procedures for their preparation. It had a significant impact on European accounting, as consolidations were previously uncommon in Continental Europe.

The Fourth Directive included comprehensive accounting rules covering the content of annual financial statements, their methods of presentation, and measurement and disclosure of information for both public and private companies. It established the "true and fair view" principle, which required financial statements to provide a true and fair view of a company's assets and liabilities, and of its financial position and profit and loss for the benefit of shareholders and third parties.

The Fourth Directive provided considerable flexibility. Dozens of provisions beginning with the expression "Member states may require or permit companies to…" allowed countries to choose from among acceptable alternatives. For example, under Dutch and British law, companies could write assets up to higher market values, whereas in Germany this was strictly forbidden. Both approaches were acceptable under the Fourth Directive. By allowing different options for a variety of accounting issues, the EU directives opened the door for noncomparability in financial statements. As an illustration of the effects of differing principles within the EU, the profits of one case study company were measured using the accounting principles of various member states. The results, presented in the following table, reveal the lack of comparability:[11]

Most Likely Profit—Case Study Company	
Country	ECUs (millions)
Spain	131
Germany	133
Belgium	135
Netherlands	140
France	149
Italy	174
United Kingdom	192

[9] Several EU members—namely, Denmark, Sweden, and the United Kingdom—have not adopted the euro as their national currency.

[10] The EU has issued numerous directives covering a broad range of business issues, including directives related to accounting, auditing, taxation, e-commerce, and the prevention of money laundering.

[11] Anthony Carey, "Harmonization: Europe Moves Forward," *Accountancy,* March 1990.

Profit measurement across EU countries differed in part because the directives failed to cover several important topics, including lease accounting, foreign currency translation, accounting changes, contingencies, income taxes, and long-term construction contracts.

Notwithstanding the flexibility afforded by the directives, their implementation into local law caused extensive change in accounting practice in several EU member countries. The following are some of the changes in German accounting practice brought about by the integration of the EU's Fourth and Seventh Directives into German law in 1985:

1. Required inclusion of notes to the financial statements.
2. Preparation of consolidated financial statements on a worldwide basis (i.e., foreign subsidiaries no longer could be excluded from consolidation).
3. Elimination of unrealized intercompany losses on consolidation.
4. Use of the equity method for investments in associated companies.
5. Disclosure of comparative figures in the balance sheet and income statement.
6. Disclosure of liabilities with a maturity of less than one year.
7. Accrual of deferred tax liabilities and pension obligations.[12]

Most of these "innovations" had been common practice in the United States for several decades.

Although the EU directives did not lead to complete comparability across member nations, they helped reduce differences in financial statements. In addition, the EU directives have served as a basic framework of accounting that has been adopted by other countries in search of an accounting model. With the economic reforms in Eastern Europe since 1989, several countries in that region found it necessary to abandon the Soviet-style accounting system previously used in favor of a Western, market-oriented system. For example, in the early 1990s, Hungary, Poland, and the Czech and Slovak Republics all passed new accounting laws primarily based on the EU directives in anticipation of securing EU membership. This is further evidence of the influence that economic ties among countries can have on accounting practice.

In 1990, the European Commission indicated that there would be no further EU directives related to accounting. Instead, the commission indicated in 1995 that it would associate the EU with efforts undertaken by the IASC toward a broader international harmonization of accounting standards. In June 2000, the European Commission issued the following communication to the European Parliament:

- Before the end of 2000, the Commission will present a formal proposal requiring all listed EU companies to prepare their consolidated accounts in accordance with one single set of accounting standards, namely International Accounting Standards (IAS).
- This requirement will go into effect, at the latest, from 2005 onwards.
- Member states will be allowed to extend the application of IAS to unlisted companies and to individual accounts.[13]

---

[12] Timothy S. Doupnik, "Recent Innovations in German Accounting Practice Through the Integration of EC Directives," *Advances in International Accounting* 5 (1992), pp. 75–103.

[13] Commission of the European Communities, "EU Financial Reporting Strategy: The Way Forward," Communication from the Commission to the Council and the European Parliament, June 13, 2000.

The International Forum on Accountancy Development (IFAD)

IFAD was created as a working group between the Basel Committee, the IFAC, IOSCO, the large accounting firms, OECD, UNCTAD, and the World Bank and regional development banks, which flowed from the East Asian crisis in the late 1990s. Its mission was to improve market security and transparency and financial stability on a global basis. The objectives of IFAD were to promote understanding by national governments of the value of transparent financial reporting, in accordance with sound corporate governance; assist in defining expectations as to how the accountancy profession (in both the public and private sectors) should carry out its responsibilities to support the public interest; encourage governments to focus more directly on the needs of developing countries (including economies in transition); help harness funds and expertise to build accounting and auditing capacity in developing countries; contribute to a common strategy and framework of reference for accountancy development; and promote cooperation among governments, the accountancy and other professions, the international financial institutions, regulators, standard-setters, capital providers, and issuers.

IFAD promoted the view that the national accounting standards of most countries should be raised, with the IAS as the benchmark. IFAD completed its work with the publication of *GAAP Convergence 2002*.

The International Accounting Standards Committee (IASC)

IASC was established in 1973 by an agreement of the leading professional accounting bodies in 10 countries (Australia, Canada, France, Germany, Ireland, Japan, Mexico, the Netherlands, the United Kingdom, and the United States) with the broad objective of formulating "international accounting standards." Prior to its dissolution, the IASC consisted of 156 professional accountancy bodies in 114 countries, representing more than 2 million accountants in public practice, education, government service, industry, and commerce. The IASC was funded by contributions from member bodies, multinational companies, financial institutions, accounting firms, and the sale of IASC publications.

The "Lowest-Common-Denominator" Approach

The IASC's harmonization efforts from 1973 to 2001 evolved in several different phases. In the initial phase, covering the first 15 years, the IASC's main activity was the issuance of 26 generic International Accounting Standards (IASs), many of which allowed multiple options. The IASC's approach to standard-setting during this phase can be described as a lowest-common-denominator approach, as the standards reflected an effort to accommodate existing accounting practices in various countries. For example, International Accounting Standard (IAS) 11, *Construction Contracts*, as originally written in 1979, allowed companies to choose between the percentage-of-completion method and the completed contract method in accounting for long-term construction contracts, effectively sanctioning the two major methods used internationally. A study conducted by the IASB in 1988 found that all or most of the companies listed on the stock exchanges of the countries included in Nobes's classification presented in Chapter 2 of this book (except for Germany and Italy) were in compliance with the International Accounting Standards.[14] Given the lowest-common-denominator approach adopted by the IASC, it was obvious that IASC standards existing in 1988 introduced little if any comparability of financial statements across countries.

[14] International Accounting Standards Committee, *Survey of the Use and Application of International Accounting Standards 1988* (London: IASC, 1988).

The Comparability Project

Two significant activities took place from 1989 to 1993, which can be described as the IASC's second phase. The first was the 1989 publication of the *Framework for the Preparation and Presentation of Financial Statements* (hereafter referred to as the *Framework*), which set out the objectives of financial statements, the qualitative characteristics of financial information, definitions of the elements of financial statements, and the criteria for recognition of financial statement elements. The second activity was the Comparability of Financial Statements Project, the purpose of which was "to eliminate most of the choices of accounting treatment currently permitted under International Accounting Standards."[15] As a result of the Comparability Project, 10 revised International Accounting Standards were approved in 1993 and became effective in 1995. As an example of the changes brought about by the Comparability Project, IAS 11 was revised to require the use of the percentage-of-completion method when certain criteria are met, thereby removing the option to avoid the use of this method altogether.

The IOSCO Agreement

The final phase in the work of the IASC began with the IOSCO agreement in 1993 and ended with the creation of the IASB in 2001. The main activity during this phase was the development of a core set of international standards that could be endorsed by IOSCO for cross-listing purposes. This period also was marked by the proposal to restructure the IASC and the proposal's final approval.

IOSCO became a member of the IASC's Consultative Group in 1987 and supported the IASC's Comparability Project. In 1993, IOSCO and the IASC agreed on a list of 30 core standards that the IASC needed to develop that could be used by companies involved in cross-border security offerings and listings. In 1995, the IASC and IOSCO agreed on a work program for the IASC to develop the set of core international standards, and IOSCO agreed to evaluate the standards for possible endorsement for cross-border purposes upon their completion.

With the publication of IAS 39, *Financial Instruments: Recognition and Measurement*, in December 1998, the IASC completed its work program to develop the set of 30 core standards. In May 2000, IOSCO's Technical Committee recommended that securities regulators permit foreign issuers to use the core IASC standards to gain access to a country's capital market as an alternative to using local standards. The Technical Committee consisted of securities regulators representing the 14 largest and most developed capital markets, including Australia, France, Germany, Japan, the United Kingdom, and the United States. IOSCO's endorsement of IASC standards was an important step in the harmonization process.[16]

U.S. Reaction to International Accounting Standards

Of the 14 countries represented on IOSCO's Technical Committee, only Canada and the United States did not allow foreign companies to use International Accounting Standards (IASs) without reconciliation to local GAAP for listing purposes.[17] In 1996, the U.S. Securities and Exchange Commission (SEC) announced

---

[15] International Accounting Standards Committee, *International Accounting Standards 1990* (London: IASC, 1990), p. 13.

[16] IOSCO, *Final Communique of the XXIXth Annual Conference of the International Organization of Securities Commissions*, Amman, May 17–20, 2004.

[17] The SEC allows foreign companies listed on U.S. stock exchanges to file annual reports based on IAS, but only if a reconciliation from IAS to U.S. GAAP for income and stockholders' equity is included in the notes to the financial statements. Many foreign companies find this reconciliation to be very costly and view this requirement as a significant barrier to entering the U.S. capital market.

three criteria IASs would have to meet to be acceptable for cross-listing purposes. Namely, IASs would have to:

- Constitute a comprehensive, generally accepted basis of accounting.
- Be of high quality, resulting in comparability and transparency, and providing for full disclosure.
- Be rigorously interpreted and applied.

Partly in response to the third criterion, the IASC created a Standing Interpretations Committee (SIC) to provide guidance on accounting issues where there is likely to be divergent or unacceptable treatment in the absence of specific guidance in an International Accounting Standard.

The SEC began its assessment of the IASC's core set of standards in 1999 and issued a concept release in 2000 soliciting comments on whether it should modify its requirement that all financial statements be reconciled to U.S. GAAP.

The FASB conducted a comparison of IASC standards and U.S. GAAP in 1996, identifying 218 items covered by both sets of standards.[18] The following table lists the degree of similarity across these items:

	Number	Percent
Similar approach and guidance	56	26%
Similar approach but different guidance	79	36
Different approach	56	26
Alternative approaches permitted	27	12
	218	100%

Although it was widely assumed that U.S. GAAP and IASs were generally consistent, the FASB's comparison showed that differences existed for 74 percent of the accounting items covered by both sets of standards.

Compliance with International Accounting Standards

Several studies investigated the extent of compliance by those firms that claimed to follow International Accounting Standards.[19] These studies found various levels of noncompliance with IAS.[20] Former IASC Secretary-General David Cairns referred to the use of IAS with exceptions as "IAS-lite."[21] In response to the use of "IAS-lite," IAS 1 was revised in 1997 to preclude a firm from claiming to be in compliance with IAS unless it complies with all requirements (including disclosure

[18] Financial Accounting Standards Board, *The IASC-U.S. Comparison Project: A Report on the Similarities and Differences between IASC Standards and U.S. GAAP*, ed. Carrie Bloomer (Norwalk, CT: FASB, 1996).

[19] See, for example, Donna L. Street, Sidney J. Gray, and Stephanie M. Bryant, "Acceptance and Observance of International Accounting Standards: An Empirical Study of Companies Claiming to Comply with IASs," *The International Journal of Accounting* 34, no. 1 (1999), pp. 11–48; and David Cairns, *Financial Times International Accounting Standards Survey* (London: FT Finance, 1999).

[20] Apparently concerned with the lack of full compliance with IFRS, one of the SEC's major requirements to allow foreign registrants to use IFRS without reconciliation to U.S. GAAP is the existence of "an infrastructure that ensures that the standards are rigorously interpreted and applied," SEC Concept Release: International Accounting Standards (2000).

[21] David Cairns, "IAS Lite Is Alive and Well," *Accountancy*, May 2001. Cairns identifies three types of IAS lite: (1) disclosed IAS lite, where companies disclose exceptions from full IAS compliance; (2) implied IAS lite, where companies refer to the use of rather than compliance with IAS; and (3) undisclosed IAS lite, where companies claim to comply with IAS but fail to comply fully with it.

requirements) of each standard and each applicable Interpretation. A number of firms that previously disclosed in the annual report their use of IAS "with exceptions" discontinued this disclosure subsequent to this revision to IAS 1.

In its accounting policies note to its 1998 financial statements, the French firm Thomson-CSF stated:

> In a February 1998 recommendation, the C.O.B. (the French Securities Regulator) observed that for operating periods starting as from July 1, 1998, a company could no longer state that it complied with the International Accounting Standards Committee (I.A.S.C.) reference system, if it did not apply all I.A.S.C. standards currently in force. Consequently, as from the 1998 operating period, the consolidated financial statements of Thomson-CSF, prepared in accordance with accounting principles applicable in France, as also the provisions of the 7th European Directive, no longer refer to the I.A.S.C. standards. (p. 82)

Prior to 1998, Thomson-CSF claimed to follow IAS when it apparently did not. From the excerpt above, it appears that Thomson-CSF elected not to fully comply with IAS and in 1998 no longer claimed to do so as required by the French Securities Regulator. Because the IASC itself did not have the power to enforce it, IAS 1 had to be enforced by national securities regulators and auditors.

Challenges to the IASC

- During the 1970s and 1980s, the UN and the OECD were concerned that the IASC lacked legitimacy because it was created by the accounting profession (private sector), with its self-interests.
- The IASC also faced problems of legitimacy with regard to constituent support, independence, and technical expertise. For example, some interested parties perceived the fact that IASC board members worked at international standard-setting only part-time and were not necessarily selected because of their technical expertise as an indication of a lack of commitment on the part of the IASC to develop i the highest-quality standards possible.
- The IFAC, arguing on the issue of who should control the international standard-setting, tried unsuccessfully on two occasions during the 1980s to bring the IASC under its control.
- In 1993–94, standard setters from the United Kingdom, the United States, Canada, and Australia began meeting quarterly to discuss issues related to international standard-setting. The group came to be known as the G4+1, the 1 being a representative, usually the secretary-general of the IASC, who attended as an observer.

CREATION OF THE IASB

Responding to these challenges, the IASC appointed a Strategy Working Party in 1996, which issued a discussion document in December 1998 entitled "Shaping IASC for the Future." This document proposed a vastly different structure and process for the development of international accounting standards.

The final recommendations of the IASC Strategy Working Party were approved at its Venice meeting in November 1999. These recommendations, designed to deal with the issue of legitimacy, attempted to balance calls for a structure based on geographic representativeness and those based on technical competence and independence. Accordingly, it was decided that representativeness would be provided by the geographic distribution of the trustees, who would be essential to ensuring the effectiveness and independence of the board, but that board members would be selected based on their expertise.

On April 1, 2001, the newly created International Accounting Standards Board (IASB) took over from the IASC as the creator of international accounting standards, which were to be called International Financial Reporting Standards (IFRS). The process of restructuring the IASC into the IASB took over five years and is summarized in Exhibit 3.1. The formation of the IASB in 2001, with a change in focus from harmonization to convergence or global standard-setting, marked the beginning of a new era in international financial reporting.

EXHIBIT 3.1
The Process of Restructuring the IASC into the IASB

Date	Activity
September 1996	IASC board approves formation of a Strategy Working Party (SWP) to consider what IASC's strategy and structure should be when it completes the Core Standards work program.
December 1998	SWP publishes a discussion paper, "Shaping IASC for the Future," and invites comments.
April to October 1999	SWP holds various meetings to discuss the comments on their initial proposal and to develop final recommendations.
December 1999	SWP issues final report, *Recommendations on Shaping IASC for the Future*. IASC board passes a resolution supporting the report and appoints a nominating committee for the initial trustees.
January 2000	Nominating committee elects SEC chairman Arthur Levitt as its chair and invites nominations from public.
March 2000	IASC board approves a new constitution reflecting the SWP proposals.
May 2000	Nominating committee announces initial trustees.
May 2000	IASC member bodies approve the restructuring and the new IASC constitution.
June 2000	Trustees appoint Sir David Tweedie as the first chairman of new IASC board.
July 1, 2000	New IASC constitution takes effect.
Starting in July 2000	Trustees invite nominations for membership on the new IASC board, narrow the list to approximately 45 finalists, and conduct interviews in London, New York, and Tokyo.
January 2001	Trustees invite nominations for membership on the new advisory council.
January 2001	Members of the IASB announced.
March 2001	IASC trustees activate Part B of IASC's constitution and establish a nonprofit Delaware corporation, named the International Accounting Standards Committee Foundation, to oversee the International Accounting Standards Board.
April 2001	On April 1, 2001, the new IASB takes over from the IASC the responsibility for setting International Accounting Standards.

EXHIBIT 3.2
The Structure of the
IASB

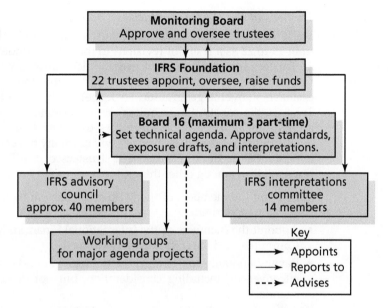

The Structure of the IASB

The IASB is organized under an independent foundation called the IFRS Foundation. Components of the structure are as follows (Exhibit 3.2) (the titles of some of the components are as changed on March 31, 2010):

1. International Accounting Standards Board (IASB).
2. IFRS Foundation (IFRSF).
3. Monitoring Board.
4. IFRS Interpretations Committee (IFRSIC).
5. IFRS Advisory Council (IFRSAC).
6. Working Groups (expert task forces for individual agenda projects).

Monitoring Board

The IASC Foundation Constitution was amended in February 2009 to create a Monitoring Board of public authorities. The Monitoring Board comprises the relevant leaders of the European Commission, the Japanese Financial Services Agency, the U.S. Securities and Exchange Commission, the Emerging Markets Committee of IOSCO, and the Technical Committee of IOSCO. The chairman of the Basel Committee on Banking Supervision is a nonvoting observer. The Monitoring Board oversees the IFRS Foundation Trustees, participates in the Trustee nomination process, and approves appointments to the Trustees. The specific functions of the Monitoring Board include the following:

- To enhance public accountability of the IASC Foundation.
- To participates in the Trustee nomination process and approval of appointments to the Trustees.
- To carry out oversight responsibilities in relation to the Trustees and their oversight of the IASB's activities, in particular the agenda-setting process and the IASB's efforts to improve the accuracy and effectiveness of financial reporting and to protect investors.

Trustees of the IFRS Foundation

The IFRS Foundation consists of 22 Trustees (the number of trustees was increased from 19 to 22 as a result of revisions to the IFRS Foundation in June 2005). These 22 Trustees represent different geographical areas (six from North America; six from Europe; six from the Asia/Oceania region; four from any area, subject to establishing overall geographical balance). With regard to the composition of the Trustees, the constitution requires an appropriate balance of professional backgrounds, including auditors, preparers, users, academics, and other officials serving the public interest. Two Trustees will normally be senior partners of prominent international accounting firms. The Trustees of the IFRS Foundation have the responsibility, among other things, to:

- Appoint the members of the IASB and establish their contracts of service and performance criteria.
- Appoint the members of the International Financial Reporting Interpretations Committee and the IFRS Advisory Council.
- Review annually the strategy of the IASC Foundation and the IASB and its effectiveness, including consideration, but not determination, of the IASB's agenda.
- Approve annually the budget of the IFRS Foundation and determine the basis for funding.
- Review broad strategic issues affecting accounting standards, promote the IASC Foundation and its work, and promote the objective of rigorous application of International Accounting Standards and International Financial Reporting Standards—provided that the Trustees shall be excluded from involvement in technical matters relating to accounting standards.
- Establish and amend operating procedures, consultative arrangements, and due process for the IASB, the International Financial Reporting Interpretations Committee, and the Standards Advisory Council.
- Review compliance with the operating procedures, consultative arrangements, and due process procedures.
- Approve amendments to the constitution after following a due process, including consultation with the IFRS Advisory Council and publication of an Exposure Draft for public comment and subject to the voting requirements.
- Exercise all powers of the IFRS Foundation, except for those expressly reserved to the IASB, the IFRS Interpretations Committee, and the IFRS Advisory Council.
- Foster and review the development of educational program and materials that are consistent with the IFRS Foundation's objectives.

International Accounting Standards Board

The IASB has sole responsibility for establishing International Financial Reporting Standards (IFRS).

The principal responsibilities of the IASB are to:

- Develop and issue International Financial Reporting Standards and Exposure Drafts.
- Approve Interpretations developed by the International Financial Reporting Interpretations Committee (IFRIC).

The Board consists of 16 members (effective February 1, 2009), of whom at least 13 serve full-time and not more than 3 part-time.

The Board members are selected on the basis of professional competence and practical experience. They are expected to represent a geographical mix, and to ensure a broad international diversity. Since July 2012, the composition of the board has been:

- Four members from the Asia/Oceania region.
- Four members from Europe.
- Four members from North America.
- One member from Africa.
- One member from South America.
- Two members appointed from any area, subject to maintaining overall geographical balance.

Due process procedures followed by the IASB include the following (the steps that are required by the IASC Foundation constitution are indicated by an asterisk*):

1. Ask the staff to identify and review the issues associated with the topic and to consider the application of the *Framework* to the issues.
2. Study national accounting requirements and practice and exchange views about the issues with national standard-setters.
3. Consult the Standards Advisory Council about the advisability of adding the topic to the IASB's agenda.*
4. Form an advisory group (generally called a "working group") to advise the IASB and its staff on the project.
5. Publish for public comment a discussion document.
6. Publish for public comment an Exposure Draft approved by the vote of at least nine IASB members, including any dissenting opinions held by IASB members (in Exposure Drafts, dissenting opinions are referred to as "alternative views").*
7. Publish within an Exposure Draft a basis for conclusions.
8. Consider all comments received within the comment period on discussion documents and Exposure Drafts.*
9. Consider the desirability of holding a public hearing and the desirability of conducting field tests and, if considered desirable, holding such hearings and conducting such tests.
10. Approve a standard by the votes of at least nine IASB members and include in the published standard any dissenting opinions.*
11. Publish within a standard a basis for conclusions, explaining, among other things, the steps in the IASB's due process and how the IASB dealt with public comments on the Exposure Draft.

In March 2006, the Trustees of the IFRS Foundation published a new *Due Process Handbook* for the IASB. The *Handbook* describes the IASB's consultative procedures.

IFRS Advisory Council

The IFRS Advisory Council provides a forum for participation by organizations and individuals with an interest in international financial reporting, having diverse geographical and functional backgrounds, with the objective of:

- Advising the IASB on agenda decisions and priorities in the IASB's work.
- Informing the IASB of the views of the organizations and individuals on the Council on major standard-setting projects.
- Giving other advice to the IASB or the Trustees.

The Advisory Council currently has about 40 members. The requirement is to have at least 30 members. Members are appointed by the Trustees for a renewable term of three years. They have diverse geographic and functional backgrounds.

IFRS Interpretations Committee

The IFRS Interpretations Committee (initially this committee was known as the Standing Interpretations Committee, and later changed to the International Financial Reporting Interpretations Committee) has 14 members appointed by the Trustees for terms of three years (in November 2007, the membership was increased from 12 to 14).

The Committee's responsibilities include the following:

- To interpret the application of International Financial Reporting Standards (IFRS) and provide timely guidance on financial reporting issues not specifically addressed in IFRS or IASs, in the context of the IASB's framework, and undertake other tasks at the request of the Board.
- To publish Draft Interpretations for public comment and consider comments made within a reasonable period before finalizing an Interpretation.
- To report to the Board and obtain Board approval for final Interpretations.

IFRS Foundation Constitution

In January 2009, the Trustees voted to revise the constitution for changes resulting from the first phase of the review, including formation of the Monitoring Board. In January 2010, the Trustees again voted to revise the constitution for changes resulting from the second phase of the review, including name changes from IASC Foundation to IFRS Foundation, from International Financial Reporting Interpretations Committee to IFRS Interpretations Committee, and from Standards Advisory Council to IFRS Advisory Council.

Review of the IASC Foundation's Constitution

The IASC Foundation's constitution states that the Trustees should undertake:

> [A] review of the entire structure of the IASC Foundation and its effectiveness, such review to include consideration of changing the geographical distribution of Trustees in response to changing global economic conditions, and publishing the proposals of that review for public comment, the review commencing three years after the coming into force of this Constitution, with the objective of implementing any agreed changes five years after the coming into force of this Constitution (6 February 2006, five years after the date of the incorporation of the IASC Foundation [Section 18 (b)]).

Consistent with Section 18 of the constitution, the IASC Foundation's Constitution Committee initiated in May 2004 a broad review of the constitution and identified 10 issues for consideration. These issues are based on the concerns expressed by important constituencies through various processes of consultation. They are as follows:

1. Whether the objectives of the IASC Foundation should expressly refer to the challenges facing small and medium-sized entities (SMEs). (*Concern:* The

language of the constitution does not adequately address the position of SMEs and emerging economies.)

2. Number of Trustees and their geographical and professional distribution. (*Concern:* Certain regions are overrepresented, while the Asia-Oceania region as well as emerging economies are underrepresented.)

3. The oversight role of the Trustees. (*Concern:* Trustees should demonstrate more clearly how they are fulfilling the oversight function.)

4. Funding of the IASC Foundation. (*Concern:* The funding structure of the IASC Foundation needs to be examined.)

5. The composition of the IASB. (*Concern:* The geographic backgrounds of the IASB members need to be examined.)

6. The appropriateness of the IASB's existing formal liaison relationships. (*Concern:* More guidance is needed in the constitution regarding the role that liaison relationships play.)

7. Consultation arrangements of the IASB. (*Concern:* Consultative arrangements need to be improved.)

8. Voting procedures of the IASB. (*Concern:* For approval of a standard, the current "simple majority" approach should be replaced with a "super majority" approach.)

9. Resources and effectiveness of the International Financial Reporting Interpretations Committee (IFRIC). (*Concern:* Given the likely increase in demand for IFRIC interpretations, the current arrangements are inadequate.)

10. The composition, role, and effectiveness of the SAC. (*Concern:* Steps should be taken to make better use of the SAC.)

A proposal published by the Trustees of the IFRS Foundation builds on governance enhancements implemented as a result of the first Constitution Review, completed in 2005 (these reviews will take place every five years). For example, in 2005, the IASC Foundation's Trustees changed the most important criterion for IASB membership from "technical expertise" to "professional competence and practical experience." Indeed, Hans Hoogervorst, who succeeded David Tweedie as IASB chairman in July 2011, was the immediate past chairman of the Dutch securities regulator, and he did not have an accounting background. The Trustees published a report on the changes to the Foundation's constitution made as a result of the second part of their 2008–2010 constitution review. They have launched a program to enhance investors' participation in the development of IFRS. In early 2009, the Trustees revised the constitution to increase the number of Board members from 14 to 16 and specified geographical quotas for membership: four from North America, four from Europe, four from Asia/Oceania, one from South America, one from Africa, and two to achieve geographical balance. Further, as many as three of the 16 members may be part-timers. Further, in response to the criticism that the IASB is a private-sector standard-setter and is not likely to act in the public interest, the Trustees created a Monitoring Board, which consisted of leading figures from regulators in the world (namely, representatives of the SEC, Japan's Financial Services Agency, the European Commission, and the Emerging Markets and Technical Committees of IOSCO) with the functions of overseeing the standard-setting activities of the IASB and approving the appointment of Trustees. One of the proposals could see the IASB become the IFRS Board (or IFRSB) in the future.

ARGUMENTS FOR AND AGAINST INTERNATIONAL CONVERGENCE OF FINANCIAL REPORTING STANDARDS

Arguments for Convergence

Proponents of accounting convergence put forward several arguments. First, they argue that comparability of financial statements worldwide is necessary for the globalization of capital markets. Financial statement comparability would make it easier for investors to evaluate potential investments in foreign securities and thereby take advantage of the risk reduction possible through international diversification. Second, it would simplify the evaluation by multinational companies of possible foreign takeover targets. Third, convergence would reduce financial reporting costs for companies that seek to list their shares on foreign stock exchanges. Cross-listing of securities would allow companies to gain access to less expensive capital in other countries and would make it easier for foreign investors to acquire the company's stock. Fourth, national differences in corporate reporting cause loss of investor confidence, which affects the availability and cost of capital. Investors often build in a premium to the required return on their investment if there is any uncertainty or lack of comparability about the figures—such premiums can be as large as 40 percent.[22] Fifth, one set of universally accepted accounting standards would reduce the cost of preparing worldwide consolidated financial statements, and the auditing of these statements also would be simplified. Sixth, multinational companies would find it easier to transfer accounting staff to other countries. This would be true for the international auditing firms as well. Finally, convergence would help raise the quality level of accounting practices internationally, thereby increasing the credibility of financial information. In relation to this argument, some point out that as a result of convergence, developing countries would be able to adopt a ready-made set of high-quality standards with minimum cost and effort.

Arguments against Convergence

The greatest obstacle to convergence is the magnitude of the differences that exist between countries and the fact that the political cost of eliminating those differences would be enormous. One of the main obstacles is nationalism. Whether out of deep-seated tradition, indifference born of economic power, or resistance to intrusion of foreign influence, some say that national entities will not bow to any international body. Arriving at principles that satisfy all of the parties involved throughout the world seems an almost impossible task. Not only is convergence difficult to achieve, but the need for such standards is not universally accepted. A well-developed global capital market exists already. It has evolved without uniform accounting standards. Opponents of convergence argue that it is unnecessary to force all companies worldwide to follow a common set of rules. They also point out that this would lead to a situation of "standards overload" as a result of requiring some enterprises to comply with a set of standards not relevant to them. The international capital market will force those companies that can benefit from accessing the market to provide the required accounting information without convergence. Yet another argument against convergence is that because of different

[22] David Illigworth, President of the Institute of Chartered Accountants in England and Wales, in a speech at the China Economic Summit 2004 of the 7th China Beijing International High-Tech Expo, May 21, 2004.

environmental influences, differences in accounting across countries might be appropriate and necessary. For example, countries that are at different stages of economic development or that rely on different sources of financing perhaps should have differently oriented accounting systems. Professor Frederick Choi refers to this as the dilemma of global harmonization: "The thesis of environmentally stimulated and justified differences in accounting runs directly counter to efforts at the worldwide harmonization of accounting. Hence, the dilemma." This applies equally to the idea of convergence.

A PRINCIPLES-BASED APPROACH TO INTERNATIONAL FINANCIAL REPORTING STANDARDS

The IASB uses a principles-based approach in developing accounting standards, rather than a rules-based approach. Principles-based standards focus on establishing general principles derived from the IASB *Framework*, providing recognition, measurement, and reporting requirements for the transactions covered by the standard. By following this approach, IFRS tend to limit guidance for applying the general principles to typical transactions and encourage professional judgment in applying the general principles to transactions specific to an entity or industry. Sir David Tweedie, IASB chairman, explained the principles-based approach taken by the IASB as follows:

> The IASB concluded that a body of detailed guidance (sometimes referred to as *brightlines*) encourages a rule-based mentality of "where does it say I can't do this?" We take the view that this is counter-productive and helps those who are intent on finding ways around standards more than it helps those seeking to apply standards in a way that gives useful information. Put simply, adding the detailed guidance may obscure, rather than highlight, the underlying principles. The emphasis tends to be on compliance with the letter of the rule rather than on the spirit of the accounting standard. We prefer an approach that requires the company and its auditors to take a step back and consider with the underlying principles. This is not a soft option. Our approach requires both companies and their auditors to exercise professional judgement in the public interest. Our approach requires a strong commitment from preparers to financial statements that provide a faithful representation of all transactions and strong commitment from auditors to resist client pressures. It will not work without those commitments. There will be more individual transactions and situations that are not explicitly addressed. We hope that a clear statement of the underlying principles will allow companies and auditors to deal with those situations without resorting to detailed rules.[23]

A report published by the Institute of Chartered Accountants in Scotland in early 2006 stated that rules-based accounting adds unnecessary complexity, encourages financial engineering, and does not necessarily lead to a true and fair view or a fair presentation. Further, it pointed out that the volume of rules would hinder the translation into different languages and cultures. The Global Accounting Alliance (GAA- This was formed in November 2005 and is an alliance of 11 leading professional accounting bodies in U.S., U.K., Canada, Hong Kong, Australia, Germany, Japan, New Zealand and South Africa. Its objective is to promote quality services, share information and collaborate on important international iussues.) supports a single set of globally accepted and principles-based accounting standards that focus on transparency and capital market needs and would be

---

[23] Excerpt from a speech delivered before the Committee on Banking, Housing and Urban Affairs of the United States Senate, Washington, DC, February 14, 2002.

ideal for all stakeholders. In February 2010, the IOSCO, in a report entitled "Principles for Periodic Disclosure by Listed Entities," provided securities regulators with a framework for establishing or reviewing their periodic disclosure regimes. According to the report, its principles-based format allows for a wide range of application and adaptation by securities regulators.

THE IASB FRAMEWORK

The Need for a Framework

With no conceptual framework, accounting standards would be developed unsystematically. As a result, accounting standards may be inconsistent and, according to *Gresham's law*,[24] bad accounting practices will triumph over good practices. In this situation, a principle or practice would be declared to be "right" because it was generally accepted, but it would not be generally accepted because it was "right." Further, it is unwise to develop standards unless there is agreement on the scope and objective of financial reporting, the type of entities that should produce financial reports, recognition and measurement rules, and qualitative characteristics of financial information. Furthermore, by adding rigor and discipline, a conceptual framework enhances public confidence in financial reports, and preparers and auditors can use the conceptual framework as a point of reference to resolve an accounting issue in the absence of a standard that specifically deals with that issue.

The *Framework for the Preparation and Presentation of Financial Statements* was first approved by the IASC board in 1989 and was reaffirmed by the newly formed IASB in 2001. The objective of the *Framework* is to establish the concepts underlying the preparation and presentation of IFRS-based financial statements. It deals with the following:

1. Objective of financial statements and underlying assumptions.
2. Qualitative characteristics that affect the usefulness of financial statements.
3. Definition, recognition, and measurement of the financial statements elements.
4. Concepts of capital and capital maintenance.

Among other things, the purpose of the *Framework* is to assist the IASB in developing future standards and revising existing standards. It also is intended to assist preparers of financial statements in applying IFRS and in dealing with topics that have not yet been addressed in IFRS. The *Framework* identifies investors, creditors, employees, suppliers, customers, government agencies, and the general public as potential users of financial statements but concludes that financial statements that are designed to meet the needs of investors will also meet most of the information needs of other users. This is an important conclusion because it sets the tone for the nature of individual IFRS, that is, that their application will result in a set of financial statements that is useful for making investment decisions.

Objective of Financial Statements and Underlying Assumptions

The *Framework* establishes that the primary objective of IFRS-based financial statements is to *provide information useful for decision making*. Financial statements also show the results of management's stewardship of enterprise resources, but that is not their primary objective. To meet the objective of decision usefulness, financial statements must be prepared on an *accrual basis*. The other underlying assumption is that the enterprise for which financial statements are being prepared is a *going concern*.

---

[24] Gresham's law is named after Sir Thomas Gresham (1519–1579), an English financier in Tudor times. It means, briefly, "Bad money drives out good."

Qualitative Characteristics of Financial Statements

The four characteristics that make financial statement information useful are *understandability, relevance, reliability,* and *comparability*. Information is relevant if it can be used to make predictions of the future or if it can be used to confirm expectations from the past. The *Framework* indicates that the relevance of information is affected by its nature and its materiality. An item of information is material if its misstatement or omission could influence the decision of a user of financial statements.

Information is reliable when it is neutral (i.e., free of bias) and represents faithfully what it purports to. The *Framework* specifically states that reflecting items in the financial statements based on their economic substance rather than their legal form is necessary for faithful representation. The *Framework* also states that while the exercise of prudence (conservatism) in measuring accounting elements is necessary, it does not allow the creation of hidden reserves or excessive provisions to deliberately understate income, as this would be biased and therefore would not have the quality of reliability.

Elements of Financial Statements: Definition, Recognition, and Measurement

Assets are defined as resources controlled by the enterprise from which future economic benefits are expected to flow to the enterprise. Note that a resource need not be owned to be an asset of an enterprise. This allows, for example, for leased resources to be treated as assets. An *asset should be recognized only when it is probable that future economic benefits will flow to the enterprise and the asset has a cost or value that can be measured reliably*. The *Framework* acknowledges that several different measurement bases may be used to measure assets, including historical cost, current cost, realizable value, and present value.

Liabilities are present obligations arising from past events that are expected to be settled through an outflow of resources. Obligations need not be contractual to be treated as a liability. Similar to assets, *liabilities should be recognized when it is probable that an outflow of resources will be required to settle them and the amount can be measured reliably*. Also as with assets, several different bases exist for measuring liabilities, including the amount of proceeds received in exchange for the obligation, the amount that would be required to settle the obligation currently, undiscounted settlement value in the normal course of business, and the present value of future cash outflows expected to settle the liabilities.

The *Framework* identifies income and expenses as the two elements that constitute profit. *Income,* which encompasses both revenues and gains, is defined as increases in equity other than from transactions with owners. *Expenses,* including losses, are decreases in equity other than through distributions to owners. *Equity* is defined as assets minus liabilities. Income should be recognized when the increase in an asset or decrease in a liability can be measured reliably. The *Framework* does not provide more specific guidance with respect to income recognition. (This topic is covered in IAS 18, *Revenue.*) Expenses are recognized when the related decrease in assets or increase in liabilities can be measured reliably. The *Framework* acknowledges the use of the matching principle in recognizing liabilities but specifically precludes use of the matching principle to recognize expenses and a related liability when it does not meet the definition of a liability. For example, it is inappropriate to recognize an expense if a present obligation arising from a past event does not exist.

Concepts of Capital Maintenance

The *Framework* describes different concepts of capital maintenance (financial capital maintenance versus physical capital maintenance) and acknowledges that each leads to a different basis for measuring assets (historical cost versus current cost). The *Framework* does not prescribe one measurement basis (and related model of accounting) over another, but indicates that it (the *Framework*) is applicable to a range of accounting models.

The IASB *Framework* is similar in content and direction to the FASB's *Conceptual Framework* embodied in *Statements of Financial Accounting Concepts 1, 2, 5,* and *6.* However, the IASB *Framework* is considerably less detailed.

INTERNATIONAL FINANCIAL REPORTING STANDARDS

As of July 2013, 41 International Accounting Standards (IAS) and 13 International Financial Reporting Standards (IFRS) had been issued (see Exhibit 3.3). Several IASs have been revised one or more times since original issuance. For example, IAS 21, *The Effects of Changes in Foreign Exchange Rates,* was originally issued in 1983 and then revised as part of the comparability project in 1993. This standard was again updated in 2003 as part of the improvements project undertaken by the IASB that resulted in revisions to 13 IASs. A minor amendment to the standard was issued in 2005, and it was amended again in 2007 as a result of the revision to IAS 1 that resulted in amendments to 23 IASs. Other IASs have been withdrawn or replaced by later standards. Of 41 IASs issued by the IASC, only 30 were still in force as of July 2013. The first IFRS was issued by the IASB in 2003, providing guidance on the important question of how a company goes about restating its financial statements when it adopts IFRS for the first time.

As Exhibit 3.3 shows, IFRS constitutes a comprehensive system of financial reporting, addressing accounting concerns ranging from accounting for income taxes, to the recognition and measurement of financial instruments, to the preparation of consolidated financial statements. Because the IASB is a private body, it does not have the ability to enforce its standards. Instead, the IASB develops IFRS for the public good, making them available to any country or company that might choose to adopt them.

PRESENTATION OF FINANCIAL STATEMENTS (IAS 1)

IAS 1, *Presentation of Financial Statements,* is a single standard providing guidelines for the preparation and presentation of financial statements. In September 2007, the IASB published a revised IAS 1, effective for annual periods beginning on or after January 1, 2009. It provides guidance in the following areas:

- *Purpose of financial statements.* To provide information for decision making.
- *Components of financial statements.* A set of financial statements must include a balance sheet, income statement, statement of cash flows, statement of changes in equity, and notes, comprising a summary of significant accounting policies and other explanatory notes.
- *Overriding principle of fair presentation.* IAS 1 states that financial statements "shall present fairly the financial position, financial performance and cash flows of an entity. Fair presentation requires the faithful representation of the effects

EXHIBIT 3.3 International Financial Reporting Standards (IFRS) as of May 2011

Title	Issued (Revised)	Effective Date
Framework for the Preparation and Presentation of Financial Statements[a]	1989	
IAS 1 Presentation of Financial Statements[a]	1975 (1997, 2003, 2007)	Jan. 1, 2009
IAS 2 Inventories[b]	1975 (1993, 2003)	Jan. 1, 2005
IAS 7 Cash Flow Statements[b]	1977 (1992, 2007)	Jan. 1, 2009
IAS 8 Accounting Policies, Changes in Accounting Estimates and Errors[b]	1978 (1993, 2003, 2007)	Jan. 1, 2009
IAS 10 Events After the Balance Sheet Date[b]	1978 (1999, 2003, 2007)	Jan. 1, 2009
IAS 11 Construction Contracts	1979 (1993, 2007)	Jan. 1, 2009
IAS 12 Accounting for Taxes on Income[b]	1979 (1997, 2000, 2007)	Jan. 1, 2009
IAS 16 Property, Plant and Equipment[b]	1982 (1993, 1998, 2003, 2007)	Jan. 1, 2009
IAS 17 Leases[b]	1982 (1997, 2003)	Jan. 1, 2005
IAS 18 Revenue[b]	1982 (1993)	Jan. 1, 1995
IAS 19 Employee Benefits[b]	1983 (1997, 2000, 2007)	Jan. 1, 2009
IAS 20 Accounting for Government Grants and Disclosure of Government Assistance	1983 (2007)	Jan. 1, 2009
IAS 21 The Effects of Changes in Foreign Exchange Rates[c]	1983 (1993, 2003, 2007)	Jan. 1, 2009
IAS 23 Borrowing Costs[b]	1984 (1993)	Jan. 1, 1995
IAS 24 Related Party Disclosures[b]	1984 (2003, 2007)	Jan. 1, 2009
IAS 26 Accounting and Reporting by Retirement Benefit Plans	1987	Jan. 1, 1988
IAS 27 Consolidated Financial Statements and Accounting for Investments in Subsidiaries[d]	1989 (2003, 2007)	Jan. 1, 2009
IAS 28 Accounting for Investments in Associates[d]	1989 (1998, 2003, 2007)	Jan. 1, 2009
IAS 29 Financial Reporting in Hyperinflationary Economies[d]	1989 (2007)	Jan. 1, 2009
IAS 31 Financial Reporting of Interests in Joint Ventures[d]	1990 (1998, 2003)	Jan. 1, 2005
IAS 32 Financial Instruments: Disclosure and Presentation[b]	1995 (2003, 2007)	Jan. 1, 2009
IAS 33 Earnings per Share[b]	1997 (2003, 2007)	Jan. 1, 2009
IAS 34 Interim Financial Reporting[b]	1998 (2007)	Jan. 1, 2009
IAS 38 Intangible Assets[b]	1998 (2004, 2007)	April 1, 2009

(continued)

EXHIBIT 3.3 *(continued)*

Title		Issued (Revised)	Effective Date
IAS 39	Financial Instruments: Recognition and Measurement[b]	1998 (2000, 2003, 2004, 2007)	Jan. 1, 2009
IAS 40	Investment Property[b]	2000 (2003, 2004, 2007)	Jan. 1, 2009
IAS 41	Agriculture	2001 (2007)	Jan. 1, 2009
IFRS 1	First-time Adoption of International Financial Reporting Standards[a]	2003 (2007)	Jan. 1, 2009
IFRS 2	Share-based Payment[b]	2004	Jan. 1, 2005
IFRS 3	Business Combinations[d]	2004	March 31, 2004
IFRS 4	Insurance Contracts	2004 (2007)	Jan. 1, 2009
IFRS 5	Non-current Assets Held for Sale and Discontinued Operations[b]	2004 (2007)	Jan. 1, 2009
IFRS 6	Exploration for and Evaluation of Mineral Resources	2004	Jan. 1, 2006
IFRS 7	Financial Instruments: Disclosures	2005	Jan. 1, 2007
IFRS 8	Operating Segments[d]	2006	Jan. 1, 2009
IFRS 9	Financial Instruments	2010	Jan. 1, 2013
IFRS 10	Consolidated Financial Statements	May 2011	Jan. 1, 2013
IFRS 11	Joint Arrangements	May 2011	Jan. 1, 2013
IFRS 12	Disclosure of Interests in Other Entities	May 2011	Jan. 1, 2013
IFRS 13	Fair Value Measurement	May 2011	Jan. 1, 2013

Standards covered in this book:
[a] Denotes standards covered in Chapter 3.
[b] Denotes standards covered in Chapter 4.
[c] Denotes standards covered in Chapters 7 and 8.
[d] Denotes standards covered in Chapter 9.

of transactions, other events and conditions in accordance with the definitions and recognition criteria for assets, liabilities, income and expenses set out in the *Framework.*"[25] Compliance with IFRS generally ensures fair presentation. In the *extremely rare* circumstance when management concludes that compliance with the requirement of a standard or interpretation would be so misleading that it would conflict with the objective of financial statements set out in the *Framework,* IAS 1 *requires* departing from that requirement, with extensive disclosures made in the notes. If the local regulatory framework will not allow departing from a requirement, disclosures must be made to reduce the misleading aspects of compliance with that requirement.

- *Accounting policies.* Management should select and apply accounting policies to be in compliance with all IASB standards and all applicable interpretations. If guidance is lacking on a specific issue, management should refer to (a) the requirements and guidance in other IASB standards dealing with similar issues; (b) the definitions, recognition, and measurement criteria for assets, liabilities, income, and expenses set out in the IASB *Framework;* and (c) pronouncements of other standard-setting bodies and accepted industry practices to the extent, but only to the extent, that these are consistent with (a) and (b). IAS 1 does *not* indicate that this is a hierarchy. It is important to note that individual country GAAP may be used to fill in the blanks, but only if consistent with other IASB standards and the IASB *Framework.*

- *Basic principles and assumptions.* IAS 1 reiterates the accrual basis and going-concern assumptions and the consistency and comparative information principles found in the *Framework.* IAS 1 adds to the guidance provided in the *Framework* by indicating that immaterial items should be aggregated. It also stipulates that assets and liabilities, and income and expenses should not be offset and reported at a net amount unless specifically permitted by a standard or interpretation.

- *Structure and content of financial statements.* IAS 1 also provides guidance with respect to: (a) current/noncurrent distinction, (b) items to be presented on the face of financial statements, and (c) items to be disclosed in the notes.

IAS 1 requires companies to classify assets and liabilities as current and non-current on the balance sheet, except when a presentation based on liquidity provides information that is reliable and more relevant. IAS 1 also provides guidance with respect to the items, at a minimum, that should be reported on the face of the income statement or balance sheet. Exhibit 3.4 presents an illustrative income statement, and Exhibit 3.5 presents an illustrative statement of financial position demonstrating minimum compliance with IAS 1. The line items comprising profit before tax must be reflected using either a nature of expense format (common in Continental Europe) or a function of expense format (commonly found in Anglo countries). Both formats are presented in Exhibit 3.4. IAS 1 specifically precludes designating items as extraordinary on the income statement or in the notes.

In Exhibit 3.5, assets are presented on one side of the balance sheet, and liabilities and equity are presented on the other side. Other formats are equally acceptable so long as the current/noncurrent distinction is clear. For example, British balance sheets commonly present noncurrent assets, net current assets (working capital), and noncurrent liabilities on one side of the balance sheet and equity on the other side. In addition, assets and liabilities may be presented in order of liquidity, as is common in North America.

---

[25] IAS 1, paragraph 13.

EXHIBIT 3.4   Illustrative IFRS Income Statement

MODEL COMPANY
Income Statement
For the year ended 31 December 20XX
(in thousands of currency units)

Nature of Expenses Format	Function of Expenses Format
Revenue	**Revenue**
Changes in inventories of finished goods and work in progress	Cost of sales
Work performed by the entity and capitalized	**Gross profit**
Raw materials and consumables used	Other income
Employee benefits expense	Distribution costs
Depreciation and amortization expense	Administrative expenses
Impairment of property, plant, and equipment	Other expenses
Other expenses	Finance costs
Finance costs	Share of profit of associates
Share of profit of associates	**Profit before tax**
Profit before tax	Income tax expense
Income tax expense	**Profit for the period from continuing operations**
Profit for the period from continuing operations	Gain (loss) from discontinued operations
Gain (loss) from discontinued operations	**Profit for the period**
Profit for the period	Attributable to:
Attributable to:	Equity holders of the parent
Equity holders of the parent	Minority interest
Minority interest	

Note: IAS 33, *Earnings per Share*, requires that basic and diluted earnings per share also be reported on the face of the income statement. Additional required disclosures must be made either on the face of the income statement or in the notes.

FIRST-TIME ADOPTION OF INTERNATIONAL FINANCIAL REPORTING STANDARDS (IFRS 1)

IFRS 1, *First-time Adoption of International Financial Reporting Standards*, issued in June 2003, was the first IFRS developed by the IASB. IFRS 1 sets out the requirements for adopting IFRS and preparing a set of IFRS financial statements for the first time. As companies make the transition from their previous GAAP to IFRS, guidance on this issue is very important.

In general, IFRS 1 requires an entity adopting IFRS to comply with each IFRS effective at the reporting date of its first IFRS financial statements. For example, if an entity is preparing IFRS financial statements for the year ended December 31, 2013, it must comply with all IFRS in force at that date. Moreover, if the entity provides comparative financial statements for the year 2012 in its 2013 IFRS financial statements, the comparative statements also must be prepared in accordance with IFRS in force at December 31, 2013. According to IFRS 1, if the entity's date of transition

EXHIBIT 3.5 Illustrative IFRS Statement of Financial Position

MODEL COMPANY
Consolidated Statement of Financial Position
As at 31 December, Year 1
(in thousands of currency units)

Assets	Equity and Liabilities
Noncurrent assets	**Equity attributable to owners of the parent**
Property, plant, and equipment	Share capital
Goodwill	Other reserves
Other intangible assets	Retained earnings
Investments in associates	
Available-for-sale financial assets	**Minority interest**
	Total equity
Current assets	
Inventories	**Noncurrent liabilities**
Trade receivables	Long-term borrowings
Other current assets	Deferred tax
Cash and cash equivalents	Long-term provisions
	Total noncurrent liabilities
Total assets	
	Current liabilities
	Trade and other payables
	Short-term borrowings
	Current portion of long-term borrowings
	Current tax payable
	Short-term provisions
	Total current liabilities
	Total liabilities
	Total equity and liabilities

Note: Additional required disclosures must be made on the face of the balance sheet or in the notes.

to IFRS is January 1, 2012, the entity should prepare an "opening IFRS balance sheet" as of that date, which becomes the starting point for accounting under IFRS.

In preparing its opening IFRS balance sheet, IFRS 1 requires an entity to do the following:

1. Recognize all assets and liabilities whose recognition is required by IFRS.
2. Derecognize items previously recognized as assets or liabilities if IFRS do not permit such recognition.
3. Reclassify items that it recognized under previous GAAP as one type of asset, liability, or component of equity, but are a different type of asset, liability, or component of equity under IFRS.
4. Apply IFRS in measuring all recognized assets and liabilities.

To understand the significance of these requirements, consider their implementation with respect to intangible assets. In preparing its opening IFRS balance sheet, an entity would need to (1) exclude previously recognized intangible assets that do not meet the recognition criteria in IAS 38, *Intangible Assets*, at the date of transition to IFRS, and (2) include intangible assets that do meet the recognition criteria in IAS 38 at that date, even if they previously had been accounted for as an expense. For example, an entity adopting IFRS must determine whether previously expensed development costs would have qualified for recognition as an intangible asset under IAS 38 at the date of transition to IFRS. If so, then an asset should be recognized in the opening IFRS balance sheet, even if the related costs had been expensed previously. Furthermore, if amortization methods and useful lives for intangible assets recognized under previous GAAP differ from those that would be acceptable under IFRS, then the accumulated amortization in the opening IFRS balance sheet must be adjusted retrospectively to comply with IFRS.

In specific areas where the cost of complying with an IFRS would likely exceed the benefits to users, IFRS 1 provides exemptions from complying with IFRS. Exemptions are allowed with respect to specific aspects of accounting in the following areas: business combinations, asset revaluations, employee benefits, cumulative translation differences, and financial instruments. Recently, IFRS 1 has been further amended to assist first-time adopters.

INTERNATIONAL CONVERGENCE TOWARD IFRS

The IASB has earned a great deal of goodwill from many interested parties. Its new approach clearly reflects a change of role from a harmonizer to a global standard-setter. According to its chairman, the IASB's strategy is to identify the best in standards around the world and build a body of accounting standards that constitute the "highest common denominator" of financial reporting. The IASB has adopted a principles-based approach to standard-setting and has obtained the support of U.S. regulators (even though U.S. standard-setters historically have taken a rules-based approach). On the other hand, the IASB's structure is similar to that of the U.S. standard-setter, recognizing that the FASB has the best institutional structure for developing accounting standards.

In 2002, the six largest public accounting firms worldwide conducted a survey of national efforts in 54 countries to promote and achieve convergence with IFRS.[26] Almost all the countries surveyed intend to converge with IFRS, indicating that the IASB is the appropriate body to develop a global accounting language. Countries indicating a plan to achieve convergence included members of the European Union, the six countries of the Western Hemisphere with the largest economies (Argentina, Brazil, Canada, Chile, Mexico, and the United States), and China, India, Malaysia, New Zealand, South Korea, and Thailand. The survey identified three different convergence strategies:

1. Replacing national GAAP with IFRS (supplemented for issues not addressed by IFRS).
2. Adopting IFRS as national GAAP on a standard-by-standard basis.
3. Eliminating differences between national GAAP and IFRS when possible and practicable.

[26] BDO, Deloitte Touche Tohmatsu, Ernst & Young, Grant Thornton, KPMG, and PricewaterhouseCoopers, *GAAP Convergence 2002: A Survey of National Efforts to Promote and Achieve Convergence with International Financial Reporting Standards.* Available at www.ifad.net.

The major concerns in achieving IFRS convergence as expressed by respondents to the 2002 survey included:

- The complicated nature of particular standards, especially those related to financial instruments and fair value accounting (51 percent of countries).
- The tax-driven nature of the national accounting regime; using IFRS as the basis for taxation is seen as a problem (47 percent of countries).
- Disagreement with certain significant IFRS, especially those related to financial statements and fair value accounting (39 percent of countries).
- Insufficient guidance on first-time application of IFRS (35 percent of countries).
- Limited capital markets, and therefore little benefit to be derived from using IFRS (30 percent of countries).
- Investor/user satisfaction with national accounting standards (21 percent of countries).
- IFRS language translation difficulties (18 percent of countries).

The IASB has taken initiatives to facilitate and enhance its role as a global standard-setter. The issuance of IFRS 1 is one such initiative. IFRS 1 was issued in response to the concern about a lack of guidance on first-time application of IFRS. The official language of the IASB is English, and IFRS are written in this language. The IASB has attempted to address the translation issue by permitting national accountancy bodies to translate IFRS into more than 30 languages, including Chinese, French, German, Japanese, Portuguese, and Spanish. In addition to the problem that IFRS have not yet been translated into very many languages, research has shown that translation can be problematic, as some terms in English have no direct equivalent in other languages.[27]

With the increasing trend in many countries, including Australia and the EU member nations, to adopt IFRS, a large number of companies (over 7,000 listed companies in Europe alone) now use IFRS in preparing their financial statements. The IASB's decision to hold a series of public roundtable forums to provide opportunities for those who have commented on an exposure draft to discuss their views on the proposals with members of the IASB is another important initiative.

A significant number of board members have direct liaison responsibility with national standard-setters.[28] As a result, unlike its predecessor, the IASB now is formally linked to national standard-setters in at least some countries, and the liaison board members are able to coordinate agendas and ensure that the IASB and those national bodies are working toward convergence.

IFAC supports the IASB's objective of convergence. For example, at its July 2003 meeting, held in Quebec, Canada, IFAC approved a Compliance Program designed to provide clear benchmarks to current and potential member organizations in ensuring high-quality performance by accountants worldwide. This program requires member bodies to implement, with appropriate investigation and disciplinary regulations, both IFAC standards and IFRS. IFAC's Auditing

---

[27] T. S. Doupnik and M. Richter, "Interpretation of Uncertainty Expressions: A Cross-National Study," *Accounting, Organizations and Society* 28, no. 1 (2003), pp. 15–35. These researchers find, for example, that German speakers do not view the English word "remote" (used in the context of the probability that a loss will occur) and its German translation "Wahrscheinlichkeit äußerst gering" as being equivalent.

[28] The IASB initially had official liaison with national standard-setters from Australia, Canada, France, Germany, Japan, New Zealand, the United Kingdom, and the United States.

and Assurance Standards Board (IAASB) also has issued new guidance clarifying when financial statements are in full compliance with IFRS. In its 2007 annual report, the IFAC highlights, among other things, the progress in achieving international convergence through IFRS.

As stated earlier in this chapter, the main objective of the IASB is to achieve international convergence with IFRS. However, Zeff[29] points out that some obstacles to comparability are likely to arise in areas of the business and financial culture, the accounting culture, the auditing culture, and the regulatory culture. He also warns that, in addition to the obstacles to convergence due to the problems of interpretation, language, and terminology, the impact of politics can create a "catch-22" situation. He states:

> The more rigorous the enforcement mechanism—that is, the more authority and the larger budget a country gives to its securities market regulator to fortify the effort to secure compliance with IFRS—the more lobbying pressure that will be brought on the IASB, because companies in such countries will know that they have no "escape valve," no way of side-stepping the adverse consequences, as they see them, of a proposed IASB standard or interpretation. If the auditor is strict and the regulator is strict, political lobbying of the standard setter, IASB, may become more intense. If a powerful company or group of companies do not like a draft standard, they will have an incentive to engage in politicking of the standard-setting body. Hence it becomes a Catch-22.

Regardless of the arguments against harmonization, substantial efforts to reduce differences in accounting practice have been ongoing for several decades. The question is no longer *whether* harmonization should be strived for, but going a step further, it is to ask *how to achieve convergence.*

THE ADOPTION OF INTERNATIONAL FINANCIAL REPORTING STANDARDS

There are a number of different ways in which a country might adopt IFRS, including requiring (or permitting) IFRS to be used by the following:

1. *All* companies; in effect, IFRS replace national GAAP.
2. Parent companies in preparing *consolidated* financial statements; national GAAP is used in parent company-only financial statements.
3. *Stock exchange listed* companies in preparing consolidated financial statements. Nonlisted companies use national GAAP.
4. *Foreign* companies listing on domestic stock exchanges. Domestic companies use national GAAP.
5. Domestic companies that list on *foreign* stock exchanges. Other domestic companies use national GAAP.

The endorsement of IFRS for cross-listing purposes by IOSCO and the EU's decision to require domestic listed companies to use IFRS for consolidated accounts beginning in 2005 have provided a major boost to the efforts of the IASB. Exhibit 3.6 shows the use of IFRS around the world as of June 2012.

IFAC supports IASB in its efforts at global standard-setting. The IFAC 2008 annual report highlights initiatives during the credit crisis and the need for convergence to global standards.

[29] S. Zeff, "Political Lobbying on Proposed Standards: A Challenge to the IASB," *Accounting Horizons* 16, no. 1 (2002), pp. 43–54.

EXHIBIT 3.6 Use of IFRS in Preparing Consolidated Financial Statements as of June 2012

IFRS Required for All Domestic Listed Companies

Abu Dhabi (UAE)	Ecuador	Kenya	Norway
Anguilla	Egypt	Korea (South)	Oman
Antigua and Barbuda	Estonia	Kuwait	Panama
Argentina	Fiji	Kyrgyzstan	Papua New Guinea
Armenia	Finland	Latvia	Peru
Australia	France	Lebanon	Poland
Austria	Georgia	Libya	Portugal
Bahamas	Germany	Liechtenstein	Qatar
Bahrain	Ghana	Lithuania	Romania
Barbados	Greece	Luxembourg	Serbia
Belgium	Grenada	Macedonia	Sierra Leone
Bosnia & Herzegovina	Guatemala	Malawi	Slovak Republic
Botswana	Guyana	Malta	Slovenia
Bulgaria	Honduras	Mauritius	South Africa
Canada	Hong Kong	Mexico	Spain
Chile	Hungary	Mongolia	St. Kitts & Nevis
Costa Rica	Iceland	Montenegro	Sweden
Croatia	Iraq	Namibia	Tajikistan
Cyprus	Ireland	Nepal	Tanzania
Czech Republic	Italy	Netherlands	Trinidad & Tobago
Denmark	Jamaica	New Zealand	United Kingdom
Dominican Republic	Jordan	Nicaragua	West Bank/Gaza
Dubai (UAE)	Kazakhstan	Nigeria	Zambia

IFRS Required for Some Domestic Listed Companies

Azerbaijan	Israel	Saudi Arabia	China
Morocco			

IFRS Permitted for Domestic Listed Companies

Aruba	Gibraltar	Mozambique	Switzerland
Bermuda	Haiti	Myanmar	Turkey
Bolivia	India	Netherlands Antilles	Uganda
Cayman Islands	Japan	Paraguay	Virgin Is. (British)
Dominican Republic	Laos	Sri Lanka	Zimbabwe
Ecuador	Lesotho	Suriname	
El Salvador	Maldives	Swaziland	

IFRS Not Permitted for Domestic Listed Companies

Bangladesh	Iran	Singapore	United States
Benin	Malaysia	Syria	Uruguay
Bhutan	Mali	Taiwan	Uzbekistan
Burkina Faso	Moldova	Thailand	Venezuela
Colombia	Niger	Togo	Vietnam
Cote d'Ivoire	Pakistan	Tunisia	
Cuba	Philippines	Turkmenistan	
Indonesia	Russia	Ukraine	

IFRSs in Your Pocket 2012, www.iasplus.com (accessed on May 22, 2012)

The IFAC G20 accountancy summit in July 2009 issued a renewed mandate for adoption of global standards in which they recommended that governments and regulators should step up initiatives to promote convergence to global accountancy and auditing standards. The latest IFAC Global Leadership Survey, which polled its membership of 157 accountancy organizations in 123 countries, emphasizes that investors and all consumers of financial information deserve simpler and more useful information, and that the adoption, implementation, and enforcement of international financial standards are crucial in this regard.

Recently, China, Japan, and Korea formed the Asian-Oceanian Standard Setters Group (AOSSG) as a forum for the countries in the region to exchange their ideas but also to have a joint voice in matters relating to IFRS and to bring together Asian-Oceanian standard-setters. The IASB has responded to concerns expressed by various parties. For example, it has issued amendments to IFRS 1, *First-time Adoption of IFRS*, that address the retrospective application of IFRS to particular situations and are aimed at ensuring that entities applying IFRS will not face undue cost or effort in the transition process. The IASB has also issued a revised version of IAS 24, *Related Party Disclosures*, that simplifies the disclosure requirements for government-related entities and clarifies the definition of a related party.

Many developing countries have adopted IFRS with little or no amendment as their national standards. For some of them, it may have been a less expensive option than developing their own standards. The need to attract foreign investment also may have been an influencing factor. Countries changing from centrally planned to market-based economies also have found IFRS attractive, as they offer a ready-made set of standards to facilitate the development of a market system.

Although many countries do not allow domestic listed companies to use IASB standards, some of these countries nevertheless allow *foreign* companies listed on domestic stock exchanges to use IFRS in accordance with IOSCO's recommendation. Japan, for example, allows foreign companies listing on the Tokyo stock exchange to file financial statements prepared in accordance with IFRS without any reconciliation to Japanese GAAP. (The same is now true in the United States.)

A global leadership survey conducted by the IFAC in late 2007 revealed that a large majority (89 percent) indicated that convergence to IFRS was "very important" or "important" for economic growth in their countries. The survey included 143 business leaders from 91 countries.[30] A majority of recent Deloitte IFRS survey respondents preferred a set date for global accounting standards. Currently, approximately 120 countries and reporting jurisdictions permit or require IFRS for domestic listed companies. However, approximately 90 countries have fully conformed with IFRS as promulgated by the IASB and include a statement in audit report to that effect.

IFRS IN THE EUROPEAN UNION

In July 2002, the European Union issued a directive (Regulation 1606/2002) requiring all listed companies of member states to prepare consolidated financial statements based on IFRS beginning January 1, 2005. The aim was to improve the quality of corporate financial reporting by increasing their comparability and transparency, and to promote the development of a single capital market in Europe.

The European Union has adopted the strategy of replacing national GAAP (supplemented for issues not addressed by IFRS) with respect to the preparation

[30]http://accountingeducation.com/index.cfm?page=newsdetails&id=145923.

of consolidated financial statements by listed companies. Nonlisted companies continue to apply national GAAP. However, several EU countries (Denmark and Estonia) also have adopted a convergence strategy with respect to nonlisted companies, by adopting a plan to converge national GAAP with IFRS. This strategy could eventually result in no substantive differences between IFRS and a country's national GAAP. In January 2003, the European Parliament approved amendments to the EU Fourth and Seventh Directives removing all inconsistencies between the directives and IFRS.

The switch to IFRS involved significant changes to the accounting policies of listed companies. With this in mind, the U.K. Institute of Chartered Accountants in England and Wales urged British companies to provide investors and analysts with clear explanations of their preparations for adopting IFRS and changes to accounting policies ahead of publication of their 2005 accounts, as this was seen as being important in securing investor confidence.

The EU decided to adopt a version of IAS 39, *Financial Instruments: Recognition and Measurement,* with two "carve outs." The EU-approved version of IAS 39 removes specific provisions related to the use of a fair value option and of hedge accounting. This was not well received internationally, including in the United Kingdom. The concerns included that this could have adverse consequences for the cost of capital of European companies if the adopted standard prevents European companies from complying with the complete standard as issued by the IASB, as it will damage the credibility of European financial reporting. Further, it was pointed out that the adopted standard includes seriously weakened hedge accounting requirements and may give rise to artificial volatility in reported profits and difficulties in application as a result of limiting the fair value option.

Some European companies are careful to disclose the fact that they are using "IFRS as adopted by the EU," meaning that IAS 39 is not applied in its entirety. The following disclosure made by the Swedish firm AB Electrolux in Note 1, Accounting and Valuation Principles of the 2006 Annual Report is an example:

> The consolidated financial statements are prepared in accordance with International Financial Reporting Standards (IFRS) as adopted by the European Union.
> Electrolux's auditor, PricewaterhouseCoopers, uses similar language in its audit opinion.

So far, no research has been conducted to examine the full effect of adopting an amended version of IAS 39 in Europe. In the area of enforcement of accounting standards, there are considerable challenges in Europe. The Committee of European Securities Regulators (CESR) issued Standard No. 1, *Financial Information: Enforcement of Standards on Financial Information in Europe,* in 2003 to provide principles that could underpin the development and implementation of a common approach to the enforcement of IFRS. However, application of the standard is not mandatory, and CESR will rely on the cooperation of member states in adopting the stated principles.

There is a wide variety of accounting enforcement systems used in Europe. Some countries, such as Germany, Finland, and the Netherlands, have no institutional oversight of financial reporting. Further, the enterprises that are expected to apply IFRS in Europe are heterogeneous in terms of jurisdiction, size, capital structure, ownership structure, and degree of accounting sophistication.[31] In pre-2005 Europe, there was a variety of national standards of varying degrees of

---

[31] K. Schipper, "The Introduction of International Accounting Standards in Europe: Implications for International Convergence," *European Accounting Review* 14, no.1 (2005), pp. 101–26.

completeness, sophistication, and authority, reflecting different national traditions and institutional arrangements.[32] Starting in 2005, although the European Union will have a single financial reporting standard-setter, securities regulation is subject to considerable cross-jurisdictional variation due to existing legal and cultural differences among EU jurisdictions. As a result, EU countries decided to evaluate existing enforcement strategies and introduce enforcement bodies.[33]

Recent IFRS (especially IAS 39) have increasingly required fair value measurements, with the intent of enhancing the relevance of reported numbers. A key issue for convergence is whether fair value measurements can be accepted as having sufficient reliability. One difficulty in developing fair value measures particularly in Europe is a lack of organized and liquid markets for many assets and obligations.

In September 2009, the EU published Commission Regulation (EC) No. 839/2009 (*Adoption of Eligible Hedged Items—Amendments to IAS 39 Financial Instruments: Recognition and Measurement*), amending Regulation (EC) No. 1226/2008, adopting certain international accounting standards in accordance with Regulation (EC) No. 1606/2002. EFRAG commented on the IASB's Exposure Draft on Fair Value Measurement, supporting most aspects of the IASB proposal to define fair value, but recommending that the proposal should apply to financial assets and financial liabilities only after there has been a public consultation and debate on its use for nonfinancial assets and liabilities. The UK FRC also supports the view that an EU focus on principles and values in corporate reporting should be adopted and suggests that "comply or explain" should remain a fundamental cornerstone of the EU framework. In February 2013, the IFRS Foundation had a Memorandum of Understanding with the International Integrated Reporting Council (IIRC) in the UK.

IFRS IN THE UNITED STATES

Support for a Principles-Based Approach

It is interesting that support for a principles-based approach has come from many quarters, including current and former U.S. regulators. It has been pointed out that as part of the commitment to convergence, the FASB and SEC should change their behavior and become more like the rest of the world. For example, a former SEC chairman, expressing preference for the IASB's principles-based standards, referred to the IASB's approach as a "Ten Commandments" approach in contrast to the FASB's "cookbook" approach.[34] The SEC chairman, in a speech made in Puerto Rico in February 2002, also expressed preference for a principles-based set of accounting standards.[35] In addition, in an editorial in the June 27, 2002, edition of *Financial Times*, titled "The World after WorldCom," the U.S. regulators were

[32] G. Whittington, "The Adoption of International Accounting Standards in the European Union," *European Accounting Review* 14, no.1 (2005), pp. 127–53.

[33] Committee of European Securities Regulators, CESR's First Initiative towards More Robust Enforcement of Financial Information in Europe, press release CESR/03-081b, 2 April, (2003). Available at www .europefesco.org/v2/default.asp.

[34] http://banking.senate.gov/02_02hrg/021202/index.htm.

[35] www.sec.gov/news/speech/spch539.htm.

urged to move to principles-based standards. The following is an extract from this editorial:

> It is time for US accounting standards to move away from prescriptive rulemaking towards the alternative used in many other countries, which focuses on "substance over form." US regulators have been suspicious of principles-based standards drafted by the International Accounting Standards Board, arguing that the US approach is superior. As the list of US accounting scandals mounts, it is hard to maintain such a position.

The 2008 financial crisis led to much soul-searching among global standard-setters and regulators for its underlying root causes, as many commentators pointed to inaccurate accounting standards and the need for improvement. Further, the standard-setters such as the IASB and FASB came under intense political pressure to accommodate the interests of the banking regulators, who required financial stability and accounting standards that would not result in "credit crunches" by depressing bank capital at a time of falling securities prices. In the United States, these efforts were driven by the SEC, FASB, and AICPA.[36] In recent years, the standard-setting activities at the international level were characterized by the efforts at converging U.S. GAAP and IFRS.

The SEC and IFRS Convergence

In November 2007, the SEC decided to remove the requirement that foreign private issuers using IFRS reconcile their financial statements to U.S. GAAP. This reflects the recognition that IFRS is a high-quality set of accounting standards which is capable of ensuring adequate disclosure for the protection of investors and the promotion of fair, orderly, and efficient markets. This decision was supported by the experience in the European markets, where there has been no market disruption or loss of investor confidence as a result of the introduction of IFRS in 2005. Substantial amounts of capital have been invested by U.S. investors in European companies which report under IFRS, thus suggesting that many U.S. investors already have concluded that IFRS is a fit-for-purpose financial reporting framework. Of the 1,100 foreign companies that file financial statements with the SEC, 180 use IFRS. Beginning in 2007, the Form 20-F filed by these companies with the SEC no longer includes a reconciliation to U.S. GAAP.

Elimination of the reconciliation requirement for foreign filers who prepare their financial reports in accordance with IFRS creates an asymmetric situation, as domestic filers do not have the option of preparing their financial reports in accordance with IFRS. In July 2007, the SEC issued a concept release soliciting public comment on the idea of allowing U.S. companies to choose between the use of IFRS and U.S. GAAP. In October 2007, the AICPA recommended that the SEC should allow American public companies to report financial results using international accounting standards. Preliminary results of a survey conducted by Deloitte & Touche LLP in November 2007 show that approximately 205 CEOs and senior finance professionals (representing approximately 300 U.S. companies) would consider adopting IFRS, if given a choice by the SEC. Even the chairmen of the FASB and Financial Accounting Foundation, which oversees the FASB, have

---

[36] Full text of the testimony is available at www.iasplus.com/index.htm.

expressed approval for a move toward the use of IFRS in the United States. They concluded that:

> Investors would be better served if all U.S. public companies used accounting standards promulgated by a single global standard setter as the basis for preparing their financial reports. This would be best accomplished by moving U.S. public companies to an improved version of International Financial Reporting Standards (IFRS).[37]

In November 2008, the SEC issued a rule called "Roadmap for the Potential Use of Financial Statements Prepared in Accordance with International Financial Reporting Standards (IFRS) by U.S. Issuers." Since 2009, the SEC has been suggesting that gradual convergence toward IFRS be engineered by the FASB, stating that a single set of high-quality, globally accepted accounting standards would benefit U.S. investors. In February 2010, the SEC issued a statement supporting global accounting standards and convergence with IFRS. That statement was based on the responses to its November 2008 proposed rule. However, the move to IFRS in the United States will be a complex, multiyear process that will involve making significant changes to the U.S. financial reporting system, including changes in auditing standards, licensing requirements, and how accountants are educated.

Further, for companies and financial professionals that have been using detailed rules associated with U.S. GAAP, the prospect of IFRS presents both opportunities and challenges.

There is widespread support for the SEC's "Roadmap for the Potential Use of Financial Statements Prepared in Accordance with International Financial Reporting Standards by U.S. Issuers"; for example, the UK FRC, the UK's independent regulator responsible for promoting confidence in corporate reporting and governance, emphasized that permitting U.S. domestic issuers to use IFRS will be significant to the future development and credibility of IFRS. U.S. executives want an option for early IFRS adoption, according to a KPMG IFRS institute survey, which found that nearly half of those polled say they would like the option for "early adoption" once the SEC decides to require or permit U.S. companies to use IFRS. However, the National Association of State Boards of Accountancy, supporting the joint effort by the IASB and the FASB to converge standards by 2011, has recommended that moving to convergence with, rather than adoption of, IFRS is the right path for the SEC to be following and that the SEC should withdraw its idea of a "road map" for adoption of IFRS. U.S. President Obama's administration has supported global standards in its financial reform proposal, which has been applauded by IFAC.

Challenges to International Convergence

- In different countries there are different views on what is or should be the primary purpose of financial statements. In the United States, the investors or their decisions are considered to be the most important; in Germany, creditors' information needs are considered the top priority; in France, the information needs of the government play a major role. This diversity has led to the use of a variety of definitions of the elements of financial statements.

- Some politicians in the United States and the United Kingdom blame IFRS, particularly fair value accounting, for the recent financial crisis.

---

[37]Letter to Ms. Nancy M. Morris, Securities and Exchange Commission, signed by Robert E. Denham, Chairman, Financial Accounting Foundation, and Robert H. Herz, Chairman, Financial Accounting Standards Board, dated November 7, 2007 (www.fasb.org/FASB_FAF_Response_SEC_Release_msw.pdf).

- Now the IASB must consider the consequences of an IFRS world without the United States, where the SEC is the world's most respected securities market regulator.
- The IASB will need to manage and balance the diverse feedback from the regional standard-setter groups. Such feedback from different parts of the world has become better organized and more persistent.
- There is a great deal of variability in the effectiveness of enforcement of IFRS in different countries, for example, within the EU and developing countries.
- In countries where IFRS are adopted as the governing set of standards for listed companies, the affirmation of compliance with IFRS by the company or the auditor, or both, may refer to the financial reporting framework in a way that makes it unclear to readers whether, and to what degree, it corresponds with IFRS as issued by the IASB.
- Taking proper cognizance of the fundamentally different ways in which business is done in different countries is necessary when developing standards. For example, in developing a standard on consolidated financial statements: in Japan, *keiretsu* are networks of affiliated companies that may not have a parent company; in China, most business is done by government-owned entities, not by private-sector enterprise.
- Impossibility of determining a clear winner between two approaches to accounting education. Some accounting educators follow a "rules-based" approach to accounting education; for example, many accounting educators in the United States seem to take this approach. Accordingly, accounting exercises have "right" and "wrong" solutions, and there exists a "correct" way to account for a certain transaction. A much lesser importance is placed on the theoretical aspects of accounting problems. An alternative approach can be described as "concept-based." The IASB has taken this approach. Accordingly, theoretical aspects of an accounting problem are first considered, and then possible alternative solutions are chosen, and finally, the solutions which are consistent with the current regulatory guidance are determined.
- Use of IFRS could be expected to have visible repercussions for the financial statements of listed firms in different countries. For example, France, which is a code law country, is presumed to have an outlook that contrasts with the dominant view in the IASB conceptual framework, which has been extensively inspired by its founding members (including Australia, Canada, the United Kingdom, and the United States).

  The differences between the French GAAP (Continental European model) and IFRS ("Anglo-American" model) can be explained by distinct features at the origin of divergent development of national accounting systems: the influence of the legal system (common law or code law), the tax system (whose degree of independence from accounting varies), the primary source of financing for businesses (stock markets or banks), and accounting rules that reflect both cultural and institutional differences.
- Overall, standardization cannot be expected to resolve dilemmas in accounting education. As noted by Baxter[38] some thirty years ago:

  > Standards are a godsend to the feebler type of writer and teacher who finds it easier to recite a creed than to analyze facts and to engage in argument. If an official

---

[38] W. T. Baxter, "Accounting Standards: Boon or Curse?" The Saxe Lectures in Accounting (1979). Available at http://newman.baruch.cuny.edu/DIGITAL/saxe/saxe_1978/baxter_79.htm.

answer is available to a problem, why should a teacher confuse examination candidates with rival views? Thus, learning by rote replaces reason; the good student of today is he who can parrot most rules. On this spare diet, accounting students are not likely to develop the habits of reasoning and skepticism that education should instill.

- There is an ongoing debate concerning the efficacy of mandating high-quality accounting standards in unsuitable contexts with inadequate institutional infrastructures. Greece provides an example of an unfavorable jurisdiction for enforcement of IFRS, due to its code law tradition, bank orientation, concentrated corporate ownership, poor shareholders' protection, and low regulatory quality.[39]

New Direction for the IASB

Recently, IASB Chairman Hans Hoogervoorst, suggesting that the IASB would no longer seek to converge with U.S. GAAP, waved goodbye to a quick convergence of IFRS and U.S. GAAP. This means that U.S. GAAP and IFRS convergence is likely to remain an elusive dream.

The IASB no longer takes the view that a failure to converge with U.S. GAAP will be fatal for the IFRS project. According to Hoogervoorst, five years ago a standstill in the United States would have had very serious consequences for the IASB, because the risk was that without the United States on board, Europe would go its own way and Asia would develop its own regional standards; but today, such risk has disappeared. However, given the importance of the United States, this is probably a setback to the IASB. On the other hand, the international weight of IFRS has grown so much that it has long since reached critical mass.

Indeed, worldwide IFRS adoption has picked up dramatically over the past few years; for example, over 100 countries now use the standards, including three-quarters of the G20, according to the IASB.

It is quite inconceivable that the formal end to convergence with U.S. GAAP will cause any IFRS adopters to reverse their decision once the cost of the transition to IFRS is behind them, and it is unlikely that they would undo this work and revert to national or regional standards.

Nonetheless, the decision to give up the objective of convergence with U.S. GAAP would not have been possible without the change at the helm of the IASB after 20 years, from Sir David Tweedie, who was a strong proponent of convergence, to Hoogervoorst, who is critical of the concept of prudence, believing that companies could be smoothing their figures under its guise, and who has pointed out that conservative accounting comes at the cost of transparency and trust in financial figures. Given the growing internationality of IFRS, the IASB must satisfy a growing constituency. It has become increasingly imperative for the IASB to listen to the voices of that constituency. Pursuing convergence with U.S. GAAP at the cost of ignoring concerns raised by the swelling constituency was becoming an increasingly costly exercise.

However, the formal end to convergence with U.S. GAAP does not mean the project is completely dead. It has merely been relegated to a lower priority level. Regular consultations between the FASB and IASB will also continue. The recent appointment of former senior SEC member Mary Tokar to the IASB board also suggests that not all hope has been discarded by the IASB.

---

[39] The wide variance between Greek accounting standards and IFRS has frequently been reported in the international accounting literature.

Both the previous EU experience and the current state of the IASB/FASB convergence process suggest that two or more sets of slightly different standards are likely to coexist in future.

The FASB and IFRS Convergence

The FASB's mission is to improve U.S. financial accounting standards for the benefit of present and potential investors, lenders, donors, and other creditors. Its ultimate goal of convergence is a single set of high-quality, international accounting standards that companies worldwide would use for both domestic and cross-border financial reporting. The FASB was of the view that these groups should benefit from the increased comparability that would result from internationally converged accounting standards, and that working cooperatively with the IASB to develop common standards would improve financial reporting in the United States and internationally, and that would foster global comparability and fulfill FASB's mission.

The Norwalk Agreement

In September 2002, at a meeting in Norwalk, Connecticut, the FASB and IASB pledged to use their best efforts (1) to make their existing financial reporting standards fully compatible as soon as is practicable, and (2) to coordinate their work program to ensure that once achieved, compatibility is maintained. This has become known as the "Norwalk Agreement." Note that this agreement does not mean that the FASB will always try to move in the direction of IASB standards to remove existing differences, but that the opposite also will occur. Significantly, the two standard-setters have agreed to work together on future issues to try to develop common solutions. In March 2003, the IASB decided to use identical style and wording in the standards issued by the FASB and IASB on joint projects.

The following are key FASB initiatives to further convergence between IFRS and U.S. GAAP:

1. *Joint projects.* Joint projects involve sharing staff resources and working on a similar time schedule. Revenue recognition, business combinations, and review of the *conceptual framework* are three major topics covered by joint projects.

2. *Short-term convergence project.* The two Boards agreed to undertake a short-term project to remove a variety of differences that exist between IFRS and U.S. GAAP. The scope of the short-term convergence project is limited to those differences between the two sets of standards in which convergence is likely to be achieved in the short term. Convergence is expected to occur by selecting either existing U.S. GAAP or IFRS requirements as the high-quality solution.

3. *Liaison IASB member.* A full-time IASB member is in residence at the FASB offices. This facilitates information exchange and cooperation between the FASB and the IASB.

4. *Monitoring of IASB projects.* The FASB monitors IASB projects according to the FASB's level of interest in the topic being addressed.

5. *The convergence research project.* The FASB staff embarked on a project to identify all the substantive differences between U.S. GAAP and IFRS and catalog differences according to the FASB's strategy for resolving them.

6. *Consideration of convergence potential in board agenda decisions.* All topics considered for addition to the FASB's agenda are assessed for the potential cooperation with the IASB.

The expectation was that through these initiatives, significant progress could be made toward convergence with IFRS in the short to medium term. Toward the end of 2004, the FASB issued three standards resulting from the short-term convergence project designed to eliminate some differences between the U.S. and IASB standards: SFAS 123 (revised 2004), *Share-based Payments*, issued in December 2004; SFAS 151, *Inventory Costs* (an amendment of ARB 43, Chapter 4), issued in November 2004; and SFAS 153, *Exchange of Non-monetary Assets* (an amendment of APB Opinion 29), issued in December 2004. SFAS 123 requires that compensation cost relating to share-based payments transactions be recognized in financial statements. The cost is to be measured on the basis of the fair value of the equity or liability instrument issued. This standard eliminates the use of the intrinsic value method, which was allowed under Opinion 25, and it is expected to result in convergence with IFRS 2. ARB 43 states that under some circumstances, items such as idle facility expenses, excessive spoilage, double freight, and rehandling costs may be so abnormal as to require treatment as current period charges. SFAS 151 eliminates the term abnormal. The term was not defined in ARB 43. The language used in SFAS 151 is similar to that in IAS 2. SFAS 153 eliminates certain narrow differences between Opinion 29 and IAS 2. Opinion 29 provided an exception to the basic measurement principle (fair value) for exchanges of similar productive assets (commercially substantive assets). SFAS 153 eliminates that exception and brings the U.S. standard closer to IAS 16.

At a conference held in New York in April 2007, the chairmen of the IASB and FASB stressed that principles-based accounting standards would best serve users of financial statements and the public interest. More recently, the joint project on business combinations resulted in the FASB issuing a new standard on this topic in December 2007. SFAS 141 (revised), *Business Combinations*, adopts the acquisition method of accounting for business combinations that was first introduced by the IASB in IFRS 3, *Business Combinations*, in 2004. The FASB and IASB worked together to agree on solutions to a number of issues related to the application of the acquisition method. The IASB issued a revised IFRS 3 adopting these solutions in January 2008. In introducing SFAS 141 (revised 2007), the FASB states:

> This Statement, together with the IASB's IFRS 3, *Business Combinations* (as revised in 2007), completes a joint effort by the FASB and the IASB to improve financial reporting about business combinations and to promote the international convergence of accounting standards.[40]

Following the global financial crisis, the Financial Crisis Advisory Group (FCAG), a high-level group of recognized leaders with broad experience in international financial markets, was formed at the request of the IASB and FASB to consider financial reporting issues arising from the crisis. The FCAG published in July 2009 a wide-ranging review of standard-setting activities following the global financial crisis. The report articulates four main principles and contains a series of recommendations to improve the functioning and effectiveness of global standard-setting. The main areas addressed in the report are:

- Effective financial reporting.
- Limitations of financial reporting.
- Convergence of accounting standards.
- Standard-setting independence and accountability.

[40] FASB Statement of Financial Accounting Standards No. 141 (revised 2007), *Business Combinations*, p. vi.

As the co-chairmen of the FCAG stated, accounting was not a root cause of the financial crisis, but it has an important role to play in its resolution. Improved financial reporting will help restore the confidence of financial market participants and serve as a catalyst for increased financial stability and sound economic growth. The independence and integrity of the standard-setting process, including wide consultation, is critical to developing high-quality, broadly accepted accounting standards responsive to the issues highlighted by the crisis.

In September 2008, at the peak of the financial crisis, the IASB and the FASB described their plans to achieve convergence, in addition to the Norwalk Agreement issued in 2002, and the Memorandum of Understanding (MoU), originally issued in 2006. They reaffirmed the list of 11 fundamental topics that would lead to accounting convergence (namely, business combinations, consolidation, fair value measurement guidance, liabilities and equities distinction, performance reporting, postretirement benefits, derecognition, financial instruments, revenue recognition, intangible assets, and leases) and stated 2011 as the deadline.

In November 2009, the IASB and FASB issued a joint statement detailing the status of the convergence process and identified two particularly controversial topics: (1) accounting for financial instruments, and (2) de recognition of assets and liabilities. With respect to accounting for financial instruments, the IASB issued a new standard in November 2009 (IFRS 9). This new standard modified extant rules on accounting for financial instruments as assets, whereas it leaves financial instruments as liabilities under the scope of the old IAS 39. Indications were that the FASB had also reached an agreement about many specifics of a new standard on financial instruments.

In 2011, the FASB and IASB completed the *Fair Value Measurement* project and issued SFAS 257 and IFRS 13, respectively. However, the FASB's activities during the aftermath of the global financial crisis were described as "riding two horses." On the one hand, it had to respond to the financial reporting crisis, and on the other hand, it needed to take timely actions to improve U.S. GAAP while also working with the IASB.

AICPA and IFRS Convergence

The AICPA announced in May 2008 that private companies were allowed to adopt IFRS ahead of publicly traded companies. This gave AICPA members the option to conduct audits in line with IFRS as an alternative to U.S. GAAP. As a result, U.S.-based private companies that were subsidiaries of foreign parent companies using IFRS were allowed to adopt IFRS in their audited financial statements.

The attempts at convergence between IFRS and U.S. GAAP have brought about an actual narrowing of differences. As a result, U.S. accounting professionals have found it much easier to work in Europe. Further, international companies no longer have to reconcile from IFRS to U.S. GAAP to be registered in the United States. In 2009, a survey conducted by KPMG and the AAA, collecting about 500 responses from U.S. accounting academics, showed 75 percent of the respondents indicating that IFRS should immediately be introduced into the accounting curriculum.

However, the 2008 financial crisis had an impact on the convergence process. In particular, it prompted debates on such fundamental issues as (1) how to report information about financial instruments, (2) the appropriateness of fair values, and (3) the perimeter of consolidation in cases of "special purpose" business combinations. These three items were already on the list of the fundamental topics considered in the MoU of 2006, and the Boards were under pressure to issue accounting standards on these controversial issues.

Revision of the Conceptual Framework

The IASB and FASB have agreed to work together to produce a conceptual framework that will be built upon the IASB's and FASB's existing frameworks and will provide a basis for developing future accounting standards by the boards. The boards have agreed to the following phases of this project:

A. Objectives and qualitative characteristics
B. Elements and recognition
C. Measurement
D. Reporting entity
E. Presentation and disclosure
F. Purpose and status
G. Application to not-for-profit entities
H. Finalization

The two boards jointly published a discussion paper, *Preliminary Views on an Improved Conceptual Framework for Financial Reporting: The Objective of Financial Reporting and Qualitative Characteristics of Decision-useful Financial Reporting Information.*[41] As part of this project, the IASB has consulted views from interested parties with the aim of converging international and U.S. accounting standards. In response, the Institute of Chartered Accountants in Scotland pointed out that the term "fair value" is used in different ways in the two sets of standards, and suggested that the IASB develop its own higher-level guidance that could be relevant to the U.S. context. They state, "The problem is that U.S. GAAP requires fair values in much more limited circumstances than IFRS, especially for financial instruments, for some of which there are efficient markets. For other types of assets and liabilities, such as stock or a straightforward loan, applying this guidance would result in numbers that bear little resemblance to economic reality."

The preceding discussion paper sets out a draft of the first chapter of their proposed improved "conceptual framework," and includes several changes. First, it proposes a decision-useful objective and argues that information relevant to assessing stewardship will be encompassed in that objective. However, it is important to note that stewardship and decision usefulness are parallel objectives with different emphases. It can be argued that they should be defined as separate objectives. For example, there is strong support in Europe for stewardship as a core objective of financial reporting. The European Financial Reporting Advisory Group (EFRAG), the Accounting Standards Board (ASB), and a number of other European accounting standard-setters have published a brief paper discussing the rationale for including stewardship or directors' accountability to shareholders as a separate objective of financial reporting.

Second, taking a stakeholder approach, the users of financial reports, other than capital providers, would be explicitly acknowledged in the proposed objective of financial reporting. This reflects an amendment to the current U.S. "conceptual framework," which takes a shareholder approach. Third, the IASB and the FASB have tentatively decided that an asset of an entity would be "a present economic resource to which, through an enforceable right or other means, the entity has access or can limit the access of others." Fourth, emphasis would be placed on

---

[41] This "preliminary views" document deals only with financial reporting by business entities in the private sector. It does not consider issues that arise in connection with not-for-profit entities (such as charities) or entities in the public sector.

developing principles and measurement guidance for *fair value* measurements in IFRS. In particular, the IASB plans to assess whether an "exit price" was the measurement basis intended by each standard, and when an exit price was not the measurement basis intended, whether additional guidance should be developed.

The question of whether financial reporting should be based on "decision usefulness" or should also recognize *stewardship* as a separate objective is not new, but it has come to the fore again as a result of the publication of this discussion paper by the IASB and the FASB.

In regard to the use of "fair values" in financial statements, in November 2006, the IASB published for public comment a discussion paper on fair value measurement in financial reports. In February 2007, the FASB issued a standard, SFAS No. 159, *The Fair Value Option for Financial Assets and Financial Liabilities,* which provides companies with an option to report selected financial assets and liabilities at fair value. SFAS 159 establishes a single definition of fair value together with a framework for measuring fair value for financial reports in accordance with U.S. GAAP. The standard requires companies to provide additional information that will help investors and other users of financial statements to more easily understand the effect of the company's choice to use fair value on its earnings. It also requires entities to display the fair value of those assets and liabilities for which the company has chosen to use fair value on the face of the balance sheet.[42]

IFRS require some assets, liabilities, and equity instruments to be measured at fair value. However, the current guidance on fair value measurement is inconsistent, incomplete, and scattered. The IASB has published its proposed changes to the accounting for financial liabilities. These proposed changes follow work completed on the classification and measurement of financial assets (IFRS 9, *Financial Instruments*). They involve limited changes to the accounting for liabilities, with changes to the fair value option. The proposals respond to the view that volatility in profit or loss resulting from changes in the credit risk of liabilities that an entity chooses to measure at fair value is counter intuitive and does not provide useful information to investors.

It is clear that the revised conceptual framework will include elements of both the IASB and FASB frameworks. For example, the IASB/FASB joint project on revenue recognition has as its objective the development of a single comprehensive set of principles for revenue recognition that is based on assets and liabilities. Under the asset and liability approach, revenue would be recognized based on changes in contract assets and liabilities, as opposed to the performance of obligations.

In a joint statement issued by the FASB and IASB in November 2009, the two boards affirmed June 2011 as the target date for completing the major projects in the 2006 Memorandum of Understanding (MoU), as updated in May 2008 through a Discussion Paper, "Preliminary Views on an Improved Conceptual Framework for Financial Reporting: The Reporting Entity." Accordingly, the two boards issued an Exposure Draft in March 2010, "Conceptual Framework for Financial Reporting—The Reporting Entity" (Exposure Draft ED/2010/2), with a view to bringing about significant improvement and convergence between IFRS and U.S. GAAP. Many aspects of IASB's and FASB's conceptual frameworks are consistent with each other. For example, neither the IASB's *Framework for the Preparation and Presentation of Financial Statements* nor FASB Concepts Statements override authoritative standards, even though some may be inconsistent with them.

---

[42] This statement is effective as of the beginning of an entity's first fiscal year beginning after November 15, 2007.

The boards focused mainly on the improvement and convergence of their existing frameworks, and they initially considered concepts applicable to business entities in the private sector. In this phase of the conceptual framework project, the boards are considering conceptual matters relating to the reporting entity. The conceptual matters considered by other phases include the objective of financial reporting and the qualitative characteristics of financial reporting information, the elements of financial statements, and measurement. Matters of presentation and disclosure, and the applicability of the concepts in earlier phases to other types of entities, are expected to be considered in later phases.

The IASB's *Framework* defines the reporting entity as "an entity for which there are users who rely on the financial statements as their major source of financial information about the entity." The FASB's *Statement of Financial Accounting Concepts* does not contain a definition of a reporting entity or a discussion of how to identify one. The Exposure Draft jointly issued by the IASB and FASB defines a reporting entity as "a circumscribed area of economic activities whose financial information has the potential to be useful to existing and potential equity investors, lenders, and other creditors who cannot directly obtain the information they need in making decisions about providing resources to the entity and in assessing whether the management and the governing board of that entity have made efficient and effective use of the resources provided."

This concept of reporting entity is intended to further the objective of financial reporting, which is to provide financial information about the reporting entity that is useful in making decisions about providing resources to the entity and in assessing whether the management and the governing board of that entity have made efficient and effective use of the resources provided. However, during late 2010, the IASB deferred further work on the joint project with the FASB on the conceptual framework until after other more urgent convergent projects were finalized. In September 2012, the IASB reactivated the conceptual framework project as an IASB-only comprehensive project.

SOME CONCLUDING REMARKS

In the quest to achieve convergence with national accounting standards, the IASB must remain alert to the potential for it to be unduly influenced by interested parties. Commenting on the IASB's strategy to engineer convergence through a process of formal liaison with leading national standard-setters, Professor Steven Zeff warns about the political pressures that may be triggered by any board initiative to prescribe specific accounting treatments, eliminate alternative treatments, impose additional disclosure requirements, or tighten interpretations.[43] Most accounting issues are politically sensitive, because the need for standards often arises where there is controversy, and accounting can have economic consequences that affect the wealth of different groups. As a result, different groups interested in a particular accounting issue can be expected to lobby for the standard most beneficial to them, or to prevent the establishment of a proposed standard which they believe would be less favorable than the status quo.

The issue of accounting standards convergence versus financial statement comparability also should not be overlooked. Convergence of standards does not necessarily produce comparable financial statements. Cultural and other factors

---

[43] S. Zeff, "Political Lobbying on Proposed Standards: A Challenge to the IASB," *Accounting Horizons* 16, no. 1 (2002), pp. 43–54.

could lead to different interpretations of standards and different levels of compliance across countries, leading to the production of financial statements that might not be entirely comparable.

Summary

1. Harmonization and convergence are processes of reducing differences in financial reporting practices across countries.

2. Unlike harmonization, convergence implies the adoption of one set of standards internationally. The major goal of both harmonization and convergence is comparability of financial statements.

3. Harmonization or convergence of accounting standards might not necessarily result in comparable financial statements internationally due to nation-specific factors such as culture.

4. Proponents of international accounting harmonization/convergence argue that cross-country comparability of financial statements is required for the globalization of capital markets. Opponents argue that globalization is occurring without harmonization/convergence and that it might be appropriate for countries with different environments to have different standards.

5. Several organizations were involved in the harmonization efforts at global and regional levels, including IOSCO, IFAC, and the EU.

6. To achieve a common capital market, the European Union (EU) attempted to harmonize accounting through the issuance of the Fourth and the Seventh Directives. Although the EU directives reduced differences in accounting in Europe, complete comparability was not achieved. Rather than developing additional directives, the European Commission decided to require the use of IFRS beginning in 2005.

7. The International Accounting Standards Committee (IASC) was formed in 1973 to develop international accounting standards universally acceptable in all countries. In 2001, the IASC was replaced by the International Accounting Standards Board (IASB).

8. The IASB has 16 members (13 full-time and 3 part-time). The IASB adheres to an open process in developing standards, which are principles-based (rather than rules-based). With the establishment of the IASB, there has been a shift in emphasis from harmonization to global standard-setting or convergence.

9. The IASB's main item is to develop a set of high-quality financial reporting standards for global use.

10. As of August 2010, International Financial Reporting Standards (IFRS) consisted of 30 IASs, 9 IFRS, and a number of interpretations. As a private organization, the IASB does not have the ability to require the use of its standards.

11. The International Organization of Securities Commissions (IOSCO) recommends that securities regulators permit foreign issuers to use IFRS for cross-listing. Most major stock exchanges are in compliance with this recommendation. In addition, a large and growing number of countries either require or allow domestic listed companies to use IFRS in preparing consolidated financial statements. The EU's adoption of IFRS in 2005 was a major boost to the IASB's legitimacy as a global accounting standard-setter.

12. The IASB's *Framework for the Preparation and Presentation of Financial Statements* establishes usefulness for decision making as the primary objective of financial

statements prepared under IFRS. Understandability, relevance, reliability, and comparability are the primary qualitative characteristics that make financial statements useful. The *Framework* also provides workable definitions of the accounting elements.

13. IAS 1 is a single standard providing guidelines for the presentation of financial statements. The standard stipulates that a set of IFRS-based financial statements must include a balance sheet, an income statement, a statement of cash flows, a statement of changes in equity, and accounting polices and explanatory notes. IAS 1 establishes the overriding principle of fair presentation and permits an override of a requirement of an IASB standard in the extremely rare situation where management concludes that compliance with a requirement of a standard would be misleading.

14. IFRS 1 provides guidance to companies that are adopting IFRS for the first time. IFRS 1 requires an entity to comply with each IFRS effective at the reporting date of its first IFRS financial statements. However, IFRS 1 provides exemptions to this rule where the cost of complying with this requirement would likely exceed the benefit to users.

15. In 2002, the FASB and IASB signed the Norwalk Agreement, in which they agreed to work toward convergence of their two sets of financial reporting standards.

16. In February 2007, the FASB issued SFAS 159, *The Fair Value Opinion for Financial Assets and Financial Liabilities*, which provides companies with an option to report selected financial assets and liabilities at fair values, bringing U.S. GAAP and IFRS closer together.

17. In November 2007, the SEC removed the requirement that foreign private issuers using IFRS must reconcile their financial statements to U.S. GAAP.

18. Although the two boards had previously agreed to revise their respective conceptual frameworks as a joint project, recently the IASB has decided to launch an IASB-only project to develop a conceptual framework.

Appendix to Chapter 3

What Is This Thing Called Anglo-Saxon Accounting?

The term *Anglo-Saxon* or *Anglo-American* is used for a group of countries that includes the United States, the United Kingdom, Canada, Australia, and New Zealand. This group often figures in international accounting textbooks and articles, particularly with regard to international classification of accounting systems and international harmonization of accounting standards. The efforts of the IASB (and its predecessor, the IASC) are usually associated with Anglo-Saxon accounting. Some even criticize the IASB for attempting to promote Anglo-Saxon accounting throughout the world. However, many non-Anglo countries are already using IFRS. Given this, it is important to examine some of the important features of Anglo-Saxon accounting, which is the basis for IFRS.

In a broad sense, the term *Anglo-Saxon accounting* refers to the accounting systems prevalent in the English-speaking countries mentioned in the preceding paragraph. Although the accounting systems in these countries are not identical, they share some fundamental features that distinguish them from other systems of accounting:

- A focus on how businesses operate at the firm level (micro orientation), with an emphasis on the importance of professional judgment (recognition of professional rules and professional self-regulation).
- An investor orientation, with the provision of information for efficient operation of the capital market as the primary aim (recognition of the importance of being transparent).
- Less emphasis on prudence and measurement of taxable income or distributable income, and willingness to go beyond superficial legal form (substance over form).[1]

There are other recognizable commonalities that are related to the above features. For example, because of the investor orientation and emphasis on transparency in accounting reports, the principle of true and fair view or fair presentation is predominant in Anglo-Saxon financial reporting. Auditors are required to report on whether, in their opinion, the financial statements have been prepared in such a way that they adhere to this principle. In the United Kingdom, the concept of *true and fair view* has not been clearly defined in legislation. The courts have placed considerable reliance on expert witnesses in developing a meaning for this concept. The UK government's view has been that this is a highly technical matter and therefore should be dealt with by the profession. This leaves open the possibility for different interpretations. There is no single true and fair view. There are also some differences in how the concept of true and fair view is applied. For example, in the United Kingdom, it is an overriding requirement. In other words, complying with the legal requirements does not necessarily lead to a true and fair view, in which case additional information should be provided. However, in Canada and Australia, a true-and-fair-view override does not apply. Further, the U.S. equivalent to true and fair view, *present fairly*, is defined in terms of conformity with U.S. GAAP. In other words, if the financial statements have been prepared in accordance with U.S. GAAP, then it is assumed that the information is presented fairly. In general, it is recognized that the application of the qualitative characteristics and appropriate accounting standards would normally result in financial statements that convey a true and fair view of such information, or that present it fairly.[2]

The use of a conceptual framework to provide guidance for developing accounting standards is another common feature among these countries. The qualitative characteristics such as understandability, relevance, reliability, and objectivity or representational faithfulness are found in the conceptual frameworks developed by all Anglo-Saxon countries and by the IASB. The IASB's conceptual framework is largely based on that of the U.S. FASB. This has been one of the reasons for the view that the IASB has been heavily influenced by Anglo-Saxon accounting. Another recognizable common feature among Anglo-Saxon countries is that they all have common law traditions rather than code law traditions. This means they all use common law legal systems, which tend to be flexible in terms of legislation

[1] Christopher W. Nobes, "On the Myth of 'Anglo-Saxon' Financial Accounting: A Comment," *International Journal of Accounting* 38 (2003), pp. 95–104.

[2] IASC, *Framework for the Preparation and Presentation of Financial Statements* (London: IASC, 1989).

and rely heavily on private-sector and market mechanisms for regulation. Related to this, all these countries have private-sector standard-setting bodies recognizing the profession's capacity to self-regulate.[3]

Some differences can be observed among Anglo-Saxon countries with regard to the recognizable common features described in the preceding paragraph. For example, the conceptual frameworks are not always used as the basis for developing accounting standards. As a case in point, SFAS 87, *Employers' Accounting for Pensions*, in the United States specifically states that it does not follow the FASB's conceptual framework. Further, a common law legal system does not necessarily lead to flexible standards. U.S. accounting standards are increasingly becoming more detailed and rigidly prescriptive as compared to accounting standards developed in the United Kingdom. With regard to private-sector standard-setting, traditionally the U.S. standard-setting system is significantly more public-sector-oriented than the UK system, because the U.S. Securities and Exchange Commission (SEC) has the ultimate responsibility for authorizing accounting standards. On the basis of these differences, some commentators have argued that Anglo-Saxon accounting is a myth.[4] However, such differences do not necessarily indicate that these countries cannot usefully be seen as members of the same group.[5]

Questions

1. How does harmonization differ from convergence?
2. What are the potential benefits that a multinational corporation could derive from the international convergence of accounting standards?
3. Were the EU directives effective in generating comparability of financial statements across companies located in member nations? Why or why not?
4. What were the three phases in the life of the IASC?
5. Why was IOSCO's endorsement of IASs so important to the IASC's efforts?
6. How does the structure of the IASB help to establish its legitimacy as a global standard-setter?
7. What is the IASB's principles-based approach to accounting standard-setting?
8. Are there any major accounting issues that have not yet been covered by IFRS?
9. Do you see a major change of emphasis in the harmonization process since the establishment of the IASB? Explain.
10. What are the different ways in which IFRS might be used within a country?
11. Would the worldwide adoption of IFRS result in worldwide comparability of financial statements? Why or why not?
12. In what way is the IASB's *Framework* intended to assist firms in preparing IFRS-based financial statements?
13. As expressed in IAS 1, what is the overriding principle that should be followed in preparing IFRS-based financial statements?

[3] Nobes (2003), op cit.

[4] David Alexander and Simon Archer, "On the Myth of 'Anglo-Saxon' Accounting," *International Journal of Accounting* 35, no. 4 (2000), pp. 539–57.

[5] Nobes (2003), op cit.

14. Under what conditions should a firm claim to prepare financial statements in accordance with IFRS?
15. To what extent have IFRS been adopted by countries around the world?
16. How has the U.S. SEC policy toward IFRS changed?

Exercises and Problems

1. "The IASB has been repeatedly accused of devising accounting standards that pay insufficient attention to the concerns and practices of companies. . . . Some European banks and insurers complain about poor due process by the IASB, and Frits Bolkestein, European commissioner responsible for accounting matters, endorsed their concerns earlier this month." (*Financial Times*, March 24, 2004, p. 20)

   Required:
   Elaborate on the concerns raised in the preceding quote, and discuss the measures that have been taken by the IASB to alleviate those concerns.

2. Since 2005, publicly traded companies in the European Union have been required to use IFRS in preparing their consolidated financial statements.

   Required:
   a. Explain the EU's objective in requiring the use of IFRS.
   b. Identify and describe two issues that might hamper the EU from achieving the objective underlying the use of IFRS.

3. Assume that you have been invited to advise the newly established accounting oversight body in one of the former Eastern European countries that became a member of the EU in May 2004. The accounting oversight body is charged with the task of identifying the main issues to be addressed in implementing the use of IFRS.

   Required:
   Prepare a report outlining the key points you would include in your advice to this accounting oversight body.

4. Refer to Exhibit 3.6 in this chapter and note the countries that do not permit domestic listed companies to use IFRS.

   Required:
   Identify three countries from this group that are likely to have different reasons for not permitting the use of IFRS by domestic listed companies. Describe those reasons.

5. On May 19, 2004, the IASB published a single volume of its official pronouncements that will be applicable from January 1, 2005.

   Required:
   Access the IASB Web site (www.iasb.org), search for these pronouncements, and prepare a list of them.

6. The professional accounting bodies in many countries have taken, or are taking, steps to adopt IFRS.

   Required:
   Go to the Web site of a professional accounting body of your choice and outline the steps it has taken so far to facilitate adoption of IFRS.

7. The appendix to this chapter describes what is commonly referred to as Anglo-Saxon accounting.

Required:
Explain why Anglo-Saxon accounting might be of interest to Chinese accounting regulators.

8. In its 2003 annual report, Honda Motor Company Ltd. states:

> Honda's manufacturing operations are principally conducted in 25 separate factories, 5 of which are located in Japan. Principal overseas manufacturing factories are located in the United States of America, Canada, the United Kingdom, France, Italy, Spain, India, Pakistan, the Philippines, Thailand, Vietnam, Brazil, and Mexico. . . . The company and its domestic subsidiaries maintain their books of account in conformity with financial accounting standards of Japan, and its foreign subsidiaries generally maintain their books of account in conformity with those of the countries of their domicile. The consolidated financial statements presented herein have been prepared in a manner and reflect the adjustments which are necessary to conform them with accounting principles generally accepted in the United States of America. (p. 59)

Required:
Discuss the possible reasons for Honda to prepare its consolidated financial statements in conformity with U.S. GAAP.

9. A list of foreign companies with shares traded on the New York Stock Exchange (NYSE) can be found on the NYSE's Web site (www.nyse.com).

Required:
a. Refer to Exhibit 3.6. Identify a developing country in Asia, Africa, and Latin America listed in Exhibit 3.6, and determine how many companies from each of these countries are listed on the NYSE. If the country you select first from a region does not have any NYSE-listed companies, identify another country included in Exhibit 3.6 from that region that does.
b. Describe the manner in which IFRS are used in each of the countries you have selected.

10. The *Financial Times,* on Tuesday, April 13, 2004, made the following comment in its editorial "Parmalat: Perennial Lessons of European Scandal: Urgent need for better enforcement and investor scepticism":

> After the accounting scandals in the US, there was an unseemly amount of crowing in Europe. As it happens, Parmalat is a much older scandal than Enron or WorldCom. It just took longer to come out at the Italian dairy company. . . . Convergence of standards—in accounting, for instance—will help spread best practice. . . . But we are nowhere near having a world super-regulator. . . . In Italy regulation has been weak because of fragmentation and lack of clout and resources. Attempts to tackle this and to ensure regulators' independence from political interference should be urgently pursued. (p. 12)

Required:
Discuss the lessons referred to above concerning the objectives of the current efforts at setting global standards for accounting and financial reporting.

11. The chapter describes different phases in the harmonization efforts of the IASC.

    Required:
    Identify one such phase and prepare a brief report describing its importance in the overall scheme of international harmonization of accounting standards. You should consult relevant literature in preparing this report.

12. The IASB's main objective is to develop a set of high-quality standards for financial reporting by companies at the international level.

    Required:
    Critically examine the possibility of achieving this objective.

13. Geneva Technology Company (GTC), a Swiss-based company founded in 1999, is considering the use of IFRS in preparing its annual report for the year ended December 31, 2013. You are the manager of GTC's fixed assets accounting department.

    Required:
    Identify the steps that you will need to take in your department to comply with the requirements of IFRS 1.

14. Recently the IASB revised IFRS 1.

    Required:
    What is the main reason for this revision?

15. The SEC lifted the requirement for foreign companies that have used IFRS as the basis for preparing their financial statements: that to be eligible to list their shares in U.S. stock exchanges, they should reconcile their financial statements using U.S. GAAP.

    Required:
    Discuss the possible reasons for this relaxation of rules.

16. The objective of convergence between IFRS and U.S. GAAP is no longer a priority for the IASB.

    Required:
    Discuss the possible reasons for, and the consequences of, the IASB's above decision.

Case 3-1

Jardine Matheson Group (Part 1)

With its broad portfolio of market-leading businesses, the Jardine Matheson Group is an Asian-based conglomerate with extensive experience in the region. Its business interests include Jardine Pacific, Jardine Motors Group, Hongkong Land, Dairy Farm, Mandarin Oriental, Cycle & Carriage, and Jardine Lloyd Thompson. These companies are leaders in the fields of engineering and construction, transport services, motor trading, property, retailing, restaurants, hotels, and insurance broking.

The Group's strategy is to build its operations into market leaders across Asia Pacific, each with the support of Jardine Matheson's extensive knowledge of the region and its long-standing relationships. Through a balance of cash-producing activities and investment in new businesses, the Group aims to produce sustained growth in shareholder value.

Incorporated in Bermuda, Jardine Matheson has its primary share listing in London, with secondary listings in Singapore and Bermuda. Jardine Matheson Limited operates from Hong Kong and provides management services to Group companies, making available senior management and providing financial, legal, human resources, and treasury support services throughout the Group.[1]

Jardine Matheson uses International Financial Reporting Standards in preparing its financial statements and has done so for a number of years.

Required

Access Jardine Matheson's most recent annual report on the company's Web site (www.jardine-matheson.com). Review the company's consolidated financial statements to evaluate whether the financial statements presented comply with the presentation requirements in IAS 1, *Presentation of Financial Statements*. Document your evaluation.

References

Alexander, David, and Simon Archer. "On the Myth of 'Anglo-Saxon' Accounting." *International Journal of Accounting* 35, no. 4 (2000), pp. 539–57.

BDO, Deloitte Touche Tohmatsu, Ernst & Young, Grant Thornton, KPMG, PricewaterhouseCoopers. *GAAP Convergence 2002: A Survey of National Efforts to Promote and Achieve Convergence with International Financial Reporting Standards.* Available at www.ifad.net.

Beresford, Dennis R. "Accounting for International Operations." *CPA Journal*, October 1988, pp. 79–80.

Cairns, David. "Compliance Must Be Enforced." *Accountancy International*, September 1998, pp. 64–65.

———. *Financial Times International Accounting Standards Survey.* London: FT Finance, 1999.

Carey, Anthony. "Harmonization: Europe Moves Forward." *Accountancy*, March 1990.

Carsberg, Sir Bryan. "Global Issues and Implementing Core International Accounting Standards: Where Lies IASC's Final Goal?" Remarks made at the 50th Anniversary Dinner, Japanese Institute of CPAs, Tokyo, October 23, 1998.

Chen, S., Z. Sun, and Y. Wang. "Evidence from China on Whether Harmonized Accounting Standards Harmonize Accounting Practices." *Accounting Horizons* 16, no. 3 (2002), pp. 183–97.

Choi, F. D. S. "A Cluster Approach to Harmonization." *Management Accounting*, August 1981, pp. 27–31.

Collins, Stephen H. "The SEC on Full and Fair Disclosure." *Journal of Accountancy*, January 1989, p. 84.

[1] www.jardine-matheson.com/profile/intro.html.

Commission of the European Communities. "EU Financial Reporting Strategy: The Way Forward." Communication from the Commission to the Council and the European Parliament, June 13, 2000.

Doupnik, Timothy S. "Recent Innovations in German Accounting Practice Through the Integration of EC Directives." *Advances in International Accounting* 5 (1992), pp. 75–103.

————, and M. Richter. "Interpretation of Uncertainty Expressions: A Cross-national Study." *Accounting, Organizations and Society* 28, no. 1 (2003), pp. 15–35.

Emenyonu, Emmanuel N., and Sidney J. Gray. "International Accounting Harmonization and the Major Developed Stock Market Countries: An Empirical Study." *International Journal of Accounting* 31, no. 3 (1996), pp. 269–79.

Ernst & Young. "Mind the GAAP: The Rise and Fall of IAS Lite." *Eye on IAS Newsletter,* June 2002, pp. 2–8.

Financial Accounting Standards Board. *The IASC-U.S. Comparison Project: A Report on the Similarities and Differences between IASC Standards and U.S. GAAP,* ed. Carrie Bloomer. Norwalk, CT: FASB, 1996.

Financial Accounting Standards Board. *The IASC-U.S. Comparison Project,* 2nd ed. Norwalk, CT: FASB, 1999.

Goeltz, Richard Karl. "International Accounting Harmonization: The Impossible (and Unnecessary?) Dream." *Accounting Horizons,* March 1991, pp. 85–86.

International Accounting Standards Committee. *Survey of the Use and Application of International Accounting Standards 1988.* London: IASC, 1988.

IOSCO. *Final Communique of the XXIXth Annual Conference of the International Organization of Securities Commissions.* Amman, May 17–20, 2004.

Nobes, Christopher W. "On the Myth of 'Anglo-Saxon' Financial Accounting: A Comment." *International Journal of Accounting* 38 (2003), pp. 95–104.

Street, Donna L., Sidney J. Gray, and Stephanie M. Bryant. "Acceptance and Observance of International Accounting Standards: An Empirical Study of Companies Claiming to Comply with IASs." *International Journal of Accounting* 34, no. 1 (1999), pp. 11–48.

"The World After WorldCom." *Financial Times,* June 27, 2002.

Zeff, S. "Political Lobbying on Proposed Standards: A Challenge to the IASB." *Accounting Horizons* 16, no. 1 (2002), pp. 43–54.

Chapter **Four**

International Financial Reporting Standards: Part I

Learning Objectives

After reading this chapter, you should be able to

- Discuss the types of differences that exist between International Financial Reporting Standards (IFRS) and U.S. generally accepted accounting principles (GAAP).
- Describe IFRS requirements related to the recognition and measurement of assets, specifically inventories; property, plant, and equipment; intangibles; and leased assets.
- Explain major differences between IFRS and U.S. GAAP on the recognition and measurement of assets.
- Describe the requirements of IFRS in a variety of disclosure and presentation standards.
- Explain major differences between IFRS and U.S. GAAP on certain disclosure and presentation issues.
- Analyze the impact that differences between IFRS and U.S. GAAP can have on the financial statements.

INTRODUCTION

As noted in Chapter 3, International Financial Reporting Standards (IFRS) have been adopted as generally accepted accounting principles (GAAP) for listed companies in many countries around the world and are accepted for cross-listing purposes by most major stock exchanges, including those in the United States.[1] Increasingly, accountants are being called on to prepare and audit, and users are finding it necessary to read and analyze, IFRS-based financial statements. With the U.S. Securities and Exchange Commission reaffirming its support for a global set of accounting standards, it is likely that IFRS will be integrated into

---

[1] The term *International Financial Reporting Standards (IFRS)* describes the body of authoritative pronouncements issued or adopted by the IASB. IFRS consist of International Accounting Standards issued by the IASC (and adopted by the IASB), International Financial Reporting Standards issued by the IASB, and interpretations developed by IFRIC or the former SIC.

the U.S. financial reporting system in the near future.[2] This chapter describes and demonstrates the requirements of selected IASB standards, particularly those relating to the recognition and measurement of assets, through numerical examples. IFRS that deal exclusively with disclosure and presentation issues also are briefly summarized.

The International Accounting Standards Committee (IASC) issued a total of 41 International Accounting Standards (IASs) during the period 1973–2001. Thirteen of these standards have been superseded or withdrawn. Most of the 28 remaining standards have been revised one or more times. Since 2001, the IASB has issued 13 International Financial Reporting Standards (IFRS). Exhibit 3.3 in Chapter 3 provides a list of IAS and IFRS issued by the IASB as of September 2013. In addition, more than 20 interpretations issued by the Standing Interpretations Committee (SIC) or International Financial Reporting Interpretations Committee (IFRIC) complement the standards to comprise the complete set of IFRS.

In this chapter, in addition to describing the guidance provided by IFRS, we make comparisons with U.S. GAAP to indicate the differences and similarities between the two sets of standards.[3] In this way, we can begin to appreciate the impact a choice between the two sets of standards has on financial statements.

TYPES OF DIFFERENCES BETWEEN IFRS AND U.S. GAAP

Numerous differences exist between IFRS and U.S. GAAP. The types of differences that exist can be classified as follows:

- *Definition differences.* Differences in definitions exist even though concepts are similar. Definition differences can lead to recognition or measurement differences.
- *Recognition differences.* Differences in recognition criteria and/or guidance are related to (1) whether an item is recognized or not, (2) how it is recognized (e.g., as a liability or as equity), and/or (3) when it is recognized (timing difference).
- *Measurement differences.* Differences in the *amount* recognized resulting from either (1) a difference in the method required or (2) a difference in the detailed guidance for applying a similar method.
- *Alternatives.* One set of standards allows a choice between two or more alternative methods; the other set of standards requires one specific method to be used.
- *Lack of requirements or guidance.* IFRS may not cover an issue addressed by U.S. GAAP, and vice versa.
- *Presentation differences.* Differences exist in the presentation of items in the financial statements.
- *Disclosure differences.* Differences in information presented in the notes to financial statements are related to (1) whether a disclosure is required and (2) the manner in which disclosures are required to be made.

In many cases, IFRS are more flexible than U.S. GAAP. For example, several IASB standards allow firms to choose between two alternative treatments in accounting for a particular item. Also, IFRS generally have less bright-line guidance

---

[2] Securities and Exchange Commission, Release Nos. 33-9109; 34-61578, *Commission Statement in Support of Convergence and Global Accounting Standards*, February 2010.

[3] It is important to remember that both IFRS and U.S. GAAP are moving targets, constantly changing. This chapter describes IFRS and makes comparisons with U.S. GAAP as of September 2013.

than U.S. GAAP; therefore, more judgment is required in applying IFRS. IFRS are said to constitute a principles-based accounting system (broad principles with limited detailed rules), whereas U.S. GAAP is a rules-based system.[4] However, for some accounting issues, IFRS are more detailed than U.S. GAAP.

Ernst & Young conducted a survey of 130 companies that provided reconciliation from IFRS to U.S. GAAP in their 2005 Form 20-F filed with the U.S. Securities and Exchange Commission.[5] Companies included in the survey were primarily located in the European Union, but it also included several companies in Switzerland, South Africa, and China. The 130 companies in the survey reported a total of 1,900 reconciling items, and 200 unique differences between IFRS and U.S. GAAP were identified. Many of the adjustments related to first-time application of IFRS. Pensions and business combinations were the two accounting issues that required adjustments by the greatest number of companies (122 companies and 100 companies, respectively). Other issues requiring adjustment by a large number of companies included provisions (74 companies), impairment of assets (62 companies), leases (49 companies), and intangibles (36 companies).

INVENTORIES

IAS 2, *Inventories,* is an example of an International Accounting Standard that provides more extensive guidance than U.S. GAAP, especially with regard to inventories of service providers and disclosures related to inventories. IAS 2 provides guidance on determining the initial cost of inventories, the cost formulas to be used in allocating the cost of inventories to expense, and the subsequent measurement of inventories on the balance sheet.

The cost of inventories includes costs of purchase, costs of conversion, and other costs:

- *Costs of purchase* include purchase price; import duties and other taxes; and transportation, handling, and other costs directly attributable to acquiring materials, services, and finished products.
- *Costs of conversion* include direct labor and a systematic allocation of variable and fixed production overhead. Fixed overhead should be applied based on a normal level of production.
- *Other costs* are included in the cost of inventories to the extent they are incurred to bring the inventories to their present location and condition. This can include the cost of designing products for specific customers. Under certain conditions, interest costs are allowed to be included in the cost of inventories for those items that require a substantial period of time to bring them to a salable condition.

Costs that are expressly excluded from the costs of inventories are:

- Abnormal amounts of wasted materials, labor, or other production costs.
- Storage costs, unless they are necessary in the production process before a further stage of production.

---

[4] In response to several accounting scandals, including those at Enron and WorldCom, the Sarbanes-Oxley Act passed by the U.S. Congress in 2002 required the FASB to investigate the desirability of U.S. GAAP shifting to a principles-based approach.

[5] Ernst & Young, *Towards Convergence—A Survey of IFRS/US GAAP Differences* (EYGM Limited, 2007). The publication is available at www.ey.com.

- Administrative overhead that does not contribute to bringing inventories to their present location and condition.
- Selling costs.

IAS 2 does not allow as much choice with regard to cost formulas as does U.S. GAAP. First-in, first-out (FIFO) and weighted-average cost are acceptable treatments, but last-in, first-out (LIFO) is not. The standard cost method and retail method also are acceptable provided that they approximate cost as defined in IAS 2. The cost of inventories of items that are not ordinarily interchangeable and goods or services produced and segregated for specific projects must be accounted for using the specific identification method. An entity must use the same cost formula for all inventories having a similar nature and use to the entity, even if they are located in different geographical locations. For inventories with a different nature or use, different cost formulas may be justified. U.S. GAAP does not require use of a uniform inventory valuation method for inventories having a similar nature. It is common for U.S. companies to use different methods in different jurisdictions for tax reasons—for example, LIFO in the United States and FIFO or average cost elsewhere.

Lower of Cost or Net Realizable Value

IAS 2 requires inventory to be reported on the balance sheet at the lower of cost or net realizable value. *Net realizable value* is defined as estimated selling price in the ordinary course of business less the estimated costs of completion and the estimated costs necessary to make the sale. This rule typically is applied on an item-by-item basis. However, the standard indicates that it may be appropriate to group similar items of inventory relating to the same product line. Write-downs to net realizable value must be reversed when the selling price increases.

U.S. GAAP requires inventory to be reported at the lower of cost or market, where market is defined as replacement cost with a ceiling (net realizable value) and a floor (net realizable value less normal profit margin). The two sets of standards will provide similar results only when replacement cost is greater than net realizable value. Application of this valuation rule may be done either item by item, by groups of inventory, or on a total inventory basis. Under U.S. GAAP, write-downs to market may not be reversed if replacement costs should subsequently increase.

Example: Application of Lower of Cost or Net Realizable Value Rule
Assume that Distributor Company Inc. has the following inventory item on hand at December 31, Year 1:

Historical cost.	$1,000.00
Replacement cost.	800.00
Estimated selling price	880.00
Estimated costs to complete and sell	50.00
Net realizable value	830.00
Normal profit margin—15%	124.50
Net realizable value less normal profit margin	$ 705.50

Net realizable value is $830, which is lower than historical cost. In accordance with IFRS, inventory must be written down by $170 ($1,000 − $830). The journal entry at December 31, Year 1, is:

Inventory Loss	$170	
Inventory		$170
To record the write-down on inventory due to decline in net realizable value.		

Under U.S. GAAP, market is replacement cost of $800 (falls between $705.50 and $830), which is lower than historical cost. Inventory must be written down by $200 ($1,000 − $800).

Assume that at the end of the first quarter in Year 2, replacement cost has increased to $900, the estimated selling price has increased to $980, and the estimated cost to complete and sell remains at $50. The item now has a net realizable value of $930. This is $100 greater than carrying amount (and $70 less than historical cost). Under IFRS, $100 of the write-down that was made at December 31, Year 1, is reversed through the following journal entry:

Inventory	$100	
Recovery of Inventory Loss (increase in income).		$100
To record a recovery of inventory loss taken in the previous period.		

Under U.S. GAAP, the new carrying amount for the item is $800, which is less than the current replacement cost of $900. However, no adjustment is made.

In effect, under IFRS, the historical cost of $1,000 is used in applying the lower of cost or net realizable value rule over the entire period the inventory is held. In contrast, under U.S. GAAP, the inventory write-down at the end of Year 1 establishes a new cost used in subsequent periods in applying the lower of cost or market rule.

Over the period of time that inventory is held by a firm, the two sets of standards result in the same amount of expenses (cost of goods sold plus any net inventory loss). However, the amount of expense recognized in any given accounting period can differ between the two rules, as can the amount at which inventory is measured on the balance sheet.

PROPERTY, PLANT, AND EQUIPMENT

IAS 16, *Property, Plant, and Equipment*, provides guidance for the following aspects of accounting for fixed assets:

1. Recognition of initial costs of property, plant, and equipment.
2. Recognition of subsequent costs.
3. Measurement at initial recognition.
4. Measurement after initial recognition.
5. Depreciation.
6. Derecognition (retirements and disposals).

Impairment of assets, including property, plant, and equipment, is covered by IAS 36, *Impairment of Assets.* Accounting for impairments is discussed later in this chapter.

Recognition of Initial and Subsequent Costs

Relying on the definition of an asset provided in the IASB's *Framework for the Preparation and Presentation of Financial Standards,* both initial costs and subsequent costs related to property, plant, and equipment should be recognized as an asset when (1) it is probable that future economic benefits will flow to the enterprise and (2) the cost can be measured reliably. Replacement of part of an asset should be capitalized if (1) and (2) are met, and the carrying amount of the replaced part should be derecognized (removed from the accounts).

Example: Replacement of Part of an Asset

Road Warriors Inc. acquired a truck with a useful life of 20 years at a cost of $150,000. At the end of the sixth year, the power train requires replacement. The remainder of the truck is perfectly roadworthy and is expected to last another 14 years. The cost of the new power train is $35,000.

The new power train will provide economic benefit to Road Warriors (it will allow the company to continue to use the truck), and the cost is measurable. The $35,000 cost of the new power train meets the asset recognition criteria and should be added to the cost of the truck. The original cost of the truck of $150,000 was not broken down by component, so the cost attributable to the original power train must be estimated. Assuming annual price increases for power trains of 5 percent, Road Warriors estimates that the cost of the original power train was $26,117 ($35,000/1.05^6). The appropriate journal entries to account for the replacement would be:

Truck	$35,000	
Cash		$35,000
Expense	$26,117	
Truck		$26,117

Measurement at Initial Recognition

Property, plant, and equipment should be initially measured at cost, which includes (1) purchase price, including import duties and taxes; (2) all costs directly attributable to bringing the asset to the location and condition necessary for it to perform as intended; and (3) an estimate of the costs of dismantling and removing the asset and restoring the site on which it is located.

An item of property, plant, and equipment acquired in exchange for a nonmonetary asset or combination of monetary and nonmonetary assets should be initially measured at fair value unless the exchange transaction lacks commercial substance. Fair value is defined as the "amount for which an asset could be exchanged between knowledgeable, willing parties in an arm's length transaction."[6] If the transaction lacks commercial substance or the fair value of the asset acquired and given up cannot be determined, then the cost of the asset acquired is measured as the carrying value of the asset given up. As a result, no gain or loss is recognized.

[6] IAS 16, paragraph 6.

Example: Dismantling and Removal Costs

Caylor Corporation constructed a powder coating facility at a cost of $3,000,000: $1,000,000 for the building and $2,000,000 for machinery and equipment. Local law requires the company to dismantle and remove the plant assets at the end of their useful life. Caylor estimates that the net cost, after deducting salvage value, for removal of the equipment is $100,000, and the net cost for dismantling and removing the building will be $400,000. The useful life of the facility is 20 years, and the company uses a discount rate of 10 percent in determining present values.

The initial cost of the machinery and equipment and the building must include the estimated dismantling and removal costs discounted to present value. The present value factor for a discount rate of 10 percent for 20 periods is 0.14864 ($1/1.10^{20}$). The calculations are as follows:

Building	
Construction cost	$1,000,000
Present value of dismantling and removal costs ($400,000 × 0.14864)	59,457
Total cost of the building	$1,059,457
Machinery and equipment	
Construction cost	$2,000,000
Present value of dismantling and removal costs ($100,000 × 0.14864)	14,864
Total cost of the machinery and equipment	$2,014,864

The journal entry to record the initial cost of the assets would be:

Building.	$1,059,457	
Machinery and Equipment.	2,014,864	
Cash		$3,000,000
Provision for dismantling and removal (long-term liability)		74,321

Measurement Subsequent to Initial Recognition

A substantive area of difference between IFRS and U.S. GAAP relates to the measurement of property, plant, and equipment subsequent to initial recognition. IAS 16 allows two treatments for reporting fixed assets on balance sheets subsequent to their acquisition: the cost model and the revaluation model.

Under the cost model, an item of property, plant, and equipment is carried on the balance sheet at cost less accumulated depreciation and any accumulated impairment losses. This is consistent with U.S. GAAP.

Under the revaluation model, an item of property, plant, and equipment is carried at a revalued amount, measured as fair value at the date of revaluation, less any subsequent accumulated depreciation and any accumulated impairment losses. If an enterprise chooses to follow this measurement model, revaluations must be made often enough that the carrying amount of assets does not differ materially from the assets' fair value. When revaluations are made, an entire class of property, plant, and equipment must be revalued. Revaluation increases are credited directly to the other comprehensive income component of equity as a revaluation surplus. Revaluation decreases are first recognized as a reduction in any related revaluation surplus, and, once the surplus is exhausted, additional revaluation decreases are recognized as an expense. The revaluation surplus may be transferred to retained earnings on disposal of the asset. Revalued assets may be presented either (1) at a gross amount less a separately reported accumulated depreciation (both revalued) or (2) at a net amount. Allowing firms the option to revalue fixed assets is one of the most substantial differences between IFRS and U.S. GAAP. Guidelines for applying this option are presented in more detail in the following paragraphs.

Determination of Fair Value

The basis of revaluation is the *fair value* of the asset at the date of revaluation. The definition in IAS 16 indicates that fair value is the amount at which an asset could be exchanged between knowledgeable, willing parties in an arm's-length transaction. The fair value of land and buildings is usually determined through appraisals conducted by professionally qualified valuers. The fair value of plant and equipment is also usually determined through appraisal. In the case of a specialized asset that is not normally sold, fair value may need to be estimated using, for example, a depreciated replacement cost approach. In 2009, the IASB issued an exposure draft, *Fair Value Measurement*, that is intended to provide considerably more guidance with respect to measuring the fair value of assets, including property, plant, and equipment, and liabilities. If approved as a final standard, this exposure draft also will substantially converge IFRS with U.S. GAAP with respect to how fair value is measured.

Frequency of Revaluation

IAS 16 requires that revalued amounts should not differ materially from fair values at the balance sheet date. The effect of this rule is that once an enterprise has opted for the revaluation model, it has an obligation to keep the valuations up to date. Although the IASB avoids mandating annual revaluations, these will be necessary in some circumstances in order to comply with the standard. In other cases, annual changes in fair value will be insignificant and revaluation may be necessary only every several years.

Selection of Assets to Be Revalued

IAS 16 requires that all assets of the same class be revalued at the same time. Selectivity *within a class* is not permitted, but selection *of a class* is. Different classes of assets described in the standard are as follows: land; land and buildings; machinery; office equipment; furniture and fixtures; motor vehicles; ships; and aircraft.

Detailed disclosures are required for each class of property, plant, and equipment (whether revalued or not). Thus, if a company divides its assets into many classes to minimize the effect of the rule about revaluing a whole class of assets, it will incur the burden of being required to make additional disclosures for each of those classes.

Accumulated Depreciation

Two alternative treatments are described in IAS 16 for the treatment of accumulated depreciation when a class of property, plant, and equipment is revalued:

1. Restate the accumulated depreciation proportionately with the change in the gross carrying amount of the asset so that the carrying amount of the asset after revaluation equals its revalued amount. The standard comments that this method is often used where an asset is revalued by means of an index and is the appropriate method for those companies using current cost accounting.
2. Eliminate the accumulated depreciation against the gross carrying amount of the asset, and restate the net amount to the revalued amount of the asset.

Example: Treatment of Accumulated Depreciation upon Revaluation

Assume that Kiely Company Inc. has buildings that cost $1,000,000, with accumulated depreciation of $600,000 and a carrying amount of $400,000 on December 31, Year 1. On that date, Kiely Company determines that the market value for these buildings is $750,000. Kiely Company wishes to carry buildings on the December 31, Year 1, balance sheet at a revalued amount. Under treatment 1, Kiely Company would restate both the buildings account and accumulated depreciation on buildings such that the ratio of net carrying amount to gross carrying amount is 40 percent ($400,000/$1,000,000) and the net carrying amount is $750,000. To accomplish this, the following journal entry would be made at December 31, Year 1:

Buildings	$875,000	
Accumulated Depreciation—Buildings		$525,000
Revaluation Surplus		350,000
To revalue buildings and related accumulated depreciation.		

	Original Cost		Revaluation		Total	%
Gross carrying amount	$1,000,000	+	$875,000	=	$1,875,000	100%
Accumulated depreciation	600,000	+	525,000	=	1,125,000	60
Net carrying amount	$ 400,000	+	$350,000	=	$ 750,000	40%

Under treatment 2, accumulated depreciation of $600,000 is first eliminated against the buildings account, and then the buildings account is increased by $350,000 to result in a net carrying amount of $750,000. The necessary journal entries are as follows:

Accumulated Depreciation—Buildings	$600,000	
Buildings		$600,000
To eliminate accumulated depreciation on buildings to be revalued.		
Buildings	$350,000	
Revaluation Surplus		$350,000
To revalue buildings.		

As a result of making these two entries, the buildings account has a net carrying amount of $750,000 ($1,000,000 − 600,000 + 350,000). Under both treatments, both assets and equity are increased by a net amount of $350,000.

Treatment of Revaluation Surpluses and Deficits

On the first revaluation after initial recording, the treatment of increases and decreases in carrying amount as a result of revaluation is very straightforward:

- Increases are credited directly to a revaluation surplus in the other comprehensive income component of equity.
- Decreases are charged to the income statement as an expense.

At subsequent revaluations, the following rules apply:

- To the extent that there is a previous revaluation surplus with respect to an asset, a decrease first should be charged against it and any excess of deficit over that previous surplus should be expensed.

- To the extent that a previous revaluation resulted in a charge to expense, a subsequent upward revaluation first should be recognized as income to the extent of the previous expense and any excess should be credited to other comprehensive income in equity.

Example: Treatment of Revaluation Surplus

Assume that Kiely Company Inc. has elected to measure property, plant, and equipment at revalued amounts. Costs and fair values for Kiely Company's three classes of property, plant, and equipment at December 31, Year 1 and Year 2, are as follows:

	Land	Buildings	Machinery
Cost.	$100,000	$500,000	$200,000
Fair value at 12/31/Y1	120,000	450,000	210,000
Fair value at 12/31/Y2	150,000	460,000	185,000

The following journal entries are made at December 31, Year 1, to adjust the carrying amount of the three classes of property, plant, and equipment to fair value:

Land	$20,000	
Revaluation Surplus—Land		$20,000
Loss on Revaluation—Buildings (expense).	$50,000	
Buildings.		$50,000
Machinery	$10,000	
Revaluation Surplus—Machinery		$10,000

At December 31, Year 2, the following journal entries are made:

Land	$30,000	
Revaluation Surplus—Land		$30,000
Buildings	$10,000	
Recovery of Loss on Revaluation—Buildings (income)		$10,000
Revaluation Surplus—Machinery	$10,000	
Loss on Revaluation—Machinery (expense)	15,000	
Machinery.		$25,000

IAS 16 indicates that the revaluation surplus in equity may be transferred to retained earnings when the surplus is realized. The surplus may be considered to be realized either through use of the asset or upon its sale or disposal. Accordingly, the revaluation surplus in equity may be transferred in one of two ways to retained earnings:

- A lump sum may be transferred at the time the asset is sold or scrapped.
- Within each period, an amount equal to the difference between depreciation on the revalued amount and depreciation on the historical cost of the asset may be transferred to retained earnings.

A third possibility apparently allowed by IAS 16 would be to do nothing with the revaluation surplus. However, this would result in a revaluation surplus being reported in equity related to assets no longer owned by the firm.

128   Chapter Four

Insight into the effect the revaluation model has on financial statements can be gained by examining the U.S. GAAP reconciliations that were required of foreign companies with shares publicly traded in the United States. With shares traded on the New York Stock Exchange, until 2007 China Eastern Airlines Corporation (CEA) was required to reconcile IFRS-based income and shareholders' equity to a U.S. GAAP basis. Exhibit 4.1 presents CEA's reconciliation to U.S. GAAP, along with the note describing significant differences between IFRS and U.S. GAAP with respect to revaluation of property, plant, and equipment. In reconciling "consolidated profit/(loss) attributable to the Company's equity holders," CEA makes an adjustment for the "reversal of net revaluation surplus, net of depreciation charges." This adjustment reflects the amount of additional depreciation expense recognized under IFRS on higher revalued amounts that would not be taken under U.S. GAAP. In 2006, profit/(loss) under IFRS was increased by 53.7 million renminbi (RMB) to adjust to a U.S. GAAP basis. CEA also makes a positive adjustment in reconciling to U.S. GAAP income for the "profit/(loss) on disposals of aircraft and related assets." Revalued assets have a higher book value than assets carried at cost. As a result, when revalued assets are sold, the gain on sale is smaller than it otherwise would be. In 2006, CEA increased U.S. GAAP income by RMB 156.5 million to include the larger gain that would have been recognized if assets had been carried at cost (under U.S. GAAP) rather than revalued amounts (under IFRS).

EXHIBIT 4.1

CHINA EASTERN AIRLINES CORPORATION LIMITED
Form 20-F
2006
Revaluation of Property, Plant, and Equipment

Notes to the Consolidated Financial Statements

Excerpt from Note 40, Significant Differences between IFRS and U.S. GAAP

Differences between IFRS and U.S. GAAP which have significant effects on the consolidated profit/(loss) attributable to equity holders and consolidated net assets of the Group are summarized as follows:

	Note	2004 RMB'000	2005 RMB'000	2006 RMB'000
Consolidated profit/(loss) attributable to the Company's equity holders				
As stated under IFRS		456,371	(438,728)	(3,452,765)
Less: Minority interests	(h)	(135,680)	(28,579)	139,340
		320,691	(467,307)	(3,313,425)
U.S. GAAP adjustments:				
Net (loss)/income after tax effect attributable to CEA Northwest and CEA Yunnan	(a)	24,424	(575,326)	—
Reversal of net revaluation surplus, net of depreciation charges	(b)	57,568	73,803	53,772
Profit/(loss) on disposals of aircraft and related assets	(b)	7,099	861	156,589
Rescission of related party lease arrangements	(c)	(133,029)	—	—
Reversal of the impact of the new overhaul accounting policy adopted in 2005	(d)	227,510	(471,756)	—
Recognition of additional write-down in relation to assets held for sale	(e)	—	—	(434,561)
Reversal of gain on sale and leaseback of aircraft recognized under IFRS	(f)	—	—	(126,470)

Others	(i)	(1,518)	(3,720)	26,997
Deferred tax effect on the U.S. GAAP adjustments	(j)	(43,598)	60,122	(23,872)
As stated under U.S. GAAP		459,147	(1,383,323)	(3,660,970)
Basic and fully diluted earning/(loss) per share under U.S. GAAP		RMB 0.094	(RMB 0.284)	(RMB 0.741)
Basic and fully diluted earning/(loss) per American Depository Share ("ADS") under U.S. GAAP		RMB 9.43	(RMB 28.42)	(RMB 74.12)
Consolidated net assets				
As stated under IFRS		7,302,086	6,918,542	3,476,643
Less: Minority interests	(h)	(820,835)	(822,477)	(661,746)
		6,481,251	6,096,065	2,814,897
U.S. GAAP adjustments:				
Impact on equity before tax effect attributable to CEA Northwest and CEA Yunnan	(a)	(1,426,741)	413,841	413,841
Reversal of net revaluation surplus net of depreciation charges and profit/(loss) on disposals of aircraft and related assets	(b)	(480,010)	(405,346)	(194,985)
Reversal of impact of the new overhaul accounting policy adopted in 2005	(d)	471,756	—	—
Recognition of additional write-down in relation to assets held for sale	(e)	—	—	(434,561)
Reversal of gain on sale-and-leaseback of aircraft recognized under IFRS	(f)	—	—	(126,470)
Recognition of the funded status of postretirement benefits obligations under U.S. GAAP	(g)	—	—	(548,428)
Others	(i)	34,453	(12,140)	(12,365)
Deferred tax effect on the U.S. GAAP adjustments	(j)	(52,993)	7,129	(16,232)
As stated under U.S. GAAP		5,027,716	6,099,549	1,895,697

(b) Revaluation of property, plant, and equipment

Under IFRS, the Group's property, plant, and equipment are initially recorded at cost and are subsequently restated at revalued amounts less accumulated depreciation. The excess depreciation charge arising from the revaluation surplus was approximately RMB57,568,000, RMB73,803,000, and RMB53,772,000 for the years ended December 31, 2004, 2005, and 2006, respectively. The additional gains arising from the revaluation surplus on disposals of revalued property, plant, and equipment were approximately gains of RMB7,099,000, RMB861,000, and RMB156,589,000 for the years ended December 31, 2004, 2005, and 2006, respectively.

Under U.S. GAAP, property, plant, and equipment are stated at cost less accumulated depreciation and impairment charges, if any. Accordingly, the revaluation surplus, the related differences in depreciation charges and gains or losses on disposals on aircraft and the related assets are reversed.

In reconciling "consolidated net assets" (stockholders' equity) from IFRS to U.S. GAAP, CEA includes an adjustment for the "reversal of net revaluation surplus net of depreciation charges and profit/(loss) on disposals of aircraft and related assets." This one-line item actually combines three different adjustments:

1. The original revaluation surplus (less accumulated depreciation) included in other comprehensive income (stockholders' equity) under IFRS is reversed. This results in a smaller amount of other comprehensive income under U.S. GAAP.

2. The difference in depreciation expense under IFRS and U.S. GAAP results in an adjustment to retained earnings; U.S. GAAP retained earnings is larger.

3. The additional amount of gain on disposal of assets that would have been recognized under U.S. GAAP also results in a larger amount of U.S. GAAP retained earnings.

The first adjustment is larger in amount than the latter two. In 2006, the sum of these three adjustments caused net assets on a U.S. GAAP basis to be RMB194 million smaller than under IFRS. This amount represents 6.9 percent of IFRS net assets.

Depreciation

Depreciation is based on estimated useful lives, taking residual value into account. The depreciation method should reflect the pattern in which the asset's future economic benefits are expected to be consumed; straight-line depreciation will not always be appropriate. IAS 16 requires estimates of useful life, residual value, and the method of depreciation to be reviewed on an annual basis. Changes in depreciation method, residual value, and useful life are treated prospectively as changes in estimates.

When an item of property, plant, and equipment is comprised of significant parts for which different depreciation methods or useful lives are appropriate, each part must be depreciated separately. This is commonly referred to as component depreciation. Components can be physical, such as an aircraft engine, or nonphysical, such as a major inspection. Component depreciation is not commonly used under U.S. GAAP.

Example: Component Depreciation

On January 1, Year 1, an entity acquires a new piece of machinery with an estimated useful life of 10 years for $120,000. The machine has an electrical motor that must be replaced every five years and is estimated to cost $10,000 to replace. In addition, by law the machine must be inspected every two years; the inspection cost is $2,000. The company has determined that the straight-line method of depreciation best reflects the pattern in which the asset's future benefits will be consumed. Assuming no residual value, depreciation of $13,800 on this machinery in Year 1 is determined in the following manner:

Component	Cost	Useful Life	Depreciation
Motor	$ 10,000	5 years	$ 2,000
Inspection	2,000	2 years	1,000
Machine	108,000	10 years	10,800
Total	$120,000		$13,800

Derecognition

Derecognition refers to the removal of an asset or liability from the balance sheet and the accounts. The carrying amount of an item of property, plant, and equipment is derecognized (1) upon disposal, or (2) when no future economic benefits are expected from its use or disposal. The gain or loss arising from the derecognition of an item of property, plant, and equipment is included in net income.

Note that an item of property, plant, and equipment should be reclassified as "noncurrent assets held for sale" when the asset's carrying amount is to be recovered by selling the asset rather than by using the asset. IFRS 5, *Noncurrent Assets Held for Sale and Discontinued Operations*, provides guidance with respect to the accounting treatment for noncurrent assets, including property, plant, and equipment, that are held for sale, as well as guidance with respect to the accounting for discontinued operations.

INVESTMENT PROPERTY

IAS 40, *Investment Property*, prescribes the accounting treatment for investment property, which is defined as land and/or buildings held to earn rentals, capital appreciation, or both. The principles related to accounting for property, plant, and equipment generally apply to investment property, including the option to use either a cost model or a fair value model in measuring investment property subsequent to acquisition. The fair value model for investment property differs from the revaluation method for property, plant, and equipment in that changes in fair value are recognized as gains or losses in current income and not as a revaluation surplus. Even if an entity chooses the cost model, it is required to disclose the fair value of investment property in the notes to financial statements. In contrast to IFRS, U.S. GAAP generally requires use of the cost model for investment property.

IMPAIRMENT OF ASSETS

IAS 36, *Impairment of Assets*, requires impairment testing and recognition of impairment losses for property, plant, and equipment; intangible assets; goodwill; and investments in subsidiaries, associates, and joint ventures. It does not apply to inventory, construction in progress, deferred tax assets, employee benefit assets, or financial assets such as accounts and notes receivable. U.S. GAAP also requires impairment testing of assets. However, several important differences exist between the two sets of standards.

Under IAS 36, an entity must assess annually whether there are any indicators that an asset is impaired. Events that might indicate an asset is impaired are:

- *External events,* such as a decline in market value, increase in market interest rate, or economic, legal, or technological changes that adversely affect the value of an asset.
- *Internal events,* such as physical damage, obsolescence, idleness of an asset, the restructuring of part of an asset, or the worse-than-expected economic performance of the asset.

If indicators of impairment are present, an entity must estimate the recoverable amount of the asset and compare that amount with the asset's carrying amount (book value).

Definition of Impairment

Under IAS 36, an asset is impaired when its carrying amount exceeds its recoverable amount.

- *Recoverable amount* is the greater of *net selling price* and *value in use.*
- *Net selling price* is the price of an asset in an active market less disposal costs.
- *Value in use* is determined as the present value of future net cash flows expected to arise from continued use of the asset over its remaining useful life and upon disposal. In calculating value in use, projections of future cash flows should be based on approved budgets and should cover a maximum of five years (unless a longer period can be justified). The discount rate used to determine present value should reflect current market assessments of the time value of money and the risks specific to the asset under review.

Under U.S. GAAP, impairment exists when an asset's carrying amount exceeds the future cash flows (undiscounted) expected to arise from its continued use and disposal. Net selling price is not involved in the test, and future cash flows are not discounted to their present value. When value in use is the recoverable amount under IAS 36, an impairment is more likely to arise under IFRS (discounted cash flows) than under U.S. GAAP (undiscounted cash flows).

Measurement of Impairment Loss

The measurement of impairment loss under IAS 36 is straightforward. It is the amount by which carrying value exceeds recoverable amount, and it is recognized in income. In the case of property, plant, and equipment carried at a revalued amount, the impairment loss is first taken against revaluation surplus and then to income.

The comparison of carrying value and undiscounted future cash flows under U.S. GAAP is done to determine whether an asset is impaired. The impairment loss is then measured as the amount by which carrying value exceeds *fair value*. Fair value may be determined by reference to quoted market prices in active markets, estimates based on the values of similar assets, or estimates based on the results of valuation techniques. It is unlikely that fair value (U.S. GAAP) and recoverable amount (IFRS) for an asset will be the same, resulting in differences in the amount of impairment loss recognized between the two sets of standards.

Example: Determination and Measurement of Impairment Loss

At December 31, Year 1, Toca Company has specialized equipment with the following characteristics:

Carrying amount	$50,000
Selling price	40,000
Costs of disposal	1,000
Expected future cash flows	55,000
Present value of expected future cash flows	46,000

In applying IAS 36, the asset's recoverable amount would be determined as follows:

Net selling price	$40,000 − 1,000 = $39,000	
Value in use	$46,000	
Recoverable amount (greater of the two)		$46,000

The determination and measurement of impairment loss would be:

Carrying amount	$50,000
Recoverable amount	46,000
Impairment loss	$ 4,000

The following journal entry would be made to reflect the impairment of this asset:

Impairment Loss	$4,000	
Equipment		$4,000
To recognize an impairment loss on equipment.		

Under U.S. GAAP, an impairment test would be carried out as follows:

Carrying value	$50,000
Expected future cash flows (undiscounted).	55,000

Because expected future cash flows exceed the asset's carrying value, no impairment is deemed to exist. The asset would be reported on the December 31, Year 1, balance sheet at $50,000.

Reversal of Impairment Losses

At each balance sheet date, a review should be undertaken to determine if impairment losses have reversed. (Indicators of impairment reversal are provided in IAS 36.) If, subsequent to recognizing an impairment loss, the recoverable amount of an asset is determined to exceed its new carrying amount, the impairment loss should be reversed. However, the loss should be reversed only if there are changes in the estimates used to determine the original impairment loss or there is a change in the basis for determining the recoverable amount (from value in use to net selling price or vice versa). The carrying value of the asset is increased, but not to exceed what it would have been if no impairment loss had been recognized. The reversal of an impairment loss should be recognized in income immediately. U.S. GAAP does not allow the reversal of a previously recognized impairment loss.

Example: Reversal of Impairment Loss

Spring Valley Water Company purchased new water filtration equipment at the beginning of Year 1 for $1,000,000. The equipment is expected to have a useful life of 40 years with no residual value. Therefore, annual depreciation is $25,000. By the end of Year 3, Spring Valley concluded that the filtration system was not performing up to expectations. The company determined that the system had a recoverable amount based on net selling price of $740,000. The carrying amount of the asset at the end of Year 3 was $925,000 [$1,000,000 − ($25,000 × 3 years)], so the company recognized an impairment loss of $185,000 in Year 3. Annual depreciation of $20,000 [$740,000/37 years] subsequently was recognized in Years 4 and 5. The carrying amount of the equipment at the end of Year 5 was $700,000 [$740,000 − ($20,000 × 2)]. The summary journal entries to account for this asset in Years 1 through 5 are shown here:

January 1, Year 1		
Equipment	$1,000,000	
Cash		$1,000,000
December 31, Year 1, Year 2, Year 3		
Depreciation Expense	$25,000	
Accumulated Depreciation—Equipment		$25,000
December 31, Year 3		
Impairment Loss	$185,000	
Equipment		$185,000
December 31, Year 4, Year 5		
Depreciation Expense	$20,000	
Accumulated Depreciation—Equipment		$20,000

In January, Year 6, a technician discovered that the filtration equipment had not been properly set up at the time of initial installation. Adjustments to the installation resulted in a significant boost in performance, which led the company to reevaluate whether the equipment was still impaired. New estimates of future cash flows to be generated through continued operation of the equipment resulted in a recoverable amount based on value in use of $900,000, and the company determined that it was appropriate to reverse the impairment loss recognized in Year 3. To determine the amount of impairment loss to reverse, the company calculates what the carrying amount of the equipment would have been if the impairment had never been recognized. Annual depreciation of $25,000 would have been taken for five years, resulting in a carrying amount of $875,000 [$1,000,000 − ($25,000 × 5 years)], which is less than the new recoverable amount of $900,000. With impairment, the carrying amount of the equipment at the end of Year 5 is $700,000. Therefore, early in Year 6, Spring Valley increased the carrying amount of the equipment by $175,000 to write it up to $875,000 and recorded a reversal of impairment loss of the same amount. The reversal of impairment loss results in an increase in income:

January, Year 6		
Equipment.	$175,000	
Reversal of Impairment Loss (increase in income).		$175,000

The shares of Lihir Gold Limited, a mining company based in Papua New Guinea, are traded on the NASDAQ market in the United States. Lihir Gold uses IFRS in preparing its financial statements. The reconciliation of net income to U.S. GAAP and the procedures followed by Lihir Gold in complying with IAS 36's impairment rules are summarized in Exhibit 4.2. The company explains that impairment losses on mine properties were recorded in 1999 and 2000 under IAS 36 and that these losses were partially reversed in 2004 in the amount of $205.7 million. This reversal of a previously recognized impairment loss (which increases income) is not acceptable under U.S. accounting rules, so IFRS income was reduced by $205.7 million in 2004 to reconcile to U.S. GAAP. IFRS stockholders' equity (retained earnings) was reduced by the same amount to reconcile to U.S. GAAP.

INTANGIBLE ASSETS

IAS 38, *Intangible Assets*, provides accounting rules for purchased intangible assets, intangible assets acquired in a business combination, and internally generated intangible assets. Goodwill is covered by IFRS 3, *Business Combinations*.

IAS 38 defines an intangible asset as an *identifiable*, nonmonetary asset without physical substance held for use in the production of goods or services, for rental to others, or for administrative purposes. As an asset, it is a resource *controlled* by the enterprise as a result of past events from which *future economic benefits are expected* to arise. If a potential intangible asset does not meet this definition (i.e., it is not identifiable, not controlled, or future benefits are not probable) or cannot be measured reliably, it should be expensed immediately, unless it is obtained in a business combination, in which case it should be included in goodwill.

EXHIBIT 4.2

LIHIR GOLD LIMITED
Form 20-F
2006
Impairment of Assets

Notes to the Financial Statements

Excerpt from Note 34. Reconciliation to U.S. GAAP

The basis of preparation of these financial statements is set out in Note 1. These accounting policies vary in certain important respects from the accounting principles generally accepted in the United States (U.S. GAAP). The material differences affecting the financial statement line items between generally accepted accounting principles followed by the Company and those generally accepted in the United States are summarized below.

	Reference	2006 US $'000	2005 US $'000	2004 US $'000
Net income under IFRS		**53,837**	**9,788**	**329,221**
Mine properties—capitalized interest	b	559	3,661	—
Depreciation of mine properties	c	9,226	9,205	2,974
Mine properties—impairment reversal	d	—	—	(205,723)
EGS—impairment reversal	e	—	—	(90,200)
Deferred mining costs	j	—	—	(3,123)
Adjustment of deferred charges to inventory	f	25,839	—	—
Recognition of deferred waste as a charge	f	(56,349)	—	—
Deferred tax benefit adjustment for U.S. GAAP	i	3,167	(808)	108,465
Net income under U.S. GAAP		**36,279**	**21,845**	**141,614**

d. Impairment: Mine properties

Under IAS 36, the impairment test for determining the recoverable amount of a noncurrent asset is the higher of net selling price and its value in use. Value in use is the net present value of cash flows expected to be realized from the asset, assessed based on the current condition of the asset. Under IFRS, impairment losses may be reversed in subsequent periods.

Under SFAS 144, an impairment loss is recognized if the carrying amount of a long-lived asset (asset group) exceeds the sum of the undiscounted cash flows expected to result from the use and eventual disposition of the asset (asset group). An impairment loss is measured as the excess of the carrying amount of the long-lived asset (asset group) over its fair value. Fair value has been estimated using present value techniques. Under U.S. GAAP, impairment reversals are not permitted.

No impairments or impairment reversals occurred in 2006 or 2005. In 2004, as a result of significant changes in the critical assumptions used to determine the value in use, including increases in the life of mine and reserves and increases in the estimated long-term gold price, the directors resolved to partially reverse impairments recognized in 2000 and 1999 to the value of $205.7 million. In determining the value in use, the Company used the long-term gold price assumptions of $380 for the year ended 2004 and a pretax real discount rate of 7 percent. As a result of the reversal in 2004, all the impairments recognized in 2000 and 1999, excluding the amount that would have been depreciated of $82.7 million, have been reversed for IFRS as the impairment write-back is limited to the amount that would have been the written-down value of the assets had there been no impairment.

Purchased Intangibles

Purchased intangibles are initially measured at cost, and their useful life is assessed as finite or indefinite. The cost of intangible assets with a finite useful life is amortized on a systematic basis over the useful life. The residual value is assumed to be zero unless (1) a third party has agreed to purchase the asset at the end of its useful life or (2) there is an active market for the asset from which a residual value can be estimated.

An intangible asset is deemed to have an indefinite life when there is no foreseeable limit to the period over which it is expected to generate cash flows for the entity. If the useful life of an intangible asset is indefinite, no amortization should be taken until the life is determined to be definite. The distinction made in IAS 38 between intangibles with a finite life and those with an indefinite life and corresponding accounting treatment is consistent with U.S. GAAP.

Intangibles Acquired in a Business Combination

Under both IAS 38 and U.S. GAAP, intangibles such as patents, trademarks, and customer lists acquired in a business combination should be recognized as assets apart from goodwill at their fair value. The acquiring company should recognize these intangibles as assets even if they were not recognized as assets by the acquiree, so long as their fair value can be measured reliably. If fair value cannot be measured reliably, the intangible is not recognized as a separate asset but is included in goodwill. Similar to purchased intangibles, intangibles acquired in a business combination must be classified as having a finite or an indefinite useful life.

A special situation arises with respect to development costs that have been incurred by the acquiree prior to the business combination, often called in-process research and development. In accordance with IAS 38, in-process development costs that meet certain criteria (described in more detail in the following subsections) must be capitalized as an intangible asset unless their fair value cannot be measured reliably, in which case they are included in goodwill. In either case, the development costs are capitalized under IFRS. Recent changes in U.S. GAAP converged the treatment of in-process research and development with IFRS.

Internally Generated Intangibles

A major difference between IFRS and U.S. GAAP lies in the treatment of internally generated intangibles. To determine whether an internally generated intangible should be recognized as an asset, IAS 38 requires the expenditures giving rise to the potential intangible to be classified as either research or development expenditures. If the two cannot be distinguished, all expenditures should be classified as research expenditures. Research expenditures must be expensed as incurred. Development expenditures, in contrast, are recognized as an intangible asset when an enterprise can demonstrate all of the following:

1. The technical feasibility of completing the intangible asset so that it will be available for use or sale.
2. Its intention to complete the intangible asset and use or sell it.
3. Its ability to use or sell the intangible asset.
4. How the intangible asset will generate probable future economic benefits. Among other things, the enterprise should demonstrate the existence of a market for the output of the intangible asset or the existence of the intangible asset itself or, if it is to be used internally, the usefulness of the intangible asset.
5. The availability of adequate technical, financial, and other resources to complete the development and to use or sell the intangible asset.
6. Its ability to reliably measure the expenditure attributable to the intangible asset during its development.

Considerable management judgment is required in determining whether development costs should be capitalized as an internally generated intangible. Managers must determine the point at which research ends and development begins. IAS 38 provides the following examples of activities generally included in research:

- Activities aimed at obtaining new knowledge.
- The search for application of research findings or other knowledge.

- The search for alternatives for materials, devices, products, processes, systems, or services.
- The formulation, design, evaluation, and selection of possible alternatives for new or improved materials, devices, products, processes, systems, or services.

Development activities typically include the following:

- The design, construction, and testing of preproduction prototypes and models.
- The design of tools, jigs, molds, and dies involving new technology.
- The design, construction, and operation of a pilot plant that is not of a scale economically feasible for commercial production.
- The design, construction, and testing of a chosen alternative for new or improved materials, devices, products, processes, systems, or services.

IAS 38 also provides a list of activities that are neither research nor development, including the following:

- Engineering follow-through in an early phase of commercial production.
- Quality control during commercial production, including routine testing of products.
- Troubleshooting in connection with breakdowns during commercial production.
- Routine efforts to refine, enrich, or otherwise improve upon the qualities of an existing product.
- Adaptation of an existing capability to a particular requirement or customer's need as part of a continuing commercial activity.
- Seasonal or other periodic design changes to existing products.
- Routine design of tools, jigs, molds, and dies.
- Activities, including design and construction engineering, related to the construction, relocation, rearrangement, or start-up of facilities or equipment other than facilities or equipment used solely for a particular research and development project.

Once the research and development phases of a project have been determined, management must assess whether all six criteria (listed earlier) for development cost capitalization have been met. Judgments of future circumstances often will be necessary and may be highly subjective. The ultimate decision can depend on the degree of optimism or pessimism of the persons making the judgment.

Development costs consist of (1) all costs directly attributable to development activities and (2) those costs that can be reasonably allocated to such activities, including:

- Personnel costs.
- Materials and services costs.
- Depreciation of property, plant, and equipment.
- Amortization of patents and licenses.
- Overhead costs, other than general administrative costs.

In other words, development costs are similar to costs incurred in producing inventory. Because the costs of some, but not all, development projects will be deferred as assets, it is necessary to accumulate costs for each development project as if it were a separate work in progress.

In accordance with IAS 23, *Borrowing Costs,* borrowing costs should be included as part of the cost of development activities to the extent that the costs of those activities constitute a "qualifying asset." IAS 23 is discussed in more detail later in this chapter.

Development costs capitalized as an internally generated intangible can only be treated as having a finite useful life. They must be amortized over their useful life using a method that best reflects the pattern in which the asset's economic benefits are consumed. Declining-balance, units-of-production, and straight-line methods are among the acceptable methods. Amortization begins when the intangible asset is available for sale or use.

Example: Deferred Development Costs

Szabo Company Inc. incurred costs to develop a specific product for a customer in Year 1, amounting to $300,000. Of that amount, $250,000 was incurred up to the point at which the technical feasibility of the product could be demonstrated, and other recognition criteria were met. In Year 2, Szabo Company incurred an additional $300,000 in costs in the development of the product. The product was available for sale on January 2, Year 3, with the first shipment to the customer occurring in mid-February, Year 3. Sales of the product are expected to continue for four years, at which time it is expected that a replacement product will need to be developed. The total number of units expected to be produced over the product's four-year economic life is 2,000,000. The number of units produced in Year 3 is 800,000. Residual value is zero.

In Year 1, $250,000 of development costs is expensed and $50,000 is recognized as an asset. The journal entry is as follows:

Development Expense	$250,000	
Deferred Development Costs (intangible asset)	50,000	
Cash, payables, etc.		$300,000
To record development expense and deferred development costs.		

In Year 2, $300,000 of development costs is recognized as an asset:

Deferred Development Costs (asset)	$300,000	
Cash, payables, etc.		$300,000
To record deferred development costs.		

Amortization of deferred development costs begins on January 2, Year 3, when the product becomes available for sale. Szabo Company determines that the units-of-production method best reflects the pattern in which the asset's economic benefits are consumed. Amortization expense for Year 3 is calculated as follows:

Carrying amount of deferred development cost		$350,000
Units produced in Year 3	800,000	
Total number of units to be produced over economic life	2,000,000	
% of total units produced in Year 3		40%
Amortization expense in Year 3		$140,000

The journal entry to record amortization of deferred development costs at December 31, Year 3, is as follows:

Amortization Expense	$140,000	
Deferred Development Costs (asset)		$140,000
To record annual amortization expense.		

If Szabo Company were unable to estimate with reasonable certainty the number of units to be produced, it would be appropriate to amortize the deferred development costs on a straight-line basis over the four-year expected life. In that case, the journal entry to record amortization in Year 3 is as follows:

Amortization Expense	$87,500	
Deferred Development Costs (asset).		$87,500
To record annual amortization expense.		

Examples of Internally Generated Intangible Assets

Items that might qualify for capitalization as internally generated intangible assets under IAS 38 include:

- Computer software costs
- Patents, copyrights
- Motion picture films
- Mortgage servicing rights
- Fishing licenses
- Franchises
- Customer or supplier relationships
- Customer loyalty
- Market share
- Marketing rights
- Import quotas

IAS 38 specifically excludes the following from being recognized as internally generated intangible assets:

- Brands
- Mastheads
- Publishing titles
- Customer lists
- Advertising costs
- Training costs
- Business relocation costs

Internally generated goodwill may *not* be recognized as an asset.

Finnish cellular telephone manufacturer Nokia Corporation is a European multinational that has used IFRS for many years. Exhibit 4.3 presents the reconciliation of net income from IFRS to U.S. GAAP provided by Nokia in its 2006 Form 20-F filed with the U.S. Securities and Exchange Commission (SEC), and the note describing the U.S. GAAP adjustment related to development costs. Adjusting for

140   Chapter Four

EXHIBIT 4.3

NOKIA
Form 20-F
2006
Development Costs

Notes to the Consolidated Financial Statements

Excerpt from Note 38. Differences between International Financial Reporting Standards and U.S. Generally Accepted Accounting Principles

The Group's consolidated financial statements are prepared in accordance with International Financial Reporting Standards, which differ in certain respects from accounting principles generally accepted in the United States of America (US GAAP). The principal differences between IFRS and US GAAP are presented below together with explanations of certain adjustments that affect consolidated net income and total shareholders' equity under US GAAP as of and for the years ended December 31:

	2006 EURm	2005 EURm	2004 EURm
Reconciliation of profit attributable to equity holders of the parent under IFRS to net income under US GAAP:			
Profit attributable to equity holders of the parent reported under IFRS	**4,306**	3,616	3,192
U.S. GAAP adjustments:			
Pensions	**(1)**	(3)	—
Development costs	**(55)**	10	42
Share-based compensation expense	**(8)**	(39)	39
Cash flow hedges	**—**	(12)	31
Amortization of identifiable intangible assets acquired	**—**	—	(11)
Impairment of identifiable intangible assets acquired	**—**	—	(47)
Amortization of goodwill	**—**	—	106
Other differences	**22**	(1)	(6)
Deferred tax effect of U.S. GAAP adjustments	**11**	11	(3)
Net income under U.S. GAAP	**4,275**	3,582	3,343

Development costs

Development costs are capitalized under IFRS after the product involved has reached a certain degree of technical feasibility. Capitalization ceases and depreciation begins when the product becomes available to customers. The depreciation period of these capitalized assets is between two and five years.

Under U.S. GAAP, software development costs are similarly capitalized after the product has reached a certain degree of technological feasibility. However, certain non-software-related development costs capitalized under IFRS are not capitalizable under U.S. GAAP and therefore are expensed as incurred.

The U.S. GAAP development cost adjustment reflects the reversal of capitalized non-software-related development costs under U.S. GAAP net of the reversal of associated amortization expense and impairments under IFRS. The adjustment also reflects differences in impairment methodologies under IFRS and U.S. GAAP for the determination of the recoverable amount and net realizable value of software-related development costs.

the capitalization of development costs under IFRS that would not be allowed under U.S. GAAP resulted in U.S. GAAP net income being €55 million less than IFRS net income in 2006. However, in 2004 and 2005, U.S. GAAP net income was €42 million and €10 million greater than IFRS income, respectively. The larger income under U.S. GAAP in these years most likely is attributable to the amount of amortization expense related to deferred development costs under IFRS exceeding the development costs expensed immediately under U.S. GAAP. Related adjustments also are made each year to reconcile stockholders' equity (retained earnings) from IFRS to U.S. GAAP. The amount of the adjustment is equal to the book value of the deferred development costs reported as an asset under IFRS; equity is smaller under U.S. GAAP.

Revaluation Model

IAS 38, *Intangible Assets,* allows the use of the revaluation model for intangible assets with finite lives, but only if the intangible has a price that is available on an active market, a condition rarely met in practice. Examples of intangible assets that may be priced on an active market include taxi licenses, fishing licenses, and production quotas. If the company chooses the revaluation method, the asset's fair value should be assessed regularly, typically annually. An increase in fair value of the asset is credited to "revaluation surplus" in equity, except to the extent it reverses a previously recorded decrease reported directly in net income. U.S. GAAP does not provide for the revaluation of intangible assets.

Impairment of Intangible Assets

Even though they are subject to amortization, finite-lived intangible assets also must be tested for impairment whenever changes in events or circumstances indicate an asset's carrying amount may not be recoverable. Goodwill and intangible assets with indefinite lives must be reviewed at least annually for impairment, regardless of the existence of impairment indicators. IAS 36, *Impairment of Assets,* allows reversals of impairment losses on intangible assets under special circumstances. However, reversal of impairment losses on goodwill is prohibited.

GOODWILL

IFRS 3, *Business Combinations,* contains the international rules related to the initial measurement of goodwill. Goodwill is recognized only in a business combination and is measured as the difference between (a) and (b):

(a) The consideration transferred by the acquiring firm plus any amount recognized as noncontrolling interest.

(b) The fair value of net assets acquired (identifiable assets acquired less liabilities assumed).

When (a) exceeds (b), goodwill is recognized as an asset. When (a) is less than (b), a "bargain purchase" is said to have taken place and the difference between (a) and (b) (sometimes called "negative goodwill") is recognized as a gain in net income by the acquiring firm.

The amount recognized as goodwill depends on the option selected to measure any noncontrolling interest in the acquired company that might exist. Under IFRS 3, noncontrolling interest may be measured at either (1) a proportionate share of the fair value of the acquired firm's net assets excluding goodwill or (2) fair value, which includes the noncontrolling interest's share of goodwill.

Example: Initial Measurement of Goodwill

George Company acquired 90 percent of the outstanding shares of Chris Company by paying $360,000 in cash. The fair value of Chris's identifiable assets is $320,000, and the liabilities assumed by George in this business combination are $40,000. George can choose between two alternatives to determine the amount to recognize as goodwill in this business combination.

Alternative 1   Noncontrolling Interest Measured at Proportionate Share of Acquired Firm's Net Assets

Fair value of Chris's identifiable net assets ($320,000 − $40,000)		$280,000
Noncontrolling interest percentage		10%
Noncontrolling interest		$ 28,000
Consideration transferred	$360,000	
Plus: Noncontrolling interest	28,000	
Subtotal.	$388,000	
Less: Fair value of Chris's identifiable net assets	280,000	
Goodwill	$108,000	

Alternative 2   Noncontrolling Interest Measured at Fair Value

Implied fair value of 100% of Chris Company ($360,000/90%)		$400,000
Noncontrolling interest percentage		10%
Noncontrolling interest		$ 40,000
Consideration transferred	$360,000	
Plus: Noncontrolling interest	40,000	
Subtotal.	$400,000	
Less: Fair value of Chris's identifiable net assets	280,000	
Goodwill	$120,000	

In Alternative 2, goodwill of $120,000 is comprised of $108,000 purchased by George plus $12,000 [$40,000 − $28,000] attributed to the noncontrolling interest.

Example: Gain on Bargain Purchase

Assume the same facts as in the previous example, except George acquires 90 percent of Chris for $240,000. Also, assume that noncontrolling interest is measured at the proportionate share of net assets (Alternative 1).

Consideration transferred	$240,000
Plus: Noncontrolling interest	28,000
Subtotal.	$268,000
Less: Fair value of Chris's identifiable net assets	280,000
Gain on bargain purchase	$ (12,000)

In this case, George would recognize a gain from a bargain purchase in net income in the year in which the acquisition takes place.

Impairment of Goodwill

As an indefinite-lived intangible asset, goodwill is not amortized. Instead, goodwill must be tested at least annually for impairment. IAS 36, *Impairment of Assets*, provides specific rules with respect to the impairment of goodwill.

Impairment testing of goodwill is performed at the level of the cash-generating unit (CGU). The CGU is the "smallest identifiable group of assets that generates cash inflows that are largely independent of the cash inflows from other assets or groups of assets." The impairment test is conducted by comparing the carrying value of the entire CGU, including goodwill attributable to that CGU, with its recoverable amount. The recoverable amount is the higher of the CGU's (1) value in use and (2) fair value less costs to sell. Under U.S. GAAP, impairment of goodwill is tested at the level of the "reporting unit," which can be different (typically larger) than a cash-generating unit.

If noncontrolling interest was originally measured at the proportionate share of net assets (Alternative 1), then the carrying value of the entire CGU must be increased by the amount of goodwill attributable to the noncontrolling interest (as if Alternative 2 had been applied). The impairment loss on the CGU is the amount by which the CGU's carrying amount, including goodwill, exceeds its recoverable amount. An impairment loss identified at the CGU level is first applied against goodwill. Once goodwill has been eliminated, any remaining impairment is allocated to the other assets of the CGU on a prorated basis based on their relative carrying amounts.

Example: Impairment of Goodwill

Continuing with the initial measurement of goodwill example presented earlier, at least annually, George Company must conduct an impairment test of the goodwill related to the acquisition of Chris Company. The assets of Chris Company are the smallest group of assets that generate cash inflows that are largely independent of the cash inflows from other assets or groups of assets. Therefore, Chris Company is a separate CGU. The goodwill related to the acquisition of Chris Company will be tested by comparing Chris Company's carrying amount with its recoverable amount. At the end of the year, George Company develops the following estimates for Chris Company:

Fair value	$280,000
Costs to sell	$ 30,000
Present value of future cash flows	$270,000

Alternative 1 Assuming that George Company adopted the proportionate share of acquired firm's net assets approach to measure noncontrolling interest, the impairment loss is determined as follows:

	Chris Co. Net Assets	Chris Co. Goodwill	Total
Carrying amount	$280,000	$108,000	$388,000
Unrecognized noncontrolling interest in goodwill. . .		12,000	12,000
Adjusted carrying amount	$280,000	$120,000	$400,000
Determination of recoverable amount:			
Fair value less costs to sell (1)			$250,000
Present value of future cash flows (2)			270,000
Recoverable amount [higher of (1) and (2)]			$270,000
Impairment loss (adjusted carrying amount less recoverable amount)			$130,000

144   Chapter Four

In terms of allocation of impairment loss, $120,000 of the impairment loss is allocated to goodwill. The goodwill impairment is shared between the controlling and noncontrolling interest. Thus, $108,000 (90 percent) is allocated to the parent's investment in Chris Company; the remaining $12,000 (10 percent) is attributable to the noncontrolling interest (but is not recognized because the noncontrolling interest's goodwill is not recognized under this alternative). The remaining $10,000 ($130,000 − $120,000) of impairment loss is allocated to Chris Company's identifiable assets on a pro rata basis.

	Chris Co. Net Assets	Chris Co. Goodwill	Total
Carrying amount	$280,000	$108,000	$388,000
Impairment loss	10,000	108,000	118,000
Carrying amount after impairment loss	$270,000	$ 0	$270,000

Alternative 2   Now assume that George Company had adopted the fair value method to measure noncontrolling interest. The impairment loss is determined in the following manner:

	Chris Co. Net Assets	Chris Co. Goodwill	Total
Carrying amount	$280,000	$120,000	$400,000
Determination of recoverable amount:			
Fair value less costs to sell (1)			$250,000
Present value of future cash flows (2)			270,000
Recoverable amount [higher of (1) and (2)]			$270,000
Impairment loss (carrying amount less recoverable amount)			$130,000

Allocation of impairment loss:

	Chris Co. Net Assets	Chris Co. Goodwill	Total
Carrying amount	$280,000	$120,000	$400,000
Impairment loss	10,000	120,000	130,000
Carrying amount after impairment loss	$270,000	$ 0	$270,000

Goodwill Not Allocable to Cash-Generating Unit under Review

In testing goodwill for impairment, the recoverable amount is determined for the CGU to which the goodwill belongs by first applying a so-called bottom-up test. In this test, goodwill is allocated to the individual CGU under review, if possible, and impairment of that CGU is then determined by comparing (1) the carrying amount plus allocated goodwill and (2) the recoverable amount. The example presented previously demonstrated application of the bottom-up test.

If goodwill cannot be allocated on a reasonable and consistent basis to the CGU under review, then both a bottom-up test and a top-down test should be applied. Under the top-down test, goodwill is allocated to the smallest group of CGUs to which it can be allocated on a reasonable and consistent basis, and impairment of the *group* of CGUs is then determined by comparing (1) the carrying amount of the group plus allocated goodwill and (2) the recoverable amount. U.S. GAAP requires only a bottom-up test and only for that goodwill associated with those assets that are being reviewed for impairment.

Example: Application of the Bottom-Up and Top-Down Tests for Goodwill

In Year 1, La Brea Company acquired another company that operates a chain of three restaurants, paying $300,000 for goodwill. By the end of Year 4, it is clear that the restaurant located in Anaheim is not generating the profit and cash flows expected at the date of purchase. Therefore, La Brea Company is required to test for impairment.

Each restaurant is a cash-generating unit, but La Brea cannot allocate the goodwill on a reasonable and consistent basis to individual restaurants. Both a bottom-up test and a top-down test must be applied.

Bottom-Up Test   A bottom-up test is applied to each restaurant by estimating the recoverable amount of the assets of each restaurant and comparing with the carrying amount of those assets excluding goodwill. An impairment loss is recognized for the amount by which a restaurant's carrying amount exceeds its recoverable amount. The loss is allocated to the impaired restaurant's assets on a pro rata basis according to the relative carrying amount of the assets. The bottom-up test checks for impairment of the assets of the individual restaurants but provides no information about the impairment of the goodwill that was purchased in the acquisition of the chain of restaurants. Assume the following carrying values and recoverable amounts for the three restaurants acquired:

Cash-Generating Unit (restaurant location)	Carrying Amount	Recoverable Amount	Impairment Loss
Anaheim	$1,000,000	$ 970,000	$30,000
Buena Park	1,000,000	1,050,000	0
Cerritos	1,000,000	1,020,000	0

An impairment loss of $30,000 is recognized, and the assets of the Anaheim restaurant are written down by that amount. The carrying amount of Anaheim's net assets is now $970,000.

Top-Down Test   La Brea determines that the smallest cash-generating unit to which goodwill can be allocated is the entire chain of restaurants. Therefore, La Brea estimates the recoverable amount of the chain of restaurants and compares this with the carrying amount (after any impairment has been recognized) of the assets of all the restaurants plus goodwill. Goodwill is considered to be impaired to the extent that the carrying amount of the assets plus goodwill exceeds the restaurant chain's recoverable amount.

Cash-Generating Unit (restaurant location)	Carrying Amount
Anaheim	$ 970,000
Buena Park	1,000,000
Cerritos	1,000,000
Subtotal	2,970,000
Goodwill	300,000
Total	$3,270,000

La Brea estimates the recoverable amount of the chain of restaurants to be $3,000,000. La Brea compares this amount with the total carrying amount of $3,270,000 to determine that goodwill is impaired. A loss on the impairment of goodwill of $270,000 must be recognized.

BORROWING COSTS

Prior to its revision in 2007, IAS 23, *Borrowing Costs,* provided two methods of accounting for borrowing costs:

1. *Benchmark treatment:* Expense all borrowing costs in the period incurred.
2. *Allowed alternative treatment:* Capitalize borrowing costs to the extent they are attributable to the acquisition, construction, or production of a qualifying asset; other borrowing costs are expensed in the period incurred.

Adoption of the benchmark treatment would not have been acceptable under U.S. GAAP. As part of the FASB-IASB convergence project, IAS 23 was revised in 2007. The benchmark treatment was eliminated, and the allowed alternative treatment has become the only acceptable treatment. Borrowing costs directly attributable to the acquisition, construction, or production of a qualifying asset must be capitalized as part of the cost of that asset; all other borrowing costs must be expensed immediately.

IAS 23 (as revised in 2007) is similar to U.S. GAAP, but some definitional and implementation differences exist. IAS 23 defines *borrowing costs* as interest and other costs incurred by an enterprise in connection with the borrowing of funds. This definition is broader in scope than the definition of *interest cost* under U.S. GAAP. Borrowing costs in accordance with IAS 23 specifically include foreign exchange gains and losses on foreign currency borrowings to the extent they are regarded as an adjustment to interest costs. An asset that qualifies for borrowing cost capitalization is one that necessarily takes a substantial period to get ready for its intended use or sale. Both IAS 23 and U.S. GAAP exclude inventories that are routinely manufactured or produced in large quantities on a repetitive basis over a short period. However, IAS 23 specifically includes inventories that require a substantial period to bring them to a marketable condition.

The amount to be capitalized is the amount of interest cost that could have been avoided if the expenditure on the qualifying asset had not been made. This is determined by multiplying the weighted-average accumulated expenditures by an appropriate interest rate. The appropriate interest rate is determined similarly under both IAS 23 and U.S. GAAP, being a weighted-average interest rate on borrowings outstanding. If a specific new borrowing can be associated with a qualifying asset, the actual interest rate is used to the extent the weighted-average accumulated expenditures are less than the amount of the specific borrowing. Interest income earned on the temporary investment of a specific new borrowing is offset against the interest cost to determine the net amount of interest to be capitalized. Netting interest income against interest cost is not acceptable under U.S. GAAP. The capitalization of borrowing costs begins when expenditures for the asset are incurred and ceases when substantially all the activities necessary to prepare the asset for sale or use are completed.

Example: Capitalization of Borrowing Costs

On January 1, Year 1, Pinquill Company borrows 30,000,000 euros (€) at an annual interest rate of 8 percent to finance the construction of a new facility in Spain. The facility is expected to cost €30,000,000 and take two years to build. Pinquill temporarily invests the euros borrowed until cash is needed to pay costs. During Year 1, expenditures of €20,000,000 are incurred; the weighted-average expenditures are €12,000,000. Pinquill makes annual interest payments on the loan and will repay the loan in full on December 31, Year 2, by converting U.S. dollars into euros, The U.S. dollar/euro exchange rate was $1.42 on January 1, Year 1, and $1.40 on December 31, Year 1. The change in exchange rate is the result of the difference in interest rates on U.S. dollar and euro borrowings. The following information relates to Year 1:

Capitalizable interest cost (€12,000,000 × 8% = €960,000 × $1.40 exchange rate on 12/31/Y1)	$1,344,000
Income earned on temporary investment of borrowing (€225,000 × $1.40)	315,000
Exchange rate gain [€12,000,000 × ($1.42 − $1.40)]	240,000

The net interest cost is $1,029,000 ($1,344,000 − $315,000). After deducting the exchange rate gain, the total amount of borrowing cost to be capitalized as part of the cost of the facility is $789,000. Under U.S. GAAP, the amount of interest cost to be capitalized would be $1,344,000.

LEASES

The discussion in this section on leases is based upon guidance in effect at the time this book went to press in late 2013. As noted at the end of this section, the accounting for leases under both IFRS and U.S. GAAP is likely to be changed and substantially converged.

IAS 17, *Leases*, distinguishes between finance (capitalized) leases and operating leases. IAS 17 provides guidance for classifying leases as finance or operating, and then describes the accounting procedures that should be used by lessees and lessors in accounting for each type of lease. IAS 17 also provides rules for sale–leaseback transactions. IAS 17 and U.S. GAAP are conceptually similar, but IAS 17 provides less specific guidance than U.S. GAAP.

Lease Classification

As a case in point, IAS 17 indicates that a lease should be classified and accounted for as a finance lease when it transfers substantially all the risks and rewards incidental to ownership to the lessee. The standard then provides examples of five situations that individually or in combination *normally would* lead to a lease being classified as a finance lease:

1. The lease transfers ownership of the asset to the lessee by the end of the lease term.
2. The lessee has the option to purchase the asset at a price less than fair market value.
3. The lease term is for the major part of the leased asset's economic life.
4. The present value of minimum lease payments at the inception of the lease is equal to substantially all the fair value of the leased asset.
5. The leased asset is of a specialized nature such that only the lessee can use it without major modifications.

IAS 17 provides three additional indicators of situations that individually or in combination *could* lead to a lease being classified as a finance lease:

6. The lessee bears the lessor's losses if the lessee cancels the lease.
7. The lessee absorbs the gains or losses from fluctuations in the fair value of the residual value of the asset.
8. The lessee may extend the lease for a secondary period at a rent substantially below the market rent.

In contrast, U.S. GAAP stipulates that if any one of four very specific criteria is met, a lease must be capitalized. These criteria are similar to 1 through 4 just listed; in fact, the first two are exactly the same. In the U.S. GAAP version of criterion 3, *major part* is specifically defined as 75 percent, and in criterion 4, *substantially all* is defined as 90 percent. Depending on the manner by which a financial statement preparer defines the terms *major part* and *substantially all*, application of IAS 17 and U.S. GAAP might or might not lead to similar classification of leases. In addition, there is nothing similar to criteria 5 through 8 in U.S. GAAP.

In assessing criterion 4, minimum lease payments include (1) periodic lease payments; (2) any amounts guaranteed by the lessee, such as a guaranteed residual value; and (3) the exercise price in a bargain renewal option. The discount rate to be used in determining the present value of minimum lease payments is the implicit interest rate earned by the lessor in the lease, if this is practicable to determine. If not, the lessee's incremental borrowing rate should be used. In contrast, U.S. GAAP requires the lessee's incremental borrowing rate to be used as the discount rate, unless the lessor's implicit interest rate can be determined and is less than the lessee's incremental borrowing rate.

Example: Classification of Leases

On January 1, Year 1, Creative Transportation Company (CTC) entered into a lease with Arnold Aircraft Inc. for a pre-owned airplane with the following terms:

- Lease term is seven years.
- Annual lease payments are $3,000, due on December 31.
- Fair value of the airplane at the inception of the lease is $20,000.
- The airplane has a 10-year remaining economic life.
- Estimated residual value (unguaranteed) is $5,124. CTC does not absorb any gains or losses in the fluctuations of the fair value of the residual value.
- CTC has the option to purchase the airplane at the end of the lease term for $8,000.

- Implicit annual interest rate is 5 percent (disclosed to CTC by Arnold).
- CTC's incremental annual borrowing rate is 4 percent.
- Ownership is not transferred at the end of the lease term.
- The lease may not be extended.

To determine the present value (PV) of minimum lease payments (MLP) the lessor's implicit interest rate of 5 percent is used because it is known, regardless of the lessee's incremental borrowing rate. The PV factor for an ordinary annuity of 7 payments at a 5 percent discount rate is 5.786373. The PV of MLP is calculated as $3,000 × 5.786373 = $17,359. The residual value is not included in the MLP because it is not guaranteed, and there is no renewal option to consider.

Based on the analysis presented in the following table, CTC most likely would not classify the lease as a finance lease under IFRS. However, this decision is not clear-cut. The company could decide that the lease term of seven years is the major part of the remaining economic life of the airplane and, as a result, treat this as a finance lease. Under U.S. GAAP, CTC definitely would not capitalize the lease because none of the four criteria are met.

Finance Lease Indicator	Indicator Present?
Ownership is transferred to the lessee by the end of the lease term.	No. Ownership is not transferred at the end of the lease term.
The lease contains a bargain purchase option.	No. The purchase option price of $8,000 is greater than the estimated residual value of $5,124.
The lease term is a major part of the estimated economic life of the leased property.	Maybe. The lease term is for 70% of the estimated economic life of the airplane, which might (or might not) be considered "a major part" by CTC.
The PV of MLP is substantially all of the fair value of the leased property.	Probably not. The PV of MLP is 87% of the fair value of the leased property ($17,359/$20,000). This does not appear to meet the threshold of "substantially all."
The leased assets are of a specialized nature such that only the lessee can use them without major modifications being made.	No. There is no indication that this is the case.
The lessee bears the lessor's losses if the lessee cancels the lease.	No. There is no indication that this is the case.
The lessee absorbs the gains or losses from fluctuations in the fair value of the residual value of the asset.	No. CTC does not guarantee the residual value.
The lessee may extend the lease for a secondary period at a rent substantially below the market rent.	No. The lease may not be extended.

Finance Leases

IAS 17 requires leases classified as finance leases to be recognized by the lessee as assets and liabilities at an amount equal to the fair value of the leased property or, if lower, at the present value of the future minimum lease payments. Initial direct costs incurred by the lessee in connection with negotiating the lease are capitalized as part of the cost of the asset under IAS 17. U.S. GAAP is silent with respect to this issue, but common practice is to defer and amortize the costs over the lease term.

Lease payments are apportioned between interest expense and a reduction in the lease obligation using an effective interest method to amortize the lease obligation. The leased asset is depreciated in a manner consistent with assets owned by the lessee. Normally, depreciable finance lease assets are depreciated over the shorter of useful life and lease term. If it is reasonably certain that the lessee will obtain ownership of the asset at the end of its lease term, the asset is depreciated over its expected useful life. IAS 36, *Impairment of Assets,* applies to finance lease assets the same as it does to assets owned by the entity.

A lease classified as a finance lease by the lessee should also be classified as a finance lease by the lessor. The leased asset is replaced by the "net investment" in the lease, which is equal to the present value of future minimum lease payments (including any unguaranteed residual value). Any profit on the "sale" is recognized at the inception of the lease, and interest is recognized over the life of the lease using an effective interest method. Under U.S. GAAP, the net investment in the lease is determined simply as the lessor's cost or carrying amount for the leased asset. Under U.S. GAAP, a lessor classifies a capital lease as either a sales-type lease (which includes the recognition of profit) or a direct-finance lease (no profit; fair value and carrying value of the leased asset are equal). IFRS does not make this distinction.

Operating Leases

Any lease not classified as a finance lease is an operating lease. With an operating lease, lease payments are recognized by the lessee as an expense and by the lessor as income. The asset remains on the books of the lessor and is accounted for in a similar fashion to any other asset owned by the lessor.

Lease payments under an operating lease are recognized as an expense on a straight-line basis over the lease term, unless another systematic basis is more representative of the time pattern of the user's benefit, in which case, that basis is used. SIC-15, *Operating Leases-Incentives,* provides guidance for situations where the lessee receives an incentive, such as a rent-free period, from the lessor to enter into the lease. In those situations, the total amount of rent to be paid over the life of the lease is allocated on a straight-line basis to the periods covered by the lease term.

Example: Operating Lease

Budget Company enters into a two-year lease for a computer with lease payments of $200 per month in the first year, and $250 per month in the second year. The total amount of lease payments will be $5,400 [($200 × 12) + ($250 × 12)]. The straight-line method accurately reflects the time pattern of the user's benefit from using the computer. On a straight-line basis, an expense in the amount of $225 ($5,400/24 months) should be recognized each month.

Sale–Leaseback Transaction

A sale–leaseback transaction involves the sale of an asset by the initial owner of the asset and the leasing of the same asset back to the initial owner. If the lease is classified as a finance lease, IAS 17 requires the initial owner to defer any gain on the sale and amortize it to income over the lease term. U.S. GAAP rules are generally similar. If the fair value of property at the time of the sale–leaseback is less than its carrying amount, IAS 17 allows recognition of a loss only if the loss is due to an impairment in the value of the asset sold. U.S. GAAP requires immediate recognition of the loss regardless of its source.

If the lease in a sale–leaseback transaction is classified as an operating lease, IAS 17 requires the difference between the fair value of the asset and its carrying amount to be recognized immediately in income. Any difference between the fair value of the asset and its selling price is amortized ratably over the lease term. In contrast, U.S. GAAP requires the seller to amortize any gain over the lease term.

Example: Gain on Sale and Leaseback

Berlin Corporation sells a building to Essen Finance Company for $2,200,000. Essen Finance then leases the building back to Berlin under a 10-year agreement, which Berlin classifies as an operating lease. On the date of sale, the carrying amount of the building on Berlin's books is $1,800,000, and the building had an appraised fair value of $2,100,000.

Under IFRS, Berlin recognizes a gain on sale and leaseback of $300,000 ($2,100,000 − $1,800,000) at the date of sale for the difference between the fair value and the carrying amount of the building. The company has a deferred gain of $100,000 ($2,200,000 − $2,100,000) for the difference between the fair value and the selling price; this will be amortized to income at the rate of $10,000 per year over the 10-year life of the lease. Under U.S. GAAP, the entire gain of $400,000 is deferred and amortized at the rate of $40,000 per year over the lease term.

The difference in accounting treatment for gains on sale–leaseback transactions between IAS 17 and U.S. GAAP is described by Swisscom AG in Exhibit 4.4. In its 2006 reconciliation to U.S. GAAP, Swisscom made an adjustment for this accounting difference that resulted in an increase in income, as stated under U.S. GAAP, of 17 million Swiss francs. This reflects the amount of original gain on sale and leaseback that was realized in 2001 that is amortized to income in 2006 under U.S. GAAP. The gain was recognized in full in 2001 under IFRS. An adjustment also is made to stockholders' equity to reverse the difference between the full amount of gain recognized under IFRS (included in IFRS retained earnings) and the portion of the gain that has been recognized through amortization under U.S. GAAP. This adjustment reduced IFRS equity by 280 million Swiss francs in 2006 to reconcile to a U.S. GAAP basis.

Disclosure

Lessees must disclose the amount of future minimum lease payments related to operating leases and related to finance leases, separately, for each of the following periods:

1. Amount to be paid within one year (Year 1).
2. Amount to be paid after one year and not later than five years (Years 2–5) as a single amount.
3. Amount to be paid later than five years (Year 6 and beyond) as a single amount.

Also, the present value of the future minimum lease payments under finance leases must be disclosed. Entities provide more detailed information under U.S. GAAP, which requires disclosure of the amount to be paid in each of the next five years (Years 1–5) by year, as well as the amount to be paid later than five years (Year 6 and beyond) as a single amount.

EXHIBIT 4.4

SWISSCOM AG
Form 20-F
2006
Sale and Leaseback Transactions

Excerpt from Note 43. Differences between International Financial Reporting Standards and U.S. Generally Accepted Accounting Principles

The consolidated financial statements of Swisscom have been prepared in accordance with International Financial Reporting Standards (IFRS), which differ in certain significant respects from generally accepted accounting principles in the United States (U.S. GAAP). Application of U.S. GAAP would have affected the shareholders' equity as of December 31, 2006, 2005, and 2004, and net income for each of the years in the three-year period ended December 31, 2006, to the extent described below. A description of the significant differences between IFRS and U.S. GAAP as they relate to Swisscom are discussed in further detail below.

Reconciliation of net income from IFRS to U.S. GAAP

The following schedule illustrates the significant adjustments to reconcile net income in accordance with IFRS to the amounts determined in accordance with U.S. GAAP for each of the three years ended December 31.

CHF in millions	2006	2005	2004
Net income according to IFRS attributable to equity holders of Swisscom AG	**1,599**	**2,022**	**1,596**
U.S. GAAP adjustments:			
a) Capitalization of interest cost	20	14	(4)
b) Retirement benefits	(16)	(27)	(21)
c) Termination benefits	—	(31)	(10)
d) Impairment of investments	—	9	—
e) Cross-border tax leases	15	(20)	49
f) Debitel purchase accounting	—	—	(23)
g) Sale of debitel	—	254	342
h) Deferred interest	—	21	(21)
i) Revenue recognition	18	35	56
j) Outsourcing contracts	(40)	16	—
k) Site restoration	(2)	3	15
l) Goodwill and other intangible assets	—	—	106
m) Sale and leaseback transaction	17	29	24
n) Onerous contracts	(5)	6	10
o) Share buyback	(17)	—	—
p) Income taxes	—	(2)	(6)
Net income according to U.S. GAAP	**1,589**	**2,329**	**2,113**

m) Sale and leaseback transaction

In March 2001 Swisscom entered into two master agreements for the sale of real estate. At the same time, Swisscom entered into agreements to lease back part of the sold property space. The gain on the sale of the properties after transaction costs of CHF 105 million and including the reversal of environmental provisions, was CHF 807 million under IFRS.

A number of the leaseback agreements are accounted for as finance leases under IFRS and the gain on the sale of these properties of CHF 129 million is deferred and released to income over the individual lease terms. The remaining gain of CHF 678 million represents the gain on the sale of buildings which were sold outright and the gain on the sale of land and buildings which qualify as operating leases under IFRS. Under IFRS, the gain on a leaseback accounted for as an operating lease is recognized immediately. Under U.S. GAAP, in general the gain is deferred and amortized over the lease term. If the leaseback was minor, the gain was immediately recognized. In addition, certain of the agreements did not qualify as sale-and-leaseback accounting under U.S. GAAP because of continuing involvement in the form of purchase options. These transactions are accounted for under the finance method and the sales proceeds are reported as a financing obligation and the properties remain on the balance sheet and continue to be depreciated as in the past. The lease payments are split between interest and amortization of the obligation.

Exhibit 4.5 shows the disclosures made by British retailer Marks and Spencer Group plc related to operating leases. Note that Marks and Spencer has elected to disaggregate the period beyond five years into five-year increments up to 25 years, even though IAS 17 does not require the company to do so.

IASB/FASB Convergence Project

In 2010, the IASB and FASB jointly issued an exposure draft for a proposed new standard on the accounting for leases. The Boards issued a revised exposure draft on leases in 2013, but provided no information about a possible effective date for a new standard. If approved, the exposure draft will result in significant changes to the accounting requirements for both lessees and lessors, and the accounting for leases under both IASB and FASB standards will be substantially converged. Under the proposal, lessees would recognize a "right-of-use" asset and a liability to make lease payments for all leases. Leases would no longer be classified as finance or operating; in essence, all leases with a maximum possible term of more than 12 months would be treated as finance leases. Lease assets and liabilities would be measured based on the longest possible lease term that is more likely than not to occur, and an expected outcome approach would be used to reflect lease payments. Lessors would recognize an asset representing the right to receive lease payments and would either derecognize the leased asset or recognize a liability, depending on exposure to the risks and rewards associated with the leased asset. On sale–leasebacks, the seller would recognize the transaction either as a sale or as a borrowing, depending on whether the transaction meets conditions for recognition as a sale as stipulated in the exposure draft.

Other Recognition and Measurement Standards

The next chapter covers IASB standards pertaining to the recognition and measurement of current liabilities, provisions, employee benefits, share-based payment,

---

EXHIBIT 4.5

MARKS AND SPENCER GROUP PLC
2012
Annual Report

Excerpt from Note 25. Contingencies and Commitments

C. Commitments under operating leases

The Group leases various stores, office, warehouses, and equipment under non-cancelable operating lease agreements. The leases have varying terms, escalation clauses, and renewal rights.

	2012 £m	2011 £m
Total future minimum rentals payable under non-cancelable operating leases are as follows:		
Within one year	257.8	242.6
Later than one year and not later than five years	997.4	923.0
Later than five years and not later than ten years	1,029.5	990.8
Later than ten years and not later than 15 years	772.7	767.4
Later than 15 years and not later than 20 years	385.1	402.9
Later than 20 years and not later than 25 years	259.3	243.1
Later than 25 years	1,210.1	1,210.3
Total	4,911.9	4,780.1

The total future sublease payments to be received are £63.3m (last year £65.8m).

income taxes, revenue, and financial instruments. IAS 21, *Foreign Currency Translation,* which provides guidance for dealing with foreign currency transactions and the translation of foreign currency financial statements, is covered in detail in Chapters 7 and 8. Standards related to financial reporting in hyperinflationary economies (IAS 29), business combinations (IFRS 3), consolidated financial statements (IAS 27), investments in associates (IAS 28), and investments in joint ventures (IAS 31) are covered in Chapter 9, Additional Financial Reporting Issues.

DISCLOSURE AND PRESENTATION STANDARDS

Several IFRS deal primarily with disclosure and presentation issues. This section summarizes some of those standards. While briefly introduced here, IFRS 8, *Operating Segments,* is discussed in greater detail in Chapter 9.

Statement of Cash Flows

IAS 7, *Statement of Cash Flows,* reiterates the requirement in IAS 1 that a company must present a statement of cash flows as an integral part of its financial statements. IAS 7 contains the following requirements:

- Cash flows must be classified as being related to operating, investing, or financing activities.
- Cash flow from operations may be presented using the direct method or the indirect method. When using the indirect method, IAS 7 does *not* specify that the reconciliation from income to cash flows must begin with any particular line item, e.g., net income. Thus, an entity could begin the reconciliation with operating income or some other measure of income. When using the direct method, there is no requirement to also present a reconciliation of income to cash from operations.
- Cash flows related to interest, dividends, and income taxes must be reported separately.
- Interest and dividends paid may be classified as operating or financing.
- Interest and dividends received may be classified as operating or investing.
- Income taxes are classified as operating unless they are specifically identified with investing or financing activities.
- Noncash investing and financing transactions are excluded from the statement of cash flows but must be disclosed elsewhere within the financial statements.
- Components of cash and cash equivalents must be disclosed and reconciled with amounts reported on the statement of financial position (balance sheet). However, the total for cash and cash equivalents in the statement of cash flows need not agree with a single line item in the balance sheet.
- IAS 7 makes an explicit distinction between bank borrowings and bank overdrafts. Overdrafts may be classified as a component (i.e., reduction) of cash and cash equivalents, if considered to be an integral part of an enterprise's cash management. Otherwise, bank overdrafts are classified as a financing activity.

Several differences exist between IFRS and U.S. GAAP in the presentation of a statement of cash flows. Under U.S. GAAP:

- Interest paid, interest received, and dividends received are all classified as operating cash flows. Dividends paid are classified as financing cash flows.
- When using the indirect method of presenting operating cash flows, the reconciliation from income to cash flows must begin with net income.

- When using the direct method of presenting operating cash flows, a reconciliation from net income to operating cash flows also must be presented.
- The cash and cash equivalents line item in the statement of cash flows must reconcile with the cash and cash equivalents line in the statement of financial position.

Example: Classification of Interest and Dividends in the Statement of Cash Flows

Star Kissed Corporation (SKC) currently reports under U.S. GAAP but is investigating the effect that the adoption of IFRS might have on its statement of cash flows. For the current year, SKC has interest received of $500, interest paid of $1,250, dividends received of $200, and dividends paid of $2,700. Under U.S. GAAP, the company classifies interest paid, interest received, and dividends received as operating activities, and dividends paid are classified as a financing activity. These items are presented in the company's U.S. GAAP statement of cash flows as follows:

Operating activities:	
Interest paid.	$(1,250)
Interest received.	500
Dividends received	200
Cash flow from operating activities	$ (550)
Investing activities:	
Nothing reported.	$ 0
Financing activities:	
Dividends paid	(2,700)
Cash flow from financing activities.	$(2,700)
Net change in cash	$(3,250)

This classification would be acceptable under IFRS. However, the following presentation, among others, also would be acceptable under IAS 7:

Operating activities:	
Nothing reported	$ 0
Investing activities:	
Interest received	$ 500
Dividends received	200
Cash flow from investing activities	$ 700
Financing activities:	
Interest paid	$(1,250)
Dividends paid	(2,700)
Cash flow from financing activities	$(3,950)
Net change in cash	$(3,250)

Events after the Reporting Period

IAS 10, *Events after the Reporting Period,* prescribes when an entity should adjust its financial statements for events occurring after the balance sheet date (referred to in the United States as "subsequent events") and the disclosures to be made related to those events. Events after the reporting period are those events, favorable and unfavorable, that occur between the balance sheet date and the date that the financial statements are *authorized for issuance.* Under U.S. GAAP, the subsequent event period runs through the date that the financial statements are issued (or are available to be issued), which is later than the date they are authorized for issuance.

There are two types of after-the-reporting-period events that are treated differently:

1. Adjusting events after the reporting period.
2. Nonadjusting events after the reporting period.

Adjusting Events

Those events that provide evidence of conditions that existed at the end of the reporting period are adjusting events. These events must be recognized through adjustment of the financial statements. For example, assume a company has recorded an estimated liability related to litigation on its December 31, Year 1, balance sheet of $2 million. On January 20, Year 2, before the board of directors has approved the financial statements for issuance, the judge orders the company to pay $3 million. The liability on the December 31, Year 1, balance sheet should be adjusted upward to $3 million. The judge's decision clarifies the value of the liability that existed at the balance sheet date.

Nonadjusting Events

Events that are indicative of conditions that arise after the balance sheet date but before the date the financial statements are authorized for issue are nonadjusting events. No adjustments are made to the financial statements related to these events. However, disclosures are required of:

1. The nature of the event.
2. An estimate of the financial effect, or a statement that an estimate cannot be made.

For example, assume inventory carried on the December 31, Year 1, balance sheet at $3 million decreases in net realizable value to $1 million due to a change in the law on February 15, Year 2. The financial statements are approved for issuance on February 20, Year 2. The decline in market value does not relate to the condition of the inventory at the balance sheet date, so no adjustment should be made. If material, the decrease in value should be disclosed in the notes to the financial statements.

IAS 10 specifically states that financial statements should not be adjusted for cash dividends declared after the balance sheet date. The same is true for stock dividends and stock splits.

Accounting Policies, Changes in Accounting Estimates, and Errors

IAS 8, *Accounting Policies, Changes in Accounting Estimates and Errors*, provides guidance with respect to (1) the selection of accounting policies, (2) accounting for changes in accounting policies, (3) dealing with changes in accounting estimates, and (4) correction of errors.

Selection of Accounting Policies

IAS 8 establishes the following hierarchy of authoritative pronouncements to be followed in selecting accounting policies to apply to a specific transaction or event:

1. IASB Standard or Interpretation that specifically applies to the transaction or event.
2. IASB Standard or Interpretation that deals with similar and related issues.

3. Definitions, recognition criteria, and measurement concepts in the IASB *Framework.*
4. Most recent pronouncements of other standard-setting bodies that use a similar conceptual framework to develop accounting standards.

Changes in Accounting Policy

To ensure comparability of financial statements over time, an entity is required to apply its accounting policies consistently. A change in accounting policy is allowed only if the change:

1. Is required by an IFRS.
2. Results in the financial statements providing more relevant and reliable information.

If practical, the change in accounting policy should be applied retrospectively. The cumulative effect of adopting the new accounting policy is treated as an adjustment to the carrying amounts of the assets and liabilities affected and as an adjustment to the beginning balance in retained earnings. The cumulative effect is *not* included in net income.

Changes in Estimates

A change in estimate due to new developments or new information should be accounted for in the period of the change or in future periods, depending on the periods affected by the change. In other words, the change in estimate should be handled prospectively.

Correction of Errors

Material, prior-period errors should be corrected retrospectively by restating all prior reported accounts (assets, liabilities, equity) affected by the error and by recording a prior-period adjustment to the beginning balance in retained earnings. When it is impractical to determine the period-specific effects of an error on comparative information for one or more prior periods, the entity restates the opening balances in assets, liabilities, and equity for the earliest period for which retrospective restatement is practicable. This might be the current period. Whereas IFRS provides an exception if it is impractical to restate financial statements for a correction of an error, U.S. GAAP does not provide such an exception but instead requires all material errors to be corrected through restatement.

Related Party Disclosures

Transactions between related parties must be disclosed in the notes to financial statements. Parties are related if one party has the ability to control or exert significant influence over the other party. Related parties can include parent companies, subsidiaries, equity method associates, individual owners, and key management personnel. Similar rules exist in U.S. GAAP.

Earnings per Share

Basic and diluted earnings per share must be reported on the face of the income statement. IAS 33, *Earnings per Share,* provides guidance for calculating earnings per share. U.S. GAAP provides more detailed guidance with respect to the calculation of diluted earnings per share. Application of this guidance would appear to be consistent with IAS 33.

Interim Financial Reporting

IAS 34, *Interim Financial Reporting*, does not mandate which companies should prepare interim statements, how frequently, or how soon after the end of an interim period. The standard defines the minimum content to be included in interim statements by those entities required by their national jurisdiction to present them and identifies the accounting principles that should be applied. With certain exceptions, IAS 34 requires interim periods to be treated as discrete reporting periods. This differs from the position in U.S. GAAP, which treats interim periods as an integral part of the full year. As an example, IAS 34 would require annual bonuses to be recognized as expense in the interim period in which bonuses are paid. Under U.S. GAAP, on the other hand, one-fourth of the expected annual bonus is accrued each quarter.

Noncurrent Assets Held for Sale and Discontinued Operations

Noncurrent assets held for sale must be reported separately on the balance sheet at the lower of (1) carrying value or (2) fair value less costs to sell. Assets held for sale are not depreciated. Similar rules exist in U.S. GAAP.

A discontinued operation is a component of an entity that represents a major line of business or geographical area of operations that either has been disposed of or has been classified as held for sale. The after-tax profit or loss and after-tax gain or loss on disposal must be reported as a single amount on the face of the income statement. Detail of the revenues, expenses, gain or loss on disposal, and income taxes comprising this single amount must be disclosed in the notes or on the face of the income statement. If presented on the face of the income statement, it must be presented in a section identified as discontinued operations. The definition of the type of operation that can be classified as discontinued is somewhat narrower than under U.S. GAAP. In addition, U.S. GAAP requires both pre-tax and after-tax profit or loss to be reported on the income statement. Otherwise, the two sets of standards are substantially similar.

Operating Segments

As part of the short-term convergence project with the FASB, the IASB issued IFRS 8, *Operating Segments*, in 2006 to replace IAS 14, *Segment Reporting*. IFRS 8 adopted the FASB's so-called management approach. Extensive disclosures are required for each separately reportable operating segment. Operating segments are components of a business (1) that generate revenues and expenses, (2) whose operating results are regularly reviewed by the chief operating officer, and (3) for which separate financial information is available. IFRS 8 provides the following guidelines with regard to segment reporting:

- An operating segment is separately reportable if it meets any of three quantitative tests (revenue test, profit or loss test, asset test). Operating segments can be defined in terms of products and services or on the basis of geography.
- Disclosures required for each operating segment include assets, capital expenditures, liabilities, profit or loss, and the following components of profit or loss: external revenues, intercompany revenues, interest income and expense, depreciation and amortization, equity method income, income tax expense, and noncash expenses. Similar disclosures are required by U.S. GAAP except that liabilities by operating segment need not be reported.
- If the revenue reported by operating segments is less than 75 percent of total revenues, additional operating segments must be reported separately—even if

they do not meet any of the three quantitative tests—until at least 75 percent of total revenue is included in reportable segments.

- In addition to disclosures by operating segment, entitywide disclosures related to products and services, geographic areas, and major customers are required.
- If operating segments are not defined on the basis of products and services, revenue derived from each major product and service must be disclosed, even if the company has only one operating segment.
- Revenues and noncurrent assets must be disclosed for the domestic country and all foreign countries combined. These two items also must be disclosed for each foreign country in which a material amount of revenues or noncurrent assets is located. Materiality is not defined.
- The existence and amount of revenue derived from major customers must be disclosed, along with the identity of the segment generating the revenue. A major customer is defined as one from which 10 percent or more of total revenues are generated.

Summary

1. Many countries currently use IFRS, and it is likely that IFRS will be integrated into the U.S. financial reporting system in the near future. An understanding of IFRS is important for accountants who prepare or audit financial statements.

2. Differences exist between IFRS and U.S. GAAP with respect to recognition, measurement, presentation, disclosure, and choice among alternatives. In some cases, IFRS are more flexible than U.S. GAAP. Several IFRS allow firms to choose between alternative treatments in accounting for a particular item. Also, IFRS generally have less bright-line guidance than U.S. GAAP; therefore, more judgment is required in applying individual IFRS. However, in some cases, IFRS are more detailed than U.S. GAAP.

3. Some of the more important asset recognition and measurement differences between IFRS and U.S. GAAP relate to the following issues: inventory valuation; revaluation of property, plant, and equipment; component depreciation; capitalization of development costs; measurement of impairment losses; and classification of leases.

4. IAS 2 requires inventory to be reported on the balance sheet at the lower of cost and net realizable value. Write-downs to net realizable value must be reversed when the selling price increases. Under U.S. GAAP, inventory is carried at the lower of cost or replacement cost (with a ceiling and floor), and the reversal of write-downs is not permitted. Unlike U.S. GAAP, IAS 2 does not allow the use of last-in, first-out (LIFO) in determining the cost of inventory.

5. IAS 16 allows property, plant, and equipment to be carried at cost less accumulated depreciation and impairment losses or at a revalued amount less any subsequent accumulated depreciation and impairment losses. Specific guidance is provided for those firms that choose the revaluation option. U.S. GAAP does not permit use of the revaluation model.

6. IAS 16 requires an item of property, plant, and equipment comprised of significant parts for which different useful lives or depreciation methods are appropriate to be split into components for purposes of depreciation. Component depreciation is uncommon in U.S. GAAP.

7. IAS 36 requires impairment testing of property, plant, and equipment; intangibles, including goodwill; and long-term investments. An asset is impaired when its carrying value exceeds its recoverable amount, which is the greater of net selling price and value in use. An impairment loss is the amount by which carrying value exceeds the recoverable amount. If, subsequent to recognizing an impairment loss, the recoverable amount of an asset exceeds its new carrying amount, the impairment loss is reversed and the asset is written back up to the carrying amount that would have existed if the impairment had never been recognized. U.S. GAAP employs a different impairment test, and impairment losses may not be reversed.

8. IAS 38 requires development costs to be capitalized as an intangible asset when six specific criteria are met. Development costs can include personnel costs; materials and services; depreciation of property, plant, and equipment; amortization of patents and licenses; and overhead costs, other than general administrative costs. Development costs generally are not capitalized under U.S. GAAP. Intangible assets (including deferred development costs) are classified as having a finite or indefinite useful life. Finite-lived intangibles are amortized over their useful lives using a straight-line method; indefinite-lived intangibles are reviewed each year to determine if the useful life still is indefinite. If not, the intangible is reclassified as having a finite life and amortization begins.

9. Goodwill is measured as the excess of the consideration transferred in a business acquisition by the acquiring firm, plus any noncontrolling interest, over the fair value of net assets acquired. IFRS 3 allows two options in measuring noncontrolling interest, which results in two possible measures of goodwill. U.S. GAAP only allows one method for measuring noncontrolling interest.

10. Indefinite-lived intangibles and goodwill must be reviewed for impairment at least once per year. Finite-lived intangibles are tested for impairment whenever changes in circumstances indicate an asset's carrying amount may not be recoverable. IAS 36 allows the reversal of impairment losses on intangibles when certain conditions are met; however, the reversal of goodwill impairment is not allowed.

11. IAS 23 requires borrowing costs to be capitalized to the extent they are attributable to the acquisition of a qualifying asset; other borrowing costs are expensed immediately. Borrowing costs include interest and other costs, such as foreign exchange gains and losses on foreign currency borrowings, incurred in connection with a borrowing. The amount of borrowing cost to be capitalized is reduced by any interest income earned from the temporary investment of the amount borrowed. U.S. GAAP has a narrower definition of capitalizable interest costs and does not allow the netting of interest income.

12. At the time this book went to press, leases were required to be classified as finance leases or operating leases under both IFRS and U.S. GAAP. However, the classification guidelines differ between the two sets of standards. While there are more finance lease indicators provided in IAS 17 than in U.S. GAAP, the guidelines in IAS 17 tend to be less prescriptive and avoid the use of bright-line thresholds.

13. A sale-and-leaseback transaction generally results in a gain or loss on the sale for the seller-lessee. IFRS and U.S. GAAP differ with regard to the timing of when the gain or loss on the sale–leaseback can be recognized.

14. In addition to IAS 1, which was described in the previous chapter, several other IASB standards primarily provide guidance with respect to disclosure and presentation of information in the financial statements.

15. IAS 7 contains requirements for the presentation of the statement of cash flows. Several differences exist from U.S. GAAP, including the option to present interest and dividends paid as either operating or financing activities and interest and dividends received as either operating or investing activities.

16. IAS 10 prescribes when financial statements should be adjusted for events occurring after the end of the reporting period. The cutoff date for adjusting events is the date financial statements are authorized for issuance. Under U.S. GAAP, the cutoff date is the date financial statements are issued or are available to be issued, which is later than the date the statements are approved.

17. IAS 8 establishes a hierarchy of authoritative pronouncements to be considered in selecting accounting policies. The lowest level in the hierarchy is guidance issued by other standard-setting bodies that use a conceptual framework similar to the IASB's. This includes standards set by the FASB.

18. Once selected, an entity must use its accounting policies consistently over time. A change in accounting policy is allowed only if the change results in the financial statements providing more relevant and reliable information or the change is required by an IASB pronouncement.

19. Other disclosure and presentation standards provide guidance with respect to related party disclosures, earnings per share, noncurrent assets held for sale and discontinued operations, interim reporting, and segment reporting.

Questions

Unless otherwise indicated, questions should be answered based on IFRS.

1. What are the types of differences that exist between IFRS and U.S. GAAP?

2. How does application of the lower of cost or market rule for inventories differ between IFRS and U.S. GAAP?

3. How are the estimated costs of removing and dismantling an asset handled upon initial recognition of the asset?

4. What are the two models allowed for measuring property, plant, and equipment at dates subsequent to original acquisition?

5. Which items of property, plant, and equipment may be accounted for under the revaluation model, and how frequently must revaluation occur?

6. How is the revaluation surplus handled under the revaluation model?

7. How is depreciation determined for an item of property, plant, and equipment that is comprised of significant parts, such as an airplane?

8. In what way does the fair value model for investment property differ from the revaluation model for property, plant, and equipment?

9. How is an impairment loss on property, plant, and equipment determined and measured under IFRS? How does this differ from U.S. GAAP?

10. When a previously recognized impairment loss is subsequently reversed, what is the maximum amount at which the affected asset may be carried on the balance sheet?

11. What are the three major types of intangible asset, and how does the accounting for them differ?

12. How are internally generated intangibles handled under IFRS? How does this differ from U.S. GAAP?

13. Which intangible assets are subject to annual impairment testing?
14. How is goodwill measured in a business combination with a noncontrolling interest?
15. What is a gain on bargain purchase?
16. What is the process for determining whether goodwill allocated to a specific cash-generating unit is impaired?
17. What is the current treatment with respect to borrowing costs?
18. What are the differences in the amount of borrowing costs that can be capitalized under IFRS and U.S. GAAP?
19. How do the criteria for determining whether a lease qualifies as a finance (capitalized) lease differ between IFRS and U.S. GAAP?
20. What is the difference between IFRS and U.S. GAAP with regard to the recognition of gains and losses on sale–leaseback transactions?
21. How does the classification of interest and dividends in the statement of cash flows differ between IFRS and U.S. GAAP?
22. What is the cutoff date for the occurrence of events after the reporting period requiring adjustment to the financial statements?
23. What are the guidelines on selecting and changing accounting policies?

Exercises and Problems

Unless otherwise indicated, exercises and problems should be solved based on IFRS.

1. A company incurred the following costs related to the production of inventory in the current year:

Cost of materials	$100,000
Cost of direct labor	60,000
Allocation of variable overhead costs	30,000
Allocation of fixed overhead costs (based on normal production levels)	25,000
Storage costs (after production, prior to sale)	2,000
Selling costs	8,000

The cost of materials included abnormal waste of $10,000. What is the cost of inventory in the current year?

a. $190,000.
b. $205,000.
c. $215,000.
d. $217,000.

2. A company determined the following values for its inventory as of the end of its fiscal year:

Historical cost	$50,000
Current replacement cost	35,000
Net realizable value	45,000
Net realizable value less a normal profit margin	40,000
Fair value	48,000

What amount should the company report for inventory on its balance sheet?

a. $35,000.
b. $40,000.
c. $45,000.
d. $48,000.

3. When an entity chooses the revaluation model as its accounting policy for measuring property, plant, and equipment, which of the following statements is correct?

a. When an asset is revalued, the entire class of property, plant, and equipment to which that asset belongs must be revalued.
b. When an asset is revalued, individual assets within a class of property, plant, and equipment to which that asset belongs may be selectively revalued.
c. Revaluations of property, plant, and equipment must be made at least every three years.
d. Increases in an asset's carrying value as a result of the first revaluation must be recognized in net income.

4. On January 1, Year 1, an entity acquires a new machine with an estimated useful life of 20 years for $100,000. The machine has an electrical motor that must be replaced every five years at an estimated cost of $20,000. Continued operation of the machine requires an inspection every four years after purchase; the inspection cost is $10,000. The company uses the straight-line method of depreciation. What is the depreciation expense for Year 1?

a. $5,000.
b. $5,500.
c. $8,000.
d. $10,000.

5. An asset is considered to be impaired when its carrying amount is greater than its

a. Net selling price.
b. Value in use.
c. Undiscounted future cash flows.
d. Recoverable amount.

6. Under IFRS, an entity that acquires an intangible asset may use the revaluation model for subsequent measurement only if

a. The useful life of the intangible asset can be reliably determined.
b. An active market exists for the intangible asset.
c. The cost of the intangible asset can be measured reliably.
d. The intangible asset has a finite life.

7. Which of the following is a criterion that must be met in order for an item to be recognized as an intangible asset?

a. The item's fair value can be measured reliably.
b. The item is part of the entity's activities aimed at gaining new scientific or technical knowledge.

    c.   The item is expected to be used in the production or supply of goods or services.

    d.   The item is identifiable and lacks physical substance.

8. An entity incurs the following costs in connection with the purchase of a trademark:

Purchase price of the trademark.	$80,000
Nonrefundable value added tax paid on the purchase of the trademark	4,000
Training sales department staff on the use of the trademark	2,000
Research expenditures incurred prior to the purchase of the trademark	15,000
Legal fees to register the trademark	8,000
Salaries of personnel who negotiated the purchase of the trademark during the period of negotiation	10,000

Assuming that the trademark meets the criteria for recognition as an intangible asset, at what amount should the trademark be initially measured?

    a. $84,000.

    b. $92,000.

    c. $104,000.

    d. $119,000.

9. Which of the following best describes the accounting for goodwill subsequent to initial recognition?

    a.   Goodwill is amortized over its expected useful life, not to exceed 20 years.

    b.   Goodwill is tested for impairment whenever impairment indicators are present.

    c.   Goodwill is tested for impairment on an annual basis.

    d.   Goodwill is revalued using a revaluation model.

10. An entity must adjust its financial statements for an event that occurs after the end of the reporting period if

    a.   The event occurs before the financial statements have been approved for issuance and it provides evidence of conditions that existed at the end of the reporting period.

    b.   The event occurs before the financial statements have been issued and it changes the value of an asset that existed at the end of the reporting period.

    c.   The event occurs before the financial statements have been audited and it changes the value of a liability that existed at the end of the reporting period.

    d.   The event occurs within 15 days of the end of the reporting period and it changes the level of ownership in another entity from a noncontrolling to a controlling interest.

11. In selecting an accounting policy for a transaction, which of the following is the first level within the hierarchy of guidance that should be considered?

    a.   The most recent pronouncements of other standard-setting bodies to the extent they do not conflict with IFRS or the IASB *Framework*.

    b.   An IASB Standard or Interpretation that specifically relates to the transaction.

c. The definitions, recognition criteria, and measurement concepts in the IASB *Framework*.

d. An IASB Standard or Interpretation that deals with similar and related issues.

12. An entity can justify a change in accounting policy if

a. The change will result in a reliable and more relevant presentation of the financial statements.

b. The entity encounters new transactions that are substantively different from existing or previous transactions.

c. The entity previously accounted for similar, though immaterial, transactions under an unacceptable accounting method.

d. An alternative accounting policy gives rise to a material change in current year net income.

13. As a result of a downturn in the economy, Optiplex Corporation has excess productive capacity. On January 1, Year 3, Optiplex signed a special order contract to manufacture custom-design generators for a new customer. The customer requests that the generators be ready for pickup by June 15, Year 3, and guarantees it will take possession of the generators by July 15, Year 3. Optiplex incurred the following direct costs related to the custom-design generators:

Cost to complete the design of the generators.	$ 3,000
Purchase price for materials and parts	80,000
Transportation cost to get materials and parts to manufacturing facility.	2,000
Direct labor (10,000 labor hours at $12 per hour)	120,000
Cost to store finished product (from June 15 to June 30)	2,000

Because of the company's inexperience in manufacturing generators of this design, the cost of materials and parts included an abnormal amount of waste totaling $5,000. In addition to direct costs, Optiplex applies variable and fixed overhead to inventory using predetermined rates. The variable overhead rate is $2 per direct labor hour. The fixed overhead rate based on a normal level of production is $6 per direct labor hour. Given the decreased level of production expected in Year 3, Optiplex estimates a fixed overhead application rate of $9 per direct labor hour in Year 3.

Required:
Determine the amount at which the inventory of custom-design generators should be reported on Optiplex Corporation's June 30, Year 3, balance sheet.

14. To determine the amount at which inventory should be reported on the December 31, Year 1, balance sheet, Monroe Company compiles the following information for its inventory of Product Z on hand at that date:

• Historical cost	$20,000
• Replacement cost	14,000
• Estimated selling price	17,000
• Estimated costs to complete and sell	2,000
• Normal profit margin as a percentage of selling price	20%

The entire inventory of Product Z that was on hand at December 31, Year 1, was completed in Year 2 at a cost of $1,800 and sold at a price of $17,150.

Required:
a. Determine the impact that Product Z has on income in Year 1 and Year 2 under (1) IFRS and (2) U.S. GAAP.
b. Summarize the difference in income, total assets, and total stockholders' equity using the two different sets of accounting rules over the two-year period.

15. Beech Corporation has three finished products (related to three different product lines) in its ending inventory at December 31, Year 1. The following table provides additional information about each product:

Product	Cost	Replacement Cost	Selling Price	Normal Profit Margin
101	$130	$140	$160	20%
202	$160	$135	$140	20%
303	$100	$ 80	$100	15%

Beech Corporation expects to incur selling costs equal to 5 percent of the selling price on each of the products.

Required:
Determine the amount at which Beech should report its inventory on the December 31, Year 1, balance sheet under (1) IFRS and (2) U.S. GAAP.

16. This is a continuation of problem 15. At December 31, Year 2, Beech Corporation still had the same three different products in its inventory. The following table provides updated information for the company's products:

Product	Cost	Replacement Cost	Selling Price	Normal Profit Margin
101	$130	$180	$190	20%
202	$160	$150	$160	20%
303	$100	$100	$130	15%

Beech Corporation still expects to incur selling costs equal to 5 percent of the selling price.

Required:
Determine the amount at which Beech should report its inventory on the December 31, Year 2, balance sheet under (1) IFRS and (2) U.S. GAAP.

17. Steffen-Zweig Company exchanges two used printing presses with a total net book value of $24,000 ($40,000 cost less accumulated depreciation of $16,000) for a new printing press with a fair value of $24,000 and $3,000 in cash. The fair value of the two used printing presses is $27,000. The transaction is deemed to lack commercial substance.

Required:
Determine the amount of gain or loss that would be recognized from this exchange of assets.

18. Stevenson Corporation acquires a one-year-old building at a cost of $500,000 at the beginning of Year 2. The building has an estimated useful life of 50 years. However, based on reliable historical data, the company believes the carpeting will need to be replaced in 5 years, the roof will need to be replaced in 15 years, and the HVAC system will need to be replaced in 10 years. On the date of acquisition, the cost to replace these items would have been carpeting, $10,000; roof, $15,000; HVAC system, $30,000. Assume no residual value.

Required:
Determine the amount to be recognized as depreciation expense in Year 2 related to this building.

19. Quick Company acquired a piece of equipment in Year 1 at a cost of $100,000. The equipment has a 10-year estimated life, zero salvage value, and is depreciated on a straight-line basis. Technological innovations take place in the industry in which the company operates in Year 4. Quick gathers the following information for this piece of equipment at the end of Year 4:

Expected future undiscounted cash flows from continued use	$59,000
Present value of expected future cash flows from continued use	51,000
Net selling price in the used equipment market	50,000

At the end of Year 6, it is discovered that the technological innovations related to this equipment are not as effective as first expected. Quick estimates the following for this piece of equipment at the end of Year 6:

Expected future undiscounted cash flows from continued use	$50,000
Present value of expected future cash flows from continued use	44,000
Net selling price in the used equipment market	42,000

Required:
a. Discuss whether Quick Company must conduct an impairment test on this piece of equipment at December 31, Year 4.
b. Determine the amount at which Quick Company should carry this piece of equipment on its balance sheet at December 31, Year 4; December 31, Year 5; and December 31, Year 6. Prepare any related journal entries.

20. Godfrey Company constructed a new, highly automated chemical plant in Year 1, which began production on January 1, Year 2. The cost to construct the plant was $5,000,000: $1,500,000 for the building and $3,500,000 for machinery and equipment. The useful life of the plant (both building and machinery) is estimated to be 20 years. Local environmental laws require the machinery and equipment to be inspected by engineers after every five years of operation. The inspectors could require Godfrey to overhaul equipment at that time to be able to continue to operate the plant. Godfrey estimates that the costs of the inspection and any required overhaul to take place in five years to be

$200,000. Environmental laws also require Godfrey to dismantle and remove the plant assets at the end of their useful life. The company estimates that the net cost, after deducting any salvage value, for removal of the equipment will be $100,000, and the net cost for dismantling and removal of the building, after deducting any salvage value, will be $1,500,000. Godfrey has determined that the straight-line method of depreciation will best reflect the pattern in which the plant's future economic benefits will be received by the company. The company uses the cost model to account for its property, plant, and equipment. The company uses a discount rate of 10 percent in determining present values.

Required:

Determine the cost of the plant assets at January 1, Year 2. Determine the amount of depreciation expense that should be recognized related to the plant assets in Year 2.

21. Jefferson Company acquired equipment on January 2, Year 1, at a cost of $10 million. The equipment has a five-year life, no residual value, and is depreciated on a straight-line basis. On January 2, Year 3, Jefferson Company determines the fair value of the asset (net of any accumulated depreciation) to be $12 million.

Required:

a. Determine the impact the equipment has on Jefferson Company's income in Years 1–5 using (1) IFRS, assuming that the revaluation model is used for measurement subsequent to initial recognition, and (2) U.S. GAAP.

b. Summarize the difference in income, total assets, and total stockholders' equity using the two different sets of accounting rules over the period of Years 1–5.

22. Madison Company acquired a depreciable asset at the beginning of Year 1 at a cost of $12 million. At December 31, Year 1, Madison gathered the following information related to this asset:

Carrying amount (net of accumulated depreciation)...............	$10 million
Fair value of the asset (net selling price)........................	$7.5 million
Sum of future cash flows from use of the asset	$10 million
Present value of future cash flows from use of the asset	$8 million
Remaining useful life of the asset............................	5 years

Required:

a. Determine the impact on Year 2 and Year 3 income from the depreciation and possible impairment of this equipment under (1) IFRS and (2) U.S. GAAP.

b. Determine the difference in income, total assets, and total stockholders' equity for the period of Years 1–6 under the two different sets of accounting rules.

Note: If the asset is determined to be impaired, there would be no adjustment to Year 1 depreciation expense of $2 million.

23. Iptat International Ltd. provided the following reconciliation from IFRS to U.S. GAAP in its most recent annual report (amounts in thousands of CHF):

	Net Income	Shareholders' Equity
As stated under IFRS	541,713	7,638,794
U.S. GAAP adjustments		
(a) Reversal of additional depreciation charges arising from revaluation of fixed assets	85,720	643,099
(b) Reversal of revaluation surplus of fixed assets	—	(977,240)
As stated under U.S. GAAP	627,433	7,305,653

Required:
a. Explain why U.S. GAAP adjustment (a) results in an addition to net income. Explain why U.S. GAAP adjustment (a) results in an addition to shareholders' equity that is greater than the addition to net income. What is the shareholders' equity account affected by adjustment (a)?
b. Explain why U.S. GAAP adjustment (b) results in a subtraction from shareholders' equity but does not affect net income. What is the shareholders' equity account affected by adjustment (b)?

24. In Year 1, in a project to develop Product X, Lincoln Company incurred research and development costs totaling $10 million. Lincoln is able to clearly distinguish the research phase from the development phase of the project. Research-phase costs are $6 million, and development-phase costs are $4 million. All of the IAS 38 criteria have been met for recognition of the development costs as an asset. Product X was brought to market in Year 2 and is expected to be marketable for five years. Total sales of Product X are estimated at more than $100 million.

Required:
a. Determine the impact research and development costs have on Lincoln Company's Year 1 and Year 2 income under (1) IFRS and (2) U.S. GAAP.
b. Summarize the difference in income, total assets, and total stockholders' equity related to Product X over its five-year life under the two different sets of accounting rules.

25. Xanxi Petrochemical Company provided the following reconciliation from IFRS to U.S. GAAP in its most recent annual report (amounts in thousands of RMB):

	Net Income	Shareholders' Equity
As stated under IFRS	938,655	4,057,772
U.S. GAAP adjustments		
(a) Reversal of amortization charge on deferred development costs	5,655	16,965
(b) Gain on sale and leaseback of building	(40,733)	(66,967)
As stated under U.S. GAAP	903,577	4,007,770

Required:
a. Explain why U.S. GAAP adjustment (a) results in an addition to net income. Explain why U.S. GAAP adjustment (a) results in an addition to shareholders' equity that is greater than the addition to net income. What is the shareholders' equity account affected by adjustment (a)?
b. Explain why U.S. GAAP adjustment (b) reduces net income. Explain why U.S. GAAP adjustment (b) reduces shareholders' equity by a larger amount than it reduces net income. What is the shareholders' equity account affected by adjustment (b)?

26. Buch Corporation purchased Machine Z at the beginning of Year 1 at a cost of $100,000. The machine is used in the production of Product X. The machine is expected to have a useful life of 10 years and no residual value. The straight-line method of depreciation is used. Adverse economic conditions develop in Year 3 that result in a significant decline in demand for Product X. At December 31, Year 3, the company develops the following estimates related to Machine Z:

Expected future cash flows	$75,000
Present value of expected future cash flows	55,000
Selling price	70,000
Costs of disposal	7,000

At the end of Year 5, Buch's management determines that there has been a substantial improvement in economic conditions, resulting in a strengthening of demand for Product Z. The following estimates related to Machine Z are developed at December 31, Year 5:

Expected future cash flows	$70,000
Present value of expected future cash flows	53,000
Selling price	50,000
Costs of disposal	7,000

Required:
Determine the carrying amounts for Machine Z to be reported on the balance sheet at the end of Years 1–5, and the amounts to be reported in the income statement related to Machine Z for Years 1–5.

27. On January 1, Year 1, Holzer Company hired a general contractor to begin construction of a new office building. Holzer negotiated a $900,000, five-year, 10 percent loan on January 1, Year 1, to finance construction. Payments made to the general contractor for the building during Year 1 amount to $1,000,000. Payments were made evenly throughout the year. Construction is completed at the end of Year 1, and Holzer moves in and begins using the building on January 1, Year 2. The building is estimated to have a 40-year life and no residual value. On December 31, Year 3, Holzer Company determines that the market value for the building is $970,000.

On December 31, Year 5, the company estimates the market value for the building to be $950,000.

Required:

Use the two alternative methods allowed by IAS 16 with respect to the measurement of property, plant, and equipment subsequent to initial recognition to determine:

a. The carrying amount of the building that would be reported on the balance sheet at the end of Years 1–5.

b. The amounts to be reported in net income related to this building for Years 1–5.

In each case, assume that the building's value in use exceeds its carrying value at the end of each year and therefore impairment is not an issue.

28. Quantacc Company began operations on January 1, Year 1, and uses IFRS to prepare its financial statements. Quantacc reported net income of $100,000 in Year 5 and had stockholders' equity of $500,000 at December 31, Year 5. The company wishes to determine what its Year 5 income and December 31, Year 5, stockholders' equity would be if it had used U.S. GAAP. Relevant information follows:

   - Quantacc carries fixed assets at revalued amounts. Fixed assets were last revalued upward by $35,000 on January 1, Year 3. At that time, fixed assets had a remaining useful life of 10 years.

   - Quantacc capitalized development costs related to a new product in Year 4 in the amount of $80,000. Quantacc began selling the new product in January, Year 5, and expects the product to be marketable for a total of five years.

   - Early in January, Year 5, Quantacc realized a gain on the sale-and-leaseback of an office building in the amount of $150,000. The lease is accounted for as an operating lease, and the term of the lease is 20 years.

   Required:

   Calculate the following for Quantacc Company using U.S. GAAP (ignore income taxes):

   a. Net income for Year 5.

   b. Stockholders' equity at December 31, Year 5.

29. Stratosphere Company acquires its only building on January 1, Year 1, at a cost of $4,000,000. The building has a 20-year life, zero residual value, and is depreciated on a straight-line basis. The company adopts the revaluation model in accounting for buildings. On December 31, Year 2, the fair value of the building is $3,780,000. The company eliminates accumulated depreciation against the building account at the time of revaluation. The company's accounting policy is to reverse a portion of the revaluation surplus account related to increased depreciation expense. On January 2, Year 4, the company sells the building for $3,500,000.

   Required:

   Determine the amounts to be reflected in the balance sheet related to this building for Years 1–4 in the following table. (Use parentheses to indicate credit amounts.)

Date	Cost	Accumulated Depreciation	Carrying Amount	Revaluation Surplus	Income	Retained Earnings
January 1, Year 1	$4,000,000		$4,000,000			
December 31, Year 1						
Balance						
December 31, Year 2						
Balance						
December 31, Year 3						
Balance						
January 2, Year 4						
Balance						

30. During Year 1, Reforce Company conducted research and development on a new product. By March 31, Year 2, the company had determined the new product was technologically feasible, and the company obtained a patent for the product in April, Year 2. The company developed an initial prototype by June 30, Year 2. Also, by June 30, Year 2, the company had developed a business plan including identification of a ready market for the product, and a commitment of resources to ready the product for market. After completion of the second prototype at the end of September, Year 2, the product was ready for commercial production and marketing. The company has tracked costs associated with the new product as follows:

Market research costs, Year 1	$ 25,000
Research costs, Year 1	100,000
Research costs, 1st quarter, Year 2	70,000
Legal fees to register patent, April, Year 2	25,000
Development costs for initial prototype, 2nd quarter, Year 2	500,000
Testing of initial prototype, June, Year 2	50,000
Management time to develop business plan, 2nd quarter, Year 2	15,000
Cost of revisions and second prototype, 3rd quarter, Year 2	175,000
Legal fees to defend patent, October, Year 2	50,000
Commercial production costs, 4th quarter, Year 2	400,000
Marketing campaign, 4th quarter, Year 2	80,000

Required:
Determine the amount related to this new product that will be reported as intangible assets on the company's December 31, Year 2, balance sheet.

31. Philosopher Stone Inc. incurred costs of $20,000 to develop an intranet Web site for internal use. The intranet will be used to store information related to company policies, customers, and products. Access to the intranet is password-protected and is restricted to company personnel. As the company's

auditor, you have been asked to determine whether Philosopher Stone can capitalize the Web site development costs as an intangible asset or whether the company must expense the costs in the period in which they were incurred. Your research finds that SIC 32, *Intangible Assets–Web Site Costs,* indicates that a Web site developed for internal or external use is an internally generated intangible asset that is subject to the requirements of IAS 38. Specifically, SIC 32 indicates that the recognition criteria in IAS 38 related to development costs must be satisfied. The criterion most in question is whether the company can demonstrate the usefulness of the intranet and how it will generate probable future economic benefits.

Required:
Develop a justification for why Philosopher Stone should, or should not, be allowed to account for the intranet development costs as an intangible asset.

32. Bartholomew Corporation acquired 80 percent of the outstanding shares of Samson Company in Year 1 by paying $5,500,000 in cash. The fair value of Samson's identifiable net assets is $5,000,000. Bartholomew uses the proportionate share of the acquired firm's net assets approach to measure noncontrolling interest. Samson is a separate cash-generating unit. At the end of Year 1, Bartholomew compiles the following information for Samson:

Amount at which the shares of Samson could be sold	$5,000,000
Costs that would be incurred to sell the shares of Samson	$ 200,000
Present value of future cash flows from continuing to control Samson . . .	$4,750,000

Required:
At what amount should Samson's identifiable net assets and goodwill from the acquisition of Samson be reported on Bartholomew's consolidated balance sheet at the end of Year 1?

33. This exercise consists of two parts.

Part A.   The following table summarizes the assets of the Rocker Division (a separate cash-generating unit) at December 31, Year 5, prior to testing goodwill for impairment. Property, Plant, and Equipment and Other Intangibles are amortized on a straight-line basis over an average useful life of 12 years and 5 years, respectively. Management has estimated the present value of future cash flows from operating the Rocker Division to be $1,560. No fair market value is available.

Required:
Complete the following table to determine the carrying amounts at 12/31/Y5 for the assets of the Rocker Division.

	Goodwill	Property, Plant, and Equipment	Other Intangibles	Total
Carrying amount, 12/31/Y4	$1,000	$1,500	$500	$3,000
Amortization expense, Year 5 . . .	0	(125)	(100)	(225)
Subtotal.	$1,000	$1,375	$400	$2,775
Impairment loss				
Carrying amount, 12/31/Y5				

Part B.   Due to favorable changes in export laws, management revises its estimate of the value in use for the Rocker Division at 12/31/Y6 to be $1,930.

Required:
Complete the following table to determine the carrying amounts at 12/31/Y6 for the assets of the Rocker Division.

	Goodwill	Property, Plant, and Equipment	Other Intangibles	Total
Carrying amount, 12/31/Y5				
Amortization expense, Year 6 . . .				
Subtotal.				
Impairment loss/recovery				
Carrying amount, 12/31/Y6				

34. This exercise consists of three parts.

Part A.   On January 1, Year 1, Complete Company acquired 60 percent of the outstanding shares of Partial Company by paying $1,200,000 in cash. The fair value of Partial's identifiable assets and liabilities is $2,000,000 and $500,000, respectively.

Required:
Determine the possible amounts at which Complete Company should recognize goodwill from this business combination.

Part B.   Assume the same facts as in part A, except Complete Company acquires 80 percent of Partial Company for $1,100,000.

Required:
Determine the possible amounts at which Complete Company should recognize goodwill from this business combination.

Part C.   Assume the same facts as in part A and that Complete Company measured noncontrolling interest at the date of acquisition at the proportionate share of fair value of Partial Company's net assets. Complete Company determines that Partial Company is a separate cash-generating unit. At the end of Year 1, Complete Company develops the following estimates for Partial Company:

Fair value.	$1,900,000
Costs to sell	$ 20,000
Present value of future cash flows	$1,860,000

Required:
Determine the amount of impairment loss, if any, to be recognized in the Year 2 consolidated income statement, and the amount at which Partial Company's net assets, goodwill, and noncontrolling interest would be carried on the consolidated balance sheet at the end of Year 2.

35. Thurstone Company, a U.S.-based company, borrows 1,500,000 British pounds (£) on January 1, Year 1, at an interest rate of 4 percent to finance the construction of a new office building for its employees in England. Construction is expected to take six months and cost £1,500,000. Thurstone temporarily invests the British pounds borrowed until cash is needed to pay costs. Interest earned in the first quarter of Year 1 is £5,000. During the first quarter of Year 1, expenditures of £500,000 are incurred; the weighted-average expenditures are £300,000. Thurstone will repay the borrowing plus interest on June 30, Year 1, by converting U.S. dollars into British pounds. The U.S. dollar/British pound exchange rate was $2.00 on January 1, Year 1, and $2.10 on March 31, Year 1. The change in exchange rate is the result of the difference in interest rates in the United States and Great Britain.

    Required:
    Determine the amount of borrowing costs (in U.S. dollars) that Thurstone should include in the cost of the new office building at March 31, Year 1.

36. Atlanta Tours Company entered into a five-year lease on January 1, Year 1, with Duck Boats Inc. for a customized duck boat. Duck Boats Inc. will provide a vehicle to Atlanta Tours Company with the words "Gone with the Wind" carved into the sides. Following are the terms of the lease arrangement:

    - Fair value of the wagon at the inception of the lease is $10,000.
    - There is an eight-year estimated economic life.
    - Estimated (unguaranteed) residual value is $3,500. Atlanta Tours Company does not absorb any gains or losses in the fluctuations of the fair value of the residual value.
    - Annual lease payments of $2,000 are due on January 1 of each year. The implicit interest rate in the lease is 6 percent.
    - There is an option to purchase at end of lease term for $4,000.
    - The lease is noncancelable and may not be extended.

    Required:
    Discuss whether Atlanta Tours Company should classify this lease as an operating lease or as a finance lease under (a) IFRS and (b) U.S. GAAP.

37. This problem is comprised of three parts.

    Part A.   Fields Company sells a building to Victory Finance Company. The selling price of the building is $500,000, which approximates its fair value, and the carrying amount is $400,000. Fields then leases the building back from Victory under an operating lease for a period of three years.

    Required:
    Determine how Fields should account for the gain or loss on sale-and-leaseback.

    Part B.   Fields Company sells a building to Victory Finance Company. The selling price of the building is $500,000, which exceeds its fair value of $470,000. The carrying amount is $400,000. Fields then leases the building back from Victory under an operating lease for a period of three years.

    Required:
    Determine how Fields should account for the gain or loss on sale-and-leaseback.

Part C.   Fields Company sells a building to Victory Finance Company. The selling price of the building is $500,000, which is equal to its fair value. The carrying amount of the building is $400,000. Fields then leases the building back from Victory under a finance lease for a period of 20 years.

Required:
Determine how Fields should account for the gain or loss on sale-and-leaseback.

38. Bridget's Bakery Inc. enters into a new operating lease for a 10-year term at a monthly rental of $2,500. To induce Bridget's Bakery into the lease, the lessor agreed to a free-rent period for the first three months.

Required:
Determine the amount of lease expense, if any, that Bridget's Bakery would recognize in the first month of the lease.

39. Indicate whether each of the following describes an accounting treatment that is acceptable under IFRS, U.S. GAAP, both, or neither, by checking the appropriate box.

	Acceptable Under			
	IFRS	U.S. GAAP	Both	Neither
• A company takes out a loan to finance the construction of a building that will be used by the company. The interest on the loan is capitalized as part of the cost of the building.				
• Inventory is reported on the balance sheet using the last-in, first-out (LIFO) cost flow assumption.				
• The gain on a sale–leaseback transaction classified as an operating lease is deferred and amortized over the lease term.				
• A company writes a fixed asset down to its recoverable amount and recognizes an impairment loss in Year 1. In a subsequent year, the recoverable amount is determined to exceed the asset's carrying value, and the previously recognized impairment loss is reversed.				
• A company pays less than the fair value of net assets acquired in the acquisition of another company. The acquirer recognizes the difference as a gain on purchase of another company.				
• A company enters into an eight-year lease on equipment that is expected to have a useful life of 10 years. The lease is accounted for as an operating lease.				
• An intangible asset with an active market that was purchased two years ago is carried on the balance sheet at fair value.				
• In preparing interim financial statements, interim periods are treated as discrete reporting periods rather than as an integral part of the full year.				
• Development costs are capitalized when certain criteria are met.				
• Interest paid on borrowings is classified as an operating activity in the statement of cash flows.				

Case 4-1

Bessrawl Corporation

Bessrawl Corporation is a U.S.-based company that prepares its consolidated financial statements in accordance with U.S. GAAP. The company reported income in 2014 of $1,000,000 and stockholders' equity at December 31, 2014, of $8,000,000.

The CFO of Bessrawl has learned that the U.S. Securities and Exchange Commission is considering requiring U.S. companies to use IFRS in preparing consolidated financial statements. The company wishes to determine the impact that a switch to IFRS would have on its financial statements and has engaged you to prepare a reconciliation of income and stockholders' equity from U.S. GAAP to IFRS. You have identified the following five areas in which Bessrawl's accounting principles based on U.S. GAAP differ from IFRS.

1. Inventory
2. Property, plant, and equipment
3. Intangible assets
4. Research and development costs
5. Sale-and-leaseback transaction

Bessrawl provides the following information with respect to each of these accounting differences.

Inventory

At year-end 2014, inventory had a historical cost of $250,000, a replacement cost of $180,000, a net realizable value of $190,000, and a normal profit margin of 20 percent.

Property, Plant, and Equipment

The company acquired a building at the beginning of 2013 at a cost of $2,750,000. The building has an estimated useful life of 25 years, an estimated residual value of $250,000, and is being depreciated on a straight-line basis. At the beginning of 2014, the building was appraised and determined to have a fair value of $3,250,000. There is no change in estimated useful life or residual value. In a switch to IFRS, the company would use the revaluation model in IAS 16 to determine the carrying value of property, plant, and equipment subsequent to acquisition.

Intangible Assets

As part of a business combination in 2011, the company acquired a brand with a fair value of $40,000. The brand is classified as an intangible asset with an indefinite life. At year-end 2014, the brand is determined to have a selling price of $35,000 with zero cost to sell. Expected future cash flows from continued use of the brand are $42,000, and the present value of the expected future cash flows is $34,000.

Research and Development Costs

The company incurred research and development costs of $200,000 in 2014. Of this amount, 40 percent related to development activities subsequent to the point at which criteria had been met indicating that an intangible asset existed. As of the end of the 2014, development of the new product had not been completed.

Sale-and-Leaseback

In January 2012, the company realized a gain on the sale-and-leaseback of an office building in the amount of $150,000. The lease is accounted for as an operating lease, and the term of the lease is five years.

Required

Prepare a reconciliation schedule to convert 2014 income and December 31, 2014, stockholders' equity from a U.S. GAAP basis to IFRS. Ignore income taxes. Prepare a note to explain each adjustment made in the reconciliation schedule.

References

Ernst & Young. "The Evolution of IAS 39 in Europe." *Eye on IFRS Newsletter*, November 2004, pp. 1–4.

Financial Accounting Standards Board. *The IASC-U.S. Comparison Project*, 2nd ed. Norwalk, CT: FASB, 1999.

Reimers, J. L. "Additional Evidence on the Need for Disclosure Reform." *Accounting Horizons*, March 1992, pp. 36–41.

U.S. Securities and Exchange Commission. Release Nos. 33-9109; 34-61578, *Commission Statement in Support of Convergence and Global Accounting Standards*, February 2010.

Chapter **Five**

International Financial Reporting Standards: Part II

Learning Objectives

After reading this chapter, you should be able to

- Describe and apply the requirements of International Financial Reporting Standards (IFRS) related to the financial reporting of current liabilities, provisions, employee benefits, share-based payment, income taxes, revenue, and financial instruments.
- Explain and analyze the effect of major differences between IFRS and U.S. GAAP related to the financial reporting of current liabilities, provisions, employee benefits, share-based payment, income taxes, revenue, and financial instruments.

INTRODUCTION

International Financial Reporting Standards (IFRS) issued by the International Accounting Standards Board (IASB) comprise a comprehensive set of standards providing guidance for the preparation and presentation of financial statements. Chapter 4 described and demonstrated the requirements of selected IASB standards, particularly those relating to the recognition and measurement of assets. This chapter continues the study of IFRS by focusing on the recognition and measurement of current liabilities, provisions, employee benefits, share-based payment, income taxes, revenue, and financial instruments.

CURRENT LIABILITIES

IAS 1, *Presentation of Financial Statements,* requires liabilities to be classified as current or noncurrent. Current liabilities are those liabilities that a company:

1. Expects to settle in its normal operating cycle.
2. Holds primarily for the purpose of trading.
3. Expects to settle within 12 months of the balance sheet date.
4. Does not have the right to defer until 12 months after the balance sheet date.

The classification and accounting for current liabilities under IFRS is very similar to U.S. GAAP. Differences relate to the following:

- *Refinanced short-term debt:* May be reclassified as long-term debt only if refinancing is completed prior to the balance sheet date. Under U.S. GAAP, a refinancing agreement must be reached, but the refinancing need not be completed by the balance sheet date.

- *Amounts payable on demand due to violation of debt covenants:* Must be classified as current unless a waiver of at least 12 months is obtained from the lender by the balance sheet date. The waiver must be obtained by the annual report issuance date under U.S. GAAP.

- *Bank overdrafts:* Are netted against cash if the overdrafts form an integral part of the entity's cash management; otherwise bank overdrafts are classified as current liabilities. Bank overdrafts are always classified as current liabilities under U.S. GAAP.

Example: Violation of Debt Covenant

On June 30, Year 1, Sprockets Inc. obtains a $100,000 loan from a bank for a manufacturing facility. The loan is due in 24 months and is subject to a number of debt covenants. In December, Year 1, Sprockets distributes too much of its cash on employee bonuses and incurs a debt covenant violation as of December 31, Year 1. As a result of the violation, the loan becomes due within 30 days. Sprockets' CFO asks the bank to waive the violation. On January 5, Year 2, the bank agrees to waive the violation, stipulating that it must be rectified within 90 days. Sprockets issues its financial statements on January 30, Year 2. In this situation, Sprockets would be required to classify the bank loan as a current liability on its December 31, Year 1, balance sheet because it did not obtain a waiver from the bank by the balance sheet date.

Now assume that Sprockets' CFO obtained a waiver from the bank on December 30, Year 1, stipulating that the debt covenant violation must be rectified within 90 days. In this case, although the waiver was obtained before the balance sheet date, Sprockets still would be required to classify the bank loan as a current liability, because the waiver is not for at least 12 months, but is for only 90 days.

PROVISIONS, CONTINGENT LIABILITIES, AND CONTINGENT ASSETS

IAS 37, *Provisions, Contingent Liabilities and Contingent Assets,* provides guidance for reporting liabilities (and assets) of uncertain timing, amount, or existence. It contains specific rules related to onerous contracts and restructuring costs. By way of examples in IAS 37, Part B, guidance also is provided with regard to issues such as environmental costs and nuclear decommissioning costs.

Contingent Liabilities and Provisions

IAS 37 distinguishes between a contingent liability, which is not recognized on the balance sheet, and a provision, which is. A *provision* is defined as a "liability of uncertain timing or amount." A provision should be recognized when

1. The entity has a *present* obligation (legal or constructive) as a result of a past event.
2. It is *probable* (more likely than not) that an outflow of resources embodying economic events will be required to settle the obligation.
3. A reliable estimate of the obligation can be made.

A *constructive obligation* exists when a company through past actions or current statements indicates that it will accept certain responsibilities and, as a result, has created a valid expectation on the part of other parties that it will discharge those responsibilities. For example, an entity has a constructive obligation to restructure when it communicates the details of the restructuring plan to those employees who will be affected by it. Another example of a constructive obligation is where a manufacturer (e.g., Sony) announces that it will honor rebates offered by a retailer that goes out of business (e.g., Circuit City) on the manufacturer's products, even though the manufacturer has no contractual obligation to do so. A constructive obligation is recognized as a provision when it meets the remaining criteria (2 and 3) just listed. U.S. GAAP does not have the concept of a constructive obligation. Thus, only legal obligations might be accrued when criteria are met.

Contingent liabilities are defined in IAS 37 as one of the following:

- *Possible* obligations that arise from past events and whose existence will be confirmed by the occurrence or nonoccurrence of a future event.
- A *present* obligation that is *not recognized* because (1) it is *not* probable that an outflow of resources will be required to settle the obligation or (2) the amount of the obligation *cannot* be measured with sufficient reliability.

Contingent liabilities are disclosed unless the possibility of an outflow of resources embodying the economic future benefits is *remote.*

The rules for recognition of a provision and disclosure of a contingent liability are generally similar to the U.S. GAAP rules related to contingent liabilities. Under U.S. GAAP, a contingent liability is neither recognized nor disclosed if the likelihood of an outflow of resources is remote; it is disclosed if such an outflow is possible but not probable; and it is recognized on the balance sheet when an outflow of resources is probable. The main difference is that U.S. GAAP requires accrual when it is probable that a loss has occurred, with no guidance as to how the word *probable* should be interpreted. Research suggests that U.S. accountants require the likelihood of occurrence to be in the range of 70 to 90 percent before recognizing a contingent liability.[1] In defining a provision, IAS 37 specifically defines *probable* as "more likely than not," which implies a threshold of just over 50 percent. Thus, in practice, the threshold for recognition of a "liability of uncertain timing or amount" is considerably lower under IFRS than under U.S. GAAP.

IAS 37 establishes guidance for measuring a provision as the *best estimate* of the expenditure required to settle the present obligation at the balance sheet date. The best estimate is the probability-weighted expected value when a range of estimates exists or the midpoint within a range if all estimates are equally likely. Provisions must be discounted to present value. Provisions also must be reviewed at the end of each accounting period and adjusted to reflect the current best estimate. Under U.S. GAAP, contingent liabilities should be recognized at the low end of the range of possible amounts when a range of estimates exists. U.S. GAAP only allows discounting of a recognized contingent liability when the amount of the liability and the timing of payments are fixed or reliably determinable.

Subsequent reduction of a provision can be made only for the expenditures for which the provision was established. For example, if a provision is created for warranties, the provision can only be reduced as warranty costs are incurred. A

---

[1] Financial Accounting Standards Board, *The IASC-US Comparison Project: A Report on the Similarities and Differences between IASC Standards and US GAAP*: 2nd ed., Norwalk, CT: FASB, 1999.

provision is reversed when it is no longer probable that an outflow of resources will occur.

With respect to disclosure of contingent liabilities, IAS 37 allows an enterprise "in extremely rare cases" to omit disclosures that "can be expected to prejudice seriously the position of the enterprise in a dispute with other parties." No such exemption exists under U.S. GAAP.

Example: Provision for Litigation Loss

Former employees of Dreams Unlimited Inc. filed a lawsuit against the company in Year 1 for alleged age discrimination. At December 31, Year 1, external legal counsel provided an opinion that it was 60 percent probable that the company would be found liable, which would result in a total payment to the former employees between $1,000,000 and $1,500,000, with all amounts in that range being equally likely.

Because it is "more likely than not" that an outflow of resources (cash) will be required as a result of the lawsuit and an amount can be reasonably estimated, Dreams Unlimited should recognize a provision. Because all amounts in the estimated range of loss are equally likely, the amount recognized would be the midpoint of the range, $1,250,000 [($1,000,000 + $1,500,000)/2]. Therefore, Dreams Unlimited would prepare the following journal entry at December 31, Year 1 to recognize a provision:

Litigation Loss	$1,250,000	
Provision for Litigation Loss		$1,250,000

Note that under U.S. GAAP, a provision probably would not be recognized because the likelihood of incurring a loss is only 60 percent. If a provision were recognized under U.S. GAAP, it would be for $1,000,000, the low end of the range.

In Year 2, Dreams Unlimited settled with the former employees, making a total payment of $1,100,000. As a result, the company would prepare the following journal entry:

Provision for Litigation Loss	$1,250,000	
Cash		$1,100,000
Reversal of Litigation Loss		150,000

The reversal of litigation loss would result in an increase in income in Year 2.

Onerous Contract

IAS 37 requires the recognition of a provision for the present obligation related to an "onerous contract," that is, a contract in which the unavoidable costs of meeting the obligation of the contract exceed the economic benefits expected to be received from it. However, recognition of a provision for expected future operating losses is not allowed. When an onerous contract exists, a provision should be recognized for the unavoidable costs of the contract, which is the lower of the cost of fulfillment and the penalty that would result from non fulfillment under the contract. When a contract becomes onerous as a result of an entity's own action, the resulting provision should *not* be recognized until that action has actually occurred.

Example: Onerous Contract

Delicious Chocolate Company produces chocolate candies. It has a noncancelable lease on a building in Ridgeway, South Carolina, that it uses for production. The lease expires on December 31, Year 2, and is classified as an operating lease for accounting purposes. The annual lease payment is $120,000. In October, Year 1, the company closed its South Carolina facility and moved production to Mexico. The company does not believe it will be possible to sublease the building located in South Carolina.

Because there is no future economic benefit expected from the lease, it is an onerous contract. The unavoidable cost of fulfilling the lease contract for Year 2 of $120,000 should be expensed and recorded as a provision on December 31, Year 1. The journal entry would be:

```
Noncancelable Lease Expense . . . . . . . . . . . . . . . . . . . . . . . . . . . . . . . . $120,000
    Provision for Future Lease Payments . . . . . . . . . . . . . . . . . . . . . . . . . . . $120,000
```

Restructuring

A restructuring is a program that is planned and controlled by management and that materially changes either

1. The scope of a business undertaken by an entity.
2. The manner in which that business is conducted.

Examples of restructurings include:

- Sale or termination of a line of business.
- Closure of business locations in a country or region.
- Change in management structure.
- Fundamental reorganization that has a material effect on the nature and focus of the entity's operations.

A difference exists between IAS 37 and U.S. GAAP with respect to when a provision should be recognized related to a restructuring plan. According to IAS 37, a restructuring provision should be recognized when an entity has a detailed formal plan for the restructuring and it has raised a valid expectation in those affected by the plan that it will carry out the restructuring, either by announcing the main features of the plan to those affected by it or by beginning to implement the plan. Also, the cost of the restructuring must be reasonably estimable and the plan must be carried out within a reasonable period of time.

U.S. GAAP does not allow recognition of a restructuring provision until a liability has been incurred. The existence of a restructuring plan and its announcement do not necessarily create a liability. Thus, the recognition of a restructuring provision and related loss may occur at a later date under U.S. GAAP than under IFRS.

Contingent Assets

A contingent asset is a probable asset that arises from past events and whose existence will be confirmed only by the occurrence or nonoccurrence of a future event. Contingent assets should not be recognized, but should be disclosed when the inflow of economic benefits is *probable*. If the realization of income from a contingency is determined to be *virtually certain,* then the related benefit is considered to meet the definition of an asset and recognition is appropriate. IAS 37 allows earlier recognition of a contingent asset (and related gain) than does U.S. GAAP, which generally requires the asset to be realized before it can be recognized.

Exhibit 5.1 provides a summary of the recognition and disclosure guidelines in IAS 37.

EXHIBIT 5.1
IAS 37 Recognition and Disclosure Guidelines

Contingent Element	Likelihood of Realization	Accounting Treatment
Uncertain liability	Probable (more likely than not)	
	—Reliably measurable	Recognize provision
	—Not reliably measurable	Disclosure
	Not probable	Disclosure
	Remote	No disclosure
Uncertain asset	Virtually certain	Recognize asset
	Probable	Disclosure
	Not probable	No disclosure

Additional Guidance

The IASB document published to accompany IAS 37 (IAS 37, Part B) provides a number of examples to demonstrate the application of the standard's recognition principles. Example 2B, for example, describes a situation involving contaminated land, which gives rise to a constructive obligation.

Example: Contaminated Land Constructive Obligation

Petrocan Company operates in the oil industry and contaminates land at a location in a foreign country. The foreign country does not have environmental legislation that will require the company to clean up the contamination. However, Petrocan has a widely published environmental policy to clean up all contamination that it causes, and the company has a record of honoring this policy.

The company applies the criteria of IAS 37 to determine whether recognition of a provision is appropriate:

1. *Present obligation as a result of a past obligating event:* The past obligating event is the contamination of the land. A present constructive obligation exists because the past conduct of the company creates a valid expectation on the part of those affected by it that the entity will clean up the contamination.

2. *An outflow of resources embodying economic benefits in settlement is probable:* Because the contamination has occurred, and the company has a policy of cleaning up all contamination, an outflow of resources to settle the constructive obligation is "more likely than not."

3. *A reliable estimate of the obligation can be made:* The company must determine whether this criterion is met. If so, a provision would be recognized for the best estimate of the costs of clean up. If not, then disclosures would be made because there is a greater than remote likelihood of an outflow of resources to settle the obligation.

EMPLOYEE BENEFITS

IAS 19, *Employee Benefits*, is a single standard that covers all forms of employee compensation and benefits other than share-based compensation (e.g., stock options), which is covered in IFRS 2. IAS 19 provides guidance with respect to four types of employee benefits:

1. Short-term employee benefits (such as compensated absences and bonuses).
2. Post-employment benefits (pensions, medical benefits, and other post-employment benefits).
3. Other long-term employee benefits (such as deferred compensation and disability benefits).
4. Termination benefits (such as severance pay and early retirement benefits).

Short-Term Benefits

An employer recognizes an expense and a liability at the time that the employee provides services. The amount recognized is undiscounted.

Compensated Absences

For short-term compensated absences (such as sick pay or vacation pay), an amount is accrued when services are provided only if the compensated absences accumulate over time and can be carried forward to future periods. In the case of nonaccumulating compensated absences, an expense and liability are recognized only when the absence occurs.

Profit-Sharing and Bonus Plans

An expense and a liability are accrued for profit-sharing or bonus plans only if:

- The company has a present legal or constructive obligation to make such payments as a result of past events.
- The amount can be reliably estimated.

Even if a company has no legal obligation to pay a bonus, it can have a constructive obligation to do so if it has no realistic alternative but to pay the bonus.

Post-employment Benefits

IAS 19 was revised in 2011 and made significant changes in the treatment of post-employment benefits. Revised IAS 19 became effective in 2013.

IAS 19 distinguishes between defined contribution plans and defined benefit plans. The accounting for a defined contribution plan is simple and straightforward. An employer:

1. Accrues an expense and a liability at the time the employee renders service for the amount the employer is obligated to contribute to the plan.
2. Reduces the liability when contributions are made.

The accounting for a defined post-employment benefit plan is considerably more complicated.

Defined Post-employment Benefit Plans

Under IFRS, the accounting for both defined benefit pension plans and other defined post-employment benefit plans (such as medical and life insurance benefits) is basically the same and is generally similar to the accounting under U.S. GAAP, but with some differences. The following discussion relates specifically to pensions, but it also is applicable to other post-employment benefits.

The two major issues in accounting for defined benefit pension plans are (1) calculation of the *net defined benefit liability (or asset)* to be reported on the balance sheet and (2) calculation of the *defined benefit cost* to be recognized in income (either net income or other comprehensive income).

Net Defined Benefit Liability (Asset)

The amount recognized on the employer's balance sheet as a *net defined benefit liability (or asset)* is calculated as:

+ Present value of the defined benefit obligation (PVDBO)
− Fair value of plan assets (FVPA)

The PVDBO is based on assumptions related to variables such as employee turnover, life expectancy, and future salary levels. The discount rate used in determining the PVDBO is determined by reference to the yield at the end of the period on high-quality corporate bonds.

When the PVDBO is greater than the FVPA, a *deficit* exists, and the employer reports this amount as a net defined benefit liability on the balance sheet. When the FVPA is greater than the PVDBO, a *surplus* arises, but the amount of the net defined benefit asset recognized is limited to the larger of:

a. the surplus, and
b. the asset ceiling, which is the present value of any economic benefits available in the form of refunds from the plan or reductions in future contributions to the plan.

Under U.S. GAAP, the amount recognized on the balance sheet also is equal to the difference between the PVDBO and the FVPA; this is known as the funded status. However, there is no asset ceiling under U.S. GAAP.

Example: Limitation on the Recognition of the Net Defined Benefit Asset

The defined benefit pension plan of Fortsen Company Inc. has the following characteristics at December 31, Year 9:

Present value of defined benefit obligation (PVDBO)	$ 10,000
Fair value of plan assets (FVPA)	(10,800)
Surplus	$ (800)
Asset ceiling (present value of reductions in future contributions)	$ 525

Fortsen recognizes a net defined benefit asset of $525 on its December 31, Year 9, balance sheet and discloses the fact that the asset ceiling reduces the carrying amount of the asset by $275 ($800 − $525). The asset limitation of $275 also is included in *the remeasurements of the net defined benefit liability (asset)*, described below. Under U.S. GAAP, Fortsen would report a net defined benefit asset of $800, equal to the difference between the PVDBO and FVPA.

Defined Benefit Cost

The defined benefit cost reported in income is comprised of four components. Three of these components are included in the computation of net income, and one is included in other comprehensive income. The components of defined benefit cost included in *net income* are:

- Current service cost
- Past service cost and gains and losses on settlements
- Net interest on the net defined benefit liability (asset)

Net interest on the net defined benefit liability (asset) (NIDBA) is determined by multiplying the net defined benefit liability (asset) by the same discount rate used to measure PVDBO. As a result, NIDBA is the difference between interest expense (PVDBO × discount rate) and interest income (FVPA × discount rate).

Past service cost arises when an employer improves the benefits to be paid to employees in a defined benefit plan. IAS 19 requires all past service costs to be recognized in net income in the period in which the benefit plan is changed, regardless of the status of the employees benefiting from the change.

In comparison, U.S. GAAP requires that the past service cost (referred to as prior service cost) be recognized in other comprehensive income (OCI) and then amortized to net income over time. The past service cost related to retirees is amortized to net income over their remaining expected life, and the past service cost related to active employees is amortized to net income over their expected remaining service period.

Example: Recognition of Past Service Cost

On January 1, Year 7, Eagle Company amends its defined benefit pension plan to increase the amount of benefits to be paid. The benefits vest after five years of service. Eagle has no retirees. At the date of the plan amendment, the increase in the present value of the defined benefit obligation (PVDBO) attributable to active employees is $18,000. The active employees have an average remaining service life of 12 years.

Under IFRS, Eagle Company recognizes the entire past service cost of $18,000 as an expense to net income in Year 7. Under U.S. GAAP, because all of the employees affected by the plan amendment are active employees, the past service cost of $18,000 would be amortized to net income over the remaining service life of those employees at the rate of $1,500 per year ($18,000/12 years).

Gains and losses on settlements arise when an employer settles a defined benefit plan by making a lump-sum cash payment to employees in exchange for their rights to receive defined future benefits. A pension plan curtailment arises when there is a material reduction in the number of employees covered by a plan (such as when a plant is closed as part of a restructuring) or when the future service by current employees will no longer qualify for pension benefits or will qualify only for reduced benefits. Gains and losses usually arise in conjunction with both plan settlements and curtailments.

IAS 19 treats gains and losses on settlements and curtailments similarly; both are recognized in net income in the period in which the settlement or curtailment takes place or when the related restructuring costs are recognized, if earlier. U.S. GAAP treats gains and losses on plan curtailments and settlements differently, with losses generally being recognized earlier than gains. Under U.S. GAAP, a curtailment gain cannot be recognized until the related employees terminate or the plan has been adopted.

Remeasurements of the net defined benefit liability (asset) are the fourth component of the net defined benefit liability (asset). Remeasurements are recognized in other comprehensive income (OCI) and are never recycled to net income. Remeasurements consist of:

1. Actuarial gains and losses.
2. The difference between the actual return on plan assets in the current period and the interest income component of NIDBA (FVPA × discount rate).
3. Any change in the effect of the asset ceiling during the period.

Actuarial gains and losses arise when an employer changes the actuarial assumptions used in determining the future benefit obligation or makes adjustments based on differences between past assumptions and past experience. In contrast to IAS 19, which requires actuarial gains and losses to be recognized immediately through OCI with no recycling to net income, U.S. GAAP allows a choice between immediate recognition in OCI or in net income. Actuarial gains and losses recognized in OCI are recycled to net income by adopting either a so-called corridor approach or a systematic method that results in faster recycling.

Other Post-employment Benefits

IAS 19 does not provide separate guidance for other post-employment benefits. The procedures described earlier for pension plans are equally applicable for other forms of post-employment benefits provided to employees, such as medical benefits and life insurance. In calculating the PVDBO for post-employment medical benefit plans, assumptions also must be made regarding expected changes in the cost of medical services.

U.S. GAAP provides considerably more guidance than IAS 19 with regard to the assumptions to be used and the measurement of the employer's obligation for post-employment medical benefits. As allowed by the IASB's *Framework*, companies using IFRS could refer to the guidance provided in U.S. GAAP to identify an appropriate method for determining the amount of expense to recognize related to post-employment benefits other than pensions.

Other Long-Term Employee Benefits

Other long-term employee benefits include, for example, long-term compensated absences (e.g., sabbatical leaves), long-term disability benefits, bonuses payable 12 months or more after the end of the period, and deferred compensation paid 12 months or more after the end of the period. A liability should be recognized for other long-term employee benefits equal to the difference between:

1. The present value of the defined benefit obligation.
2. The fair value of plan assets (if any).

SHARE-BASED PAYMENT

The IASB and the FASB worked closely in developing new standards related to accounting for share-based payments. Concurrent with the IASB's issuance of IFRS 2, the FASB published an exposure draft in March 2004 and subsequently issued a final standard on this topic in December 2004. Although a number of minor differences exist between the two standards, IFRS 2 and U.S. GAAP are substantially similar.

IFRS 2, *Share-based Payment*, sets out measurement principles and specific requirements for three types of share-based payment transactions:

1. *Equity-settled share-based payment transactions,* in which the entity receives goods or services as consideration for equity instruments of the entity (including stock options granted to employees).
2. *Cash-settled share-based payment transactions,* in which the entity acquires goods or services by incurring liabilities to the supplier of those goods or services for amounts that are based on the price (or value) of the entity's shares or other equity instruments of the entity (e.g., share appreciation rights).
3. *Choice-of-settlement share-based payment transactions,* in which the terms of the arrangement provide either the entity or the supplier of goods or services with a choice of whether the entity settles the transaction in cash or by issuing equity instruments.

IFRS 2 applies to share-based transactions with both employees and nonemployees and requires an entity to recognize all share-based payment transactions in its financial statements; there are no exceptions.

The standard applies a *fair value approach* in accounting for share-based payment transactions. In some situations, these transactions are recognized at the fair value of the goods or services obtained; in other cases, at the fair value of the equity instrument awarded. Fair value of shares and stock options is based on market prices, if available; otherwise a generally accepted valuation model should be used. IFRS 2, Part B, contains extensive application guidance with respect to estimating the "fair value of equity instruments granted."

Equity-Settled Share-Based Payment Transactions

Share-based payment transactions entered into by an entity that will be settled by the entity issuing equity shares are accounted for as equity transactions. Typically, a debit is made to either an asset (goods acquired) or an expense (service received), and a credit is made to paid-in capital.

Share-Based Payments to Nonemployees

Entities sometimes will acquire goods or services from external suppliers using shares of the entity's stock as payment. Share-based payments to nonemployees are measured at the fair value of the goods or services received. If the fair value of the goods or services received cannot be reliably determined, then the fair value of the equity instruments is used. If the fair value of the equity instruments is used, the measurement date is the date the entity obtains the goods or services. If the goods or services are received on a number of dates over a period, the fair value at each date should be used.

Under U.S. GAAP, when the transaction is accounted for using the fair value of the equity instruments, the earlier of either the date at which a commitment for performance is reached or when the performance is completed is used as the measurement date for determining the fair value of the equity instruments.

Share-Based Payments to Employees

For share-based payments to employees (including stock options), the transaction should be measured at the fair value of the equity instruments granted because the fair value of the service provided by the employees generally is not reliably measurable. The fair value of stock options must be determined at the date the options are granted (grant date).

Stock option plans typically contain vesting conditions that must be met in order for the options to become exercisable. The entity issuing stock options must estimate the number of options that are expected to vest. The product of the number of options expected to vest multiplied by the fair value of those options is the total compensation cost that will be recognized as compensation expense over the vesting period. The estimate of options expected to vest should be revised throughout the vesting period, with corresponding adjustments to compensation expense. As compensation expense is recognized, it is offset by an increase in additional paid-in capital.

Compensation expense associated with stock options that vest on a single date (cliff vesting) is recognized on a straight-line basis over the service period. When stock options vest in installments (graded vesting), the compensation expense associated with each installment (or tranche) must be amortized over that installment's vesting period. U.S. GAAP allows a choice in recognizing compensation cost related to graded-vesting stock options. Entities may choose to amortize compensation cost on an accelerated basis by tranche (similar to IFRS); alternatively, compensation cost may be amortized on a straight-line basis over the vesting period.

Example: Graded-Vesting Stock Options

Glackin Corporation grants stock options with a fair value of $100,000 to select employees at the beginning of Year 1; 50 percent vest at the end of Year 1 and 50 percent vest at the end of Year 2. Under IFRS, compensation cost associated with the first tranche is fully allocated to expense in Year 1, and compensation cost associated with the second tranche is amortized to expense 50 percent in Year 1 and 50 percent in Year 2. As a result, the amount of compensation expense recognized in Year 1 is $75,000 [$50,000 + (50% × $50,000)], and the amount of compensation expense recognized in Year 2 is $25,000 [50% × $50,000]. The same pattern of compensation expense recognition would be acceptable under U.S. GAAP. Alternatively, U.S. GAAP allows the company to simply amortize the $100,000 compensation cost on a straight-line basis over the two-year vesting period, recognizing compensation expense of $50,000 in each of Year 1 and Year 2.

Modification of Stock Option Plans

Entities that grant stock options sometimes make modifications to the terms and conditions under which equity instruments were granted. For example, an entity might change the length of the vesting period or change the exercise price, which could change the fair value of the stock options. If an entity modifies the terms and conditions of a stock option, IFRS 2 requires the entity to recognize, at a minimum, the original amount of compensation cost as measured at the grant date. If the fair value of the options is reduced as a result of the modification, then there is no change in the total compensation cost to be recognized. If the modification results in an increase in the fair value of the options, then total compensation cost must be increased by the increase in fair value (the difference between the fair value at the original grant date and the fair value at the modification date). Under U.S. GAAP, when modifications are made to stock options, the fair value of the options at the date of modification determines the total amount of compensation expense to be recognized. There is no minimum amount of compensation cost to recognize as there is under IFRS.

Cash-Settled Share-Based Payment Transactions

An entity might provide employees with stock appreciation rights in which they are entitled to receive a cash payment when the entity's stock price increases above a predetermined level. Stock appreciation rights are an example of a cash-settled share-based payment transaction. This type of transaction results in the recognition of a liability (because there will be a future outflow of cash) and an expense. The liability (and expense) is measured at the fair value of the share appreciation rights using an option-pricing model. Until the liability is settled, it must be remeasured at each balance sheet date, with the change in fair value reflected in net income. Under U.S. GAAP, certain cash-settled share-based payment transactions are classified as equity; these transactions would be classified as a liability under IFRS.

Choice-of-Settlement Share-Based Payment Transactions

When the terms of a share-based payment transaction allow the *entity to choose* between equity settlement and cash settlement, the entity must treat the transaction as a cash-settled share-based payment transaction only if it has a present obligation to settle in cash; otherwise the entity treats the transaction as an equity-settled share-based payment transaction.

When the terms of a share-based payment transaction allow the *supplier of goods and services to choose* between equity settlement and cash settlement, the entity has issued a compound financial instrument the fair value of which must be split into separate debt and equity components. The debt component must be remeasured at fair value at each balance sheet date, with the change in fair value reflected in net income. If the supplier of goods and services chooses to receive settlement in cash, the cash payment is applied only against the debt component (reduces the liability). The equity component remains in equity. If the supplier chooses to receive settlement in equity, the debt component (liability) is transferred to equity.

Example: Choice-of-Settlement Share-Based Payment Transaction (Supplier Has Choice)

On January 1, Year 1, Leiyu Company issued 100 stock options with an exercise price of $18 each to five employees (500 options in total). The employees can choose to settle the options either (1) in shares of stock ($1 par value) or (2) in cash equal to the intrinsic value of the options on the vesting date. The options vest on December 31, Year 2, after the employees have completed two years of service. Leiyu Company expects that only four of the employees will remain with the company for the next two years and vest in the options. One employee resigns in Year 1, and the company continues to assume an overall forfeiture rate of 20 percent at December 31, Year 1. As expected, four employees vest on December 31, Year 2, and exercise their stock options. Share prices and fair values of the two settlement alternatives over the vesting period are:

Date	Share Price	Fair Value of Cash-Settlement Alternative	Fair Value of Share-Settlement Alternative
January 1, Year 1	$20	$10.00	$10.00
December 31, Year 1	$26	$11.00	$11.00
December 31, Year 2	$30	$12.00	$12.00

Because Leiyu has granted employees stock options that can be settled either in cash or in shares of stock, this is a compound financial instrument. Because this is a transaction with employees, Leiyu must determine the fair value of the compound financial instrument at the measurement date, taking into account the terms and conditions on which the rights to cash or equity instruments are granted. To determine the fair value of a compound financial instrument, the company first measures the fair value of the debt component (i.e., the cash-settlement alternative) and then measures the fair value of the equity component (i.e., the equity-settlement alternative), taking into account that the employee must forfeit the right to receive cash in order to receive the shares of stock. The fair value of the compound financial instrument is the sum of the fair values of the two components.

The stand-alone fair value of the cash-settlement alternative at the grant date (January 1, Year 1) is $5,000 (500 options × $10 per option). The stand-alone fair value of the equity-settlement alternative at the grant date also is $5,000 (500 options × $10 per option). IFRS 2 indicates that this type of share-based payment often is structured such that the fair value of the debt component and the fair value of the equity component are the same. In such cases, the fair value of the equity component is zero. Thus, the fair value of the compound financial instrument is $5,000 ($5,000 + $0).

For equity-settled share-based payment transactions, the services received and equity recognized is measured at the fair value of the equity instrument at grant date. Because the fair value of the equity component in this case is zero, there is no compensation expense recognized related to the equity component. For cash-settled share-based payment transactions, the services received and the liability incurred are initially measured at the fair value of the liability at grant date. The fair value of the liability, adjusted to reflect the number of options expected to vest, is recognized as expense over the period that the services are rendered. At each reporting date, and ultimately at settlement date, the fair value of the liability is remeasured, with the change in fair value affecting the amount recognized as compensation expense. As a result, the total amount of expense recognized will be the amount paid to settle the liability.

Compensation expense for Year 1 is calculated as follows:

Fair value per option at December 31, Year 1	$11.00
Number of options	500
Subtotal	$5,500
Percentage of options expected to vest	80%
Total compensation expense	$4,400
Vesting period (number of years)	2
Compensation expense, Year 1	$2,200

The journal entry on December 31, Year 1, to recognize Year 1 compensation expense is:

Compensation Expense	$2,200	
Share-based Payment Liability		$2,200

At December 31, Year 2, the fair value of each option is equal to its intrinsic value of $12.00 ($30 share price − $18 exercise price). The fair value of the liability is $6,000 ($12.00 × 500 options). The total compensation expense is $4,800 ($6,000 × 80%).

The amount to be recognized as compensation expense in Year 2 is $2,600 ($4,800 – 2,200). The journal entry on December 31, Year 2, is:

Compensation Expense.		$2,600
Share-based Payment Liability.		$2,600

Accounting for the exercise of the stock options:

- *Cash-Settlement Alternative:* If the four employees choose the cash-settlement alternative upon exercise of their stock options, they will receive a total of $4,800, the intrinsic value of the 400 options that they exercise. The journal entry on December 31, Year 2, would be:

Share-based Payment Liability.		$4,800
Cash.		$4,800

- *Share-Settlement Alternative:* If the four employees choose the share-settlement alternative upon exercise of their stock options, they will receive a total of 400 shares of stock with a fair value of $12,000 in exchange for $7,200 (400 shares × Exercise price of $18.00 per share). The journal entry on December 31, Year 2, would be:

Cash.		$7,200
Share-based Payment Liability.		4,800
Common Stock ($1 par × 400).		$ 400
Additional Paid-in Capital ($29 × 400).		11,600

INCOME TAXES

IAS 12, *Income Taxes,* and U.S. GAAP take a similar approach to accounting for income taxes. Both standards adopt an asset-and-liability approach that recognizes deferred tax assets and liabilities for temporary differences and for operating loss and tax credit carry forwards. However, differences do exist. The accounting for income taxes is a very complex topic, and only some of the major issues are discussed here.

Tax Laws and Rates

IAS 12 requires that current and deferred taxes be measured on the basis of tax laws and rates that have been enacted or *substantively enacted* by the balance sheet date. The interpretation of substantively enacted will vary from country to country. To help make this assessment, the IASB has published guidelines that address the point in time when a tax law change is substantively enacted in many of the jurisdictions that apply IFRS. The IASB's exposure draft (ED) on income taxes would clarify that "substantively enacted" occurs when any future steps in the enactment process cannot change the outcome. The ED notes, for example, that the point of substantive enactment in the United States is when a tax law is passed. U.S. GAAP requires measurement of income taxes using actually enacted tax laws and rates.

To minimize the double taxation of corporate dividends (tax paid by both the company and its shareholders), some countries apply a lower tax rate to profits that are distributed to shareholders than to profits that are retained by the company. Therefore, companies doing business in these countries need to know which tax rate (distributed profits versus undistributed profits) should be applied when measuring the amount of current and deferred taxes. Examples provided in IAS 12 indicate that the tax rate that applies to undistributed profits should be used to measure tax expense.

Example: Undistributed Profits

Multinational Corporation owns a subsidiary in a foreign jurisdiction where income taxes are payable at a higher rate on undistributed profits than on distributed profits. For the year ending December 31, Year 1, the foreign subsidiary's taxable income is $150,000. The foreign subsidiary also has net taxable temporary differences amounting to $50,000 for the year, thus creating the need for a deferred tax liability. The tax rate paid in the foreign country on distributed profits is 40 percent, and the rate on undistributed profits is 50 percent. A tax credit arises when undistributed profits are later distributed. As of the balance sheet date, no distributions of dividends have been proposed or declared. On March 15, Year 2, Multinational's foreign subsidiary distributes dividends of $75,000 from the profit earned in Year 1.

The tax rate on undistributed profits (50 percent) is used to recognize the current and deferred tax liabilities related to earnings of the foreign subsidiary in Year 1:

Current Tax Expense		$75,000
Taxes Payable ($150,000 × 50%)		$75,000
Deferred Tax Expense		$25,000
Deferred Tax Liability ($50,000 × 50%)		$25,000

On March 15, Year 2, when the foreign subsidiary distributes a dividend of $75,000, a tax credit receivable from the government of $7,500 [$75,000 × (50% − 40%)] is recognized, with an offsetting reduction in the current tax expense:

Tax Credit Receivable	$7,500
Current Tax Expense	$7,500

Recognition of Deferred Tax Asset

IAS 12 requires recognition of a deferred tax asset if future realization of a tax benefit is probable, where *probable* is undefined. Under U.S. GAAP, a deferred tax asset must be recognized if its realization is more likely than not. If the word *probable* is interpreted as a probability of occurrence that is greater than the phrase *more likely than not*, then IAS 12 provides a more stringent threshold for the recognition of a deferred tax asset.

Example: Deferred Tax Asset

During the fiscal year ended December 31, Year 1, Janeiro Corporation had a net operating loss of $450,000. Because the company has experienced losses in the last several years, it cannot utilize a net operating loss carry back. However, Janeiro has negotiated several new contracts, and management expects that it is slightly more than 50 percent likely that it will be able to utilize one-third of the net operating loss in future years. The company's effective tax rate is 40 percent.

Depending on the degree of likelihood the company assigns to the word *probable*, either it would not recognize a tax asset, or it would recognize an asset related to the amount of the net operating loss that it expects to be able to use. In the latter case, the deferred tax asset and income tax benefit would be $60,000 [$450,000 $\times$ 1/3 $\times$ 40%].

Deferred Tax Asset	$60,000
Income Tax Benefit	$60,000

Disclosures

IAS 12 requires extensive disclosures to be made with regard to income taxes, including disclosure of the current and deferred components of tax expense. The standard also requires an explanation of the relationship between hypothetical tax expense based on statutory tax rates and reported tax expense based on the effective tax rate using one of two approaches: (1) a numerical reconciliation between tax expense based on the statutory tax rate in the home country and tax expense based on the effective tax rate or (2) a numerical reconciliation between tax expense based on the weighted-average statutory tax rate across jurisdictions in which the company pays taxes and tax expense based on the effective tax rate.

Exhibit 5.2 demonstrates these two approaches. Tesco plc uses approach 1, showing that accounting profit multiplied by the UK statutory income tax rate of 28.2 percent would have resulted in tax expense of £833 in 2009. However, the actual tax expense was only £788, resulting in an effective tax rate of 26.7 percent. One of the reasons that the effective tax rate is different from the UK statutory tax rate is the fact that profits earned in foreign countries are taxed at different rates (differences in overseas taxation rates).

Nestlé SA uses approach 2 in reconciling its total tax expense. The reconciliation begins with the amount that would be recognized as tax expense after multiplying the profit earned in each country in which the company operates by the statutory tax rate in that country and then summing across all countries. Nestlé's effective tax rate can be measured by dividing the amount reported as taxes on continuing operations by pre-tax profit on continuing operations (not shown in Exhibit 5.2).

The expected tax expense at the weighted-average applicable tax rate results from applying the domestic statutory tax rates to profits before taxes of each entity in the country it operates. For the Nestlé, the weighted-average applicable tax rate varies from one year to another, depending on the relative weight of the profit of each individual entity in the Nestlé Group, profit as well as the changes in the statutory tax rates.

IFRS versus U.S. GAAP

Application of IFRS can create temporary differences unknown under U.S. GAAP. For example, the revaluation of property, plant, and equipment for financial statement purposes (in accordance with IAS 16's revaluation model) with no equivalent

EXHIBIT 5.2

RECONCILIATION OF ACCOUNTING PROFIT TO EFFECTIVE TAX RATE
Tesco plc
2009
Annual Report

Note 6. Taxation

Reconciliation of effective tax charge

	2009 £m	2008 £m
Profit before tax	2,954	2,803
Effective tax charge at 28.2% (2008 at 30.0%)	(833)	(841)
Effect of:		
Non-deductible expenses	(189)	(180)
Differences in overseas taxation rates	111	41
Adjustments in respect of prior years	67	215
Share of results of joint ventures and associates	3	123
Change in tax rate	25	69
Total income tax charge for the year	(788)	(673)
Effective tax rate	**26.7%**	**24.0%**

NESTLÉ
2009
Annual Report

Note 7. Taxes

Reconciliation of taxes

In millions of CHF

	2009	2008
Expected tax expense at weighted average applicable tax rate	2,789	3,142
Tax effect of non-deductible or non-taxable items	(168)	(105)
Prior years' taxes	(17)	68
Transfers to unrecognized deferred tax assets	58	61
Transfers from unrecognized deferred tax assets	(44)	(14)
Changes in tax rates	(1)	(2)
Withholding taxes levied on transfers of income	340	347
Other, including taxes on capital	130	190
Taxes on continuing operations	**3,087**	**3,687**

adjustment for tax purposes will result in a temporary difference that cannot exist under U.S. GAAP. Other differences between IFRS and U.S. GAAP can create different amounts of temporary differences. For example, because of different definitions of impairment, differences in the amount of an impairment loss can exist under the two sets of standards. With no equivalent tax adjustment, the amount of temporary difference related to the impairment loss will be different in a set of IFRS-based financial statements from the amount recognized under U.S. GAAP.

Financial Statement Presentation

Under U.S. GAAP, deferred tax assets and liabilities generally are classified as current or noncurrent based on the classification of the related asset or liability, or for tax losses and credit carry-forwards, based on the expected timing of realization.

The net deferred tax amount arising from current assets and liabilities is classified as a current asset or liability; the net deferred tax amount arising from noncurrent assets and liabilities is reported as a noncurrent asset or liability. IAS 1, *Presentation of Financial Statements,* stipulates that deferred taxes may *not* be classified as a current asset or current liability, but only as noncurrent.

REVENUE RECOGNITION

IAS 18, *Revenue,* is a single standard that covers most revenues, in particular revenues from the sale of goods; the rendering of services; and interest, royalties, and dividends. There is no equivalent single standard in U.S. GAAP. U.S. rules related to revenue recognition are found in more than 200 different authoritative pronouncements, making a direct comparison between IAS 18 and U.S. GAAP difficult.

General Measurement Principle

IAS 18 requires revenue to be measured at the fair value of the consideration received or receivable.

Identification of the Transaction Generating Revenue

Revenue recognition criteria normally are applied to each transaction generating revenue. However, if a transaction consists of multiple elements, it may be appropriate to split the transaction into separate units of account and recognize revenue from each element separately. For example, if a sale of computer software is accompanied by an agreement to provide maintenance (post-contract support) for a period of time, it might be appropriate to allocate the proceeds from the sale into an amount applicable to the sale of software (revenue recognized at the time of sale) and an amount applicable to the post-contract support (revenue recognized over the period of support). Conversely, there may be situations where it is necessary to treat two or more separate transactions as one economic transaction to properly reflect their true economic substance.

Sale of Goods

Five conditions must be met in order for revenue from the sale of goods to be recognized:

1. The significant risks and rewards of ownership of the goods have been transferred to the buyer.
2. Neither continuing managerial involvement normally associated with ownership nor effective control of the goods sold is retained.
3. The amount of revenue can be measured reliably.
4. It is probable that the economic benefits associated with the sale will flow to the seller.
5. The costs incurred or to be incurred with respect to the sale of goods can be measured reliably.

Evaluating whether significant risks and rewards of ownership have been transferred to the buyer can sometimes be difficult and require the exercise of judgment.

IAS 18 provides a list of examples in which significant risks and rewards might be retained by the seller. These include the following:

- The seller assumes an obligation for unsatisfactory performance not covered by normal warranty provisions.
- Receipt of revenue by the seller is contingent on the buyer generating revenue through its sale of the goods.
- Goods sold are subject to installation, installation is a significant part of the contract, and installation has not yet been completed.
- The sales contract gives the buyer the right to rescind the purchase, and the probability of return is uncertain.

Similarly, in determining whether the seller has relinquished managerial involvement or control over the goods sold, a careful evaluation is required for some types of sales.

Example: Sale of Goods with Right of Return

Qwilleran Products Inc. is a manufacturer of lighting fixtures. Qwilleran enters into an agreement with a company in Mexico which will import and distribute Qwilleran's products locally. In December, Year 1, the first month of the agreement, Qwilleran ships $2,000,000 of lighting fixtures to the Mexican distributor to cover anticipated demand in Mexico. The distributor has the right to return products to Qwilleran if they cannot be sold in Mexico. Qwilleran has extensive experience selling its products in the United States but no experience in Mexico or other foreign countries.

Qwilleran must determine whether it is appropriate to recognize revenue in December, Year 1, when products are shipped to the Mexican distributor. The most important question is whether the significant risks and rewards of ownership of the goods have been transferred to the buyer. IAS 18 indicates that this might not be the case when the buyer has the right to return the purchase, and the probability of return is uncertain. Because Qwilleran has no experience selling products in Mexico, it has no basis for estimating whether the Mexican distributor will make returns. Thus, Qwilleran should conclude that it has not transferred all the significant risks of ownership to the Mexican distributor, and it should defer revenue recognition until this criterion has been met.

Example: Sale of Goods with Contingent Payment

Victoria Enterprises sells small motors to Gamma Company. Gamma mounts these motors in its water pumps and sells the completed pumps to plumbing supply distributors. When Gamma receives payment from its customers, it pays Victoria for the motors. Gamma has the right to return any unused motors at the end of the year. Historically, these returns have averaged 2 percent of sales. In the month of September, Year 1, Victoria Enterprises made sales of $500,000 to Gamma Company.

IAS 18 indicates that five conditions must be met to recognize revenue from the sale of goods. In this case, it appears that conditions 2, 3, and 5 are met. It is unclear, however, whether conditions 1 and 4 are met. Because payment for the motors is only made if Gamma is able to sell its water pumps, it appears that a significant risk of ownership might have been retained by Victoria, and therefore condition 1 might not be met. This is reinforced by paragraph 16 of IAS 18, which indicates that an entity may retain significant risks and rewards of ownership "when the receipt of the revenue from a particular sale is contingent on the derivation of revenue by the buyer from its sale of the goods."

With respect to condition 4, from past experience, it is probable that almost all (98 percent) of "the economic benefits associated with the transaction will flow to the entity." This suggests that condition 4 is met. IAS 18, paragraph 17, indicates that when the seller retains only an insignificant risk of ownership, the transaction is a sale and revenue is recognized. The last sentence of IAS 18, paragraph 17 states: "Revenue in such cases is recognized at the time of sale provided the seller can reliably estimate future returns and recognizes a liability for returns based on previous experience and other relevant factors." As a result, it appears Victoria Enterprises would be justified in recognizing revenue for 98 percent of the sales price and would prepare the following journal entry in September, Year 1 to account for its sales to Gamma Company:

Accounts Receivable	$500,000	
Sales Revenue [$500,000 × 98%]		$490,000
Deferred Revenue (liability)		10,000

Rendering of Services

When (1) the outcome of a service transaction can be estimated reliably and (2) it is probable that economic benefits of the transaction will flow to the enterprise, revenue should be recognized in proportion to some measure of the extent of services rendered (i.e., on a stage-of-completion basis). The outcome of a transaction can be estimated reliably when (1) the amount of revenue, (2) the costs incurred and the costs to be incurred, and (3) the stage of completion can all be measured reliably. The stage of completion can be estimated in a number of ways, including on the basis of the percentage of total services to be performed, percentage of total costs to be incurred, and surveys of work performed. Guidelines provided in IAS 11, *Construction Contracts,* related to the application of the percentage-of-completion method on construction projects are generally applicable to the recognition of revenue for service transactions. U.S. GAAP does not allow the percentage-of-completion method to be used with service contracts.

When the outcome of a service transaction cannot be estimated reliably, revenue should be recognized only to the extent that expenses incurred are probable of recovery. If such underlying expenses are not probable of recovery, the expense should be recognized, but not the revenue.

Example: Recognition of Service Revenue

Seese & Associates, an information technology (IT) consulting firm, contracted with Drexel Manufacturing Company on January 1, Year 1, to provide services over a period of 18 months for a fixed fee of $180,000. Seese is unable to specify upfront the type and number of services that it will provide. However, based on past experience, Seese can reliably estimate the cost it will incur to fulfill its contractual obligation as $150,000. Seese incurred actual costs of $90,000 in Year 1 and received monthly payments of $10,000 from Drexel Manufacturing.

The criteria for recognizing revenue on a stage-of-completion basis are met in this situation. Drexel is making monthly payments, so the criterion of probable inflow of economic benefits is met. Because this is a fixed-fee contract, the amount of revenue to be earned is known with certainty, and Seese is able to reliably estimate the stage of completion on the basis of total costs to be incurred. In Year 1, the company has incurred 60 percent [$90,000/$150,000] of the total estimated costs and therefore would recognize service revenue of $108,000 [$180,000 × 60%] with the following journal entry:

Cash [$10,000 × 12]		$120,000
Service Revenue		$108,000
Deferred Revenue		12,000

Interest, Royalties, and Dividends

If it is probable that the economic benefits of interest, royalties, and dividends will flow to the enterprise and the amounts can be measured reliably, revenue should be recognized on the following bases:

- Interest income is recognized on an effective yield basis.
- Royalties are recognized on an accrual basis in accordance with the terms of the relevant agreement.
- Dividends are recognized when the shareholders' right to receive payment is established.

Exchanges of Goods or Services

In an exchange of goods or services, if the exchanged items are similar in nature and value, no revenue (i.e., no gain or loss) is recognized. If the exchanged goods or services are dissimilar in nature, revenue is recognized at the fair value of the goods or services received, adjusted for the amount of any cash paid or received. When the fair value of the goods or services received cannot be measured reliably, revenue should be measured as the fair value of the goods or services given up, adjusted for the amount of any cash paid or received.

IAS 18, Part B

The IASB document published to accompany IAS 18 (IAS 18, Part B) provides examples illustrating the application of the standard to major types of revenue-generating transactions. Most of the examples are self-explanatory, and the relationships of the examples to the underlying provisions of the standard are straightforward. The examples accompany IAS 18 but technically are not part of the standard. Issues covered in the examples include:

- *Sales transactions:* Bill-and-hold sales, goods shipped subject to conditions, layaway sales, sale and repurchase agreements, subscription sales, installment sales, and real estate sales.
- *Service transactions:* Installation fees; servicing fees included in the price of a product; advertising commissions; insurance agency commissions; financial service fees; admission fees; initiation, entrance, and membership fees; franchise fees; and fees from the development of customized software.
- *Interest, royalties, and dividends:* License fees and royalties.

We summarize the guidance provided in two of these examples next.

Bill-and-Hold Sales

The first illustrative example describes a "bill-and-hold sale" as a sale "in which delivery is delayed at the buyer's request but the buyer takes title and accepts billing." Bill-and-hold sales have been used by entities (such as Sunbeam) to shift sales to be made in future periods into the current period—a type of earnings management. To make sure that a bill-and-hold sale is truly a sale in substance, IAS 18, Part B suggests that revenue may be recognized by the seller when the buyer takes title only if four conditions are met:

1. It is probable that delivery will be made.
2. The item is on hand, identified, and ready for delivery to the buyer at the time the sale is recognized.
3. The buyer specifically acknowledges the deferred delivery instructions.
4. The usual payment terms apply.

Servicing Fees Included in the Price of the Product

The sales price of a product sometimes includes an identifiable amount for subsequent servicing. An example is after-sales support provided by a software company for a specified period of time. In such a case, IAS 18, Part B indicates a portion of the sales price should be deferred and recognized as revenue over the period during which the service is performed. The amount deferred must be sufficient to cover the expected costs of the services under the agreement and provide a reasonable profit on those services. Judgment must be applied in determining the amount to be deferred, since a reasonable amount of profit is not defined in the standard.

Customer Loyalty Programs

A growing number of entities use customer loyalty programs to provide customers with incentives to buy their goods and services. In many of these programs, "points" are awarded at the time a customer makes a purchase. The question arises as to whether the entity's obligation to provide a free or discounted good or service should be recognized and measured by (1) allocating a portion of the consideration received from the sale transaction or (2) establishing a provision for the estimated future costs of providing the award.

IFRIC 13, *Customer Loyalty Programmes,* stipulates that award credits should be treated as a separately identifiable component of the sales transaction in which they are granted. The fair value of the consideration received on the sale must be allocated between the award credits and the other components of the sale. The amount allocated to the award credits is based on their fair value. If the entity supplies the award itself, it recognizes the amount allocated to award credits as revenue when award credits are redeemed and the obligation to provide a free or discounted good or service is fulfilled. The amount of revenue to be recognized is based on the number of award credits that have been redeemed, relative to the total number expected to be redeemed.

Example: Frequent-Flyer Awards Program

Redjet Airways, a regional air carrier, has a frequent-flyer program in which customers receive one point for each mile flown on Redjet flights. Frequent-flyer program members can redeem 30,000 points for a free domestic flight, which, on average, would otherwise cost $600. During Year 1, Redjet awarded 1,000,000 points to its customers on flights with total ticket sales of $600,000. Frequent-flyer points expire two years after they are awarded. By the end of Year 1, frequent-flyer program members had redeemed 300,000 points for free tickets. Redjet expects that only 10 percent of points will expire unredeemed.

Redjet must allocate the $600,000 collected in ticket sales in Year 1 between flight revenue and frequent-flyer awards (deferred revenue) based on the fair value of the points awarded. The amount to be allocated to the frequent-flyer awards is determined as follows:

Points awarded in Year 1	1,000,000
Percentage expected to be redeemed	× 90%
Points expected to be redeemed	900,000
Points needed for a free flight	÷ 30,000
Expected number of free flights	30
Average value per flight	× $600
Fair value of points awarded	$18,000

The journal entry to recognize revenue from ticket sales in Year 1 is as follows:

```
Cash. . . . . . . . . . . . . . . . . . . . . . . . . . . . . . . . . . . . . . . . . . .$600,000
    Revenue . . . . . . . . . . . . . . . . . . . . . . . . . . . . . . . . . . . . . . .$582,000
    Deferred Revenue. . . . . . . . . . . . . . . . . . . . . . . . . . . . . . . . . .18,000
```

During Year 1, 300,000 points were redeemed for 10 free flights, with a value of $6,000. The journal entry to recognize revenue from providing free flights under the awards program is:

```
Deferred Revenue. . . . . . . . . . . . . . . . . . . . . . . . . . . . . . . . . $6,000
    Revenue . . . . . . . . . . . . . . . . . . . . . . . . . . . . . . . . . . . . . . . .$6,000
```

Construction Contracts

IAS 11, *Construction Contracts,* identifies two types of construction contracts: a fixed-price contract and a cost-plus contract. Revenues and expenses related to both types of contracts should be recognized using the percentage-of-completion method when the outcome of the contract can be estimated reliably. The outcome of a cost-plus contract can be estimated reliably when (1) it is probable that the economic benefits associated with the contract will flow to the entity and (2) the contract costs can be clearly identified and reliably measured. Two additional criteria must be met for a fixed-price contract to qualify for percentage-of-completion accounting treatment: (1) total contract revenues must be reliably measurable and (2) the costs to complete the contract and the stage of completion at the balance sheet date must be reliably measurable. If the outcome of a construction contract cannot be estimated reliably, a cost recovery method should be used to recognize revenue. Under this method, contract costs are expensed as incurred and revenue is recognized to the extent that contract costs incurred are likely to be recovered. If, during the construction period, the uncertainties that prevented the outcome of the contract from being estimated reliably no longer exist, then the accounting for the contract should be changed to the percentage-of-completion method.

U.S. GAAP also requires use of the percentage-of-completion method when certain criteria are met. When the percentage-of-completion method is not appropriate, the completed contract method is used, which is a departure from IAS 11. Under both IAS 11 and U.S. GAAP, when the outcome of a construction contract is expected to be a loss, the loss should be recognized immediately.

IASB–FASB Revenue Recognition Project

Revenue recognition is an issue for which neither the IASB nor the FASB believes it has adequate authoritative literature that is coherent and comprehensive. In 2002, the two boards began work on a joint project to develop a single standard to deal with this important issue. The main reasons for undertaking this project are to (1) eliminate weaknesses in existing concepts and standards and (2) converge IFRS and U.S. GAAP.

In June 2010, the IASB and FASB published a joint Exposure Draft, *Revenue from Contracts with Customers,* which proposes a contract-based revenue recognition model to be applied across a wide range of transactions and industries. The boards published a revised Exposure Draft in November 2011. The proposed model requires an entity to apply the following five steps in the recognition of revenue:

1. *Identify the contract with a customer.* It might be appropriate to treat a single contract with a customer as two or more contracts when the single contract contains multiple elements that are priced independently. On the other hand, it might be appropriate to treat two or more separate contracts that are priced interdependently as a single contract.

2. *Identify the separate performance obligations in the contract.* Performance obligation is defined as "an enforceable promise (whether explicit or implicit) in a contract with a customer to transfer a good or service to the customer." The entity must evaluate all of the goods and/or services promised in a contract to determine whether there are separate performance obligations.

3. *Determine the transaction price.* If material, the time value of money should be considered in determining the transaction price in a deferred payment contract. When future payments for goods or services are not fixed in amount, the expected value should be used to determine the transaction price. A probability-weighted approach should be used to adjust the transaction price to reflect the customer's credit risk. In effect, the customer's credit risk affects how much, but not whether, revenue should be recognized.

4. *Allocate the transaction price to the separate performance obligations.* The transaction price should be allocated to the separate performance obligations in proportion to the stand-alone selling price of each element of the contract. When goods or services are not sold separately, the transaction price must be allocated to the separate performance obligations using a reasonable approach.

5. *Recognize the revenue allocated to each performance obligation when the entity satisfies each performance obligation.* An entity satisfies a performance obligation and recognizes revenue when control of a promised good or service is transferred to the customer. The general principle is that a customer obtains control of a good or service when the customer has the ability to direct the use of, and receive the benefit from, the good or service. For many revenue-generating transactions, transfer of control will occur at a specific point in time, often when the good or service is delivered to the customer. However, transfer of control also can occur over a period of time. In this latter case, use of a percentage-of-completion method to recognize revenue will be acceptable when certain conditions are met.

In mid-2013, the boards announced that if approved, the proposed revenue recognition standard would not become effective until reporting periods beginning on or after January 1, 2017. Early application of the new standard would not be allowed.

204   Chapter Five

FINANCIAL INSTRUMENTS

Current IFRS guidance for the financial reporting of financial instruments is located in the following three standards:

IAS 32, *Financial Instruments: Presentation*
IAS 39, *Financial Instruments: Recognition and Measurement*
IFRS 7, *Financial Instruments: Disclosure*

In addition, the IASB issued IFRS 9, *Financial Instruments,* in November 2009 to begin the process of replacing IAS 39; IFRS 9 becomes effective in 2015.

It should be noted that the adoption of IAS 39 met with considerable resistance in the European Union. The European Commission ultimately decided in 2004 to endorse IAS 39, but with exceptions. The Commission modified the version of IAS 39 to be applied by publicly traded companies in the EU with respect to certain provisions on the use of a full fair value option and on hedge accounting. According to the European Commission, these "carve-outs" are temporary, in effect only until the IASB modifies IAS 39 in line with European requests.[2]

Definitions

IAS 32 defines a *financial instrument* as any contract that gives rise to both a financial asset of one entity and a financial liability or equity instrument of another entity. A *financial asset* is defined as any asset that is:

- Cash.
- A contractual right
  - to receive cash or another financial asset.
  - to exchange financial assets or financial liabilities under potentially favorable conditions.
- An equity instrument of another entity.
- A contract that will or may be settled in the entity's own equity instruments and is not classified as an equity instrument of the entity.

Examples of financial assets include cash, receivables, loans made to other entities, investments in bonds and other debt instruments, and investments in equity instruments of other entities. Investments in equity instruments that are accounted for under the equity method (associates, joint ventures), or are consolidated [subsidiaries and special-purpose entities (SPEs)] do not fall within the scope of IAS 32 and IAS 39. Only those investments in equity instruments that result in less than significant influence over the other entity (sometimes labeled as "marketable securities") are accounted for in accordance with IAS 32 and IAS 39.

A *financial liability* is defined as:

- A contractual obligation
  - to deliver cash or another financial asset.
  - to exchange financial assets or financial liabilities under potentially unfavorable conditions.
- A contract that will or may be settled in the entity's own equity instruments.

---

[2] Ernst & Young, "The Evolution of *IAS 39* in Europe," *Eye on IFRS Newsletter,* November 2004, pp. 1–4.

Examples of financial liabilities include payables, loans from other entities (including banks), issued bonds and other debt instruments, and obligations to deliver the entity's own shares for a fixed amount of cash. *Derivative financial instruments* also are financial assets or financial liabilities.

An *equity* instrument is defined as:

- Any contract that evidences a residual interest in the assets of an entity after deducting all of its liabilities.

Liability or Equity

IAS 32 requires financial instruments to be classified as financial liabilities or equity or both in accordance with the substance of the contractual arrangement and the definitions of financial liability and equity. If an equity instrument contains a contractual obligation that meets the definition of a financial liability, it should be classified as a liability even though its legal form is that of an equity instrument. For example, if an entity issues preferred shares that are redeemable by the shareholder and the entity cannot avoid the payment of cash to shareholders if they redeem their shares, the preferred shares should be accounted for as a liability. Preferred shares that are contingently redeemable based on future events outside the control of either the issuer or the shareholder also would be classified as a financial liability.

Example: Redeemable Preferred Shares

On October 29, Year 1, Griglia Company issued $1,000,000 of 5 percent preferred shares at par value. The preferred shareholders have the right to force the company to redeem the shares at par value if the Federal Reserve Bank interest rate rises above 5 percent. On December 10, Year 3, the Federal Reserve Bank interest rate reaches that level.

Because the future event that triggers redemption of the preferred shares is outside the control of both the company and the shareholders, the 5 percent preferred shares must be classified as a liability under IFRS. The journal entry to record issuance of the shares on October 29, Year 1, is:

```
Cash. . . . . . . . . . . . . . . . . . . . . . . . . . . . . . . . . . . . . . . . . $1,000,000
       Redeemable Preferred Shares Liability . . . . . . . . . . . . . . . . . . . . . . . . . . $1,000,000
```

Under U.S. GAAP, the preferred shares initially would be classified as equity. On December 10, Year 3, when the event triggering redemption occurs, the preferred shares would be reclassified as a liability.

Compound Financial Instruments

If a financial instrument contains both a liability element and an equity element, it is a *compound financial instrument* and should be split into two components that are reported separately. This is referred to as "split accounting." For example, a bond that is convertible into shares of common stock at the option of the bondholder is a compound financial instrument. From the perspective of the issuer, the bond is comprised of two components:

1. A contractual obligation to make cash payments of interest and principal as long as the bond is not converted. This meets the definition of a financial liability.
2. A call option that grants the bondholder the right to convert the bond into a fixed number of common shares. This meets the definition of an equity instrument.

Under split accounting, the initial carrying amounts of the liability and equity components are determined using what can be called the with-and-without method. The fair value of the financial instrument with the conversion feature is determined (i.e., the selling price of the instrument). Then the fair value of the financial instrument without the conversion feature is determined. This becomes the carrying amount of the financial liability component. The difference between the fair value of the instrument as a whole and the amount separately determined for the liability component is allocated to the equity component. Note that a compound financial instrument is a financial asset for the holder of the instrument.

Example: Convertible Bonds

Sharma Corporation issued $2 million of 4 percent convertible bonds at par value. The bonds have a five-year life with interest payable annually. Each bond has a face value of $1,000 and is convertible at any time up to maturity into 250 shares of common stock. At the date of issue, the interest rate for similar debt without a conversion feature is 6 percent.

The fair value of the convertible bonds is their selling price of $2 million. The fair value of the liability is calculated using the prevailing interest rate for nonconvertible bonds:

Present value of $2,000,000, n = 5, i = 6%	$2,000,000 × 0.7473 = $1,494,516
Present value of ordinary annuity of $80,000, n = 5, i = 6%	$80,000 × 4.2124 = 336,989
Fair value of liability	$1,831,505

The present value of the bond at 6 percent is $1,831,505; this is the fair value of the liability component of the compound financial instrument. The remaining $168,495 from the proceeds of the bond issuance is allocated to the equity component.

Cash. $2,000,000	
Bonds Payable $1,831,505	
Additional Paid-in Capital 168,495	

Classification of Financial Assets and Financial Liabilities

IAS 39 establishes categories into which all financial assets and liabilities must be classified. The classification of a financial asset or financial liability determines how the item will be measured. A financial asset must be classified into one of the following four categories:

- *Financial assets at fair value through profit or loss (FVPL):* This includes financial assets that an entity either (1) holds for trading purposes or (2) has elected to classify into this category under the so-called fair value option (discussed in more detail later).

- *Held-to-maturity investments:* This category includes financial assets with fixed or determinable payments and fixed maturity that the entity has the intention and ability to hold to maturity. If an entity sells or reclassifies more than an insignificant amount of held-to-maturity investments prior to maturity, the entity normally will be disqualified from using this classification during the following two-year period. The entity's intentions are said to be "tainted" in this case.

- *Loans and receivables:* This includes financial assets with fixed or determinable payments that do not have a price that is quoted in an active market.
- *Available-for-sale financial assets:* This category includes all financial assets that (1) are not classified in one of the other categories or (2) the entity has elected to classify as available-for-sale. Financial assets held for trading purposes may not be classified as available-for-sale.

A financial liability must be classified as one of the following:

- *Financial liabilities at fair value through profit or loss (FVPL):* This includes financial liabilities that are held for trading or that the entity has opted to classify into this category under the "fair value option." An example of a liability held for trading is a debt instrument that the issuer intends to repurchase in the short term to make a gain from short-term changes in interest rates.
- *Financial liabilities measured at amortized cost:* This is the default category for most financial liabilities, including accounts payables, notes payable, bonds payable, and deposits from customers.

Fair Value Option

According to IAS 39, the option to designate financial assets or financial liabilities as FVPL may be applied only if one of the following conditions is met:

1. It eliminates or significantly reduces a measurement or recognition inconsistency (sometimes referred to as "an accounting mismatch") that would otherwise arise from measuring assets or liabilities or recognizing the gains and losses on them on different bases.
2. A group of financial assets, financial liabilities, or both that is managed and its performance is evaluated on a fair value basis, in accordance with a documented risk management or investment strategy, and information about the group of instruments is provided internally on that basis to the entity's key management personnel.

Example: Fair Value Option

St. John's Inc. issued $1,000 in 5 percent bonds at par value on January 1, Year 1. The cash proceeds were used to invest in $1,000 of corporate bonds (at a fixed rate of 6 percent). The bond investment is classified as FVPL. By year-end, interest rates have increased. As a result, the fair value of the investment in bonds is $900 and the fair value of the bonds payable is $900.

The bonds payable and investment in bonds are linked. As interest rates change, the economic loss on the asset will be offset by a gain on the liability, and vice versa. However, for accounting purposes, without a fair value option, there would be a mismatch because the bonds payable are carried at amortized cost and are not revalued, whereas the bond investment is classified as FVPL and, therefore, is carried at fair value with gains/losses recognized in net income. The company would prepare the following journal entries in Year 1:

January 1		
Cash		$1,000
Bonds Payable		$1,000
Investment in Bonds (FVPL)		$1,000
Cash		$1,000

December 31

Interest Expense [$1,000 × 5%]...................................	$50
Cash..	.$50
Cash..	$60
Interest Income [$1,000 × 6%]	.$60
Loss on Investment in Bonds [$1,000 – $900].......................	$100
Investment in Bonds (FVPL).................................	.$100

The company's Year 1 income statement would report the following:

Interest income (expense), net...	$ 10
Gain (loss) on financial instruments, net....................................	(100)
Total	$ (90)

Under IAS 39, St. John's may use the fair value option to designate the bonds payable as FVPL to remove the accounting mismatch. If the fair value option is used, both the asset and the liability will be measured at fair value with gains/losses on both recognized in income. The company would prepare the following additional journal entry on December 31:

Bonds Payable	$100
Gain on Bonds Payable....................................	$100

As a result, the company's Year 1 income statement would reflect the following:

Interest income (expense), net..	$ 10
Gain (loss) on financial instruments, net.................................	0
Total	$(10)

A net increase in income of $10 more accurately reflects the economic substance of holding these two financial instruments at the same time.

Transfers between Categories of Financial Assets and Financial Liabilities

To reduce the ability to "manage earnings," IAS 39 severely restricts the ability to reclassify financial assets and liabilities. Financial instruments may not be reclassified into or out of the FVPL category. Reclassification between the available-for-sale and held-to-maturity categories is possible, but as noted above, reclassification of more than an insignificant amount of held-to-maturity investments results in a two-year ban on its use.

Measurement of Financial Instruments

Initial Measurement

Financial assets and financial liabilities are initially recognized on the balance sheet at their fair value, which normally will be equal to the amount paid or received. Except for FVPL assets and liabilities, transaction costs are capitalized as part of the fair value of a financial asset or as a reduction in the fair value of a liability. Transaction costs associated with FVPL assets and liabilities are expensed as incurred.

Subsequent Measurement

Subsequent to initial recognition, financial assets and liabilities are measured using one of three values: (1) cost, (2) amortized cost, or (3) fair value. The only financial asset measured at cost is an unquoted investment in equity instruments that cannot be reliably measured at fair value. This type of asset affects income only when dividends are received (dividend income is recognized) or the asset is sold (gain or loss is realized and recognized). Unrealized gains and losses are not recognized.

Three types of financial assets and liabilities are measured at amortized cost: held-to-maturity investments, loans and receivables, and liabilities measured at amortized cost. Amortized cost is the cost of an asset or liability adjusted to achieve a constant effective interest rate over the life of the asset or liability. The effective interest rate is the internal rate of return of the cash flows of the asset or liability. Equity investments cannot be measured at amortized cost because there are no fixed cash flows; therefore, there is no constant effective interest rate.

Three categories of financial assets and liabilities normally are measured at fair value: (1) FVPL financial assets, (2) FVPL financial liabilities, and (3) available-for-sale financial assets. The carrying amount of these items is adjusted to fair value at each balance sheet date. The unrealized gains and losses (changes in fair value) on FVPL assets and liabilities are recognized in net income. The unrealized gains and losses on available-for-sale financial assets are deferred as a separate component of equity until they are realized (or impairment occurs).

IFRS 9 (effective January 1, 2015)

IFRS 9, *Financial Instruments,* issued in November 2009, simplifies the classification of financial assets into two categories:

1. *Financial assets measured at amortized cost:* Financial assets that are held with the objective to collect contractual cash flows that are solely in the form of principal and interest.

2. *Financial assets measured at fair value:* All other financial assets.

IFRS 9 does not affect the classification of financial liabilities.

Example: Financial Liabilities Measured at Amortized Cost (Bonds Payable)

On January 1, Year 1, Keane Corp. issued $1,000,000 of 5 percent bonds at face value. The bonds pay interest annually and mature on December 31, Year 2. The company incurred bank and legal fees of $70,000 in conjunction with issuing the bonds.

Under IFRS, the debt issuance costs reduce the fair value of the liability. The fair value of the bonds payable at the date of issuance is $930,000 [$1,000,000 − $70,000]. The entry to initially recognize the liability is:

January 1, Year 1	
Cash	$930,000
Bonds Payable	$930,000

Subsequent to initial recognition, the bonds payable are measured at amortized cost. The difference between the fair value of the bonds at the date of issuance and their face value is amortized to expense over the life of the bonds using the effective interest rate method. The effective interest rate is 8.98 percent, calculated as the internal rate of return of the following stream of payments:

January 1, Year 1: Proceeds from debt issuance $930,000
December 31, Year 1: Interest payment [$1,000,000 × 5%] ($50,000)
December 31, Year 2: Interest and principal payment ($1,050,000)

The following journal entries are made over the life of the bonds:

December 31, Year 1

Interest Expense [$930,000 × 8.98%]	$83,496	
Cash		$50,000
Bonds Payable		33,496

December 31, Year 2

Interest Expense [$963,496 × 8.98%]	$86,504	
Cash		$50,000
Bonds Payable		36,504

Bonds Payable	$1,000,000	
Cash		$1,000,000

Under U.S. GAAP, debt issuance costs are deferred as an asset and amortized on a straight-line basis over the life of the debt. Total expense in Year 1 and in Year 2 would be determined as follows:

Interest expense [$1,000,000 × 5%]	$50,000
Amortization of debt issuance costs [$70,000/2]	35,000
Total	$85,000

Available-for-Sale Financial Asset Denominated in a Foreign Currency

Financial assets classified as available for sale are measured at fair value on each balance sheet date, with changes in fair value recognized as part of other comprehensive income. When an entity holds an available-for-sale financial asset that is denominated in a foreign currency, the asset's fair value in foreign currency must be translated into fair value in the entity's reporting currency. The change in fair value in the entity's reporting currency is comprised of two components, which must be accounted for separately. The two components are (1) the change in fair value in the foreign currency and (2) a foreign exchange gain or loss from changes in the exchange rate over time. IAS 39 indicates that these components are determined by treating the financial asset as if it were carried at amortized cost in the foreign currency. The foreign exchange gain or loss resulting from changes in the translated value of the amortized cost of the asset is recognized in net income, and the remaining change in fair value on the available-for-sale financial asset is recognized in other comprehensive income.

Example: Foreign Currency Financial Asset Classified as Available-for-Sale

On October 29, Year 1, Jacob Industries Inc., a U.S.-based company, purchased a Swiss treasury bond for 10,000 Swiss francs (CHF) when the exchange rate was $1.80 per Swiss franc. The bond investment has a cost of $18,000 [CHF 10,000 × $1.80] and is classified as available for sale. On December 31, Year 1, the bond has a fair value of 10,200 Swiss francs, and the exchange rate is $1.92 per Swiss franc. The bond investment now has a fair value of $19,584 [CHF 10,200 × $1.92]. Jacob must determine how to account for the $1,584 [$19,584 − $18,000] increase in the U.S. dollar fair value of this financial asset.

A foreign exchange gain or loss is recognized for the change in exchange rate applied to the amortized cost of the bond: CHF 10,000 × ($1.92 − $1.80) = $1,200 foreign exchange gain. The change in fair value in the foreign currency is then translated using the current exchange rate: (CHF 10,200 − CHF 10,000) × $1.92 = $384 fair value gain. The journal entry recorded at December 31, Year 1, is:

Investment in Bonds $1,584	
Foreign Exchange Gain	$1,200
Other Comprehensive Income	384

Impairment

IAS 39 requires an entity, at each balance sheet date, to assess whether there is any objective evidence that a financial asset is impaired. For available-for-sale equity investments, a significant or prolonged decline in the fair value below the original cost is objective evidence of impairment. FVPL financial assets are not subject to impairment testing because they already are measured at fair value, with unrealized gains and losses recognized in net income.

When an investment in a loan is determined to be impaired, the creditor writes down its financial asset for the difference between (1) the investment in the loan (principal and interest) and (2) the expected future cash flows discounted at the loan's historical effective interest rate. If the loan is secured, the expected future cash flows can be estimated as the fair value of the collateral securing the loan. The investment in the loan can be written down either directly or through an allowance account. The write-down is recognized as an impairment loss in net income. If in a subsequent period, the impairment loss decreases, the financial asset (investment in loan) is written back up to what its carrying amount would have been if the impairment had not been recognized. The reversal of the impairment loss is recognized as a gain in net income. (Note that the counterparty debtor is not allowed to reduce the carrying amount of its financial liability due to its inability to pay unless its contractual obligation has been legally reduced by the creditor.)

Derecognition

Derecognition refers to the process of removing an asset or liability from the balance sheet. Under IAS 39, derecognition of a *financial asset* is appropriate if either of the following criteria is met:

1. The contractual rights to the cash flows of the financial asset have expired.
2. The financial asset has been transferred and the transfer qualifies for derecognition based on an evaluation of the extent to which risks and rewards of ownership have been transferred.

Application of the second criterion is often complex. IAS 39, Appendix A, Application Guidance, provides a flowchart to be followed in evaluating whether a financial asset may be derecognized.

IAS 39 also provides specific guidance with respect to a so-called pass-through arrangement, which is a contractual arrangement in which an entity continues to collect cash flows from a financial asset it holds, but immediately transfers those payments to other parties. This arrangement can qualify for derecogniton of the financial asset when certain conditions listed in IAS 39 are met. If a financial asset meets the criteria for derecognition, its carrying amount is removed from the balance sheet and any difference between that amount and consideration received, if any, is recognized as a gain or loss in net income. Application of IAS 39's derecognition requirements to receivables is described in more detail later.

Derecognition of a *financial liability* is appropriate only when the obligation is extinguished—that is, when the obligation is paid, canceled, or expired. The difference between the carrying amount of the debt and the amount paid to extinguish it is recognized as a gain or loss in net income. Costs incurred in the extinguishment of debt are included as part of the gain or loss. A so-called troubled debt restructuring, in which a debtor is relieved of its obligation to the creditor due to financial hardship, is treated as a debt extinguishment.

A substantial modification of the terms of existing debt should be treated as an extinguishment of old debt and the issuance of new debt. A less-than-substantial modification of the terms of existing debt is not treated as an extinguishment, but instead the modification is handled prospectively. An example would be the renegotiation of the interest rate on existing debt. Costs associated with a less-than-substantial debt modification that is not treated as an extinguishment are subtracted from the carrying amount of the debt and are amortized over the remaining term of the debt.

Under U.S. GAAP, debt modification costs are expensed as incurred. Debt extinguishment costs also are expensed as incurred, except when new debt is issued for old debt, in which case the costs are deferred and amortized over the term of the new debt.

Example: Debt Extinguishment/Modification

Champaign Company issued $10 million in 12 percent bonds several years ago at a discount. The bonds currently have a carrying amount of $9.8 million. The bond agreement allows for early extinguishment by Champaign beginning in the current year. Champaign's investment bank has arranged for the company to issue $10 million of new 10 percent bonds at face value to a group of European investors. The proceeds will be used to extinguish the 12 percent bonds. The investment banking, legal, and accounting costs to execute the transaction total $400,000.

This is a *debt extinguishment*. The costs associated with issuing the new debt are reflected in the calculation of the gain or loss on extinguishment of the old debt as follows:

Carrying amount of old debt	$ 9,800,000
Fair value of new debt	(10,000,000)
Subtotal	(200,000)
New debt issuance costs	(400,000)
Loss on extinguishment of old debt	$ (600,000)

The debt extinguishment is recognized as follows:

Bonds Payable—12% (old debt)	$9,800,000	
Loss on Extinguishment of 12% Bonds	600,000	
Bonds Payable—10% (new debt)		$10,000,000
Cash		400,000

Now assume the investment bank has negotiated a reduction in the interest rate with the 12 percent bondholder, who agrees to lower the interest rate to 10 percent based on current market conditions. Fees for the reduction in interest rate total $250,000. This is a *less- than-substantial debt modification.* The costs incurred adjust the carrying amount of the debt and are amortized prospectively to interest expense over the remaining life of the bonds.

Bonds Payable—12% (now 10%) $250,000
      Cash $250,000

Derivatives

Derivatives are financial instruments such as options, forwards, futures, and swaps whose value changes in response to the change in a specified interest rate, financial instrument price, commodity price, foreign exchange rate, index, credit rating, or other variable. IFRS 39 requires derivatives to be measured at fair value. Whether the change in fair value over time is recognized in net income or deferred in stockholders' equity (i.e., other comprehensive income) depends on whether the derivative is designated as a hedge or not, and if so, what kind of a hedge. If a derivative is not designated as a hedge, the change in fair value must be recognized in net income when the fair value change occurs.

Hedge accounting results in the change in fair value on the derivative being recognized in net income in the same accounting period as gains and losses on the underlying hedged item are recognized in net income. Hedge accounting is optional and is only permitted when certain conditions are met. Similar to U.S. GAAP, IAS 39 identifies three types of hedging relationships: (1) fair value hedge, (2) cash flow hedge, and (3) hedge of a net investment in a foreign operation. We discuss fair value hedges and cash flow hedges in the context of foreign currency risks in Chapter 7 and hedges of a net investment in a foreign operation in Chapter 8.

Receivables

The accounting for receivables is governed by IAS 39, which identifies "loans and receivables" as one of four categories of financial assets. Receivables are measured initially at fair value. Subsequently, they are measured at amortized cost using an effective interest method.

Impairment of Receivables

If there is objective evidence that receivables are impaired, a loss should be recognized. Individually significant receivables should be tested for impairment individually. Individually insignificant receivables are assessed for impairment as a portfolio group. A bad debt loss and provision (allowance) for uncollectible receivables is estimated. IAS 39 states that the loss should be measured as the difference between the carrying amount of the portfolio of receivables and the present value of future cash flows expected to be received. Implementation guidance in IAS 39 suggests that the aging method of estimating the provision for uncollectible receivables is not appropriate.

Sale of Receivables

When an entity sells receivables to a third party, there is a question as to whether the sale is truly a sale of an asset or simply a borrowing secured by the accounts receivable. In the former case, it is appropriate to recognize a sale and derecognize the receivables—that is, remove them from the accounting records. In the latter case, the receivables are not derecognized and the transaction is accounted for as a borrowing. The general principle in IAS 39 is that a financial asset may be derecognized when the significant risks and rewards associated with ownership of the asset have been transferred to another entity. In some cases, the seller of receivables retains significant risks, for example, by guaranteeing the collectibility of the receivables through right of recourse, and derecognition of the receivables is not appropriate. Instead, the cash received from the sale of receivables is treated as a loan payable.

A so-called pass-through arrangement exists when an entity retains the right to collect cash flows from a receivable but is obligated to transfer those cash flows to a third party. In this type of arrangement, derecognition is appropriate only if each of the following criteria is met:

1. The entity has no obligation to pay cash to the buyer of the receivables unless it collects equivalent amounts from the receivables.
2. The entity is prohibited by the terms of the transfer contract from selling or pledging the receivables.
3. The entity has an obligation to remit any cash flows it collects on the receivables to the eventual recipient without material delay. In addition, the entity is not entitled to reinvest such cash flows. An exception exists for investments in cash equivalents during the short settlement period from the collection date to the date of remittance to the eventual recipients, as long as interest earned on such investments also is passed to the eventual recipients.

The following excerpt from Fiat Group's notes to the 2009 consolidated financial statements demonstrates the impact of IAS 39's derecognition requirements with respect to receivables:

> At 31 December 2009, Current receivables include receivables sold and financed through both securitization and factoring transactions of €6,588 million (€6,190 million at 31 December 2008) which do not meet IAS 39 derecognition requirements. These receivables are recognized as such in the Group financial statements even though they have been legally sold; a corresponding financial liability is recorded in the consolidated statement of financial position as Asset-backed financing (see Note 27).

Example: Derecognition of Receivables

Edwards Inc. has receivables from unrelated parties with a face value of $1,000. Edwards transfers these receivables to Main Street Bank for $900, without recourse. The discount reflects the fact that the bank has assumed the credit risk. Edwards will continue to collect the receivables, depositing them in a non-interest-bearing bank account with the cash flows remitted to the bank at the end of each month. Edwards is not allowed to sell or pledge the receivables to anyone else and is under no obligation to repurchase the receivables from Main Street Bank.

This is a pass-through arrangement, and Edwards appears to meet the three criteria required for derecognition: (1) the company is under no obligation to pay any more than it collects, (2) it may not pledge or resell the receivables, and (3) it has agreed to remit the money collected in a timely manner. There is no interest earned on the short-term bank deposits, so there is no question whether Edwards passes on the interest to Main Street Bank. The receivables may be derecognized, as follows:

Cash		$900
Expense		100
Accounts Receivable		$1,000

Now assume that Edwards collects the receivables and deposits collections in its interest-bearing bank account. At the end of each month, Edwards remits to Main Street Bank only the amount collected on the receivables; interest earned on the short-term deposits is retained by Edwards. Because Edwards retains the interest on short-term bank deposits, the third pass-through criterion has not been met. Edwards would not be allowed to derecognize the accounts receivable. Instead, the cash received from Main Street Bank would be treated as a secured borrowing.

Cash.	$900
Expense	100
Notes Payable.	$1,000

Summary

1. IAS 1 requires liabilities to be classified as current or noncurrent. The classification and accounting for current liabilities under IFRS is very similar to U.S. GAAP. Differences relate to refinancing short-term debt, amounts payable on demand due to debt covenant violations, and bank overdrafts.

2. IAS 37 defines a provision as a liability of uncertain timing or amount. A provision is recognized when there is a present obligation that can be reliably estimated and for which it is probable (more likely than not) that an outflow of resources will be made. U.S. GAAP has similar requirements but does not provide guidance for the degree of likelihood needed to meet the threshold of being probable.

3. A provision should be recognized for an onerous contract, which is a contract in which the unavoidable costs of fulfilling the contract exceed the benefit expected to be received. A provision should be recognized for a restructuring when an entity has created a constructive obligation—that is, when it has raised a valid expectation in those affected by the plan that it will carry out the restructuring. U.S. GAAP does not allow recognition of a restructuring until a liability has been incurred.

4. IFRS and U.S. GAAP differ in the accounting for defined post-retirement benefit plans with respect to the periods of time over which past service cost and actuarial gains and losses are recognized, and measurement of the amount of benefit liability or asset reported on the balance sheet.

5. Under IAS 19, the amount reported on the balance sheet related to a defined post-employment benefit plan is equal to the present value of the defined benefit obligation (PVDBO) minus the fair value of plan assets minus unrecognized past service cost plus (minus) unrecognized actuarial gains (losses). Under U.S. GAAP, the amount recognized is PVDBO minus the fair value of plan assets.

6. IFRS 2 distinguishes between three types of share-based payments. Equity-settled share-based payments are treated as equity transactions; cash-settled and choice-of-settlement share-based payment transactions result in the recognition of a liability. The standard applies a fair value approach to all three types of share-based payment.

7. In a stock option plan that vests in installments, compensation cost associated with each installment is amortized over that installment's vesting period under IFRS. This approach also is acceptable under U.S. GAAP, but a simpler straight-line method also may be used.

8. Similar to U.S. GAAP, IAS 12 uses an asset-and-liability approach that requires recognition of deferred tax assets and liabilities for temporary differences and for operating loss and tax credit carry-forwards. A deferred tax asset is recognized only if it is probable that a tax benefit will be realized.

9. IFRS contain two standards specifically related to revenue recognition: IAS 18 and IAS 11. U.S. GAAP, on the other hand, has many more separate pieces of authoritative guidance that are now codified in FASB Accounting Standards Codification Topic 605. The IASB and FASB jointly issued an Exposure Draft in 2010, which was revised in 2011, with the intent to converge their rules with regard to revenue recognition.

10. IAS 18 provides general principles for the recognition and measurement of revenue generated from the sale of goods; rendering of services; and interest, royalties, and dividends. The general measurement principle is that revenue should be measured at the fair value of the consideration received or receivable.

11. Five conditions must be met before revenue may be recognized from the sale of goods, including the criterion that the significant risks and rewards of ownership of the goods have been transferred to the buyer.

12. IAS 18 allows use of the stage-of-completion method for recognition of service revenue when several criteria are met. This method of revenue recognition is not used for service transactions under U.S. GAAP.

13. Entities that use customer loyalty programs to provide customers with incentives to purchase their goods and services must treat the award credits as a separate component of the sale transaction and recognize a portion of the sales price as deferred revenue.

14. The accounting for financial instruments is covered by IAS 32, IAS 39, IFRS 7, and IFRS 9 (which goes into effect in 2015). Financial instruments are contracts that give rise to both a financial asset for one party and either a financial liability or equity for another party.

15. IAS 32 requires financial instruments to be classified as financial liabilities or equity or both in accordance with the substance of the contractual arrangement. If an equity instrument contains a contractual obligation that meets the definition of a financial liability, it should be classified as such. Preferred shares that are redeemable at the option of the shareholders are an example of a financial liability.

16. Compound financial instruments, such as convertible bonds, must be split into a liability element and an equity element. This so-called split accounting is not followed under U.S. GAAP.

17. IAS 39 establishes four categories of financial assets and two categories of financial liabilities; both categories include the classification "at fair value through profit or loss" (FVPL). Financial assets and liabilities that otherwise would be classified in a different category may be classified as FVPL under certain conditions, such as to eliminate an accounting mismatch.

18. Financial assets and financial liabilities are initially measured at their fair value. Subsequent to initial recognition, they are measured at one of three possible values: (a) cost (unquoted equity investments), (b) amortized cost (loans and receivables, held-to-maturity investments, and liabilities measured at amortized cost), or (c) fair value (FVPL financial assets, FVPL financial liabilities, and available-for-sale financial assets).

19. Under IFRS, costs associated with the issuance or modification of debt are subtracted in determining the carrying amount of the related liability. These costs are then allocated over the life of the debt as part of interest expense. Under U.S. GAAP, debt issuance costs are treated as an asset that is amortized over the life of the debt, and debt modification costs are expensed immediately.

20. According to IAS 39, the sale of receivables can be recognized as such and the receivables may be derecognized only if the significant risks and rewards from owning the receivables are transferred to the buyer. If this is not the case, the sale of receivables is treated as a borrowing with the accounts receivable acting as collateral.

Questions

Answer questions based on IFRS unless indicated otherwise.

1. What is a provision, and when must a provision be recognized?
2. What is a contingent liability? What is the financial reporting treatment for contingent liabilities?
3. What is a constructive obligation?
4. What is an onerous contract? How are onerous contracts accounted for?
5. How does a company measure the net pension benefit liability (asset) to report on the balance sheet under IFRS and U.S. GAAP?
6. In accounting for post-employment benefits, when are past service costs and actuarial gains and losses recognized in income?
7. What is the basis for determining compensation cost in an equity-settled share-based payment transaction with nonemployees? With employees?
8. What is the difference in measuring compensation expense associated with stock options that vest on a single date (cliff vesting) and in installments (graded vesting)?
9. How does an entity account for a choice-of-settlement share-based payment transaction?
10. Which income tax rates should be used in accounting for income taxes?
11. What are the rules related to the recognition of a deferred tax asset?
12. What approaches are available for disclosing the relationship between tax expense and accounting profit?
13. How are deferred taxes classified on the balance sheet?
14. What are the criteria that must be met in order to recognize revenue from the sale of goods?
15. What approaches are used to recognize revenue from the rendering of services? Under what conditions is each of these approaches used?
16. How is an exchange of goods that are similar in nature and value accounted for?
17. Under what conditions may revenue be recognized on a "bill-and-hold" sale?
18. What is a customer loyalty program, and how is such a program accounted for?
19. What are the five steps to follow in revenue recognition as proposed in the IASB/FASB Exposure Draft on revenue from contracts with customers?

20. What are the four classes of financial assets?

21. Under what conditions should preferred shares be recognized as a liability on the balance sheet?

22. How are convertible bonds measured initially on the balance sheet?

23. How can use of the "fair value option" solve the problem of an accounting mismatch?

24. What happens if a significant amount of held-to-maturity investments is reclassified as available- for-sale?

25. How are costs associated with the issuance of bonds payable accounted for?

26. What is the accounting treatment for debt extinguishment costs? Debt modification costs?

27. In a sale of receivables described as a pass-through arrangement, under what conditions can receivables be derecognized?

Exercises and Problems

Solve exercises and problems based on IFRS unless indicated otherwise.

1. Halifax Corporation has a December 31 fiscal year-end. As of December 31, Year 1, the company has a debt covenant violation that results in a 10-year note payable to Nova Scotia Bank becoming due on March 1, Year 2. Halifax will be required to classify the 10-year note payable as a current liability unless it obtains a waiver from the bank

   a. Prior to issuance of its Year 1 financial statements that gives the company until January 1, Year 3, to rectify the debt covenant violation.

   b. Prior to December 31, Year 1, that gives the company until January 1, Year 3, to rectify the debt covenant violation.

   c. Prior to issuance of its Year 1 financial statements, that gives the company until June 30, Year 2, to rectify the debt covenant violation.

   d. Prior to December 31, Year 1, that gives the company until June 30, Year 2, to rectify the debt covenant violation.

2. Bull Arm Company has the following items at December 31, Year 1:

   • $200,000, 5 percent note payable, due March 15, Year 2. The company has reached an agreement with the bank to refinance the note for two years, but the refinancing has not yet been completed.

   • $1,000,000, 4 percent bonds payable, due December 31, Year 5. The company has violated an agreement with the bondholders to maintain a minimum balance in retained earnings, which causes the bonds to come due on January 31, Year 2.

   • $50,000 overdraft on a bank account. Overdrafts are a normal part of the company's cash management plan.

   Required:
   Related to these items, what amount should Bull Arm Company report as current liabilities on its December 31, Year 1, balance sheet?

   a. $50,000.

   b. $250,000.

   c. $1,050,000.

   d. $1,200,000.

3. Melbourne Inc. became involved in a tax dispute with the national tax authority. Melbourne's legal counsel indicates that there is a 70 percent likelihood that the company will lose this dispute and estimates that the amount the company will have to pay is between $500,000 and $700,000, with all amounts in that range being equally likely. What amount, if any, should Melbourne recognize as a provision related to this tax dispute?

   a. $0.

   b. $500,000.

   c. $600,000.

   d. $700,000.

4. Which of the following is not a criterion that must be met before an entity recognizes a provision related to a restructuring program?

   a. The entity has a detailed formal plan for the restructuring.

   b. The entity has begun implementation of the restructuring.

   c. The restructuring plan indicates that the restructuring will be carried out in a reasonable period of time.

   d. The cost of the restructuring is reasonably estimable.

5. Past service cost related to nonvested employees should be recognized as expense

   a. In the period the cost is incurred.

   b. Over the nonvested employees' remaining vesting period.

   c. Over the nonvested employees' estimated remaining working life.

   d. Over the nonvested employees' estimated life expectancy.

6. When stock options are granted to employees, what is the basis for determining the amount of compensation cost that will be recognized as expense?

   a. The fair value of the service provided by the employees receiving the options at the grant date.

   b. The fair value of the stock options at the exercise date.

   c. The fair value of the stock options at the grant date.

   d. There is no recognition of expense related to stock options.

7. Which of the following types of share-based payment (SBP) transactions always results in the recognition of a liability?

   a. Equity-settled SBP transaction with employees.

   b. Equity-settled SBP transaction with nonemployees.

   c. Cash-settled SBP transaction with employees.

   d. Choice-of-settlement SBP transaction in which the entity chooses the form of settlement.

8. Sandoval Company operates in a country in which distributed profits are taxed at 25 percent and undistributed profits are taxed at 30 percent. In Year 1, Sandoval generated pre-tax profit of $100,000 and paid $20,000 in dividends from its Year 1 earnings. In Year 2, Sandoval generated pre-tax profit of $120,000 and paid dividends of $40,000 from its Year 1 earnings. What amounts should Sandoval recognize as current tax expense in Years 1 and 2, respectively?

220   Chapter Five

     a. $29,000 and $34,000.

     b. $30,000 and $34,000.

     c. $25,000 and $30,000.

     d. $30,000 and $36,000.

9. Which of the following is not a criterion that must be met to recognize revenue from the sale of goods?

     a. The amount of revenue can be measured reliably.

     b. The significant risks and rewards of ownership of the goods have been transferred to the buyer.

     c. The costs incurred or to be incurred with respect to the sale of the goods can be measured reliably.

     d. It is certain that the economic benefits associated with the sale will flow to the seller.

10. Manometer Company sells accounts receivable of $10,000 to Eck Bank for $9,000 in cash. The sale does not qualify for derecognition of a financial asset. As a result, Manometer's balance sheet will be different in which of the following ways?

     a. $1,000 more in assets than under derecognition.

     b. $9,000 more in assets than under derecognition.

     c. $9,000 more in liabilities than under derecognition.

     d. $10,000 less in equity than under derecognition.

11. Sinto Bem Company issues a two-year note paying 5 percent interest on January 1, Year 1. The note sells for its par value of $1,000,000, and the company incurs issuance costs of $22,000. Which of the following amounts best approximates the amount of interest expense Sinto Bem will recognize in Year 1 related to this note?

     a. $48,900.

     b. $50,000.

     c. $58,680.

     d. $60,670.

12. Costs incurred to accomplish a less- than-substantial debt modification, such as an interest rate adjustment, are treated in which of the following ways?

     a. Expensed immediately.

     b. Increase the carrying amount of the debt that has been modified.

     c. Decrease the carrying amount of the debt that has been modified.

     d. Decrease the gain on the debt modification.

13. On December 31, Year 1, Airways Corp. issued $1 million in bonds at 5 percent annual interest, due December 31, Year 6, at a discount of $100,000. Airways incurred bank fees of $100,000, legal fees of $50,000, and salaries of $25,000 for its employees in conjunction with issuing the bonds. What is the original carrying amount for these bonds?

     a. $725,000.

     b. $750,000.

     c. $850,000.

     d. $900,000.

14. In Year 1, Better Sleep Company began to receive complaints from physicians that patients were experiencing unexpected side effects from the company's sleep apnea drug. The company took the drug off the market near the end of Year 1. During Year 2, the company was sued by 1,000 customers who had had a severe allergic reaction to the company's drug and required hospitalization. At the end of Year 2, the company's attorneys estimated a 60 percent chance the company would need to make payments in the range of $1,000 to $5,000 to settle each claim, with all amounts in that range being equally likely. At the end of Year 3, while none of the cases had been resolved, the company's attorneys now estimated an 80 percent probability the company would be required to make payments in the range of $2,000 to $7,000 to settle each claim. In Year 4, 400 claims were settled at a total cost of $1.2 million. Based on this experience, the company believes 30 percent of the remaining cases will be settled for $3,000 each, 50 percent will be settled for $5,000, and 20 percent will be settled for $10,000.

Required:

Prepare journal entries for Years 1–4 related to this litigation.

15. On June 1, Year 1, Charley Horse Company entered into a contract with Good Feed Company to purchase 1,000 bales of organic hay on January 30, Year 2, at a price of $30 per bale. The hay will be grown especially for Charley Horse and is needed to feed the company's herd of buffalos. On December 1, Year 1, Charley Horse sells its herd of buffalos. As a result, the company no longer has a need for the organic hay that will be delivered on January 30, Year 2, and the company does not believe it will be able to sell the hay to a third party. Charley Horse is able to cancel the contract with Good Feed for a cancellation fee of $20,000.

Required:

Determine what accounting entries, if any, Charley Horse Company should make on December 31, Year 1, related to the contract to purchase 1,000 bales of hay on January 30, Year 2.

16. The board of directors of Chestnut Inc. approved a restructuring plan on November 1, Year 1. On December 1, Year 1, Chestnut publicly announced its plan to close a manufacturing division in New Jersey and move it to China, and the company's New Jersey employees were notified that their jobs would be eliminated. Also on December 1, Year 1, to ensure an orderly transition, management promised a termination bonus of $10,000 to any employee who remains with the company until his or her position is terminated in the fourth quarter of Year 2. Chestnut estimates it will pay termination bonuses to 120 employees at the end of Year 2, for a total of $1,200,000. The present value of the estimated termination bonus is $1,000,000.

Required:

Determine the provision that should be recognized for Chestnut's restructuring plan. Identify the dates on which journal entries should be made and the amounts to be recorded.

17. The Kissel Trucking Company Inc. has a defined benefit pension plan for its employees. At December 31, Year 1, the following information is available regarding Kissel's plan:

Fair value of plan assets	$30,000,000
Present value of defined benefit obligation	38,000,000
Service costs	4,000,000
Interest costs	1,200,000
Actuarial gains	150,000
Past service costs	375,000

Required:

Determine the amount that Kissel will report on the balance sheet as of December 31, Year 1, for this pension plan under IFRS.

18. On January 1, Year 1, the Hoverman Corporation made amendments to its defined benefit pension plan, resulting in $150,000 of past service costs. The plan has 100 active employees with an average expected remaining working life of 10 years. There currently are no retirees under the plan.

Required:

Determine the amount of past service costs to be amortized in Year 1 and subsequent years under (a) IFRS and (b) U.S. GAAP.

19. The Baton Rouge Company compiled the following information for the current year related to its defined benefit pension plan:

Present value of defined benefit obligation, beginning of year	$1,000,000
Fair value of plan assets, beginning of year	800,000
Service cost, current year	50,000
Actuarial gain, current year	8,000
Actual return on plan assets, current year	55,000
Effective yield on high-quality corporate bonds, current year	5%

Required:

Determine the amount of defined benefit cost for the current year to be reported in (a) net income and (b) other comprehensive income.

20. White River Company has a defined benefit pension plan in which the fair value of plan assets (FVPA) exceeds the present value of defined benefit obligations (PVDBO). The following information is available at December 31, Year 1 (amounts in millions):

PVDBO	$3,200
FVPA	3,700

Because the FVPA exceeds the PVDBO, White River will be able to reduce future contributions to the plan for several years. The present value of reductions in future contributions is $100 million.

Required:

Determine the amount at which White River Company will report a defined pension benefit asset on its December 31, Year 1, balance sheet under (a) IFRS and (b) U.S. GAAP.

21. On January 2, Year 1, Argy Company's board of directors granted 12,000 stock options to a select group of senior employees. The requisite service period is three years, with one-third of the options vesting at the end of each calendar year (graded vesting). An option-pricing model was used to calculate a fair value of $5 for each option on the grant date. The company assumes all 12,000 options will vest (i.e., there will be no forfeitures).

    Required:
    Determine the amount to be recognized as compensation expense in Year 1, Year 2, and Year 3 under (a) IFRS and (b) U.S. GAAP. Prepare the necessary journal entries.

22. SC Masterpiece Inc. granted 1,000 stock options to certain sales employees on January 1, Year 1. The options vest at the end of three years (cliff vesting) but are conditional upon selling 20,000 cases of barbecue sauce over the three-year service period. The grant-date fair value of each option is $30. No forfeitures are expected to occur. The company is expensing the cost of the options on a straight-line basis over the three-year period at $10,000 per year (1,000 options $\times$ $30 $\div$ 3 = $10,000).

    On January 1, Year 2, the company's management believes the original sales target of 20,000 units will not be met because only 5,000 cases were sold in Year 1. Management modifies the sales target for the options to vest to 15,000 units, which it believes is reasonably achievable. The fair value of each option at January 1, Year 2, is $28.

    Required:
    Determine the amount to be recognized as compensation expense in Year 1, Year 2, and Year 3 under (a) IFRS and (b) U.S. GAAP. Prepare the necessary journal entries.

23. Updike and Patterson Investments Inc. (UPI) holds equity investments with a cost basis of $250,000. UPI accounts for these investments as available-for-sale securities. As such, the investments are carried on the balance sheet at fair value, with unrealized gains and losses reported in other comprehensive income.

    At the end of Year 1, the fair value of these investments has declined to $220,000. Consequently, UPI reports an unrealized loss for financial reporting purposes of $30,000 in other comprehensive income, which creates a temporary tax difference. As of December 31, Year 1, UPI management determines that it is more likely than not that the company will be able to deduct capital losses on these investments for tax purposes if they are realized.

    As of December 31, Year 2, UPI management evaluates its assessment of tax position and determines that it is more likely than not that the company will not be able to take a deduction for any capital loss on these investments. UPI's tax rate is 40 percent.

    Required:
    Prepare journal entries to account for income taxes in Year 1 and Year 2.

24. Gotti Manufacturing Inc., a U.S.-based company, operates in three countries in addition to the United States. The following table reports the company's pretax income and the applicable tax rate in these countries for the year ended December 31, Year 1. Gotti does not have any temporary tax differences, but it does have two permanent differences: (1) nontaxable municipal bond interest

of $20,000 in the United States and (2) nondeductible expenses of $5,000 in the United States.

Country	Pre-tax Income	Applicable Tax Rate
United States.	$1,450,000	35%
Country One	400,000	40%
Country Two	500,000	20%
Country Three	600,000	25%
Total	$2,950,000	
Permanent differences	15,000	
Book income	$2,965,000	

Required:

Prepare the numerical reconciliation between tax expense and accounting profit that would appear in Gotti's income tax note in the Year 1 financial statements. Show two different ways in which this reconciliation may be presented.

25. Mishima Technologies Company introduced Product X to the market on December 1. The new product carries a one-year warranty. In its first month on the market, Mishima sold 1,000 units of the new product for a total of $1,000,000. Customers have an unconditional right of return for 90 days if they are not completely satisfied with the product. During the month of December, customers returned 200 units of the new product that they had purchased for $200,000.

Required:

Determine when it would be appropriate for Mishima Technologies Company to recognize revenue from the December sales of the new product.

26. Ultima Company offers its customers discounts to purchase goods and take title before they actually need the goods. The company offers to hold the goods for the customers until they request delivery. This relieves the customers from making room in their warehouses for merchandise not yet needed. The goods are on hand and ready for delivery to the buyer at the time the sale is made. Ultima Company pays the cost of storage and insurance prior to shipment. Customers are billed at the time of sale and are given the normal credit period (90 days) to pay.

Required:

Determine whether Ultima Company should recognize revenue from the sale of goods at the time title passes to the customer or whether it should defer revenue recognition until the goods are delivered to the customer.

27. The Miller-Porter Company sells powder coating equipment at a sales price of $50,000 per unit. The sales price includes delivery, installation, and initial testing of the equipment, as well as a monthly service call for one year in which a technician checks to make sure that the equipment is working properly and makes adjustments as needed. After the first year, customers are given the

opportunity to enter into an extended service agreement; Miller-Porter prices these extended service agreements to earn an expected gross profit of 50 percent. Given the wages paid to technicians and the time required to make a service call, the company estimates that the cost of providing each monthly service call is $200.

Required:

Develop a revenue recognition policy consistent with IAS 18 for The Miller-Porter Company for its sales of power coating equipment.

28. Cypress Company enters into a fixed-fee contract to provide architectural services to the Gervais Group for $240,000. The Gervais Group, which will make monthly payments of $40,000, is a new client for Cypress Company. Cypress has agreed to provide Gervais with plans and drawings for a new manufacturing facility that will qualify for a LEED (Leadership in Energy and Environmental Design) green building certification. Cypress has no experience in designing green buildings, but it has guaranteed Gervais that the plans and drawings will be completed in six months.

Required:

Evaluate whether it would be appropriate for Cypress Company to account for its contract with Gervais Group on a stage-of-completion basis.

29. Phil's Sandwich Company sells sandwiches at several locations in the northeastern part of the country. Phil's customers receive a card on their first visit that allows them to receive one free sandwich for every eight sandwiches purchased in a three-month period. Customers must redeem their cards in the month after the three-month period is completed. Each time a customer purchases a sandwich, his or her card is stamped. Past experience shows that only 50 percent of customers accumulate enough stamps within a three-month period to qualify for a free sandwich, and only 80 percent of those customers actually redeem their card to receive a free sandwich. In the first quarter of the current year, Phil's sold 12,000 sandwiches at an average price of $7.00. Phil's only accepts payment in cash.

Required:

Prepare the summary journal entry Phil's Sandwich Company should make to recognize revenue from the sale of sandwiches for the first quarter of the current year.

30. Saffron Enterprises Inc., a U.S.-based company, purchases a 4 percent bond denominated in euros for $1,500 on January 1, Year 1, when the exchange rate is $1.50 per euro. (In other words, the purchase price was 1,000 euros.) The bond was purchased at par value. At December 31, Year 1, the fair value of the bond in the marketplace is 1,050 euros and the exchange rate is $1.40 per euro. Saffron classifies its investment in bonds as available for sale.

Required:

Prepare the journal entries that Saffron Enterprises should record in Year 1 related to its investment in euro-denominated bonds.

31. On January 1, Year 1, Spectrum Fabricators Inc. issues $20 million of convertible bonds at par value. The bonds have a stated annual interest rate of 6 percent, pay interest annually, and come due December 31, Year 5. The bonds

are convertible at any time after issuance at the rate of 10 shares of common stock for each $1,000 of the face value of the convertible bonds. Issuance costs total $100,000. The current market interest rate for nonconvertible bonds is 8 percent.

Required:
Prepare the journal entries to record the issuance of the convertible bonds (round to the nearest dollar). Determine the amount of expense related to the convertible bonds that the company should recognize each year (round to the nearest dollar). [Note: You will need to calculate the effective interest rate on the bonds to determine interest expense. One way to do this is to solve for the internal rate of return (IRR) of the cash flows using Excel.]

32. The Bockster Company issues $20 million of preferred shares on January 1, Year 1, at par value. The preferred shares have a 5 percent fixed annual cash dividend.

    Part A. The preferred shareholders have the option to redeem the preferred shares for cash equal to par value any time after January 1, Year 2.

    Required:
    Discuss how Bockster should account for these redeemable preferred shares.

    Part B. The preferred shareholders do not have the option to redeem the preferred shares, but instead have the option to convert the preferred shares into a fixed number of shares of common stock any time after January 1, Year 2.

    Required:
    Discuss how Bockster should account for these convertible preferred shares.

33. On January 1, Year 1, Tempe extinguishes $10 million of 10 percent bonds payable due December 31, Year 2, that were originally issued at a discount by calling them at par value. The current carrying amount of the bonds payable is $9,950,000. To finance the debt extinguishment, management issues new debt at par with a new lender in the amount of $10 million. The new debt matures on December 31, Year 2, and has a 9 percent annual interest rate. Management incurs $100,000 in legal costs to negotiate the issuance of the new long-term bonds payable.

    Required:
    Prepare the journal entries to record the extinguishment of the debt and interest expense for Year 1.

34. Five years ago, Macro Arco Corporation (MAC) borrowed $12 million from Friendly Neighbor Bank (FNB) to finance the purchase of a new factory to be able to meet an expected increase in demand for its products. The expected increase in demand never materialized, and due to a downturn in the economy, MAC is no longer able to make its monthly payments to FNB. After a lengthy negotiation process, which cost MAC $50,000 in legal fees, MAC will transfer the factory to the bank, along with a cash payment of $1.5 million. This will discharge MAC from the debt. The carrying amount and fair value of the factory is $8 million, and the current balance due to the bank is $10 million.

Required:

Prepare the journal entries to be recorded by MAC and FNB related to this troubled debt restructuring.

35. On November 1, Year 1, Farley Corporation sells receivables due in six months with a carrying amount of $100,000 to Town Square Bank for a cash payment of $95,000, subject to full recourse. Under the right of recourse, Farley Corporation is obligated to compensate Town Square Bank for the failure of any debtor to pay when due. In addition to the recourse, Town Square Bank is entitled to sell the receivables back to Farley Corporation in the event of unfavorable changes in interest rates or credit rating of the underlying debtors.

Required:

Determine the appropriate accounting by Farley Corporation for the sale of receivables. Prepare any necessary journal entries for Year 1.

36. On December 1, Year 1, Traylor Company sells $100,000 of short-term trade receivables to Main Street Bank for $98,000 in cash by guaranteeing to buy back the first $15,000 of defaulted receivables. Traylor's historic rate of noncollection on receivables is 5 percent. Traylor notifies the customers affected that they should make payment on their accounts directly to Main Street Bank.

Required:

Determine whether the sale of receivables by Traylor Company qualifies for derecognition.

37. The Campolino Company has a defined benefit post-retirement health-care plan for its employees. To fund the plan, Campolino makes an annual cash contribution to a health-care benefit fund on December 31 of each year. At the beginning of Year 5, Campolino amended the plan to provide additional benefits to all employees. Assume that the health-care benefit fund pays benefits to employees on December 31 of each year.

The following facts apply to the plan for the year ended December 31, Year 5:

Present value of defined benefit obligation (PVDBO) on January 1	$650,000
Plan assets at fair value (FVPA) on January 1.........................	420,000
Service cost	46,000
Past service cost...	16,000
Actual return on plan assets...................................	28,000
Employer cash contribution to post-retirement benefit fund.............	50,000
Benefit paid by post-retirement benefit fund	42,000
Discount rate..	5 percent
Plan assets at fair value (FVPA) on December 31.....................	456,000

Required:

Use the following template to determine the post-retirement defined benefit cost to be recognized in (a) net income and (b) other comprehensive income for the year ended December 31, Year 5, and the post-retirement defined benefit liability (asset) at December 31, Year 5, to be reported by Campolino Company under IFRS. Prepare a summary journal entry to reflect the recognition of these amounts.

228   Chapter Five

(Amounts in parentheses represent credits.)

	Campolino Company General Ledger				Benefit Fund General Ledger	
	Defined benefit cost recognized in net income	Defined benefit cost recognized in OCI	Cash	Defined benefit asset (liability)	PVDBO	FVPA
Balance at January 1				$(230,000)	$(650,000)	$420,000
Service cost						
Interest expense						
Interest income						
Net interest						
Excess of actual return on plan assets over interest income						
Past service costs						
Actuarial loss						
Contributions						
Benefits paid						
Balance at December 31						$456,000

38. This problem consists of two parts.

Part A.   On January 1, Year 1, Stone Company issued 100 stock options with an exercise price of $38 each to 10 employees (1,000 options in total). The employees can choose to settle the options either (a) in shares of stock ($1 par value) or (b) in cash equal to the intrinsic value of the options on the vesting date. The options vest on December 31, Year 3, after the employees have completed three years of service. Stone Company expects that only seven employees will remain with the company for three years and vest in the options. Two employees resign in Year 1, and the company continues to assume an overall forfeiture rate of 30 percent at December 31, Year 1. In Year 2, one more employee resigns. As expected, seven employees vest on December 31, Year 3, and exercise their stock options.

The following represents the share price and fair value at the relevant dates:

Date	Share Price	Fair Value of Cash Alternative	Fair Value of Stock Alternative
January 1, Year 1	$43	$6.00	$6.00
December 31, Year 1, Year 2	$45	$8.00	$8.00
December 31, Year 3	$47	$9.00	$9.00

Required:
Determine the fair value of the stock options at the grant date and the amount to be recognized as compensation expense in Year 1, Year 2, and Year 3. Prepare journal entries assuming that the vested employees choose (a) the cash alternative and (b) the stock alternative.

Part B.   Now assume that if the employees choose to settle the stock options in shares of stock, the employees receive a 10 percent discount on the exercise price (i.e., the exercise price would be $34.20). As a result, the fair value of the share alternative on the grant date is $8.80.

Required:
Determine the fair value of the stock options at the grant date and the amount to be recognized as compensation expense in Year 1.

39. Indicate whether each of the following describes an accounting treatment that is acceptable under IFRS, U.S. GAAP, both, or neither by checking the appropriate box.

	Acceptable Under			
	IFRS	**U.S. GAAP**	**Both**	**Neither**
• Bank overdrafts are netted against cash rather than being recognized as a liability when overdrafts are a normal part of cash management.				
• Uncertain legal obligations, but not constructive obligations, contingent upon a future event are recognized as liabilities when certain criteria are met.				
• A defined benefit pension liability is measured as the excess of the present value of the defined benefit obligation (PVDBO) over the fair value of plan assets (FVPA).				
• Actuarial gains and losses in a defined benefit pension plan are amortized to net income over a period of time.				
• The compensation cost associated with graded-vesting stock options is amortized to expense on a straight-line basis over the vesting period.				
• The minimum amount recognized as compensation expense on a stock option plan is the compensation cost as measured at the grant date, even if a subsequent modification to the plan decreases the total compensation cost.				
• Deferred taxes are classified as current or noncurrent based on the classification of the related asset or liability.				
• The stage-of-completion method is used to recognize revenue from service transactions when specified criteria are met.				
• Nonredeemable preferred shares are classified as a liability on the balance sheet.				
• Costs associated with the issuance of debt are amortized on a straight-line basis over the life of the debt.				

Case 5-1

S. A. Harrington Company

S. A. Harrington Company is a U.S.-based company that prepares its consolidated financial statements in accordance with U.S. GAAP. The company reported income in 2015 of $5,000,000 and stockholders' equity at December 31, 2015, of $40,000,000.

The CFO of S. A. Harrington has learned that the U.S. Securities and Exchange Commission is considering requiring U.S. companies to use IFRS in preparing consolidated financial statements. The company wishes to determine the impact that a switch to IFRS would have on its financial statements and has engaged you to prepare a reconciliation of income and stockholders' equity from U.S. GAAP to IFRS. You have identified the following five areas in which S. A. Harrington's accounting principles based on U.S. GAAP differ from IFRS.

1. Restructuring
2. Pension plan
3. Stock options
4. Revenue recognition
5. Bonds payable

The CFO provides the following information with respect to each of these accounting differences.

Restructuring Provision

The company publicly announced a restructuring plan in 2015 that created a valid expectation on the part of the employees to be terminated that the company will carry out the restructuring. The company estimated that the restructuring would cost $300,000. No legal obligation to restructure exists as of December 31, 2015.

Pension Plan

In 2013, the company amended its pension plan, creating a past service cost of $60,000. The past service cost was attributable to already vested employees who had an average remaining service life of 15 years. The company has no retired employees.

Stock Options

Stock options were granted to key officers on January 1, 2015. The grant date fair value per option was $10, and a total of 9,000 options were granted. The options vest in equal installments over three years: one-third vest in 2014, one-third in 2015, and one-third in 2016. The company uses a straight-line method to recognize compensation expense related to stock options.

Revenue Recognition

The company entered into a contract in 2015 to provide engineering services to a long-term customer over a 12-month period. The fixed price is $250,000, and the company estimates with a high degree of reliability that the project is 30 percent complete at the end of 2015.

Bonds Payable

On January 1, 2014, the company issued $10,000,000 of 5 percent bonds at par value that mature in five years on December 31, 2018. Costs incurred in issuing the bonds were $500,000. Interest is paid on the bonds annually.

Required

Prepare a reconciliation schedule to reconcile 2015 net income and December 31, 2015, stockholders' equity from a U.S. GAAP basis to IFRS. Ignore income taxes. Prepare a note to explain each adjustment made in the reconciliation schedule.

Chapter **Seven**

Foreign Currency Transactions and Hedging Foreign Exchange Risk

Learning Objectives

After reading this chapter, you should be able to

- Provide an overview of the foreign exchange market.
- Explain how fluctuations in exchange rates give rise to foreign exchange risk.
- Demonstrate the accounting for foreign currency transactions.
- Describe how foreign currency forward contracts and foreign currency options can be used to hedge foreign exchange risk.
- Describe the concepts of cash flow hedges, fair value hedges, and hedge accounting.
- Demonstrate the accounting for forward contracts and options used as cash flow hedges and fair value hedges to hedge foreign currency assets and liabilities, foreign currency firm commitments, and forecasted foreign currency transactions.

INTRODUCTION

International trade (imports and exports) constitutes a significant portion of the world economy. According to the World Trade Organization, more than $18 trillion worth of merchandise was exported (and imported) in 2011.[1] Recent growth in trade has been phenomenal. From 1990 to 2001, global exports increased by 75 percent while global gross domestic product increased by only 27 percent.

The number of companies involved in trade also has grown substantially. From 1987 to 1999, the number of U.S. companies making export sales rose by 233 percent to a total of 231,420 companies.[2] Raytheon Company is a U.S.-based electronics and defense systems company with more than $6.2 billion of annual export

---

[1] World Trade Organization, *International Trade Statistics 2012*, Table I.7: Leading Exporters and Importers in World Merchandise Trade, 2012 (www.wto.org).

[2] U.S. Department of Commerce, International Trade Administration, "Small and Medium-Sized Enterprises Play an Important Role," *Export America*, September 2001, pp. 26–29.

sales. In 2012, 25 percent of Raytheon's sales were outside of the United States.[3] Even small businesses are significantly involved in exporting. Companies with fewer than 500 workers comprise 97 percent of U.S. exporters.

Collections from export sales or payments for imports are not always made in a company's domestic currency; they may be made in a foreign currency depending on the negotiated terms of the transaction. As the exchange rate for the foreign currency fluctuates, so does the domestic currency value of these export sales and import purchases. Companies often find it necessary to engage in some form of hedging activity to reduce losses arising from fluctuating exchange rates. For example, at the end of 2012, Raytheon reported having "foreign currency forward contracts with commercial banks to fix the foreign currency exchange rates on specific commitments, payments, and receipts."[4] At December 31, 2012, the company had outstanding foreign currency contracts to buy or sell foreign currency in the amount of $1,305 million. At year-end 2012, Italian automaker Fiat SpA reported having contracts to hedge foreign exchange risks amounting to 10.5 billion euros (approximately $13.8 billion at the time).

This chapter covers accounting issues related to foreign currency transactions and foreign currency hedging activities. To provide background for subsequent discussion of the accounting issues, we begin with a description of foreign exchange markets. We then discuss the accounting for import and export transactions, followed by coverage of various types of hedging techniques. The discussion concentrates on forward contracts and options because these are the most popular types of hedging instruments. Understanding how to account for these items is important for any company engaged in international transactions.

FOREIGN EXCHANGE MARKETS

Each country uses its own currency as the unit of value for the purchase and sale of goods and services. The currency used in the United States is the U.S. dollar, the currency used in Japan is the Japanese yen, and so on. If a U.S. citizen travels to Japan and wishes to purchase local goods, Japanese merchants require payment to be made in Japanese yen. To make the purchase, a U.S. citizen has to purchase yen using U.S. dollars. The price at which the foreign currency can be acquired is known as the *foreign exchange rate.* A variety of factors determine the exchange rate between two currencies; unfortunately for those engaged in international business, the exchange rate fluctuates.[5] In some cases, a change in the exchange rate is quite large and unexpected.

Exchange Rate Mechanisms

Exchange rates have not always fluctuated. During the period 1945–1973, countries fixed the par value of their currency in terms of the U.S. dollar, and the value of the U.S. dollar was fixed in terms of gold. Countries agreed to maintain the value of their currency within 1 percent of the par value. If the exchange rate for a particular currency began to move outside of this 1 percent range, the country's

---

[3] Raytheon Company, 2012 Annual Report, p. 122.

[4] Ibid., p. 90.

[5] Several theories attempt to explain exchange rate fluctuations, but with little success, at least in the short run. A discussion of exchange rate determination can be found in any international finance textbook. An understanding of the causes of exchange rate changes is not necessary for an understanding of the concepts underlying the accounting for changes in exchange rates.

central bank was required to intervene by buying or selling its currency in the foreign exchange market. Due to the law of supply and demand, the purchase of currency by a central bank would cause the price of the currency to stop falling, and the sale of currency would cause the price to stop rising.

The integrity of the system hinged on the ability of the U.S. dollar to maintain its value in terms of gold and the ability of foreign countries to convert their U.S.-dollar holdings into gold at the fixed rate of $35 per ounce. As the United States began to incur balance-of-payment deficits in the 1960s, a glut of U.S. dollars arose worldwide, and foreign countries began converting their U.S. dollars into gold. This resulted in a decline in the U.S. government's gold reserve from a high of $24.6 billion in 1949 to a low of $10.2 billion in 1971. In the latter year, the United States suspended the convertibility of the U.S. dollar into gold, signaling the beginning of the end for the fixed exchange rate system. In March 1973, most currencies were allowed to float in value.

Today, several different currency arrangements exist. The following are some of the more important ones and the countries they affect:

1. *Independent float.* The value of the currency is allowed to fluctuate freely according to market forces, with little or no intervention from the central bank (Australia, Brazil, Canada, Japan, Mexico, Sweden, Switzerland, United States).
2. *Pegged to another currency.* The value of the currency is fixed (pegged) in terms of a particular foreign currency, and the central bank intervenes as necessary to maintain the fixed value. For example, several countries peg their currency to the U.S. dollar (including the Bahamas and Ecuador).
3. *European Monetary System (euro).* In 1998, the countries comprising the European Monetary System adopted a common currency called the euro and established the European Central Bank.[6] Until 2002, local currencies such as the German mark and French franc continued to exist but were fixed in value in terms of the euro. On January 1, 2002, local currencies disappeared and the euro became the currency in 12 European countries. In 2013, 17 countries were members of the "euro zone." The value of the euro floats against other currencies such as the U.S. dollar.

Foreign Exchange Rates

Exchange rates between the U.S. dollar and most foreign currencies are published daily in major U.S. newspapers. Current and past exchange rates are readily obtainable from a variety of Web sites, such as OANDA.com and X-rates.com. U.S. dollar exchange rates at various dates for selected foreign currencies are presented in Exhibit 7.1. These are interbank rates, or wholesale prices, that banks charge one another when exchanging currencies. Prices charged when selling foreign currency to retail customers such as companies engaged in international business are higher, and prices offered to buy foreign currency from retail customers are lower. The difference between the buying and selling rates is the spread through which banks and other foreign exchange brokers earn a profit on foreign exchange trades.

The exchange rates in Exhibit 7.1 reflect the U.S. dollar price for one unit of foreign currency. These are known as direct quotes. The direct quote for the UK pound on May 24, 2013, was $1.511701; in other words, one British pound could be purchased for $1.511701. Indirect quotes indicate the number of foreign currency

---

[6] Most long-term members of the European Union (EU) are euro-zone countries. The major exception is the United Kingdom, which decided not to participate. Switzerland is another important European country that is not part of the euro zone because it is not a member of the EU.

units that can be purchased with one U.S. dollar. Indirect quotes are simply the inverse of direct quotes. If one British pound costs $1.511701, then $1.00 can purchase only 0.661506 (1/1.511701) British pounds; the indirect quote would be 0.661506. To avoid confusion, direct quotes are used exclusively in this chapter.

Exhibit 7.1 shows the U.S. dollar price for one unit of foreign currency at four dates: April 23, 2012, one year later on April 23, 2013, one month later on May 23, 2013, and one day later on May 24, 2013. The percentage changes from one date to the next also are presented. Four of the currencies presented in Exhibit 7.1 increased in price or appreciated against the U.S. dollar from May 23 to May 24, 2013 (Bahraini dinar, Brazilian real, Chinese yuan, and Swiss franc), and five of the currencies depreciated against the U.S. dollar on that same day (euro, Mexican peso, Taiwanese new dollar, Thai baht, and British pound). However, the percentage change by which foreign currencies appreciated or depreciated against the U.S. dollar varied considerably, from 0.02 percent for the Chinese yuan to 5.8 percent for the Swiss franc. Other than the Chinese yuan, all of the currencies in Exhibit 7.1 weakened against the U.S. dollar in the month from April 23 to May 23, 2013, with the Thai baht experiencing the greatest percentage decrease (−3.70%). Over the year April 23, 2012, to April 23, 2013, five currencies fell against the U.S. dollar, with the Brazilian real experiencing the greatest percentage decrease (−6.43%), and four currencies strengthened against the U.S. dollar, with both the Mexican peso and Thai baht experiencing a greater than 7 percent increase in value over the year. The percentage changes reported in Exhibit 7.1 demonstrate the great variability that exists in exchange rate changes in terms of both magnitude and direction; exchange rates fluctuate constantly.

EXHIBIT 7.1
Foreign Exchange Rates
U.S. Dollar per Foreign Currency
(Direct Quotes)

Country (currency)	Apr. 23, 2012 $ per FC	Apr. 23, 2013 $ per FC	May 23, 2013 $ per FC	May 24, 2013 $ per FC
Bahrain (dinar)	2.652350	2.652876	2.651821	2.653227
Brazil (real)	0.530104	0.496020	0.486914	0.487346
China (yuan)	0.158550	0.161760	0.163014	0.163049
Euro	1.312792	1.301400	1.295479	1.291670
Mexico (peso)	0.075705	0.081665	0.080217	0.079843
Switzerland (franc)	1.092499	1.060788	1.033976	1.093979
Taiwan (new dollar)	0.033887	0.033568	0.033424	0.033399
Thailand (baht)	0.032230	0.034686	0.033401	0.033361
United Kingdom (pound)	1.610086	1.526615	1.512983	1.511701

Country (currency)	% Change for the Year[a]	% Change for the Month[b]	% Change for the Day[c]
Bahrain (dinar)	0.02	−0.04	0.05
Brazil (real)	−6.43	−1.84	0.09
China (yuan)	2.02	0.78	0.02
Euro	−0.87	−0.45	−0.29
Mexico (peso)	7.87	−1.77	−0.47
Switzerland (franc)	−2.90	−2.53	5.80
Taiwan (new dollar)	−0.94	−0.43	−0.07
Thailand (baht)	7.62	−3.70	−0.12
United Kingdom (pound)	−5.18	−0.89	−0.08

[a] From April 23, 2012, to April 23, 2013.
[b] From April 23, 2013, to May 23, 2013.
[c] From May 23, 2013, to May 24, 2013.

Fluctuating exchange rates introduce considerable uncertainty with respect to the cash flows associated with foreign currency transactions. Assume that a U.S. exporter sold parts to a Brazilian customer on April 23, 2013, with payment of 100,000 Brazilian reals (BRL) to be received on May 23, 2013. On April 23, 2013, the U.S. dollar equivalent value of the sale was $49,602 (BRL 100,000 × $0.49602). On May 23, 2013, the U.S. exporter receives BRL 100,000 from the customer and sells them at the spot exchange rate of $0.486914, receiving $48,692, which is $910 less than would have been received on April 23, 2013, when the parts were sold. The important point to understand is that, because of fluctuating exchange rates, on April 23, when the sale is made, the U.S. exporter does not know how many U.S. dollars it will receive on May 23 as a result of the sale.

Spot and Forward Rates

Foreign currency trades can be executed on a *spot* or *forward* basis. The *spot rate* is the price at which a foreign currency can be purchased or sold today. In contrast, the *forward rate* is the price today at which foreign currency can be purchased or sold sometime in the future. Because many international business transactions take some time to be completed, the ability to lock in a price today at which foreign currency can be purchased or sold at some future date has definite advantages.

The *Wall Street Journal* publishes forward rates quoted by New York banks for several major currencies (Canadian dollar, Japanese yen, Swiss franc, and British pound) on a daily basis. This is only a partial listing of possible forward contracts. A firm and its bank can tailor forward contracts in other currencies and for other time periods to meet the needs of the firm. There is no up-front cost to enter into a forward contract.

The forward rate can exceed the spot rate on a given date, in which case the foreign currency is said to be selling at a *premium* in the forward market, or the forward rate can be less than the spot rate, in which case it is selling at a *discount*. Currencies sell at a premium or a discount because of differences in interest rates between two countries. When the interest rate in the foreign country exceeds the interest rate domestically, the foreign currency sells at a discount in the forward market. Conversely, if the foreign interest rate is less than the domestic rate, the foreign currency sells at a premium.[7] Forward rates are said to be unbiased predictors of the future spot rate.

The spot rate for Swiss francs on April 15, 2013, was $1.0738, indicating that 1 franc could have been purchased on that date for $1.0738. On the same day, the one-month forward rate was $1.0741. The Swiss franc was selling at a premium in the one-month forward market. By entering into a forward contract on April 15, it was possible to guarantee that Swiss francs could be purchased one month later at a price of $1.0741 per franc, regardless of what the spot rate turned out to be on that date. Entering into the forward contract to purchase francs would have been beneficial if the spot rate in one month turned out to be greater than $1.0741. However, such a forward contract would have been detrimental if the future spot rate turned out to be less than $1.0741. In either case, the forward contract must be honored and Swiss francs must be purchased at $1.0741.

On the same day that the Swiss franc was selling at a premium in the forward market, the British pound was selling at a discount. On April 15, 2013, when the British pound spot rate was $1.5284, a U.S. importer of British goods could have locked in a rate of only $1.5282 to purchase British pounds in one month. This

---

[7] This relationship is based on the theory of interest rate parity, which indicates that the difference in national interest rates should be equal to but opposite in sign to the forward rate discount or premium. This topic is covered in detail in international finance textbooks.

action would eliminate the risk to the importer that the British pound might actually appreciate against the U.S. dollar over the next month, which would increase the U.S.-dollar cost of the British imports.[8]

Option Contracts

To provide companies more flexibility than exists with a forward contract, a market for *foreign currency options* has developed. A foreign currency option gives the holder of the option *the right but not the obligation* to trade foreign currency in the future. A *put option* is for the sale of foreign currency by the holder of the option; a *call option* is for the purchase of foreign currency by the holder of the option. The *strike price* is the exchange rate at which the option will be executed if the holder of the option decides to exercise the option. The strike price is similar to a forward rate. There are generally several strike prices to choose from at any particular time. Most foreign currency options are purchased directly from a bank in the so-called over-the-counter market, but they also may be purchased on the Philadelphia Stock Exchange and the Chicago Mercantile Exchange.

Unlike forward contracts, where banks earn their profit through the spread between buying and selling rates, options must actually be purchased by paying an *option premium*. The option premium is a function of two components: intrinsic value and time value. The *intrinsic value* of an option is equal to the gain that could be realized by exercising the option immediately. For example, if the spot rate for a foreign currency is $1.00, a call option (to purchase foreign currency) with a strike price of $0.97 has an intrinsic value of $0.03, whereas a put option (to sell foreign currency) with a strike price of $1.00 or less has an intrinsic value of zero. An option with a positive intrinsic value is said to be "in the money."

The *time value* of an option relates to the fact that the spot rate can change over time and cause the option to become in the money. Even though a 90-day call option with a strike price of $1.00 has zero intrinsic value when the spot rate is $1.00, it will still have a positive time value because there is a chance that the spot rate could increase over the next 90 days and bring the option into the money.

The value of a foreign currency option can be determined by applying an adaptation of the Black-Scholes option pricing formula. This formula is discussed in detail in international finance books. In very general terms, the value of an option is a function of the difference between the current spot rate and strike price, the difference between domestic and foreign interest rates, the length of time to expiration, and the potential volatility of changes in the spot rate. In this book, we will give the premium originally paid for a foreign currency option and its subsequent fair value up to the date of expiration derived from applying the pricing formula.

FOREIGN CURRENCY TRANSACTIONS

Export sales and import purchases are international transactions. When two parties from different countries enter into a transaction, they must decide which of the two countries' currencies to use to settle the transaction. For example, if a U.S. computer manufacturer sells to a customer in Japan, the parties must decide whether the transaction will be denominated (i.e., whether payment will be made) in U.S. dollars or Japanese yen. In some cases, a third country's currency might be used to denominate the transaction.

---

[8] As it turned out, the spot rate for British pounds on May 15, 2013, was $1.5210, so entering into a forward contract on April 15 to purchase pounds at $1.5282 on May 15 would not have been beneficial.

Assume that a U.S. exporter (Eximco) sells goods to a Spanish customer with payment to be made in euros. In this situation, Eximco has entered into a foreign currency transaction. It must restate the euro amount that actually will be received into U.S. dollars to account for this transaction. This is because Eximco keeps its books and prepares financial statements in U.S. dollars. Although the Spanish importer has entered into an international transaction, it does not have a foreign currency transaction (payment will be made in its home currency) and no restatement is necessary.

Assume that, as is customary in its industry, Eximco does not require immediate payment and allows its Spanish customer three months to pay for its purchases. By doing this, Eximco runs the risk that from the date the sale is made until the date of payment, the euro might decrease in value (depreciate) against the U.S. dollar and the actual number of U.S. dollars generated from the sale will be less than expected. In this situation, Eximco is said to have an *exposure to foreign exchange risk*. Specifically, Eximco has a *transaction exposure*.

Transaction exposure can be summarized as follows:

- *Export sale.* A transaction exposure exists when the exporter allows the buyer to pay in a foreign currency and also allows the buyer to pay sometime after the sale has been made. The exporter is exposed to the risk that the foreign currency might decrease in value between the date of sale and the date of payment, thereby decreasing the amount of domestic currency (U.S. dollars for Eximco) into which the foreign currency can be converted.

- *Import purchase.* A transaction exposure exists when the importer is required to pay in foreign currency and is allowed to pay sometime after the purchase has been made. The importer is exposed to the risk that the foreign currency might increase in price (appreciate) between the date of purchase and the date of payment, thereby increasing the amount of domestic currency that has to be paid for the imported goods.

Accounting Issue

The major issue in accounting for foreign currency transactions is how to deal with the change in the domestic-currency value of the sales revenue and account receivable resulting from the export when the foreign currency changes in value. The corollary issue is how to deal with the change in the domestic-currency value of the foreign currency account payable and goods being acquired in an import purchase.

Assume that Eximco sells goods to a Spanish customer at a price of 1 million euros (€) when the spot exchange rate is $1.50 per euro. If payment were received at the date of sale, Eximco could have converted €1,000,000 into $1,500,000, and this amount clearly would be the amount at which the sales revenue would be recognized. Instead, Eximco allows the Spanish customer three months to pay for its purchase. At the end of three months, the euro has depreciated to $1.48, and Eximco is able to convert the €1,000,000 received on that date into only $1,480,000. How should Eximco account for this $20,000 decrease in value?

Accounting Alternatives

Conceptually, the two methods of accounting for changes in the value of a foreign currency transaction are the one-transaction perspective and the two-transaction perspective. The *one-transaction perspective* assumes that an export sale is not complete until the foreign currency receivable has been collected and converted into U.S. dollars. Any change in the U.S.-dollar value of the foreign currency will be accounted for as an adjustment to Accounts Receivable and to Sales. Under this perspective, Eximco would ultimately report Sales at $1,480,000 and an increase in the Cash account of the same amount. This approach can be criticized because it hides the fact that the company could have received $1,500,000 if the Spanish customer had been required to pay at the date of sale. The company incurs a $20,000 loss because of the depreciation in the euro, but that loss is buried in an adjustment to Sales. This approach is not acceptable under either International Financial Reporting Standards (IFRS) or U.S. GAAP.

Instead, both International Accounting Standard (IAS) 21, *The Effects of Changes in Foreign Exchange Rates*, and FASB ASC 830, *Foreign Currency Matters*, require companies to use a *two-transaction perspective* in accounting for foreign currency transactions. This perspective treats the export sale and the subsequent collection of cash as two separate transactions. Because management has made two decisions—(1) to make the export sale, and (2) to extend credit in foreign currency to the customer— the income effect from each of these decisions should be reported separately.

Under the two-transaction perspective, Eximco records the U.S. dollar value of the sale at the date the sale occurs. At that point, the sale has been completed; there are no subsequent adjustments to the Sales account. Any difference between the number of U.S. dollars that could have been received at the date of sale and the number of U.S. dollars actually received at the date of payment due to fluctuations in the exchange rate is a result of the decision to extend foreign currency credit to the customer. This difference is treated as a Foreign Exchange Gain or Loss that is reported separately from Sales in the income statement. Using the two-transaction perspective to account for its export sale to Spain, Eximco would make the following journal entries:

Date of Sale:	Accounts Receivable (€)......................	1,500,000	
	Sales................................		1,500,000
	To record the sale and euro receivable at the spot rate of $1.50.		
Date of Payment:	Foreign Exchange Loss.......................	20,000	
	Accounts Receivable (€)		20,000
	To adjust the U.S.-dollar value of the euro receivable to the new spot rate of $1.48 and record a foreign exchange loss resulting from the depreciation in the euro.		
	Cash......................................	1,480,000	
	Accounts Receivable (€)		1,480,000
	To record the receipt of €1,000,000 and conversion into U.S. dollars at the spot rate of $1.48.		

Sales are reported in income at the amount that would have been received if the customer had not been given three months to pay the €1,000,000, that is, $1,500,000. A separate Foreign Exchange Loss of $20,000 is reported in income to indicate that because of the decision to extend foreign currency credit to the Spanish customer and because the euro decreased in value, fewer U.S. dollars are actually received.[9]

[9] Note that the foreign exchange loss results because the customer is allowed to pay in euros and is given 30 days to pay. If the transaction were denominated in U.S. dollars, no loss would result. There would also be no loss if the euros had been received at the date the sale was made.

Note that Eximco keeps its Account Receivable (€) account separate from its U.S.-dollar receivables. Companies engaged in international trade need to keep separate payable and receivable accounts in each of the currencies in which they have transactions. Each foreign currency receivable and payable should have a separate account number in the company's chart of accounts.

We can summarize the relationship between fluctuations in exchange rates and foreign exchange gains and losses as follows:

		Foreign Currency (FC)	
Transaction	**Type of Exposure**	**Appreciates**	**Depreciates**
Export sale	Asset	Gain	Loss
Import purchase	Liability	Loss	Gain

A foreign currency receivable arising from an export sale creates an *asset exposure* to foreign exchange risk. If the foreign currency appreciates, the foreign currency asset increases in terms of domestic-currency value and a foreign exchange gain arises; depreciation of the foreign currency causes a foreign exchange loss. A foreign currency payable arising from an import purchase creates a *liability exposure* to foreign exchange risk. If the foreign currency appreciates, the foreign currency liability increases in domestic-currency value and a foreign exchange loss results; depreciation of the currency results in a foreign exchange gain.

Balance Sheet Date before Date of Payment

The question arises as to what accounting should be done if a balance sheet date falls between the date of sale and the date of payment. For example, assume that Eximco shipped goods to its Spanish customer on December 10, Year 1, with payment to be received on March 1, Year 2. Assume that at December 10 the spot rate for euros is $1.50, but by December 31 the euro has appreciated to $1.51. Is any adjustment needed at December 31, Year 1, when the books are closed to account for the fact that the foreign currency receivable has changed in U.S. dollar value since December 10?

The general consensus worldwide is that a foreign currency receivable or foreign currency payable should be revalued at the balance sheet date to account for the change in exchange rates. Under the two-transaction perspective, this means that a foreign exchange gain or loss arises at the balance sheet date. The next question, then, is what should be done with these foreign exchange gains and losses that have not yet been realized in cash. Should they be included in net income?

The two approaches to accounting for unrealized foreign exchange gains and losses are the deferral approach and the accrual approach. Under the *deferral approach,* unrealized foreign exchange gains and losses are deferred on the balance sheet until cash is actually paid or received. When cash is paid or received, a *realized* foreign exchange gain or loss would be included in income. This approach is not acceptable under either IFRS or U.S. GAAP.

IAS 21 (as well as FASB ASC 830) requires companies to use the *accrual approach* to account for unrealized foreign exchange gains and losses. Under this approach, a firm reports unrealized foreign exchange gains and losses in net income in the period in which the exchange rate changes. The FASB justified this approach by saying: "This is consistent with accrual accounting; it results in reporting the effect of a rate change that will have cash flow effects when the event causing the effect takes place."[10] Thus, any change in the exchange rate from the date of sale to the balance sheet date would result in a foreign exchange gain or loss to be reported in income in that period. Any change in the exchange rate from the balance sheet date to the date of payment would result in a second foreign exchange gain or loss that would be reported in the second accounting period. The journal entries Eximco would make under the accrual approach would be as follows:

12/1/Y1	Accounts Receivable (€)............................	1,500,000	
	Sales.....................................		1,500,000
	To record the sale and euro receivable at the spot rate of $1.50.		
12/31/Y1	Accounts Receivable (€)............................	10,000	
	Foreign Exchange Gain......................		10,000
	To adjust the value of the euro receivable to the new spot rate of $1.51 and record a foreign exchange gain resulting from the appreciation in the euro since December 10.		
3/1/Y2	Foreign Exchange Loss............................	30,000	
	Accounts Receivable (€).....................		30,000
	To adjust the value of the euro receivable to the new spot rate of $1.48 and record a foreign exchange loss resulting from the depreciation in the euro since December 31.		
	Cash...................................	1,480,000	
	Accounts Receivable (€).....................		1,480,000
	To record the receipt of €1,000,000 and conversion at the spot rate of $1.48.		

The net impact on income in Year 1 includes Sales of $1,500,000 and a Foreign Exchange Gain of $10,000; in Year 2, a Foreign Exchange Loss of $30,000 is recorded. This results in a net increase in Retained Earnings of $1,480,000 that is balanced by an equal increase in Cash.[11]

One criticism of the accrual approach is that it leads to a *violation of conservatism* when an unrealized foreign exchange gain arises at the balance sheet date. In fact, this is one of only two situations in U.S. GAAP (the other relates to trading marketable securities reported at market value) where it is acceptable to recognize an unrealized gain in income. Historically, several European Union (EU) countries (such as Germany and Austria) more strictly adhered to the concept of conservatism. In those countries, if at the balance sheet date the exchange rate had changed such that an unrealized gain had arisen, the change in exchange rate was ignored and the foreign currency account receivable or payable continued to be carried on the balance sheet at the exchange rate that existed at the date of the transaction. In contrast, if the exchange rate had changed to cause a foreign exchange loss, the account receivable would have been revalued and an unrealized loss would have been recorded and reported in income. This is a classic application of conservatism. With

[10] FASB Statement No. 52, *Foreign Currency Translation* (Stamford, CT, 1981), para. 124.

[11] Note that the journal entries recorded at March 1, Year 2, could have been combined into the following single entry:

3/1/Y2	Foreign Exchange Loss............................	30,000	
	Cash...................................	1,480,000	
	Accounts Receivable (€).....................		1,510,000

the introduction of the requirement to use IFRS, this practice is no longer used by EU-based companies in preparing consolidated financial statements.

All foreign currency assets and liabilities carried on a company's books must be restated at the balance sheet date. In addition to foreign currency payables and receivables arising from import and export transactions, companies also might have dividends receivable from foreign subsidiaries, loans payable to foreign lenders, lease payments receivable from foreign customers, and so on that are denominated in a foreign currency and therefore must be restated at the balance sheet date. Each of these foreign-currency-denominated assets and liabilities is exposed to foreign exchange risk; therefore, fluctuations in the exchange rate will result in foreign exchange gains and losses.

Many U.S. companies report foreign exchange gains and losses on the income statement in a line item often titled "Other Income (Expense)." Other incidental gains and losses such as gains and losses on sales of assets would be included in this line item as well. Companies must disclose the magnitude of foreign exchange gains and losses if material. For example, in the Notes to Financial Statements in its 2012 annual report, Merck & Company Inc. indicated that the income statement item "Other (Income) Expense, Net" included exchange losses of $185 million in 2012, $143 million in 2011, and $214 million in 2010.[12]

HEDGING FOREIGN EXCHANGE RISK

In the preceding example, Eximco has an asset exposure in euros when it sells goods to the Spanish customer and it allows the customer three months to pay for its purchase. If the euro depreciates over the next three months, Eximco incurs a foreign exchange loss. For many companies, the uncertainty of not knowing exactly how much domestic currency will be received on this export sale is of great concern. To avoid this uncertainty, companies often use foreign currency derivatives to hedge against the effect of unfavorable changes in the value of foreign currencies.[13] The two most common derivatives used to hedge foreign exchange risk are foreign currency forward contracts and foreign currency options. Through a forward contract, Eximco can lock in the price at which it will sell the euros it receives in three months. An option establishes a price at which Eximco will be able, but is not required, to sell the euros it receives in three months. If Eximco enters into a forward contract or purchases an option on the date the sale is made, the derivative is being used as a *hedge of a recognized foreign-currency-denominated asset* (the euro account receivable).

Companies engaged in foreign currency activities often enter into hedging arrangements as soon as a noncancelable sales order is received or a noncancelable purchase order is placed. A noncancelable order that specifies the foreign currency price and date of delivery is a known as a *foreign currency firm commitment*. Assume that, on April 1, Eximco accepts an order to sell parts to a customer in Thailand at a price of 20 million Thai baht. The parts will be delivered and payment will be received on May 15. On April 1, before the sale has been made, Eximco enters into a forward contract to sell 20 million Thai baht on May 15. In this case, Eximco is using a foreign currency derivative as a *hedge of an unrecognized foreign currency firm commitment*.

[12] Merck & Company, Inc., Form 10-K, 2012, Note 15, Other (Income) Expense, Net, p. 126.

[13] A derivative is a financial instrument whose value changes in response to the change in a specified interest rate, security price, commodity price, index of prices or rates, or other variable. The value of a foreign currency derivative changes in response to changes in foreign exchange rates.

Some companies have foreign currency transactions that occur on a regular basis and can be reliably forecast. For example, Eximco regularly purchases components from a supplier in Singapore, making payment in Singapore dollars. Even if Eximco has no contract to make future purchases, it has an exposure to foreign currency risk if it plans to continue making purchases from the Singapore supplier. Assume that, on October 1, Eximco forecasts that it will make a purchase from the Singapore supplier in one month. To hedge against a possible increase in the price of the Singapore dollar, Eximco acquires a call option on October 1 to purchase Singapore dollars in one month. The foreign currency option represents a *hedge of a forecasted foreign-currency-denominated transaction.*

ACCOUNTING FOR DERIVATIVES

In the development of a core set of standards for global use, the International Organization of Securities Commissions (IOSCO) required the International Accounting Standards Board (IASB) to include a standard on the recognition and measurement of financial instruments, off-balance-sheet items, and hedging activities. In 1988, the IASB embarked on a joint project with the Canadian Institute of Chartered Accountants to develop a comprehensive standard in this area. Due to the critical response to an early Exposure Draft, the project was subsequently divided into two parts, and IAS 32, *Financial Instruments: Disclosure and Presentation,* was issued in 1995. Work continued on the recognition and measurement dimensions of the project, with a discussion paper published in 1997. Comments on the discussion paper raised numerous issues that caused the IASB to conclude that developing a final standard in the near term was not possible. Therefore, to provide users of IFRS with some guidance in this area, an interim statement, IAS 39, *Financial Statements: Recognition and Measurement,* was issued in 1999. The IASB continues to work on an integrated standard on financial instruments.[14] IAS 39 provides the following general principles with respect to the accounting for derivatives:

1. All derivatives should be reported on the balance sheet at fair value (off-balance-sheet treatment is not acceptable).
2. "Hedge accounting" is acceptable for those derivatives used for hedging purposes provided the hedging relationship is clearly defined, measurable, and actually effective.

Hedge accounting is described in more detail later in this chapter.

IAS 39 (as well as FASB ASC 830) provides guidance for hedges of the following sources of foreign exchange risk:

1. Recognized foreign-currency-denominated assets and liabilities.
2. Unrecognized foreign currency firm commitments.
3. Forecast foreign-currency-denominated transactions.
4. Net investments in foreign operations.

Different accounting applies to each of these different types of foreign currency hedge. This chapter demonstrates the accounting for the first three types of hedge. Hedges of net investments in foreign operations are covered in Chapter 8.

---

[14] The IASB completed the first phase of its project to replace IAS 39 in November 2009 by issuing IFRS 9, *Financial Instruments.* IFRS 9 does not cover financial instruments used in hedging activities.

Fundamental Requirement of Derivatives Accounting

In accounting for derivative financial instruments, the fundamental requirement is that all derivatives must be carried on the balance sheet at their fair value. Derivatives are reported on the balance sheet as assets when they have a positive fair value and as liabilities when they have a negative fair value. The first issue in accounting for derivatives is the determination of fair value.

The fair value of derivatives can change over time, causing adjustments to be made to the carrying values of the assets and liabilities. The second issue in accounting for derivatives is the treatment of the unrealized gains and losses that arise from these adjustments.

Determining the Fair Value of Derivatives

The *fair value of a foreign currency forward contract* is determined by reference to changes in the forward rate over the life of the contract, discounted to the present value. Three pieces of information are needed to determine the fair value of a forward contract at any time:

1. The forward rate when the forward contract was entered into.
2. The current forward rate for a contract that matures on the same date as the forward contract entered into.
3. A discount rate—typically, the company's incremental borrowing rate.

Assume that Interco enters into a forward contract on November 1 to sell 1 million South African rand on May 1 at a forward rate of $0.15 per rand, or a total of $150,000. There is no cost to Interco to enter into the forward contract, and the forward contract has no value on November 1. On December 31, when Interco closes its books to prepare financial statements, the forward rate to sell South African rand on May 1 has changed to $0.147. On that date, a forward contract for the delivery of 1 million South African rand could be negotiated that would result in a cash inflow on May 1 of only $147,000. This represents a favorable change in the value of Interco's forward contract of $3,000 ($150,000 − $147,000). The fair value of the forward contract on December 31 is $3,000, discounted to its present value. Assuming that the company's incremental borrowing rate is 12 percent per annum, the fair value of the forward contract must be discounted at the rate of 1 percent per month for four months (from the current date of December 31 to the settlement date of May 1). The fair value of the forward contract at December 31 is $2,883 ($3,000 × 0.96098).[15]

The manner in which the *fair value of a foreign currency option* is determined depends on whether the option is traded on an exchange or has been acquired in the over-the-counter market. The fair value of an exchange-traded foreign currency option is its current market price quoted on the exchange. For over-the-counter options, fair value can be determined by obtaining a price quote from an option dealer (such as a bank). If dealer price quotes are unavailable, the company can estimate the value of an option using the modified Black-Scholes option pricing model (briefly mentioned earlier in this chapter). Regardless of who does the calculation, principles similar to those in the Black-Scholes pricing model will be used in determining the fair value of the option.

Accounting for Changes in the Fair Value of Derivatives

Changes in the fair value of derivatives must be included in comprehensive income. *Comprehensive income* is defined as all changes in equity from nonowner

---

[15] The present value factor for four months at 1 percent per month is calculated as $1/1.01^4$, or 0.96098.

sources and consists of two components: net income and other comprehensive income. *Other comprehensive income* consists of unrealized income items that accounting standards require to be deferred in stockholders' equity, such as gains and losses on available-for-sale marketable securities. Other comprehensive income is accumulated and reported as a separate line in the stockholders' equity section of the balance sheet. The account title *Accumulated Other Comprehensive Income* is used in this chapter to describe this stockholders' equity line item.

Gains and losses arising from changes in the fair value of derivatives are recognized initially either (1) on the income statement as a part of net income or (2) on the balance sheet as a component of other comprehensive income. Recognition treatment partly depends on whether the derivative is used for hedging purposes or for speculation.[16] For speculative derivatives, the change in the fair value of the derivative (the unrealized gain or loss) is recognized immediately in net income.[17] The accounting for changes in the fair value of derivatives used for hedging depends on the nature of the foreign exchange risk being hedged, and whether the derivative qualifies for hedge accounting.

HEDGE ACCOUNTING

Companies enter into hedging relationships to minimize the adverse effect that changes in exchange rates have on cash flows and net income. As such, companies would like to account for hedges in such a way that the gain or loss from the hedge is recognized in net income in the same period as the loss or gain on the risk being hedged. This approach is known as *hedge accounting.* Hedge accounting for foreign currency derivatives may be used only if three conditions are satisfied:

1. The derivative is used to hedge either a fair value exposure or cash flow exposure to foreign exchange risk.
2. The derivative is highly effective in offsetting changes in the fair value or cash flows related to the hedged item.
3. The derivative is properly documented as a hedge.

Each of these conditions is discussed in turn.

Nature of the Hedged Risk

A *fair value exposure* exists if changes in exchange rates can affect the fair value of an asset or liability reported on the balance sheet. To qualify for hedge accounting, the fair value risk must have the potential to affect net income if it is not hedged. For example, there is a fair value risk associated with a foreign currency account receivable. If the foreign currency depreciates, the receivable must be written down, with an offsetting loss recognized in net income. A fair value exposure also exists for foreign currency firm commitments.

---

[16] Companies can acquire derivative financial instruments as investments for speculative purposes. For example, assume the three-month forward rate for Swiss francs is $1.03, and a speculator believes the Swiss franc spot rate in three months will be $1.00. In that case, the speculator would enter into a three-month forward contract to sell Swiss francs. At the future date, the speculator purchases francs at the spot rate of $1.00 and sells them at the contracted forward rate of $1.03, reaping a gain of $0.03 per franc. Of course, such an investment might just as easily generate a loss if the spot rate does not move in the expected direction.

[17] In the next section, we will see that the change in fair value of a derivative designated as the fair value hedge of a foreign-currency-denominated asset or liability also is recognized immediately in net income.

A *cash flow exposure* exists if changes in exchange rates can affect the amount of cash flow to be realized from a transaction, with changes in cash flow reflected in net income. A cash flow exposure exists for (1) recognized foreign currency assets and liabilities, (2) foreign currency firm commitments, and (3) forecasted foreign currency transactions.

Derivatives for which companies wish to use hedge accounting must be designated as either a *fair value hedge* or a *cash flow hedge*. For hedges of recognized foreign currency assets and liabilities and hedges of foreign currency firm commitments, companies must choose between the two types of designation. Hedges of forecasted foreign currency transactions can qualify only as cash flow hedges. Accounting procedures differ for the two types of hedge. In general, gains and losses on fair value hedges are recognized immediately in net income, whereas gains and losses on cash flow hedges are included in other comprehensive income.[18]

Hedge Effectiveness

For hedge accounting to be used initially, the hedge must be expected to be highly effective in generating gains and losses that offset losses and gains on the item being hedged. The hedge actually must be effective in generating offsetting gains and losses for hedge accounting to continue to be applied.

At inception, a foreign currency derivative can be considered an effective hedge if the critical terms of the hedging instrument match those of the hedged item. Critical terms include the currency type, currency amount, and settlement date. For example, a forward contract to purchase 1 million Japanese yen in 30 days would be an effective hedge of a liability of 1 million Japanese yen that is payable in 30 days. Assessing hedge effectiveness on an ongoing basis can be accomplished using a cumulative dollar offset method.

Hedge Documentation

For hedge accounting to be applied, the hedging relationship must be formally documented at the inception of the hedge, that is, on the date a foreign currency forward contract is entered into or a foreign currency option is acquired. The hedging company must prepare a document that identifies the hedged item, the hedging instrument, the nature of the risk being hedged, how the hedging instrument's effectiveness will be assessed, and the risk management objective and strategy for undertaking the hedge.

HEDGING COMBINATIONS

The specific entries required to account for a foreign currency hedging relationship are determined by a combination of the following factors:

1. The type of item being hedged:
   a. Foreign-currency-denominated asset/liability,
   b. Foreign currency firm commitment, or
   c. Forecasted foreign currency transaction.

---

[18] Many companies choose not to designate derivatives used to hedge recognized foreign currency assets and liabilities as hedges per se. In that case, the derivative is accounted for in exactly the same manner as if it had been designated as a fair value hedge; gains and losses are recognized immediately. As a result, designating a hedge of a recognized foreign currency asset/liability as a fair value hedge is of no importance.

2. The nature of the item being hedged:
   a. Existing (or future) asset, or
   b. Existing (or future) liability.
3. The type of hedging instrument being used:
   a. Forward contract, or
   b. Option.
4. The nature of the hedged risk:
   a. Fair value exposure, or
   b. Cash flow exposure.

To measure the fair value of a firm commitment, a choice must be made between using

1. Changes in the spot rate, or
2. Changes in the forward rate.

We do not have enough space in this chapter to demonstrate the accounting for over 20 different combinations of hedging relationships. However, it is important to see the differences in accounting for (1) foreign-currency-denominated assets/ liabilities, (2) firm commitments, and (3) forecasted transactions. We show this by focusing on the accounting that would be done by an exporter who has an existing or future foreign currency asset. We also demonstrate the use of both forward contracts and options for different types of items being hedged, and we selectively demonstrate the accounting for fair value and cash flow hedges. The appendix to this chapter demonstrates the accounting for hedges entered into by an importer who has existing and future foreign currency liabilities.

HEDGES OF FOREIGN-CURRENCY-DENOMINATED ASSETS AND LIABILITIES

Hedges of foreign-currency-denominated assets and liabilities, such as accounts receivable and accounts payable, can qualify as either *cash flow hedges* or *fair value hedges*. To qualify as a cash flow hedge, the hedging instrument must completely offset the variability in the cash flows associated with the foreign currency receivable or payable. If the hedging instrument does not qualify as a cash flow hedge, or if the company elects not to designate the hedging instrument as a cash flow hedge, the hedge is designated as a fair value hedge. The following lists summarize the basic accounting for the two types of hedges.

Cash Flow Hedge

At each balance sheet date:

1. The hedged asset or liability is adjusted to fair value according to changes in the spot exchange rate, and a foreign exchange gain or loss is recognized in net income.
2. The derivative hedging instrument is adjusted to fair value (resulting in an asset or liability reported on the balance sheet), with the counterpart recognized as a change in accumulated other comprehensive income (AOCI).
3. An amount equal to the foreign exchange gain or loss on the hedged asset or liability is then transferred from AOCI to net income; the net effect is to offset any gain or loss on the hedged asset or liability.

4. An additional amount is removed from AOCI and recognized in net income to reflect (*a*) the current period's amortization of the original discount or premium on the forward contract (if a forward contract is the hedging instrument) or (*b*) the change in the *time value* of the option (if an option is the hedging instrument).

Fair Value Hedge
At each balance sheet date:

1. The hedged asset or liability is adjusted to fair value according to changes in the spot exchange rate, and a foreign exchange gain or loss is recognized in net income.
2. The derivative hedging instrument is adjusted to fair value (resulting in an asset or liability reported on the balance sheet), with the counterpart recognized as a gain or loss in net income.

FORWARD CONTRACT USED TO HEDGE A RECOGNIZED FOREIGN-CURRENCY-DENOMINATED ASSET

We now return to the Eximco example in which the company has a foreign currency account receivable to demonstrate the accounting for a hedge of a recognized foreign-currency-denominated asset. In the preceding example, Eximco has an asset exposure in euros when it sells goods to the Spanish customer and allows the customer three months to pay for its purchase. To hedge its exposure to a decline in the U.S. dollar value of the euro, Eximco decides to enter into a forward contract.

Assume that on December 1, Year 1, the three-month forward rate for euros is $1.485 and Eximco signs a contract with First National Bank to deliver €1,000,000 in three months in exchange for $1,485,000. No cash changes hands on December 1. Given that the spot rate on December 1 is $1.50, the euro is selling at a discount in the three-month forward market (the forward rate is less than the spot rate). Because the euro is selling at a discount of $0.015 per euro, Eximco receives $15,000 less than if payment had been received at the date the goods are delivered ($1,485,000 vs. $1,500,000). This $15,000 reduction in cash flow can be seen as an expense; it is the cost of extending foreign currency credit to the foreign customer.[19] Conceptually, this expense is similar to the transaction loss that arises on the export sale. It exists only because the transaction is denominated in a foreign currency. The major difference is that Eximco knows the exact amount of the discount expense at the date of sale, whereas, if the receivable is left unhedged, Eximco does not know the size of the transaction loss until three months pass. In fact, it is possible that the unhedged receivable could result in a transaction gain rather than a transaction loss.

Given that the future spot rate turns out to be only $1.48, selling euros at a forward rate of $1.485 is obviously better than leaving the euro receivable unhedged—Eximco will receive $5,000 more as a result of the hedge. This can be viewed as a gain resulting from the use of the forward contract. Unlike the discount expense, the exact size of this gain is not known until three months pass. (In fact, it is possible that use of the forward contract could result in an additional loss. This would occur if the spot rate on March 1, Year 2, is higher than the forward rate of $1.485.)

---

[19] This should not be confused with the cost associated with normal credit risk; that is, the risk that the customer will not pay for its purchase. That is a separate issue unrelated to the currency in which the transaction is denominated.

356   Chapter Seven

EXHIBIT 7.2   Hedge of a Foreign Currency Account Receivable with a Forward Contract

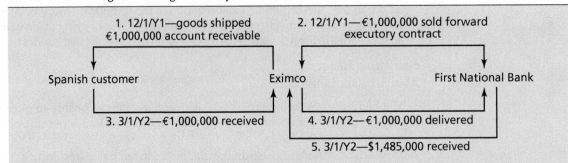

Steps on December 1, Year 1

1. Eximco ships the goods to the Spanish customer, thereby creating a €1,000,000 account receivable.

2. Eximco sells €1,000,000 three months forward to First National Bank, creating an executory contract to pay €1,000,000 and receive $1,485,000.

Steps on March 1, Year 2

3. The Spanish customer sends €1,000,000 to Eximco to settle the account receivable; Eximco now has €1,000,000 in foreign currency.

4. Eximco delivers €1,000,000 to First National Bank.

5. First National Bank pays Eximco $1,485,000.

Eximco must account for its foreign currency transaction and the related forward contract simultaneously but separately. The process can be better understood by referring to the steps involving the three parties—Eximco, the Spanish customer, and First National Bank—shown in Exhibit 7.2.

Because the settlement date, currency type, and currency amount of the forward contract match the corresponding terms of the account receivable, the hedge is expected to be highly effective. If Eximco properly designates the forward contract as a hedge of its euro account receivable position, hedge accounting may be applied. Because it completely offsets the variability in the cash flows related to the accounting receivable, the forward contract may be designated as a cash flow hedge. Alternatively, Eximco may elect to account for this forward contract as a fair value hedge.

In either case, Eximco determines the fair value of the forward contract by referring to the change in the forward rate for a contract maturing on March 1, Year 2. The relevant exchange rates, U.S.-dollar value of the euro receivable, and fair value of the forward contract are determined as follows:

		Account Receivable (€)		Forward Contract		
Date	Spot Rate	U.S.-Dollar Value	Change in U.S.-Dollar Value	Forward Rate to 3/1/Y2	Fair Value	Change in Fair Value
12/1/Y1	$1.50	$1,500,000	—	$1.485	$0	—
12/31/Y1	$1.51	$1,510,000	+$10,000	$1.496	$(10,783)*	−$10,783
3/1/Y2	$1.48	$1,480,000	−$30,000	$1.480	$5,000†	+$15,783

* $1,485,000 − $1,496,000 = $(11,000) × 0.9803 = $(10,783), where 0.9803 is the present value factor for two months at an annual interest rate of 12% (1% per month) calculated as $1/1.01^2$.
† $1,485,000 − $1,480,000 = $5,000.

Eximco pays nothing to enter into the forward contract at December 1, Year 1, and the forward contract has a fair value of zero on that date. At December 31, Year 1, the forward rate for a contract to deliver euros on March 1, Year 2, is $1.496. A forward contract could be entered into on December 31, Year 1, to sell €1,000,000 for $1,496,000 on March 1, Year 2. Because Eximco is committed to sell €1,000,000 for $1,485,000, the nominal value of the forward contract is negative $11,000. The fair value of the forward contract is the present value of this amount. Assuming that Eximco has an incremental borrowing rate of 12 percent per year (1 percent per month), and discounting for two months (from 12/31/Y1 to 3/1/Y2), the fair value of the forward contract at December 31, Year 1, is negative $10,783 (a liability). On March 1, Year 2, the forward rate to sell euros on that date is the spot rate—$1.48. At that rate, €1,000,000 could be sold for $1,480,000. Because Eximco has a contract to sell euros for $1,485,000, the fair value of the forward contract on March 1, Year 2, is $5,000. This represents an increase in fair value from December 31, Year 1, of $15,783. The original discount on the forward contract is determined by the difference in the euro spot rate and three-month forward rate on December 1, Year 1: ($1.485 − $1.50) × €1,000,000 = $15,000.

Forward Contract Designated as Cash Flow Hedge

Assume that Eximco designates the forward contract as a *cash flow hedge* of a foreign-currency-denominated asset. In this case, the original forward discount or premium is allocated to net income over the life of the forward contract using an effective interest method. The company would prepare the following journal entries to account for the foreign currency transaction and the related forward contract:

Year 1 Journal Entries—Forward Contract Designated as a Cash Flow Hedge

12/1/Y1	Accounts Receivable (€)	$1,500,000	
	Sales		$1,500,000
	To record the sale and €1,000,000 account receivable at the spot rate of $1.50 (Step 1 in Exhibit 7.2).		

There is no formal entry for the forward contract, as it is an executory contract (no cash changes hands) and has a fair value of zero (Step 2 in Exhibit 7.2).

A memorandum would be prepared designating the forward contract as a hedge of the risk of changes in the cash flow to be received on the foreign currency account receivable resulting from changes in the U.S. dollar–euro exchange rate.

12/31/Y1	Accounts Receivable (€)	$10,000	
	Foreign Exchange Gain		$10,000
	To adjust the value of the euro receivable to the new spot rate of $1.51 and record a foreign exchange gain resulting from the appreciation of the euro since December 1.		
	Accumulated Other Comprehensive Income (AOCI)	$10,783	
	Forward Contract[20]		$10,783
	To record the forward contract as a liability at its fair value of $10,783 with a corresponding debit to AOCI.		

[20] "Forward Contract" is a generic account title. In practice, the balance sheet line item in which forward contract assets and liabilities are recognized will differ across companies. Chevron Corporation, for example, indicates that the fair values of forward contracts "are reported on the Consolidated Balance Sheet as "Accounts and notes receivable, net" or "Accrued liabilities," with gains and losses reported in "Other income" (2009 Form 10-K, Note 10: Financial and Derivative Instruments).

Loss on Forward Contract	$10,000	
Accumulated Other Comprehensive Income (AOCI) . . .		$10,000
To record a loss on forward contract to offset the foreign exchange gain on account receivable with a corresponding credit to AOCI.		
Discount Expense.	$5,017	
Accumulated Other Comprehensive Income (AOCI).		$5,017
To allocate the forward contract discount to net income over the life of the contract using the effective interest method with a corresponding credit to AOCI.		

The first entry on 12/31/Y1 ensures that the foreign-currency-denominated asset is reported on the balance sheet at its current US$ value of $1,510,000 and that its change in US$ value is reflected as a $10,000 gain in income. The forward contract should be reported on the balance sheet as a liability. Thus, the second entry makes a credit of $10,783 to Forward Contract. Under cash flow hedge accounting, the change in the fair value of the forward contract, which has gone from $0 to $(10,783), is not recognized immediately in income, but is instead deferred in stockholders' equity. Thus, the debit of $10,783 in the second entry is made to AOCI. The third entry achieves the objective of hedge accounting by transferring $10,000 from AOCI to a loss on forward contract. As a result of this entry, the loss on forward contract of $10,000 and the foreign exchange gain on the account receivable of $10,000 exactly offset one another, and the net impact on income is zero—this is the essence of hedge accounting. As a result of the second and third entries, the forward contract is reported on the balance sheet as a liability at its fair value of $(10,783); a loss on forward contract is recognized in the amount of $10,000 to offset the foreign exchange gain; and AOCI has a negative (debit) balance of $783. The second and third entries could be combined into one entry as follows:

Loss on Forward Contract	10,000	
Accumulated Other Comprehensive Income (AOCI)	783	
Forward Contract		10,783

The negative balance in AOCI of $783 can be understood as that portion of the loss on the forward contract (decrease in fair value of the forward contract) that is not recognized in net income, but instead is deferred in stockholders' equity. Under cash flow hedge accounting, a loss on the hedging instrument (forward contract) is recognized only to the extent that it offsets a gain on the item being hedged (account receivable).

The last entry uses the effective interest method to allocate a portion of the $15,000 forward contract discount as an expense to net income. The company calculates the implicit interest rate associated with the forward contract by considering the fact that the forward contract will generate cash flow of $1,485,000 from a foreign currency asset with an initial value of $1,500,000. Because the discount of $15,000 accrues over a three-month period, the effective interest rate is calculated as $1 - \sqrt[3]{\$1,485,000/\$1,500,000} = 0.003345$. The amount of discount to be allocated to net income for the month of December Year 1 is $1,500,000 \times 0.3345\% = \$5,017$. A debit of $5,017 is made to Discount Expense in the last journal entry on 12/31/Y1. By making the credit in this journal entry to AOCI, the theoretically correct amounts are reported in net income and on the balance sheet, and the balance sheet remains in balance, as is shown next.

The impact on Year 1 net income is as follows:

Sales		$1,500,000
Foreign Exchange Gain	$10,000	
Loss on Forward Contract	(10,000)	
Net gain (loss)		0
Discount Expense		(5,017)
Impact on net income		$1,494,983

The effect on the December 31, Year 1, balance sheet is as follows:

Assets		Liabilities and Stockholders' Equity	
Accounts receivable (€)	$1,510,000	Forward contract	$ 10,783
		Retained earnings	1,494,983
		AOCI	4,234
			$1,510,000

Year 2 Journal Entries—Forward Contract Designated as Cash Flow Hedge

3/1/Y2	Foreign Exchange Loss	$30,000	
	Accounts Receivable (€)		$30,000
	To adjust the value of the euro receivable to the new spot rate of $1.48 and record a foreign exchange loss resulting from the depreciation of the euro since December 31.		
	Forward Contract	$15,783	
	Accumulated Other Comprehensive Income (AOCI)		$15,783
	To adjust the carrying value of the forward contract to its current fair value of $5,000 with a corresponding credit to AOCI.		
	Accumulated Other Comprehensive Income (AOCI)	$30,000	
	Gain on Forward Contract		$30,000
	To record a gain on forward contract to offset the foreign exchange loss on account receivable with a corresponding debit to AOCI.		
	Discount Expense	$9,983	
	Accumulated Other Comprehensive Income (AOCI)		$9,983
	To allocate the remaining forward contract discount to net income ($15,000 − $5,017 = $9,983) with a corresponding credit to AOCI.		

As a result of these entries, the balance in AOCI is zero: $4,234 − $30,000 + $15,783 + $9,983 = $0.

	Foreign Currency (€)	$1,480,000	
	Accounts Receivable (€)		$1,480,000
	To record receipt of €1,000,000 from the Spanish customer as an asset (Foreign Currency) at the spot rate of $1.48 (Step 3 in Exhibit 7.2).		
	Cash	$1,485,000	
	Foreign Currency (€)		$1,480,000
	Forward Contract		5,000

> To record settlement of the forward contract, that is, record receipt of $1,485,000 in exchange for delivery of €1,000,000, and remove the forward contract from the accounts (Steps 4 and 5 in Exhibit 7.2).

The impact on Year 2 net income is:

Foreign Exchange Loss.................................	$(30,000)
Gain on Forward Contract	30,000
Net gain (loss).......................................	0
Discount Expense	(9,983)
Impact on net income	$(9,983)

The net effect on the balance sheet over the two years is an increase in cash of $1,485,000 with a corresponding increase in retained earnings of $1,485,000 ($1,494,983 − $9,983). The cumulative Discount Expense of $15,000 reflects the cost of extending credit to the Spanish customer.

The net benefit from having entered into the forward contract is $5,000. Eximco has a cash inflow of $1,485,000 rather than only the $1,480,000 that would have been received without a forward contract. This "gain" is reflected in net income as the difference between the net Gain on Forward Contract and the cumulative Discount Expense ($20,000 − $15,000 = $5,000) recognized over the two periods.

Effective Interest versus Straight-Line Methods

Use of the effective interest method results in allocation of the forward contract discount of $5,017 at the end of the first month and $9,983 at the end of the next two months. Straight-line allocation on a monthly basis of the $15,000 discount would result in a reasonable approximation of these amounts:

12/31/Y1	$15,000 \times \frac{1}{3} = \$5,000$
3/1/Y2	$15,000 \times \frac{2}{3} = \$10,000$

Determining the effective interest rate is complex, and no conceptual insights are gained by its use. For the remainder of this chapter, we use straight-line allocation of forward contract discounts and premiums, as is allowed by the FASB. The important thing to keep in mind in this example is that, with a cash flow hedge, an expense equal to the original forward contract discount is recognized in net income over the life of the contract.

What if the forward rate on December 1, Year 1, had been $1.506 (i.e., the euro was selling at a premium in the forward market)? In that case, Eximco would receive $6,000 more through the forward sale of euros ($1,506,000) than if the euros had been received and converted into dollars at the date of sale ($1,500,000). The forward contract premium would be allocated as an increase in net income at the rate of $2,000 per month; $2,000 at 12/31/Y1 and $4,000 at 3/1/Y2.

Forward Contract Designated as Fair Value Hedge

Assume that Eximco decides not to designate the forward contract as a cash flow hedge, but instead elects to treat it as a fair value hedge. In that case, the gain or loss on the forward contract is taken directly to net income and there is no separate amortization of the original discount on the forward contract.

Year 1 Journal Entries—Forward Contract Designated as a Fair Value Hedge

12/1/Y1	Accounts Receivable (€)........................	$1,500,000	
	Sales....................................		$1,500,000
	To record the sale and €1,000,000 account receivable at the spot rate of $1.50 (Step 1 in Exhibit 7.2).		

There is no formal entry for the forward contract (Step 2 in Exhibit 7.2). A memorandum would be prepared designating the forward contract as a hedge of the risk of changes in the fair value of the foreign currency account receivable resulting from changes in the U.S. dollar–euro exchange rate.

12/31/Y1	Accounts Receivable (€).............................	$10,000	
	Foreign Exchange Gain		$10,000
	To adjust the value of the euro receivable to the new spot rate of $1.51 and record a foreign exchange gain resulting from the appreciation of the euro since December 1.		
	Loss on Forward Contract	$10,783	
	Forward Contract		$10,783
	To record the forward contract as a liability at its fair value of $10,783 and record a forward contract loss for the change in the fair value of the forward contract since December 1.		

The impact on Year 1 net income is:

Sales		$1,500,000
Foreign Exchange Gain	$10,000	
Loss on Forward Contract	(10,783)	
Net gain (loss)		(783)
Impact on net income		$1,499,217

The effect on the December 31, Year 1, balance sheet is:

Assets		Liabilities and Stockholders' Equity	
Accounts receivable (€)	$1,510,000	Forward contract	$ 10,783
		Retained earnings	1,499,217
			$1,510,000

Year 2 Journal Entries—Forward Contract Designated as a Fair Value Hedge

3/1/Y2	Foreign Exchange Loss	$ 30,000	
	Accounts Receivable (€)		$ 30,000
	To adjust the value of the euro receivable to the new spot rate of $1.48 and record a foreign exchange loss resulting from the depreciation of the euro since December 31.		
	Forward Contract	$ 15,783	
	Gain on Forward Contract		$ 15,783
	To adjust the carrying value of the forward contract to its current fair value of $5,000 and record a forward contract gain for the change in the fair value since December 31.		
	Foreign Currency (€)	$1,480,000	
	Accounts Receivable (€)		$1,480,000
	To record receipt of €1,000,000 from the Spanish customer as an asset at the spot rate of $1.48 (Step 3 in Exhibit 7.2).		
	Cash	$1,485,000	
	Foreign Currency (€).		$1,480,000
	Forward Contract		5,000
	To record settlement of the forward contract, that is, record receipt of $1,485,000 in exchange for delivery of €1,000,000 and remove the forward contract from the accounts (Steps 4 and 5 in Exhibit 7.2).		

The impact on Year 2 net income is as follows:

Foreign Exchange Loss	$(30,000)
Gain on Forward Contract	15,783
Impact on Net Income	$(14,217)

The net effect on the balance sheet for the two years is an increase in cash of $1,485,000 with a corresponding increase in retained earnings of $1,485,000 ($1,499,217 − $14,217).

Under fair value hedge accounting, the original forward contract discount is not amortized systematically over the life of the contract. Instead, it is recognized in income as the difference between the Foreign Exchange Gain (Loss) on the account receivable and the Gain (Loss) on the Forward Contract, that is, $(783) in Year 1 and $(14,217) in Year 2. The net impact on net income over the two years is $(15,000), which reflects the cost of extending credit to the Spanish customer. The net Gain on Forward Contract of $5,000 ($10,783 loss in Year 1 and $15,783 gain in Year 2) reflects the net benefit—that is increase in cash inflow—from Eximco's decision to hedge the euro receivable.

The accounting for a fair value hedge of a foreign-currency-denominated asset or liability is the same as if the forward contract were not designated as a hedging instrument; changes in the fair value of the forward contract are immediately recognized in net income. Exhibit 7.3 provides an excerpt from the Coca-Cola Company annual report describing the accounting for forward contracts used as

EXHIBIT 7.3

COCA-COLA COMPANY
Annual Report
2009

Notes to the Consolidated Financial Statements

Excerpt from Note 4: Hedging Transactions and Derivative Financial Instruments

Cash Flow Hedging Strategy

The Company uses cash flow hedges to minimize the variability in cash flows of assets or liabilities or forecasted transactions caused by fluctuations in foreign currency exchange rates, commodity prices or interest rates. The changes in the fair values of derivatives designated as cash flow hedges are recorded in AOCI and are reclassified into the line item in the consolidated income statement in which the hedged items are recorded in the same period the hedged items affect earnings. The changes in fair values of hedges that are determined to be ineffective are immediately reclassified from AOCI into earnings. The Company did not discontinue any cash flow hedging relationships during the year ended December 31, 2009. The maximum length of time over which the Company hedges its exposure to future cash flows is typically three years.

The Company maintains a foreign currency cash flow hedging program to reduce the risk that our eventual U.S. dollar net cash inflows from sales outside the United States and U.S. dollar net cash outflows from procurement activities will be adversely affected by changes in foreign currency exchange rates. We enter into forward contracts and purchase foreign currency options (principally euros and Japanese yen) and collars to hedge certain portions of forecasted cash flows denominated in foreign currencies. When the dollar strengthens against the foreign currencies, the decline in the present value of future foreign currency cash flows is partially offset by gains in the fair value of the derivative instruments. Conversely, when the dollar weakens, the increase in the present value of future foreign currency cash flows is partially offset by losses in the fair value of the derivative instruments. The total notional value of derivatives that have been designated and qualify for the Company's foreign currency cash flow hedging program as of December 31, 2009, was approximately $3,679 million.

Economic Hedging Strategy

In addition to derivative instruments that are designated and qualify for hedge accounting, the Company also uses certain derivatives as economic hedges. Although these derivatives were not designated and/ or did not qualify for hedge accounting, they are effective economic hedges. The Company primarily uses economic hedges to offset the earnings impact that fluctuations in foreign currency exchange rates have on certain monetary assets and liabilities denominated in nonfunctional currencies. The changes in fair values of these economic hedges are immediately recognized into earnings in the line item other income (loss)—net. The total notional value of derivatives related to our economic hedges of this type as of December 31, 2009, was approximately $651 million. The Company's other economic hedges are not significant to the Company's consolidated financial statements.

hedges of foreign-currency-denominated assets and liabilities that demonstrates this point. Coca-Cola uses the term *remeasurement* to refer to the process of adjusting the value of foreign currency "monetary assets and liabilities," that is, receivables and payables.

FOREIGN CURRENCY OPTION USED TO HEDGE A RECOGNIZED FOREIGN-CURRENCY-DENOMINATED ASSET

As an alternative to a forward contract, Eximco could hedge its exposure to foreign exchange risk arising from the euro account receivable by purchasing a foreign currency put option. A put option would give Eximco the right but not the obligation to sell €1,000,000 on March 1, Year 2, at a predetermined strike price. Assume that on December 1, Year 1, Eximco purchases an over-the-counter option from its bank with a strike price of $1.50 when the spot rate is $1.50 and pays a premium of $0.009 per euro.[21] Thus, the purchase price for the option is $9,000 (€1,000,000 × $0.009).

Because the strike price and spot rate are the same, there is no intrinsic value associated with this option. The premium is based solely on time value; that is, it is possible that the euro will depreciate and the spot rate on March 1, Year 2, will be less than $1.50, in which case the option will be in the money. If the spot rate for euros on March 1, Year 2, is less than the strike price of $1.50, Eximco will exercise its option and sell its €1,000,000 at the strike price of $1.50. If the spot rate for euros in three months is greater than the strike price of $1.50, Eximco will not exercise its option and instead will sell euros at the higher spot rate. By purchasing this option, Eximco is guaranteed a minimum cash flow from the export sale of $1,491,000 ($1,500,000 from exercising the option less the $9,000 cost of the option). There is no limit to the maximum number of U.S. dollars that could be received.

As is true for other derivative financial instruments, foreign currency options must be reported on the balance sheet at fair value. The fair value of a foreign currency option at the balance sheet date is determined by reference to the premium quoted by banks on that date for an option with a similar expiration date. Banks (and other sellers of options) determine the current premium by incorporating relevant variables at the balance sheet date into the modified Black-Scholes option pricing model. Changes in value for the euro account receivable and the foreign currency option are summarized as follows:

		Account Receivable (€)			Foreign Currency Option	
Date	Spot Rate	U.S.-Dollar Value	Change in U.S.-Dollar Value	Option Premium for 3/1/Y2	Fair Value	Change in Fair Value
12/1/Y1	$1.50	$1,500,000	—	$0.009	$9,000	—
12/31/Y1	$1.51	$1,510,000	+$10,000	$0.006	$6,000	−$3,000
3/1/Y2	$1.48	$1,480,000	−$30,000	$0.020	$20,000	+$14,000

The fair value of the foreign currency option can be decomposed into its intrinsic value and time value components as follows:

Date	Fair Value	Intrinsic Value	Time Value	Change in Time Value
12/1/Y1	$9,000	$0	$9,000	—
12/31/Y1	$6,000	$0	$6,000	−$3,000
3/1/Y2	$20,000	$20,000	$0	−$6,000

Because the option strike price is less than or equal to the spot rate at both December 1 and December 31, the option has no intrinsic value at those dates. The entire fair value is attributable to time value only. On March 1, the date of expiration, there is no time value remaining and the entire amount of fair value is attributable to intrinsic value.

---

[21] The price of the option (the premium) was determined by the seller of the option through the use of a variation of the Black-Scholes option pricing formula.

Option Designated as Cash Flow Hedge

Assume that Eximco designates the foreign currency option as a *cash flow hedge* of a foreign-currency-denominated asset. In this case, the change in the option's time value is recognized immediately in net income. The company prepares the following journal entries to account for the foreign currency transaction and the related foreign currency option:

Year 1 Journal Entries—Option Designated as a Cash Flow Hedge

Date	Entry	Debit	Credit
12/1/Y1	Accounts Receivable (€)	$1,500,000	
	Sales		$1,500,000
	To record the sale and €1,000,000 account receivable at the spot rate of $1.50.		
	Foreign Currency Option	$9,000	
	Cash		$9,000
	To record the purchase of the foreign currency option as an asset at its fair value of $9,000.		
12/31/Y1	Accounts Receivable (€)	$10,000	
	Foreign Exchange Gain		$10,000
	To adjust the value of the euro receivable to the new spot rate of $1.51 and record a foreign exchange gain resulting from the appreciation of the euro since December 1.		
	Accumulated Other Comprehensive Income (AOCI)	$3,000	
	Foreign Currency Option		$3,000
	To adjust the fair value of the option from $9,000 to $6,000 with a corresponding debit to AOCI.		
	Loss on Foreign Currency Option	$10,000	
	Accumulated Other Comprehensive Income (AOCI)		$10,000
	To record a loss on foreign currency option to offset the foreign exchange gain on the euro account receivable with a corresponding credit to AOCI.		
	Option Expense	$3,000	
	Accumulated Other Comprehensive Income (AOCI)		$3,000
	To recognize the change in the time value of the option as a decrease in net income with a corresponding credit to AOCI.		

The impact on Year 1 net income is as follows:

Sales		$1,500,000
Foreign Exchange Gain	$10,000	
Loss on Foreign Currency Option	(10,000)	
Net gain (loss)		0
Option Expense		(3,000)
Impact on net income		$1,497,000

The effect on the December 31, Year 1, balance sheet is:

Assets		Liabilities and Stockholders' Equity	
Cash	$ (9,000)	Retained earnings	$1,497,000
Accounts receivable (€)	1,510,000	AOCI	10,000
Foreign currency option	6,000		$1,507,000
	$1,507,000		

At March 1, Year 2, the option has increased in fair value by $14,000—time value decreases by $6,000, and intrinsic value increases by $20,000. The accounting entries made in Year 2 are as follows:

Year 2 Journal Entries—Option Designated as a Cash Flow Hedge

3/1/Y2	Foreign Exchange Loss	$30,000	
	Accounts Receivable (€)		$30,000
	To adjust the value of the euro receivable to the new spot rate of $0.98 and record a foreign exchange loss resulting from the depreciation of the euro since December 31.		
	Foreign Currency Option	$14,000	
	Accumulated Other Comprehensive Income (AOCI)		$14,000
	To adjust the fair value of the option from $6,000 to $20,000 with a corresponding credit to AOCI.		
	Accumulated Other Comprehensive Income (AOCI)	$30,000	
	Gain on Foreign Currency Option		$30,000
	To record a gain on foreign currency option to offset the foreign exchange gain on account receivable with a corresponding debit to AOCI.		
	Option Expense	$6,000	
	Accumulated Other Comprehensive Income (AOCI)		$6,000
	To recognize the change in the time value of the option as a decrease in net income with a corresponding credit to AOCI.		
	Foreign Currency (€)	$1,480,000	
	Accounts Receivable (€)		$1,480,000
	To record receipt of €1,000,000 from the Spanish customer as an asset at the spot rate of $1.48.		
	Cash	$1,500,000	
	Foreign Currency (€)		$1,480,000
	Foreign Currency Option		20,000
	To record exercise of the option, that is, record receipt of $1,500,000 in exchange for delivery of €1,000,000, and remove the foreign currency option from the accounts.		

The impact on Year 2 net income is as follows:

Foreign Exchange Loss	$(30,000)	
Gain on Foreign Currency Option	30,000	
Net gain (loss)		0
Option Expense		(6,000)
Impact on net income		$(6,000)

Over the two accounting periods, Eximco would report Sales of $1,500,000 and a cumulative Option Expense of $9,000. The net effect on the balance sheet is an increase in cash of $1,491,000 ($1,500,000 − $9,000) with a corresponding increase in retained earnings of $1,491,000 ($1,497,000 − $6,000).

The net benefit from having acquired the option is $11,000. Eximco has a net cash inflow of $1,491,000 rather than only $1,480,000 if the option had not been purchased. This "gain" is reflected in net income as the net Gain on Foreign Currency Option less the cumulative Option Expense ($20,000 − $9,000 = $11,000) recognized over the two accounting periods.

Spot Rate Exceeds Strike Price

If the spot rate at March 1, Year 2, had been greater than the strike price of $1.50, Eximco would allow its option to expire unexercised. Instead it would sell its foreign currency (€) at the spot rate. The fair value of the foreign currency option on March 1, Year 2, would be zero. The journal entries for Year 1 to reflect this scenario would be the same as above. The option would be reported as an asset on the December 31, Year 1, balance sheet at $6,000, and the euro receivable would have a carrying value of $1,510,000. The entries on March 1, Year 2, assuming a spot rate on that date of $1.505 (rather than $1.48), would be as follows:

3/1/Y2	Foreign Exchange Loss	$5,000	
	Accounts Receivable (€)		$5,000
	To adjust the value of the euro receivable to the new spot rate of $1.505 and record a foreign exchange loss resulting from the depreciation of the euro since December 31.		
	Loss on Foreign Currency Option	$6,000	
	Foreign Currency Option		$6,000
	To adjust the fair value of the option from $6,000 to $0 and record a loss on foreign currency option for the change in fair value since December 31.		
	Accumulated Other Comprehensive Income (AOCI)	$5,000	
	Gain on Foreign Currency Option		$5,000
	To record a gain on foreign currency option to offset the foreign exchange loss on account receivable with a corresponding debit to AOCI.		
	Foreign Currency (€)	$1,505,000	
	Accounts Receivable (€)		$1,505,000
	To record receipt of €1,000,000 from the Spanish customer as an asset at the spot rate of $1.505.		
	Cash	$1,505,000	
	Foreign Currency (€)		$1,505,000
	To record the sale of €1,000,000 at the spot rate of $1.505.		

The preceding entries result in a credit balance in AOCI of $5,000. The following entry must be made to close AOCI and recognize a corresponding increase in net income.

AOCI	$5,000	
Adjustment to Net Income		$5,000
To close the balance in accumulated other comprehensive income as an adjustment to net income.		

As a result of the last entry, net income related to this hedged transaction is a total of $1,496,000 ($1,500,000 Sales − $9,000 Option Expense + $5,000 Adjustment to Net Income), which is exactly equal to the net increase in cash ($1,505,000 − $9,000). In practice, companies might use a variety of account titles for the adjustment to net income that results from closing AOCI.

Option Designated as Fair Value Hedge

If Eximco had decided to designate the foreign currency option as a fair value hedge, the gain or loss on the option would have been taken directly to net income and there would have been no separate recognition of the change in the time value of the option. The net gain (loss) recognized in Year 1 and Year 2 would be different from the amounts recognized under the cash flow hedge, but over the two-year period, the same amount of net income would be recognized. The accounting method (fair value hedge or cash flow hedge) has no impact on cash flows or on the net amount of income recognized.

HEDGES OF UNRECOGNIZED FOREIGN CURRENCY FIRM COMMITMENTS

In the examples thus far, Eximco does not enter into a hedge of its export sale until the sale is actually made. Assume now that on December 1, Year 1, Eximco receives and accepts an order from a Spanish customer to deliver goods on March 1, Year 2, at a price of €1,000,000. Assume further that under the terms of the sales agreement, Eximco will ship the goods to the Spanish customer on March 1, Year 2, and will receive immediate payment on delivery. In other words, Eximco will not allow the Spanish customer time to pay. Although Eximco will not make the sale until March 1, Year 2, it has a firm commitment to make the sale and receive €1,000,000 in three months. This creates a euro asset exposure to foreign exchange risk as of December 1, Year 1. On that date, Eximco wants to hedge against an adverse change in the value of the euro over the next three months. This is known as a hedge of a foreign currency firm commitment. Because the results of fair value hedge accounting are intuitively more appealing, we do not cover cash flow hedge accounting for firm commitments.

Under fair value hedge accounting, (1) the gain or loss on the hedging instrument is recognized currently in net income and (2) the gain or loss (i.e., the change in fair value) on the firm commitment attributable to the hedged risk is also recognized currently in net income. This accounting treatment requires (1) measurement of the fair value of the firm commitment, (2) recognizing the change in fair value in net income, and (3) reporting the firm commitment on the balance sheet as an asset or liability. This raises the conceptual question of how the fair value of the firm commitment should be measured. Two possibilities are (1) through reference to changes in the spot exchange rate or (2) through reference to changes in the forward rate. These two approaches are demonstrated in the examples that follow.

Forward Contract Used as Fair Value Hedge of a Firm Commitment

To hedge its firm commitment exposure to a decline in the U.S.-dollar value of the euro, Eximco decides to enter into a forward contract on December 1, Year 1. Assume that on December 1, Year 1, the three-month forward rate for euros is $1.485 and Eximco signs a contract with New Manhattan Bank to deliver €1,000,000 in three months in exchange for $1,485,000. No cash changes hands on December 1, Year 1. Eximco elects to measure the fair value of the firm commitment through changes in the forward rate. As the fair value of the forward contract is also measured using changes in the forward rate, the gains and losses on the firm commitment and forward contract exactly offset. The fair value of the forward contract and firm commitment are determined as follows:

Date	Forward Rate to 3/1/Y2	Forward Contract		Firm Commitment	
		Fair Value	Change in Fair Value	Fair Value	Change in Fair Value
12/1/Y1	$1.485	$0	—	$0	—
12/31/Y1	$1.496	$(10,783)*	−$10,783	$10,783*	+$10,783
3/1/Y2	$1.48 (spot)	$5,000†	+$15,783	$(5,000)†	−$15,783

* ($1,485,000 − $1,496,000) = $(11,000) × 0.9803 = $(10,783), where 0.9803 is the present value factor for two months at an annual interest rate of 12% (1% per month) calculated as $1/1.01^2$.
† ($1,485,000 − $1,480,000) = $5,000.

Eximco pays nothing to enter into the forward contract at December 1, Year 1. Both the forward contract and the firm commitment have a fair value of zero on that date. At December 31, Year 1, the forward rate for a contract to deliver euros on March 1, Year 2, is $1.496. A forward contract could be entered into on December 31, Year 1, to sell €1,000,000 for $1,496,000 on March 1, Year 2. Because Eximco is committed to sell €1,000,000 for $1,485,000, the value of the forward contract is negative $11,000; present value is negative $10,783 (a liability). The fair value of the firm commitment is also measured through reference to changes in the forward rate. As a result, the fair value of the firm commitment is equal in amount but of opposite sign to the fair value of the forward contract. At December 31, Year 1, the firm commitment is an asset of $10,783.

On March 1, Year 2, the forward rate to sell euros on that date is the spot rate—$1.48. At that rate, €1,000,000 could be sold for $1,480,000. Because Eximco has a contract to sell euros for $1,485,000, the fair value of the forward contract on March 1, Year 2, is $5,000 (an asset). The firm commitment has a value of negative $5,000 (a liability). The journal entries to account for the forward contract fair value hedge of a foreign currency firm commitment are as follows:

Year 1 Journal Entries—Forward Contract Fair Value Hedge of Firm Commitment

12/1/Y1	There is no entry to record either the sales agreement or the forward contract, as both are executory contracts. A memorandum would be prepared designating the forward contract as a hedge of the risk of changes in the fair value of the firm commitment resulting from changes in the U.S. dollar–euro forward exchange rate.		
12/31/Y1	Loss on Forward Contract	$10,783	
	Forward Contract		$10,783
	To record the forward contract as a liability at its fair value of $(10,783) and record a forward contract loss for the change in the fair value of the forward contract since December 1.		

Firm Commitment	$10,783
Gain on Firm Commitment	$10,783
To record the firm commitment as an asset at its fair value of $10,783 and record a firm commitment gain for the change in the fair value of the firm commitment since December 1.	

Consistent with the objective of hedge accounting, the gain on the firm commitment offsets the loss on the forward contract and the impact on Year 1 net income is zero. The Forward Contract is reported as a liability and the Firm Commitment is reported as an asset on the 12/31/Y1 balance sheet. This achieves the objective of making sure that derivatives are recognized on the balance sheet and at the same time ensures that there is no impact on net income.

Year 2 Journal Entries—Forward Contract Fair Value Hedge of Firm Commitment

3/1/Y2	Forward Contract	$15,783
	Gain on Forward Contract	$15,783
	To adjust the fair value of the forward contract from $(10,783) to $5,000 and record a forward contract gain for the change in fair value since December 31.	
	Loss on Firm Commitment	$15,783
	Firm Commitment	$15,783
	To adjust the fair value of the firm commitment from $10,783 to $(5,000) and record a firm commitment loss for the change in fair value since December 31.	
	Foreign Currency (€)	$1,480,000
	Sales	$1,480,000
	To record the sale and the receipt of €1,000,000 as an asset at the spot rate of $1.48.	
	Cash	$1,485,000
	Foreign Currency (€)	$1,480,000
	Forward Contract	5,000
	To record settlement of the forward contract (receipt of $1,485,000 in exchange for delivery of €1,000,000), and remove the forward contract from the accounts.	
	Firm Commitment	$5,000
	Adjustment to Net Income	$5,000
	To close the firm commitment as an adjustment to net income.	

Once again, the gain on forward contract and the loss on firm commitment offset. As a result of the last entry, the export sale increases Year 2 net income by $1,485,000 ($1,480,000 in Sales plus a $5,000 Adjustment to Net Income). This is exactly equal to the amount of cash received. In practice, companies might use a variety of account titles for the adjustment to net income that results from closing the firm commitment account.

The net Gain on Forward Contract of $5,000 ($10,783 loss in Year 1 plus $15,783 gain in Year 2) measures the net benefit to the company from hedging its firm commitment. Without the forward contract, Eximco would have sold the €1,000,000 received on March 1, Year 2, at the spot rate of $1.48, generating cash flow of $1,480,000. Through the forward contract, Eximco is able to sell the euros for $1,485,000, a net gain of $5,000.

Option Used as Fair Value Hedge of Firm Commitment

Now assume that to hedge its exposure to a decline in the U.S.-dollar value of the foreign currency firm commitment, Eximco purchases a put option to sell €1,000,000 on March 1, Year 2, at a strike price of $1.50. The premium for such an option on December 1, Year 1, is $0.009 per euro. With this option, Eximco is guaranteed a minimum cash flow from the export sale of $1,491,000 ($1,500,000 from option exercise less $9,000 cost of the option).

Eximco elects to measure the fair value of the firm commitment through reference to changes in the U.S. dollar–euro spot rate. In this case, the fair value of the firm commitment must be discounted to its present value. The fair value and changes in fair value for the firm commitment and foreign currency option are summarized as follows:

Date	Option Premium for 3/1/Y2	Foreign Currency Option		Spot Rate	Firm Commitment	
		Fair Value	Change in Fair Value		Fair Value	Change in Fair Value
12/1/Y1	$0.009	$9,000	—	$1.50	—	—
12/31/Y1	$0.006	$6,000	−$3,000	$1.51	$9,803*	+$9,803
3/1/Y2	$0.020	$20,000	+$14,000	$1.48	$(20,000)†	−$29,803

* $1,510,000 − $1,500,000 = $10,000 × 0.9803 = $9,803, where 0.9803 is the present value factor for two months at an annual interest rate of 12% (1% per month) calculated as $1/1.01^2$.
† $1,480,000 − $1,500,000 = $(20,000).

At December 1, Year 1, given the spot rate of $1.50, the firm commitment to receive €1,000,000 in three months would generate a cash flow of $1,500,000. At December 31, Year 1, the cash flow that could be generated from the firm commitment increases by $10,000 to $1,510,000. The fair value of the firm commitment at December 31, Year 1, is the present value of $10,000 discounted at 1 percent per month for two months. The fair value of the firm commitment on March 1, Year 2, is determined through reference to the change in the spot rate from December 1, Year 1, to March 1, Year 2. Because the spot rate declines by $0.02 over that period, the firm commitment to receive €1,000,000 has a fair value of negative $20,000 on March 1, Year 2. The journal entries to account for the foreign currency option and related foreign currency firm commitment are as follows:

Year 1 Journal Entries—Option Fair Value Hedge of Firm Commitment

12/1/Y1	Foreign Currency Option	$9,000	
	Cash.		$9,000
	To record the purchase of the foreign currency option as an asset.		

There is no entry to record the sales agreement, as it is an executory contract. A memorandum would be prepared designating the option as a hedge of the risk of changes in the fair value of the firm commitment resulting from changes in the spot exchange rate.

12/31/Y1	Firm Commitment	$9,803	
	Gain on Firm Commitment		$9,803
	To record the firm commitment as an asset at its fair value of $9,803 and record a firm commitment gain for the change in the fair value of the firm commitment since December 1.		
	Loss on Foreign Currency Option	$3,000	
	Foreign Currency Option		$3,000
	To adjust the fair value of the option from $9,000 to $6,000 and record the change in the value of the option as a loss.		

The impact on Year 1 net income is as follows:

Gain on Firm Commitment	$9,803
Loss on Foreign Currency option	(3,000)
Impact on net income	$6,803

The effect on the December 31, Year 1, balance sheet is as follows:

Assets		Liabilities and Stockholders' Equity	
Cash	$(9,000)	Retained earnings.	$6,803
Foreign currency option	6,000		
Firm commitment	9,803		
	$ 6,803		

Year 2 Journal Entries—Option Fair Value Hedge of Firm Commitment

3/1/Y2	Loss on Firm Commitment	$ 29,803	
	Firm Commitment		$ 29,803
	To adjust the fair value of the firm commitment from $9,803 to $(20,000) and record a firm commitment loss for the change in fair value since December 31.		
	Foreign Currency Option	$ 14,000	
	Gain on Foreign Currency Option		$ 14,000
	To adjust the fair value of the foreign currency option from $6,000 to $20,000 and record a gain on foreign currency option for the change in fair value since December 31.		
	Foreign Currency (€)	$1,480,000	
	Sales		$1,480,000
	To record the sale and the receipt of €1,000,000 as an asset at the spot rate of $1.48.		

Cash	$1,500,000	
Foreign Currency (€)		$1,480,000
Foreign Currency Option		20,000
To record exercise of the foreign currency option (receipt of $1,500,000 in exchange for delivery of €1,000,000), and remove the foreign currency option from the accounts.		
Firm Commitment	$ 20,000	
Adjustment to Net Income		$ 20,000
To close the firm commitment as an adjustment to net income.		

The impact on Year 2 net income is as follows:

Sales	$1,480,000
Loss on Firm Commitment	(29,803)
Gain on Foreign Currency Option	14,000
Adjustment to Net Income	20,000
Impact on net income	$1,484,197

The net increase in net income over the two accounting periods is $1,491,000 ($6,803 in Year 1 plus $1,484,197 in Year 2), which is exactly equal to the net cash flow realized on the export sale ($1,500,000 from exercising the option less $9,000 to purchase the option). The net gain on option of $11,000 (loss of $3,000 in Year 1 plus gain of $14,000 in Year 2) reflects the net benefit from having entered into the hedge. Without the option, Eximco would have sold the €1,000,000 received on March 1, Year 2, at the spot rate of $1.48 for $1,480,000.

HEDGE OF FORECASTED FOREIGN-CURRENCY-DENOMINATED TRANSACTION

Cash flow hedge accounting is used for foreign currency derivatives that hedge the cash flow risk associated with a forecasted foreign currency transaction. For hedge accounting to apply, the forecasted transaction must be probable (likely to occur), the hedge must be highly effective in offsetting fluctuations in the cash flow associated with the foreign currency risk, and the hedging relationship must be properly documented.

The accounting for a hedge of a forecasted transaction differs from the accounting for a hedge of a foreign currency firm commitment in two ways:

1. Unlike the accounting for a firm commitment, there is no recognition of the forecasted transaction or gains and losses on the forecasted transaction.

2. The hedging instrument (forward contract or option) is reported at fair value, but because there is no gain or loss on the forecasted transaction to offset against, changes in the fair value of the hedging instrument are not reported as gains and losses in net income. Instead they are reported in other comprehensive income. On the projected date of the forecasted transaction, the cumulative change in the fair value of the hedging instrument is transferred from other comprehensive income (balance sheet) to net income (income statement).

Option Designated as a Cash Flow Hedge of a Forecasted Transaction

To demonstrate the accounting for a hedge of a forecasted foreign currency transaction, assume that Eximco has a long-term relationship with its Spanish customer and can reliably forecast that the customer will require delivery of goods costing €1,000,000 in March of Year 2. Confident that it will receive €1,000,000 on March 1, Year 2, Eximco hedges its forecasted foreign currency transaction by purchasing a €1,000,000 put option on December 1, Year 1. The facts are essentially the same as for the option hedge of a firm commitment, except that Eximco does not receive a sales order from the Spanish customer until late February, Year 2.

The option, which expires on March 1, Year 2, has a strike price of $1.50 and a premium of $0.009 per euro. The fair value of the option at relevant dates is as follows:

Date	Option Premium for 3/1/Y2	Foreign Currency Option				
		Fair Value	Change in Fair Value	Intrinsic Value	Time Value	Change in Time Value
12/1/Y1	$0.009	$9,000	—	$0	$9,000	—
12/31/Y1	$0.006	$6,000	−$3,000	$0	$6,000	−$3,000
3/1/Y2	$0.020	$20,000	−$14,000	$20,000	$0	−$6,000

Year 1 Journal Entries—Option Hedge of a Forecasted Transaction

12/1/Y1	Foreign Currency Option	$9,000	
	Cash		$9,000
	To record the purchase of the foreign currency option as an asset.		

There is no entry to record the forecasted sale. A memorandum would be prepared designating the foreign currency option as a hedge of the risk of changes in the cash flows related to the forecasted sale.

12/31/Y1	Option Expense	$3,000	
	Foreign Currency Option		$3,000
	To adjust the carrying value of the option to its fair value and recognize the change in the time value of the option as an expense.		

The impact on Year 1 net income is as follows:

Option Expense	$(3,000)
Impact on net income	$(3,000)

A Foreign Currency Option of $6,000 is reported as an asset on the December 31, Year 1, balance sheet. Cash decreases by $9,000, and retained earnings decreases by $3,000.

Year 2 Journal Entries—Option Hedge of a Forecasted Transaction

3/1/Y2	Foreign Currency Option	$14,000	
	Option Expense	6,000	
	Accumulated Other Comprehensive Income (AOCI). . .		$20,000
	To adjust the carrying value of the option to its fair value and recognize the change in the time value of the option as an expense, with a corresponding credit to AOCI.		
	Foreign Currency (€)	$1,480,000	
	Sales		$1,480,000
	To record the sale and the receipt of €1,000,000 as an asset at the spot rate of $0.98.		
	Cash	$1,500,000	
	Foreign Currency (€)		$1,480,000
	Foreign Currency Option		20,000
	To record exercise of the foreign currency option (receipt of $1,000,000 in exchange for delivery of €1,000,000), and remove the foreign currency option from the accounts.		
	Accumulated Other Comprehensive Income (AOCI)	$20,000	
	Adjustment to Net Income		$20,000
	To close AOCI as an adjustment to net income.		

The impact on Year 2 net income is as follows:

Sales	$1,480,000
Option Expense	(6,000)
Adjustment to Net Income	20,000
Impact on net income	$1,494,000

Over the two-year period, net income increases by $1,491,000 ($1,494,000 in Year 2 minus $3,000 in Year 1), equal to the net cash inflow realized from the export sale.

USE OF HEDGING INSTRUMENTS

There probably are as many different corporate strategies regarding hedging foreign exchange risk as there are companies exposed to that risk. Some companies simply require hedges of all foreign currency transactions. Others require the use of a forward contract hedge when the forward rate results in a greater cash inflow or smaller cash outflow than with the spot rate. Still other companies have proportional hedging policies that require hedging on some predetermined percentage (e.g., 50 percent, 60 percent, or 70 percent) of transaction exposure.

It is quite common for companies to use foreign currency derivatives to hedge the exposure to foreign exchange risk arising from forecasted foreign currency

EXHIBIT 7.4
Hedges of
Forecasted
Foreign Currency
Transactions

INTERNATIONAL BUSINESS MACHINES CORPORATION Annual Report 2012

Excerpt from Note D. Financial Instruments

Anticipated Royalties and Cost Transactions

The company's operations generate significant nonfunctional currency, third-party vendor payments and intercompany payments for royalties and goods and services among the company's non-U.S. subsidiaries and with the parent company. In anticipation of these foreign currency cash flows and in view of the volatility of the currency markets, the company selectively employs foreign exchange forward contracts to manage its currency risk. These forward contracts are accounted for as cash flow hedges. The maximum length of time over which the company is hedging its exposure to the variability in future cash flows is approximately four years. At December 31, 2012, the total notional amount of forward contracts designated as cash flow hedges of forecasted royalty and cost transactions was $10.7 billion, with a weighted-average remaining maturity of 0.7 years.

THE BOEING COMPANY Annual Report 2012

Excerpt from Note 18—Derivative Financial Instruments

Cash Flow Hedges

Our cash flow hedges include foreign currency forward contracts, foreign currency option contracts, and commodity purchase contracts. *We use foreign currency forward and option contracts to manage currency risk associated with certain transactions, specifically forecasted sales and purchases made in foreign currencies. Our foreign currency contracts hedge forecasted transactions principally occurring within five years in the future, with certain contracts hedging transactions up to 2021.*

Derivative Instruments Not Receiving Hedge Accounting Treatment

We also hold certain derivative instruments, primarily foreign currency forward contracts, for risk management purposes that are not receiving hedge accounting treatment.

Author's note: Emphasis added.

transactions. Exhibit 7.4 presents information provided by two U.S.-based companies with respect to hedging forecasted transactions. International Business Machines Corporation (IBM) uses forward contracts to hedge transactions that are anticipated to take place in no longer than four years. In contrast, Boeing Company uses both forward contracts and options to hedge future transactions principally occurring up to five years in the future, with certain contracts hedging transactions up to the year 2021.

The notes to financial statements of multinational companies also indicate the magnitude of foreign exchange risk and the importance of hedging contracts. Exhibit 7.5 presents information extracted from Abbott Laboratories' 2012 Annual Report. At December 31, 2012, Abbott had $1.6 billion in foreign currency forward contracts related to anticipated foreign currency transactions and $18.2 billion in forward contracts used to hedge foreign-currency-denominated payables and receivables. To better appreciate the significance of these amounts, consider that Abbott had assets of $67.2 billion, sales of $39.9 billion, and net earnings of $6.0 billion in 2012.

EXHIBIT 7.5

ABBOTT LABORATORIES
Annual Report
2012

Notes to Consolidated Financial Statements

Note 3—Financial Instruments, Derivatives and Fair Value Measures

Certain Abbott foreign subsidiaries enter into foreign currency forward exchange contracts to manage exposures to changes in foreign exchange rates for anticipated intercompany purchases by those subsidiaries whose functional currencies are not the U.S. dollar. These contracts, totaling $1.6 billion at December 31, 2012 and 2011 and $1.3 billion at December 31, 2010, are designated as cash flow hedges of the variability of the cash flows due to changes in foreign exchange rates and are recorded at fair value. Accumulated gains and losses as of December 31, 2012 will be included in Cost of products sold at the time the products are sold, generally through the next twelve months.

Abbott enters into foreign currency forward exchange contracts to manage currency exposures for foreign currency denominated third-party trade payables and receivables, and for intercompany loans and trade accounts payable where the receivable or payable is denominated in a currency other than the functional currency of the entity. For intercompany loans, the contracts require Abbott to sell or buy foreign currencies, primarily European currencies and Japanese yen, in exchange for primarily U.S. dollars and other European currencies. For intercompany and trade payables and receivables, the currency exposures are primarily the U.S. dollar, European currencies and Japanese yen. At December 31, 2012, 2011, and 2010, Abbott held $18.2 billion, $15.7 billion, and $10.8 billion, respectively, of such foreign currency forward exchange contracts.

Dell Inc. uses "foreign currency option contracts and forward contracts to hedge our exposure on forecasted transactions and firm commitments for certain currencies. During Fiscal 2013, we hedged our exposures on more than 20 currencies."[22] The Coca-Cola Company reports using a combination of forward contracts, options, and collars in its foreign currency hedging strategy.[23]

FOREIGN CURRENCY BORROWING

In addition to the receivables and payables that arise from import and export activities, companies often must account for foreign currency borrowings, another type of foreign currency transaction. Companies borrow foreign currency from foreign lenders either to finance foreign operations or perhaps to take advantage of more favorable interest rates. Accounting for a foreign currency borrowing is complicated by the fact that both the principal and interest are denominated in foreign currency and both create an exposure to foreign exchange risk.

To demonstrate the accounting for foreign currency debt, assume that on July 1, Year 1, Mapleleaf International (a company based in Canada) borrowed 1 billion Japanese yen (¥) on a one-year note at a per annum interest rate of

---

[22] Dell Inc., 2013 Form 10-K, p. 59.

[23] A foreign currency collar can be created by simultaneously purchasing a call option and selling a put option to fix a range of prices at which foreign currency can be purchased at a predetermined future date.

5 percent. Interest is payable and the note comes due on July 1, Year 2. The following exchange rates apply:

Date	Canadian Dollars (C$) per Japanese Yen (¥) Spot Rate
July 1, Year 1	C$0.00921
December 31, Year 1	0.00932
July 1, Year 2	0.00937

On July 1, Year 1, Mapleleaf borrows ¥1,000,000,000 and converts it into C$9,210,000 in the spot market. Over the life of the note, Mapleleaf must record accrued interest expense at year-end and interest payments on the anniversary date of July 1. In addition, the Japanese yen note payable must be revalued at year-end, with foreign exchange gains and losses reported in income. The journal entries to account for this foreign currency borrowing are as follows:

July 1, Year 1	Dr. Cash.	9,210,000	
	Cr. Note Payable (¥).		9,210,000
	To record the yen note payable at the spot rate of C$0.00921 and the conversion of ¥1,000,000,000 into Canadian dollars.		
December 31, Year 1	Dr. Interest Expense	233,000	
	Cr. Accrued Interest Payable (¥).		233,000
	To accrue interest for the period July 1–December 31, Year 2: (¥1,000,000,000 × 5% × $\frac{1}{2}$ year = ¥25,0000,000 × C$0.00932 = C$233,0000.		
	Dr. Foreign Exchange Loss . . . . :	110,000	
	Cr. Note Payable (¥).		110,000
	To revalue the yen note payable at the spot rate of C$0.00932 and record a foreign exchange loss of C$110,000 (¥1,000,000,000 × [C$0.00932 − C$0.00921]).		
July 1, Year 2	Dr. Interest Expense	234,250	
	Accrued Interest Payable (¥).	233,000	
	Foreign Exchange Loss	1,250	
	Cr. Cash		468,500
	To record the interest payment of ¥50,000,000 acquired at the spot rate of C$0.00937 for C$468,500; interest expense for the period January 1–July 1, Year 2 (¥25,000,000 × C$0.00937); and a foreign exchange loss on the yen accrued interest payable (¥ 25,000,000 × [C$0.00937 − C$0.00932]).		
	Dr. Foreign Exchange Loss	50,000	
	Cr. Note Payable (¥).		50,000
	To revalue the yen note payable at the spot rate of C$0.00937 and record a foreign exchange loss of C$50,000 (¥1,000,000,000 × [C$0.00937 − C$0.00932]).		

Dr. Note Payable (¥) . . . . , ...	9,370,000
Cr. Cash	9,370,000
To record repayment of the ¥1,000,000,000 note through purchase of yen at the spot rate of C$0.00937.	

Foreign Currency Loan

At times companies might lend foreign currency to related parties, creating the opposite situation to that with a foreign currency borrowing. The accounting will involve keeping track of a note receivable and interest receivable, both of which are denominated in foreign currency. Fluctuations in the U.S.-dollar value of the principal and interest will generally give rise to foreign exchange gains and losses, which would be included in income. Under U.S. GAAP, an exception arises when the foreign currency loan is being made on a long-term basis to a foreign branch, subsidiary, or equity method affiliate. Foreign exchange gains and losses on "intercompany foreign currency transactions that are of a long-term investment nature (that is, settlement is not planned or anticipated in the foreseeable future)" are reported in other comprehensive income until the loan is repaid. Only the foreign exchange gains and losses related to the interest receivable would be recorded currently in net income.

Summary

1. There are a variety of exchange rate mechanisms in use around the world. A majority of national currencies are allowed to fluctuate in value against other currencies over time.

2. Exposure to foreign exchange risk exists when a payment to be made or received is denominated in terms of a foreign currency. Appreciation in a foreign currency will result in a foreign exchange gain on a foreign currency receivable and a foreign exchange loss on a foreign currency payable. Conversely, a decrease in the value of a foreign currency will result in a foreign exchange loss on a foreign currency receivable and a foreign exchange gain on a foreign currency payable.

3. Foreign exchange gains and losses on foreign currency balances are recorded in income in the period in which an exchange rate change occurs; this is a two-transaction perspective, accrual approach. Foreign currency balances must be revalued to their current domestic-currency equivalent using current exchange rates whenever financial statements are prepared. This approach violates the conservatism principle when unrealized foreign exchange gains are recognized as income.

4. Exposure to foreign exchange risk can be eliminated through hedging. Hedging involves establishing a price today at which a foreign currency to be received in the future can be sold in the future or at which a foreign currency to be paid in the future can be purchased in the future.

5. The two most popular instruments for hedging foreign exchange risk are foreign currency forward contracts and foreign currency options. A forward contract is a binding agreement to exchange currencies at a predetermined rate. An

option gives the buyer the right, but not the obligation, to exchange currencies at a predetermined rate.

6. Derivative financial instruments must be reported on the balance sheet at their fair value. Hedge accounting is appropriate if the derivative is (a) used to hedge an exposure to foreign exchange risk, (b) highly effective in offsetting changes in the fair value or cash flows related to the hedged item, and (c) properly documented as a hedge. Under hedge accounting, gains and losses on the hedging instrument are reported in net income in the same period as gains and losses on the item being hedged.

7. Accounting standards provide guidance for hedges of (a) recognized foreign-currency-denominated assets and liabilities, (b) unrecognized foreign currency firm commitments, and (c) forecasted foreign-currency-denominated transactions. Cash flow hedge accounting can be used for all three types of hedges; fair value hedge accounting can be used only for (a) and (b).

Appendix to Chapter 7

Illustration of the Accounting for Foreign Currency Transactions and Hedging Activities by an Importer

This appendix provides illustrations of the accounting for the following types of hedges used by an importing company:

1. Forward contract cash flow hedge of a recognized foreign currency liability.
2. Forward contract fair value hedge of a recognized foreign currency liability.
3. Option cash flow hedge of a recognized foreign currency liability.
4. Forward contract fair value hedge of a foreign currency firm commitment.
5. Option fair value hedge of a foreign currency firm commitment.
6. Option cash flow hedge of a forecasted foreign currency transaction.

BASIC FACTS

Telectro Company is a U.S. company that produces electronic switches for the telecommunications industry. Telectro regularly imports component parts from a supplier located in Guadalajara, Mexico, with payments made in Mexican pesos (Mex$). The following spot exchange rates, forward exchange rates, and call option premiums for Mexican pesos exist during the period August to October.

| | US$ per Mexican Peso | | |
Date	Spot Rate	Forward Rate to October 31	Call Option Premium for October 31 (strike price $0.080)
August 1	$0.080	$0.085	$0.0052
September 30	0.086	0.088	0.0095
October 31	0.091	0.091	0.0110

1. Forward Contract Cash Flow Hedge of a Recognized Foreign Currency Liability

On August 1, Telectro imports parts from its Mexican supplier at a price of Mex$1,000,000. The parts are received on August 1, but are not paid for until October 31. In addition, on August 1, Telectro enters into a forward contract to purchase Mex$1,000,000 on October 31. The forward contract is appropriately designated as a *cash flow hedge* of the Mexican peso liability exposure. Telectro's incremental borrowing rate is 12 percent per annum (1 percent per month), and the company uses a straight-line method on a monthly basis for allocating forward discounts and premiums.

Journal Entries and Impact on the September 30 and October 31 Trial Balances

8/1	Parts Inventory	$80,000	
	Accounts Payable (Mex$)		$80,000
	To record the purchase of parts and a Mexican peso account payable at the spot rate of $0.080.		

There is no formal entry for the forward contract. A memorandum would be prepared designating the forward contract as a hedge of the risk of changes in the cash flow to be paid on the foreign currency payable resulting from changes in the U.S. dollar–Mexican peso exchange rate.

9/30	Foreign Exchange Loss	$6,000	
	Accounts Payable (Mex$)		$6,000
	To adjust the value of the peso payable to the new spot rate of $0.086 and record a foreign exchange loss resulting from the appreciation of the peso since August 1.		
	Forward Contract	$2,970	
	Accumulated Other Comprehensive Income (AOCI)		$2,970
	To record the forward contract as an asset at its fair value of $2,970 with a corresponding credit to AOCI.		
	Accumulated Other Comprehensive Income (AOCI)	$6,000	
	Gain on Forward Contract		$6,000
	To record a gain on forward contract to offset the foreign exchange loss on account payable with a corresponding debit to AOCI.		

The fair value of the forward contract is determined by reference to the change in the forward rate for a contract that settles on October 31: ($0.088 − $0.085) × Mex$1,000,000 = $3,000. The present value of $3,000 discounted for one month (from October 31 to September 30) at an interest rate of 12 percent per year (1 percent per month) is calculated as follows: $3,000 × 0.9901 = $2,970.

	Premium Expense	$3,333	
	Accumulated Other Comprehensive Income (AOCI)		$3,333
	To allocate the forward contract premium to income over the life of the contract using a straight-line method on a monthly basis ($5,000 × $\frac{2}{3}$ = $3,333).		

The original premium on the forward contract is determined by the difference in the Mexican peso spot rate and three-month forward rate on August 1: ($0.085 − $0.080) × Mex$1,000,000 = $5,000.

Trial Balance—September 30	Debit	Credit
Parts Inventory	$80,000	
Accounts Payable (Mex$)		$86,000
Forward Contract (asset)	2,970	
AOCI		303
Foreign Exchange Loss	6,000	
Gain on Forward Contract		6,000
Premium Expense	3,333	
	$92,303	$92,303

			Debit	Credit
10/31	Foreign Exchange Loss		$5,000	
	Accounts Payable (Mex$)			$5,000
	To adjust the value of the peso payable to the new spot rate of $0.091 and record a foreign exchange loss resulting from the appreciation of the peso since September 30.			
	Forward Contract		$3,030	
	Accumulated Other Comprehensive Income (AOCI)			$3,030
	To adjust the carrying value of the forward contract to its current fair value of $6,000 with a corresponding credit to AOCI.			
	Accumulated Other Comprehensive Income (AOCI)		$5,000	
	Gain on Forward Contract			$5,000
	To record a gain on forward contract to offset the foreign exchange loss on account payable with a corresponding debit to AOCI.			

The current fair value of the forward contract is determined by reference to the difference in the spot rate on October 31 and the original forward rate: ($0.091 − $0.085) × Mex$1,000,000 = $6,000. The forward contract adjustment on October 31 is calculated as the difference in the current fair value and the carrying value at September 30: $6,000 − $2,970 = $3,030.

	Debit	Credit
Premium Expense	$1,667	
Accumulated Other Comprehensive Income (AOCI)		$1,667
To allocate the forward contract premium to income over the life of the contract using a straight-line method on a monthly basis ($5,000 × $\frac{1}{3}$ = $1,667).		
Foreign Currency (Mex$)	$91,000	
Cash		$85,000
Forward Contract		6,000

> To record settlement of the forward contract: record payment of $85,000 in exchange for Mex$1,000,000, record the receipt of Mex$1,000,000 as an asset at the spot rate of $0.091, and remove the forward contract from the accounts.

Accounts Payable (Mex$)	$91,000	
Foreign Currency (Mex$)		$91,000

> To record remittance of Mex$1,000,000 to the Mexican supplier.

Trial Balance—October 31	Debit	Credit
Cash		$85,000
Parts Inventory	$80,000	
Retained Earnings, 9/30	3,333	
Foreign Exchange Loss	5,000	
Gain on Forward Contract		5,000
Premium Expense	1,667	
	$90,000	$90,000

2. Forward Contract Fair Value Hedge of a Recognized Foreign Currency Liability

The facts are the same as in (1), with the exception that Telectro designates the forward contract as a *fair value hedge* of the Mexican peso liability exposure.

Journal Entries and Impact on the September 30 and October 31 Trial Balances

8/1	Parts Inventory	$80,000	
	Accounts Payable (Mex$)		$80,000

> To record the purchase of parts and a Mexican peso account payable at the spot rate of $0.080.

There is no formal entry for the forward contract. A memorandum would be prepared designating the forward contract as a hedge of the risk of changes in the cash flow to be paid on the foreign currency payable resulting from changes in the U.S. dollar–Mexican peso exchange rate.

9/30	Foreign Exchange Loss	$6,000	
	Accounts Payable (Mex$)		$6,000

> To adjust the value of the peso payable to the new spot rate of $0.086 and record a foreign exchange loss resulting from the appreciation of the peso since August 1.

	Forward Contract	$2,970	
	Gain on Forward Contract		$2,970

> To record the forward contract as an asset at its fair value of $2,970 and record a forward contract gain for the change in the fair value of the forward contract since August 1.

384   Chapter Seven

Trial Balance—September 30	Debit	Credit
Parts Inventory	$80,000	
Accounts Payable (Mex$)		$86,000
Forward Contract (asset)	2,970	
Foreign Exchange Loss	6,000	
Gain on Forward Contract		2,970
	$88,970	$88,970

			Debit	Credit
10/31	Foreign Exchange Loss		$5,000	
		Accounts Payable (Mex$)		$5,000
	To adjust the value of the peso payable to the new spot rate of $0.091 and record a foreign exchange loss resulting from the appreciation of the peso since September 30.			
	Forward Contract		$3,030	
		Gain on Forward Contract		$3,030
	To adjust the carrying value of the forward contract to its current fair value of $6,000 and record a forward contract gain for the change in fair value since September 30.			
	Foreign Currency (Mex$)		$91,000	
		Cash		$85,000
		Forward Contract		6,000
	To record settlement of the forward contract: record payment of $85,000 in exchange for Mex$1,000,000, record the receipt of Mex$1,000,000 as an asset at the spot rate of $0.091, and remove the forward contract from the accounts.			
	Accounts Payable (Mex$)		$91,000	
		Foreign Currency (Mex$)		$91,000
	To record remittance of Mex$1,000,000 to the Mexican supplier.			

Trial Balance—October 31	Debit	Credit
Cash		$85,000
Parts Inventory	$80,000	
Retained Earnings, 9/30	3,030	
Foreign Exchange Loss	5,000	
Gain on Forward Contract		3,030
	$88,030	$88,030

3. Option Cash Flow Hedge of a Recognized Foreign Currency Liability

On August 1, Telectro imports parts from its Mexican supplier at a price of Mex$1,000,000. The parts are received on August 1 but are not paid for until October 31. In addition, on August 1, Telectro purchases a three-month call option on Mex$1,000,000 with a strike price of $0.080. The option is appropriately designated as a *cash flow hedge* of the Mexican peso liability exposure.

The following schedule summarizes the changes in the components of the fair value of the Mexican peso call option with a strike price of $0.080:

Date	Spot Rate	Option Premium	Fair Value	Change in Fair Value	Intrinsic Value	Time Value	Change in Time Value
8/1	$0.080	$0.0052	$5,200	—	$0	$5,200[a]	—
9/30	$0.086	$0.0095	$9,500	+$4,300	$6,000[b]	$3,500[b]	−$1,700
10/31	$0.091	$0.0110	$11,000	+$1,500	$11,000	$0[c]	−$3,500

[a] Because the strike price and spot rate are the same, the option has no intrinsic value. Fair value is attributable solely to the time value of the option.
[b] With a spot rate of $0.086 and a strike price of $0.080, the option has an intrinsic value of $6,000. The remaining $3,500 of fair value is attributable to the time value.
[c] The time value of the option at maturity is zero.

Journal Entries and Impact on the September 30 and October 31 Trial Balances

8/1	Parts Inventory	$80,000	
	Accounts Payable (Mex$)		$80,000
	To record the purchase of parts and a Mexican peso account payable at the spot rate of $0.080.		
	Foreign Currency Option	$5,200	
	Cash		$5,200
	To record the purchase of a foreign currency option as an asset.		
9/30	Foreign Exchange Loss	$6,000	
	Accounts Payable (Mex$)		$6,000
	To adjust the value of the peso payable to the new spot rate of $0.086 and record a foreign exchange loss resulting from the appreciation of the peso since August 1.		
	Foreign Currency Option	$4,300	
	Accumulated Other Comprehensive Income (AOCI)		$4,300
	To adjust the fair value of the option from $5,200 to $9,500 with a corresponding credit to AOCI.		
	Accumulated Other Comprehensive Income (AOCI)	$6,000	
	Gain on Foreign Currency Option		$6,000
	To record a gain on foreign currency option to offset the foreign exchange loss on account payable with a corresponding debit to AOCI.		

	Debit	Credit
Option Expense	$1,700	
Accumulated Other Comprehensive Income (AOCI)		$1,700
To recognize the change in the time value of the foreign currency option as an expense with a corresponding credit to AOCI.		

Trial Balance—September 30	Debit	Credit
Parts Inventory	$80,000	
Accounts Payable (Mex$)		$86,000
Foreign Currency Option (asset)	9,500	
Cash		5,200
Foreign Exchange Loss	6,000	
Gain on Foreign Currency Option		6,000
Option Expense	1,700	
	$97,200	$97,200

		Debit	Credit
10/31	Foreign Exchange Loss	$5,000	
	Accounts Payable (Mex$)		$5,000
	To adjust the value of the peso payable to the new spot rate of $0.091 and record a foreign exchange loss resulting from the appreciation of the peso since September 30.		
	Foreign Currency Option	$1,500	
	Accumulated Other Comprehensive Income (AOCI)		$1,500
	To adjust the carrying value of the foreign currency option to its current fair value of $11,000 with a corresponding credit to AOCI.		
	Accumulated Other Comprehensive Income (AOCI)	$5,000	
	Gain on Foreign Currency Option		$5,000
	To record a gain on foreign currency option to offset the foreign exchange loss on account payable with a corresponding debit to AOCI.		
	Option Expense	$3,500	
	Accumulated Other Comprehensive Income (AOCI)		$3,500
	To recognize the change in the time value of the foreign currency option as an expense with a corresponding credit to AOCI.		
	Foreign Currency (Mex$)	$91,000	
	Cash		$80,000
	Foreign Currency Option		11,000
	To record exercise of the foreign currency option: record payment of $80,000 in exchange for Mex$1,000,000, record the receipt of Mex$1,000,000 as an asset at the spot rate of $0.091, and remove the option from the accounts.		
	Accounts Payable (Mex$)	$91,000	
	Foreign Currency (Mex$)		$91,000
	To record remittance of Mex$1,000,000 to the Mexican supplier.		

Trial Balance—October 31	Debit	Credit
Cash ($5,200 credit + $80,000 credit)		$85,200
Parts Inventory	$80,000	
Retained Earnings, 9/30	1,700	
Foreign Exchange Loss	5,000	
Gain on Foreign Currency Option		5,000
Option Expense.......................................	3,500	
	$90,200	$90,200

4. Forward Contract Fair Value Hedge of a Foreign Currency Firm Commitment

On August 1, Telectro orders parts from its Mexican supplier at a price of Mex$1,000,000. The parts are received and paid for on October 31. On August 1, Telectro enters into a forward contract to purchase Mex$1,000,000 on October 31. The forward contract is designated as a *fair value hedge* of the Mexican peso firm commitment. The fair value of the firm commitment is determined through reference to changes in the forward exchange rate.

Journal Entries and Impact on the September 30 and October 31 Trial Balances

8/1	There is no formal entry for the forward contract or the purchase order. A memorandum would be prepared designating the forward contract as a fair value hedge of the foreign currency firm commitment.		
9/30	Forward Contract	$2,970	
	Gain on Forward Contract		$2,970
	To record the forward contract as an asset at its fair value of $2,970 and record a forward contract gain for the change in the fair value of the forward contract since August 1.		
	Loss on Firm Commitment	$2,970	
	Firm Commitment		$2,970
	To record the firm commitment as a liability at its fair value of $2,970 based on changes in the forward rate and record a firm commitment loss for the change in fair value since August 1.		

Trial Balance—September 30	Debit	Credit
Forward Contract (asset)	$2,970	
Firm Commitment (liability)		$2,970
Gain on Forward Contract		2,970
Loss on Firm Commitment	2,970	
	$5,940	$5,940

10/31	Forward Contract	$3,030	
	Gain on Forward Contract		$3,030
	To adjust the carrying value of the forward contract to its current fair value of $6,000 and record a forward contract gain for the change in fair value since September 30.		
	Loss on Firm Commitment	$3,030	
	Firm Commitment		$3,030
	To adjust the value of the firm commitment to $6,000 based on changes in the forward rate and record a firm commitment loss for the change in fair value since September 30.		
	Foreign Currency (pesos)	$91,000	
	Cash		$85,000
	Forward Contract		6,000
	To record settlement of the forward contract: record payment of $85,000 in exchange for Mex$1,000,000, record the receipt of 1 million pesos as an asset at the spot rate of $0.091, and remove the forward contract from the accounts.		
	Parts Inventory	$91,000	
	Foreign Currency (Mex$)		$91,000
	To record the purchase of parts through the payment of Mex$1,000,000 to the Mexican supplier.		
	Firm Commitment	$6,000	
	Adjustment to Net Income		$6,000
	To close the firm commitment account as an adjustment to net income.		

Note that the final entry to close the Firm Commitment as an Adjustment to Net Income will be made only in the period in which the Parts Inventory affects net income through Cost of Goods Sold. The Firm Commitment remains on the books as a liability until that time.

Trial Balance—October 31	Debit	Credit
Cash		$85,000
Parts Inventory (Cost of Goods Sold)	$91,000	
Gain on Forward Contract		3,030
Loss on Firm Commitment	3,030	
Adjustment to Net Income		6,000
	$94,030	$94,030

5. Option Fair Value Hedge of a Foreign Currency Firm Commitment

On August 1, Telectro orders parts from its Mexican supplier at a price of Mex$1,000,000. The parts are received and paid for on October 31. On August 1, Telectro purchases a three-month call option on Mex$1,000,000 with a strike price of $0.080. The option is appropriately designated as a *fair value hedge* of the

Mexican peso firm commitment. The fair value of the firm commitment is determined through reference to changes in the spot exchange rate.

Journal Entries and Impact on the September 30 and October 31 Trial Balances

8/1	Foreign Currency Option	$5,200	
	Cash		$5,200
	To record the purchase of a foreign currency option as an asset.		
9/30	Foreign Currency Option	$4,300	
	Gain on Foreign Currency Option		$4,300
	To adjust the fair value of the option from $5,200 to $9,500 and record an option gain for the change in fair value since August 1.		
	Loss on Firm Commitment	$5,940	
	Firm Commitment		$5,940
	To record the firm commitment as a liability at its fair value of $5,940 based on changes in the spot rate and record a firm commitment loss for the change in fair value since August 1.		

The fair value of the firm commitment is determined through reference to changes in the spot rate from August 1 to September 30: ($0.080 − $0.086) × Mex$1,000,000 = $(6,000). This amount must be discounted for one month at 12 percent per annum (1 percent per month): $(6,000) × 0.9901 = $(5,940).

Trial Balance—September 30	Debit	Credit
Cash		$ 5,200
Foreign Currency Option (asset)	$ 9,500	
Firm Commitment (liability)		5,940
Gain on Foreign Currency Option		4,300
Loss on Firm Commitment	5,940	
	$15,440	$15,440

10/31	Foreign Currency Option	$1,500	
	Gain on Foreign Currency Option		$1,500
	To adjust the fair value of the option from $9,500 to $11,000 and record an option gain for the change in fair value since September 30.		
	Loss on Firm Commitment	$5,060	
	Firm Commitment		$5,060
	To adjust the fair value of the firm commitment from $5,940 to $11,000 and record a firm commitment loss for the change in fair value since September 30.		

The fair value of the firm commitment is determined through reference to changes in the spot rate from August 1 to October 31: ($0.080 − $0.091) × Mex$1,000,000 = $(11,000).

Foreign Currency (Mex$)	$91,000	
Cash		$80,000
Foreign Currency Option		11,000
To record exercise of the foreign currency option; record payment of $80,000 in exchange for Mex$1,000,000, record the receipt of Mex$1,000,000 as an asset at the spot rate of $0.091, and remove the option from the accounts.		
Parts Inventory	$91,000	
Foreign Currency (Mex$)		$91,000
To record the purchase of parts through the payment of Mex$1,000,000 to the Mexican supplier.		
Firm Commitment	$11,000	
Adjustment to Net Income		$11,000
To close the firm commitment account as an adjustment to net income.		

Note that the final entry to close the Firm Commitment as an Adjustment to Net Income will be made only in the period in which the Parts Inventory affects net income through Cost of Goods Sold. The Firm Commitment remains on the books as a liability until that point in time.

Trial Balance—October 31	Debit	Credit
Cash ($5,200 credit + $80,000 credit)		$85,200
Parts Inventory (Cost of Goods Sold)	$91,000	
Retained Earnings, 9/30	1,640	
Gain on Foreign Currency Option		1,500
Loss on Firm Commitment	5,060	
Adjustment to Net Income		11,000
	$97,700	$97,700

6. Option Cash Flow Hedge of a Forecasted Foreign Currency Transaction

Telectro anticipates that it will import component parts from its Mexican supplier in the near future. On August 1, Telectro purchases a three-month call option on Mex$1,000,000 with a strike price of $0.080. The option is appropriately designated as a *cash flow hedge* of a forecasted Mexican peso transaction. Parts costing Mex$1,000,000 are received and paid for on October 31.

Journal Entries and Impact on the September 30 and October 31 Trial Balances

8/1	Foreign Currency Option	$5,200	
	Cash		$5,200
	To record the purchase of a foreign currency option as an asset.		

9/30	Foreign Currency Option	$4,300	
	Accumulated Other Comprehensive Income (AOCI)		$4,300
	To adjust the fair value of the option from $5,200 to $9,500 with a corresponding adjustment to AOCI.		
	Option Expense	$1,700	
	Accumulated Other Comprehensive Income (AOCI)		$1,700
	To recognize the change in the time value of the foreign currency option as an expense with a corresponding credit to AOCI.		

Trial Balance—September 30	Debit	Credit
Cash		$ 5,200
Foreign Currency Option (asset)	$ 9,500	
Accumulated Other Comprehensive Income		6,000
Option Expense	1,700	
	$11,200	$11,200

10/31	Foreign Currency Option	$1,500	
	Accumulated Other Comprehensive Income (AOCI)		$1,500
	To adjust the fair value of the option from $9,500 to $11,000 with a corresponding adjustment to AOCI.		
	Option Expense	$3,500	
	Accumulated Other Comprehensive Income (AOCI)		$3,500
	To recognize the change in the time value of the foreign currency option as an expense with a corresponding credit to AOCI.		
	Foreign Currency (Mex$)	$91,000	
	Cash		$80,000
	Foreign Currency Option		11,000
	To record exercise of the foreign currency option: record payment of $80,000 in exchange for Mex$1,000,000, record the receipt of Mex$1,000,000 as an asset at the spot rate of $0.091, and remove the option from the accounts.		
	Parts Inventory	$91,000	
	Foreign Currency (Mex$)		$91,000
	To record the purchase of parts through the payment of Mex$1,000,000 to the Mexican supplier.		
	Accumulated Other Comprehensive Income (AOCI)	$11,000	
	Adjustment to Net Income		$11,000
	To close AOCI as an adjustment to net income.		

Note that the final entry to close AOCI as an Adjustment to Net Income is made at the date that the forecasted transaction was expected to occur, regardless of when the Parts Inventory affects net income.

Trial Balance—October 31	Debit	Credit
Cash ($5,200 credit + $80,000 credit)		$85,200
Parts Inventory (Cost of Goods Sold)	$91,000	
Retained Earnings, 9/30	1,700	
Loss on Foreign Currency Option	3,500	
Adjustment to Net Income		11,000
	$96,200	$96,200

Questions

1. What is the concept underlying the two-transaction perspective to accounting for foreign currency transactions?

2. A company makes an export sale denominated in a foreign currency and allows the customer one month to pay. Under the two-transaction perspective, accrual approach, how does the company account for fluctuations in the exchange rate for the foreign currency?

3. What factors create a foreign exchange gain on a foreign currency transaction? What factors create a foreign exchange loss?

4. What does the word *hedging* mean? Why do companies hedge foreign exchange risk?

5. How does a foreign currency option differ from a foreign currency forward contract?

6. How does the timing of hedges of the following differ?

   a. Foreign-currency-denominated assets and liabilities.

   b. Foreign currency firm commitments.

   c. Forecasted foreign currency transactions.

7. Why might a company prefer a foreign currency option rather than a forward contract in hedging a foreign currency firm commitment? Why might a company prefer a forward contract over an option in hedging a foreign currency asset or liability?

8. How are foreign currency derivatives such as forward contracts and options reported on the balance sheet?

9. How is the fair value of a foreign currency forward contract determined? How is the fair value of an option determined?

10. What is hedge accounting?

11. Under what conditions can hedge accounting be used to account for a foreign currency option used to hedge a forecasted foreign currency transaction?

12. What are the differences in accounting for a forward contract used as (a) a cash flow hedge and (b) a fair value hedge of a foreign-currency-denominated asset or liability?

13. What are the differences in accounting for a forward contract used as a fair value hedge of (a) a foreign-currency-denominated asset or liability and (b) a foreign currency firm commitment?

14. What are the differences in accounting for a forward contract used as a cash flow hedge of (a) a foreign-currency-denominated asset or liability and (b) a forecasted foreign currency transaction?

15. How are changes in the fair value of an option accounted for in a cash flow hedge? In a fair value hedge?

16. In what way is the accounting for a foreign currency borrowing more complicated than the accounting for a foreign currency account payable?

Exercises and Problems

1. Which of the following combinations correctly describes the relationship between foreign currency transactions, exchange rate changes, and foreign exchange gains and losses?

	Type of Transaction	Foreign Currency	Foreign Exchange Gain or Loss
a.	Export sale	Appreciates	Loss
b.	Import purchase	Appreciates	Gain
c.	Import purchase	Depreciates	Gain
d.	Export sale	Depreciates	Gain

2. Gracie Corporation had a Japanese yen receivable resulting from exports to Japan and a Brazilian real payable resulting from imports from Brazil. Gracie recorded foreign exchange gains related to both its yen receivable and real payable. Did the foreign currencies increase or decrease in dollar value from the date of the transaction to the settlement date?

	Yen	Real
a.	Increase	Increase
b.	Decrease	Decrease
c.	Decrease	Increase
d.	Increase	Decrease

3. On December 1, Year 1, Tackett Company (a U.S.-based company) entered into a three-month forward contract to purchase 1 million Mexican pesos on March 1, Year 2. The following U.S. dollar per peso exchange rates apply:

Date	Spot Rate	Forward Rate (to March 1, Year 2)
December 1, Year 1	$0.088	$0.084
December 31, Year 1	0.080	0.074
March 1, Year 2	0.076	

Tackett's incremental borrowing rate is 12 percent. The present value factor for two months at an annual interest rate of 12 percent (1 percent per month) is 0.9803.

Which of the following correctly describes the manner in which Tackett Company will report the forward contract on its December 31, Year 1, balance sheet?

a. As an asset in the amount of $3,921.20.

b. As an asset in the amount of $7,842.40.

c. As a liability in the amount of $13,724.20.

d. As a liability in the amount of $9,803.00.

Use the following information for Exercises 4 and 5: Reiter Corp. (a U.S.-based company) sold parts to an Israeli customer on December 1, Year 1, with payment of 100,000 Israeli shekels to be received on March 31, Year 2. The following exchange rates apply:

Date	Spot Rate	Forward Rate (to March 31, Year 2)
December 1, Year 1	$0.24	$0.23
December 31, Year 1	0.22	0.20
March 31, Year 2	0.25	

Reiter's incremental borrowing rate is 12 percent. The present value factor for three months at an annual interest rate of 12 percent (1 percent per month) is 0.9706.

4. Assuming no forward contract was entered into, how much foreign exchange gain or loss should Reiter report on its Year 1 income statement with regard to this transaction?

   a. A $5,000 gain.

   b. A $3,000 gain.

   c. A $2,000 loss.

   d. A $1,000 loss.

5. Assuming a forward contract to sell 100,000 Israeli shekels was entered into on December 1, Year 1, as a fair value hedge of a foreign currency receivable, what would be the net impact on net income in Year 1 resulting from a fluctuation in the value of the shekel?

   a. No impact on net income.

   b. A $58.80 decrease in net income.

   c. A $2,000 decrease in income.

   d. A $911.80 increase in income.

Use the following information for Exercises 6 through 8: On September 1, Year 1, Keefer Company received an order to sell a machine to a customer in Canada at a price of 100,000 Canadian dollars. The machine was shipped and payment was received on March 1, Year 2. On September 1, Year 1, Keefer Company purchased a put option giving it the right to sell 100,000 Canadian dollars on March 1, Year 2, at a price of $75,000. Keefer Company properly designates the option as a fair value hedge of the Canadian-dollar firm commitment. The option cost $1,700 and had a fair value of $2,800 on December 31, Year 1. The fair value of the firm commitment is measured through reference to changes in the spot rate. The following spot exchange rates apply:

Date	U.S. Dollar per Canadian Dollar
September 1, Year 1	$0.75
December 31, Year 1	0.73
March 1, Year 2	0.71

Keefer Company's incremental borrowing rate is 12 percent. The present value factor for two months at an annual interest rate of 12 percent (1 percent per month) is 0.9803.

6. What was the net impact on Keefer Company's Year 1 income as a result of this fair value hedge of a firm commitment?

   a. $0.

   b. An $860.60 decrease in income.

   c. An $1,100.00 increase in income.

   d. A $1,960.60 increase in income.

7. What was the net impact on Keefer Company's Year 2 income as a result of this fair value hedge of a firm commitment?

   a. $0.

   b. An $839.40 decrease in income.

   c. A $74,160.60 increase in income.

   d. A $76,200.00 increase in income.

8. What was the net increase or decrease in cash flow from having purchased the foreign currency option to hedge this exposure to foreign exchange risk?

   a. $0.

   b. A $1,000 increase in cash flow.

   c. A $1,700 decrease in cash flow.

   d. A $2,300 increase in cash flow.

Use the following information for Problems 9 and 10: On November 1, Year 1, Black Lion Company forecasts the purchase of raw materials from an Argentinian supplier on February 1, Year 2, at a price of 200,000 Argentinian pesos. On November 1, Year 1, Black Lion pays $1,200 for a three-month call option on 200,000 Argentinian pesos with a strike price of $0.35 per peso. The option is properly designated as a cash flow hedge of a forecasted foreign currency transaction. On December 31, Year 1, the option has a fair value of $900. The following spot exchange rates apply:

Date	U.S. Dollar per Argentinian Peso
November 1, Year 1	$0.35
December 31, Year 1	0.30
February 1, Year 2	0.36

9. What is the net impact on Black Lion Company's Year 1 net income as a result of this hedge of a forecasted foreign currency purchase?

   a. $0.

   b. A $200 increase in net income.

   c. A $300 decrease in net income.

   d. An $800 decrease in net income.

10. What is the net impact on Black Lion Company's Year 2 net income as a result of this hedge of a forecasted foreign currency purchase? Assume that the raw materials are consumed and become a part of cost of goods sold in Year 2.

   a. A $70,000 decrease in net income.

   b. A $70,900 decrease in net income.

   c. A $71,100 decrease in net income.

   d. A $72,900 decrease in net income.

11. Garden Grove Corporation made a sale to a foreign customer on September 15, Year 1, for 100,000 foreign currency units (FCU). Payment was received on October 15, Year 1. The following exchange rates apply:

Date	U.S. Dollar per FCU
September 15, Year 1	$0.40
September 30, Year 1	0.42
October 15, Year 1	0.37

Required:
Prepare all journal entries for Garden Grove Corporation in connection with this sale, assuming that the company closes its books on September 30 to prepare interim financial statements.

12. On December 1, Year 1, El Primero Company purchases inventory from a foreign supplier for 40,000 coronas. Payment will be made in 90 days after El Primero has sold this merchandise. Sales are made rather quickly, and El Primero pays this entire obligation on February 15, Year 2. The following exchange rates for 1 corona apply:

Date	U.S. Dollar per Corona
December 1, Year 1	$0.87
December 31, Year 1	0.82
February 15, Year 2	0.91

Required:
Prepare all journal entries for El Primero in connection with the purchase and payment.

13. On September 30, Year 1, the Lester Company negotiated a two-year loan of 1,000,000 markkas from a foreign bank at an interest rate of 2 percent per annum. Interest payments are made annually on September 30, and the principal will be repaid on September 30, Year 3. Lester Company prepares U.S.-dollar financial statements and has a December 31 year-end. Prepare all journal entries related to this foreign currency borrowing, assuming the following exchange rates for 1 markka:

Date	U.S. Dollars per Markka
September 30, Year 1	$0.20
December 31, Year 1	0.21
September 30, Year 2	0.23
December 31, Year 2	0.24
September 30, Year 3	0.27

Required:
Prepare all journal entries for the Lester Company in connection with the foreign currency borrowing. What is the effective annual cost of borrowing in dollars in each of the three years Year 1, Year 2, and Year 3?

14. The Budvar Company sells parts to a foreign customer on December 1, Year 1, with payment of 20,000 crowns to be received on March 1, Year 2. Budvar enters into a forward contract on December 1, Year 1, to sell 20,000 crowns on March 1, Year 2. Relevant exchange rates for the crown on various dates are as follows:

Date	Spot Rate	Forward Rate (to March 1, Year 2)
December 1, Year 1	$1.00	$1.04
December 31, Year 1	1.05	1.10
March 1, Year 2	1.12	

Budvar's incremental borrowing rate is 12 percent. The present value factor for two months at an annual interest rate of 12 percent (1 percent per month) is 0.9803. Budvar must close its books and prepare financial statements at December 31.

Required:
a. Assuming that Budvar designates the forward contract as a cash flow hedge of a foreign currency receivable, prepare journal entries for these transactions in U.S. dollars. What is the impact on Year 1 net income? What is the impact on Year 2 net income? What is the impact on net income over the two accounting periods?
b. Assuming that Budvar designates the forward contract as a fair value hedge of a foreign currency receivable, prepare journal entries for these transactions in U.S. dollars. What is the impact on Year 1 net income? What is the impact on Year 2 net income? What is the impact on net income over the two accounting periods?

15. The same facts apply as in Exercise 14 except that Budvar Company purchases parts from a foreign supplier on December 1, Year 1, with payment of 20,000 crowns to be made on March 1, Year 2. On December 1, Year 1, Budvar enters into a forward contract to purchase 20,000 crowns on March 1, Year 2. The parts purchased on December 1, Year 1, become a part of the cost of goods sold on March 15, Year 2.

Required:
a. Assuming that Budvar designates the forward contract as a cash flow hedge of a foreign currency payable, prepare journal entries for these transactions in U.S. dollars. What is the impact on Year 1 net income? What is the impact on Year 2 net income? What is the impact on net income over the two accounting periods?
b. Assuming that Budvar designates the forward contract as a fair value hedge of a foreign currency payable, prepare journal entries for these transactions in U.S. dollars. What is the impact on Year 1 net income? What is the impact on Year 2 net income? What is the impact on net income over the two accounting periods?

16. On November 1, Year 1, Alexandria Company sold merchandise to a foreign customer for 100,000 francs with payment to be received on April 30, Year 2. At the date of sale, Alexandria Company entered into a six-month forward contract to sell 100,000 francs. The forward contract is properly designated as

a cash flow hedge of a foreign currency receivable. Relevant exchange rates for the franc are:

Date	Spot Rate	Forward Rate (to April 30, Year 2)
November 1, Year 1	$0.23	$0.22
December 31, Year 1	0.20	0.18
April 30, Year 2	0.19	

Alexandria Company's incremental borrowing rate is 12 percent. The present value factor for four months at an annual interest rate of 12 percent (1 percent per month) is 0.9610.

Required:
Prepare all journal entries, including December 31 adjusting entries, to record the sale and forward contract. What is the impact on net income in Year 1? What is the impact on net income in Year 2?

17. Artco Inc. engages in various transactions with companies in the country of Santrica. On November 30, Year 1, Artco sold artwork at a price of 400,000 ricas to a Santrican customer, with payment to be received on January 31, Year 2. In addition, on November 30, Year 1, Artco purchased art supplies from a Santrican supplier at a price of 300,000 ricas; payment will be made on January 31, Year 2. The art supplies are consumed by the end of November, Year 1. To hedge its net exposure in ricas, Artco entered into a two-month forward contract on November 30, Year 1, wherein Artco will deliver 100,000 ricas to the foreign currency broker in exchange for U.S dollars at the agreed-on forward rate. Artco properly designates its forward contract as a fair value hedge of a foreign currency receivable. The following rates for the rica apply:

Date	Spot Rate	Forward Rate (to January 31, Year 2)
November 30, Year 1	$0.13	$0.12
December 31, Year 1	0.10	0.08
January 31, Year 2	0.09	

Artco Inc.'s incremental borrowing rate is 12 percent. The present value factor for one month at an annual interest rate of 12 percent (1 percent per month) is 0.9901.

Required:
Prepare all journal entries, including December 31 adjusting entries, to record these transactions and forward contract. What is the impact on net income in Year 1? What is the impact on net income in Year 2?

18. On October 1, Year 1, Butterworth Company entered into a forward contract to sell 100,000 rupees in four months (on January 31, Year 2). Relevant exchange rates for the rupee are as follows:

Date	Spot Rate	Forward Rate (to January 31, Year 2)
October 1, Year 1	$0.069	$0.065
December 31, Year 1	0.071	0.074
January 31, Year 2	0.072	

Butterworth Company's incremental borrowing rate is 12 percent. The present value factor for one month at an annual interest rate of 12 percent (1 percent per month) is 0.9901. Butterworth must close its books and prepare financial statements on December 31.

Required:

a. Prepare journal entries assuming the forward contract was entered into as a fair value hedge of a 100,000-rupee receivable arising from a sale made on October 1, Year 1. Include entries for both the sale and the forward contract.

b. Prepare journal entries assuming the forward contract was entered into as a fair value hedge of a firm commitment related to a 100,000-rupee sale that will be made on January 31, Year 2. Include entries for both the firm commitment and the forward contract. The fair value of the firm commitment is measured through reference to changes in the forward rate.

19. On August 1, Year 1, Huntington Corporation placed an order to purchase merchandise from a foreign supplier at a price of 100,000 dinars. The merchandise is received and paid for on October 31, Year 1, and is fully consumed by December 31, Year 1. On August 1, Huntington entered into a forward contract to purchase 100,000 dinars in three months at the agreed-on forward rate. The forward contract is properly designated as a fair value hedge of a foreign currency firm commitment. The fair value of the firm commitment is measured through reference to changes in the forward rate. Relevant exchange rates for the dinar are as follows:

Date	Spot Rate	Forward Rate (to October 31, Year 1)
August 1	$1.300	$1.310
September 30	1.305	1.325
October 31	1.320	

Huntington's incremental borrowing rate is 12 percent. The present value factor for one month at an annual interest rate of 12 percent (1 percent per month) is 0.9901. Huntington Corporation must close its books and prepare its third-quarter financial statements on September 30, Year 1.

Required:

Prepare journal entries for the forward contract and firm commitment. What is the impact on net income in Year 1? What is the net cash outflow on the purchase of merchandise from the foreign customer?

20. On June 1, Year 1, Tsanumis Corporation (a U.S.-based manufacturing firm) received an order to sell goods to a foreign customer at a price of 1 million euros. The goods will be shipped and payment will be received in three months on September 1, Year 1. On June 1, Tsanumis Corporation purchased an option to sell 1 million euros in three months at a strike price of $1.00. The option is properly designated as a fair value hedge of a foreign currency firm commitment. The fair value of the firm commitment is measured through reference to changes in the spot rate. Relevant exchange rates and option premiums for the euro during Year 1 are as follows:

Date	Spot Rate	Call Option Premium for September 1, Year 1 (strike price $1.00)
June 1	$1.00	$0.010
June 30	0.99	0.015
September 1	0.97	

Tsanumis Corporation's incremental borrowing rate is 12 percent. The present value factor for two months at an annual interest rate of 12 percent (1 percent per month) is 0.9803. Tsanumis Corporation must close its books and prepare its second-quarter financial statements on June 30.

Required:
Prepare journal entries for the foreign currency option and firm commitment. What is the impact on Year 1 net income? What is the net cash inflow resulting from the sale of goods to the foreign customer?

21. The Zermatt Company ordered parts from a foreign supplier on November 20 at a price of 100,000 francs when the spot rate was $0.80 per peso. Delivery and payment were scheduled for December 20. On November 20, Zermatt acquired a call option on 100,000 francs at a strike price of $0.80, paying a premium of $0.008 per franc. The option is designated as a fair value hedge of a foreign currency firm commitment. The fair value of the firm commitment is measured through reference to changes in the spot rate. The parts are delivered and paid for according to schedule. Zermatt does not close its books until December 31.

Required:
a. Assuming a spot rate of $0.83 per franc on December 20, prepare all journal entries to account for the option and firm commitment.

b. Assuming a spot rate of $0.78 per franc on December 20, prepare all journal entries to account for the option and firm commitment.

22. Given its experience, Garnier Corporation expects that it will sell goods to a foreign customer at a price of 1 million lire on March 15, Year 2. To hedge this forecasted transaction, a three-month put option to sell 1 million lire is acquired on December 15, Year 1. Garnier selects a strike price of $0.15 per lire, paying a premium of $0.005 per unit, when the spot rate is $0.15. The spot rate decreases to $0.14 at December 31, Year 1, causing the fair value of the option to increase to $12,000. By March 15, Year 2, when the goods are delivered and payment is received from the customer, the spot rate has fallen to $0.13, resulting in a fair value for the option of $20,000.

Required:
Prepare all journal entries for the option hedge of a forecasted transaction and for the export sale, assuming that December 31 is Garnier Corporation's year-end. What is the overall impact on net income over the two accounting periods? What is the net cash inflow from this export sale?

Case 7-1

Zorba Company

Zorba Company, a U.S.-based importer of specialty olive oil, placed an order with a foreign supplier for 500 cases of olive oil at a price of 100 crowns per case. The total purchase price is 50,000 crowns. Relevant exchange rates are as follows:

Date	Spot Rate	Forward Rate (to January 31, Year 2)	Call Option Premium for January 31, Year 2 (strike price $1.00)
December 1, Year 1	$1.00	$1.08	$0.04
December 31, Year 1	1.10	1.17	0.12
January 31, Year 2	1.15	1.15	0.15

Zorba Company has an incremental borrowing rate of 12 percent (1 percent per month) and closes the books and prepares financial statements on December 31.

Required

1. Assume the olive oil was received on December 1, Year 1, and payment was made on January 31, Year 2. There was no attempt to hedge the exposure to foreign exchange risk. Prepare journal entries to account for this import purchase.

2. Assume the olive oil was received on December 1, Year 1, and payment was made on January 31, Year 2. On December 1, Zorba Company entered into a two-month forward contract to purchase 50,000 crowns. The forward contract is properly designated as a fair value hedge of a foreign currency payable. Prepare journal entries to account for the import purchase and foreign currency forward contract.

3. The olive oil was ordered on December 1, Year 1. It was received and paid for on January 31, Year 2. On December 1, Zorba Company entered into a two-month forward contract to purchase 50,000 crowns. The forward contract is properly designated as a fair value hedge of a foreign currency firm commitment. The fair value of the firm commitment is measured through reference to changes in the forward rate. Prepare journal entries to account for the foreign currency forward contract, firm commitment, and import purchase.

4. The olive oil was received on December 1, Year 1, and payment was made on January 31, Year 2. On December 1, Zorba Company purchased a two-month call option for 50,000 crowns. The option was properly designated as a cash flow hedge of a foreign currency payable. Prepare journal entries to account for the import purchase and foreign currency option.

5. The olive oil was ordered on December 1, Year 1. It was received and paid for on January 31, Year 2. On December 1, Zorba Company purchased a two-month call option for 50,000 crowns. The option was properly designated as a fair value hedge of a foreign currency firm commitment. The fair value of the firm commitment is measured through reference to changes in the spot rate. Prepare journal entries to account for the foreign currency option, firm commitment, and import purchase.

Case 7-2

Portofino Company

Portofino Company made purchases on account from three foreign suppliers on December 15, 2012, with payment made on January 15, 2013. Information related to these purchases is as follows:

Supplier	Location	Invoice Price
Beija Flor Ltda.	São Paulo, Brazil	65,000 Brazilian reals
Quetzala SA	Guatemala City, Guatemala	250,000 Guatemalan quetzals
Mariposa SA de CV	Guadalajara, Mexico	400,000 Mexican pesos

Portofino Company's fiscal year ends December 31.

Required

1. Use historical exchange rate information available on the Internet at www.oanda.com to find interbank exchange rates between the U.S. dollar and each foreign currency for the period December 15, 2012, to January 15, 2013.
2. Determine the foreign exchange gains and losses that Portofino would have recognized in net income in 2012 and 2013, and the overall foreign exchange gain or loss for each transaction. Determine for which transaction it would have been most important for Portofino to hedge its foreign exchange risk.
3. Portofino could have acquired a one-month call option on December 15, 2012, to hedge the foreign exchange risk associated with each of the three import purchases. In each case, the option would have had an exercise price equal to the spot rate at December 15, 2012, and would have cost $200. Determine for which hedges, if any, Portofino would have recognized a net gain on the foreign currency option.

Case 7-3

Better Food Corporation

Better Food Corporation (BFC) regularly purchases nutritional supplements from a supplier in Japan with the invoice price denominated in Japanese yen. BFC has experienced several foreign exchange losses in the past year due to increases in the U.S.-dollar price of the Japanese currency. As a result, BFC's CEO, Harvey Carlisle, has asked you to investigate the possibility of using derivative financial instruments, specifically foreign currency forward contracts and foreign currency options, to hedge the company's exposure to foreign exchange risk.

Required

Draft a memo to CEO Carlisle comparing the advantages and disadvantages of using forward contracts and options to hedge foreign exchange risk. Make a recommendation for which type of hedging instrument you believe the company should employ, and provide your justification for this recommendation.

References

U.S. Department of Commerce, International Trade Administration. "Small and Medium-Sized Enterprises Play an Important Role." *Export America,* September 2001.

World Trade Organization. *International Trade Statistics 2012* (www.wto.org).

Chapter **Eight**

Translation of Foreign Currency Financial Statements

Learning Objectives

After reading this chapter, you should be able to

- Describe the conceptual issues involved in translating foreign currency financial statements.
- Explain balance sheet exposure and how it differs from transaction exposure.
- Describe the concepts underlying the current rate and temporal methods of translation.
- Apply the current rate and temporal methods of translation and compare the results of the two methods.
- Describe the requirements of applicable International Financial Reporting Standards (IFRS) and U.S. generally accepted accounting principles (GAAP).
- Discuss hedging of balance sheet exposure.

INTRODUCTION

In today's global business environment, many companies have operations in foreign countries. In its 2012 10-K report, Ford Motor Company provided a list of subsidiaries located in some 20 different countries around the world. The German automaker Volkswagen AG reports having wholly owned subsidiaries in more than 50 countries other than Germany. Many operations located in foreign countries keep their accounting records and prepare financial statements in the local currency using local accounting principles. To prepare consolidated financial statements, parent companies must restate their foreign subsidiaries' financial statements in terms of the parent company's reporting generally accepted accounting principles (GAAP) and then translate the statements into the parent company's reporting currency. The diversity in national accounting standards and the problems associated with that diversity (such as the GAAP reconciliation for consolidation purposes) are discussed in Chapter 2.

This chapter focuses on the *translation* of foreign currency financial statements for the purpose of preparing consolidated financial statements. We begin by examining the conceptual issues related to translation and then describe the manner in which these issues have been addressed by the International Accounting

Standards Board (IASB) and by the Financial Accounting Standards Board (FASB) in the United States. We then illustrate application of the two methods prescribed by those standard-setters and compare the results from applying the two different methods. We also discuss hedging the net investment in foreign operations to avoid the adverse impact the translation of foreign currency financial statements can have on the consolidated accounts.

TWO CONCEPTUAL ISSUES

In translating foreign currency financial statements into the parent company's reporting currency, two questions must be addressed:

1. What is the appropriate exchange rate to be used in translating each financial statement item?
2. How should the translation adjustment that inherently arises from the translation process be reflected in the consolidated financial statements?

We introduce these issues and the basic concepts underlying the translation of financial statements through the following example.

Example

Parentco, a U.S.-based company, establishes a wholly owned subsidiary, Foreignco, in Foreign Country on January 1 by investing US$600 when the exchange rate between the U.S. dollar and the foreign currency (FC) is FC1 = US$1.00. The equity investment of US$600 is physically converted into FC600. In addition, Foreignco borrows FC400 from local banks on January 2. Foreignco purchases inventory that costs FC900 and maintains FC100 in cash. Foreignco's opening balance sheet appears as follows:

FOREIGNCO
Opening Balance Sheet

Cash	FC 100	Liabilities	FC 400
Inventory	900	Common stock	600
Total	FC1,000	Total	FC1,000

To prepare a consolidated balance sheet at the date of acquisition, all FC balances on Foreignco's balance sheet are translated at the exchange rate of US$1.00 per FC. There is no other exchange rate that possibly could be used on that date. A partial consolidation worksheet at the date of acquisition would appear as follows:

Consolidation Worksheet at Date of Acquisition for Parentco and Its Subsidiary Foreignco

	Parentco US$	Foreignco FC	Foreignco Exchange Rate	Foreignco US$	Eliminations Dr.	Eliminations Cr.	Consolidated Balance Sheet US$
Investment	600	—				(1) 600*	0
Cash	(600)	100	$1.00	100			(500)
Inventory	xx	900	$1.00	900			900
Total	xxx	1,000		1,000			400
Liabilities	xx	400	$1.00	400			400
Common stock	xx	600	$1.00	600	(1) 600		0
Total	xxx	1,000		1,000			400

* The elimination entry eliminates Parentco's Investment in Subsidiary account against Foreignco's Common Stock account.

By translating each FC balance on Foreignco's balance sheet at the same exchange rate (US$1.00), Foreignco's US$ translated balance sheet reflects an equal amount of total assets and total liabilities and equity.

Three Months Later

During the period January 1 to March 31, Foreignco engages in no transactions. However, during that period the FC appreciates in value against the US$ such that the exchange rate at March 31 is US$1.20 per FC.

In preparing the March 31 interim consolidated financial statements, Parentco now must choose between the current exchange rate of US$1.20 and the past (historical) exchange rate of US$1.00 to translate Foreignco's balance sheet into U.S. dollars. Foreignco's stockholders' equity must be translated at the historical rate of US$1.00 so that Parentco's Investment account can be eliminated against the subsidiary's common stock in the consolidation worksheet. Two approaches exist for translating the subsidiary's assets and liabilities:

1. All assets and liabilities are translated at the *current exchange rate* (the spot exchange rate on the balance sheet date).
2. Some assets and liabilities are translated at the current exchange rate, and other assets and liabilities are translated at *historical exchange rates* (the exchange rates that existed when the assets and liabilities were acquired).

All Assets and Liabilities Are Translated at the Current Exchange Rate

If the first approach is adopted, in which all assets and liabilities are translated at the current exchange rate, the consolidation worksheet on March 31 would appear as follows:

Consolidation Worksheet Three Months after Date of Acquisition for Parentco and Its Subsidiary Foreignco

	Parentco US$	Foreignco FC	Exchange Rate	US$	Change in US$ Value Since January 1	Eliminations Dr.	Cr.	Consolidated Balance Sheet US$
Investment	600	—					600	0
Cash	(600)	100	$1.20	120	+20			(480)
Inventory	xx	900	$1.20	1,080	+180			1,080
Total	xxx	1,000		1,200	+200			600
Liabilities	xx	400	$1.20	480	+80			480
Common stock	xx	600	$1.00	600	0	600		0
Subtotal	xxx	1,000		1,080	+80			480
Translation adjustment				120	+120			120
Total				1,200	+200			600

By translating all assets at the higher current exchange rate, assets are written up in terms of their U.S.-dollar value by US$200. Liabilities are also written up by US$80. To keep the U.S.-dollar translated balance sheet in balance, a *positive* (credit) translation adjustment of US$120 must be recorded. As a result, total assets on the consolidated balance sheet are US$120 greater than on January 1, as are consolidated total liabilities and stockholders' equity.

Translating foreign currency balances at the current exchange rate is similar to revaluing foreign currency receivables and payables at the balance sheet date. The translation adjustment is analogous to the *net* foreign exchange gain or loss caused by a change in the exchange rate:

$20 gain on cash + $180 gain on inventory − $80 loss on liabilities = $120 net gain

The net foreign exchange gain (positive translation adjustment) is *unrealized*, that is, it does not result in a cash inflow of US$120 for Parentco. However, the gain can be *realized* by selling Foreignco at the book value of its net assets (FC600) and converting the proceeds into U.S. dollars at the current exchange rate (FC600 × $1.20 = US$720). In that case, Parentco would realize a gain from the sale of its investment in Foreignco that would be due solely to the appreciation in value of the foreign currency:

Proceeds from the sale	$720
Original investment	600
Realized gain	$120

The translation adjustment reflects the *change in the dollar value of the net investment* in Foreignco if the subsidiary were to be sold. In addition, a *positive* translation adjustment signals that the appreciation of the foreign currency will result in an increase in the U.S. dollar value of future foreign currency dividends to be paid by Foreignco to its parent. For example, a dividend of FC10 distributed on March 31 can be converted into US$12, whereas the same amount of foreign currency dividend would have been worth only US$10 at the beginning of the year.

Monetary Assets and Liabilities Are Translated at the Current Exchange Rates

Now assume that only monetary assets (cash and receivables) and monetary liabilities (most liabilities) are translated at the current exchange rate. The worksheet to translate Foreignco's financial statements into U.S. dollars on March 31 appears as follows:

Consolidation Worksheet Three Months after Date of Acquisition for Parentco and Its Subsidiary Foreignco

	Parentco US$	Foreignco FC	Exchange Rate	US$	Change in US$ Value Since January 1	Eliminations Dr.	Cr.	Consolidated Balance Sheet US$
Investment	600	—					600	0
Cash	(600)	100	$1.20	120	+20			(480)
Inventory	xx	900	$1.00	900	0			900
Total	xxx	1,000		1,020	+20			420
Liabilities	xx	400	$1.20	480	+80			480
Common stock	xx	600	$1.00	600	0	600		0
Subtotal	xxx	1,000		1,080	+80			480
Translation adjustment				(60)	−60			(60)
Total				1,020	+20			420

Using this approach, cash is written up by US$20 and liabilities are written up by US$80. To keep the balance sheet in balance, a *negative* (debit) translation adjustment of US$60 must be recorded. As a result, both total assets and total liabilities and stockholders' equity on the consolidated balance sheet are US$20 greater than on January 1.

The translation adjustment is analogous to the *net* foreign exchange gain or loss caused by a change in the exchange rate:

$$\$20 \text{ gain on cash} - \$80 \text{ loss on liabilities} = \$60 \text{ net loss}$$

This net foreign exchange loss (negative translation adjustment) also is *unrealized*. However, the loss can be *realized* through the following process:

1. The subsidiary uses its cash (FC100) to pay its liabilities to the extent possible.
2. The parent sends enough U.S. dollars to the subsidiary to pay its remaining liabilities (FC300). At January 1, the parent would have sent US$300 to pay FC300 of liabilities (at the $1.00/FC1 exchange rate). At March 31, the parent must send US$360 to pay FC300 of liabilities (at the $1.20/FC1 exchange rate). A foreign exchange loss (negative translation adjustment) of US$60 (US$360 − US$300) arises on the net monetary liability position because the foreign currency has appreciated from January 1 to March 31.

Note that under this translation approach, the *negative* translation adjustment does not reflect the change in the U.S.-dollar value of the net investment in Foreignco. Moreover, the *negative* translation adjustment is not consistent with the change in the U.S.-dollar value of future foreign currency dividends. As the foreign currency appreciates, the U.S.-dollar value of foreign currency dividends received from Foreignco increases.

Balance Sheet Exposure

As exchange rates change, assets and liabilities translated at the *current* exchange rate change in value from balance sheet to balance sheet in terms of the parent company's reporting currency (for example, U.S. dollar). These items are *exposed* to translation adjustment. Balance sheet items translated at *historical* exchange rates do not change in parent currency value from one balance sheet to the next. These items are *not* exposed to translation adjustment. Exposure to translation adjustment is referred to as balance sheet, translation, or accounting exposure. *Balance sheet exposure* can be contrasted with the *transaction exposure* discussed in Chapter 7 that arises when a company has foreign currency receivables and payables in the following way:

> Transaction exposure gives rise to foreign exchange gains and losses that are ultimately realized in cash; translation adjustments that arise from balance sheet exposure do not directly result in cash inflows or outflows.

Each item translated at the current exchange rate is exposed to translation adjustment. In effect, a separate translation adjustment exists for each of these exposed items. However, positive translation adjustments on assets when the foreign currency appreciates are offset by negative translation adjustments on liabilities. If total exposed assets are equal to total exposed liabilities throughout the year, the translation adjustments (although perhaps significant on an individual basis) net to a zero balance. The *net* translation adjustment needed to keep the consolidated balance sheet in balance is based solely on the net asset or net liability exposure.

A foreign operation will have a *net asset balance sheet exposure* when assets translated at the current exchange rate are greater in amount than liabilities translated at the current exchange rate. A *net liability balance sheet exposure* exists when liabilities translated at the current exchange rate are greater than assets translated at the current exchange rate. The relationship between exchange rate fluctuations, balance sheet exposure, and translation adjustments can be summarized as follows:

Balance Sheet Exposure	Foreign Currency (FC)	
	Appreciates	**Depreciates**
Net asset	Positive translation adjustment	Negative translation adjustment
Net liability	Negative translation adjustment	Positive translation adjustment

Exactly how the translation adjustment should be reported in the consolidated financial statements is a matter of some debate. The major question is whether the translation adjustments should be treated as a *translation gain or loss reported in income* or whether the translation adjustment should be treated as a *direct adjustment to owners' equity without affecting income.* This issue is considered in this chapter in more detail after first examining different methods of translation.

TRANSLATION METHODS

Four major methods of translating foreign currency financial statements have been used worldwide: (1) the current/noncurrent method, (2) the monetary/non-monetary method, (3) the temporal method, and (4) the current rate (or closing rate) method.

Current/Noncurrent Method

The rules for the current/noncurrent method are as follows: current assets and current liabilities are translated at the current exchange rate; noncurrent assets, noncurrent liabilities, and stockholders' equity accounts are translated at historical exchange rates. There is no theoretical basis underlying this method. Although once the predominant method, the current/noncurrent method has been unacceptable in the United States since 1975, has never been allowed under International Financial Reporting Standards, and is seldom used in other countries.

Monetary/Nonmonetary Method

To remedy the lack of theoretical justification for the current/noncurrent method, Hepworth developed the monetary/nonmonetary method of translation in 1956.[1] Under this method, monetary assets and liabilities are translated at the current exchange rates; nonmonetary assets, nonmonetary liabilities, and stockholders' equity accounts are translated at historical exchange rates. Monetary assets are those assets whose value does not fluctuate over time—primarily cash and receivables. Nonmonetary assets are assets whose monetary value can fluctuate. They consist of marketable securities, inventory, prepaid expenses, investments, fixed assets, and intangible assets; that is, all assets other than cash and receivables.

---

[1] Samuel R. Hepworth, *Reporting Foreign Operations* (Ann Arbor: University of Michigan, Bureau of Business Research, 1956).

Monetary liabilities are those liabilities whose monetary value cannot fluctuate over time, which is true for most payables.

Under the monetary/nonmonetary method, cash, receivables, and payables carried on the foreign operation's balance sheet are exposed to foreign exchange risk. There is a net asset exposure when cash plus receivables exceed payables, and a net liability exposure when payables exceed cash plus receivables.

$$\text{Cash} + \text{Receivables} > \text{Payables} \rightarrow \text{Net asset exposure}$$

$$\text{Cash} + \text{Receivables} < \text{Payables} \rightarrow \text{Net liability exposure}$$

The previous example in which Foreignco's monetary assets and monetary liabilities were translated at the current exchange rate demonstrates the monetary/nonmonetary method. In that example, Foreignco had a net liability exposure that, when coupled with an appreciation in the foreign currency, resulted in a negative translation adjustment.

One way to understand the concept of exposure underlying the monetary/nonmonetary method is to assume that the foreign operation's cash, receivables, and payables are actually foreign currency assets and liabilities of the parent company. For example, consider the Japanese subsidiary of a New Zealand parent company. The Japanese subsidiary's yen receivables that result from sales in Japan may be thought of as Japanese yen receivables of the New Zealand parent resulting from export sales to Japan. If the New Zealand parent had yen receivables on its balance sheet, an increase in the value of the yen would result in a foreign exchange gain. There also would be a foreign exchange gain on the Japanese yen held in cash by the parent. These foreign exchange gains would be offset by a foreign exchange loss on the parent's Japanese yen payables resulting from foreign purchases. Whether a net gain or a net loss exists depends on the relative size of yen cash and receivables versus yen payables. Under the monetary/nonmonetary method, the translation adjustment measures the net foreign exchange gain or loss on the foreign operation's cash, receivables, and payables as if those items were actually carried on the books of the parent.

Temporal Method

The basic objective underlying the temporal method of translation is to produce a set of parent currency translated financial statements as if the foreign subsidiary had actually used the parent currency in conducting its operations. For example, land carried on the books of a foreign subsidiary should be translated such that it is reported on the consolidated balance sheet at the amount of parent currency that would have been spent if the parent had sent parent currency to the subsidiary to purchase the land. Assume that a piece of land costs ¥12,000,000 and is acquired at a time when one yen costs NZ$0.016. A New Zealand parent would send NZ$192,000 to its Japanese subsidiary to acquire the land—this is the land's historical cost in parent currency terms.

Consistent with the temporal method's underlying objective, assets and liabilities reported on the foreign operation's balance sheet at historical cost are translated at historical exchange rates to yield an equivalent historical cost in parent currency terms. Conversely, assets and liabilities reported on the foreign operation's balance sheet at a current (or future) value are translated at the current exchange rate to yield an equivalent current value in parent currency terms. (As is true under any translation method, equity accounts are translated at historical exchange rates.) Application of these rules maintains the underlying valuation method (historical cost or current value) used by the foreign subsidiary in accounting for its assets and liabilities.

Cash, receivables, and most liabilities are carried at current or future values under the traditional historical cost model of accounting. These balance sheet accounts are translated at the current exchange rate under the temporal method. By coincidence, the temporal method and the monetary/nonmonetary method produce similar results in this situation. The two methods diverge from one another only when nonmonetary assets are carried at current value. Many national accounting standards require inventory to be carried on the balance sheet at the lower of historical cost or current market value. Although inventory is a nonmonetary asset, the temporal method requires its translation at the current exchange rate when it is written down to market value. In those jurisdictions in which marketable securities are carried at current market value, as is required by International Financial Reporting Standards (IFRS) and U.S. GAAP, marketable securities are also translated at the current exchange rate.

The temporal method generates either a net asset or a net liability balance sheet exposure depending on whether assets carried at current value are greater than or less than liabilities carried at current value. This can be generalized as follows:

Cash + Marketable securities + Receivables + Inventory (when carried at current value) > Liabilities → Net asset exposure

Cash + Marketable securities + Receivables + Inventory (when carried at current value) < Liabilities → Net liability exposure

Because liabilities (current plus long-term) usually are greater than assets translated at current rates, *a net liability exposure generally exists when the temporal method is used.*

Under the temporal method, income statement items are translated at exchange rates that exist when the revenue is generated or the expense is incurred. For most items, an assumption can be made that the revenue or expense is incurred evenly throughout the accounting period and an average-for-the-period exchange rate can be used for translation. Some expenses—such as cost of goods sold, depreciation of fixed assets, and amortization of intangibles—are related to assets carried at historical cost. Because these assets are translated at historical exchange rates, the expenses related to them must be translated at historical exchange rates as well.

The major difference between the translation adjustment resulting from the use of the temporal method and a foreign exchange gain or loss on a foreign currency transaction is that the translation adjustment is not necessarily realized through inflows or outflows of cash. The translation adjustment *could be realized* as a gain or loss only (1) if the foreign subsidiary collects all its receivables in yen cash and then uses its cash to pay off liabilities to the extent possible, and (2) *if there is a net asset exposure,* the excess of cash over liabilities is remitted to the parent, where it is converted into parent currency, or *if there is a net liability exposure,* the parent sends parent currency to its foreign subsidiary which is converted into foreign currency to pay the remaining liabilities.

Current Rate Method

The fourth major method used in translating foreign currency financial statements is the current rate method. The fundamental concept underlying the current rate method is that a parent's entire investment in a foreign operation is exposed to foreign exchange risk, and translation of the foreign operation's financial statements should reflect this risk. To measure the net investment's exposure to foreign exchange risk:

- All assets and liabilities of the foreign operation are translated using the *current exchange rate.*
- Equity accounts are translated at *historical exchange rates.*

The balance sheet exposure measured by the current rate method is equal to the foreign operation's net asset position (total assets minus total liabilities).

$$\text{Total assets} > \text{Total liabilities} \rightarrow \text{Net asset exposure}$$

A positive translation adjustment results when the foreign currency appreciates, and a negative translation adjustment results when the foreign currency depreciates (assuming that assets exceed liabilities). The translation adjustment arising when the current rate method is used also is unrealized. It can become a realized gain or loss if the foreign operation is sold (for its book value) and the foreign currency proceeds from the sale are converted into parent currency.

Under the current rate method, revenues and expenses are translated using the exchange rate in effect at the date of accounting recognition. In most cases an assumption can be made that the revenue or expense is incurred evenly throughout the year, and an average-for-the-period exchange rate is used. However, when an income item, such as a gain or loss on the sale of an asset, occurs at a specific point in time, the exchange rate at that date should be used for translation. Alternatively, all income statement items may be translated at the current exchange rate.

The example above in which all of Foreignco's assets and liabilities were translated at the current exchange rate demonstrates the current rate method. Foreignco has a net asset exposure that, because of the appreciation in the foreign currency, resulted in a positive translation adjustment. The positive translation adjustment that arises under the current rate method becomes a realized foreign exchange gain if the foreign subsidiary is sold at its foreign currency book value and the foreign currency proceeds are converted into parent currency.

The current rate method and the temporal method are the two methods required to be used under IAS 21, *The Effects of Changes in Foreign Exchange Rates,* and FASB ASC 830, *Foreign Currency Matters.* A summary of the appropriate exchange rate for selected financial statement items under these two methods is presented in Exhibit 8.1.

Translation of Retained Earnings

Stockholders' equity items are translated at historical exchange rates under both the temporal and current rate methods. This creates somewhat of a problem in translating retained earnings, which is a composite of many previous transactions: revenues, expenses, gains, losses, and declared dividends occurring over the life of the company. At the end of the first year of operations, foreign currency (FC) retained earnings are translated as follows:

Net income in FC	[Translated per method used to translate income statement items]	= + Net income in PC
−Dividends in FC	× Historical exchange rate	= − Dividends in PC
Ending R/E in FC	when declared	Ending R/E in PC

412 Chapter Eight

EXHIBIT 8.1
Exchange Rates
Used under the
Current Rate
Method and the
Temporal Method
for Selected
Financial Statement
Items

Balance Sheet		
	Exchange Rate Used under the Current Rate Method	Exchange Rate Used under the Temporal Method
Assets		
Cash and receivables	Current	Current
Marketable securities	Current	Current*
Inventory at market	Current	Current
Inventory at cost	Current	Historical
Prepaid expenses	Current	Historical
Property, plant, and equipment	Current	Historical
Intangible assets	Current	Historical
Liabilities		
Current liabilities	Current	Current
Deferred income	Current	Historical
Long-term debt	Current	Current
Stockholders' Equity		
Capital stock	Historical	Historical
Additional paid-in capital	Historical	Historical
Retained earnings	Historical	Historical
Dividends	Historical	Historical
Income Statement		
	Exchange Rate Used under the Current Rate Method	Exchange Rate Used under the Temporal Method
Revenues	Average	Average
Most expenses	Average	Average
Cost of goods sold	Average	Historical
Depreciation of property, plant, and equipment	Average	Historical
Amortization of intangibles	Average	Historical

*Marketable debt securities classified as hold-to-maturity are carried at cost and therefore are translated at the historical exchange rate under the temporal method.

The ending parent currency retained earnings in Year 1 becomes the beginning parent currency retained earnings for Year 2, and the translated retained earnings in Year 2 (and subsequent years) is then determined as follows:

Beginning R/E in FC	(from last year's translation)	=	Beginning R/E in PC
+ Net income in FC	[Translated per method used to translate income statement items]		
		=	+ Net income in FC
− Dividends in FC	× Historical exchange rate when declared		
		=	− Dividends in PC
Ending R/E in PC			Ending R/E in PC

The same approach is used for translating retained earnings under both the current rate and the temporal methods. The only difference is that translation of the current period's net income is done differently under the two methods.

Complicating Aspects of the Temporal Method

Under the temporal method, it is necessary to keep a record of the exchange rates that exist when inventory, prepaid expenses, fixed assets, and intangible assets are acquired because these assets, carried at historical cost, are translated at historical exchange rates. Keeping track of the historical rates for these assets is not necessary under the current rate method. Translating these assets at historical rates makes application of the temporal method more complicated than the current rate method.

Calculation of Cost of Goods Sold (COGS)

Under the *current rate method,* cost of goods sold (COGS) in foreign currency (FC) is simply translated into the parent currency (PC) using the average-for-the-period exchange rate (ER):

$$\text{COGS in FC} \times \text{Average ER} = \text{COGS in PC}$$

Under the *temporal method,* COGS must be decomposed into beginning inventory, purchases, and ending inventory, and each component of COGS must then be translated at its appropriate historical rate. For example, if beginning inventory (FIFO basis) in Year 2 was acquired evenly throughout the fourth quarter of Year 1, then the average exchange rate in the fourth quarter of Year 1 will be used to translate beginning inventory. Likewise, the fourth-quarter (4thQ) Year 2 exchange rate will be used to translate Year 2 ending inventory. If purchases were made evenly throughout Year 2, then the average Year 2 exchange rate will be used to translate purchases:

Beginning inventory in FC	× Historical ER (e.g., 4thQ Year 1)	= Beginning inventory in PC
+ Purchases in FC	× Average ER, Year 2	= + Purchases in PC
− Ending inventory in FC	× Historical ER (e.g., 4thQ Year 2)	= − Ending inventory in PC
COGS in FC		COGS in PC

There is no single exchange rate that can be used to directly translate COGS in FC into COGS in PC.

Application of the Lower of Cost or Market Rule

Under the *current rate method,* the ending inventory reported on the foreign currency balance sheet is translated at the current exchange rate regardless of whether it is carried at cost or at a lower market value. Application of the *temporal method* requires the foreign currency cost and foreign currency market value of the inventory to be translated into parent currency at appropriate exchange rates, and the *lower of the parent currency cost or parent currency market value* is reported on the consolidated balance sheet. As a result of this procedure, it is possible for inventory to be carried at cost on the foreign currency balance sheet and at market value on the parent currency consolidated balance sheet, and vice versa.

Fixed Assets, Depreciation, Accumulated Depreciation

Under the *temporal method,* fixed assets acquired at different times must be translated at different (historical) exchange rates. The same is true for depreciation of fixed assets and accumulated depreciation related to fixed assets.

For example, assume that a company purchases a piece of equipment on January 1, Year 1, for FC1,000 when the exchange rate is $1.00 per FC1. Another item of equipment is purchased on January 1, Year 2, for FC4,000 when the exchange rate is $1.20 per FC1. Both pieces of equipment have a five-year useful life. Under the temporal method, the amount at which equipment would be reported on the consolidated balance sheet on December 31, Year 2, when the exchange rate is $1.50 per FC1, would be:

$$FC1,000 \times \$1.00 = \$1,000$$
$$\underline{FC4,000} \times \$1.20 = \underline{\$4,800}$$
$$FC5,000 \qquad\qquad \$5,800$$

Depreciation expense for Year 2 under the temporal method would be calculated as follows:

$$FC \ \ 200 \times \$1.00 = \$ \ \ 200$$
$$\underline{FC \ \ 800} \times \$1.20 = \underline{\$ \ \ 960}$$
$$FC1,000 \qquad\qquad \$1,160$$

Accumulated depreciation at December 31, Year 2, under the temporal method would be calculated as follows:

$$FC \ \ 400 \times \$1.00 = \$ \ \ 400$$
$$\underline{FC \ \ 800} \times \$1.20 = \underline{\$ \ \ 960}$$
$$FC1,200 \qquad\qquad \$1,360$$

Similar procedures apply for intangible assets as well.

Under the *current rate method,* equipment would be reported on the December 31, Year 2, balance sheet at FC5,000 × $1.50 = $7,500. Depreciation expense would be translated at the average Year 2 exchange rate of $1.40: FC1,000 × $1.40 = $1,400, and accumulated depreciation would be FC1,200 × $1.50 = $1,800.

In this example, the foreign subsidiary has only two fixed assets that require translation. For subsidiaries that own hundreds and thousands of fixed assets, the temporal method, versus the current rate method, can require substantial additional work.

DISPOSITION OF TRANSLATION ADJUSTMENT

The first issue related to the translation of foreign currency financial statements is selection of the appropriate method. The second issue in financial statement translation relates to *where the resulting translation adjustment should be reported in the consolidated financial statements.* There are two prevailing schools of thought with regard to this issue:

1. *Translation gain or loss in net income.* Under this treatment, the translation adjustment is considered to be a gain or loss analogous to the gains and losses that

arise from foreign currency transactions and should be reported in income in the period in which the fluctuation in exchange rate occurs.

The first of two conceptual problems with treating translation adjustments as gains/losses in net income is the gain or loss is unrealized; that is, there is no accompanying cash inflow or outflow. The second problem is the gain or loss may not be consistent with economic reality. For example, the depreciation of a foreign currency may have a *positive* impact on the foreign operation's export sales and income, but the particular translation method used gives rise to a translation *loss*.

2. *Cumulative translation adjustment in stockholders' equity (other comprehensive income).* The alternative to reporting the translation adjustment as a gain or loss in net income is to include it in stockholders' equity as a component of other comprehensive income. In effect, this treatment defers the gain or loss in stockholders' equity until it is realized in some way. As a balance sheet account, other comprehensive income is not closed at the end of the accounting period and will fluctuate in amount over time.

The two major translation methods and the two possible treatments for the translation adjustment give rise to four possible combinations:

Combination	Translation Method	Disposition of Translation Adjustment
A	Temporal	Gain or loss in net income
B	Temporal	Deferred in stockholders' equity (other comprehensive income)
C	Current rate	Gain or loss in net income
D	Current rate	Deferred in stockholders' equity (other comprehensive income)

U.S. GAAP

Prior to 1975, there were no authoritative rules in the United States as to which translation method to use or where the translation adjustment should be reported in the consolidated financial statements. Different companies used different combinations, creating a lack of comparability across companies. In 1975, to eliminate this noncomparability, the FASB issued SFAS 8, *Accounting for the Translation of Foreign Currency Transactions and Foreign Currency Financial Statements.* SFAS 8 mandated use of the temporal method with translation gains/losses reported in income by all companies for all foreign operations (Combination A).

U.S. multinational companies were strongly opposed to SFAS 8. Specifically, they considered reporting translation gains and losses in income to be inappropriate given that the gains and losses are unrealized. Moreover, because currency fluctuations often reverse themselves in subsequent quarters, artificial volatility in quarterly earnings resulted.

After releasing two Exposure Drafts proposing new translation rules, the FASB finally issued SFAS 52, *Foreign Currency Translation,* in 1981. This resulted in a complete overhaul of U.S. GAAP with regard to foreign currency translation. SFAS 52 was approved by a narrow four-to-three vote of the FASB, indicating how contentious the issue of foreign currency translation has been. The guidance provided in SFAS 52 was incorporated into FASB ASC 830, *Foreign Currency Matters,* in 2009.

FASB ASC 830

Implicit in the *temporal method* is the assumption that foreign subsidiaries of U.S. multinational corporations have very close ties to their parent company and would actually carry out their day-to-day operations and keep their books in the U.S. dollar if they could. To reflect the integrated nature of the foreign subsidiary with its U.S. parent, the translation process should create a set of U.S.-dollar translated financial statements as if the dollar had actually been used by the foreign subsidiary. This is described as the *U.S.-dollar perspective* to translation.

Subsequently, the FASB recognized that, whereas some foreign entities are closely integrated with their parent and do in fact conduct much of their business in U.S. dollars, other foreign entities are relatively self-contained and integrated with the local economy and primarily use a foreign currency in their daily operations. For the first type of entity, the FASB determined that the U.S.-dollar perspective still applies.

For the second relatively independent type of entity, a *local-currency perspective* to translation is applicable. For this type of entity, the FASB determined that a different translation methodology is appropriate; namely, the *current rate method* should be used for translation, and translation adjustments should be reported as a separate component in other comprehensive income (Combination D in the preceding table).

Functional Currency

To determine whether a specific foreign operation is (1) integrated with its parent or (2) self-contained and integrated with the local economy, the FASB developed the concept of the functional currency. The *functional currency* is the primary currency of the foreign entity's operating environment. It can be either the parent's currency (US$) or a foreign currency (generally the local currency). The functional currency orientation results in the following rule:

Functional Currency	Translation Method	Translation Adjustment
U.S. dollar	Temporal method	Gain (loss) in income
Foreign currency	Current rate method	Separate component of stockholders' equity (accumulated other comprehensive income)

When a foreign operation is sold or otherwise disposed of, the cumulative translation adjustment related to it that has been deferred in a separate component of stockholders' equity is transferred to income as a realized gain or loss.

In addition to introducing the concept of the functional currency, the FASB also introduced some new terminology. The *reporting currency* is the currency in which the entity prepares its financial statements. For U.S.-based corporations, this is the U.S. dollar. If a foreign operation's functional currency is the U.S. dollar, foreign currency balances must be *remeasured* into U.S. dollars using the temporal method, with translation adjustments reported as remeasurement gains and losses in income. When a foreign currency is the functional currency, foreign currency balances are *translated* using the current rate method and a translation adjustment is reported on the balance sheet.

The functional currency is essentially a matter of fact. However, the FASB states that for many cases, "management's judgment will be required to determine the functional currency in which financial results and relationships are measured with the greatest degree of relevance and reliability" (FASB ASC 830-10-55-4).

EXHIBIT 8.2
U.S. GAAP
Indicators for
Determining the
Functional Currency

	Indication That the Functional Currency Is the:	
Indicator	**Foreign Currency (FC)**	**Parent's Currency**
Cash flow	Primarily in FC and does not affect parent's cash flows	Directly impacts parent's cash flows on a current basis
Sales price	Not affected on short-term basis by changes in exchange rates	Affected on short-term basis by changes in exchange rates
Sales market	Active local sales market	Sales market mostly in parent's country or sales denominated in parent's currency
Expenses	Primarily local costs	Primarily costs for components obtained from parent's country
Financing	Primarily denominated in FC, and FC cash flows are adequate to service obligations	Primarily obtained from parent or denominated in parent currency, or FC cash flows not adequate to service obligations
Intercompany transaction	Low volume of intercompany transactions; no extensive interrelationships with parent's operations	High volume of intercompany transactions and extensive interrelationships with parent's operations

U.S. GAAP provides a list of indicators to guide parent company management in its determination of a foreign entity's functional currency (see Exhibit 8.2). However, no guidance is provided as to how these indicators are to be weighted in determining the functional currency. Leaving the decision about identifying the functional currency up to management allows some leeway in this process.

Different companies approach the selection of functional currency in different ways: "For us it was intuitively obvious" versus "It was quite a process. We took the six criteria and developed a matrix. We then considered the dollar amount and the related percentages in developing a point scheme. Each of the separate criteria was given equal weight (in the analytical methods applied)."[2]

Research has shown that the weighting schemes used by U.S. multinationals for determining the functional currency might be biased toward selection of the foreign currency as the functional currency.[3] This would be rational behavior for multinationals given that, when the foreign currency is the functional currency, the translation adjustment is reported on the balance sheet and does not affect net income.

Highly Inflationary Economies

For those foreign entities located in a *highly inflationary economy*, U.S. GAAP mandates use of the *temporal method* with *translation gains/losses reported in income*. A country is defined as a highly inflationary economy if its cumulative three-year inflation exceeds 100 percent. With compounding, this equates to an average of approximately 26 percent per year for three years in a row. Countries that have met this definition in the past include Argentina, Brazil, Israel, Mexico, Turkey, and Zimbabwe. In any given year, a country may or may not be classified as highly inflationary in accordance with U.S. GAAP, depending on its most recent three-year experience with inflation.

---

[2] Jerry L. Arnold and William W. Holder, *Impact of Statement 52 on Decisions, Financial Reports and Attitudes* (Morristown, NJ: Financial Executives Research Foundation, 1986), p. 89.

[3] Timothy S. Doupnik and Thomas G. Evans, "Functional Currency as a Strategy to Smooth Income," *Advances in International Accounting*, Vol. 2, 1988, pp. 171–182.

One reason for this rule is to avoid a "disappearing plant problem" that exists when the current rate method is used in a country with high inflation. Remember that under the current rate method, all assets (including fixed assets) are translated at the current exchange rate. To see the problem this creates in a highly inflationary economy, consider the following hypothetical example: the Brazilian subsidiary of a U.S. parent purchased land at the end of 1984 for 10,000,000 cruzeiros (CR$) when the exchange rate was $0.001 per CR$1. Under the *current rate method*, the land would be reported in the parent's consolidated balance sheet at $10,000.

	Historical Cost		Current Exchange Rate		Consolidated Balance Sheet
1984	CR$10,000,000	×	$0.001	=	$10,000

In 1985, Brazil experienced roughly 200 percent inflation. Accordingly, with the forces of purchasing power parity at work, the cruzeiro plummeted against the U.S. dollar to a value of $0.00025 at the end of 1985. Under the current rate method, land now would be reported in the parent's consolidated balance sheet at $2,500 and a negative translation adjustment of $7,500 would result.

	Historical Cost		Current Exchange Rate		Consolidated Balance Sheet
1985	CR$10,000,000	×	$0.00025	=	$2,500

Using the current rate method, land has lost 75 percent of its U.S.-dollar value in one year, and land is not even a depreciable asset!

High rates of inflation continued in Brazil, reaching the high point of roughly 1,800 percent in 1993. As a result of applying the current rate method, the land, which was originally reported on the 1984 consolidated balance sheet at $10,000, was carried on the 1993 balance sheet at less than $1.00.

In an Exposure Draft preceding the issuance of current authoritative guidance, the FASB proposed requiring companies with operations in highly inflationary countries to first *restate* the historical costs for inflation and then *translate* using the current rate method. For example, with 200 percent inflation in 1985, the land would have been written up to CR$40,000,000 and then translated at the current exchange rate of $0.00025. This would have produced a translated amount of $10,000, the same as in 1984.

Companies objected to making inflation adjustments, however, because of a lack of reliable inflation indexes in many countries. The FASB backed off from requiring the restate/translate approach. Instead, current U.S. GAAP requires that the temporal method be used in highly inflationary countries. In our example, land would be translated at the historical rate of $0.001 at each balance sheet date and carried at $10,000, thus avoiding the disappearing plant problem.

INTERNATIONAL FINANCIAL REPORTING STANDARDS

IAS 21, *The Effects of Changes in Foreign Exchange Rates*, contains guidance for the translation of foreign currency financial statements. To determine the appropriate translation method, IAS 21 originally required foreign subsidiaries to be classified as either (1) foreign operations that are integral to the operations of the reporting enterprise or (2) foreign entities. As part of a comprehensive improvements project, IAS 21 was revised in 2003, adopting the functional currency approach developed years earlier by the FASB. The revised standard defines *functional currency* as the currency of the primary economic environment in which a subsidiary operates. It can either be the same as the currency in which the parent presents its financial statements or be a different, foreign currency. IAS 21 provides a list of factors that should be considered in determining the functional currency (shown in Exhibit 8.3). Unlike U.S. GAAP, IAS 21 provides a hierarchy of primary and secondary factors to be considered in determining the functional currency of a foreign subsidiary. In addition, there are several differences in the factors to be considered under IFRS and U.S. GAAP. As a result of these differences, it is possible that a foreign subsidiary could be viewed as having one functional currency under IFRS but a different functional currency under U.S. GAAP.

IAS 21 requires the financial statements of a foreign subsidiary that has a functional currency different from the reporting currency of the parent to be translated using the current rate method, with the resulting translation adjustment reported as a separate component of stockholders' equity. Upon disposal of a foreign subsidiary, the cumulative translation adjustment related to that particular foreign subsidiary is transferred to income in the same period in which the gain or loss on disposal is recognized. The financial statements of a foreign subsidiary whose functional currency is the same as the parent's reporting currency are translated using the temporal method, with the resulting translation adjustment reported currently as a gain or loss in income. The same combinations are required under U.S. GAAP.

For foreign subsidiaries whose functional currency is the currency of a hyperinflationary economy, IAS 21 requires the parent first to restate the foreign financial statements for inflation using rules in IAS 29, *Financial Reporting in Hyperinflationary Economies,* and then translate the statements into parent company currency using the current exchange rate. All balance sheet accounts, including stockholders' equity, and all income statement accounts are translated at the

EXHIBIT 8.3
IAS 21 Functional Currency Indicators

Factors Considered in Determining the Functional Currency

In accordance with IAS 21, *The Effects of Changes in Foreign Exchange Rates,* the following factors should be considered first in determining an entity's functional currency:

1. The currency (a) that mainly influences sales prices for goods and services and (b) of the country whose competitive forces and regulations mainly determine the sales price of its goods and services.
2. The currency that mainly influences labor, material, and other costs of providing goods and services.

If the primary factors listed above are mixed and the functional currency is not obvious, the following secondary factors must be considered:

3. The currency in which funds from financing activities are generated.
4. The currency in which receipts from operating activities are usually retained.
5. Whether the activities of the foreign operation are an extension of the parent's or are carried out with a significant amount of autonomy.
6. Whether transactions with the parent are a large or a small proportion of the foreign entity's activities.
7. Whether cash flows generated by the foreign operation directly affect the cash flow of the parent and are available to be remitted to the parent.
8. Whether operating cash flows generated by the foreign operation are sufficient to service existing and normally expected debt or whether the foreign entity will need funds from the parent to service its debt.

current exchange rate. This approach is substantively different from U.S. GAAP, which requires translation of financial statements of a foreign subsidiary operating in a highly inflationary economy using the temporal method. IAS 29 provides no specific definition for hyperinflation but suggests that a cumulative three-year inflation rate approaching or exceeding 100 percent is evidence that an economy is hyperinflationary. We describe the process of adjusting financial statements for inflation under IAS 29 in Chapter 9.

THE TRANSLATION PROCESS ILLUSTRATED

To provide a basis for demonstrating the translation procedures prescribed by both IFRS and U.S. GAAP, assume that Multico (a U.S.-based company) forms a wholly owned subsidiary in Italy (Italco) on December 31, Year 0. On that date, Multico invests $1,350,000 in exchange for all of the subsidiary's capital stock. Given the exchange rate of €1.00 = $1.35, the initial capital investment is €1,000,000, of which €600,000 is immediately invested in inventory and the remainder is held in cash. Thus, Italco begins operations on January 1, Year 1, with stockholders' equity (net assets) of €1,000,000 and net monetary assets of €400,000. Italco's beginning balance sheet on January 1, Year 1, is shown in Exhibit 8.4.

During Year 1, Italco purchased property and equipment, acquired a patent, and made additional purchases of inventory, primarily on account. A five-year loan was negotiated to help finance the purchase of equipment. Sales were made, primarily on account, and expenses were incurred. Income after taxes of €825,000 was generated, with dividends of €325,000 declared on December 1, Year 1. Financial statements for Year 1 (in euros) appear in Exhibit 8.5.

To properly translate the euro financial statements into U.S. dollars, we must gather exchange rates between the euro and the U.S. dollar at various times. Relevant exchange rates are as follows:

January 1, Year 1	$1.35
Rate when property and equipment were acquired and long-term debt was incurred, January 15, Year 1	1.33
Rate when patent was acquired, February 1, Year 1	1.32
Average Year 1	1.30
Rate when dividends were declared, December 1, Year 1	1.27
Average for the month of December	1.26
December 31, Year 1	1.25

As can be seen, the euro steadily declined in value against the U.S. dollar during the year.

EXHIBIT 8.4

ITALCO			
Beginning Balance Sheet			
January 1, Year 1			
Assets	**€**	**Liabilities and Equity**	**€**
Cash	400,000	Capital stock	1,000,000
Inventory	600,000		1,000,000
	1,000,000		

EXHIBIT 8.5
Italco's Financial
Statements, Year 1

Income Statement
Year 1

	€
Sales	8,000,000
Cost of goods sold	6,000,000
Gross profit	2,000,000
Selling and administrative expenses	500,000
Depreciation expense	200,000
Amortization expense	20,000
Interest expense	180,000
Income before income taxes	1,100,000
Income taxes	275,000
Net income	825,000

Statement of Retained Earnings
Year 1

	€
Retained earnings, 1/1/Y1	0
Net income, Y1	825,000
Less: Dividends, 12/1/Y1	(325,000)
Retained earnings, 12/31/Y1	500,000

Balance Sheet
December 31, Year 1

Assets	€	Liabilities and Equity	€
Cash	550,000	Accounts payable	330,000
Accounts receivable	600,000	Total current liabilities . .	330,000
Inventory*	800,000	Long-term debt	2,000,000
Total current assets	1,950,000	Total liabilities	2,330,000
Property and equipment . . .	2,000,000	Capital stock	1,000,000
Less: Accumulated		Retained earnings	500,000
depreciation	(200,000)	Total	3,830,000
Patents, net	80,000		
Total assets	3,830,000		

* Inventory is carried at first-in, first-out (FIFO) cost; ending inventory was acquired evenly throughout the month of December.

TRANSLATION OF FINANCIAL STATEMENTS: CURRENT RATE METHOD

The first step in translating foreign currency financial statements is the determination of the functional currency. Assuming that the euro is the functional currency, the income statement and statement of retained earnings would be translated into U.S. dollars using the current rate method, as shown in Exhibit 8.6.

All revenues and expenses are translated at the exchange rate in effect at the date of accounting recognition. The weighted-average exchange rate for Year 1 is used because each revenue and expense in this illustration would have been recognized evenly throughout the year. However, when an income account, such as

EXHIBIT 8.6
Translation of
Income Statement
and Statement of
Retained Earnings:
Current Rate
Method

Income Statement Year 1			
	€	Translation Rate*	US$
Sales	8,000,000	$1.30 (A)	10,400,000
Cost of goods sold	6,000,000	1.30 (A)	7,800,000
Gross profit	2,000,000		2,600,000
Selling and administrative expenses ..	500,000	1.30 (A)	650,000
Depreciation expense	200,000	1.30 (A)	260,000
Amortization expense	20,000	1.30 (A)	26,000
Interest expense	180,000	1.30 (A)	234,000
Income before income taxes	1,100,000		1,430,000
Income taxes	275,000	1.30 (A)	357,500
Net income	825,000		1,072,500

Statement of Retained Earnings Year 1			
	€	Translation Rate*	US$
Retained earnings, 1/1/Y1	0		0
Net income, Year 1	825,000	From income statement	1,072,500
Less: Dividends, 12/1/Y1	(325,000)	1.27 (H)	(412,750)
Retained earnings, 12/31/Y1	500,000		659,750

* Indicates the exchange rate used and whether the rate is the current rate (C), the average rate (A), or a historical rate (H).

a gain or loss, occurs at a specific time, the exchange rate as of that date is applied. Depreciation and amortization expense are also translated at the average rate for the year. These expenses accrue evenly throughout the year even though the journal entry may have been delayed until year-end for convenience.

The translated amount of net income for Year 1 is transferred from the income statement to the statement of retained earnings. Dividends are translated at the exchange rate that exists on the date of declaration.

Translation of the Balance Sheet

Italco's translated balance sheet is shown in Exhibit 8.7. All assets and liabilities are translated at the current exchange rate. Capital stock is translated at the exchange rate that existed when the capital stock was originally issued. Retained earnings at December 31, Year 1, is brought down from the statement of retained earnings. Application of these procedures results in total assets of $4,787,500 and total liabilities and equities of $4,922,250. The balance sheet is brought back into balance by creating a negative translation adjustment of $134,750, which is treated as a decrease in stockholders' equity.

Note that the translation adjustment for Year 1 is a *negative* $134,750 (debit balance). The sign of the translation adjustment (positive or negative) is a function of two factors: (1) the nature of the balance sheet exposure (asset or liability) and (2) the direction of change in the exchange rate (appreciation or depreciation). In this illustration, Italco has a *net asset exposure* (total assets translated at the current

EXHIBIT 8.7
Translation of
Balance Sheet:
Current Rate
Method

Balance Sheet December 31, Year 1			
Assets	**€**	**Translation Rate***	**US$**
Cash	550,000	$1.25 (C)	687,500
Accounts receivable	600,000	1.25 (C)	750,000
Inventory	800,000	1.25 (C)	1,000,000
Total current assets	1,950,000		2,437,500
Property and equipment	2,000,000	1.25 (C)	2,500,000
Less: Accumulated depreciation.	(200,000)	1.25 (C)	(250,000)
Patents, net	80,000	1.25 (C)	100,000
Total assets	3,830,000		4,787,500
Liabilities and Equity			
Accounts payable	330,000	$1.25 (C)	412,500
Total current liabilities	330,000		412,500
Long-term debt	2,000,000	1.25 (C)	2,500,000
Total liabilities	2,330,000		2,912,500
Capital stock	1,000,000	1.35 (H)	1,350,000
Retained earnings	500,000	From statement of retained earnings	659,750
Cumulative translation adjustment . . .	—	To balance	(134,750)
Total equity	1,500,000		1,875,000
	3,830,000		4,787,500

exchange rate are greater than total liabilities translated at the current exchange rate), and the euro has *depreciated,* creating a *negative translation adjustment.*

The translation adjustment can be derived as a balancing figure that brings the balance sheet back into balance. The translation adjustment also can be calculated by considering the impact of exchange rate changes on the beginning balance and subsequent changes in the net asset position. The following steps are applied:

1. The net asset balance of the subsidiary at the beginning of the year is translated at the exchange rate in effect on that date.

2. Individual increases and decreases in the net asset balance during the year are translated at the rates in effect when those increases and decreases occur. Only a few events actually change net assets (e.g., net income, dividends, stock issuance, and the acquisition of treasury stock). Transactions such as the acquisition of equipment or the payment of a liability have no effect on total net assets.

3. The translated beginning net asset balance (*a*) and the translated value of the individual changes (*b*) are then combined to arrive at the relative value of the net assets being held prior to the impact of any exchange rate fluctuations.

4. The ending net asset balance is then translated at the current exchange rate to determine the reported value after all exchange rate changes have occurred.

5. The translated value of the net assets prior to any rate changes (*c*) is compared with the ending translated value (*d*). The difference is the result of exchange rate changes during the period. If (*c*) is greater than (*d*), then a negative (debit) translation adjustment arises. If (*d*) is greater than (*c*), a positive (credit) translation adjustment results.

Computation of Translation Adjustment

According to the process just described, determination of the translation adjustment to be reported for Italco in this example is calculated as follows:

	€				US$
Net asset balance, 1/1/Y1	1,000,000	×	1.35	=	1,350,000
Change in net assets:					
Net income, Year 1	825,000	×	1.30	=	1,072,500
Dividends, 12/1/Y1	(325,000)	×	1.27	=	(412,750)
Net asset balance, 12/31/Y1	1,500,000				2,009,750
Net asset balance, 12/31/Y1, at current exchange rate	1,500,000	×	1.25	=	1,875,000
Translation adjustment, Year 1 (negative) . . .					134,750

Since this subsidiary began operations at the beginning of the current year, $134,750 is the amount of cumulative translation adjustment reported on the consolidated balance sheet. The translation adjustment is reported as a separate component of equity only until the foreign operation is sold or liquidated. In the period in which a sale or liquidation occurs, the cumulative translation adjustment related to the particular foreign subsidiary must be removed from equity and reported as part of the gain or loss on the sale of the investment.

REMEASUREMENT OF FINANCIAL STATEMENTS: TEMPORAL METHOD

Now assume that a careful examination of the functional currency indicators leads Multico's management to conclude that Italco's functional currency is the U.S. dollar. In that case, the euro financial statements will be remeasured into U.S. dollars using the temporal method and the remeasurement gain or loss will be reported in income. To ensure that the remeasurement gain or loss is reported in income, it is easier to remeasure the balance sheet first (as shown in Exhibit 8.8).

According to the procedures outlined in Exhibit 8.1, under the temporal method, cash, receivables, and liabilities are remeasured into U.S. dollars using the current exchange rate of $1.25. Inventory, carried at first-in, first-out (FIFO) cost; property and equipment; patents; and the capital stock account are remeasured at historical rates. These procedures result in total assets of $4,945,100, and liabilities and capital stock of $4,262,500. In order for the balance sheet to balance, retained earnings must be $682,600. The accuracy of this amount is verified below.

Remeasurement of Income Statement

The remeasurement of Italco's income statement and statement of retained earnings is demonstrated in Exhibit 8.9. Revenues and expenses incurred evenly throughout the year (sales, selling and administrative expenses, interest expense, and income taxes) are remeasured at the average exchange rate. Expenses related to assets remeasured at historical exchange rates (depreciation expense and amortization expense) are themselves remeasured at relevant historical rates.

EXHIBIT 8.8
Translation of
Balance Sheet:
Temporal Method

Balance Sheet December 31, Year 1			
Assets	**€**	**Translation Rate***	**US$**
Cash	550,000	$1.25 (C)	687,500
Accounts receivable	600,000	1.25 (C)	750,000
Inventory	800,000	1.26 (H)	1,008,000
Total current assets	1,950,000		2,445,500
Property and equipment	2,000,000	1.33 (H)	2,660,000
Less: Accumulated depreciation	(200,000)	1.33 (H)	(266,000)
Patents, net	80,000	1.32 (H)	105,600
Total assets	3,830,000		4,945,100
Liabilities and Equity			
Accounts payable	330,000	$1.25 (C)	412,500
Total current liabilities	330,000		412,500
Long-term debt	2,000,000	1.25 (C)	2,500,000
Total liabilities	2,330,000		2,912,500
Capital stock	1,000,000	1.35 (H)	1,350,000
Retained earnings	500,000	To balance	682,600
Total equity	1,500,000		2,032,600
	3,830,000		4,945,100

EXHIBIT 8.9
Translation of
Income Statement
and Statement of
Retained Earnings:
Temporal Method

Income Statement Year 1			
	€	**Translation Rate***	**US$**
Sales	8,000,000	$1.30 (A)	10,400,000
Cost of goods sold	6,000,000	calculation (H)	7,862,000
Gross profit	2,000,000		2,538,000
Selling and administrative expenses	500,000	1.30 (A)	650,000
Depreciation expense	200,000	1.33 (H)	266,000
Amortization expense	20,000	1.32 (H)	26,400
Interest expense	180,000	1.30 (A)	234,000
Income before income taxes	1,100,000		1,361,600
Income taxes	(275,000)	1.30 (A)	(357,500)
Remeasurement gain	—	To balance	91,250
Net income	825,000		1,095,350

Statement of Retained Earnings Year 1			
	€	**Translation Rate***	**US$**
Retained earnings, 1/1/Y1	0		0
Net income, Year 1	825,000	From income statement	1,095,350
Less: Dividends, 12/1/Y1	(325,000)	1.27 (H)	(412,750)
Retained earnings, 12/31/Y1	500,000		682,600

Cost of goods sold is remeasured at historical exchange rates using the following procedure. Beginning inventory was acquired on January 1 and is remeasured at the exchange rate from that date ($1.35). Purchases were made evenly throughout the year and are therefore remeasured at the average rate for the year ($1.30). Ending inventory (at FIFO cost) was purchased evenly throughout the month of December, and the average exchange rate for that month ($1.26) is used to remeasure that component of cost of goods sold. These procedures result in cost of goods sold of $7,862,000, calculated as follows:

	€				US$
Beginning inventory	600,000	×	$1.35	=	810,000
Plus: Purchases.	6,200,000	×	$1.30	=	8,060,000
Less: Ending inventory	(800,000)	×	$1.26	=	(1,008,000)
Cost of goods sold.	6,000,000				7,862,000

The ending balance in retained earnings on the balance sheet and in the statement of retained earnings must reconcile with one another. Given that dividends are remeasured into a U.S.-dollar equivalent of $412,750 and the ending balance in retained earnings on the balance sheet is $682,600, net income must be $1,095,350.

In order for the amount of income reported in the statement of retained earnings and in the income statement to reconcile with one another, a remeasurement gain of $91,250 is required in the calculation of income. Without this remeasurement gain, the income statement, statement of retained earnings, and balance sheet will not be consistent with one another.

The remeasurement gain can be calculated by considering the impact of exchange rate changes on the subsidiary's balance sheet exposure. Under the temporal method, Italco's balance sheet exposure is defined by its net monetary asset or net monetary liability position. Italco began Year 1 with net monetary assets (cash) of €400,000. During the year, however, expenditures of cash and the incurrence of liabilities caused monetary liabilities (Accounts payable + Long-term debt = €2,330,000) to exceed monetary assets (Cash + Accounts receivable = €1,150,000). A net monetary liability position of €1,180,000 exists at December 31, Year 1. The remeasurement gain is computed by translating the beginning net monetary asset position and subsequent changes in monetary items at appropriate exchange rates and then comparing this with the U.S.-dollar value of net monetary liabilities at year-end based on the current exchange rate.

Computation of Remeasurement Gain

	€	Translation Rate	US$
Net monetary assets, 1/1/Y1	400,000	$1.35	540,000
Increase in monetary items:			
Sales, Year 1	8,000,000	1.30	10,400,000
Decrease in monetary items:			
Purchases of inventory, Year 1	(6,200,000)	1.30	(8,060,000)
Selling and administrative expenses,			
Year 1	(500,000)	1.30	(650,000)
Payment of interest, Year 1	(180,000)	1.30	(234,000)

	€	Translation Rate	US$
Income taxes, Year 1	(275,000)	1.30	(357,500)
Purchase of property and equipment, 1/15/Y1	(2,000,000)	1.33	(2,660,000)
Acquisition of patent, 2/1/Y1	(100,000)	1.32	(132,000)
Dividends, 12/1/Y1	(325,000)	1.27	(412,750)
Net monetary liabilities, 12/31/Y1	(1,180,000)		(1,566,250)
Net monetary liabilities, 12/31/Y1, at the current exchange rate	(1,180,000)	1.25	(1,475,000)
Remeasurement gain			(91,250)

If Italco had maintained its net monetary asset position (cash) of €400,000 for the entire year, a remeasurement loss of $40,000 would have resulted. (The euro amount held in cash was worth $540,000 [€400,000 × $1.35] at the beginning of the year and $500,000 [€400,0000 × $1.25] at year-end.) However, the net monetary asset position is not maintained. Indeed, a net monetary liability position arises. The *depreciation* of the foreign currency coupled with an increase in *net monetary liabilities* generates a *remeasurement gain* for the year.

NONLOCAL CURRENCY BALANCES

An additional issue relates to how nonlocal currency balances in the foreign currency financial statements of foreign operations are reported in the consolidated financial statements. For example, if any of the accounts of the Italian subsidiary are denominated in a currency other than the euro, those balances would first have to be restated into euros in accordance with the rules discussed in the previous chapter. Both the foreign currency balance and any related foreign exchange gain or loss would then be translated (or remeasured) into U.S. dollars. For example, assume that Italco borrows 100,000 Swiss francs on January 1, Year 1, and has a 100,000 Swiss franc note payable throughout Year 1. Exchange rates in Year 1 between the Swiss franc (CHF) and the euro (€) and between the euro and the U.S. dollar ($) are as follows:

	€ per CHF	$ per €
January 1, 2013.	€0.80	$1.35
Average 2013	€0.82	$1.30
December 31, 2013.	€0.85	$1.25

On December 31, Year 1, Italco remeasures the CHF 100,000 note payable into CHF using the current exchange rate as follows: CHF 100,000 × €0.85 = €85,000. Italco also recognizes a foreign exchange loss of €5,000 [CHF 100,000 × (€0.85 − €0.80)] on the Swiss franc note payable due to the appreciation of the Swiss franc against the euro. To consolidate Italco's Swiss franc financial statements with those of its parent, the note payable remeasured in euros is then translated into U.S. dollars using the current exchange rate and the related foreign exchange loss in euros is translated into U.S. dollars using the average exchange rate as follows:

Note payable	€85,000 × $1.25 (C) = $106,250
Foreign exchange loss	€5,000 × $1.30 (A) = $6,500

A note payable of $106,250 will be reported on the consolidated balance sheet, and a loss of $6,500 will be reflected in the measurement of consolidated net income.

COMPARISON OF THE RESULTS FROM APPLYING THE TWO DIFFERENT METHODS

The use of different translation methods can have a significant impact on Multico's consolidated financial statements. The chart below shows differences for Italco in several key items under the two different translation methods:

Item	Translation Method		Difference
	Current Rate	Temporal	
Net income	$1,072,500	$1,095,350	+2.1%
Total assets	$4,787,500	$4,945,100	+3.3%
Total equity	$1,875,000	$2,032,600	+8.4%
Return on ending equity	57.2%	53.9%	−5.8%

If the temporal method is applied, net income is 2.1 percent greater, total assets are 3.3 percent greater, and total equity is 8.4 percent greater than if the current rate method is applied. Because of the larger amount of equity under the temporal method, return on ending equity (net income/total equity) is only 53.9 percent as opposed to 57.2 percent using the current rate method.

It should be noted that the temporal method does not always result in larger net income (and a greater amount of equity) than the current rate method. For example, if Italco had maintained its net monetary asset position throughout the year, a remeasurement loss would have been computed under the temporal method, leading to lower income than under the current rate method. Moreover, if the euro had appreciated during Year 1, the current rate method would have resulted in higher net income.

The important point is that selection of translation method can have a significant impact on the amounts reported by a parent company in its consolidated financial statements. Different functional currencies selected by different companies in the same industry could have a significant impact on the comparability of financial statements within that industry.

In addition to differences in amounts reported in the consolidated financial statements, the results of the Italco illustration can be used to demonstrate several conceptual differences between the two translation methods.

Underlying Valuation Method

Using the temporal method, Italco's property and equipment was remeasured as follows:

Property and equipment	€2,000,000	×	$1.33 H	=	$2,660,000

By multiplying the historical cost in euros by the historical exchange rate, $2,660,000 represents the U.S.-dollar equivalent historical cost of this asset. It is the amount of U.S. dollars that the parent company would have had to pay to acquire assets having a cost of €2,000,000 when the exchange rate was $1.33 per euro.

Property and equipment was translated under the current rate method as follows:

Property and equipment	€2,000,000	×	$1.25 C	=	$2,500,000

The $2,500,000 amount is not readily interpretable. It does not represent the U.S.-dollar equivalent historical cost of the asset; that amount is $2,660,000. It also does not represent the U.S.-dollar equivalent current cost of the asset, because €2,000,000 is not the current cost of the asset in Italy. The $2,500,000 amount is simply the product of multiplying two numbers together!

Underlying Relationships

The following table reports the values for selected financial ratios calculated from the original foreign currency financial statements and from the U.S.-dollar translated statements using the two different translation methods.

		US$	
Ratio	€	Current Rate	Temporal
Current ratio (Current assets/Current liabilities)	5.91	5.91	5.93
Debt/equity ratio (Total liabilities/Total equity)	1.55	1.55	1.43
Gross profit ratio (Gross profit/Sales)	25.0%	25.0%	24.4%
Return on equity (Net income/Total equity)	55.0%	57.2%	53.9%

The temporal method distorts all of the ratios as measured in the foreign currency. The subsidiary appears to be more liquid, less highly leveraged, and less profitable than it does in euro terms.

The current rate method maintains the first three ratios, but return on equity is distorted. This distortion occurs because income was translated at the average-for-the-period exchange rate, whereas total equity was translated at the current exchange rate. In fact, any ratio that combines balance sheet and income statement figures, such as turnover ratios, will be distorted because of the use of the average rate for income and the current rate for assets and liabilities.

Conceptually, when the current rate method is employed, income statement items can be translated either at exchange rates in effect when sales are made and expenses are incurred (approximated by the average rate) or at the current exchange rate at the balance sheet date. IFRS and U.S. GAAP require the average exchange rate to be used. In this illustration, if revenues and expenses had been translated at the current exchange rate, net income would have been $1,031,250 (€825,000 × $1.25), and the return on equity would have been 55.0 percent ($1,031,250/$1,875,000), exactly the amount reflected in the euro financial statements.

HEDGING BALANCE SHEET EXPOSURE

When a foreign operation is determined to have the parent's reporting currency as its functional currency or is located in a highly inflationary economy, remeasurement gains and losses will be reported in the consolidated income statement. Management of multinational companies might wish to avoid reporting remeasurement losses in income because of the perceived negative impact this has on the company's stock price or the adverse effect on incentive compensation. Likewise, when the foreign operation has a foreign currency as its functional currency, management might wish to avoid reporting negative translation adjustments in stockholders' equity because of the adverse impact on ratios such as the debt-to-equity ratio.

Translation adjustments and remeasurement gains/losses are a function of two factors: (1) changes in the exchange rate and (2) balance sheet exposure. While individual companies have no influence over exchange rates, there are several techniques that parent companies can use to hedge the balance sheet exposures of their foreign operations. Each of these techniques involves creating an equilibrium between foreign currency asset and foreign currency liability balances that are translated at current exchange rates.

Balance sheet exposure can be hedged through the use of a derivative financial instrument such as a forward contract or foreign currency option, or through the use of a nonderivative hedging instrument such as a foreign currency borrowing. To illustrate, assume that Italco's functional currency is the euro; this creates a *net asset balance sheet exposure*. Multico believes that the euro will lose value over the course of the next year, thereby generating a negative translation adjustment that will reduce consolidated stockholders' equity. Multico can hedge this balance sheet exposure by borrowing euros for a period of time, thus creating an offsetting euro liability exposure. As the euro depreciates, a foreign exchange gain will arise on the euro liability that offsets the negative translation adjustment arising from the translation of Italco's financial statements.

As an alternative to the euro borrowing, Multico might have acquired a euro call option to hedge its balance sheet exposure. As the euro depreciates, the fair value of the call option should increase, resulting in a gain. Both IFRS and U.S. GAAP provide that the gain or loss on a hedging instrument that is designated and effective as a *hedge of the net investment in a foreign operation* should be reported in the same manner as the translation adjustment being hedged. Thus, the foreign exchange gain on the euro borrowing or the gain on the foreign currency option would be included in other comprehensive income along with the negative translation adjustment arising from the translation of Italco's financial statements. This is an exception to the general rule that foreign currency gains and losses are taken directly to net income. In the event that the gain on the hedging instrument is greater than the translation adjustment being hedged, the excess is taken to net income. Exhibit 8.10 contains disclosures made by International Business Machines Corporation (IBM) in its 2012 annual report with respect to hedging net investments in foreign operations.

The paradox of hedging a balance sheet exposure is that in the process of avoiding an unrealized translation adjustment, realized foreign exchange gains and losses can result. Consider Multico's foreign currency borrowing to hedge a euro exposure. At initiation of the loan, Multico will convert the borrowed euros into U.S. dollars at the spot exchange rate. When the liability matures,

EXHIBIT 8.10

INTERNATIONAL BUSINESS MACHINES CORPORATION
Annual Report
2012

Excerpt from Note D. Financial Instruments

Long-Term Investments in Foreign Subsidiaries (Net Investment)

A large portion of the company's foreign currency denominated debt portfolio is designated as a hedge of net investment in foreign subsidiaries to reduce the volatility in stockholders' equity caused by changes in foreign currency exchange rates in the functional currency of major foreign subsidiaries with respect to the U.S. dollar. The company also uses cross-currency swaps and foreign exchange forward contracts for this risk management purpose. At December 31, 2012 and 2011, the total notional amount of derivative instruments designated as net investment hedges was $3.3 billion and $5.0 billion, respectively.

Multico will purchase euros at the spot rate prevailing at that date to repay the loan. The change in exchange rate over the life of the loan will generate a realized gain or loss. If the euro depreciates as expected, the result will be a realized foreign exchange gain that will offset the negative translation adjustment in other comprehensive income. Although the net effect on other comprehensive income is zero, there is a net increase in cash as a result of the hedge. If the euro unexpectedly appreciates, a realized foreign exchange loss will occur. This will be offset by a positive translation adjustment in other comprehensive income, but a net decrease in cash will arise. While a hedge of a net investment in a foreign operation eliminates the possibility of reporting a negative translation adjustment in other comprehensive income, the result can be realized gains and losses that affect cash flow.

Exhibit 8.11 presents an excerpt from the notes to the consolidated financial statements in Nokia Corporation's 2012 annual report filed on Form 20-F. Nokia prepares its financial statements in accordance with IFRS, and the excerpt describes Nokia's compliance with IAS 39 with respect to hedging of net investments. Nokia uses forward contracts, options, and foreign currency borrowings to hedge its balance sheet exposures. Hedge accounting is applied when hedges are properly documented and effective. Changes in fair value of forward contracts attributable to changes in the spot rate, changes in the intrinsic value of options, and foreign exchange gains and losses on foreign currency borrowings are deferred in stockholders' equity until the subsidiary whose balance sheet exposure is being hedged is sold or liquidated. This also is consistent with the guidance provided under U.S. GAAP.

EXHIBIT 8.11

NOKIA CORPORATION
Form 20-F
2012

Excerpt from Note 1. Accounting Principles

Hedges of Net Investments in Foreign Operations

The Group also applies hedge accounting for its foreign currency hedging on net investments. Qualifying hedges are those properly documented hedges of the foreign exchange rate risk of foreign currency-denominated net investments that are effective both prospectively and retrospectively.

For qualifying foreign exchange forwards the change in fair value that reflects the change in spot exchange rates is deferred in translation differences within consolidated shareholders' equity. The change in fair value that reflects the change in forward exchange rates less the change in spot exchange rates is recognized in profit and loss in financial income and expenses. For qualifying foreign exchange options the change in intrinsic value is deferred in translation differences within consolidated shareholders' equity. Changes in the time value are at all times recognized directly in profit and loss account as financial income and expense. If a foreign currency–denominated loan is used as a hedge, all foreign exchange gains and losses arising from the transaction are recognized in translation differences within consolidated shareholders' equity. In all cases, the ineffective portion is recognized immediately in profit and loss as financial income and expenses.

Accumulated changes in fair value from qualifying hedges are released from translation differences on the disposal of all or part of a foreign group company by sale, liquidation, repayment of share capital, or abandonment. The cumulative amount or proportionate share of the changes in the fair value from qualifying hedges deferred in translation differences is recognized as income or as expense when the gain or loss on disposal is recognized.

DISCLOSURES RELATED TO TRANSLATION

Accounting standards require an analysis of the change in the cumulative translation adjustment account to be presented in the financial statements or notes thereto. Many U.S. companies comply with this requirement by providing information on the current year's translation adjustment in their statement of comprehensive income and including a column titled "Accumulated Other Comprehensive Income" in their statement of stockholders' equity. Exhibit 8.12 demonstrates this method of disclosure as used by McDonald's Corporation. In 2012, McDonald's has three items that affect AOCI, including one labeled *Foreign currency translation*. McDonald's Consolidated Statement of Comprehensive Income reported negative foreign currency translation adjustments in 2010 and 2011 of $3.0 million and $285.1 million, respectively. From the negative signs of these adjustments, we can infer that the currencies in which McDonald's foreign subsidiaries operate, on average, depreciated against the U.S. dollar in those years; the rate of depreciation was considerably higher in 2011 than in 2010. In 2012, the foreign currency translation adjustment was a positive $274.6 million, implying an appreciation of foreign currencies against the U.S. dollar. Note that in 2011, the company reported reclassifying $25.4 million of cumulative translation adjustment to net income as a loss. This was related to the disposal of one or more foreign operations. In effect, the cumulative negative translation adjustment related to those foreign operations that had been deferred in AOCI was recognized as a loss in net income in that year. McDonald's Consolidated Statement of Shareholders' Equity reports the balances in the cumulative foreign currency translation account that, although not shown, are included on the Consolidated Balance Sheet within the shareholders' equity line item labeled *Accumulated other comprehensive income*. McDonald's had a positive cumulative translation adjustment of $852.0 million included in AOCI at the end of 2012.

IAS 21 also requires companies to provide information related to their cumulative translation adjustments. Exhibit 8.13 presents a portion of the Germany-based BASF Group's Statement of Income and Expense Recognized in Equity, which

EXHIBIT 8.12

MCDONALD'S CORPORATION			
Annual Report			
2012			

Excerpt from Consolidated Statement of Comprehensive Income

	Years ended December 31, In millions		
	2012	**2011**	**2010**
Other comprehensive income (loss), net of tax			
Foreign currency translation adjustments:			
Gain (loss) recognized in accumulated other comprehensive income (AOCI), including net investment hedges	$274.7	$(310.5)	$(3.0)
Reclassification of (gain) loss to net income	(0.1)	25.4	—
Foreign currency translation adjustments–net of tax benefit (expense) of $(47.9), $61.0 and $52.2	$274.6	$(285.1)	$(3.0)

EXHIBIT 8.12   *(Concluded)*

Excerpt from Consolidated Statement of Shareholders' Equity

	Accumulated other comprehensive income (loss)		
In millions, except per share data	**Pensions**	**Cash flow hedges**	**Foreign currency translation**
Balance at December 31, 2009	$(134.6)	$16.5	$865.5
Other comprehensive income (loss), net of tax	10.0	(1.5)	(3.0)
Balance at December 31, 2010	(124.6)	15.0	862.5
Other comprehensive income (loss), net of tax	(7.7)	(10.4)	(285.1)
Balance at December 31, 2011	(132.3)	4.6	577.4
Other comprehensive income (loss), net of tax	41.5	30.6	274.6
Balance at December 31, 2012	$(90.8)	$35.2	$852.0

EXHIBIT 8.13

BASF GROUP
Annual Report
2012

Statement of Income and Expense Recognized in Equity

Development of income and expense recognized directly in equity of shareholders of BASF SE (million €)

	Retained earnings		Other comprehensive Income					
	Actuarial gains/ losses; asset ceiling	**Foreign currency translation adjustment**	**Fair value changes in available-for-sale securities**	**Cash flow hedges**	**Hedges of net investments in foreign operations**	**Revaluation due to acquisition of majority of shares**	**Total of other comprehensive income**	**Total income and expense recognized directly in equity**
As of January 1, 2012	(2,108)	373	10	(71)	(2)	4	314	(1,794)
Additions	(2,813)	—	7	—	—	—	7	(2,806)
Releases	—	(211)	—	12	2	(3)	(200)	(200)
Deferred taxes	874	3	=	(14)	=	=	(11)	863
As of December 31, 2012	(4,047)	165	17	(73)	=	1	110	(3,937)
As of January 1, 2011	(1,526)	190	1,009	(3)	(7)	6	1,195	(331)
Additions	(763)	186	—	(71)	—	—	115	(648)
Releases	—	—	(1,014)	—	5	(2)	(1,011)	(1,011)
Deferred taxes	181	(3)	15	3	=	=	15	196
As of December 31, 2011	(2,108)	373	10	(71)	(2)	4	314	(1,794)

details the "development of income and expenses recognized directly in equity." This statement shows that BASF had a cumulative translation adjustment with a positive balance of €190 million on January 1, 2011, recorded a positive translation adjustment of €186 million (€183 net of tax) for the year 2011, and ended 2011 with a positive cumulative translation adjustment of €33 million. A negative translation adjustment of €211 million arose in 2012, which caused the positive balance in the cumulative translation adjustment to be only €165 million at December 31, 2012.

Although there is no specific requirement to do so, many companies include a description of their translation procedures in their "summary of significant accounting policies" in the notes to the financial statements. The following excerpt from IBM's 2012 annual report illustrates this type of disclosure:

Translation of Non-U.S. Currency Amounts

Assets and liabilities of non-U.S. subsidiaries that have a local functional currency are translated to United States (U.S.) dollars at year-end exchange rates. Translation adjustments are recorded in OCI. Income and expense items are translated at weighted-average rates of exchange prevailing during the year.

Inventories, property, plant, and equipment—net, and other nonmonetary assets and liabilities of non-U.S. subsidiaries and branches that operate in U.S. dollars are translated at the approximate exchange rates prevailing when the company acquired the assets or liabilities. All other assets and liabilities denominated in a currency other than U.S. dollars are translated at year-end exchange rates with the transaction gain or loss recognized in other (income) and expense. Income and expense items are translated at the weighted-average rates of exchange prevailing during the year. These translation gains and losses are included in net income for the period in which exchange rates change.[4]

Summary

1. The two major issues related to the translation of foreign currency financial statements are (*a*) which method should be used, and (*b*) where the resulting translation adjustment should be reported in the consolidated financial statements.

2. Translation methods differ on the basis of which accounts are translated at the current exchange rate and which are translated at historical rates. Accounts translated at the current exchange rate are exposed to translation adjustment. Different translation methods give rise to different concepts of balance sheet exposure and translation adjustments of differing sign and magnitude.

3. Under the current rate method, all assets and liabilities are translated at the current exchange rate, giving rise to a net asset balance sheet exposure. Appreciation in the foreign currency will result in a positive translation adjustment. Depreciation in the foreign currency will result in a negative translation adjustment. By translating assets carried at historical cost at the current exchange rate, the current rate method maintains relationships that exist among account balances in the foreign currency financial statements but distorts the underlying valuation method used by the foreign operation.

4. Under the temporal method, assets carried at current or future value (cash, marketable securities, receivables) and liabilities are translated (remeasured) at the current exchange rate. Assets carried at historical cost and stockholders' equity are translated (remeasured) at historical exchange rates. When liabilities are greater than the sum of cash, marketable securities, and receivables, a net liability balance sheet exposure exists. Appreciation in the foreign currency will result

---

[4] IBM Corporation, 2012 Annual Report, Note A. Significant Accounting Policies, p. 83.

in a negative translation adjustment (remeasurement loss). Depreciation in the foreign currency will result in a positive translation adjustment (remeasurement gain). By translating (remeasuring) assets carried at historical cost at historical exchange rates, the temporal method maintains the underlying valuation method used by the foreign operation but distorts relationships that exist among account balances in the foreign currency financial statements.

5. The appropriate combination of translation method and disposition of translation adjustment is determined under both IFRS and U.S. GAAP by identifying the functional currency of a foreign operation. The financial statements of foreign operations whose functional currency is different from the parent's reporting currency are translated using the current rate method, with the translation adjustment included in stockholders' equity. The financial statements of foreign operations whose functional currency is the same as the parent's reporting currency are translated using the temporal method, with the resulting translation gain or loss reported currently in net income.

6. The only substantive difference in translation rules between IFRS and U.S. GAAP relates to foreign operations that report in the currency of a hyperinflationary economy. IAS 21 requires the parent first to restate the foreign financial statements for inflation using rules in IAS 29 and then to translate the statements into parent-company currency using the current rate method. FASB ASC 830 requires the financial statements of foreign operations that report in the currency of a highly inflationary economy to be translated using the temporal method, as if the U.S. dollar were the functional currency. A country is considered highly inflationary if its cumulative three-year inflation rate exceeds 100 percent.

7. Some companies hedge their balance sheet exposures to avoid reporting remeasurement losses in income and/or negative translation adjustments in stockholders' equity. Foreign exchange gains and losses on foreign currency borrowings or foreign currency derivatives employed to hedge translation-based exposure (under the current rate method) are treated as part of the cumulative translation adjustment in stockholders' equity. Foreign exchange gains and losses on balance sheet hedges used to hedge remeasurement-based exposure (under the temporal method) are offset against remeasurement gain and losses on the income statement.

Questions

1. What are the two major conceptual issues that must be resolved in translating foreign currency financial statements?

2. What factors create a balance sheet (or translation) exposure to foreign exchange risk? How does balance sheet exposure compare with transaction exposure?

3. What is the concept underlying the current rate method of translation? What is the concept underlying the temporal method of translation? How does balance sheet exposure differ under these two methods?

4. What are the major procedural differences in applying the current rate and temporal methods of translation?

5. How does a parent company determine the appropriate method for translating the financial statements of a foreign subsidiary?

6. What are the major differences between IFRS and U.S. GAAP in the translation of foreign currency financial statements?

7. What does the term *functional currency* mean? How is the functional currency determined under IFRS and under U.S. GAAP?

8. Which translation method does U.S. GAAP require for operations in highly inflationary countries? What is the rationale for mandating use of this method?

9. Why might a company want to hedge its balance sheet exposure? What is the paradox associated with hedging balance sheet exposure?

10. How are gains and losses on foreign currency borrowings used to hedge the net investment in a foreign subsidiary reported in the consolidated financial statements?

Exercises and Problems

1. Which of the following items is normally translated the same way under both the current rate and temporal methods of translation?
   a. Inventory
   b. Equipment
   c. Sales revenue ✓
   d. Depreciation expense

2. In translating the financial statements of a foreign subsidiary into the parent's reporting currency under the current rate method, which of the following statements is true?
   a. Expenses are translated using a combination of current and historical exchange rates.
   b. Intangible assets are translated at the historical exchange rates in effect on the date the assets are purchased.
   c. The translation adjustment is a function of the foreign subsidiary's net assets.
   d. The translation adjustment is a function of the relative amount of monetary assets and monetary liabilities held by the foreign subsidiary.

3. A foreign subsidiary of Wampoa Ltd. has one asset (inventory) and no liabilities. The subsidiary operates with a significant degree of autonomy from Wampoa and primarily uses the local currency (the won) in carrying out its transactions. Since the date the inventory was acquired, the won has decreased in value in relation to Wampoa's reporting currency. In translating the foreign subsidiary's won financial statements into the parent's reporting currency, which of the following is true?
   a. A translation gain must be reported in net income.
   b. A positive translation adjustment must be reported in stockholders' equity.
   c. A negative translation adjustment must be reported in stockholders' equity.
   d. A translation loss must be reported in net income.

4. Which of the following best explains how a translation loss arises when the temporal method of translation is used to translate the foreign currency financial statements of a foreign subsidiary?
   a. The foreign subsidiary has more monetary assets than monetary liabilities, and the foreign currency appreciates in value.
   b. The foreign subsidiary has more monetary liabilities than monetary assets, and the foreign currency depreciates in value.
   c. The foreign subsidiary has more monetary assets than monetary liabilities, and the foreign currency depreciates in value.

d. The foreign subsidiary has more total assets than total liabilities, and the foreign currency appreciates in value.

5. Which method of translation maintains, in the translated financial statements, the underlying valuation methods used in the foreign currency financial statements?

    a. Current rate method; income statement translated at average exchange rate for the year.

    b. Current rate method; income statement translated at exchange rate at the balance sheet date.

    ✓c. Temporal method.

    d. Monetary/nonmonetary method.

6. In accordance with U.S. generally accepted accounting principles (GAAP), which translation combination would be appropriate for a foreign operation whose functional currency is the U.S. dollar?

	Method	Treatment of Translation Adjustment
a.	Temporal	Separate component of stockholders' equity
✓b.	Temporal	Gain or loss in income statement
c.	Current rate	Separate component of stockholders' equity
d.	Current rate	Gain or loss in income statement

7. The functional currency of Garland Inc.'s Japanese subsidiary is the Japanese yen. Garland borrowed Japanese yen as a partial hedge of its investment in the subsidiary. How should the transaction gain on the foreign currency borrowing be reported in Garland's consolidated financial statements?

    a. The transaction gain is reported as an adjustment to interest expense in the income statement.

    b. The transaction gain is reported as an extraordinary item in the income statement.

    c. The transaction gain is offset against the negative translation adjustment related to the Japanese subsidiary in the stockholders' equity section of the balance sheet.

    d. The transaction gain is offset against the negative translation adjustment related to the Japanese subsidiary on the income statement.

8. Selected balance sheet accounts of a foreign subsidiary of the Pacter Company have been translated into parent currency (F) as follows:

	Translated at	
	Current Rates	**Historical Rates**
Accounts receivable	₣100,000	₣120,000
Marketable securities, at cost	200,000	240,000
Prepaid insurance	120,000	130,000
Goodwill	250,000	300,000
	₣670,000	₣790,000

Required:

a. Assuming that the foreign subsidiary is determined to have the foreign currency as its functional currency in accordance with IAS 21, determine the total amount that should be included in Pacter's consolidated balance sheet for the assets listed in accordance with International Financial Reporting Standards (IFRS).

b. Assuming that the foreign subsidiary is determined to have Pacter's reporting currency as its functional currency in accordance with IAS 21, determine the total amount that should be included in Pacter's consolidated balance sheet for the assets listed in accordance with IFRS.

9. The Year 1 financial statements of the Brazilian subsidiary of Artemis Corporation (a Canadian company) revealed the following:

	Brazilian Reals (BRL)
Beginning inventory	100,000
Purchases	500,000
Ending inventory	150,000
Cost of goods sold	450,000

Canadian dollar (C$) exchange rates for 1 BRL are as follows:

January 1, Year 1	C$0.45
Average, Year 1	0.42
December 31, Year 1	0.38

The beginning inventory was acquired in the last quarter of the previous year, when the exchange rate was C$0.50 = BRL 1; ending inventory was acquired in the last quarter of the current year, when the exchange rate was C$0.40 = BRL 1.

Required:

a. Assuming that the current rate method is the appropriate method of translation, determine the amounts at which the Brazilian subsidiary's ending inventory and cost of goods sold should be included in Artemis's Year 1 consolidated financial statements.

b. Assuming that the temporal method is the appropriate method of translation, determine the amounts at which the Brazilian subsidiary's ending inventory and cost of goods sold should be included in Artemis's Year 1 consolidated financial statements.

10. Simga Company's Turkish subsidiary reported the following amounts in Turkish lire (TL) on its December 31, Year 4, balance sheet:

Equipment	TL 100,000,000,000
Accumulated depreciation (straight-line)	32,000,000,000

Additional information related to the equipment is as follows:

Date	Amount Purchased	Useful Life	US$/TL Exchange Rate
1/1/Y1	TL 60,000,000,000	10 years	$0.0000070 = TL 1
1/1/Y3	TL 40,000,000,000	10 years	$0.0000020 = TL 1

U.S.-dollar exchange rates for the Turkish lira for Year 4 are as follows:

January 1, Year 4	$0.0000010
December 31, Year 4	0.0000006

Required:

a. Assume that Turkey is a highly inflationary economy. Determine the amounts at which the Turkish subsidiary's equipment and accumulated depreciation should be reported on Simga Company's December 31, Year 4, consolidated balance sheet in accordance with U.S. GAAP. Determine the net book value for equipment.

b. Now assume that Turkey is not a highly inflationary economy and that the Turkish subsidiary primarily uses Turkish lire in conducting its operations. Determine the amounts at which the Turkish subsidiary's equipment and accumulated depreciation should be reported on Simga Company's December 31, Year 4, consolidated balance sheet in accordance with U.S. GAAP. Determine the net book value for equipment.

11. Alliance Corporation (an Australian company) invests 1,000,000 marks in a foreign subsidiary on January 1, Year 1. The subsidiary commences operations on that date, and generates net income of 200,000 marks during its first year of operations. No dividends are sent to the parent this year. Relevant exchange rates between Alliance's reporting currency (A$) and the mark are as follows:

January 1, Year 1	A$0.15
Average, Year 1	0.17
December 31, 1997................	0.21

Required:

Determine the amount of translation adjustment that Alliance will report on its December 31, Year 1, balance sheet.

12. Zesto Company (a U.S. company) establishes a subsidiary in Mexico on January 1, Year 1. The subsidiary begins the year with 1,000,000 Mexican pesos (MXN) in cash and no other assets or liabilities. It immediately uses MXN600,000 to acquire equipment. Inventory costing MXN300,000 is acquired evenly throughout the year and sold for Mex$500,000 cash. A dividend of MXN100,000 is paid to the parent on October 1, Year 1. Depreciation on the equipment for the year is MXN60,000. Currency exchange rates between the U.S. dollar and MXN for Year 1 are as follows:

January 1........................	U.S.$0.090
October 1	0.080
December 31.....................	0.078
Average for the year	0.085

Required:

Determine the amount of remeasurement loss under the temporal method to be recognized in the Year 1 consolidated income statement.

13. Alexander Corporation (a U.S.-based company) acquired 100 percent of a Swiss company for 8.2 million Swiss francs on December 20, Year 1. At the date

of acquisition, the exchange rate was $0.70 per franc. The acquisition price is attributable to the following assets and liabilities denominated in Swiss francs:

Cash	1,000,000
Inventory	2,000,000
Fixed assets	7,000,000
Notes payable	(1,800,000)

Alexander Corporation prepares consolidated financial statements on December 31, Year 1. By that date, the Swiss franc appreciated to $0.75. Because of the year-end holidays, no transactions took place between the date of acquisition and the end of the year.

Required:

a. Determine the translation adjustment to be reported on Alexander's December 31, Year 1, consolidated balance sheet, assuming that the Swiss franc is the Swiss subsidiary's functional currency? What is the economic relevance of this translation adjustment?

b. Determine the remeasurement gain or loss to be reported in Alexander's Year 1 consolidated income, assuming that the U.S. dollar is the functional currency. What is the economic relevance of this remeasurement gain or loss?

14. Gramado Company was created as a wholly owned subsidiary of Porto Alegre Corporation on January 1, Year 1. On that date, Porto Alegre invested $42,000 in Gramado's capital stock. Given the exchange rate on that date of $0.84 per cruzeiro, the initial investment of $42,000 was converted into 50,000 cruzeiros (Cz). Other than the capital investment on January 1, there were no transactions involving stockholders' equity in Year 1. Gramado's cruzeiro-denominated financial statements for Year 2 are as follows:

Income Statement
Year 2

	Cz
Sales	540,000
Cost of goods sold	(310,000)
Gross profit	230,000
Operating expenses	(108,000)
Income before tax	122,000
Income taxes	(40,000)
Net income	82,000

Statement of Retained Earnings
Year 2

	Cz
Retained earnings, 1/1/Y2	154,000
Net income	82,000
Dividends (paid on 12/1/Y2)	(20,000)
Retained earnings, 12/31/Y2	216,000

Balance Sheet
December 31, Year 2

	Cz
Cash	50,000
Receivables	100,000
Inventory	72,000
Plant and equipment (net)	300,000
Less: Accumulated depreciation	(70,000)
Total assets	452,000
Liabilities	186,000
Capital stock	50,000
Retained earnings, 12/31/Y2	216,000
Total liabilities and stockholders' equity	452,000

The cruzeiro is the primary currency that Gramado uses in its day-to-day operations. The cruzeiro has steadily fallen in value against the dollar since Porto Alegre made the investment in Gramado on January 1, Year 1. Relevant exchange rates for the cruzeiro for Years 1 and 2 are as follows:

January 1, Year 1	$0.84
Average for Year 1.	0.80
December 31, Year 1	0.75
Average for Year 2.	0.72
December 1, Year 2	0.71
December 31, Year 2	0.70

Required:

a. Translate Gramado Company's Year 2 financial statements into dollars.

b. Compute the translation adjustment for Year 1 and for Year 2 and reconcile these amounts to the cumulative translation adjustment reported on the translated balance sheet at December 31, Year 2.

15. Brookhurst Company (a U.S.-based company) established a subsidiary in South Africa on January 1, Year 1, by investing 300,000 South African rand (ZAR) when the exchange rate was US$0.09/ZAR 1. On that date, the foreign subsidiary borrowed ZAR 500,000 from local banks on a 10-year note to finance the acquisition of plant and equipment. The subsidiary's opening balance sheet (in ZAR) was as follows:

Balance Sheet
January 1, Year 1

Cash	300,000	Long-term debt	500,000
Plant and equipment	500,000	Capital stock	300,000
Total	800,000	Total	800,000

During Year 1, the foreign subsidiary generated sales of ZAR 1,000,000 and net income of ZAR 110,000. Dividends in the amount of ZAR 20,000 were paid to the parent on June 1 and December 1. Inventory was acquired evenly throughout the year, with ending inventory acquired on November 15, Year 1. The subsidiary's ZAR financial statements for the year ended December 31, Year 1, are as follows:

Income Statement
Year 1

	ZAR
Sales	1,000,000
Cost of goods sold	(600,000)
Gross profit	400,000
Depreciation expense	(50,000)
Other operating expenses	(150,000)
Income before tax	200,000
Income taxes	(90,000)
Net income	110,000

Statement of Retained Earnings
Year 1

	ZAR
Retained earnings, 1/1/Y1	0
Net income	110,000
Dividends	(40,000)
Retained earnings, 12/31/Y1	70,000

Balance Sheet
December 31, Year 1

	ZAR
Cash	80,000
Receivables	150,000
Inventory	270,000
Plant and equipment (net)	450,000
Total assets	950,000
Accounts payable	80,000
Long-term debt	500,000
Common stock	300,000
Retained earnings, 12/31/Y1	70,000
Total liabilities and stockholders' equity	950,000

Relevant exchange rates for Year 1 are as follows (US$ per ZAR):

January 1, Year 1	$0.090
June 1, Year 1	0.095
Average for Year 1	0.096
November 15, Year 1	0.100
December 1, Year 1	0.105
December 31, Year 1	0.110

Required:

a. Translate the South African subsidiary's financial statements into U.S. dollars, assuming that the South African rand is the functional currency. Compute the translation adjustment by considering the impact of exchange rate changes on the subsidiary's net assets.

b. Translate (remeasure) the South African subsidiary's financial statements into U.S. dollars, assuming that the U.S. dollar is the functional currency. Compute the translation adjustment (remeasurement gain or loss) by considering the impact of exchange rate changes on the subsidiary's net monetary asset or liability position.

16. Access the most recent annual report for a U.S.-based multinational company with which you are familiar to complete the requirements of this exercise.

Required:

a. Determine whether the company's foreign operations have a predominant functional currency.

b. If possible, determine the amount of remeasurement gain or loss, if any, reported in net income in each of the three most recent years.

c. Determine the amount of translation adjustment, if any, reported in other comprehensive income in each of the three most recent years. Explain the sign (positive or negative) of the translation adjustment in each of the three most recent years.

d. Determine whether the company hedges net investments in foreign operations. If so, determine the type(s) of hedging instrument(s) used.

17. To complete the requirements of this exercise, access the most recent Form 10-K for both Exxon Mobil and Chevron.

Required:

a. Determine whether each company's foreign operations have a predominant functional currency. Discuss the implication this has for the comparability of financial statements between the two companies.

b. Determine the amount of translation adjustment, if any, reported in other comprehensive income in each of the three most recent years. Explain the sign (positive or negative) of the translation adjustment in each of the three most recent years. Compare the relative magnitude of the translation adjustments between the two companies.

c. Determine whether each company hedges the net investment in foreign operations. If so, determine the type(s) of hedging instrument(s) used.

d. Prepare a brief report comparing and contrasting the foreign currency translation and foreign currency hedging policies of these two companies.

Case 8-1

Columbia Corporation

Columbia Corporation, a U.S.-based company, acquired a 100 percent interest in Swoboda Company in Lodz, Poland, on January 1, Year 1, when the exchange rate for the Polish zloty (PLN) was $0.25. The financial statements of Swoboda as of December 31, Year 2, two years later, are as follows:

Balance Sheet
December 31, Year 2

Assets

Cash	PLN 1,000,000
Accounts receivable (net)	1,650,000
Inventory	4,250,000
Equipment.	12,500,000
Less: Accumulated depreciation	(4,250,000)
Building	36,000,000
Less: Accumulated depreciation	(15,150,000)
Land	3,000,000
Total assets	PLN 39,000,000

Liabilities and Stockholders' Equity

Accounts payable	PLN 1,250,000
Long-term debt	25,000,000
Common stock	2,500,000
Additional paid-in capital	7,500,000
Retained earnings	2,750,000
Total liabilities and stockholders' equity	PLN 39,000,000

Statement of Income and Retained Earnings
For the Year Ending December 31, Year 2

Sales	PLN 12,500,000
Cost of goods sold.	(6,000,000)
Depreciation expense—equipment	(1,250,000)
Depreciation expense—building.	(900,000)
Research and development expense.	(600,000)
Other expenses (including taxes)	(500,000)
Net income	PLN 3,250,000
Plus: Retained earnings, 1/1/Y2	250,000
Less: Dividends, Year 2.	(750,000)
Retained earnings, 12/31/Y2	PLN 2,750,000

Additional information:

- The January 1, Year 2, beginning inventory of PLN 3,000,000 was acquired on December 15, Year 1, when the exchange rate was $0.215. Purchases of inventory during Year 2 were acquired uniformly throughout the year. The December 31, Year 2, ending inventory of PLN 4,250,000 was acquired evenly throughout the fourth quarter of Year 2 when the exchange rate was $0.16.

- All fixed assets were on the books when the subsidiary was acquired except for PLN 2,500,000 of equipment which was acquired on January 3, Year 2 when the exchange rate was $0.18 and PLN 6,000,000 in buildings which was acquired on August 5, Year 2, when the exchange rate was $0.17. Equipment is depreciated on a straight-line basis over 10 years. Buildings are depreciated on a straight-line basis over 40 years. A full year's depreciation is taken in the year of acquisition.

- Dividends were declared and paid on December 15, Year 2, when the exchange rate was $0.155.
- Other exchange rates for Year 2 are:

January 1.	$0.200
Average for the year	0.175
December 31.	0.150

Required

1. Translate Swoboda's financial statements into U.S. dollars in accordance with U.S. GAAP at December 31, Year 2:

   a. Assuming the Polish zloty is the functional currency. (The December 31, Year 1, retained earnings that appeared in Swoboda's translated financial statements was $56,250. The December 31, Year 1, cumulative translation adjustment that appeared in Swoboda's translated balance sheet was negative $506,250.)

   b. Assuming the U.S. dollar is the functional currency. (The December 31, Year 1, retained earnings that appeared in Swoboda's remeasured financial statements was $882,500.)

   c. The same as (b) except Swoboda has no long-term debt. Instead, Swoboda has common stock of PLN 10,000,000 and additional paid-in capital of PLN 25,000,000. The December 31, Year 1, retained earnings that appeared in Swoboda's remeasured financial statements was negative $367,500.

2. Explain why the sign of the translation adjustments in (1*a*), (1*b*), and (1*c*) is positive or negative.

Case 8-2

Palmerstown Company

Palmerstown Company established a subsidiary in a foreign country on January 1, Year 1, by investing 8,000,000 pounds when the exchange rate was $1.00/pound. Palmerstown negotiated a bank loan of 4,000,000 pounds on January 5, Year 1, and purchased plant and equipment in the amount of 10,000,000 pounds on January 8, Year 1. Plant and equipment is depreciated on a straight-line basis over a 10-year useful life. The first purchase of inventory in the amount of 1,000,000 pounds was made on January 10, Year 1. Additional inventory of 12,000,000 pounds was acquired at three points in time during the year at an average exchange rate of $0.86/pound. Inventory on hand at year-end was acquired when the exchange rate was $0.83/pound. The first-in, first-out (FIFO) method is used to determine cost of goods sold. Additional exchange rates for the pound during Year 1 are as follows:

January 1–31, Year 1	$1.00
Average Year 1	0.90
December 31, Year 1	0.80

The foreign subsidiary's income statement for Year 1 and balance sheet at December 31, Year 1, are as follows:

Income Statement
For the Year Ended December 31, Year 1

	Pounds (in thousands)
Sales	15,000
Cost of goods sold	9,000
Gross profit	6,000
Selling and administrative expenses	3,000
Depreciation expense	1,000
Income before tax	2,000
Income taxes	600
Net income	1,400
Retained earnings, 1/1/Y1	0
Retained earnings, 12/31/Y1	1,400

Balance Sheet
At December 31, Year 1

	Pounds (in thousands)
Cash	2,400
Inventory	4,000
Fixed assets	10,000
Less: Accumulated depreciation	(1,000)
Total assets	15,400
Current liabilities	2,000
Long-term debt	4,000
Contributed capital	8,000
Retained earnings	1,400
Total liabilities and stockholders' equity	15,400

As the controller for Palmerstown Company, you have evaluated the characteristics of the foreign subsidiary to determine that the pound is the subsidiary's functional currency.

Required

1. Use an electronic spreadsheet to translate the foreign subsidiary's financial statements into U.S. dollars at December 31, Year 1, in accordance with U.S. GAAP. Insert a row in the spreadsheet after retained earnings and before total liabilities and stockholders' equity for the cumulative translation adjustment. Calculate the translation adjustment separately to verify the amount obtained as a balancing figure in the translation worksheet.

2. Use an electronic spreadsheet to remeasure the foreign subsidiary's financial statements into U.S. dollars at December 31, Year 1, assuming that the U.S. dollar is the subsidiary's functional currency. Insert a row in the spreadsheet after depreciation expense and before income before taxes for the remeasurement gain (loss).

3. Prepare a report for the chief executive officer of Palmerstown Company summarizing the differences that will be reported in the Year 1 consolidated financial statements because the pound, rather than the U.S. dollar, is the foreign subsidiary's functional currency. In your report, discuss the relationship between the current ratio, the debt-to-equity ratio, and the profit margin calculated from the foreign currency financial statements and from the translated U.S.-dollar financial statements. Also, include a discussion of the meaning of the translated U.S.-dollar amounts for inventory and for fixed assets.

References   Arnold, Jerry L., and William W. Holder. *Impact of Statement 52 on Decisions, Financial Reports and Attitudes.* Morristown, NJ: Financial Executives Research Foundation, 1986.

Doupnik, Timothy S., and Thomas G. Evans. "Functional Currency as a Strategy to Smooth Income." *Advances in International Accounting*, 1988.

Hepworth, Samuel R. *Reporting Foreign Operations.* Ann Arbor: University of Michigan, Bureau of Business Research, 1956.